REPAIR MANUAL

DODGE CARAVAN PLMOUTH VOYAGER 1984-91

Covers all U.S and Canadian Models

ONE OF THE DIVERSIFIED PUBLISHING COMPANIES, A PART OF CAPITAL CITIES/ABC, INC.

CONTENTS

GENERAL INFORMATION and MAINTENANCE

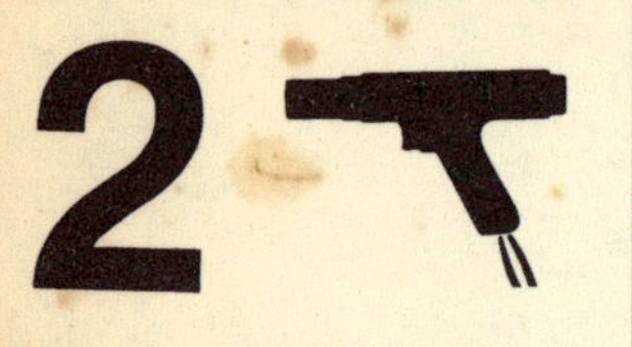

ENGINE PERFORMANCE and TUNE-UP

ENGINE and ENGINE OVERHAUL

EMISSION CONTROLS

FUEL SYSTEM

CHASSIS ELECTRICAL

DRIVE TRAIN

SUSPENSION and STEERING

BRAKES

BODY

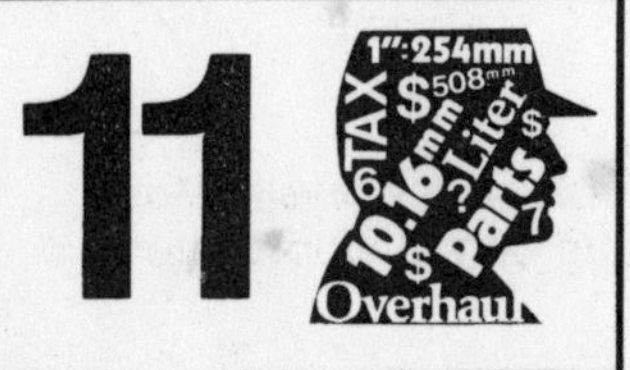

MECHANIC'S DATA

SAFETY NOTICE

Proper service and repair procedures are vital to the safe, reliable operation of all motor vehicles, as well as the safety of those performing repairs. This book outlines procedures for servicing and repairing vehicles using safe effective methods. The procedures contain many NOTES, CAUTIONS and WARNINGS which should be followed along with standard safety procedures to eliminate the possibility of personal injury or improper service which could damage the vehicle or compromise its safety.

It is important to note that repair procedures and techniques, tools and parts for servicing motor vehicles, as well as the skill and experience of the individual performing the work vary widely. It is not possible to anticipate all of the conceivable ways or conditions under which vehicles may be serviced, or to provide cautions as to all of the possible hazards that may result. Standard and accepted safety precautions and equipment should be used during cutting, grinding, chiseling, prying, or any other process that can cause material removal or projectiles.

Some procedures require the use of tools specially designed for a specific purpose. Before substituting another tool or procedure, you must be completely satisfied that neither your personal safety, nor the performance of the vehicle will be endangered.

Although the information in this guide is based on industry sources and is as complete as possible at the time of publication, the possibility exists that the manufacturer made later changes which could not be included here. While striving for total accuracy, Chilton Book Company cannot assume responsibilty for any errors, changes, or omissions that may occur in the compilation of this data.

PART NUMBERS

Part numbers listed in the reference are not recommendations by Chilton for any product by brand name. They are references that can be used with interchange manuals and aftermarket supplier catalogs to locate each brand supplier's discrete part number.

SPECIAL TOOLS

Special tools are recommended by the vehicle manufacturer to perform their specific job. Use has been kept to a minimum, but where absolutely necessary, they are referred to in the text by the part number of the tool manufacturer. These tools can be purchased, under the appropiate part number, from Owatonna Tool Company, Owatonna, MN 55060 or an equivalent tool can be purchased locally from a tool supplier or parts outlet. Before substituting any tool for the one recommended, read the SAFETY NOTICE at the top of this page.

ACKNOWLEDGEMENTS

Chilton Book Company expresses appreciation to Chrysler Plymouth Division, Chrysler Motor Corporation, Detroit, Michigan and the Dodge Division, Chrysler Motors Corporation, Detroit, Michigan for their generous assistance

Published in Radnor, Pennsylvania 19089 by Chilton Book Company
*ONE OF THE **ABC PUBLISHING COMPANIES,** A PART OF **CAPITAL CITIES/ABC, INC.***

Manufactured in the United States of America
67890 09876

Chilton's Repair Manual: Dodge Caravan/Plymouth Voyager 1984–91
ISBN 0-8019-8156-5 pbk.
Library of Congress Catalog Card No. 90-056090

General Information and Maintenance

1

HOW TO USE THIS BOOK

Chilton's Repair Manual for the Dodge Caravan/Plymouth Voyager is intended to teach you about the inner workings of your van and save you money on its upkeep.

The first two Chapters will be the most used, since they contain maintenance, tune-up information and service procedures. Studies have shown that a properly tuned and maintained vehicle will get better gas mileage (which translates into lower operating costs) and periodic maintenance will catch minor problems before they turn into major repair bills. The other Chapters deal with the more complex systems of your car. Operating systems from engine through brakes are covered. It will give you the detailed instructions to help you change your own brake pads and shoes, tune-up the engine, replace spark plugs and filters, and do many more jobs that will save you money, give you personal satisfaction and help you avoid expensive problems.

Before attempting any repairs or service on your vehicle, read through the entire procedure outlined in the appropriate Chapter. This will give you the overall view of what tools and supplies will be required. Many times a description of the system function and operation is given, helping you to understand what repairs must be done.

Two basic mechanic's rules should be mentioned here. First, whenever the LEFT side of the car or engine is referred to, it is meant to specify the DRIVER'S side of the car. Conversely, the RIGHT side of the car means the PASSENGER'S side. Second, all screws and bolts are removed by turning counterclockwise, and tightened by turning clockwise (unless otherwise noted).

Safety is always the most important rule. Constantly be aware of the dangers involved in working on or around an automobile, and take proper precautions to avoid the risk of personal injury or damage to the vehicle. See the section, Servicing Your Vehicle Safely, and the SAFETY NOTICE on the acknowledgment page before attempting any service procedures. Pay special attention to the instructions provided.

There are 3 common mistakes in mechanical work:

1. Incorrect order of assembly, disassembly or adjustment. When taking something apart or putting it together, doing things in the wrong order usually just costs you extra time; however, it CAN break something. Read the entire procedure before beginning disassembly. Do everything in the order in which the instructions say you should do it, even if you can't immediately see a reason for it. When you're taking apart something that is very intricate (for example a carburetor), you might want to draw a picture of how it looks when assembled at one point in order to make sure you get everything back in its proper position. We will supply exploded views whenever possible, but sometimes the job requires more attention to detail than an illustration provides. When making adjustments (especially tune-up adjustments), do them in order. One adjustment often affects another, and you cannot expect satisfactory results unless each adjustment is made in accordance with its sequence.

2. Overtorquing (or undertorquing) nuts and bolts. While it is more common for overtorquing to cause damage, undertorquing can cause a fastener to vibrate loose and cause serious damage, especially when dealing with aluminum parts. Pay attention to torque specifications and utilize a torque wrench in assembly. If a torque figure is not available remember that, if you are using the right tool to do the job, you will probably not have to strain your-

self to get a fastener tight enough. The pitch of most threads is so slight that the tension you put on the wrench will be multiplied many times in actual force on what you are tightening. A good example of how critical torque is can be seen in the case of spark plug installation, especially where you are putting the plug into an aluminum cylinder head. Too little torque can fail to crush the gasket, causing leakage of combustion gases, and consequent overheating of the plug and engine parts. Too much torque can damage the threads or distort the plug, which changes the spark gap. Since more and more manufacturers are using aluminum in their engine and chassis parts to save weight, a torque wrench should be in any serious do-it-yourselfer's tool box.

NOTE: *There are many commercial chemical products available for ensuring that fasteners won't come loose, even if they are not torqued just right (a very common brand is Loctite®). If you're worried about getting something together tight enough to hold, but loose enough to avoid mechanical damage during assembly, one of these products might offer substantial insurance. Read the label on the package and make sure the product is compatible with the materials, fluids, etc. involved before choosing one.*

3. Cross Threading. This occurs when a part such as a bolt is screwed into a nut or casting at the wrong angle and forced, causing the threads to become damaged. Crossthreading is more likely to occur if access is difficult. It helps to clean and lubricate fasteners, and to start threading with the part to be installed going straight in, using your fingers. If you encounter resistance, unscrew the part and start over again at a different angle until it can be inserted and turned several times without much effort. Keep in mind that many parts, especially spark plugs, use tapered threads so that gentle turning will automatically bring the part you're threading to the proper angle if you don't force it or resist a change in angle. Don't put a wrench on the part until it's been turned in a couple of times by hand. If you suddenly encounter resistance and the part has not seated fully, don't force it. Pull it back out and make sure it's clean and threading properly.

Always take your time and be patient; once you have some experience, working on your car will become an enjoyable hobby.

TOOLS AND EQUIPMENT

Naturally, without the proper tools and equipment it is impossible to properly service your vehicle. It would be impossible to catalog each tool that you would need to perform each or every operation in this book. It would also be unwise for the amateur to rush out and buy an expensive set of tools, on the theory that he may need one or more of them at sometime.

The best approach is to proceed slowly, gathering together a good quality set of those tools that are used most frequently. Don't be misled by the low cost of bargain tools. It is far better to spend a little more for better quality. Forged wrenches, 6- or 12-point sockets and fine tooth ratchets are by far preferable to their less expensive counterparts. As any good mechanic can tell you, there are few worse experiences than trying to work on a car with bad tools. Your monetary savings will be far outweighed by frustration and mangled knuckles.

Begin accumulating those tools that are used most frequently; those associated with routine maintenance and tune-up.

In addition to the normal assortment of screwdrivers and pliers you should have the following tools for routine maintenance jobs:

1. SAE/Metric wrenches, sockets and combination open end/box end wrenches in sizes from 1/8 in. (3mm) to 3/4 in. (19mm), and a spark plug socket (13/16 in. or 5/8 in.). If possible, buy various length socket drive extensions. One break in this department is that the metric sockets available in the U.S. will all fit the ratchet handles and extensions you may already have (1/4, 3/8, and 1/2 in. drive).
2. Jackstands for support.
3. Oil filter wrench.
4. Oil filler spout or funnel.
5. Grease gun for chassis lubrication.
6. Hydrometer for checking the battery.
7. A low flat pan for draining oil.
8. Lots of rags for wiping up the inevitable mess.

In addition to the above items there are several others that are not absolutely necessary, but handy to have around. These include oil-dry, a transmission fluid funnel and the usual supply of lubricants, antifreeze and fluids, although these can be purchased as needed. This is a basic list for routine maintenance, but only your personal needs and desires can accurately determine your list of necessary tools.

The second list of tools is for tune-ups. While the tools involved here are slightly more sophisticated, they need not be outrageously expensive. A basic list of tune-up equipment could include:

1. Tachometer
2. Spark plug wrench
3. Timing light
4. Wire spark plug gauge/adjusting tools

In addition to these basic tools, there are sev-

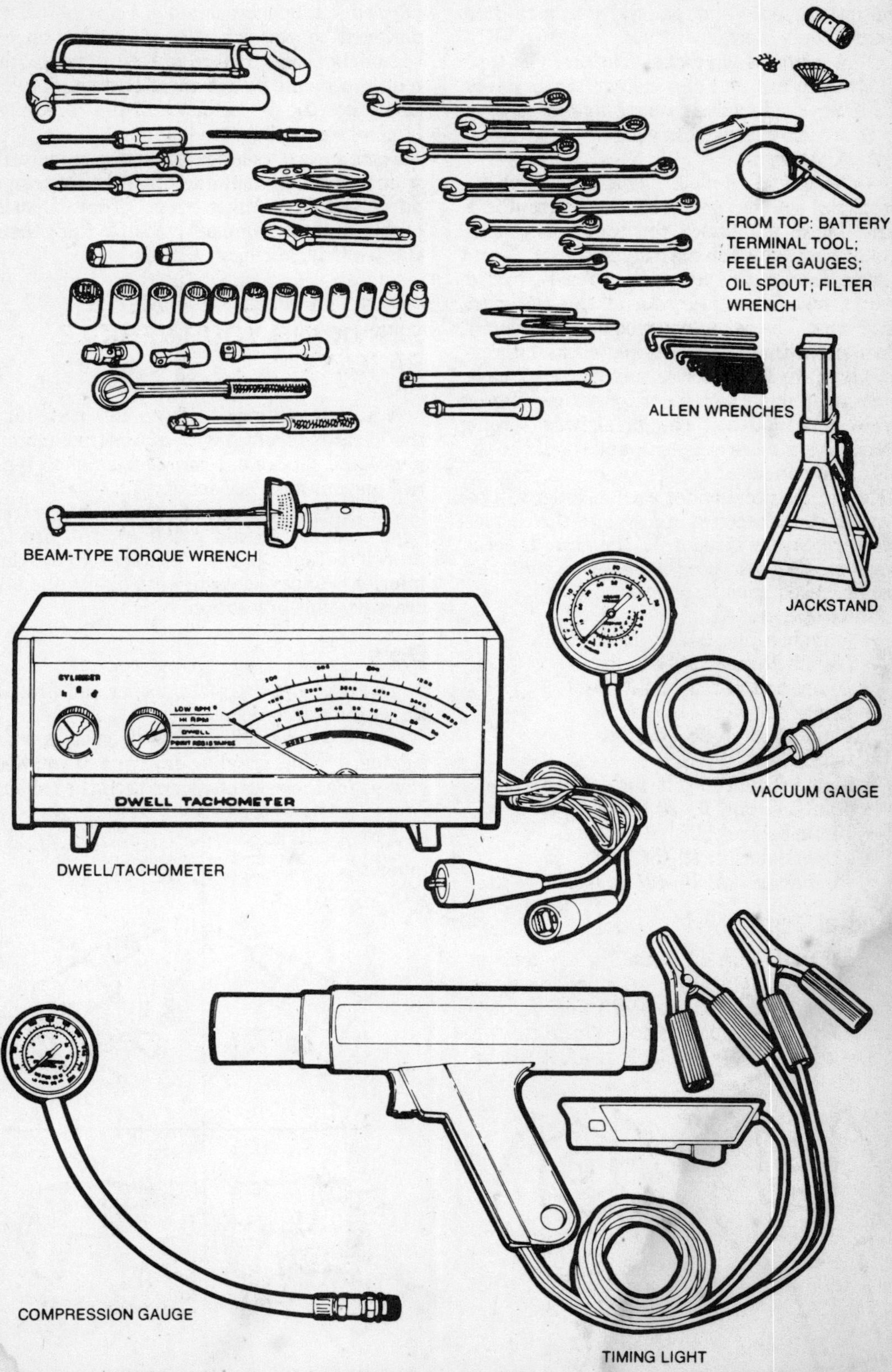

This basic collection of tools and test instruments is all you need for most maintenance on your truck.

eral other tools and gauges you may find useful. These include:

1. A compression gauge. The screw-in type is slower to use, but eliminates the possibility of a faulty reading due to escaping pressure
2. A manifold vacuum gauge
3. A test light
4. An induction meter. This is used for determining whether or not there is current in a wire. These are handy for use if a wire is broken somewhere in a wiring harness.

As a final note, you will probably find a torque wrench necessary for all but the most basic work. The beam type models are perfectly adequate, although the newer click (breakaway) type are more precise, and you don't have to crane your neck to see a torque reading in awkward situations. The breakaway torque wrenches are more expensive and should be recalibrated periodically.

Torque specification for each fastener will be given in the procedure in any case that a specific torque value is required. If no torque specifications are given, use the following values as a guide, based upon fastener size:

Bolts marked 6T

- 6mm bolt/nut: 5–7 ft. lbs.
- 8mm bolt/nut: 12–17 ft. lbs.
- 10mm bolt/nut: 23–34 ft. lbs.
- 12mm bolt/nut: 41–59 ft. lbs.
- 14mm bolt/nut: 56–76 ft. lbs.

Bolts marked 8T

- 6mm bolt/nut: 6–9 ft. lbs.
- 8mm bolt/nut: 13–20 ft. lbs.
- 10mm bolt/nut: 27–40 ft. lbs.
- 12mm bolt/nut: 46–69 ft. lbs.
- 14mm bolt/nut: 75–101 ft. lbs.

Special Tools

Normally, the use of special factory tools is avoided for repair procedures, since these are not readily available for the do-it-yourselfer mechanic. When it is possible to perform the job with more commonly available tools, it will be pointed out, but occasionally, a special tool was designed to perform a specific function and should be used. Before substituting another tool, you should be convinced that neither your safety nor the performance of the vehicle will be compromised.

Some special tools are available commercially from major tool manufacturers. Others can be purchased from Miller Special Tools; Division of Utica Tool Company, 32615 Park Lane, Garden City, Michigan 48135.

Use the proper size wrench and place it properly on the flats of the nut or bolt

SERVICING YOUR VEHICLE SAFELY

It is virtually impossible to anticipate all of the hazards involved with automotive maintenance and service but care and common sense will prevent most accidents.

The rules of safety for mechanics range from "don't smoke around gasoline", to "use the proper tool for the job." The trick to avoiding injuries is to develop safe work habits and take every possible precaution.

Do's

- Do keep a fire extinguisher and first aid kit within easy reach.
- Do wear safety glasses or goggles when cutting, drilling, grinding or prying. If you wear glasses for the sake of vision, then they should

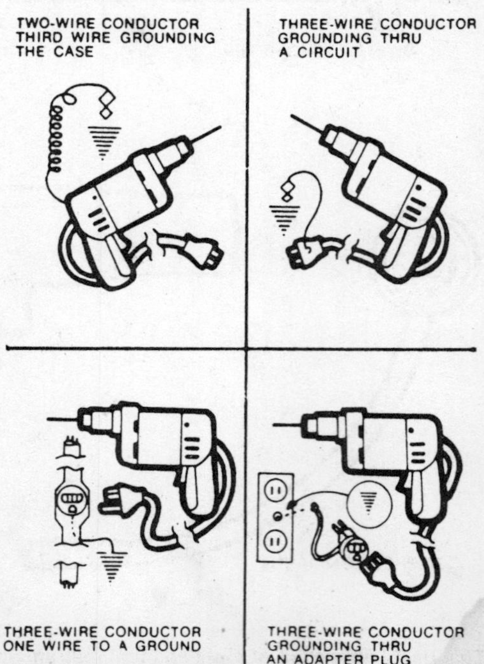

Power tools should always be properly grounded

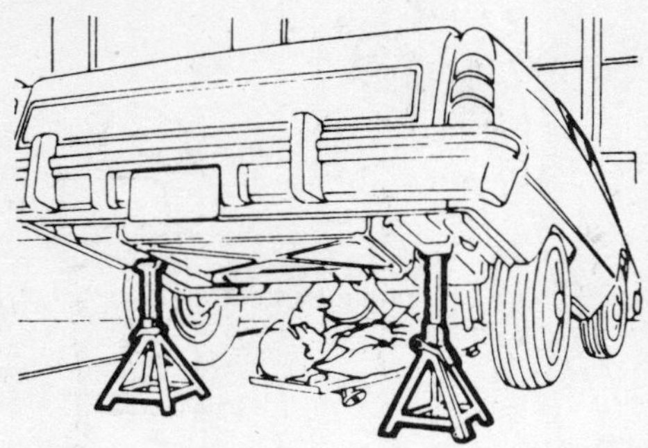

Always use jackstands when working under the vehicle

be made of hardened glass that can serve also as safety glasses, or wear safety goggles over your regular glasses.

• Do shield your eyes whenever you work around the battery. Batteries contain sulfuric acid. In case of contact with the eyes or skin, flush the area with water or a mixture of water and baking soda and get medical attention immediately.

• Do use safety stands for any under-car service. Jacks are for raising vehicles; safety stands are for making sure the vehicle stays raised until you want it to come down. Whenever the vehicle is raised, block the wheels remaining on the ground and set the parking brake.

• Do use adequate ventilation when working with any chemicals. Asbestos dust resulting from brake lining wear cause cancer.

• Do disconnect the negative battery cable when working on the electrical system.

• Do follow manufacturer's directions whenever working with potentially hazardous materials. Both brake fluid and antifreeze are poisonous if taken internally.

• Do properly maintain your tools. Loose hammerheads, mushroomed punches and chisels, frayed or poorly grounded electrical cords, excessively worn screwdrivers, spread wrenches (open end), cracked sockets, slipping ratchets, or faulty droplight sockets can cause accidents.

• Do use the proper size and type of tool for the job being done.

• Do when possible, pull on a wrench handle rather than push on it, and adjust you stance to prevent a fall.

• Do be sure that adjustable wrenches are tightly adjusted on the nut or bolt and pulled so that the face is on the side of the fixed jaw.

• Do select a wrench or socket that fits the nut or bolt. The wrench or socket should sit straight, not cocked.

• Do strike squarely with a hammer. avoid glancing blows.

• Do set the parking brake and block the wheels if the work requires that the engine be running.

Don'ts

• Don't run an engine in a garage or anywhere else without proper ventilation—EVER! Carbon monoxide is poisonous. It is absorbed by the body 400 times faster than oxygen. It takes a long time to leave the human body and you can build up a deadly supply of it in your system by simply breathing in a little every day. You may not realize you are slowly poisoning yourself. Always use power vents, windows, fans or open the garage doors.

• Don't work around moving parts while wearing a necktie or other loose clothing. Short sleeves are much safer than long, loose sleeves. Hard-toed shoes with neoprene soles protect your toes and give a better grip on slippery surfaces. Jewelry such as watches, fancy belt buckles, beads, or body adornment of any kind is not safe while working around a car. Long hair should be hidden under a hat or cap.

• Don't use pockets for toolboxes. A fall or bump can drive a screwdriver deep into you body. Even a wiping cloth hanging from the back pocket can wrap around a spinning shaft or fan.

• Don't smoke when working around gasoline, cleaning solvent or other flammable material.

• Don't smoke when working around the battery. When the battery is being charged, it gives off explosive hydrogen gas.

• Don't use gasoline to wash your hands. There are excellent soaps available. Gasoline may contain lead, and lead can enter the body through a cut, accumulating in the body until you are very ill. Gasoline also removes all the natural oils from the skin so that bone dry hands will suck up oil and grease.

• Don't service the air conditioning system unless you are equipped with the necessary tools and training. The refrigerant, R-12, is extremely cold and when exposed to the air, will instantly freeze any surface it comes in contact with, including your eyes. Although the refrigerant is normally non-toxic, R-12 becomes a deadly poisonous gas in the presence of an open flame. One good whiff of the vapors from burning refrigerant can be fatal.

NOTE: *The Dodge and Plymouth vehicles described in this manual are metric-specified. While some inch-standard parts are used, body panels, fasteners, drivetrain components, and tires are all specified according to the Metric System. Dimensions and performance data are also expressed in metric units.*

MODEL IDENTIFICATION

The Caravan and Voyager models covered in this manual have remained much the same since their introduction. There are a few variations on the basic model, these include the Mini Ram Van, the 1991 Chrysler Town & Country and the Plymouth Grand Voyager. All of these models are still based on the Caravan and Voyager, and are only different in trim configurations.

For 1991 Chrysler is offering both anti-lock brakes and All Wheel Drive (AWD) as an option on the entire Caravan and Voyager line.

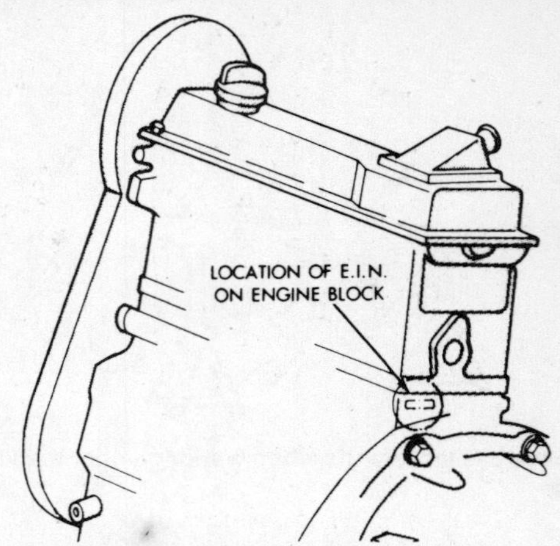

EIN location on 2.2L and 2.5L engines

SERIAL NUMBER IDENTIFICATION

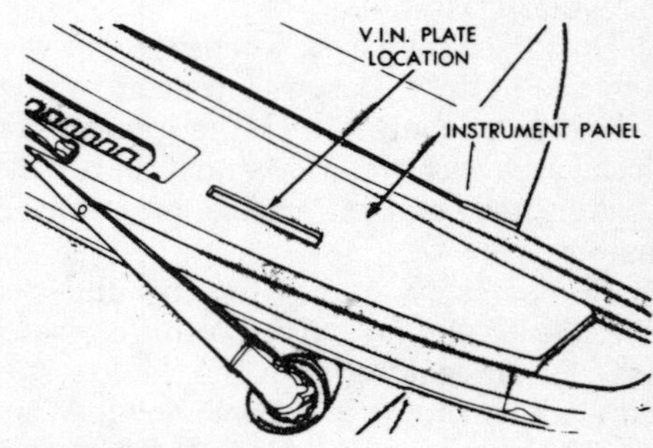

Location of VIN plate

Vehicle Identification Number (V.I.N.)

The vehicle identification number (VIN) consists of seventeen numbers and letters embossed on a plate, located on the upper left corner of the instrument panel, near the windshield.

Engine Identification Number (E.I.N.)

All engine assemblies carry an engine identification number (E.I.N.). On 2.2 liter and 2.5 liter engines, the E.I.N. is located on the face of the engine block, directly under the cylinder head (left side of vehicle).

On the 2.6 liter, 3.0 liter and 3.3 liter engines, the E.I.N. is located on the left side of the

ENGINE APPLICATION CHART

Years	Engine Code	No. Cyl.	Actual Displacement Cu. In.	cc	Liters	Type	Fuel System	Built By
1984	C	4	135	2,212	2.2	OHC	2BBL	Chrysler
	G	4	156	2,556	2.6	OHC	2BBL	Mitsubishi
1985	C	4	135	2,212	2.2	OHC	2BBL	Chrysler
	G	4	156	2,556	2.6	OHC	2BBL	Mitsubishi
1986	C	4	135	2,212	2.2	OHC	2BBL	Chrysler
	G	4	156	2,556	2.6	OHC	2BBL	Mitsubishi
1987	C	4	135	2,212	2.2	OHC	2BBL	Chrysler
	K	4	153	2,507	2.5	OHC	EFI	Chrysler
	G	4	156	2,556	2.6	OHC	2BBL	Mitsubishi
1988	K	4	153	2,507	2.5	OHC	EFI	Chrysler
	3	6	181	2,966	3.0	OHC	EFI	Mitsubishi
1989	K	4	153	2,507	2.5	OHC	EFI	Chrysler
	J	4	153	2,507	2.5	OHC	EFI ①	Chrysler
	3	6	181	2,966	3.0	OHC	EFI	Mitsubishi
1990	K	4	153	2,507	2.5	OHC	EFI	Chrysler
	J	4	153	2,507	2.5	OHC	EFI ①	Chrysler
	3	6	181	2,966	3.0	OHC	EFI	Mitsubishi
	R	6	201	3,294	3.3	OHV	EFI	Chrysler
1991	K	4	153	2,507	2.5	OHC	EFI	Chrysler
	3	6	181	2,966	3.0	OHC	EFI	Mitsubishi
	R	6	201	3,294	3.3	OHV	EFI	Chrysler

① Turbocharged Engine

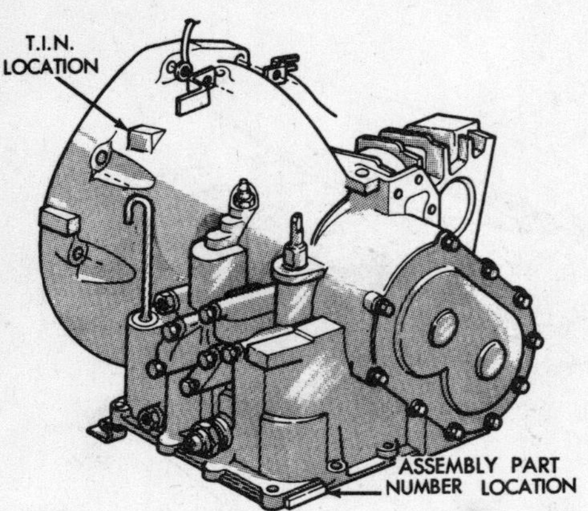

Location of Transaxle Identification Number (T.I.N.) on transaxle and assembly part number location (automatic)

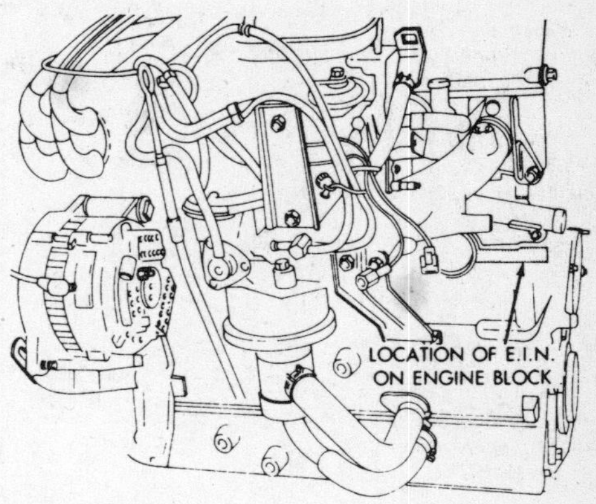

EIN location on 2.6L and 3.0L engines

engine block between the core plug and the rear face of the block (radiator side of vehicle).

Engine Serial Number

In addition to the previously covered E.I.N., each engine assembly carries an engine serial number which must be referenced when ordering engine replacement parts.

On the 2.2 liter, and 2.5 liter engines, the engine serial number is located on the rear face of the engine block, directly below the cylinder head (below E.I.N.). On 2.6 liter, 3.0 and 3.3 liter engines, the engine serial number is located on the exhaust manifold stud (dash panel side of vehicle).

Transaxle

The transaxle identification number (T.I.N.) is stamped on a boss that is located on the left upper transaxle housing.

In addition to the T.I.N., each transaxle carries an assembly part number. On manual transaxles, the assembly part number is located on a metal tag at the front of the transaxle. On automatic transaxles, the assembly part number is located just above the oil pan at the rear of the assembly.

ROUTINE MAINTENANCE

Air Cleaner

The air cleaner element on vehicles equipped with 2.2 liter engine should be replaced every 52,000 miles. Vehicles equipped with 2.5L, 2.6L, 3.0L and 3.3L engines should be replaced every 30,000 miles. However, if the vehicle is operated frequently through dusty areas; it will require periodic inspection at least every 15,000 miles.

AUTOMATIC TRANSMISSION APPLICATION CHART

Years	Transmission	Models
1984-91	A-413 3 speed	Caravan, Voyager
1984-87	A-470 4 speed	Caravan, Voyager
1988-91	A-670 3 speed	Caravan, Voyager
1989-91	A-604 4 speed	Caravan, Voyager
1991	A-604 4 speed	Town & Country

MANUAL TRANSMISSION APPLICATION CHART

Years	Transmission	Models
1984-87	A-460 4 speed	Caravan, Voyager
1984-85	A-465 5 speed	Caravan, Voyager
1984-86	A-525 5 speed	Caravan, Voyager
1987-89	A-520 5 speed	Caravan, Voyager
1989	A-555 5 speed	Caravan, Voyager
1990	A-523 5 speed	Caravan, Voyager
1990	A-568 5 speed	Caravan, Voyager

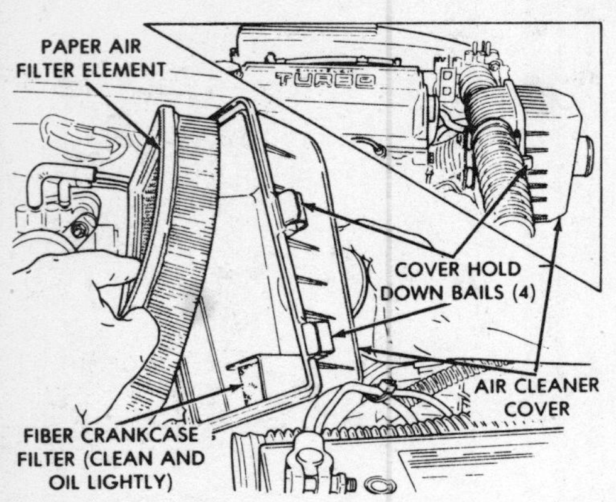

Air cleaner assembly – 2.5L Turbo engine

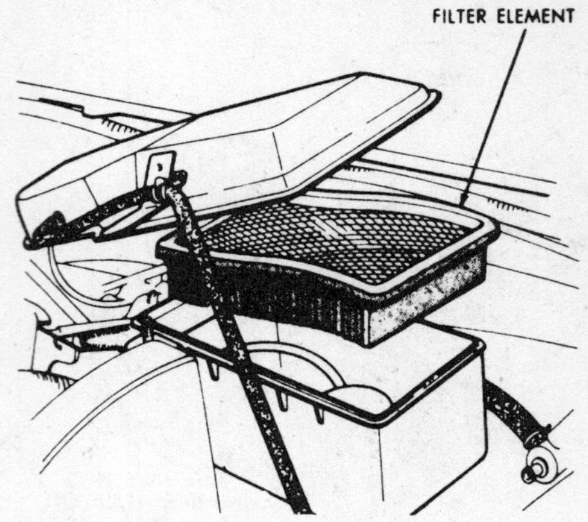

2.2L engine air cleaner filter

REMOVAL AND INSTALLATION

2.2L Engine

1. Unfasten the three hold down clips and remove the three wing nuts that retain the top of the air cleaner housing.
2. Remove the top of the air cleaner housing and position out of the way with the breather hose attached.
3. Remove the air cleaner element from the housing.
4. Clean the inside of the housing but take care not to allow the dirt to enter the carburetor air intake.
5. Install a new air cleaner element with the screen side up into the plastic housing.
6. Position the steel top cover so that the hold down clips and support bracket studs are aligned.

NOTE: *The procedures in the next steps should be followed as stated to prevent loosening and air leaks.*

7. Install the wing nuts on both carburetor studs and tighten them to 14 inch lbs. Install the wing nut that attaches the air cleaner tab to the support bracket and tighten to 14 inch lbs.
8. Fasten the hold down clips.

2.5L, 2.6L, 3.0L and 3.3L Engines

1. Unfasten the hold down clips that retain the air cleaner cover.
2. Remove the air cleaner housing cover with intake hose attached and position out of the way.
3. Remove the air cleaner element from the housing.
4. Clean the inside of the air cleaner housing.
5. Install a new cleaner element and position the cover on the air cleaner housing. Secure the hold down clips.

Fuel Filter

CAUTION: *Don't smoke when working around gasoline, cleaning solvent or other flammable material.*

2.6L engine air cleaner filter

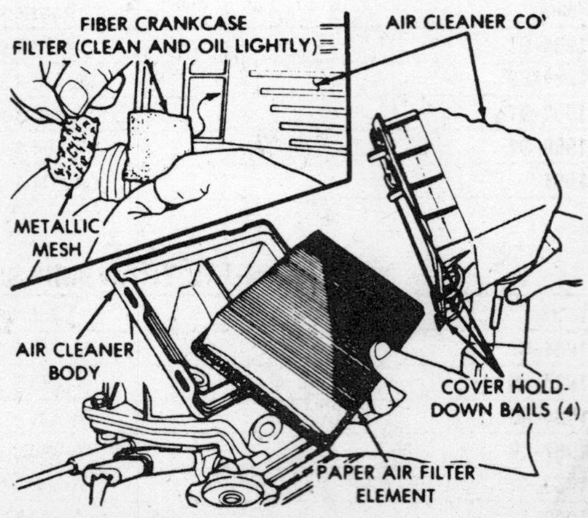

2.5L air cleaner assembly

The fuel system on all vehicles incorporate two fuel filters. One is part of the fuel gauge unit; located inside the fuel tank at the fuel suction tube. Routine servicing of this filter is not necessary. However, if limited vehicle speed or hard starting is exhibited, it should be inspected.

The second filter is located in the fuel line between the fuel pump and the carburetor or fuel injector rail. Replacement of this filter is recommended every 52,000 miles.

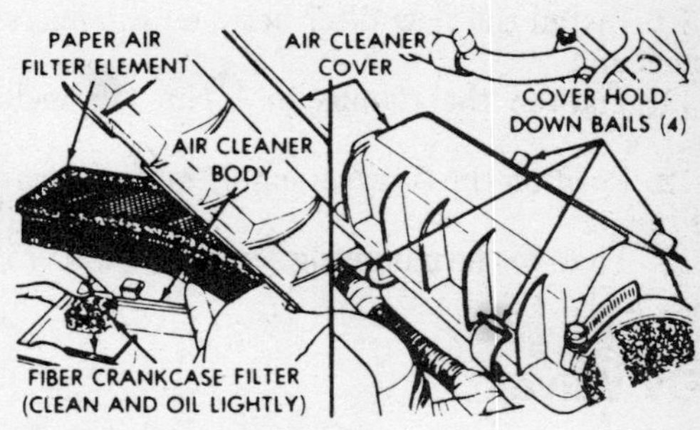

3.0L air cleaner assembly

REMOVAL AND INSTALLATION

2.2L and 2.6L Engines

1. Clean the area at the filter and clamps with a suitable solvent
2. Loosen the clamps on both ends of filter.
3. Wrap a shop towel or clean rag around the hoses to absorb fuel.
4. Remove the hoses from the filter, and discard the clamps and filter.
5. Install the new filter between the fuel lines and clamp.
6. Tighten the clamps to 1 Nm (10 inch lbs.)

2.5L, 3.0L and 3.3L Engines

The fuel filter on these vehicles is located along the chassis, mounted just ahead of the fuel tank. To remove the filter, the vehicle will have to be raised slightly.

CAUTION: *Before servicing any components within the fuel system, the system pressure must first be released.*

1. Loosen the gas cap to release tank pressure.
2. On the 2.5L engine, disconnect the harness connector from the injector
3. On the 3.0L and 3.3L engines, disconnect the harness connector from any injector
4. Ground one terminal of the injector.
5. Connect a jumper to the other terminal and momentarily touch the positive terminal of the battery for no longer than 10 seconds. This releases the system pressure.
6. Raise the vehicle slightly and safely support it. Remove the retaining screw and filter assembly from the chassis rail.
7. Loosen the clamps on both ends of the fuel filter.
8. Wrap a shop towel or clean rag around the hoses to absorb fuel
9. Remove the hoses from the filter, and discard clamps and filter.

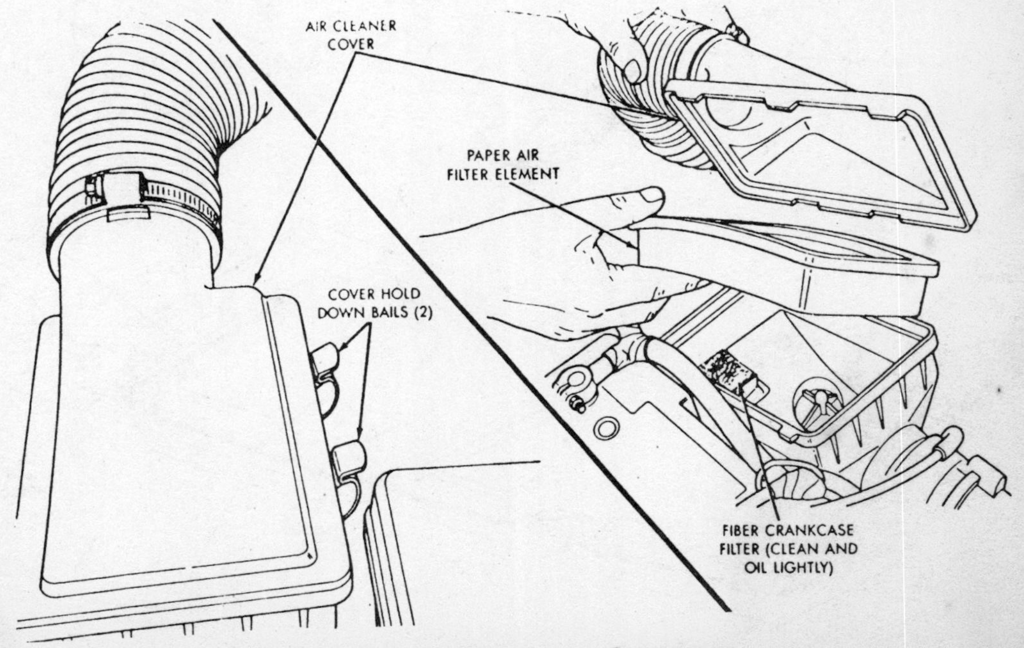

Air cleaner assembly — 3.3L engine

10. Install the new filter between the hoses and clamp.
11. Tighten the clamps to 1 Nm (10 inch lbs.).
12. Position the filter assembly on the chassis rail.
13. Tighten the mounting screw to 8 Nm (75 inch lbs.)

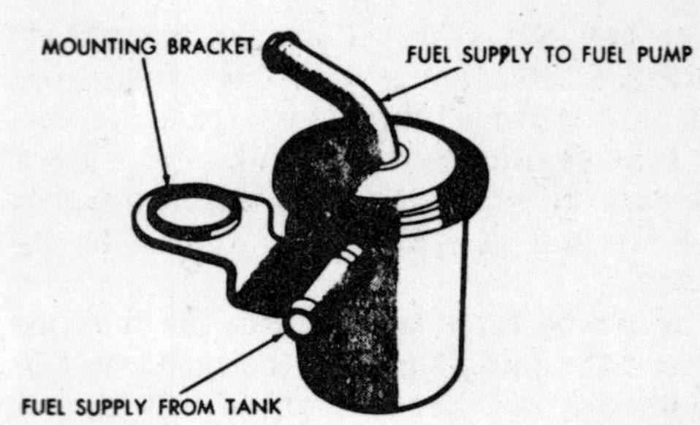

Typical inline filter

PCV Valve

2.2L, 2.5L, 3.0L and 3.3L Engines

Crankcase vapors and piston blow-by are removed from the engine by intake manifold vacuum. The emissions are drawn through the PCV valve (usually located in the top of the engine valve cover) into the intake manifold where they become part of the air/fuel mixture. Crankcase vapors are then burned and pass through the exhaust system. When there are not enough vapors or blow-by pressure in the engine, air is drawn from the air cleaner. With this system no outside air enters the crankcase.

The PCV valve is used to control the rate at which crankcase vapors are returned to the intake manifold. The action of the valve plunger is controlled by intake manifold vacuum and the spring. During deceleration and idle, when manifold vacuum is high, it over-

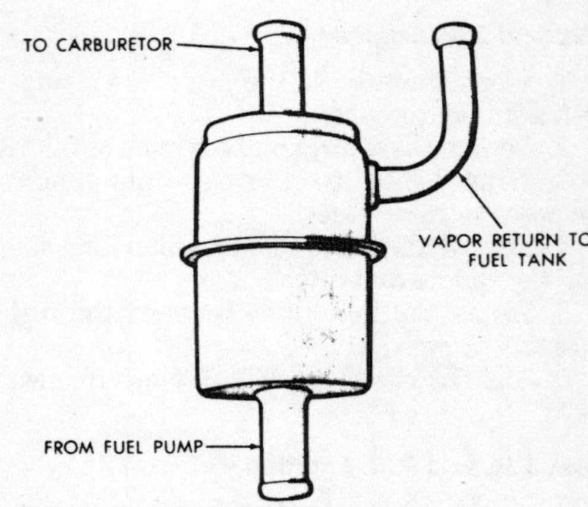

Fuel filter vapor separator 2.2L engine

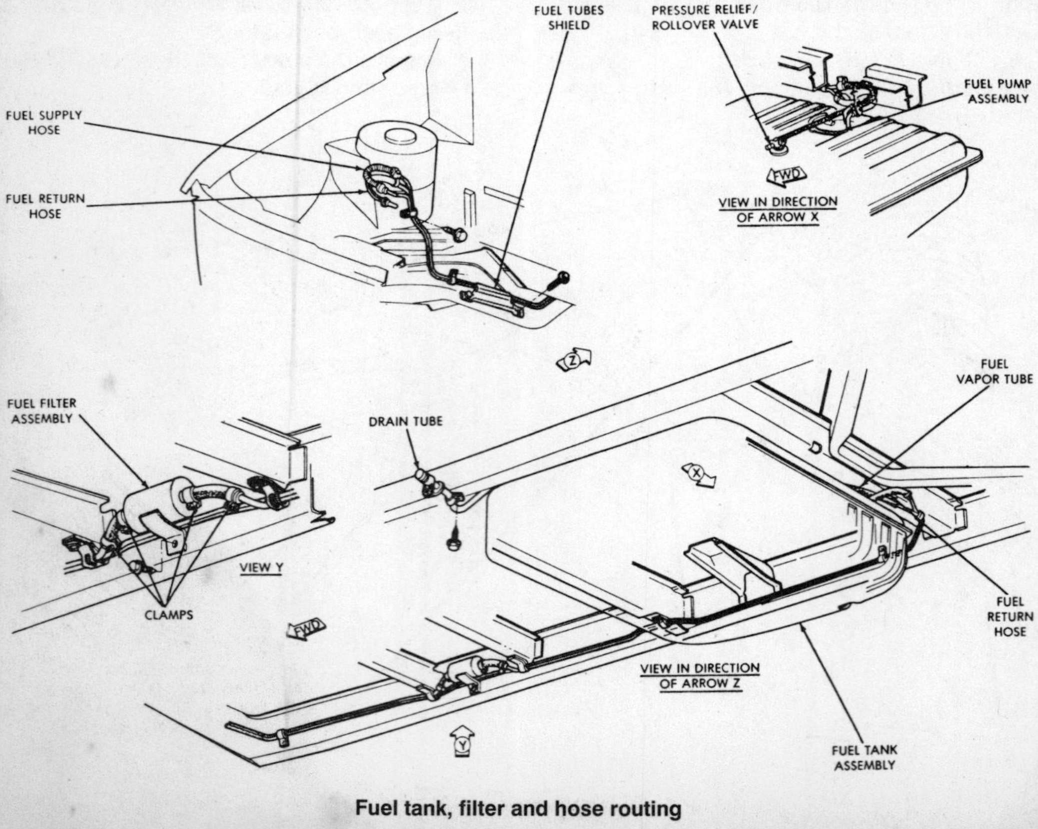

Fuel tank, filter and hose routing

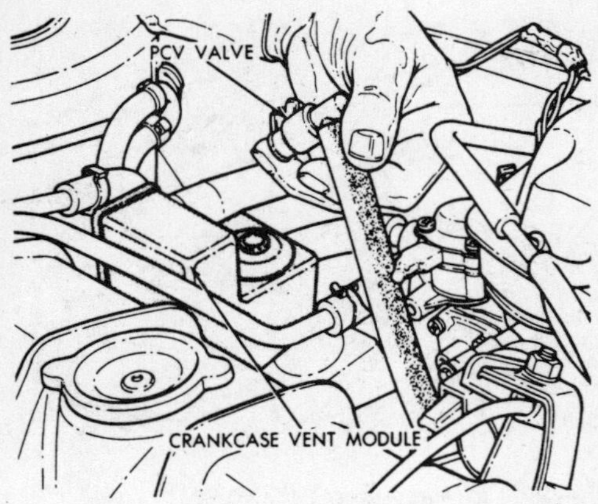

2.2L engine crankcase module and PCV valve

comes the tension of the valve spring and the plunger bottoms in the manifold end of the valve housing. Because of the valve construction, it reduces, but does not stop, the passage of vapors to the intake manifold. When the engine is lightly accelerated or operated at constant speed, spring tension matches intake manifold vacuum pull and the plunger takes a mid-position in the valve body, allowing more vapors to flow into the manifold.

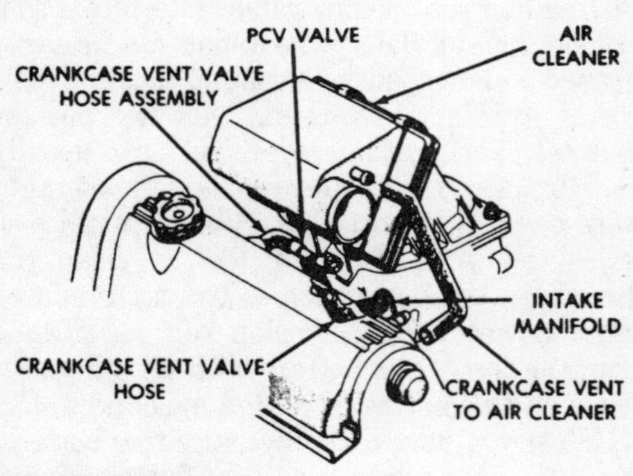

2.5L PCV system

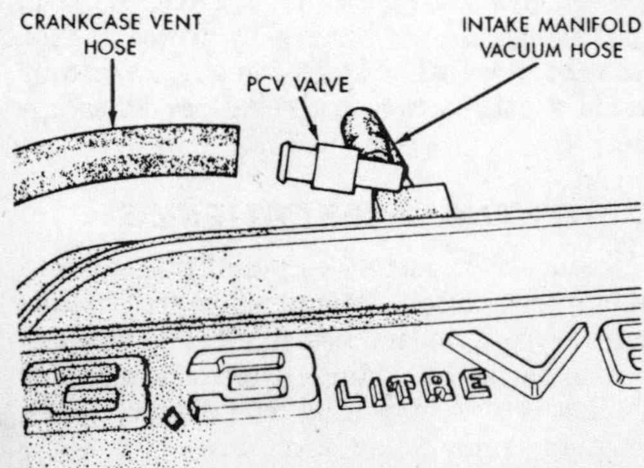

PCV system – 3.3L engine

2.6L Engine

Intake manifold vacuum draws air from the air cleaner through the valve cover into the engine, the outside air is mixed with crankcase vapors and piston blow-by and drawn through the PCV valve (located in the top end of the engine cover) and into the intake manifold where it becomes part of the air/fuel mixture. The vapors are burned and expelled with exhaust gases.

TESTING

1. Place the vehicle in Park, or Neutral (if manual transaxle). Set the parking brake and block the wheels.
2. Start the engine and allow to idle until normal operating temperature is reached.
3. With the engine idling, remove the PCV valve, with hose attached, from its rubber molded connector.
4. When the PCV valve is free of its mounting, a hissing noise will be heard and a strong vacuum felt when a finger is placed over the valve inlet. When the engine is turned off, the valve should rattle when shaken. If the valve is not operating properly it must be replaced.

REMOVAL AND INSTALLATION

1. With the engine off, clean PCV valve area with a suitable solvent.
2. Remove the PCV valve from the mounting grommet on the top cover (2.6L, 2.5L, 3.0L and 3.3L) or from the vent module (2.2L) engines. Disconnect the hose from the valve.
3. Examine the vacuum hose and replace if the hose is cracked, broken or dried out. Always check the vent hose for clogging. If clogged, replace or clean as necessary.
4. Install a new PCV valve into the hose and install into mounting grommet.

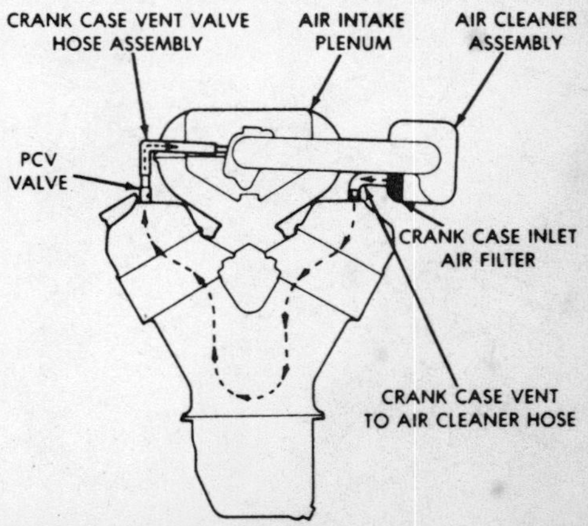

3.0L PCV system

Crankcase Vent Filter

All engines, except the 3.3L, are equipped with a crankcase vent filter which is used to filter the outside air before it enters the PCV system. The filter is located in the air cleaner housing on 2.6L and 2.5L, or in the vent module on 2.2L engines. The filter is located inside the filter element box on 3.0L engines. Replacement should be performed every 52,000 miles.

VENT FILTER SERVICE

1. On models equipped with the 2.2L engine, remove the PCV valve from the vent module and remove the vent module from the engine cover. Wash the module thoroughly in kerosene or safe solvent.
2. Lubricate or wet the filter with SAE 30 weight oil. Reinstall the module, PCV valve and hose.
3. On models equipped with the 2.5L and 2.6L engine, remove the vent filter from the air cleaner housing. Replace with a new element. Wet the new element slightly with SAE 30 weight oil before installation.
4. Models equipped with the 3.0L engine, remove the filter from the filter element box. Renew filter.

Evaporative Charcoal Canister

All vehicles are equipped with a sealed, maintenance free charcoal canister, located in the wheel well area of the engine compartment. Fuel vapors, from the carburetor float chamber and from the gas tank, are temporarily held in the canister until they can be drawn into the intake manifold and burned in the engine.

SERVICING

Periodic inspection of the vent hoses is required. Replace any hoses that are cracked, torn or become hard. Use only fuel resistant hose if replacement becomes necessary.

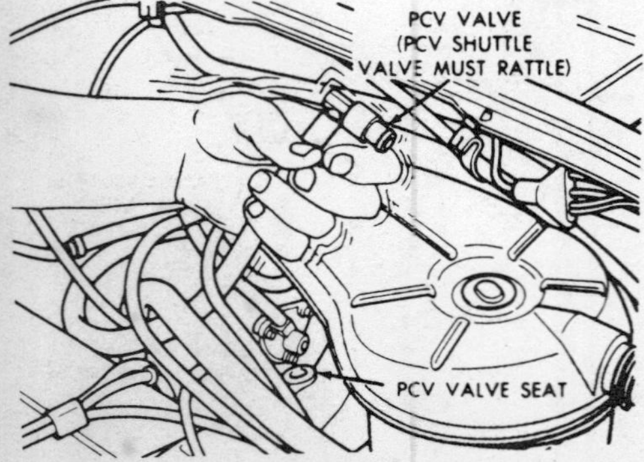

To be considered serviceable, the PCV valve must rattle when shaken

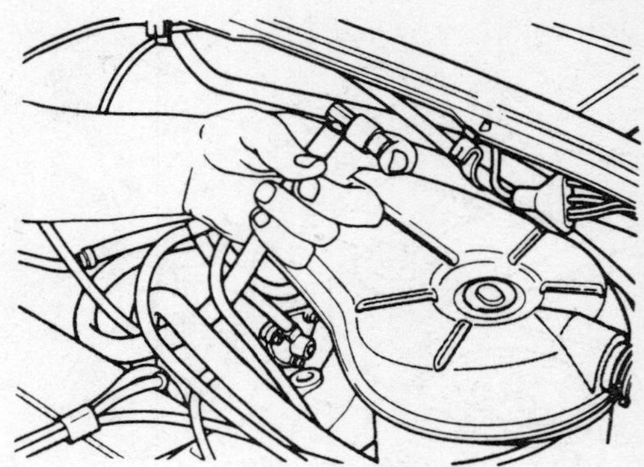

Checking for vacuum at PCV valve

Battery

Loose, dirty, or corroded battery terminals are a major cause of "no-start." Every 3 months or so, remove the battery terminals and clean them, giving them a light coating of petroleum jelly when you are finished. This will help to retard corrosion.

Check the battery cables for signs of wear or chafing and replace any cable or terminal that looks marginal. Battery terminals can be easily cleaned and inexpensive terminal cleaning tools are an excellent investment that will pay for themselves many times over. They can usually be purchased from any well-equipped auto store or parts department. Side terminal batteries require a different tool to clean the threads in the battery case. The accumulated white powder and corrosion can be cleaned from the top of the battery with an old toothbrush and a solution of baking soda and water.

Unless you have a maintenance-free battery, check the electrolyte level (see Battery under Fluid Level Checks) and check the specific gravity of each cell. Be sure that the vent holes in each cell cap are not blocked by grease or dirt. The vent holes allow hydrogen gas, formed by the chemical reaction in the battery, to escape safely.

MAINTENANCE FREE BATTERIES

All models are factory equipped with a maintenance free battery. Maintenance free batteries are as the name implies, totally free of maintenance as far as adding water is concerned. The battery is generally completely sealed except for some small vent holes that allow gases, produced in the battery, to escape. Battery terminal and cable end connector maintenance is required. Also, the cables should be

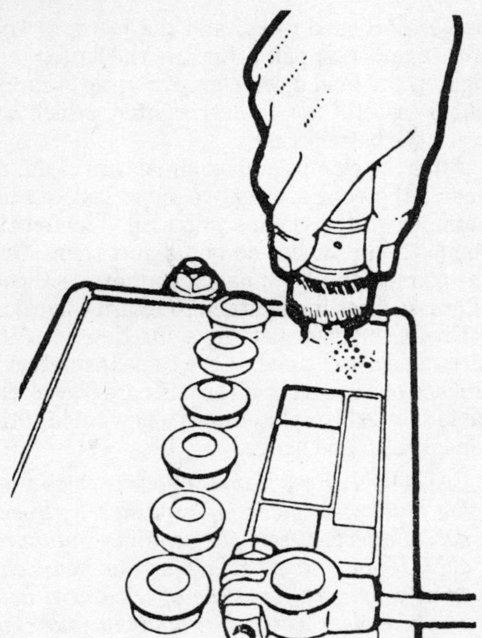

Clean the battery posts with a wire brush; or the special tool shown

disconnected, and the terminals and clamps cleaned at least once a year.

The factory installed battery contains a visual test indicator which signals when an adequate charge level exists. The test indicator is a built-in hydrometer that is equipped with a sight glass and is permanently installed in the battery cover. The sight glass indicator will show green when the battery has from a 75% to full charge. The glass will appear dark if the battery needs recharging and show yellow when replacement may be needed.

CAUTION: *Batteries contain electrolyte, a mixture of sulphuric acid and distilled water. The use of adequate eye protection, and a suitable pair of rubber gloves is strongly recommended when working with batteries. In any event, if battery acid comes in contact with the skin or eyes, flush the affected area with plenty of clear water, and seek medical attention.*

REPLACEMENT BATTERIES EXCEPT MAINTENANCE FREE

If a replacement battery of the non-maintenance free type has been installed in your vehicle, be sure to check the fluid level at least once a month. During warm weather or during periods of extended service, more frequent checking is necessary.

The fluid level can be checked through the case on translucent polypropylene batteries. The cell caps must be removed on other styles. The fluid (electrolyte) level should be kept filled

The battery is equipped with a built in test indicator

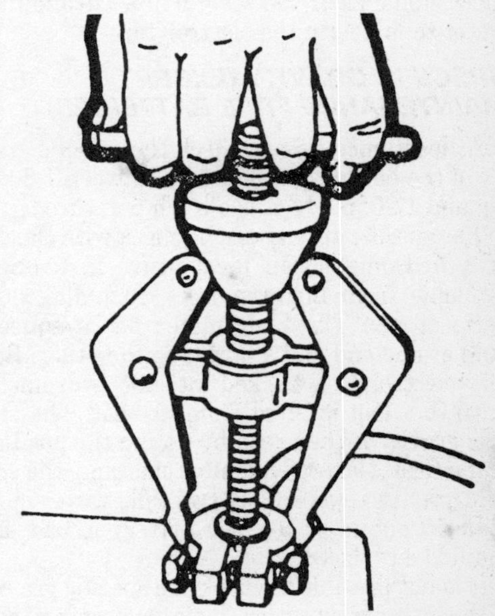

Special pullers are available to remove cable clamps

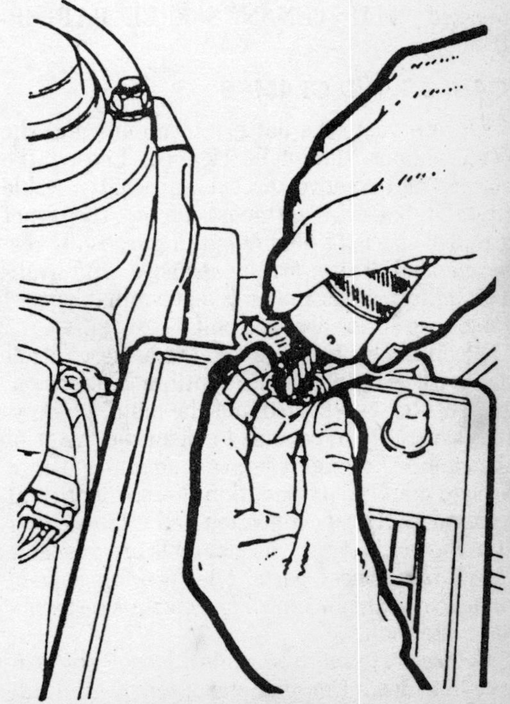

Clean the inside of the clamps with a wire brush; or the special tool

to the split ring inside each cell filler opening, or to the line marked or molded on the outside of the battery case.

If the fluid level is low, add water (distilled water only) through the top openings until the correct level is reached. Each cell is separated and must be checked and filled individually.

If water is added in freezing weather, the vehicle should be driven several miles to allow the water to mix with the electrolyte.

SPECIFIC GRAVITY (EXCEPT MAINTENANCE FREE BATTERIES)

At least once a year, check the specific gravity of the battery. It should be between 1.20 in. Hg and 1.26 in. Hg at room temperature.

The specific gravity can be check with the use of a hydrometer, an inexpensive instrument available from many sources, including auto parts stores. The hydrometer has a squeeze bulb at one end and a nozzle at the other. Battery electrolyte is sucked into the hydrometer until the float is lifted from its seat. The specific gravity is then read by noting the position of the float. Generally, if after charging, the specific gravity between any two cells varies more than 50 points (0.50), the battery is bad and should be replaced.

It is not possible to check the specific gravity in this manner on sealed (maintenance free) batteries. Instead, the indicator built into the top of the case must be relied on to display any signs of battery deterioration. Refer to section marked "MAINTENANCE FREE BATTERIES".

CABLES AND CLAMPS

Once a year, the battery terminals and the cable clamps should be cleaned. Loosen the clamps and remove the cables, negative cable first. On batteries with posts on top, the use of a puller specially made for the purpose is recommended. These are inexpensive, and available in auto parts stores. Side terminal battery cables are secured with a bolt.

Clean the cable lamps and the battery terminal with a wire brush, until all corrosion, grease, etc., is removed and the metal is shiny. It is especially important to clean the inside of the clamp thoroughly, since a small deposit of foreign material or oxidation there will prevent a sound electrical connection and inhibit either starting or charging. Special tools are available for cleaning these parts, one type for conventional batteries and another type for side terminal batteries.

Before installing the cables, loosen the battery hold down clamp or strap, remove the battery and check the battery tray. Clear it of any debris, and check it for soundness. Rust should be wire brushed away, and the metal given a coat of anti-rust paint. Replace the battery and tighten the hold down clamp or strap securely, but be careful not to over tighten, which will crack the battery case.

After the clamps and terminals are clean, reinstall the cables, negative cable last; do not hammer on the clamps to install. Tighten the clamps securely, but do not distort them. Give the clamps and terminals a thin external coat of grease after installation, to retard corrosion.

Check the cables at the same time that the terminals are cleaned. If the cable insulation is cracked or broken, or if the ends are frayed, the cable should be replaced with a new cable of the same length and gauge.

CAUTION: *Keep flame or sparks away from the battery; it gives off explosive hydrogen gas. Battery electrolyte contains sulphuric acid. If you should splash any on your skin or in your eyes, flush the affected area with plenty of clear water. If it lands in your eyes, get medical help immediately.*

Drive Belts

INSPECTION

Check the condition and tension of all drive belts every 12,000 miles, or at least once a year. Loose drive belts can lead to poor engine cooling and diminished alternator, power steering pump, air conditioning compressor, or emission air pump output. A belt that is too tight places a strain on the bearings in the driven component.

Replace any drive belt that is glazed, worn, cracked, or stretched to the point where correct adjustment tension is impossible. If two belts are used to drive a component, always replace both belts when replacement is necessary. After installing a new belt, run the engine for ten minutes, shut off the engine and recheck the belt tension. Readjust if necessary.

CHECKING DRIVE BELT ADJUSTMENT

Two popular methods of checking drive belt adjustment are; the Belt Tension Gauge Method and the Belt Deflection Method. The former requires a special gauge and the latter requires a straight edge and scale or just a good eye for measurement. The deflection method will be used in the following belt replacement instructions. A rule of thumb for checking belt tension by the deflection method is to determine the midpoint between two pulleys of the drive belt and press down at that point with moderate thumb pressure. The belt should deflect to the measurement indicated in the following installation procedures. Adjustment is

HOW TO SPOT WORN V-BELTS

V-Belts are vital to efficient engine operation—they drive the fan, water pump and other accessories. They require little maintenance (occasional tightening) but they will not last forever. Slipping or failure of the V-belt will lead to overheating. If your V-belt looks like any of these, it should be replaced.

Cracking or weathering

This belt has deep cracks, which cause it to flex. Too much flexing leads to heat build-up and premature failure. These cracks can be caused by using the belt on a pulley that is too small. Notched belts are available for small diameter pulleys.

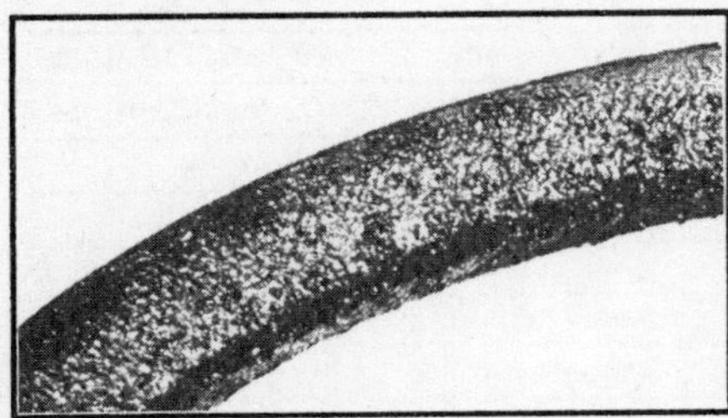
Softening (grease and oil)

Oil and grease on a belt can cause the belt's rubber compounds to soften and separate from the reinforcing cords that hold the belt together. The belt will first slip, then finally fail altogether.

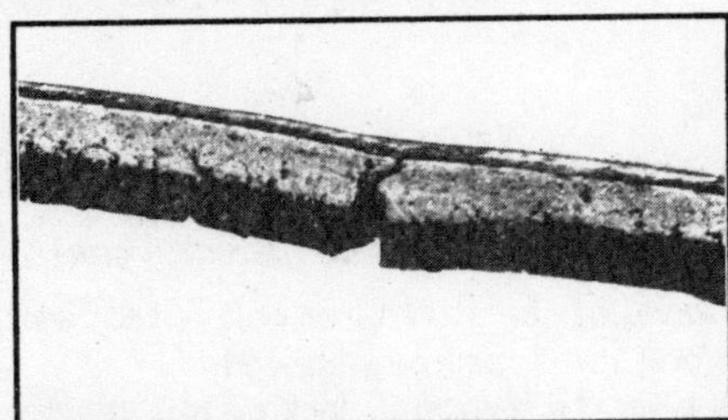
Glazing

Glazing is caused by a belt that is slipping. A slipping belt can cause a run-down battery, erratic power steering, overheating or poor accessory performance. The more the belt slips, the more glazing will be built up on the surface of the belt. The more the belt is glazed, the more it will slip. If the glazing is light, tighten the belt.

Worn cover

The cover of this belt is worn off and is peeling away. The reinforcing cords will begin to wear and the belt will shortly break. When the belt cover wears in spots or has a rough jagged appearance, check the pulley grooves for roughness.

Separation

This belt is on the verge of breaking and leaving you stranded. The layers of the belt are separating and the reinforcing cords are exposed. It's just a matter of time before it breaks completely.

2.2L Engine BELTS—TENSION CHART and REMOVE/INSTALL-ADJUST

Accessory Drive Belt		Gauge	Deflection	Torque
Air Conditioning Compressor	New	105 lb.	8mm (5/16 in.)	54 N·m (40 ft. lbs.)
	Used	80 lb.	9mm (7/16 in.)	41 N·m (30 ft. lbs.)
Air Pump	New	—	5mm (3/16 in.)	61 N·m (45 ft. lbs.)
	Used	—	6mm (1/4 in.)	47 N·m (35 ft. lbs.)
Alternator/Water Pump "V" Belt and Poly "V"	New	115 lb.	3mm (1/8 in.)	149 N·m (110 ft. lbs.)
	Used	80 lb.	6mm (1/4 in.)	108 N·m (80 ft. lbs.)
Power Steering Pump	New	105 lb.	6mm (1/4 in.)	102 N·m (75 ft. lbs.)
	Used	80 lb.	11mm (7/16 in.)	75 N·m (55 ft. lbs.)

2.6L Engine BELTS-TENSION CHART and REMOVE/INSTALL-ADJUST

Accessory Drive Belt		Gauge	Deflection	Torque
Power Steering Pump	New	95 lb.	6mm (¼ in.)	149 N·m (110 ft. lbs.)
	Used	80 lb	9mm (⅜ in.)	102 N·m (75 ft. lbs.)
Alternator	New	115 lb	4mm (3/16 in.)	—
	Used	80 lb.	6mm (¼ in.)	—
Alternator/Air Conditioning Compressor	New	115 lb.	6mm (¼ in.)	—
	Used	80 lb.	8mm (5/16 in.)	—
Water Pump	New	—	8mm (5/16 in.)	—
	Used	—	9mm (⅜ in.)	—

necessary if the belt is either too loose or too tight.

REMOVAL AND INSTALLATION

NOTE: *Jack up the front of the vehicle, support on jack stands and remove the lower splash shield if access is hampered due to space limitations when changing drive belts.*

A/C Compressor Drive Belt 2.2L Engine

1. Loosen the idler pulley bracket pivot screw and the locking screw.
2. Remove the belt and install replacement.
3. Using a breaker bar and socket apply torque to welded nut provided on the mounted bracket to obtain proper tension.
4. Tighten the locking screw first, followed by pivot screw. Tighten to 40 ft. lbs.

Alternator Drive Belt 2.2L Engines (Chrysler Type)

If removal of the alternator belt is required, the A/C belt must first be removed.

1. Loosen the pivot nut, locking screw, and the adjusting screw.
2. Remove the belt and install replacement.
3. Adjust to specification by tightening the adjusting screw.
4. Tighten the locking screw to 25 ft. lbs.
5. Tighten the pivot nut to 30 ft. lbs.

Alternator Belt 2.2L Engines (Bosch Type)

If removal of the alternator belt is required, the A/C belt must first be removed.

1. Loosen the pivot nut, locking nut, and adjusting screw.
2. Remove the belt and install replacement.
3. Adjust to specification by tightening the adjusting screw.
4. Tighten the locking nut to 25 ft. lbs.
5. Tighten the pivot nut to 30 ft. lbs.

Power Steering Belt 2.2L Engine

If removal of the power steering belt is required, the A/C and alternator belts must first be removed.

1. Loosen the locking screw, and pivot screw.
2. Remove the belt and install replacement.
3. Install a 1/2 in. breaker bar into the pump bracket slot, apply pressure with the breaker bar and adjust the belt to specification.
4. Tighten the locking screw first, then the pivot screw. Tighten to 40 ft. lbs.

Air Pump — 2.2L Engine

NOTE: *When servicing the air pump, use the square holes provided in the pulley to pre-*

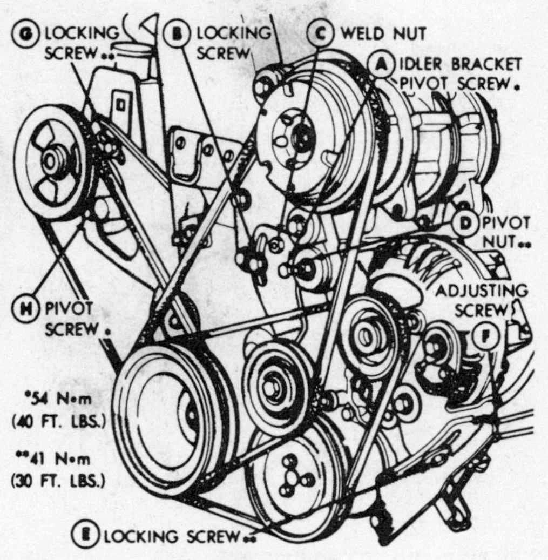

2.2L drive belt adjusting points

vent camshaft rotation.

1. Remove the nuts and bolts retaining the drive pulley cover.
2. Remove the locking bolt and pivot bolt from the pump bracket, and remove the pump.
3. Remove the belt and install replacement.
4. Position the pump, and install the locking bolt and pivot bolt finger tight.
5. Install a 1/2 in. breaker bar into the bracket assembly (block the drive pulley to prevent camshaft rotation), and adjust the belt to specification.
6. Tighten locking bolt and pivot bolt to 25 ft. lbs.

Air Conditioning Compressor – 2.5L Engine

1. Loosen the idler bracket pivot screw and the locking screws to replace, or adjust belt.
2. Remove the belt and install replacement.
3. Adjust the belt to specification by applying torque to weld nut on the idler bracket.
4. Tighten locking screw first, followed by the pivot screw. Tighten to 40 ft. lbs.

Alternator Belt 2.5L Engine

If replacement of the alternator belt is required, the A/C drive belt must first be removed.

1. Loosen the pivot nut, locking nut, and adjusting screw.
2. Remove the belt and install replacement.
3. Adjust the belt to specification by tightening the adjusting screw.
4. Tighten the locking nut to 25 ft. lbs.

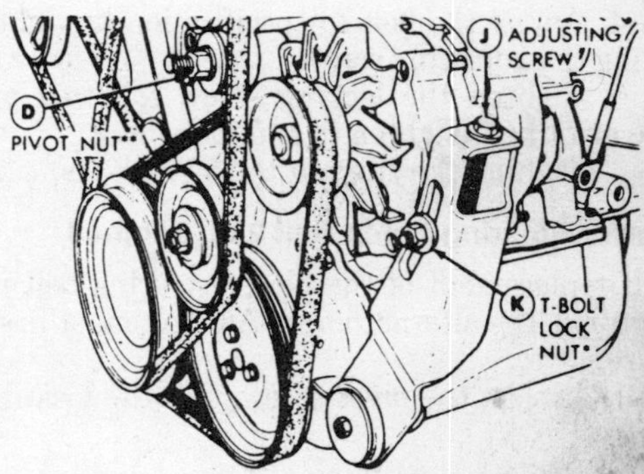

2.2L alternator belt adjustment

2.5L Engine BELTS—TENSION CHART and REMOVE/INSTALL-ADJUST

Accessory Drive Belt		Gauge	Deflection	Torque
Air Conditioning	New	105 lb.	8mm (5/16 in.)	54 N·m (40 ft. lbs.)
Compressor	Used	80 lb.	11mm (7/16 in.)	41 N·m (30 ft. lbs.)
Alternator/Water Pump	New	115 lb.	3mm (1/8 in.)	149 N·m (110 ft. lbs.)
Poly "V"	Used	80 lb.	6mm (1/4 in.)	108 N·m (80 ft. lbs.)
Power Steering Pump	New	105 lb.	6mm (1/4 in.)	102 N·m (75 ft. lbs.)
	Used	80 lb.	11mm (7/16 in.)	75 N·m (55 ft. lbs.)

3.0L Engine BELTS—TENSION CHART and REMOVE/INSTALL-ADJUST

Accessory Drive Belt		Gauge	Deflection
Air Conditioning	New	125 lb.	8mm (5/16 in.)
Compressor	Used	80 lb.	8mm (5/16 in.)
Alternator/Water Pump/	New	Dynamic Tensioner	
Power Steering Pump	Used		

5. Tighten the pivot nut to 30 ft. lbs.

Power Steering Pump 2.5L Engines

If replacement of the power steering belt is required, the A/C and alternator belts must first be remove.

1. Loosen the locking screw and pivot screw to replace, or adjust the belt.
2. Remove the belt and install replacement.
3. Using a 1/2 in. breaker bar positioned in adjusting bracket slot, adjust the belt to specification.
4. Tighten the locking screw followed by the pivot screw. Tighten to 40 ft. lbs.

Alternator/Air Conditioning Compressor 2.6L Engine

1. Loosen the locking screw, jam nut, and pivot nut.
2. Loosen the adjusting screw.
3. Remove the belt and install replacement.
4. Adjust the belt to specification by tightening the adjusting screw.
5. Tighten the locking screw followed by the pivot nut. Tighten to 195 inch lbs.
6. Tighten the jam nut to 250 inch lbs.

Power Steering Pump Belt 2.6L Engines

If replacement of the power steering belt is required, the alternator and A/C belt must first be remove.

1. Loosen the pivot screw, and the locking screw.
2. Remove the timing pickup.
3. Remove the belt and install replacement.
4. Install a 1/2 in. breaker bar in the adjusting bracket slot, torque to specification.
5. Tighten the locking screw, followed by the pivot screw. Tighten to 40 ft. lbs.
6. Install the timing pick-up, and tighten to 160 inch lbs.

Air Conditioning Compressor Belt 3.0L Engine

1. Loosen the locknut on the idler pulley.
2. Loosen the adjusting screw on the idler pulley.
3. Remove the belt and install replacement.
4. Adjust to specification by tightening the adjusting screw.
5. Tighten the idler pulley locknut to 40 ft. lbs.

Alternator/Power Steering Pump Belt 3.0L Engine

If replacement of the alternator/power steering drive belt is required, the air conditioner drive belt must first be removed.

1. Install a 1/2 in. breaker bar into the tensioner slot, and rotate counterclockwise to release belt tension.
2. Remove the belt and install replacement.
3. Proper belt tension is maintain by the dynamic tensioner.

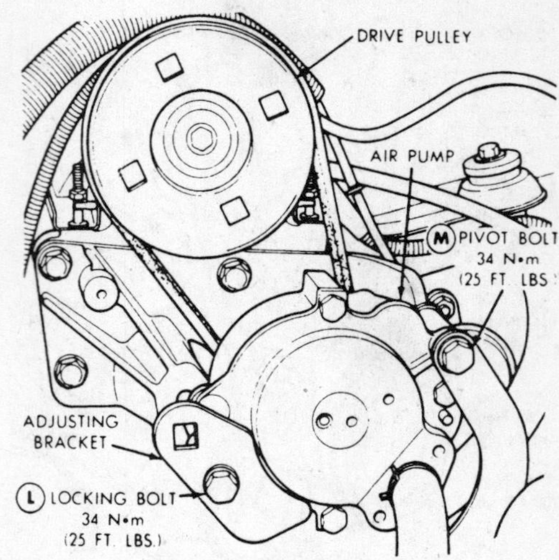

2.2L air pump belt adjustment

Accessory Drive Belt – 3.3L Engine

All of the belt driven accessories on the 3.3L engine are driven by a single serpentine belt. The belt tension is maintained by am automatic tensioner.

1. Raise the front of the vehicle and safely support it with jack stands.
2. Remove the right front splash shield.
3. Install a 1/2 in. breaker bar into the tensioner slot, and rotate counterclockwise to release belt tension.
4. Remove the belt and install replacement.
5. Proper belt tension is maintain by the dynamic tensioner.

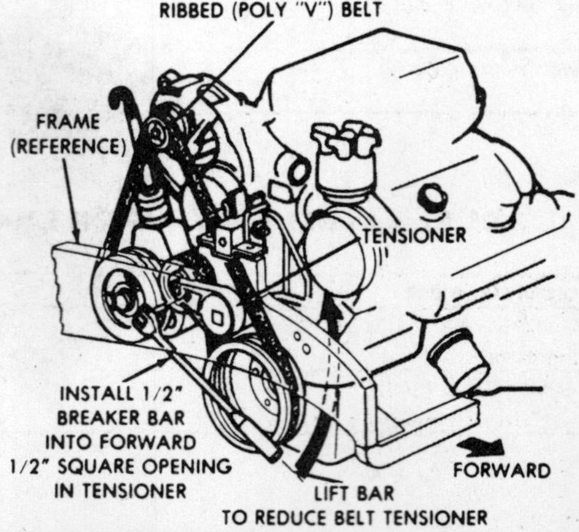

3.0L belt tensioner release

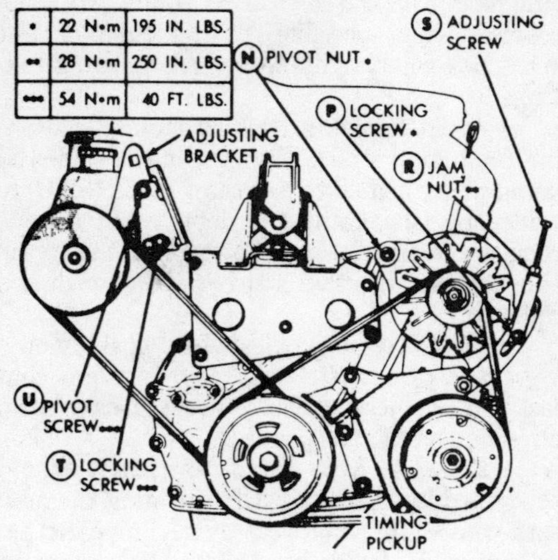

2.6L drive belt adjustment points

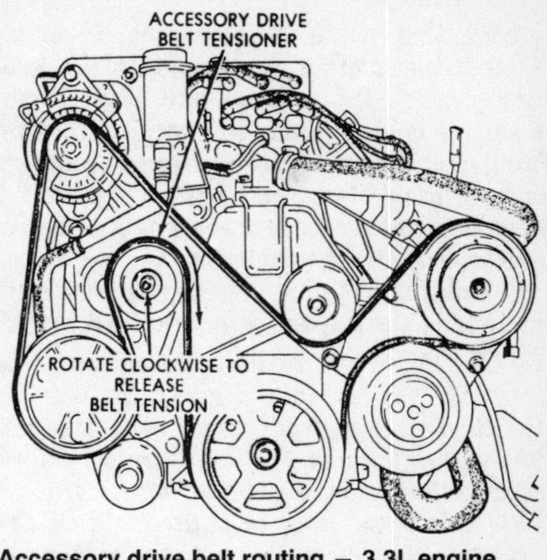

Accessory drive belt routing – 3.3L engine

ALTERNATOR

ADJUSTING SCREW

POWER STEERING PUMP

TENSIONER

LOCK NUT 57 N.m (40 FT. LBS.)

AIR CONDITIONING COMPRESSOR

3.0L drive belt adjustment points

6. Install the right front splash shield. Lower the front of the vehicle.

Hoses

On models equipped with an electric cooling fan, disconnect the negative battery cable, or fan motor wiring harness connector before replacing any radiator/heater hose. The fan may come on, under certain circumstances, even though the ignition is Off.

REMOVAL AND INSTALLATION

Inspect the condition of the radiator and heater hoses periodically. Early spring and at

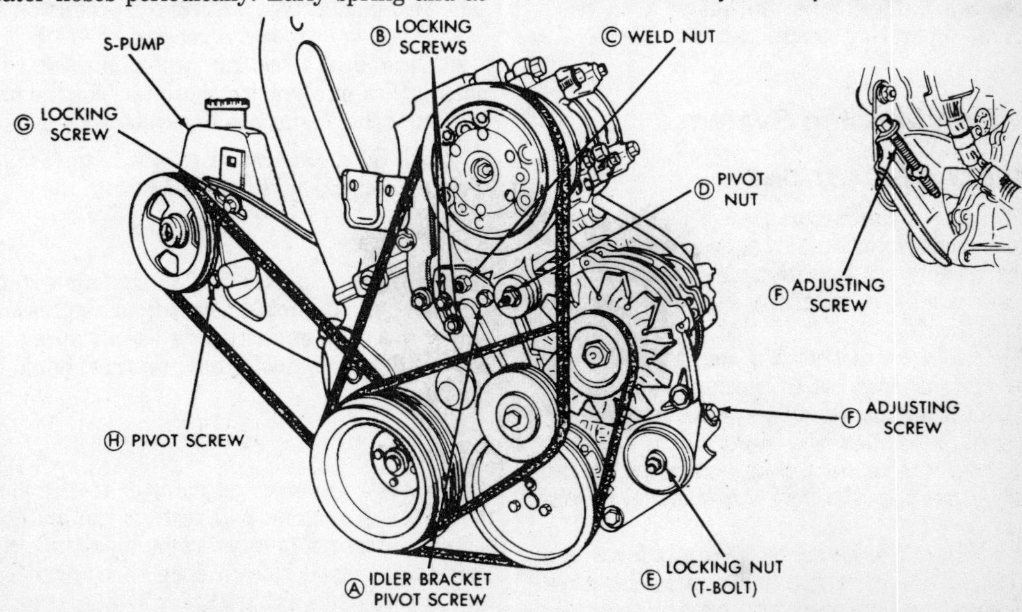

2.5L drive belt adjustment points

the beginning of the fall or winter, when you are performing other maintenance, are good times. Make sure the engine and cooling system are cold. Visually inspect for cracking, rotting or collapsed hoses, replace as necessary. Run your hand along the length of the hose. If a weak or swollen spot is noted when squeezing the hose wall, replace the hose.

1. Drain the cooling system into a suitable container (if the coolant is to be reused).

CAUTION: *When draining the coolant, keep in mind that cats and dogs are attracted by the ethylene glycol antifreeze, and are quite likely to drink any that is left in an uncovered container or in puddles on the ground. This will prove fatal in sufficient quantity. Always drain the coolant into a sealable container. Coolant should be reused unless it is contaminated or several years old.*

2. Loosen the hose clamps at each end of the hose that requires replacement.
3. Twist, pull and slide the hose off the radiator, water pump, thermostat or heater connection.
4. Clean the hose mounting connections. Position the hose clamps on the new hose.
5. Coat the connection surfaces with a water resistant sealer and slide the hose into position. Make sure the hose clamps are located beyond the raised bead of the connector (if equipped) and centered in the clamping area of the connection.
6. Tighten the clamps to 20–30 inch lbs. Do not over tighten.
7. Fill the cooling system.
8. Start the engine and allow it to reach normal operating temperature. Check for leaks.

Air Conditioning System

SAFETY PRECAUTIONS

Because of the importance of the necessary safety precautions that must be exercised when working with air conditioning systems and R-12 refrigerant, a list of the safety precautions are outlined.

- Avoid contact with a charged refrigeration system, even when working on another part of the air conditioning system or vehicle. If a heavy tool comes into contact with a section of copper tubing or a heat exchanger, it can easily cause the relatively soft material to rupture.
- When it is necessary to apply force to a fitting which contains refrigerant, as when checking that all system couplings are securely tightened, use a wrench on both parts of the fitting involved, if possible. This will avoid putting torque on the refrigerant tubing. (It is advisable, when possible, to use tube or line wrenches when tightening these flare nut fittings.)
- Avoid applying heat to any refrigerant line or storage vessel. Charging may be aided by using water heated to less than 125°F (52°C) to warm the refrigerant container. Never allow a refrigerant storage container to sit out in the sun, or near any other source of heat, such as a radiator.
- Always wear goggles when working on a system to protect the eyes. If refrigerant contacts the eye, it is advisable in all cases to see a physician as soon as possible.
- Frostbite from liquid refrigerant should be treated by first gradually warming the area with cool water, and then gently applying petroleum jelly. A physician should be consulted.
- Always keep refrigerant can fittings capped when not in use. Avoid sudden shock to the can which might occur from dropping it, or from banging a heavy tool against it. Never carry a refrigerant can in the passenger compartment of a van.
- Always completely discharge the system before painting the vehicle (if the paint is to be baked on), or before welding anywhere near the refrigerant lines.

PREVENTIVE MAINTENANCE CHECKS

Antifreeze

In order to prevent heater core freeze-up during A/C operation, it is necessary to maintain permanent type antifreeze protection of +15°F (–9°C) or lower. A reading of –15°F (–26°C) is ideal since this protection also supplies sufficient corrosion inhibitors for the protection of the engine cooling system.

WARNING: *Do not use antifreeze longer than specified by the manufacturer.*

Radiator Cap

For efficient operation of an cooling system, the radiator cap should have a holding pressure which meets manufacturer's specifications. A cap which fails to hold these pressure should be replaced.

Condenser

Any obstruction of or damage to the condenser configuration will restrict the air flow which is essential to its efficient operation. It is therefore, a good rule to keep this unit clean and in proper physical shape.

NOTE: *Bug screens are regarded as obstructions.*

HOW TO SPOT BAD HOSES

Both the upper and lower radiator hoses are called upon to perform difficult jobs in an inhospitable enviorment. They are subject to nearly 18 psi at under hood temperature often over 280F., and must circulate an hour-3 good reasons to have good hoses.

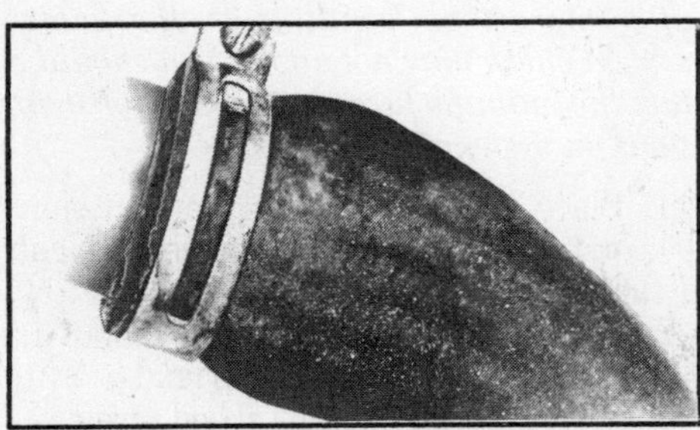

Swollen hose

A good test for any hose is to feel it for soft or spongy spots. Frequently these will appear as swollen areas of the hose. The most likely cause is oil soaking. This hose could burst at any time, when hot or under pressure.

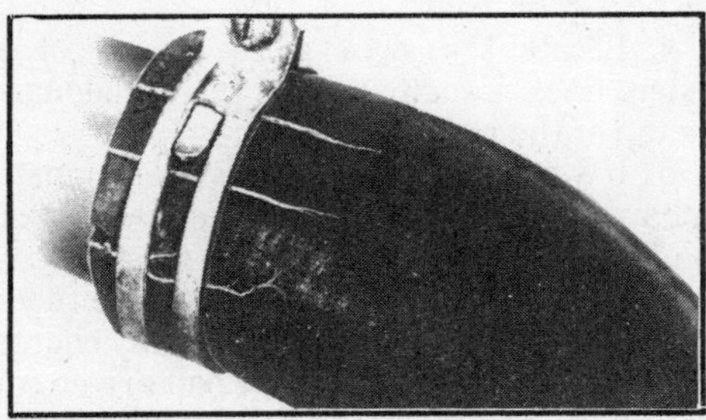

Cracked hose

Cracked hoses can usually be seen but feel the hoses to be sure they have not hardened; a prime cause of cracking. This hose has cracked down to the reinforcing cords and could split at any of the cracks.

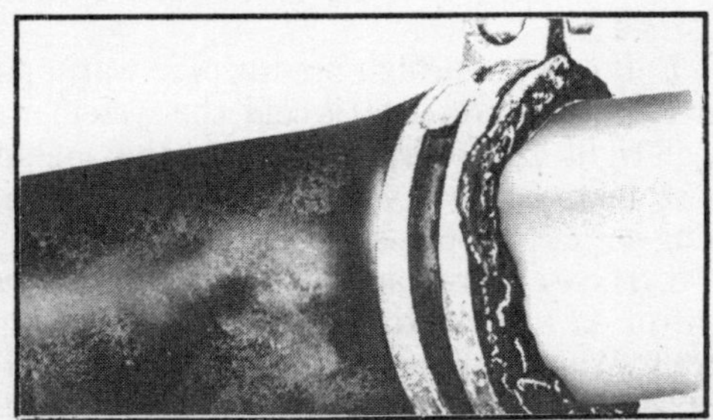

Frayed hose end (due to weak clamp)

Weakened clamps frequently are the cause of hose and cooling system failure. The connection between the pipe and hose has deteriorated enough to allow coolant to escape when the engine is hot.

Debris in cooling system

Debris, rust and scale in the cooling system can cause the inside of a hose to weaken. This can usually be felt on the outside of the hose as soft or thinner areas.

Condensation Drain Tube

This single molded drain tube expels the condensation, which accumulates on the bottom of the evaporator housing, into the engine compartment.

If this tube is obstructed, the air conditioning performance can be restricted and condensation buildup can spill over onto the vehicle's floor.

TEST GAUGES

Most of the service work performed in air conditioning requires the use of a set of two gauges, one for the high (head) pressure side of the system, the other for the low (suction) side.

The low side gauge records both pressure and vacuum. Vacuum readings are calibrated from 0 to 30 inches Hg and the pressure graduations read from 0 to no less than 150 psi.

The high side gauge measures pressure from 0 to at least 300 psi.

With the gauge set you can perform the following procedures:

1. Test high and low side pressures.
2. Charge the system with refrigerant.

All gauge sets must have 3 hoses, with 1 being for center manifold outlet.

WARNING: *When connecting the hoses to the compressor service ports, the manifold gauge valves must be closed!*

The suction gauge valve is opened to provide a passage between the suction gauge and the center manifold outlet. The discharge gauge valve is opened to provide a passage between the discharge pressure gauge and the center manifold outlet.

SYSTEM INSPECTION

CAUTION: *The compressed refrigerant used in the air conditioning system expands into the atmosphere at a temperature of –21.7°F (–30°C) or lower. This will freeze any surface, including your eyes, that it contacts. In addition, the refrigerant decomposes into a poisonous gas in the presence of a flame. Do not open or disconnect any part of the air conditioning system.*

Sight Glass Check

You can safely make a few simple checks to determine if your air conditioning system needs service. The tests work best if the temperature is warm (about 70°F [21°C]).

NOTE: *If your vehicle is equipped with an after market air conditioner, the following system check may not apply. You should contact the manufacturer of the unit for instructions on systems checks.*

1. Place the automatic transmission in Park or the manual transmission in Neutral. Set the parking brake.
2. Run the engine at a fast idle (about 1,500 Rpm) either with the help of a friend or by temporarily readjusting the idle speed screw.
3. Set the controls for maximum cold with the blower on High.
4. Locate the sight glass in one of the system lines. Usually it is on the left alongside the top of the radiator.
5. If you see bubbles, the system must be recharged. Very likely there is a leak at some point.
6. If there are no bubbles, there is either no refrigerant at all or the system is fully charged. Feel the two hoses going to the belt driven compressor. If they are both at the same temperature, the system is empty and must be recharged.
7. If one hose (high pressure) is warm and the other (low pressure) is cold, the system may be all right. However, you are probably making these tests because you think there is something wrong, so proceed to the next step.
8. Have an assistant in the van turn the fan control on and off to operate the compressor clutch. Watch the sight glass.
9. If bubbles appear when the clutch is dis-

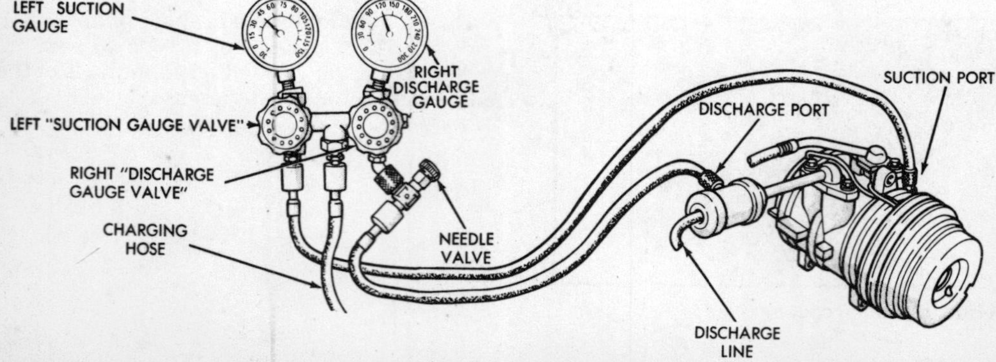

Manifold gauge set connections

engaged and disappear when it is engaged, the system is properly charged.

10. If the refrigerant takes more than 45 seconds to bubble when the clutch is disengaged, the system is overcharged. This usually causes poor cooling at low speeds.

WARNING: *If it is determined that the system has a leak, it should be corrected as soon as possible. Leaks may allow moisture to enter and cause a very expensive rust problem. Exercise the air conditioner for a few minutes, every two weeks or so, during the cold months. This avoids the possibility of the compressor seals drying out from lack of lubrication.*

TESTING THE SYSTEM

1. Connect a gauge set.
2. Close (clockwise) both gauge set valves.
3. Park the van in the shade, at least 5 feet from any walls. Start the engine, set the parking brake, place the transmission in **N** and establish an idle of 1100–1300 Rpm.
4. Run the air conditioning system for full cooling, in the **MAX** or **COLD** mode.
5. The low pressure gauge should read 5–20 psi; the high pressure gauge should indicate 120–180 psi.

WARNING: *These pressures are the norm for an ambient temperature of 70–80°F (21–27°C). Higher air temperatures along with high humidity will cause higher system pressures. At idle speed and an ambient temperature of 110°F (43°C), the high pressure reading can exceed 300 psi. Under these extreme conditions, you can keep the pressures down by directing a large electric floor fan through the condenser.*

LEAK TESTING

Some leak tests can be performed with a soapy water solution. There must be at least a 1/2 lb. charge in the system for a leak to be detected. The most extensive leak tests are performed with either a Halide flame type leak tester or the more preferable electronic leak tester.

In either case, the equipment is expensive, and, the use of a Halide detector can be **extremely** hazardous!

CHARGING THE SYSTEM

CAUTION: *Never open the high pressure side with a can of refrigerant connected to the system! Opening the high pressure side will over pressurize the can, causing it to explode!*

1. Connect the gauge set.
2. Close (clockwise) both gauge set valves.
3. Connect the center hose to the refrigerant can opener valve.
4. Make sure the can opener valve is closed, that is, the needle is raised, and connect the valve to the can. Open the valve, puncturing the can with the needle.
5. Loosen the center hose fitting at the pressure gauge, allowing refrigerant to purge the hose of air. When the air is bled, tighten the fitting.

CAUTION: *If the low pressure gauge set hose is not connected to the accumulator/drier, keep the can in an upright position!*

6. Start the engine and move the air conditioning controls to the low blower position.
7. Open the low side gauge set valve and the can valve.
8. Allow refrigerant to be drawn into the system. Adjust the valve so that charging pressure does not exceed 50 psi.

NOTE: *The low pressure (cycling) cut-out switch will prevent the compressor clutch from energizing until refrigerant is added to the system. If the clutch does not engage, replace the switch.*

9. When no more refrigerant is drawn into the system, start the engine and run it at about 1,300 Rpm. Turn on the system and operate it at the full high position. The compressor will operate and pull refrigerant gas into the system.

NOTE: *To help speed the process, the can may be placed, upright, in a pan of warm water, not exceeding 125°F (52°C).*

10. If more than one can of refrigerant is needed, close the can valve and gauge set low side valve when the can is empty and connect a new can to the opener. Repeat the charging process until the sight glass indicates a full charge. The frost line on the outside of the can will indicate what portion of the can has been used.

CAUTION: *Never allow the high pressure side reading to exceed 240 psi.*

11. When the charging process has been completed, close the gauge set valve and can valve. Remove the jumper wire and reconnect the cycling clutch wire. Run the system for at least five minutes to allow it to normalize. Low pressure side reading should be 4–25 psi; high pressure reading should be 120–210 psi at an ambient temperature of 70–90°F (21–32°C).
12. Loosen both service hoses at the gauges to allow any refrigerant to escape. Remove the gauge set and install the dust caps on the service valves.

NOTE: *Multi-can dispensers are available which allow a simultaneous hook-up of up to four 1 lb. cans of R-12.*

Windshield Wipers

Wiper blades exposed to the weather over a period of time tend to lose their wiping effectiveness. Clean the wiping surface of the blade with a sponge and a mild solution of water and detergent. If the blades continue to smear, they should be replaced with either a new blade or refill.

BLADE REFILLS

1. Turn the wiper switch to the ON position. Turn the ignition switch ON. When the blades reach a convenient place on the windshield, turn the ignition switch to OFF, thus stopping the blades.
2. Lift the wiper arm to raise the blade from the windshield.
3. Insert a small blade type tool into the release slot of wiper blade and pry slightly upward.
4. Pinch lock on each end of blade and slide wiping element out of blade.
5. Install a new wiping element into blade. Make certain each release points are properly locked in position.
6. Install blade on wiper arm.

Most Anco® styles uses a release button that is pushed down to allow the refill to slide out of the yoke jaws. The new refill slides in and locks in place. Some Trico® refills are removed by locating where the metal backing strip of the refill is wider. Insert a small screwdriver blade between the frame and metal backing strip. Press down to release the refill from the retaining tab.

The Trico® style is unlocked at one end by squeezing 2 metal tabs, and the refill is slide out of the frame jaws. When the new refill is installed, the tabs will click into place, locking the refill.

The polycarbonate type is held in place by a locking lever that is pushed downward out of the groove in the arm to free the refill. When the new refill is installed, it will lock in place automatically.

The Tridon® refill has a plastic backing strip with a notch about 1 in. (25mm) from the end. Hold the blade (frame) on a hard surface so that the frame is tightly bowed. Grip the tip of the backing strip and pull up while twisting counter clockwise. The backing strip will snap out of the retaining tab. Do this for the remaining tabs until the refill is free of the arm. The length of these refills is molded into the end and they should be replaced with identical types.

No matter which type of refill you use, be sure that all of the frame claws engage the refill. Before operating the wiper, be sure that no part of the metal frame is contacting the windshield.

Tires and Wheels

TIRE ROTATION

Tires installed on the front or rear of any vehicle are subjected to different loads, breaking, or steering functions. Because of these conditions, tires develop uneven wear patterns. Rotating the tires every 6000 miles or so will result in increased thread life. Use the correct pattern for tire rotation. Refer to Tire Rotation Patterns chart.

Most automotive experts are in agreement that radial tires are better all around performers, giving prolonged wear and better handling. An added benefit which you should consider when purchasing tires is that radials have less rolling resistance and can give up to a 10% increase in fuel economy over a bias-ply tire.

TIRE INFLATION

Check the air pressure in your vehicle's tires every few weeks. Make sure that the tires are cool. Air pressure increases with higher temperature, and will indicate false reading. A decal located on the glove box door or side door frame will tell you the proper tire pressure for the standard equipment tires.

NOTE: *Never exceed the maximum inflation pressure on the side of the tire. Also never mixed tires of different size or construction (Belted vs Bias-ply, or Radial vs Belted etc.).*

It pays to buy a tire pressure gauge to keep in your vehicle, since those of service stations are often inaccurate or broken. While you are checking the tire pressure, take a look at the tread. The tread should be wearing evenly across the tire. Excessive wear in the center of the tread indicates over inflation. Excessive wear on the outer edges indicates under inflation. An irreg-

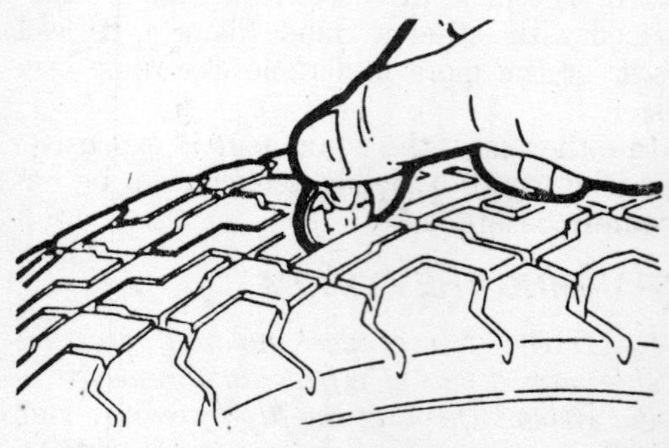

A penny works as well as anything when checking tread depth; when the top of Lincoln's head is visible, it's time for new tires

ular wear pattern is usually a sign of incorrect front wheel alignment or wheel balance.

A front end that is out of alignment will usually pull to one side when the steering wheel is released. Conditions which relate to front end alignment are associated by tire wear patterns. Tire treads being worn on one side more than the other, or wear on the tread edges may be noticeable. Front wheels which are incorrectly balance, is usually accompanied by high speed vibration.

TIRE ROTATION

It is recommended that you have the tires rotated and the balance checked every 6,000 miles. There is no way to give a tire rotation diagram for every combination of tires and vehicles, but the accompanying diagrams are a general rule to follow. Radial tires should not be cross-switched; they last longer if their direction of rotation is not changed. Truck tires and some high-performance tires sometimes have directional tread, indicated by arrows on the sidewalls; the arrow shows the direction of rotation. They will wear very rapidly if reversed. Studded snow tires will lose their studs if their direction of rotation is reversed.

NOTE: *Mark the wheel position or direction of rotation on radial tires or studded snow tires before removing them.*

If your van is equipped with tires having different load ratings on the front and the rear, the tires should not be rotated front to rear. Rotating these tires could affect tire life (the tires with the lower rating will wear faster, and could become overloaded), and upset the handling of the van.

When installing the wheels on the vehicle, tighten the lug nuts in a criss-cross pattern. Lug nuts should be torqued to 85 ft. lbs.

TIRE USAGE

The tires on your van were selected to provide the best all around performance for normal operation when inflated as specified. Oversize tires will not increase the maximum carrying capacity of the vehicle, although they will provide an extra margin of tread life. Be sure to check overall height before using larger size tires which may cause interference with suspension components or wheel wells. When replacing conventional tire sizes with other tire size designations, be sure to check the manufacturer's recommendations. Interchangeability is not always possible because of differences in load ratings, tire dimensions, wheel well clearances, and rim size. Also due to differences in handling characteristics, 70 Series and 60 Series tires should be used only in pairs on the same axle; radial tires should be used only in sets of four.

NOTE: *Many states have vehicle height restrictions; some states prohibit the lifting of vehicles beyond their design limits.*

The wheels must be the correct width for the tire. Tire dealers have charts of tire and rim compatibility. A mismatch can cause sloppy handling and rapid tread wear. The old rule of thumb is that the tread width should match the rim width (inside bead to inside bead) within 1 in. (25mm). For radial tires, the rim width should be 80% or less of the tire (not tread) width.

The height (mounted diameter) of the new tires can greatly change speedometer accuracy, engine speed at a given road speed, fuel mileage, acceleration, and ground clearance. Tire manufacturers furnish full measurement specifications. Speedometer drive gears are available for correction.

NOTE: *Dimensions of tires marked the same size may vary significantly, even among tires from the same manufacturer.*

The spare tire should be of the same size, construction and design as the tires on the vehicle. It's not a good idea to carry a spare of a different construction.

TIRE DESIGN

For maximum satisfaction, tires should be used in sets of five. Mixing or different types (radial, bias-belted, fiberglass belted) should be avoided. Conventional bias tires are constructed so that the cords run bead-to-bead at an angle. Alternate plies run at an opposite angle. This type of construction gives rigidity to both tread and sidewall. Bias-belted tires are similar in construction to conventional bias ply tires. Belts run at an angle and also at a 90° angle to the bead, as in the radial tire. Tread life is improved considerably over the conventional bias tire. The radial tire differs in construction, but instead of the carcass plies running at an angle of 90° to each other, they run at an angle of 90° to the bead. This gives the tread a great deal of rigidity and the sidewall a great deal of flexibility and accounts for the characteristic bulge associated with radial tires.

When radial tires are used, tire sizes and wheel diameters should be selected to maintain ground clearance and tire load capacity equivalent to the minimum specified tire. Radial tires should always be used in sets of five, but in an emergency, radial tires can be used with caution on the rear axle only. If this is done, both tires on the rear should be of radial design.

WARNING: *Radial tires should never be used on only the front axle!*

FLUIDS AND LUBRICANTS

Fuel Recommendations

Chrysler recommends that unleaded fuel only with a minimum octane rating of at least 87 be used in your vehicle, if equipped with a catalytic converter. The use of unleaded gasoline is required in order to meet all emission regulations, and provide excellent fuel economy.

Fuels of the same octane rating have varying anti-knock qualities. Thus, if your engine knocks or pings, try switching brands of gasoline before trying a more expansive higher octane fuel.

Your engine's fuel requirements can change with time, due to carbon buildup which changes the compression ratio. If switching brands or grades of gas doesn't work, check the ignition timing. If it is necessary to retard timing from specifications, don't change it more than about 4°. Retarded timing will reduce power output and fuel mileage and increase engine temperature.

Engine

OIL RECOMMENDATIONS

A high quality heavy-duty detergent oil having the proper viscosity for prevailing temperatures and an SG/CC service rating should be used in your vehicle. A high quality SG/CC rated oil should be used for heavy duty service or turbocharged equipped engines. The SG/CC and SG/CD rated oil contain sufficient chemical additives to provide maximum engine protection.

Pick an oil with the viscosity that matches the anticipated temperature of the region your vehicle will be operated in before the next oil change. A chart is provided to help you with your selection. Choose the oil viscosity for the lowest expected temperature and you will be assured of easy cold weather starting and sufficient engine protection.

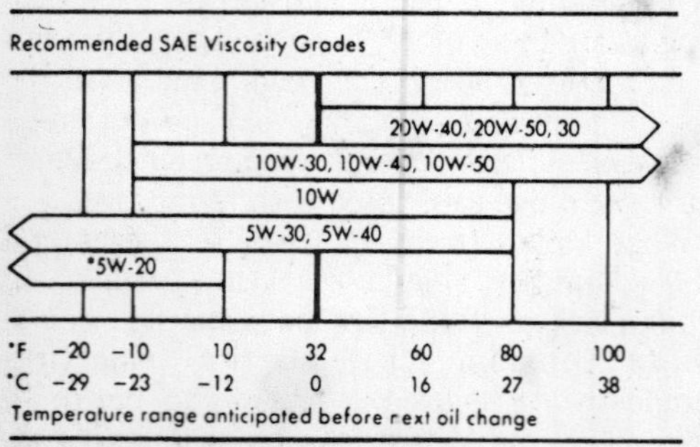

Oil viscosity chart

OIL LEVEL CHECK

The engine oil level is checked with the dipstick which is located on the radiator side of the engine.

NOTE: *The oil should be checked before the engine is started or five minutes after the engine has shut off. This gives the oil time to drain back to the oil pan and prevents an inaccurate oil level reading.*

Remove the dipstick from the tube, wipe it clean, and insert it back into the tube. Remove it again and observe the oil level. It should be maintained within the full range on the dipstick.

NOTE: *Do not overfill the crankcase. This will cause oil aeration and loss of oil pressure.*

OIL AND FILTER CHANGE

The recommended mileage figures for oil and filter changes are 7,500 miles or 12 months whichever comes first, assuming normal driving conditions. If your vehicle is being used under dusty conditions, frequent trailer pulling, excessive idling, or stop and go driving, it is recommended to change the oil and filter at 3,000 miles.

NOTE: *Improper disposing of all lubricants (engine, trans., and differential), can result in environmental problems. Contact your local dealerships of service stations for advice on proper disposal.*

Always drain the oil after the engine has been running long enough to bring it to operating temperature. Hot oil will flow easier and more contaminants will be removed along with the oil than if it were drained cold.

Chrysler recommends changing both the oil and filter during the first oil change and the filter every other oil change thereafter. For the small price of an oil filter, it's cheap insurance

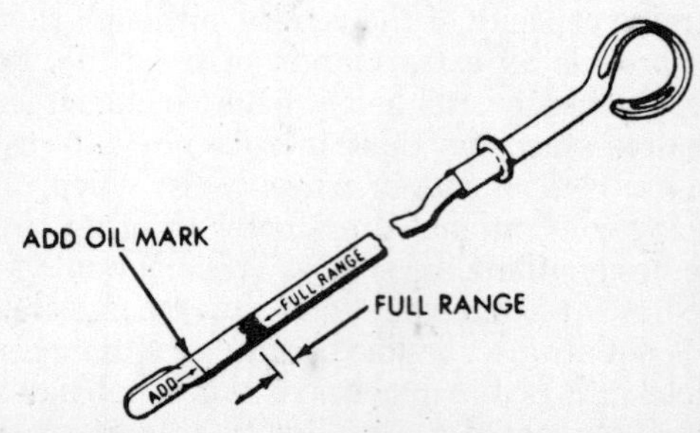

Oil dipstick

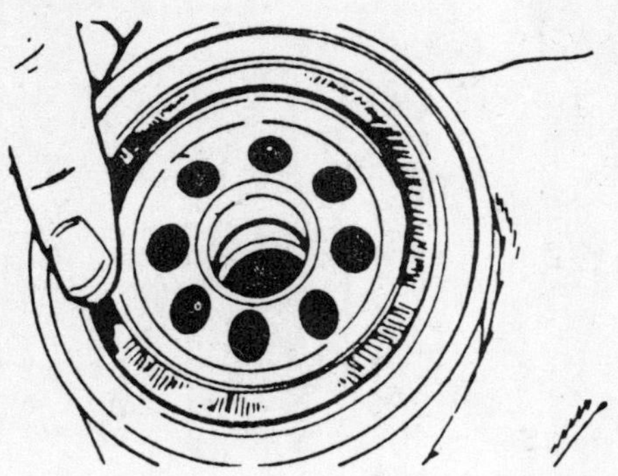

Lubricate the gasket on the new filter with clean engine oil. A dry gasket may not make as good a seal and could allow the filter to leak

to replace the filter at every oil change. One of the larger filter manufacturers points out in its advertisements that not changing the filter leaves one quart of dirty oil in the engine. This claim is true and should be kept in mind when changing your oil.

1. Run the engine until it reaches normal operating temperature.
2. Jack up the front of the vehicle and support on jack stands, remove the shield if it will cause interference.
3. Slide a drain pan of at least 6 quarts capacity under the oil pan.

CAUTION: *The engine oil will be hot! Keep your arms, face and hands away from the oil as it drains out!*

4. Loosen the drain plug. It is located in the lowest point of the oil pan. Turn the plug out by hand. By keeping an inward pressure on the plug as you unscrew it, oil won't escape past the threads and you can remove it without being burned by hot oil.
5. Allow the oil to drain completely and then install the drain plug. Don't over tighten the plug, it will result in stripped threads.
6. Using a strap wrench, remove the oil filter. Keep in mind that it's holding about one quart of dirty, hot oil.

CAUTION: *The EPA warns that prolonged contact with used engine oil may cause a number of skin disorders, including cancer! You should make every effort to minimize your exposure to used engine oil. Protective gloves should be worn when changing the oil. Wash your hands and any other exposed skin areas as soon as possible after exposure to used engine oil. Soap and water, or waterless hand cleaner should be used.*

7. Empty the old filter into the drain pan and dispose of the filter.
8. Using a clean rag, wipe off the filter adapter on the engine block. Be sure that the rag doesn't leave any lint which could clog an oil passage.
9. Coat the rubber gasket on the filter with fresh oil. Spin it onto the engine by hand; when the gasket touches the adapter surface give it another $1/2$–$3/4$ turn. No more, or you'll squash the gasket and it will leak.
10. Refill the engine with the correct amount of fresh oil. See the Capacities Chart.
11. Run the engine at idle for approximately one minute. Shut the engine off. Wait a few minutes and recheck oil level. Add oil, as necessary to bring the level up to **Fill**.
12. Shut the engine off and lower the vehicle.

CAUTION: *You now have 4 quarts of used engine oil. Please store this oil in a secure container, such as a 1 gallon windshield washer fluid bottle. Locate a service station or garage which accepts used oil for recycling and dispose of it there.*

Transaxle

FLUID RECOMMENDATION

Both the manual (4- or 5-speed) and the automatic transaxles use Dexron®II type automatic transmission fluid. Under normal operating conditions, periodic fluid change is not required. If the vehicle is operating under severe operating conditions change the fluid, or fluid and filter every 15,000 miles.

FLUID LEVEL CHECK

Manual Transaxle

1. The fluid level is checked by removing the fill plug on the end cover side of the transaxle.
2. The fluid level should be between the top of the fill hole and a point not more than $1/8$ in. (3mm) below the bottom of the fill hole.
3. Add Dexron®II type fluid as necessary. Secure the fill plug.

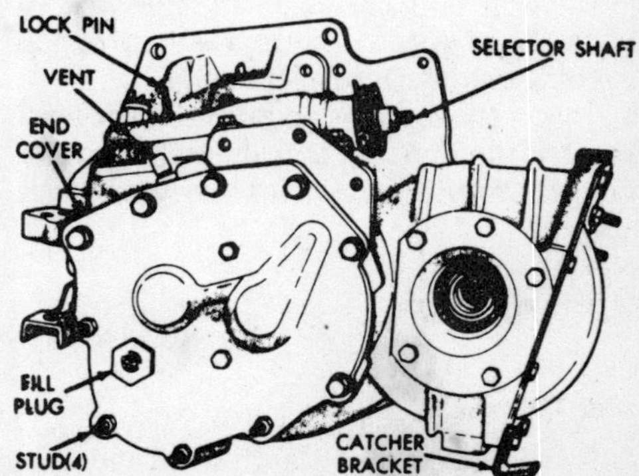

Manual transaxle filler plug location

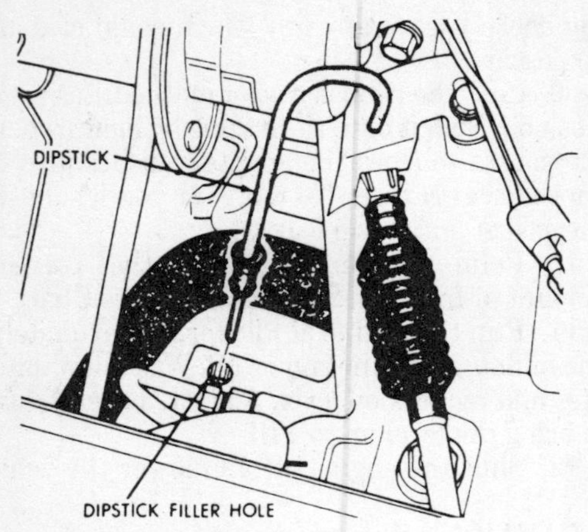

Automatic transaxle dipstick location

Automatic Transaxle

NOTE: *When checking the fluid level, the condition of the fluid should be observed. If severe darkening of the fluid and a strong odor are present, the fluid, filter and pan gasket (RTV sealant) should be changed and the bands readjusted.*

1. Make sure the vehicle is on level ground. The engine should be at normal operating temperatures, if possible.
2. Apply the parking brake, start the engine and move the gear selector through each position. Place the selector in the PARK position.
3. Remove the dipstick and determine if the fluid is warm or hot.
4. Wipe the dipstick clean and reinsert until fully seated. Remove and take note of the fluid level.
5. If the fluid is hot, the reading should be in the crosshatched area marked **HOT**.
6. If the fluid is warm, the fluid level should be in the area marked **WARM**.
7. If the fluid level checks low, add enough fluid (Dexron®II®) through the fill tube, to bring the level within the marks appropriate for average temperature of the fluid.
8. Insert the dipstick and recheck the level. Make sure the dipstick is fully seated to prevent dirt from entering. Do not overfill the transaxle.

DRAIN AND REFILL

Manual Transaxle

1. Raise and support the front of the vehicle on jack stands.
2. Remove the undercarriage splash shield

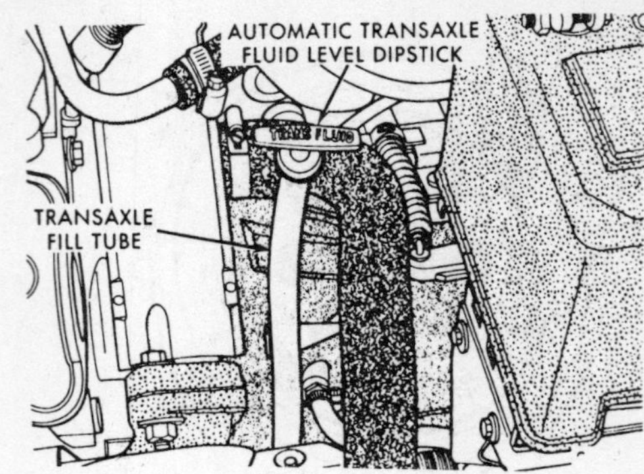

Automatic transaxle fill tube – A604 Ultradrive transaxle

if it will interfere with fluid change.

3. Position a drain pan underneath the end of the transaxle and remove the differential end cover where the fill plug is located. Loosen the bolt slightly and pry the lower edge away so that the fluid will drain.
4. Remove the cover completely. Clean the gasket surfaces of the case and cover. Clean the magnet located on the cover.
5. Use an even $^{1}/_{8}$ in. (3mm) bead of RTV sealant to form a gasket on the cover and reinstall on the transaxle case.
6. Refill the transaxle with Dexron®II.

Automatic Transaxle

NOTE: *Band readjustment and filter replacement are recommended when the fluid is changed. Refer to "Drive Train" for required procedures.*

Differential

The transmission and differential share a common housing. Fluid check and change procedures are covered in the "Drive" Train Chapter.

Power Transfer Unit (PTU)

On models with All Wheel Drive (AWD), a power transfer unit is used that is connected to the transaxle. This unit is separate from the other drive train components.

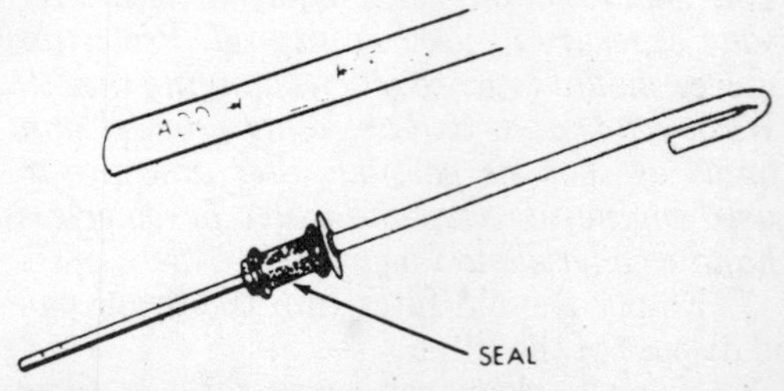

Automatic transaxle dipstick markings

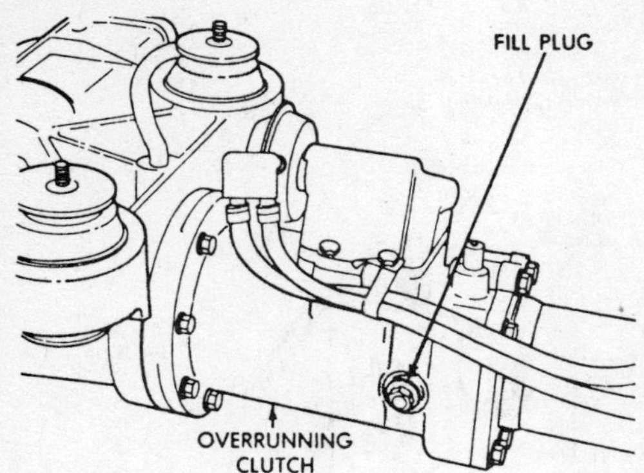

Overrunning clutch fill plug – All Wheel Drive equipped models

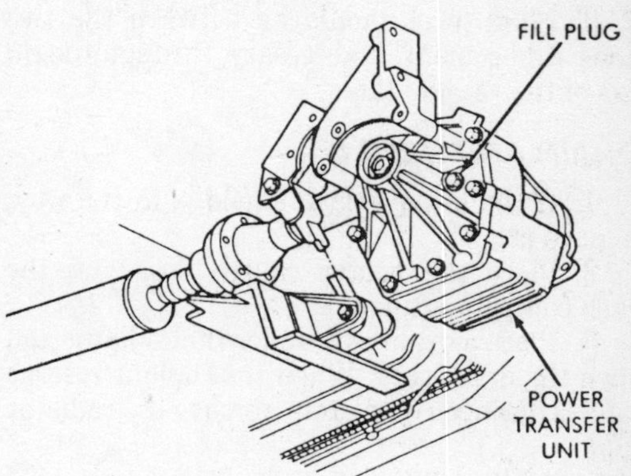

Power Transfer Unit (PTU) – fill plug location

FLUID RECOMMENDATION

Chrysler recommends the use of Mopar® Gear Lube, SAE 85W–90 or equivalent. The correct quantity of oil is 1.22 qts.

DRAIN AND REFILL

The PTU cannot be serviced. If fluid leakage is detected, the unit must be disassembled and the seals replaced.

Drive Line Module

On models with All Wheel Dive (AWD), the rear wheels are driven by shafts from the Drive Line Module. This module serves as the rear drive axle.

As well as containing the rear differential, this module contains a set of overrunning clutches in their own case. This clutch assembly serves to control differences in drive line speed and traction.

FLUID RECOMMENDATION

Drive Line Module

Chrysler recommends the use of Mopar® Gear Lube, SAE 85W–90 or equivalent. The module is full when the fluid level is 1/8 in. (3mm) below the fill plug.

Overrunning Clutch

Chrysler recommends the use of Mopar® ATF type 7176 or equivalent. The oil level should be at the bottom of the oil fill opening.

Cooling System

FLUID RECOMMENDATION

A 50/50 mixture of water and ethylene glycol type antifreeze (containing Alguard or silicate type inhibiter) that is safe for use in aluminum components is recommended. The 50/50 mixture offers protection to –34°F (–37°C). If addition cold weather protection is necessary a concentrate of 65% antifreeze may be used.

LEVEL CHECK

All vehicles are equipped with a transparent coolant reserve container. A minimum and maximum level mark are provided for a quick visual check of the coolant level.

1. Run the engine until normal operating temperature is reached.
2. Open the hood and observe the level of the coolant in the reserve.

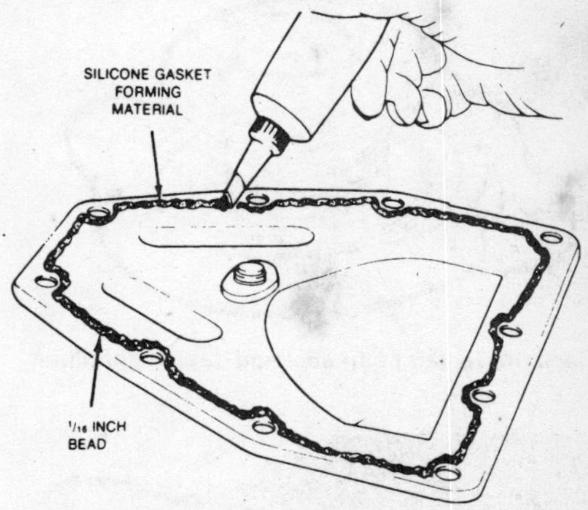

Form a silicone gasket as shown

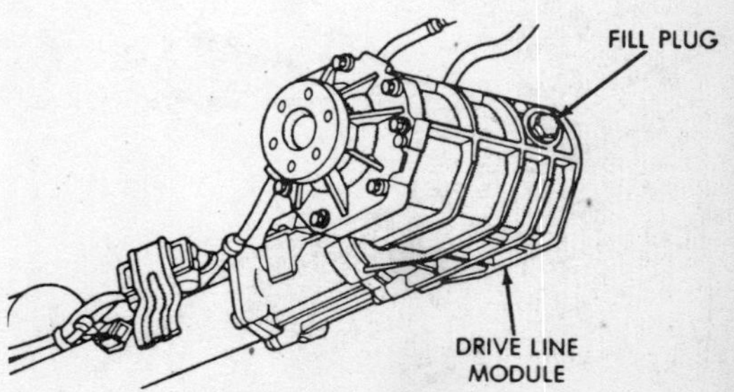

Drive line module fill plug – All Wheel Drive equipped models

3. Fluid level should be between the two lines. Add coolant, if necessary, through the fill cap of the reserve tank.

DRAIN AND REFILL

1. If the lower splash shield is in the way, remove it.
2. Place the heater control lever on the dash control to full on.
3. Place a drain pan under the radiator and open the drain cock. When the coolant reserve tank is drained completely, remove the radiator cap.

CAUTION: *When draining the coolant, keep in mind that cats and dogs are attracted by the ethylene glycol antifreeze, and are quite likely to drink any that is left in an uncovered container or in puddles on the ground. This will prove fatal in sufficient quantity. Always drain the coolant into a sealable container. Coolant should be reused unless it is contaminated or several years old.*

4. If your vehicle is equipped with the 2.2L engine, removal of the vacuum valve (located above the thermostat housing), is necessary to provide air displacement. If your vehicle is equipped with the 2.5L engine, removal of the drain/fill plug (located above the thermostat housing), is necessary to provide air displacement.

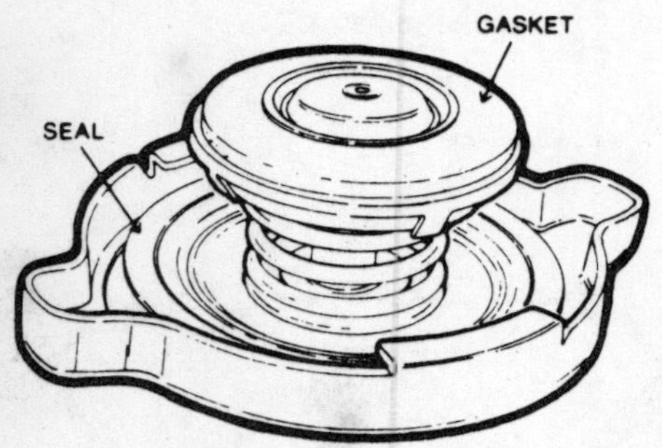

Check the radiator cap seal and gasket condition

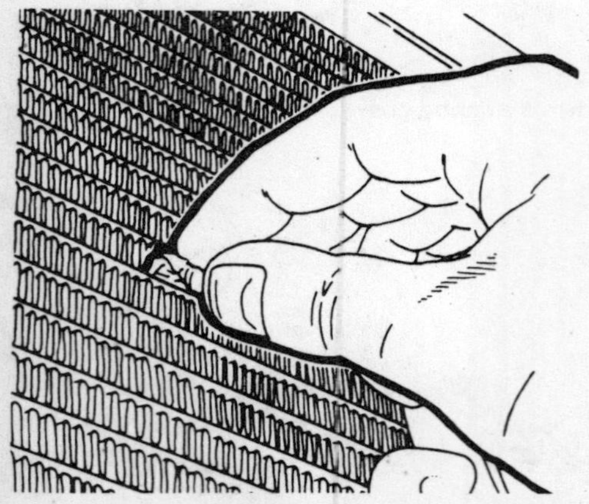
Clean the radiator fins of any debris which impedes air flow

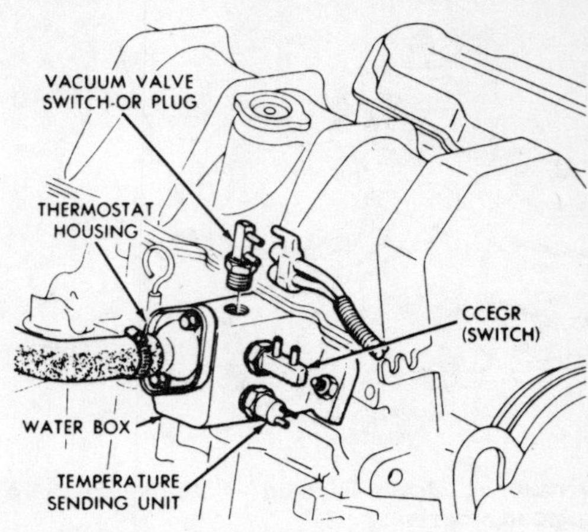

2.2L engine vacuum valve location

5. To remove the vacuum valve, disconnect the hose connector plug, and carefully unscrew the valve using the proper size wrench.
6. After draining the system, refill with water and run the engine until normal operating temperature is reached. (See the following refill procedures). Drain the system again, repeat procedure until the drained water runs clear.
7. Close the radiator drain cock.
8. Fill the system with a 50/50 mixture of ethylene glycol type antifreeze.
9. When the coolant reaches the hole in the water box at thermostat housing (2.2L and 2.5L engines), install the vacuum valve or drain/fill plug to 20 N.m (15 ft. lbs.)
10. Continue filling system until full.
11. Install the radiator cap, start the engine, and run until normal operating temperature is reached. Fill the coolant reserve tank to **Max** mark. Stop engine and allowed to cool.

NOTE: *It may be necessary to warm up and cool down engine several times to remove trapped air. Recheck level in reserve tank, and adjust level if necessary.*

CHECK THE RADIATOR CAP

While you are checking the coolant level, check the radiator cap for a worn or cracked gasket. If the cap doesn't seal properly, fluid will be lost in the form of steam and the engine will overheat. Replace the cap with a new one, if necessary.

CLEAN RADIATOR OF DEBRIS

Periodically clean any debris—leaves, paper, insects, etc.—from the radiator fins. Pick the large pieces off by hand. The smaller pieces can be washed away with water pressure from a hose.

Carefully straighten any bent radiator fins with a pair of needle nose pliers. Be careful – the fins are very soft! Don't wiggle the fins back and forth too much. Straighten them once and try not to move them again.

Master Cylinder

FLUID RECOMMENDATION

Use only a DOT 3 approved brake fluid in your vehicle. Always use fresh fluid when servicing or refilling the brake system.

LEVEL CHECK

The fluid level in both reservoirs of the master cylinder should be maintained at the bottom of the fill split rings visible after removing the covers. Add the necessary fluid to maintain proper level. A drop in the fluid level should be expected as the brake pads and shoes wear. However, if an unusual amount of fluid is required, check for system leaks.

Power Steering Pump

FLUID RECOMMENDATIONS

Power steering fluid such as Mopar Power Steering Fluid (Part Number 4318055) or equivalent should be used. Only petroleum fluids formulated for minimum effect on the rubber hoses should be added. Do not use automatic transmission fluid.

CAUTION: *Check the power steering fluid level with engine off, to avoid injury from moving parts.*

LEVEL CHECK

1. Wipe off the power steering pump reservoir cap with a cloth before removal.
2. A dipstick is built into the cover. Remove the reservoir cover cap and wipe the dipstick with a cloth.

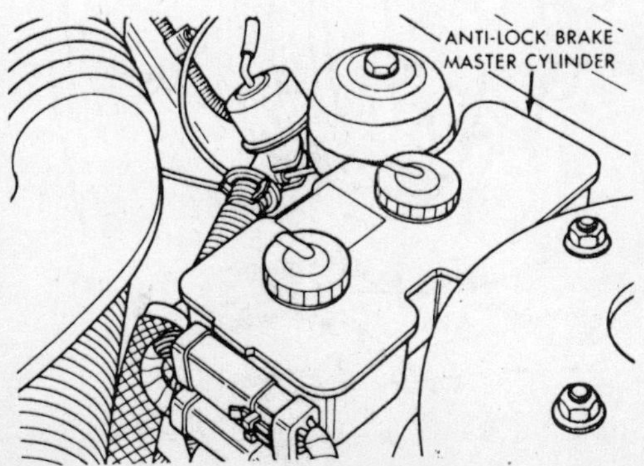

Anti-lock brake system fluid reservoir

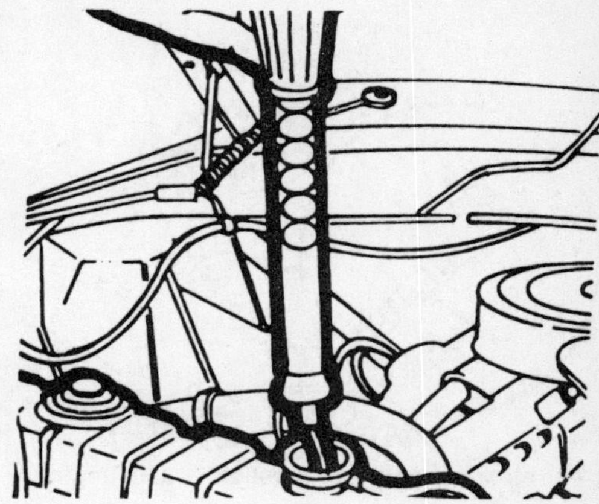

The freezing protection rating can be checked with an antifreeze tester

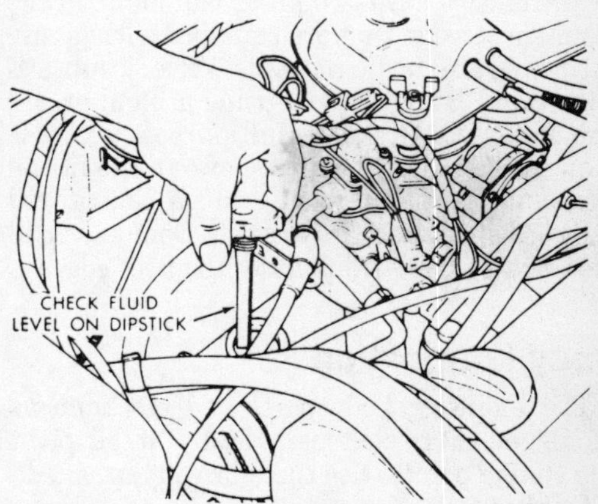

Check the power steering fluid level

3. Reinstall the dipstick and check the level indicated.
4. Add fluid as necessary, but do not overfill.

Steering Gear

NOTE: *The steering gear is lubricated and sealed at the factory, periodic lubrication is not necessary.*

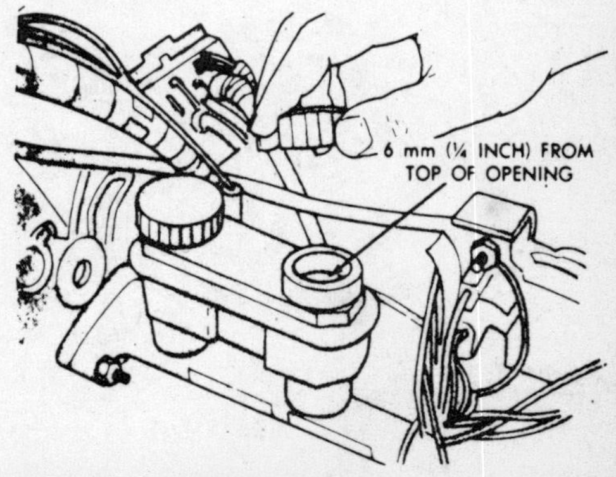

Check the master cylinder fluid level

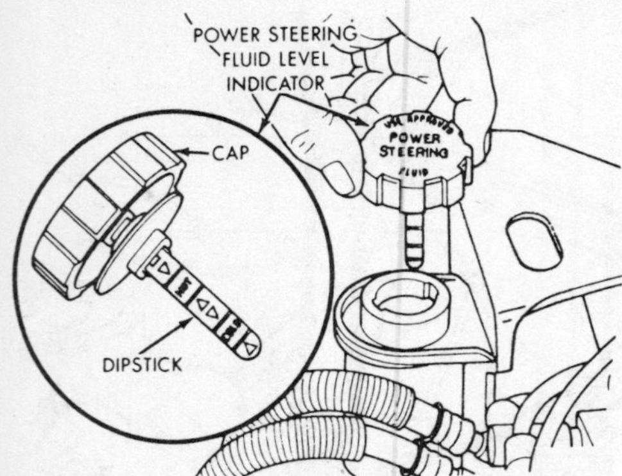

Power steering reservoir dipstick — 3.3L engine

Chassis Lubrication

All vehicles have two lower ball joints in the front suspension that are equipped with grease fittings as are the tie rod ends. Periodic lubrication (every 24,000 miles) using a hand grease gun and NLGI Grade 2, Multipurpose grease is required. Connect the grease gun to the fitting and pump until the boot seal on the tie rod ends or ball joints start to swell. Do not overfill until grease flows from under the boot edges.

Body Lubrication

The following body parts and mechanisms should be lubricated periodically at all pivot and sliding points. Use the lubricant specified;

Engine Oil:

- Door Hinges at pin and pivot contact area.
- Hinges
- Liftgate Hinges
- Sliding Door at center hinge pivot.

White Spray Lube:

- Hood Hinge cam and slide
- Lock cylinders
- Parking Brake Mechanisms
- Window Regulator: remove trim panel

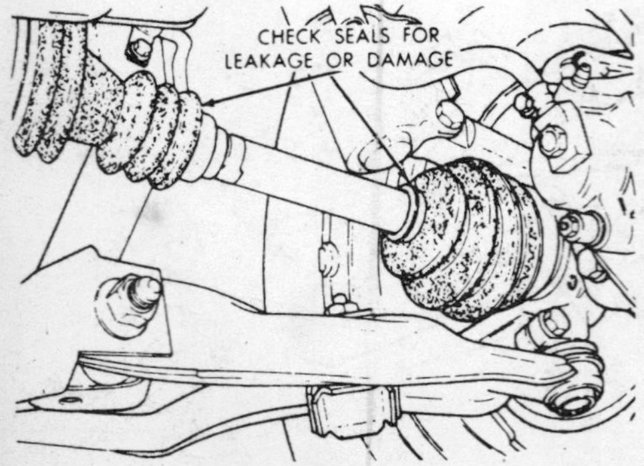

Inspect U-joint seal for leakage

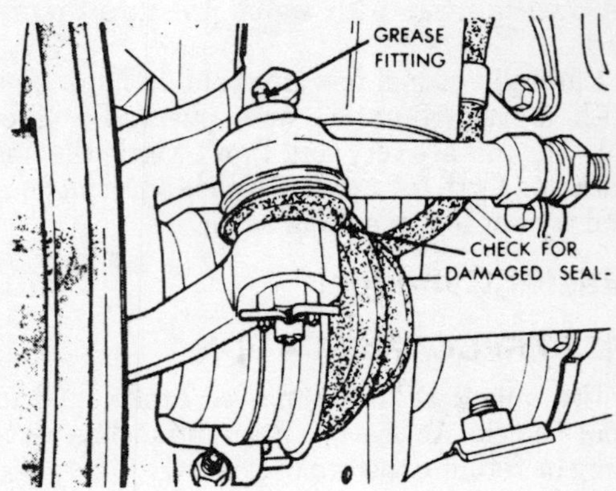

Check the tie rod end ball joint seals

- Liftgate Latches
- Liftgate Prop Pivots
- Ash Tray Slide

Multi-purpose Lubricant (Water Resistant):

- Door Latch, Lock control Linkage and Remote Control Mechanism (trim panel must be removed)
- Latch Plate and Bolt

Multi-purpose Grease, NLGI Grade 2:

- Sliding Door: lower, center and upper tracks. Open position striker spring.
- Fuel Tank Door

Rear Wheel Bearings Front Wheel Drive Only

SERVICING

NOTE: *Sodium-based grease is not compatible with lithium-based grease. Read the package labels and be careful not to mix the two types. If there is any doubt as to the type of*

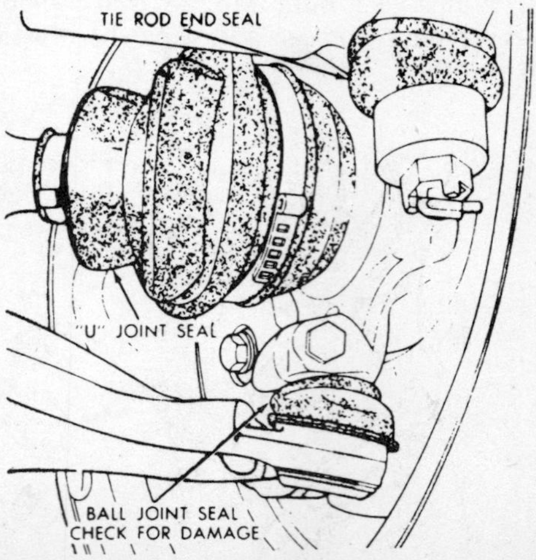

Check the ball joints for damaged seals

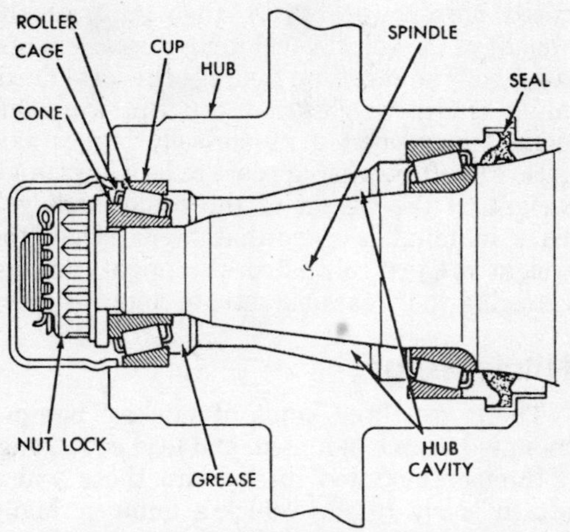

Rear wheel bearing assembly — component view

grease used, completely clean the old grease from the bearing and hub before replacing.

Before handling the bearings, there are a few things that you should remember to do and not to do.

Remember to DO the following:

- Remove all outside dirt from the housing before exposing the bearing.
- Treat a used bearing as gently as you would a new one.
- Work with clean tools in clean surroundings.
- Use clean, dry canvas gloves, or at least clean, dry hands.
- Clean solvents and flushing fluids are a must.
- Use clean paper when laying out the bearings to dry.
- Protect disassembled bearings from rust and dirt. Cover them up.
- Use clean rags to wipe bearings.
- Keep the bearings in oil-proof paper when they are to be stored or are not in use.
- Clean the inside of the housing before replacing the bearing.

Do NOT do the following:

- Don't work in dirty surroundings.
- Don't use dirty, chipped or damaged tools.
- Try not to work on wooden work benches or use wooden mallets.
- Don't handle bearings with dirty or moist hands.
- Do not use gasoline for cleaning; use a safe solvent.
- Do not spin-dry bearings with compressed air. They will be damaged.
- Do not spin dirty bearings.
- Avoid using cotton waste or dirty cloths to wipe bearings.
- Try not to scratch or nick bearing surfaces.
- Do not allow the bearing to come in contact with dirt or rust at any time.

The rear wheel bearings should be inspected and relubricated whenever the rear brakes are serviced or at least every 30,000 miles. Repack the bearings with high temperature multi-purpose grease.

Check the lubricant to see if it is contaminated. If it contains dirt or has a milky appearance indicating the presence of water, the bearings should be cleaned and repacked.

Clean the bearings in kerosene, mineral spirits or other suitable cleaning fluid. Do not dry them by spinning the bearings. Allow them to air dry.

1. Raise and support the vehicle with the rear wheels off the floor.
2. Remove the wheel grease cap, cotter pin, nut-lock and bearing adjusting nut.
3. Remove the thrust washer and bearing.
4. Remove the drum from the spindle.
5. Thoroughly clean the old lubricant from the bearings and hub cavity. Inspect the bearing rollers for pitting or other signs of wear. Light discoloration is normal.
6. Repack the bearings with high temperature multi-purpose EP grease and add a small amount of new grease to the hub cavity. Be sure to force the lubricant between all rollers in the bearing.
7. Install the drum on the spindle after coating the polished spindle surfaces with wheel bearing lubricant.
8. Install the outer bearing cone, thrust washer and adjusting nut.
9. Tighten the adjusting nut to 20–25 ft. lbs. while rotating the wheel.
10. Back off the adjusting nut to completely release the preload from the bearing.
11. Tighten the adjusting nut finger-tight.
12. Position the nut-lock with one pair of slots in line with the cotter pin hole. Install the cotter pin.
13. Clean and install the grease cap and wheel.
14. Lower the vehicle.

TOWING

The vehicle can be towed from either the front or rear. If the vehicle is towed from the front for an extended distance make sure the parking brake is completely released.

Manual transmission vehicles may be towed on the front wheels at speeds up to 30 Mph, for a distance not to exceed 15 miles, provided the transmission is in neutral and the drive line has not been damaged. The steering wheel must be clamped in a straight ahead position.

WARNING: *Do not use the steering column lock to secure front wheel position for towing.*

Automatic transmission vehicles may be towed on the front wheels at speeds not to exceed 25 Mph for a period of 15 miles.

WARNING: *If this requirement cannot be met the front wheels must be placed on a dolly.*

JACKING

The standard jack utilizes special receptacles located at the body sills. They accept the scissors jack supplied with the vehicle, for emergency road service only. The jack supplied with the vehicle should never be used for any service operation other then tire changing. Never get under the vehicle while it is supported by only a jack. Always block the wheels when changing tires.

The service operations in this book often require that one end or the other, or both, of the vehicle be raised and safely supported. The ideal method, of course, would be a hydraulic hoist. Since this is beyond both the resource and requirement of the do-it-yourselfer, a small hydraulic floor jack is recommended for certain procedures in this guide. Two sturdy jack stands should be acquired if you intend to work under the vehicle at any time. An alternate method of raising the vehicle would be drive-on ramps, Which are available commercially. Be sure to block the wheels when using ramps.

CAUTION: *Concrete blocks are not recommended for supporting the vehicle. They are likely to crumble if the load is not evenly distributed. Boxes and milk crates of any description must not be used to support the vehicle!*

TRAILER TOWING

Factory trailer towing packages are available on most vans. However, if you are installing a trailer hitch and wiring on your van, there are a few thing that you ought to know.

Trailer Weight

Trailer weight is the first, and most important, factor in determining whether or not your vehicle is suitable for towing the trailer you have in mind. The horsepower-to-weight ratio should be calculated. The basic standard is a ratio of 35:1. That is, 35 pounds of GVW for every horsepower.

To calculate this ratio, multiply you engine's rated horsepower by 35, then subtract the weight of the vehicle, including passengers and luggage. The resulting figure is the ideal maximum trailer weight that you can tow. One point to consider: a numerically higher axle ratio can offset what appears to be a low trailer weight. If the weight of the trailer that you have in mind is somewhat higher than the weight you just calculated, you might consider changing your rear axle ratio to compensate.

Hitch Weight

There are three kinds of hitches: bumper mounted, frame mounted, and load equalizing.

Bumper mounted hitches are those which attach solely to the vehicle's bumper. Many states prohibit towing with this type of hitch, when it attaches to the vehicle's stock bumper, since it subjects the bumper to stresses for which it was not designed. Aftermarket rear step bumpers, designed for trailer towing, are acceptable for use with bumper mounted hitches.

Frame mounted hitches can be of the type which bolts to two or more points on the frame, plus the bumper, or just to several points on the frame. Frame mounted hitches can also be of the tongue type, for Class I towing, or, of the receiver type, for Classes II and III.

Load equalizing hitches are usually used for large trailers. Most equalizing hitches are welded in place and use equalizing bars and chains to level the vehicle after the trailer is hooked up.

The bolt-on hitches are the most common, since they are relatively easy to install.

Check the gross weight rating of your trailer. Tongue weight is usually figured as 10% of gross trailer weight. Therefore, a trailer with a maximum gross weight of 2,000 lb. will have a maximum tongue weight of 200 lb. Class I trailers fall into this category. Class II trailers are those with a gross weight rating of 2,000–3,500 lb., while Class III trailers fall into the 3,500–6,000 lb. category. Class IV trailers are those over 6,000 lb. and are for use with fifth wheel trucks, only.

When you've determined the hitch that you'll need, follow the manufacturer's installation instructions, exactly, especially when it comes to fastener torques. The hitch will subjected to a lot of stress and good hitches come with hardened bolts. Never substitute an inferior bolt for a hardened bolt.

Wiring

Wiring the van for towing is fairly easy. There are a number of good wiring kits available and these should be used, rather than

JUMP STARTING A DEAD BATTERY

The chemical reaction in a battery produces explosive hydrogen gas. This is the safe way to jump start a dead battery, reducing the chances of an accidental spark that could cause an explosion.

Jump Starting Precautions

1. Be sure both batteries are of the same voltage.
2. Be sure both batteries are of the same polarity (have the same grounded terminal).
3. Be sure the vehicles are not touching.
4. Be sure the vent cap holes are not obstructed.
5. Do not smoke or allow sparks around the battery.
6. In cold weather, check for frozen electrolyte in the battery. Do not jump start a frozen battery.
7. Do not allow electrolyte on your skin or clothing.
8. Be sure the electrolyte is not frozen.

CAUTION: *Make certain that the ignition key, in the vehicle with the dead battery, is in the OFF position. Connecting cables to vehicles with on-board computers will result in computer destruction if the key is not in the OFF position.*

Jump Starting Procedure

1. Determine voltages of the two batteries; they must be the same.
2. Bring the starting vehicle close (they must not touch) so that the batteries can be reached easily.
3. Turn off all accessories and both engines. Put both cars in Neutral or Park and set the handbrake.
4. Cover the cell caps with a rag—do not cover terminals.
5. If the terminals on the run-down battery are heavily corroded, clean them.
6. Identify the positive and negative posts on both batteries and connect the cables in the order shown.
7. Start the engine of the starting vehicle and run it at fast idle. Try to start the car with the dead battery. Crank it for no more than 10 seconds at a time and let it cool off for 20 seconds in between tries.
8. If it doesn't start in 3 tries, there is something else wrong.
9. Disconnect the cables in the reverse order.
10. Replace the cell covers and dispose of the rags.

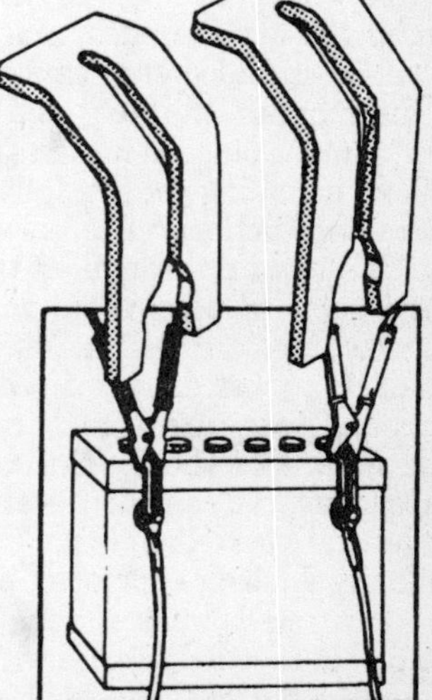

Side terminal batteries oc casionally pose a problem when connecting jumper cables. There frequently isn't enough room to clamp the cables without touching sheet metal .Side terminal adaptors are available to alleviate this problem and should be removed after use.

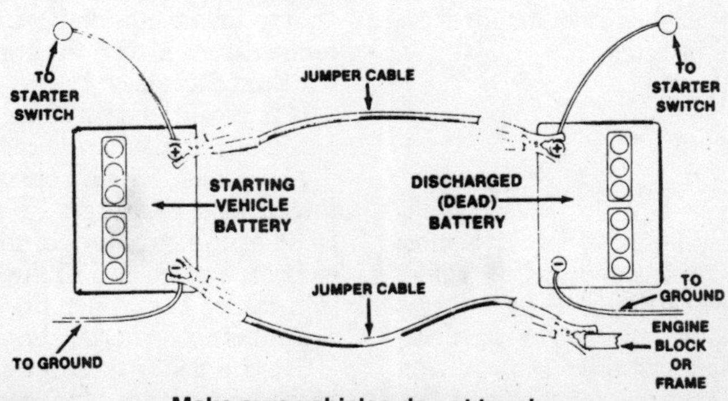

Make sure vehicles do not touch

This hook–up for negative ground cars only

trying to design your own. All trailers will need brake lights and turn signals as well as tail lights and side marker lights. Most states require extra marker lights for overly wide trailers. Also, most states have recently required back-up lights for trailers, and most trailer manufacturers have been building trailers with back-up lights for several years.

Additionally, some Class I, most Class II and just about all Class III trailers will have electric brakes.

Add to this number an accessories wire, to operate trailer internal equipment or to charge the trailer's battery, and you can have as many as seven wires in the harness.

Determine the equipment on your trailer and buy the wiring kit necessary. The kit will contain all the wires needed, plus a plug adapter set which included the female plug, mounted on the bumper or hitch, and the male plug, wired into, or plugged into the trailer harness.

When installing the kit, follow the manufacturer's instructions. The color coding of the wires is standard throughout the industry.

One point to note, some domestic vehicles, and most imported vehicles, have separate turn signals. On most domestic vehicles, the brake lights and rear turn signals operate with the same bulb. For those vehicles with separate turn signals, you can purchase an isolation unit so that the brake lights won't blink whenever the turn signals are operated, or, you can go to your local electronics supply house and buy four diodes to wire in series with the brake and turn signal bulbs. Diodes will isolate the brake and turn signals. The choice is yours. The isolation units are simple and quick to install, but far more expensive than the diodes. The diodes, however, require more work to install properly, since they require the cutting of each bulb's wire and soldering in place of the diode.

One final point, the best kits are those with a spring loaded cover on the vehicle mounted socket. This cover prevents dirt and moisture from corroding the terminals. Never let the vehicle socket hang loosely. Always mount it securely to the bumper or hitch.

Cooling

ENGINE

One of the most common, if not THE most common, problem associated with trailer towing is engine overheating.

With factory installed trailer towing packages, a heavy duty cooling system is usually included. Heavy duty cooling systems are available as optional equipment on most vans, with or without a trailer package. If you have one of these extra-capacity systems, you shouldn't have any overheating problems.

If you have a standard cooling system, without an expansion tank, you'll definitely need to get an aftermarket expansion tank kit, preferably one with at least a 2 quart capacity. These kits are easily installed on the radiator's overflow hose, and come with a pressure cap designed for expansion tanks.

Another helpful accessory is a Flex Fan. These fan are large diameter units are designed to provide more airflow at low speeds, with blades that have deeply cupped surfaces. The blades then flex, or flatten out, at high speed, when less cooling air is needed. These fans are far lighter in weight than stock fans, requiring less horsepower to drive them. Also, they are far quieter than stock fans.

If you do decide to replace your stock fan with a flex fan, note that if your van has a fan clutch, a spacer between the flex fan and water pump hub will be needed.

Aftermarket engine oil coolers are helpful for prolonging engine oil life and reducing overall engine temperatures. Both of these factors increase engine life.

While not absolutely necessary in towing Class I and some Class II trailers, they are recommended for heavier Class II and all Class III towing.

Engine oil cooler systems consist of an adapter, screwed on in place of the oil filter, a remote filter mounting and a multi-tube, finned heat exchanger, which is mounted in front of the radiator or air conditioning condenser.

TRANSMISSION

An automatic transmission is usually recommended for trailer towing. Modern automatics have proven reliable and, of course, easy to operate, in trailer towing.

The increased load of a trailer, however, causes an increase in the temperature of the automatic transmission fluid. Heat is the worst enemy of an automatic transmission. As the temperature of the fluid increases, the life of the fluid decreases.

It is essential, therefore, that you install an automatic transmission cooler.

The cooler, which consists of a multi-tube, finned heat exchanger, is usually installed in front of the radiator or air conditioning compressor, and hooked in line with the transmission cooler tank inlet line. Follow the cooler manufacturer's installation instructions.

Select a cooler of at least adequate capacity, based upon the combined gross weights of the van and trailer.

Cooler manufacturers recommend that you

Lubrication and Maintenance Schedules

SCHEDULED MAINTENANCE FOR EMISSION CONTROL AND PROPER VEHICLE PERFORMANCE
Inspection and Service should also be performed any time a malfunction is observed or suspected. O = Except California Vehicles

Component / Service Interval		Mileage in thousands	7.5	15	22.5	30	37.5	45	52.5	60	67.5	75	82.5	90	97.5	105	112.5	120
		Kilometers in thousands	12	24	36	48	60	72	84	96	108	120	132	144	156	168	180	192
Change engine oil every 12 months	Or		X	X	X	X	X	X	O	O	O	O	O	O	O	O	O	O
Change engine oil filter every second oil change (1)	Or			X		X		X		O		O		O		O		O
Inspect & adjust drive belts tension; replace as necessary	At			O		X		O		O		O		O		O		O
Replace spark plugs	At					X				O				O				O
Replace engine air filter	At					X				O				O				O
Replace oxygen sensor	At								O							O		
Replace EGR valve & tube & clean passages at 60 months	Or								O							O		
Replace PCV filter	At					X				O				O				O
Replace PCV valve at 60 months	Or									O						O		
Replace vacuum operated emission components at 60 months	Or								O							O		
Inspect timing belt 3.0L only	At								O							O		
Adjust ignition timing if not to specifications	At									O								O
Replace ignition cables, distributor cap & rotor	At									O								O
Flush & replace engine coolant at 36 months & 24 months or 30,000 miles (48 000 Km) thereafter	Or								O									
Replace alternator brushes	At											O						
Check engine coolant condition, coolant hoses & clamps every 12 months																		

(1) Note: If mileage is less than 7,500 miles (12 000km) each 12 months, replace oil filter at each oil change.

use an aftermarket cooler in addition to, and not instead of, the present cooling tank in your van's radiator. If you do want to use it in place of the radiator cooling tank, get a cooler at least two sizes larger than normally necessary.

NOTE: *A transmission cooler can, sometimes, cause slow or harsh shifting in the transmission during cold weather, until the fluid has a chance to come up to normal operating temperature. Some coolers can be purchased with or retrofitted with a temperature bypass valve which will allow fluid flow through the cooler only when the fluid has reached operating temperature, or above.*

GENERAL MAINTENANCE SERVICES FOR PROPER VEHICLE PERFORMANCE

General Maintenance	Service Intervals		Mileage in Thousands	7.5	15	22.5	30	37.5	45
			Kilometers in Thousands	12	24	36	48	60	72
Cooling System	Check & Service As Required Every 12 Months								
	Drain Flush, and Refill At 36 Months Or 52,500 Miles (84 000 Kilometers) And Every 24 Months Or 30,000 Miles (48 000 Kilometers) Thereafter								
Brake Hoses	Inspect For Deterioration And Leaks Whenever Brake System is Serviced And Every 7,500 Miles (12 000 km) Or 12 Months, Whichever Occurs First, For Non-turbocharged Vehicles and 7,500 Miles (12 000 km) or 6 Months, Whichever Occurs First, For Turbocharged Vehicles, Replace if Necessary.								
Brake Linings—Front	Inspect	At				X			X
Brake Linings—Rear	Inspect	At				X			X
Rear Wheel Bearings	Inspect	At				X			X
Tie Rod Ends and Steering Linkage	Lubricate Every 3 Years	Or					X		
Drive Shaft Boots	Inspect For Deterioration And Leaks Every Oil Change. Replace if Necessary	Or		X	X	X	X	X	X

CAPACITIES CHART

Year	Vin	Engine No. Cyl. Liters	Crankcase Includes Filter (qts)	Transmission (pts) 4-sp	5-sp	Auto	Fuel Tank (Gal)	Cooling System (qts) ③
1984	C	4-2.2L	4	8	—	①	15②	8.5
	G	4-2.6L	5	—	9	①	15②	9.5
1985	C	4-2.2L	4	8	—	①	15②	8.5
	G	4-2.6L	5	—	9	①	15②	9.5
1986	C	4-2.2L	4	8	—	①	15②	8.5
	G	4-2.6L	5	—	9	①	15②	9.5
1987	C	4-2.2L	4	8	—	①	15②	8.5
	K	4-2.5L	4	—	9	①	15②	8.5
	G	4-2.6L	5	—	9	①	15②	9.5
1988	K	4-2.5L	4	—	9	①	15②	8.5
	3	6-3.0L	4	—	—	①	15②	10.5
1989	K	4-2.5L	4	—	9	①	15②	8.5
	J	4-2.5L	4	—	9	①	15②	8.5
	3	6-3.0L	4	—	—	①	15②	10.5
1990	K	4-2.5L	4	—	9	①	15②	8.5
	J	4-2.5L	4	—	9	①	15②	8.5
	3	6-3.0L	4	—	—	①	15②	10.5
	R	6-3.3L	4	—	—	①	15②	10.5
1991	K	4-2.5L	4	—	—	①	15②	8.5
	3	6-3.0L	4	—	—	①	15②	10.5
	R	6-3.3L	4	—	—	①	15②	10.5

① A413/A470 Transaxles (except Fleet): 17.8 pts.
A413/A470 Transaxles (Fleet): 18.4 pts.
A413/A460 Transaxles with Lockup Converter: 17.0 pts.
A604 Transaxles: 18.2 pts
② Standard: 15 Gal.
Optional: 20 Gal.
③ Add 1 qt. when equipped with rear heater

SEVERE SERVICE MAINTENANCE*

	Service Intervals	Mileage in Thousands / Kilometers In Thousands	3 / 4.8	6 / 9.6	9 / 14	12 / 19	15 / 24	18 / 29	21 / 34	24 / 38	27 / 43	30 / 48	33 / 53	36 / 58	39 / 62	42 / 67	45 / 72	48 / 77
Brake Linings (Front & Rear) and Rear Wheel Bearings	Inspect				X			X			X			X			X	
Constant Velocity Universal Joints	Inspect at every oil change																	
Engine Oil	Change every 3 months or		X	X	X	X	X	X	X	X	X	X	X	X	X	X	X	X
Engine Oil Filter	Change at every second oil change																	
Front Suspension Ball Joints	Inspect at every oil change																	
Transmission Fluid and Filter—Automatic	Change at (adjust bands at time of fluid and filter change)						X					X					X	
Steering Linkage Tie Rod Ends	Lubricate every 18 months or						X					X					X	
Engine Air Filter	Inspect and replace if required						X					X					X	

*Driving under any of the following operating conditions: Stop and go driving in dusty conditions, extensive idling, frequent short trips, operating at sustained high speeds during hot weather (above +90°F, +30°C)

Engine Performance and Tune-Up

2

TUNE-UP PROCEDURES

Neither tune-up nor troubleshooting can be considered independently since each has a direct relationship with the other.

It is advisable to follow a definite and thorough tune-up procedure. Tune-up consists of three separate steps: Analysis, (the process of determining whether normal wear is responsible for performance loss, and whether parts require replacement or service); Parts Replacement or Service; and Adjustment, (where engine adjustments are performed).

The manufacturer's recommended interval for tune-ups on non-catalyst vehicles is 15,000 miles. Models with a converter, every 30,000 miles. Models equipped with a 2.6L engine require a valve lash adjustment every 15,000 miles. this interval should be shortened if the vehicle is subjected to severe operating conditions such as trailer pulling or stop and start driving, or if starting and running problems are noticed. It is assumed that the routine maintenance has been kept up, as this will have an effect on the result of the tune-up. All the applicable tune-up steps should be followed, as each adjustment complements the effects of the other. If the tune-up (emission control) sticker in the engine compartment disagrees with the information presented in the Tune-up

TUNE-UP SPECIFICATIONS CHART

Years	VIN	Engine No. Cyl. Liters	Spark Plugs Type	Spark Plugs Gap (in.)	Ignition Timing (deg.) MT	Ignition Timing (deg.) AT	Compression Pressure (psi)	Fuel Pump (psi)	Idle Speed (rpm) MT	Idle Speed (rpm) AT	Valve Clearance In.	Valve Clearance Ex.
1984	C	4-2.2L	65PR	0.035	12B	12B	100 ②	4.5–6.0	850	900	Hyd.	Hyd.
	G	4-2.6L	65PR	0.041 ①	—	12B	100 ②	4.5–6.0	—	800	0.005	0.010
1985	C	4-2.2L	65PR	0.035	12B	12B	100 ②	4.5–6.0	850	900	Hyd.	Hyd.
	G	4-2.6L	65PR	0.041 ①	—	12B	100 ②	4.5–6.0	—	800	0.005	0.010
1986	C	4-2.2L	65PR	0.035	12B	12B	100 ②	4.5–6.0	850	900	Hyd.	Hyd.
	G	4-2.6L	65PR	0.041 ①	—	12B	100 ②	4.5–6.0	—	800	0.005	0.010
1987	C	4-2.2L	RN12YC	0.035	6B	6B	100 ②	4.5–6.0	850	900	Hyd.	Hyd.
	K	4-2.5L	RN12YC	0.035	12B	12B	100 ②	15	—	800	Hyd.	Hyd.
	G	4-2.6L	RN12YC	0.040	—	7B	100 ②	4.5–6.0	—	800	0.005	0.010
1988	K	4-2.5L	RN12YC	0.035	6B	—	100 ②	15	850	—	Hyd.	Hyd.
	3	6-3.0L	RN11YC4	0.040	—	12B	100 ②	48	—	700	Hyd.	Hyd.
1989	K	4-2.5L	RN12YC	0.035	12B	12B	100 ②	15	850	850	Hyd.	Hyd.
	J	4-2.5L	RN12YC	0.035	12B	12B	100 ②	55	900	900	Hyd.	Hyd.
	3	6-3.0L	RN11YC4	0.040	—	12B	100 ②	48	—	700	Hyd.	Hyd.
1990	K	4-2.5L	RN12YC	0.035	12B	12B	100 ②	15	850	850	Hyd.	Hyd.
	J	4-2.5L	RN12YC	0.035	12B	12B	100 ②	55	900	900	Hyd.	Hyd.
	3	6-3.0L	RN11YC4	0.040	—	12B	100 ②	48	—	700	Hyd.	Hyd.
	R	6-3.3L	RN16YC5	0.050	—	16B	100 ②	43–53	—	750	Hyd.	Hyd.
1991	K	4-2.5L	RN12YC	0.035	—	12B	100 ②	55	900	900	Hyd.	Hyd.
	3	6-3.0L	RN11YC4	0.040	—	12B	100 ②	48	—	700	Hyd.	Hyd.
	R	6-3.3L	RN16YC5	0.050	—	16B	100 ②	43–53	—	750	Hyd.	Hyd.

① Canada 0.030
② Minimum compression pressure

Specifications chart in this Chapter, the sticker figures must be followed. The sticker information reflects running changes made by the manufacturer during production.

Troubleshooting is a logical sequence of procedures designed to locate a particular cause of trouble. While the apparent cause of trouble, in many cases, is worn or damaged parts, performance problems are less obvious. The first job is to locate the problem and cause. Once the problem has been isolated, repairs, removal or adjustment procedures can be performed.

It is advisable to read the entire Chapter before beginning a tune-up, although those who are more familiar with tune-up procedures may wish to go directly to the instructions.

Spark Plugs

A typical spark plug consists of a metal shell surrounding a ceramic insulator. A metal electrode extends downward through the center of the insulator and protrudes a small distance. Located at the end of the plug and attached to the side of the outer metal shell is the side electrode. The side electrode bends in at a 90° angle so that its tip is even with, and parallel to, the tip of the center electrode. The distance between these two electrodes (measured in thousandths of an inch) is called the spark plug gap. The spark plug in no way produces a spark but merely provides a gap across which the current can arc. The coil produces anywhere from 20,000 to 40,000 volts which travels to the distributor where it is distributed through the spark plug wires to the spark plugs. The current passes along the center electrode and jumps the gap to the side electrode, and, in do doing, ignites the air/fuel mixture in the combustion chamber.

SPARK PLUG HEAT RANGE

Spark plug heat range is the ability of the plug to dissipate heat. The longer the insulator (or the farther it extends into the engine), the hotter the plug will operate; the shorter the insulator the cooler it will operate. A plug that absorbs little heat and remains too cool will quickly accumulate deposits of oil and carbon since it is not hot enough to burn them off. This leads to plug fouling and consequently to misfiring. A plug that absorbs too much heat will have no deposits, but, due to the excessive heat, the electrodes will burn away quickly and in some instances, preignition may result. Preignition takes place when plug tips get so hot that they glow sufficiently to ignite the fuel/air mixture before the actual spark occurs. This early ignition will usually cause a pinging during low speeds and heavy loads.

The general rule of thumb for choosing the correct heat range when picking a spark plug is: if most of your driving is long distance, high speed travel, use a colder plug; if most of your driving is stop and go, use a hotter plug. Original equipment plugs are compromise plugs, but most people never have occasion to change their plugs from the factory-recommended heat range.

REMOVAL AND INSTALLATION

1. Before removing the spark plugs, number the plug wires so that the correct wire goes on the plug when replaced. This can be done with pieces of adhesive tape.
2. Next, clean the area around the plugs by blowing with compressed air. You can also loosen the plugs a few turns and crank the engine to blow the dirt away.

CAUTION: *Wear safety glasses to avoid possible eye injury due to flying dust particles.*

3. Disconnect the plugs wires by twisting and pulling on the rubber cap, not on the wire.
4. Remove each plug with a rubber insert spark plug socket. make sure that the socket is all the way down on the plug to prevent it from slipping and cracking the porcelain insulator.
5. After removing each plug, evaluate its condition. A spark plug's useful life is approximately 30,000 miles. Thus, it would make sense to replace a plug if it has been in service that long.
6. If the plugs are to be reused, file the center and side electrodes flat with a fine, flat point file. Heavy or baked on deposits can be carefully scraped off with a small knife blade, or the scraper tool of a combination spark plug tool. However, it is suggested that plugs be test and cleaned on a service station sandblasting machine. Check the gap between the electrodes with a round wire spark plug gapping gauge. Do not use a flat feeler gauge; it will give an inaccurate reading. If the gap is not as specified, use the bending tool on the spark plug gap gauge to bend the outside electrode. Be careful not to bend the electrode tool far or too often, because excessive bending may cause the electrode to break off and fall into the combustion chamber. This would require removing the cyl-

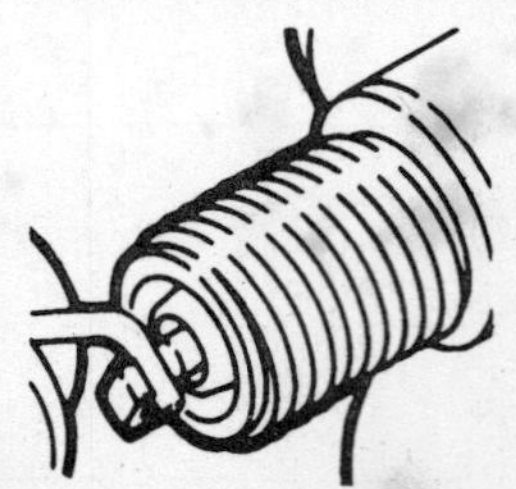

Check the spark plug gap with a feeler gauge

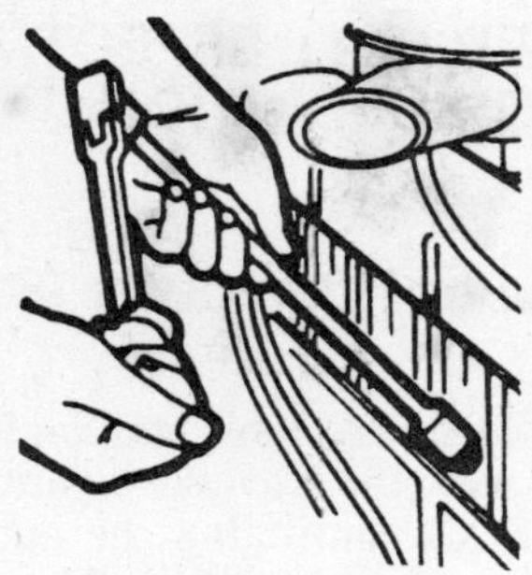

Remove the spark plugs with a ratchet and long extension

inder head to reach the broken piece, and could also result in cylinder wall, piston ring, or valve damage.

7. Clean the threads of old plugs with a wire brush. Lubricate the threads with a drop of oil.

8. Screw the plugs in finger tight, and then tighten them with the spark plug socket to 26 ft. lbs. Be very careful not to over tighten them.

9. Reinstall the wires. If, by chance, you have forgotten to number the plug wires, refer to the Firing Order illustrations.

Spark Plug Wires

Check the spark plug wire connections at the coil, distributor cap towers, and at the spark plugs. Be sure they are fully seated, and the boot covers are not cracked or split. Clean the cables with a cloth and a non-flammable solvent. Check for brittle or cracked insulation, replace wires as necessary. If a wire is suspected of failure, test it with an ohmmeter. Test as follows:

CABLE RESISTANCE CHART	
Minimum	Maximum
250 Ohms Per Inch	600 Ohms Per Inch
3000 Ohms Per Foot	7200 Ohms Per Foot

Spark plug cable resistance

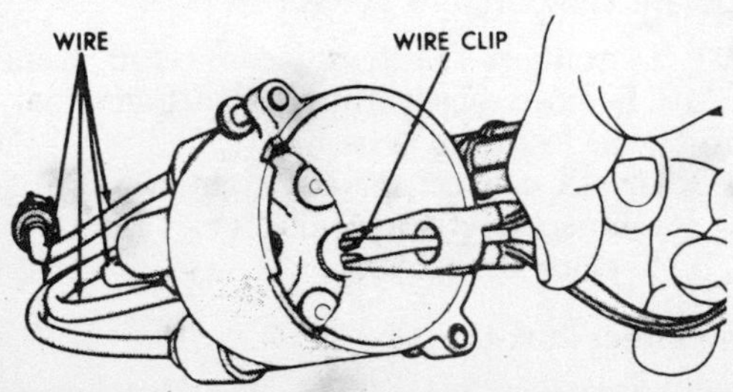

Removing the plug wires from the distributor cap

1. Remove the plug wire from the spark plug. Twist the boot and pull. Never apply pressure to the wire itself.

NOTE: *The 3.3L engine is equipped with a distributorless electronic ignition system. The plug wires run directly from the coil pack to the spark plugs.*

2. Remove the distributor cap from the distributor with all wires attached.

NOTE: *Do not pull plugs wires from distributor cap, they must first be released from inside of cap.*

3. Connect the ohmmeter between the spark plug terminal, and the corresponding electrode inside the distributor cap. Resistance should be within limits of the cable resistance chart. If resistance is not within specs, remove the wire from the distributor cap and retest. If still not within specs, replace the wire.

4. Install the new wire into cap tower, then squeeze the wire nipple to release any trapped air between the cap tower and nipple.

5. Push firmly to properly seat wire electrode into cap.

6. Install plug end of wire onto plug until it snaps into place.

WARNING: *Do not allowed plug wires to contact exhaust manifold or any moving parts.*

FIRING ORDERS

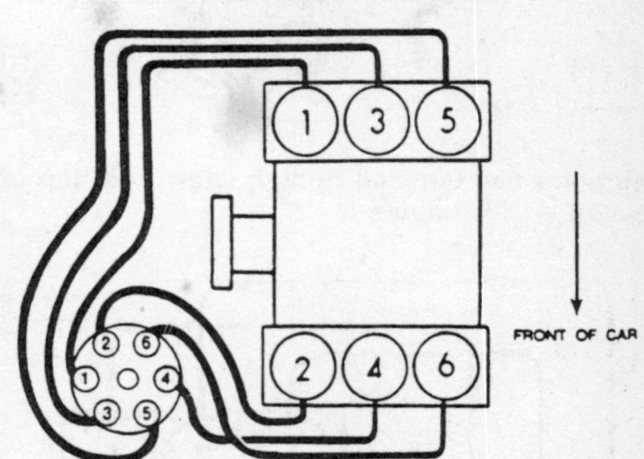

Chrysler Corp. (Mitsubishi) 2.6L engine
Engine firing order: 1-3-4-2
Distributor rotation: clockwise

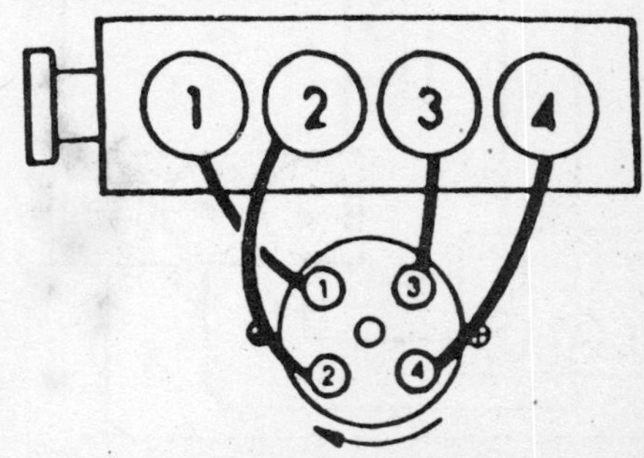

Chrysler Corp. 2.2L and 2.5L engines
Engine firing order: 1-3-4-2
Distributor rotation: clockwise

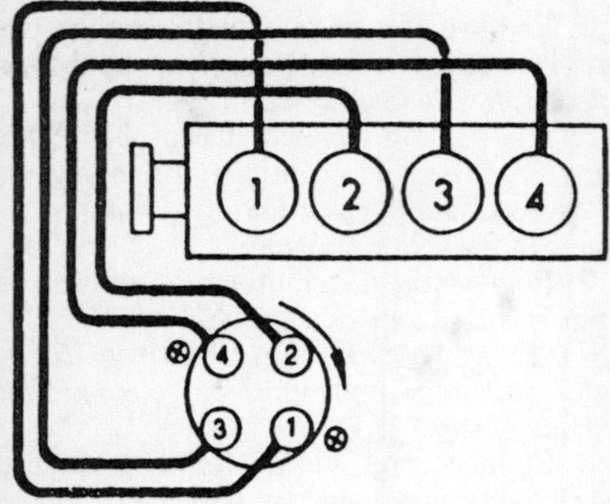

Chrysler Corp. (Mitsubishi) 2.6L engine
Engine firing order: 1-3-4-2
Distributor rotation: clockwise

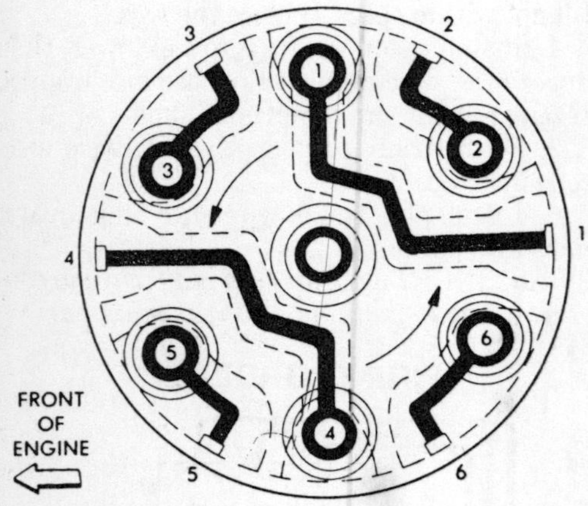

Distributor cap terminal routing (view from top of the cap) — 3.0L engine

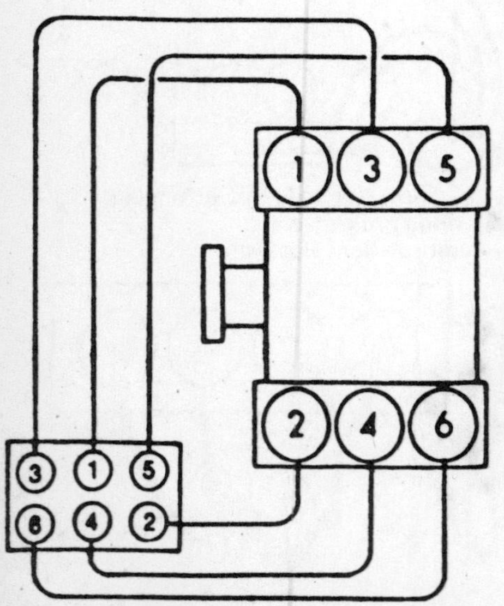

Chrysler Corp. 3.3L engine
Engine firing order: 1-2-3-4-5-6
Distributorless Ignition System

CHRYSLER HALL EFFECT ELECTRONIC IGNITION

Spark Control Computer (SCC) System

The Hall Effect electronic ignition is used in conjunction with the Chrysler Spark Control Computer (SCC) controlling the entire ignition. It consists of a sealed Spark Control Computer, specially calibrated carburetor and various engine sensors, such as the vacuum transducer, coolant switch, Hall Effect pick-up assembly, oxygen sensor and carburetor switch.

Spark Control Computer (SCC) System Component Replacement

REMOVAL AND INSTALLATION

Spark Control Computer

1. Disconnect 10-way and 14-way dual connectors and outside air duct from SCC. Remove vacuum line from transducer.
2. Remove 4 mounting screws that hold computer in place.
3. Install new computer and secure mounting screws.
4. Reconnect vacuum line to transducer, making sure vacuum line is not pinched. Reconnect dual connectors and outside air duct to SCC unit.

NOTE: *Do not remove grease from 10-way or 14-way dual connector or connector cavities in spark control computer. The grease is used to prevent moisture from corroding terminals. If there isn't at least 1/8 in. grease on bottom of computer connector cavities, apply multi-purpose grease over entire end of connector plug before reinstalling.*

Vacuum Transducer

If vacuum transducer fails, complete computer unit (SCC) must be replaced.

Coolant Temperature Sensor

1. Disconnect electrical connector from sensor. Remove sensor from engine. Some coolant may be lost from system.
2. Install new sensor and tighten to 20 ft lbs. Reconnect electrical connector.
3. Replace lost coolant.

Hall Effect Pick-Up

1. Remove splash shield from distributor and remove distributor cap.

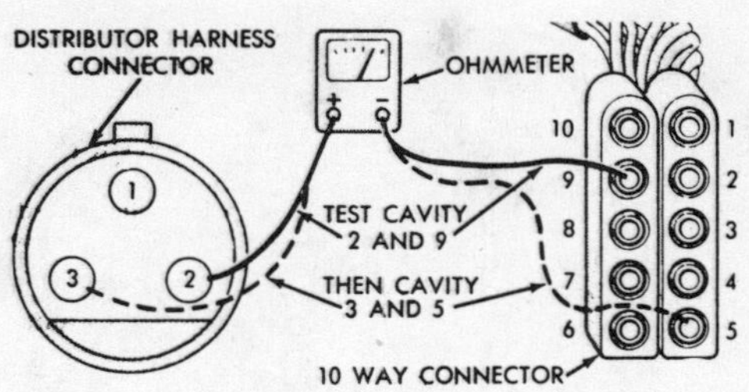

Testing cavities 2 and 9, then cavities 3 and 5 for continuity

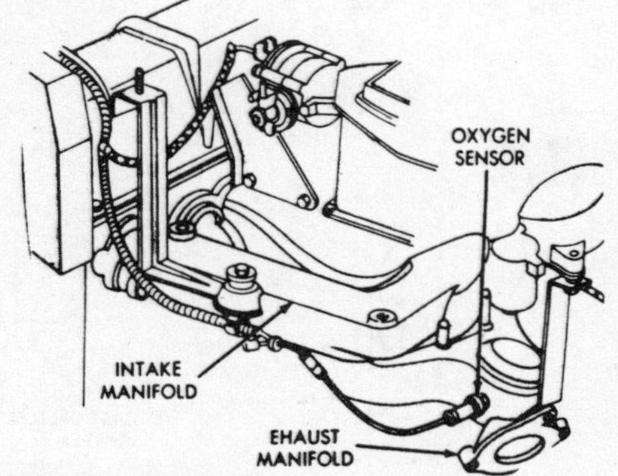

2.2L oxygen sensor

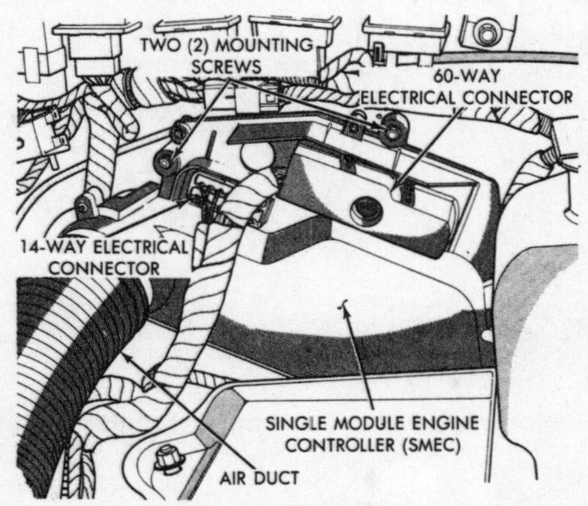

Single Module Engine Controller (SMEC) mounting location

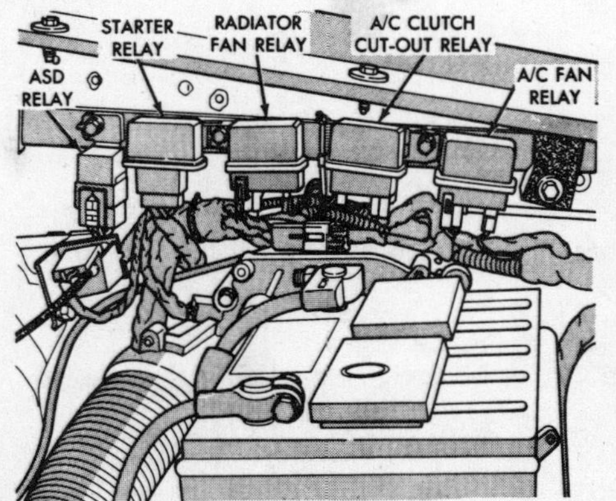

Relay identification

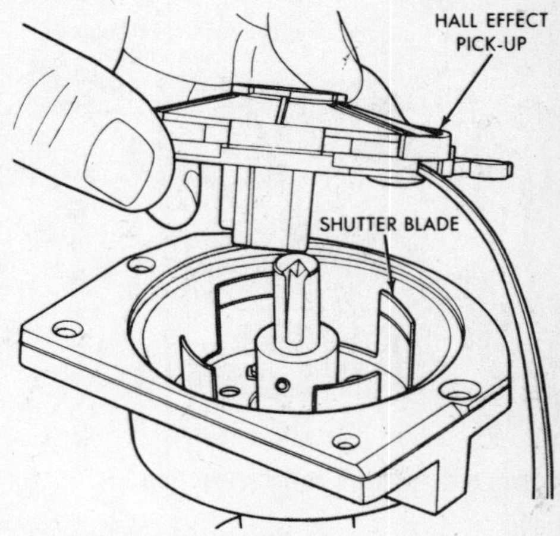

Hall Effect pick-up – SMEC system

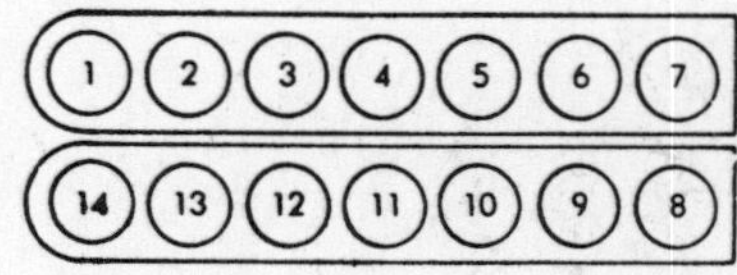

14 way connector terminal identification

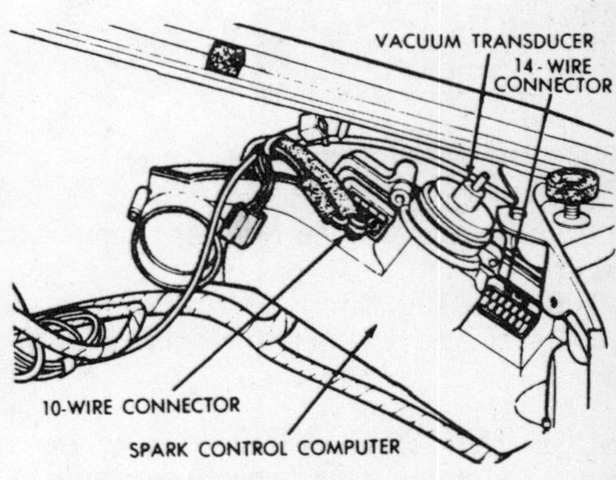

2.2L spark control vacuum transducer

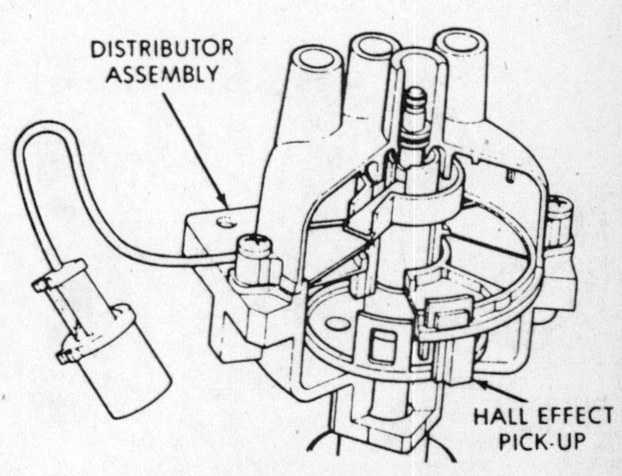

Hall Effect Distributor for carbureted vehicles

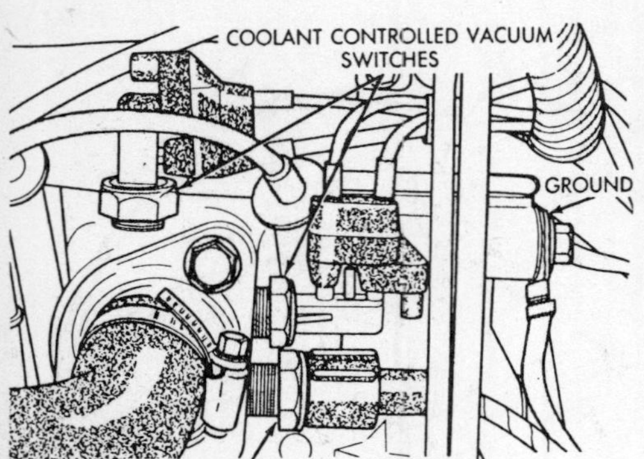

Coolant temperature sensor location

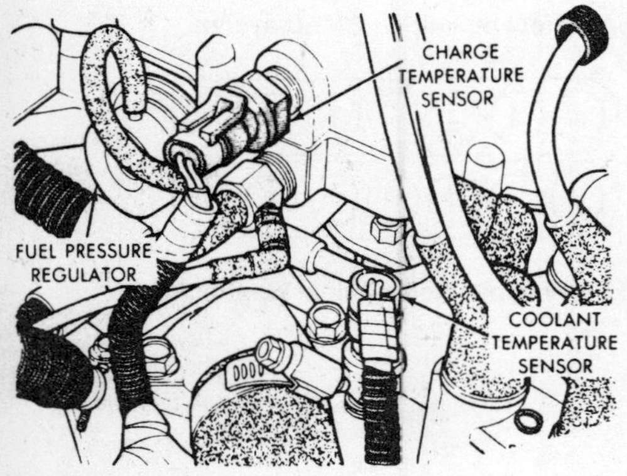

3.0L coolant temperature sensor

2. Pull straight up on rotor and remove it from shaft.
3. Remove Hall Effect pick-up assembly.
4. Install new pick-up assembly onto distributor.

NOTE: *Hall Effect assembly wiring leads may be damaged if not properly reinstalled.*

5. Install distributor rotor.
6. Install distributor cap and splash shield.

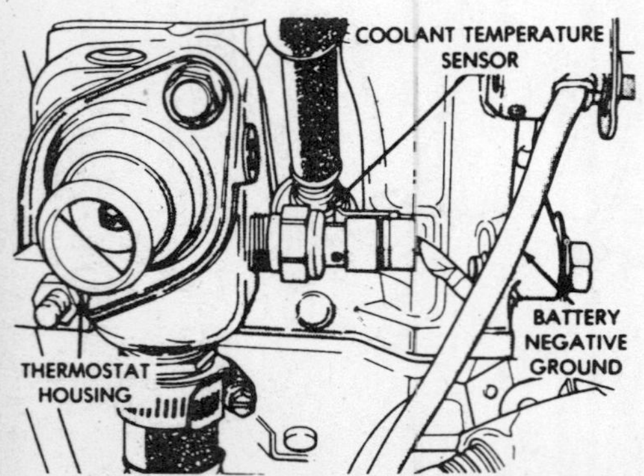

2.5L coolant temperature sensor

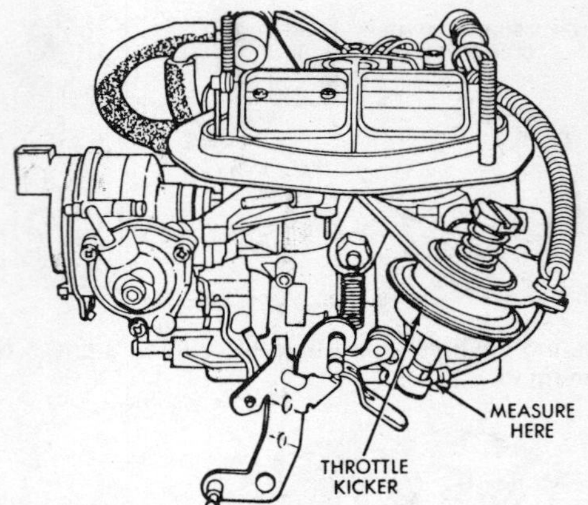

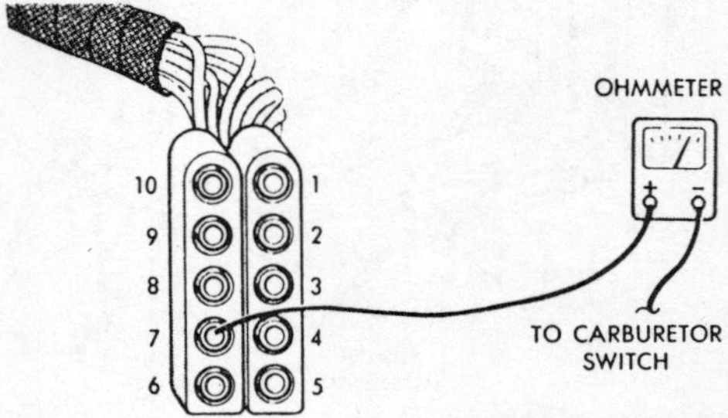

Testing carburetor switch

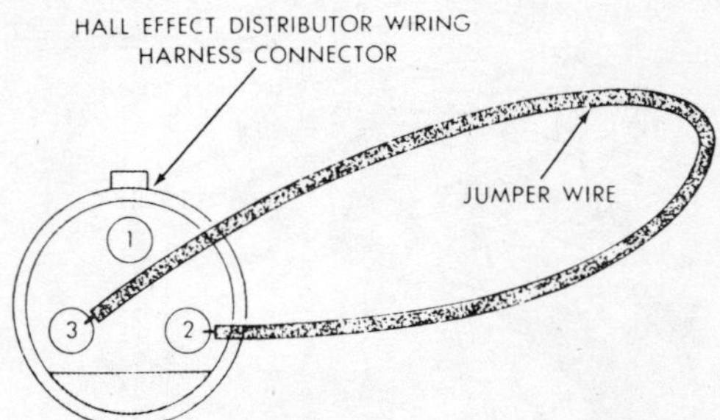

Jumping cavities 2 and 3 of the distributor harness

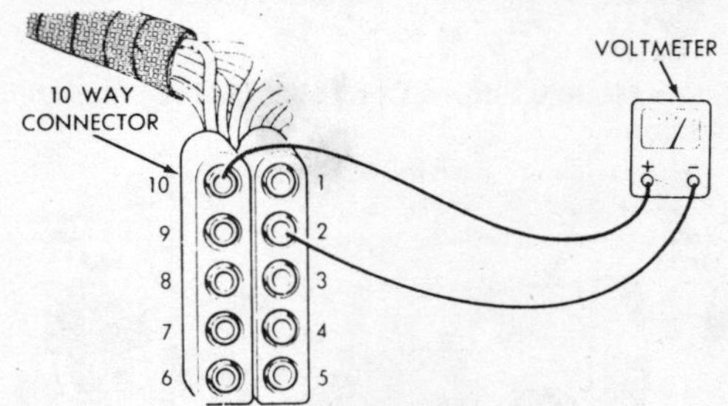

Checking voltage between cavities 2 and 10

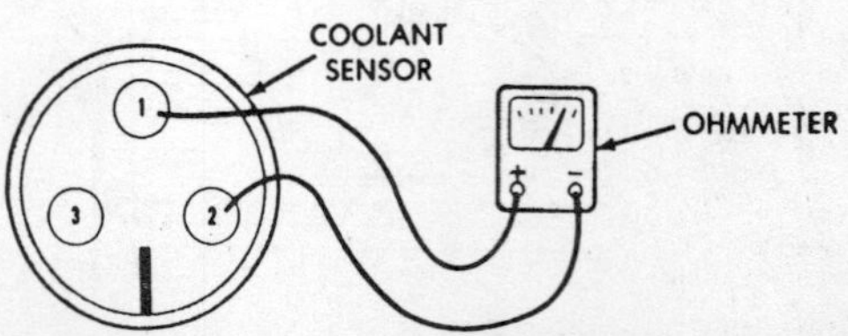

Testing coolant temperature sensor

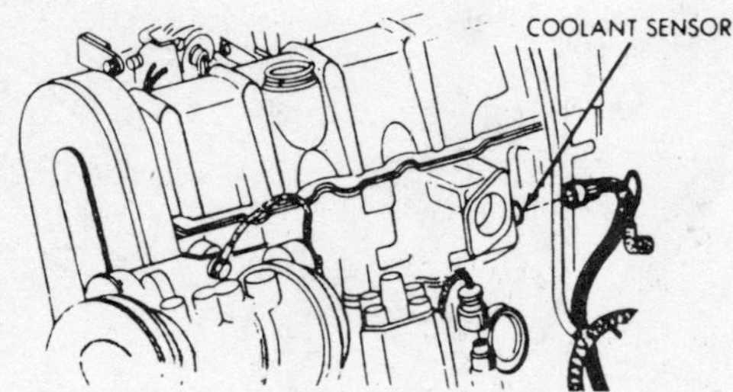

2.2L coolant temperature sensor location

Single Module Engine Controller (SMEC) System Component Replacement

REMOVAL AND INSTALLATION

Single Module Engine Control Unit

1. Disconnect the negative battery cable.
2. Disconnect the air cleaner duct from the SMEC unit.
3. Carefully disconnect the connectors from the unit.

NOTE: *Make sure there is at least an 1/8 in. of grease in the connectors.*

4. Install the connectors on the replacement unit.
5. Mount the unit in position and make sure the connectors are secure.
6. Install the air cleaner duct and connect the battery cable.

Hall Effect Pick-Up

1. Disconnect the negative battery cable.
2. Remove the distributor cap and remove the rotor.
3. Remove the screws that retain the pick-up assembly. Disconnect the electrical lead from the pick-up.
4. Carefully remove the assembly from the distributor.
5. Install the new pick-up assembly and connect the electrical lead.
6. Install the retaining screws. Install the cap and rotor.
7. Connect the negative battery cable.

Coolant Temperature Sensor

1. Disconnect electrical connector from sensor. Remove sensor from engine. Some coolant may be lost from system.
2. Install new sensor and tighten to 20 ft lbs. Reconnect electrical connector.
3. Replace lost coolant.

CHRYSLER OPTICAL DISTRIBUTOR SYSTEM

This ignition system is used in vehicles with the 3.0L engine. The system is similar to the SMEC system in operation except that it uses a different type of distributor. The computer receives its input from an optical distributor. The signals are used to control fuel injection, ignition timing and engine idle speed.

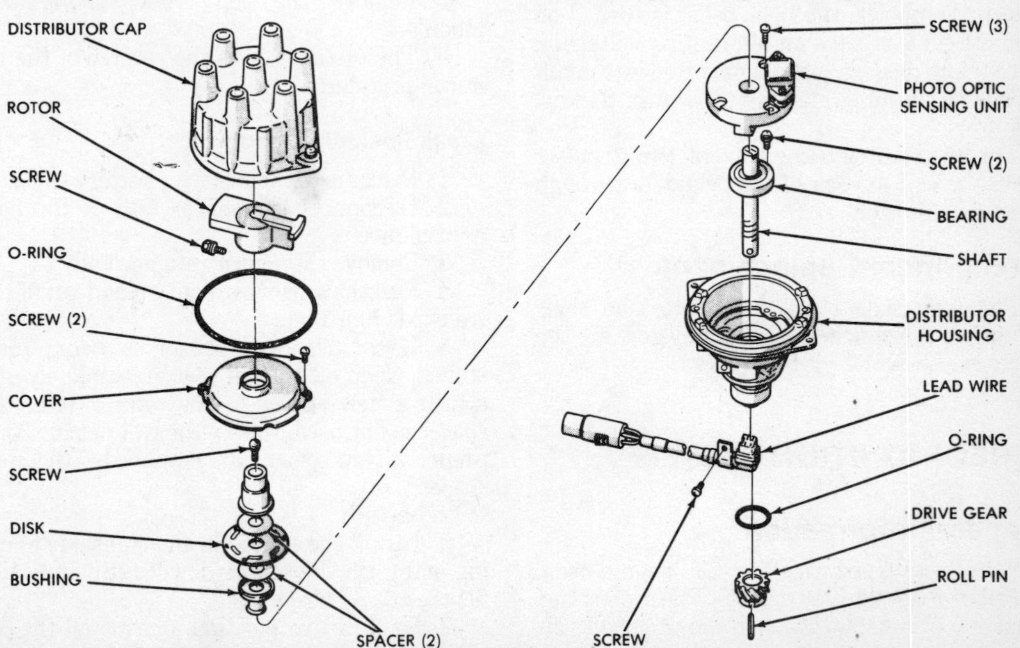

3.0L distributor assembly

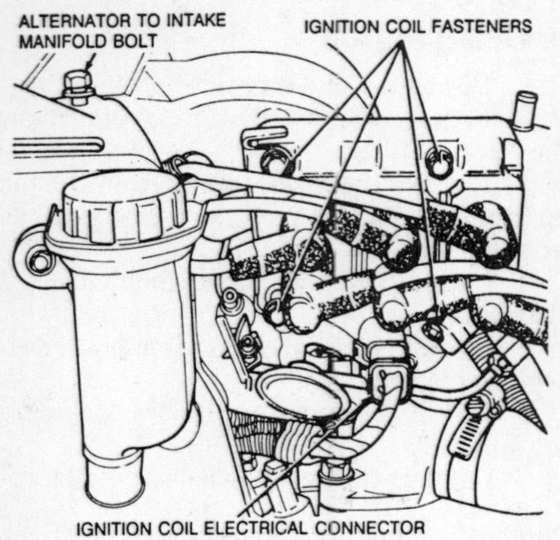

Ignition coil removal and installation – 3.3L engine

The timing member in the distributor is a thin disk, driven at half the speed of the engine, from the left camshaft. The disk has 2 sets of slots in it. The outer, high data rate slots, occur at 2 degrees of engine rotation. They are used for ignition timing at engine speed of up to 1200 Rpm.

The inner, or low data rate set, contains 6 slots which are correlated to TDC of each cylinder. This is used to trigger the fuel injection system. At engine speed over 1200 Rpm, this set also controls the ignition timing.

Light emitting diodes and photo sensors are mounted in facing positions on opposite sides of the disk in the distributor. Masks over the LED's and the diodes focus the light beams onto the photo diodes. As each slot passes between the diodes, the light beam is turned on and off. This creates an alternating voltage in each photo diode, which is converted into on/off pulses by an integrated circuit within the distributor.

The distributor also delivers firing pulses from the coil to each of the cylinders through the cap and rotor.

Component Replacement

The replacement of components and their testing in the optical distributor system are the same as the SMEC system.

DIRECT IGNITION SYSTEM

General Information

Vehicle equipped with the 3.3L engine use a distributorless ignition system. The system has 3 main components, the coil, the camshaft reference sensor and the crankshaft timing sensor.

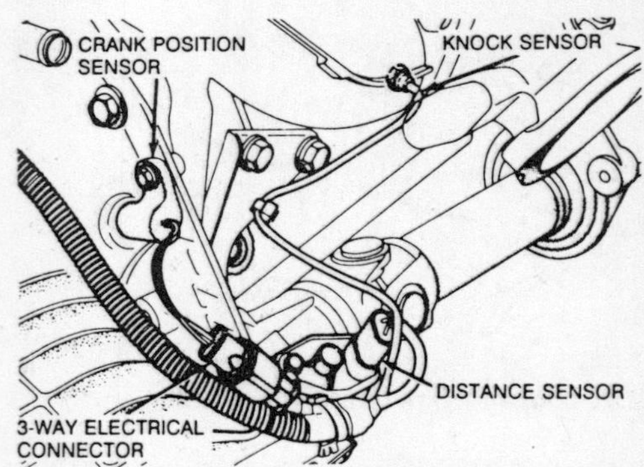

Crankshaft position sensor location – 3.3L engine

The Single Board Engine Controller (SBEC) receives its engine speed and crankshaft position signal from a sensor located in the transaxle housing. This crankshaft position sensor senses slots located around an extension on the torque converter drive plate. A camshaft sensor located in the timing case cover, supplies cylinder identification to the SBEC, by sensing slots located on the camshaft sprocket.

Component Replacement

REMOVAL AND INSTALLATION

Ignition Coil

1. Disconnect the negative battery cable.
2. Remove the spark plug wires from the coil.
3. Disconnect the electrical connector.
4. Remove the coil fasteners.
5. Remove the coil from the ignition module.
6. The installation is the reverse of the removal procedure.

Crank Position Sensor

1. Disconnect the negative battery cable.
2. Disconnect the sensor lead at the harness connector.
3. Remove the sensor retainer bolt.
4. Pull the sensor straight up and out of the transaxle housing.
5. If the removed sensor is being reinstalled, clean off the old spacer completely and attach a new spacer to the sensor. If a new spacer is not used, the sensor will not function properly. New sensors are equipped with a new spacer.

To install:

6. Install the sensor in the transaxle housing and push the sensor down until contact is made with the drive plate.
7. Hold in this position and install the retaining bolt. Torque to 9 ft. lbs. (12 Nm).
8. Connect the sensor lead wire.

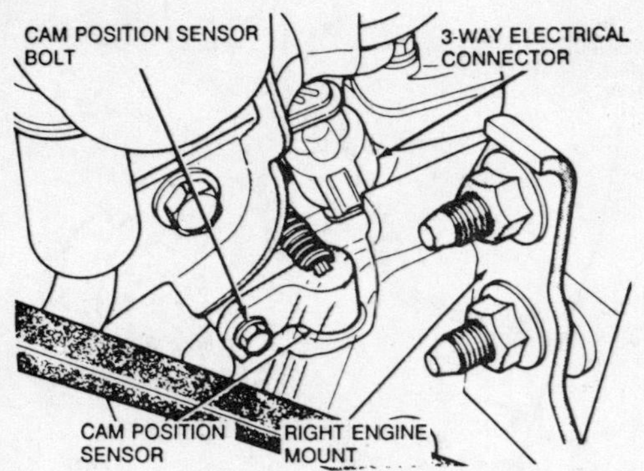

Camshaft position sensor location – 3.3L engine

Cam Position Sensor

1. Disconnect the negative battery cable.
2. Disconnect the sensor lead at the harness connector.
3. Loosen the sensor retaining bolt enough to allow the slot to slide past the bolt.
4. Pull the sensor (not by the wire) straight up and out of the chain case cover. Resistance may be high due to the presence of the rubber O-ring.
5. If the removed sensor is being reinstalled, clean off the old spacer completely and attach a new spacer to the sensor. If a new spacer is not used, the sensor will not function properly. New sensors are equipped with a new spacer.

To install:

6. Inspect the O-ring for damage and replace if necessary.
7. Lubricate the O-ring lightly with oil. Install the sensor to the chain case cover and push the sensor into its bore in the chain case cover until contact is made with the cam timing gear.
8. Hold in this position and tighten the bolt to 9 ft. lbs. (12 Nm).
9. Connect the connector and rout it away from the belt.

IGNITION TIMING

Basic timing should be checked at each tune-up in order to gain maximum engine performance. While timing isn't likely to change very much with electronic ignition system, it become a critical factor necessary to reduce engine emission and improve driveability.

A stroboscopic (dynamic) timing light must be used, because static lights are too inaccurate for emission controlled engines.

Some timing light have other features built into them, such as dwell meters or tachometers. These are nice, in that they reduce the tangle of wires under the hood when you're

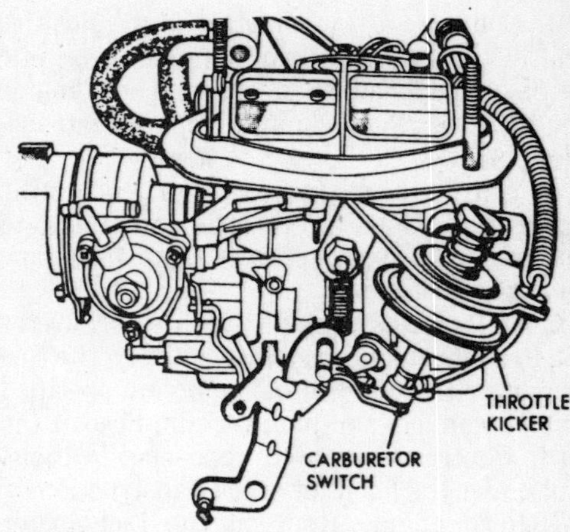

2.2L carburetor switch

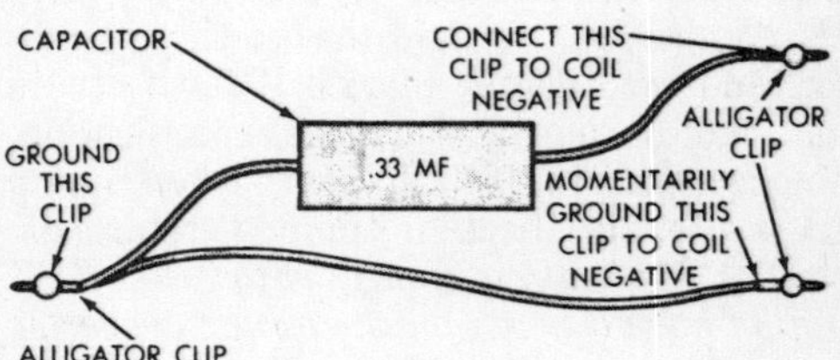

Special jumper wire construction for grounding the coil

working, but may duplicate the functions of tools your already have. One worthwhile feature, which is becoming more of a necessity with higher voltage ignition systems, is an inductive pickup. The inductive pickup clamps around the No. 1 spark plug wire, sensing the surges of high voltage electricity as they are sent to the plug. The advantage is that no mechanical connection is inserted between the wire and the plug, which eliminates false signals to the timing light. A timing light with an inductive pickup should be used on electronic ignition systems

IGNITION TIMING ADJUSTMENT

CAUTION: *Always apply parking brake and block wheels before performing any engine running tests.*

2.2L and 2.6L Engines

1. With engine off, clean off the timing marks.
2. Mark the pulley or damper notch and the timing scale with white chalk or paint. If the timing notch on the damper or pulley is not visible, bump the engine around with the starter or turn the crankshaft with a wrench on the front pulley bolt to get it to an accessible position.
3. Connect a suitable inductive timing light to number one cylinder plug wire.

4. Connect a tachometer unit, Positive Lead to the negative terminal of the coil and the Negative Lead to a known good engine ground. Select the tachometer appropriate cylinder position.

5. Warm the engine to normal operating temperature. Open the throttle and release to make sure idle speed screw is against its stop, and not on fast idle.

6. On vehicles equipped with a carburetor switch, connect a jumper wire between the carburetor switch and ground to obtain specified Rpm. Disconnect and plug vacuum hose at the Spark Control Computer. (See specifications decal under the hood for specific instructions).

7. Read engine Rpm on the tachometer 1,000 Rpm scale, and adjust curb idle to specification noted on the under hood label.

8. Aim the timing light toward timing indicator, and read degree marks. If flash occurs when timing mark is before specification, timing is advanced. If flash occurs when timing mark is after specification, timing is retarded.

NOTE: *Models equipped with the 2.2L engine have a notch on the torque converter or flywheel, with the numerical timing marks on the bell housing. Models equipped with the 2.6L engine have the timing marks on the front crankshaft pulley.*

9. If adjustment is necessary, loosen the distributor hold down screw. Turn the distributor slowly to specified value, and tighten hold down screw. Recheck timing and curb idle. If curb idle have change, readjust to specified value and reset ignition timing. Repeat curb idle setting, and ignition timing until both are within specification.

10. Disconnect timing light, and reconnect all vacuum hoses necessary.

11. Turn engine off and remove jumper wire, and tachometer.

2.5L and 3.0L Engines

1. With the engine off, clean off the timing marks.

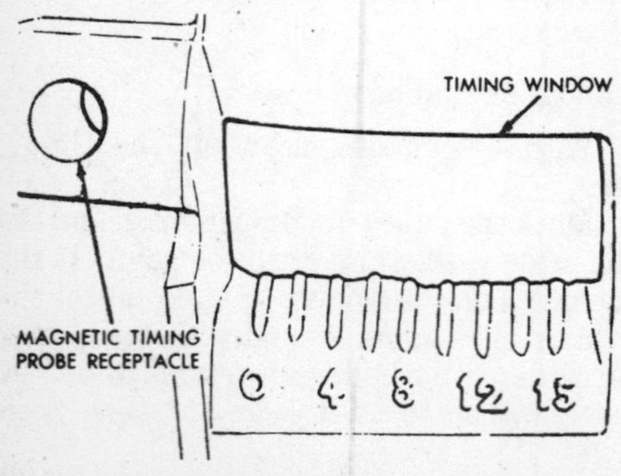

2.2L timing mark location

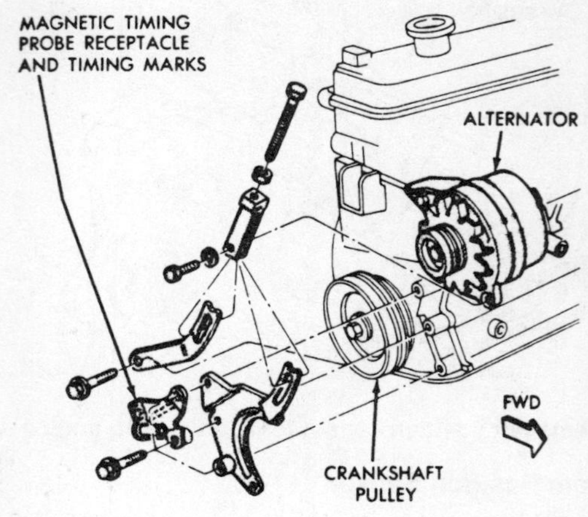

2.6L timing marks

2. Mark the pulley or damper notch and the timing scale with white chalk or paint. If the timing notch on the damper or pulley is not visible, bump the engine around with the starter or turn the crankshaft with a wrench on the front pulley bolt to get it to an accessible position.

3. Connect a suitable inductive timing light to number one cylinder plug wire.

4. Connect a tachometer unit, positive lead to the negative terminal of the coil and the negative lead to a known good engine ground. Select the tachometer appropriate cylinder position.

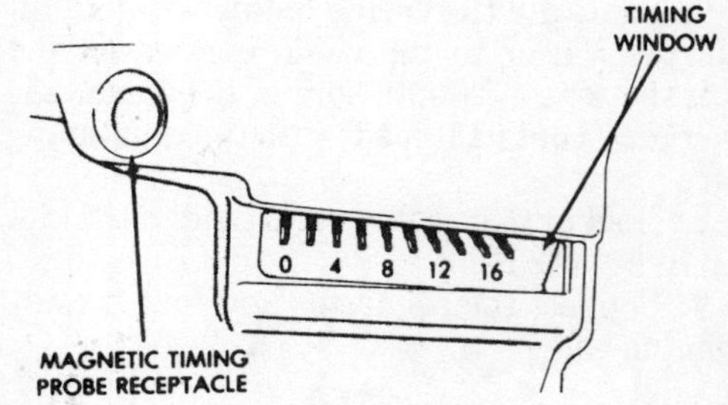

2.5L timing marks

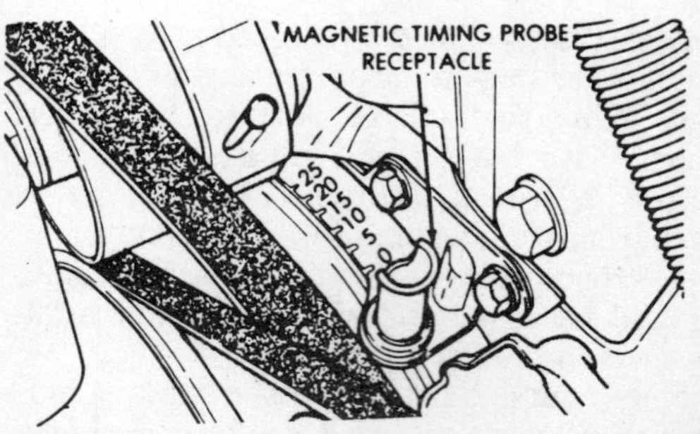

3.0L timing marks

5. Warm the engine to normal operating temperature.

6. With engine at normal operating temperature, disconnect coolant temperature sensor. Radiator fan and instrument panel check engine lamp should come on. (See specifications decal under the hood for specific instructions).

7. Read engine Rpm on the tachometer 1,000 Rpm scale, and adjust curb idle to specification noted on the under hood label.

8. Aim the timing light toward timing indicator, and read degree marks. If flash occurs when timing mark is before specification, timing is advanced. If flash occurs when timing mark is after specification, timing is retarded.

NOTE: *Models equipped with the 2.5L engine have the timing marks visible through a window on the transaxle housing. Models equipped with the 3.0L engine have the timing marks on the front crankshaft pulley.*

9. If adjustment is necessary, loosen the distributor hold down screw. Turn the distributor

HALL EFFECT ELECTRONIC SPARK ADVANCE SYSTEM DIAGNOSIS

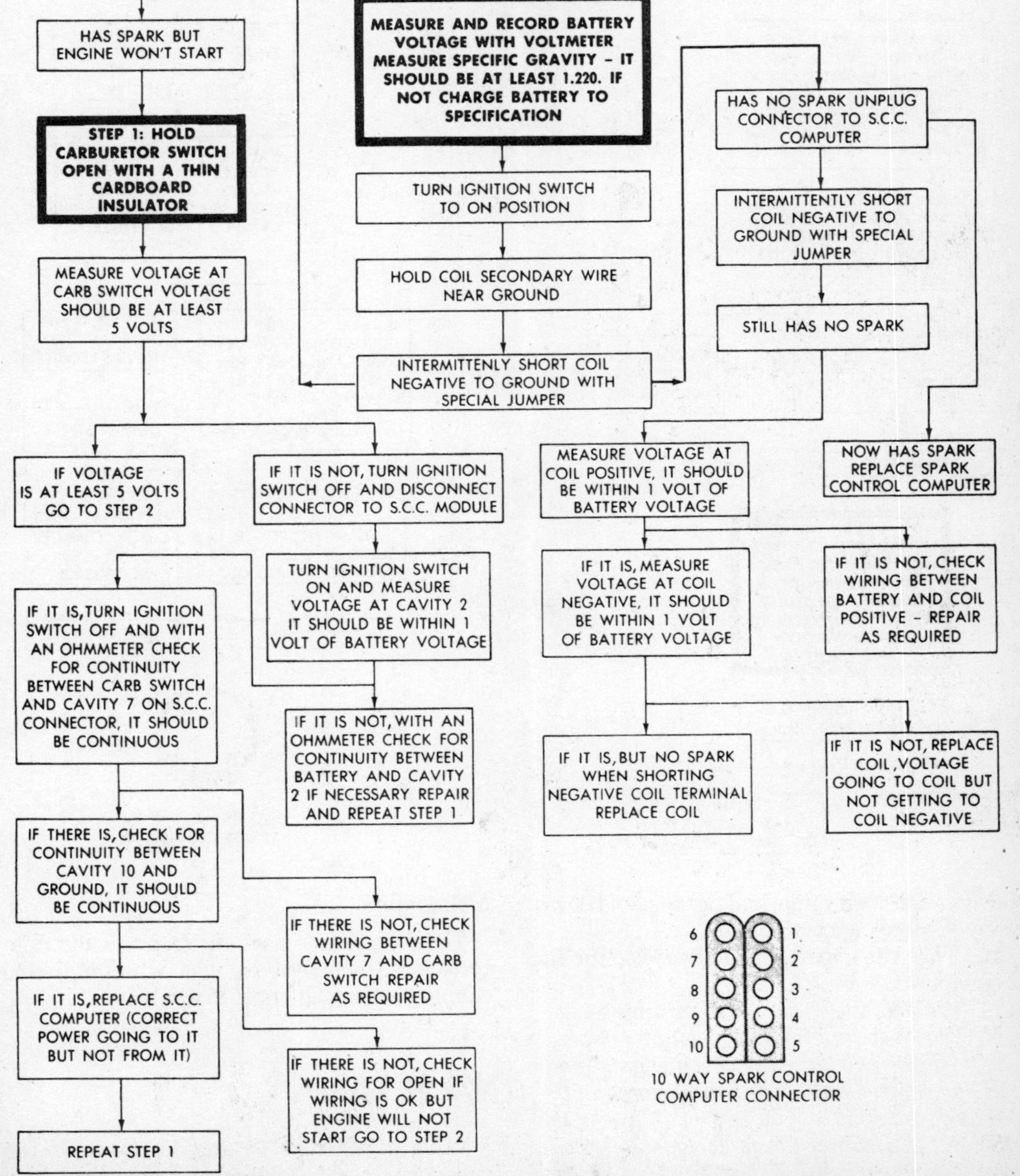

HALL EFFECT ELECTRONIC SPARK ADVANCE SYSTEM DIAGNOSIS

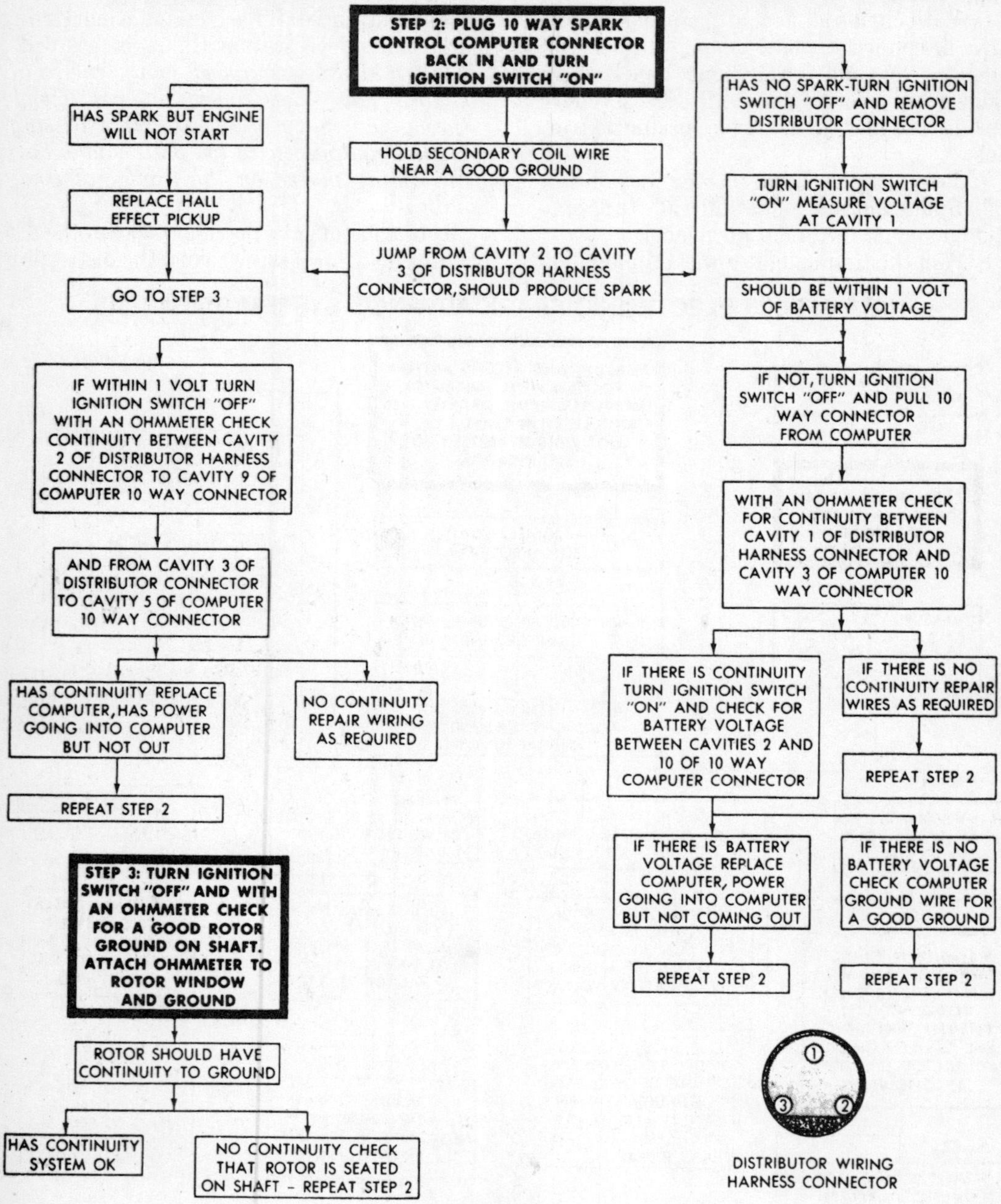

STEP 2: PLUG 10 WAY SPARK CONTROL COMPUTER CONNECTOR BACK IN AND TURN IGNITION SWITCH "ON"

HOLD SECONDARY COIL WIRE NEAR A GOOD GROUND

JUMP FROM CAVITY 2 TO CAVITY 3 OF DISTRIBUTOR HARNESS CONNECTOR, SHOULD PRODUCE SPARK

HAS SPARK BUT ENGINE WILL NOT START

REPLACE HALL EFFECT PICKUP

GO TO STEP 3

HAS NO SPARK-TURN IGNITION SWITCH "OFF" AND REMOVE DISTRIBUTOR CONNECTOR

TURN IGNITION SWITCH "ON" MEASURE VOLTAGE AT CAVITY 1

SHOULD BE WITHIN 1 VOLT OF BATTERY VOLTAGE

IF WITHIN 1 VOLT TURN IGNITION SWITCH "OFF" WITH AN OHMMETER CHECK CONTINUITY BETWEEN CAVITY 2 OF DISTRIBUTOR HARNESS CONNECTOR TO CAVITY 9 OF COMPUTER 10 WAY CONNECTOR

AND FROM CAVITY 3 OF DISTRIBUTOR CONNECTOR TO CAVITY 5 OF COMPUTER 10 WAY CONNECTOR

HAS CONTINUITY REPLACE COMPUTER, HAS POWER GOING INTO COMPUTER BUT NOT OUT

REPEAT STEP 2

NO CONTINUITY REPAIR WIRING AS REQUIRED

IF NOT, TURN IGNITION SWITCH "OFF" AND PULL 10 WAY CONNECTOR FROM COMPUTER

WITH AN OHMMETER CHECK FOR CONTINUITY BETWEEN CAVITY 1 OF DISTRIBUTOR HARNESS CONNECTOR AND CAVITY 3 OF COMPUTER 10 WAY CONNECTOR

IF THERE IS CONTINUITY TURN IGNITION SWITCH "ON" AND CHECK FOR BATTERY VOLTAGE BETWEEN CAVITIES 2 AND 10 OF 10 WAY COMPUTER CONNECTOR

IF THERE IS BATTERY VOLTAGE REPLACE COMPUTER, POWER GOING INTO COMPUTER BUT NOT COMING OUT

REPEAT STEP 2

IF THERE IS NO BATTERY VOLTAGE CHECK COMPUTER GROUND WIRE FOR A GOOD GROUND

REPEAT STEP 2

IF THERE IS NO CONTINUITY REPAIR WIRES AS REQUIRED

REPEAT STEP 2

STEP 3: TURN IGNITION SWITCH "OFF" AND WITH AN OHMMETER CHECK FOR A GOOD ROTOR GROUND ON SHAFT. ATTACH OHMMETER TO ROTOR WINDOW AND GROUND

ROTOR SHOULD HAVE CONTINUITY TO GROUND

HAS CONTINUITY SYSTEM OK

NO CONTINUITY CHECK THAT ROTOR IS SEATED ON SHAFT - REPEAT STEP 2

1 3 2

DISTRIBUTOR WIRING HARNESS CONNECTOR

slowly to specified value, and tighten hold down screw. Recheck ignition timing.

10. Turn the engine off and removed the tachometer and timing light.

11. Connect the coolant temperature sensor. NOTE: *Reconnecting the coolant temperature sensor will turn the check engine lamp off; however, a fault code will be stored in the SMEC. After 50 to 100 key on/off cycles the SMEC will cancel the fault code. The code can also be canceled by disconnecting the battery.*

3.3L Engine

The 3.3L engine uses an electronic distributorless ignition system. The ignition timing cannot be changed or set in any way.

VALVE LASH

Valve adjustment determines how far the valves enter the cylinder and how long they stay open and closed.

Exhaust Valve Closing	Adjust
No. 1 Cylinder	No. 4 Cylinder Valves
No. 2 Cylinder	No. 3 Cylinder Valves
No. 3 Cylinder	No. 2 Cylinder Valves
No. 4 Cylinder	No. 1 Cylinder Valves

If the valve clearance is too large, part of the lift of the camshaft will be used in removing the excess clearance. Consequently, the valve will not be opening as far as it should. This condition has two effects: the valve train components will emit a tapping sound as they take up the excessive clearance and the engine will perform poorly because the valves does not open fully and allow the proper amount of gases to flow in and out of the engine.

If the valve clearance is too small, the intake valve and the exhaust valves will open too far and they will not fully seat on the cylinder head when they close. As a result, the valves will also become overheated and will warp, since they cannot transfer heat unless they are touching the valve seat in the cylinder head.

NOTE: *While all valve adjustments must be made as accurately as possible, it is better to have the valve adjustment slightly loose then slightly tight as a burned valve may result from overly tight adjustments.*

Valve Adjustment

Valve adjustment must be performed after any engine overhaul or when the valve train components emit a tapping sound requiring valve adjustment service.

CAUTION: *Always apply parking brake and block wheels before performing any engine running tests.*

2.2L, 2.5L, 3.0L and 3.3L Engines

The 2.2L, 2.5L and 3.0L engines use hydraulic lash adjusters. No periodic adjustment or checking is necessary.

2.6L Engine (With Jet Valves)

A jet valve is added on some models. The jet valve adjuster is located on the intake valve rocker arm and must be adjusted before the intake valve.

1. Start the engine and allow it to reach normal operating temperature.
2. Stop the engine and remove the air cleaner and its hoses. Remove any other cables, hoses, wires, etc., which are attached to the valve cover, and remove the valve cover.
3. Disconnect the high tension coil-to-distributor wire at the distributor, and allow it to contact a known good engine ground.
4. Torque the cylinder head bolts.
5. Have a helper bump the ignition switch. Watch the rocker arms until piston No. 4 cylinder is at Top Dead Center (TDC) and adjust jet valves as follow.
6. Back out the intake valve adjusting screw two or three turns.
7. Loosen the locknut on the jet valve and back out jet valve adjusting screw.
8. Install a 0.15mm feeler gauge between the jet valve stem and the jet valve adjusting screw.
9. Turn in jet valve adjusting screw until it slightly makes contact with the jet valve stem. While holding jet valve adjusting screw in place tighten jet valve lock nut. Recheck clearance.
10. Complete the adjustment by adjusting intake and exhaust valve clearance on the same cylinder as jet valve you've finished. Refer to Valve Clearance Specification Chart.

2.6L Engine (Without Jet Valves)

1. Start the engine and allow it to reach normal operating temperature.
2. Stop the engine and remove the air cleaner and its hoses. Remove any other cables, hoses, wires, etc., which are attached to the valve cover, and remove the valve cover.
3. Disconnect the high tension coil-to-distributor wire at the distributor, and allow it to contact a known good engine ground.
4. Torque cylinder head bolts.
5. Have a helper bump the ignition switch. Watch the rocker arms until piston is at Top Dead Center (TDC) of the compression stroke (both valves closed).
6. Loosen valve adjuster lock nut. Back out valve adjusting screw and install a feeler gauge between adjusting screw and valve stem.
7. Turn in valve adjusting screw until it

Adjusting the valve lash on the 2.6L engine

slightly touches the feeler gauge. While holding the adjusting screw in place tighten adjusting screw lock nut. Refer to Valve Clearance Specification Chart.

8. Perform Step 5 thru 7 on the remaining three cylinders.

IDLE SPEED AND MIXTURE ADJUSTMENTS

IDLE SPEED ADJUSTMENT

CAUTION: *Always apply the parking brake and block wheels before performing idle adjustment, or any engine running tests.*

Holley 5220/6520—2.2L Engine

1. Check and adjust the ignition timing.
2. Disconnect and plug the vacuum connector at the Coolant Vacuum Switch Cold Closed (CVSCC) located on the top of the thermostat housing.
3. Unplug the connector at the radiator fan and connect a jumper wire so that the cooling fan will run constantly. Remove the PCV valve from the engine and allow it to draw under hood air.
4. Connect a tachometer to the engine.
5. Ground the carburetor switch with a jumper wire.
6. On models equipped with a 6250 carburetor (6250 models are equipped with an oxygen sensor) disconnect the oxygen system test connector on the left fender shield.
7. Start the engine and run until normal operating temperature is reached.
8. Turn the idle adjustment screw until required Rpm is reached. (Refer to the Under hood Specification Label or Tune-Up Chart). Shut off engine.
9. Reconnect the PCV valve, oxygen connector, vacuum connector (CVSCC) and remove the carb switch jumper. Remove the radiator fan jumper and reconnect harness.

NOTE: *After Step 9 is completed, the idle speed might change, this is normal and the engine speed should not be readjusted.*

10. Refer to Fuel System Chapter for fast idle, air conditioning idle speed check and choke kick adjustment procedures.

Mikuni Carburetor — 2.6L Engine

1. Connect a tachometer to the engine.
2. Check and adjust the ignition timing.
3. Start and run the engine until normal operating temperature is reached.
4. Disconnect the cooling fan harness connector.
5. Run at 2500 Rpm for 10 seconds. Return the engine to idle.
6. Wait two minutes and check engine Rpm indicated on the tachometer. If the idle speed is

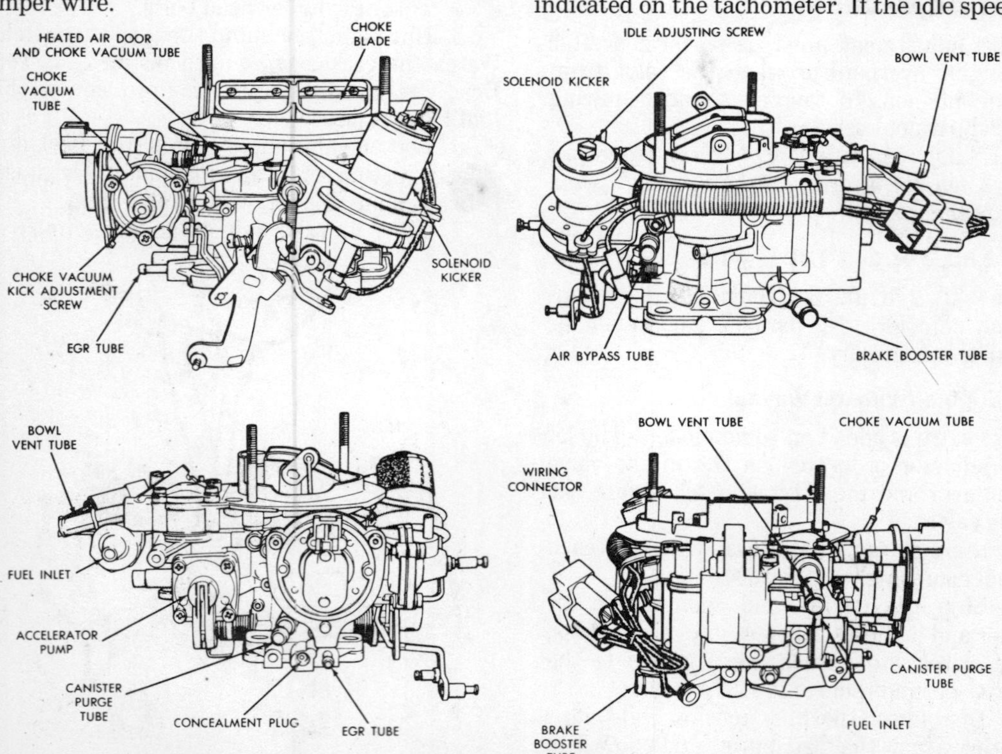

Model 5220 carburetor

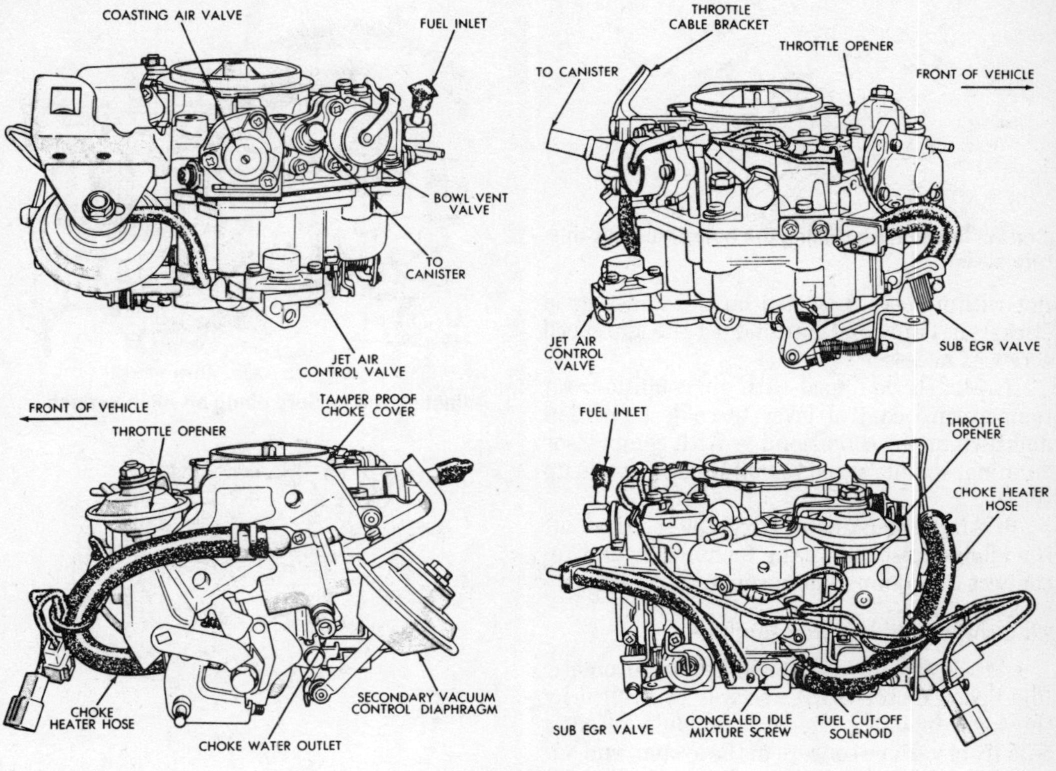

Mikuni carburetor

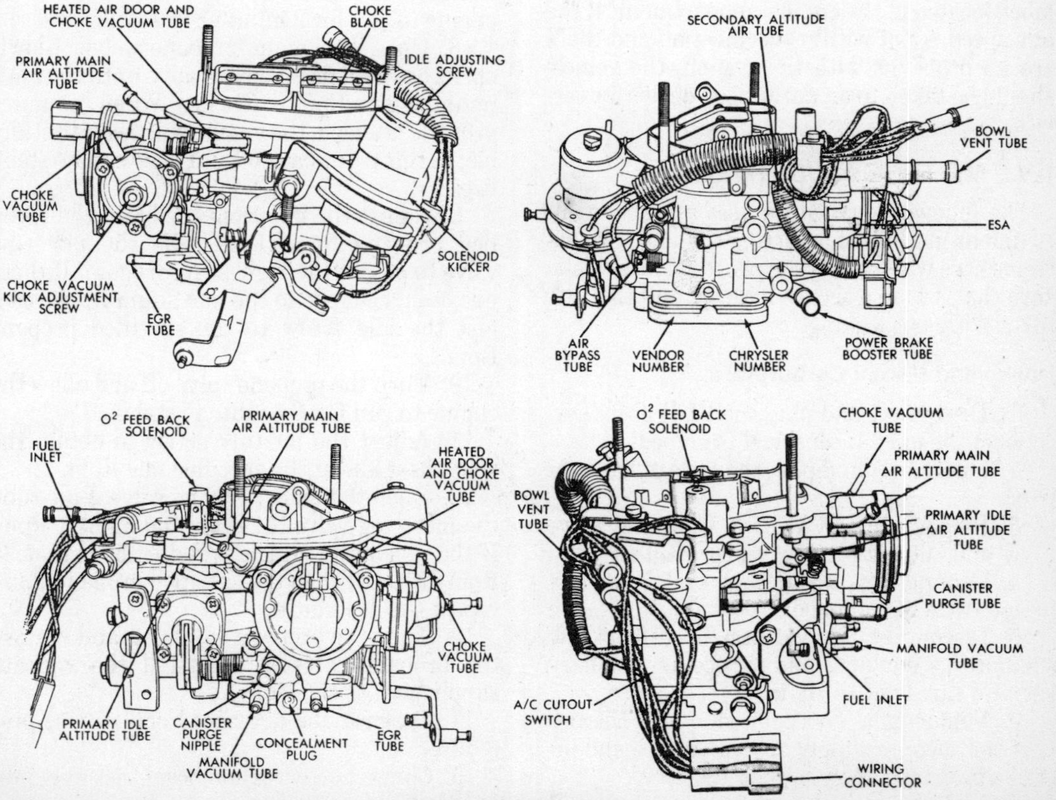

Model 6520 carburetor

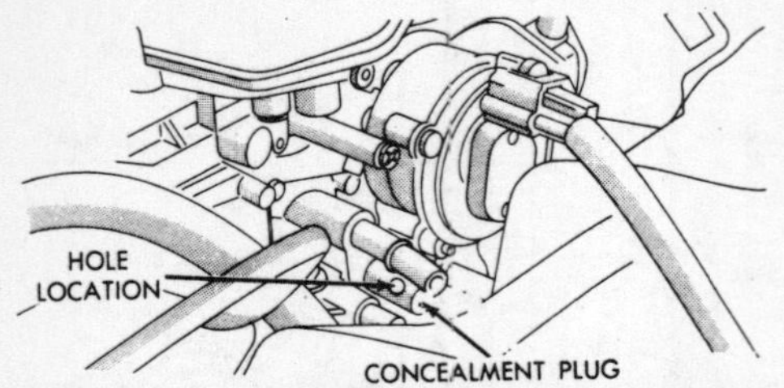

Correct location for drilling the hole at the idle mixture screw

not within specs indicated on the under hood sticker or Tune-Up Chart, adjust the idle speed screw as necessary.

7. Models equipped with air condition, set temperature control lever to coldest position and turn on air conditioning. With compressor running, set idle speed to 900 Rpm with idle up screw.

8. After adjustment is complete, shut off the engine, disconnect the tachometer and reconnect the cooling fan harness.

Electronic Fuel Injected Engines

The idle speed is controlled by the Automatic Idle Speed motor (AIS) which is controlled by the logic module. The logic module receives data from various sensors in the system and adjusts the engine idle to a predetermined speed. Idle speed specifications can be found on the Vehicle Emission Control Information (VECI) label, located in the engine compartment. If the idle speed is not within specification and there are no problems with the system, the vehicle should be taken to an authorized dealer for service.

IDLE MIXTURE ADJUSTMENT

The following procedure uses a propane enrichment method of adjusting the idle. Use extreme care when using the propane tank. Make sure that it is in a secure location and that the fittings are not leaking.

Holley and Mikuni Carburetors

1. Disconnect and plug the EGR hose. Disconnect the oxygen sensor, if equipped.

2. Disconnect and plug the hose at the canister.

3. Remove the PCV hose from the valve cover and allow it to draw under hood air.

4. Ground the carburetor switch with a jumper wire, if equipped.

5. Disconnect the vacuum hose from the computer, if equipped and connect an auxiliary vacuum supply of 16 Hg in.

6. Remove the concealment plug. Disconnect the vacuum supply hose to the tee and install a propane supply hose in its place.

7. Make sure all accessories are off. Install a tachometer and start the engine. Allow the engine to run for 2 minutes to stabilize.

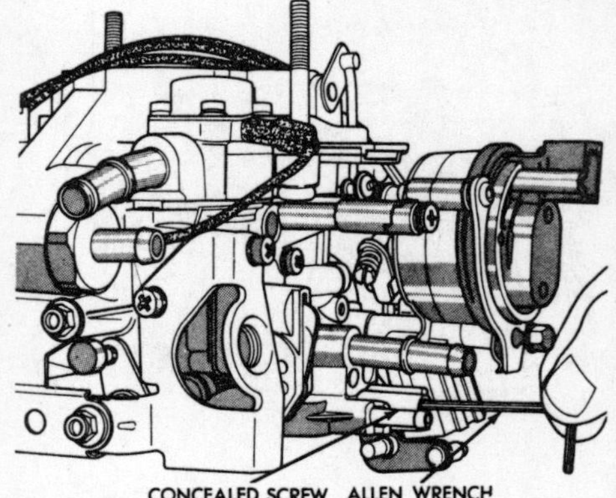

Adjusting the mixture using an Allen wrench

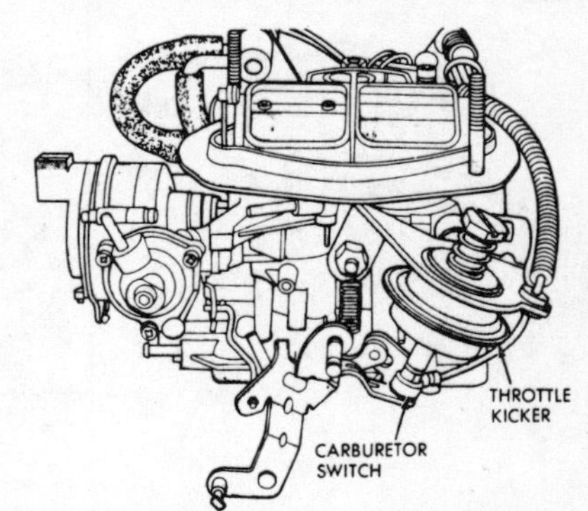

Carburetor switch location — 2.2L engine

8. Open the main propane valve. Slowly open the propane metering valve until the maximum engine Rpm is reached. When too much propane is added, the engine will begin to stumble; at this point back off until the engine stabilizes.

9. Adjust the idle Rpm to obtain the specified propane Rpm. Fine tune the metering valve to obtain the highest Rpm again. If there has been a change to the maximum Rpm, readjust the idle screw to the specified propane Rpm.

10. Turn the propane valve off and allow the engine to run for 1 minute to stabilize.

11. Adjust the mixture screw to obtain the smoothest idle at the specified idle Rpm.

12. Open the main propane valve. Fine tune the metering valve to obtain the highest Rpm. If the maximum engine speed is more that 25 Rpm different than the specified propane Rpm, repeat the procedure.

13. Turn the propane valves off and remove the propane canister. Reinstall the vacuum supply hose to the tee.

14. Perform the idle speed adjustment procedure.

15. Connect all wires and hoses that were previously disconnected.

Engine and Engine Overhaul

3

ENGINE ELECTRICAL

NOTE: *Refer to Chapter 2 for further ignition system component replacement.*

Ignition Coil

TESTING

All Models

NOTE: *On models equipped with the 3.3L engine, the spark at the coil is tested in the same ways as models with a distributor. But each of the coils towers must be checked for spark.*

1. Remove the coil wire from the distributor cap. Hold the end of the wire about $^1/_4$ in. away from a good engine ground point.
2. Have a helper crank the engine. Check for a spark between the coil wire end and the ground point.
3. If there is a spark, it must be constant and bright blue in color.
4. Continue to crank the engine. Slowly move the wire away from the ground point. If arching at the coil tower occurs, replace the coil.
5. If the spark is good and no arching at the coil tower occurs, the ignition system is producing the necessary high secondary voltage.
6. Check to make sure that the voltage is getting to the spark plugs. Inspect the distributor cap, rotor, spark plug wires and spark plugs.
7. If all of the components check okay, the ignition system is probably not the reason why the engine does not start.
8. Check the fuel system and engine mechanical items such as the timing belt.

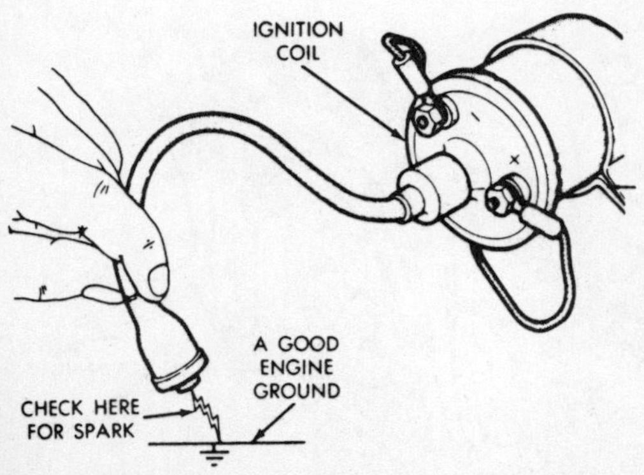

Checking for spark

Ignition Coil

REMOVAL AND INSTALLATION

All Engines Except 3.3L

1. Disconnect the negative battery cable.
2. Remove the coil wire from the top of the coil.
3. Remove the wires from the top of the coil.
4. Remove the coil mounting bolt and remove the coil.
5. Mount the replacement coil in position and reconnect all of the wires.
6. Connect the battery cable.

3.3L Engine

1. Disconnect the negative battery cable.
2. Remove the electrical connector from the coil assembly. Tag and disconnect the spark plug wires from the coil assembly.
3. Remove the coil mounting bolts and remove the coil assembly from the engine.
4. Mount the coil in position and connect all of the wires. Tighten the coil assembly mounting bolts to 105 inch lbs. (12 Nm).
5. Connect the negative battery cable.

Distributor Cap

REMOVAL AND INSTALLATION

1. Remove the splash shield retaining screws and the splash shield.
2. Loosen the distributor cap retaining screws.
3. Remove the distributor cap
4. Inspect the inside, of the cap, for spark flash over (burnt tracks on cap or terminals), center carbon button wear or cracking, and worn terminals. Replace the cap if any of these problems are present or suspected.

Light deposits on the terminals can be cleaned with a knife, heavy deposits or scaling will require cap replacement.

Wash the cap with a solution of warm water and mild detergent, scrub with a soft brush and dry with a clean soft cloth to remove dirt and grease.

5. If cap replacement is necessary, take notice of cap installed position in relationship to distributor assembly.
6. Number each plug wire so that the correct wire goes on the proper cap terminal when replaced. This can be done with pieces of adhesive tape.

NOTE: *Do not pull plugs wires from distributor cap, they must first be released from inside of cap.*

7. Position the replacement cap on the distributor assembly, and tighten the distributor cap retaining screws.
8. Push the wire terminals firmly to properly seat the wires into the cap.
9. Reinstall the splash shield.

Distributor Rotor

With the distributor cap removed, remove the rotor. Inspect the rotor for cracks, excessive wear or burn marks and sufficient spring tension of the spring to cap carbon button terminal. Clean light deposits, replace the rotor if scaled or burnt heavily. Clean the ground strap on the inner side of the shaft mount. Take care not to bend any of the shutter blades, if blades are bent replace the rotor.

Distributor

REMOVAL AND INSTALLATION

NOTE: *Although not absolutely necessary, it is probably easier (for reference reinstallation, especially if the engine is rotated after distributor removal) to bring the engine to No. 1 cylinder at TDC (top dead center) before removing the distributor.*

1. Disconnect the distributor lead wires, and vacuum hose as necessary.

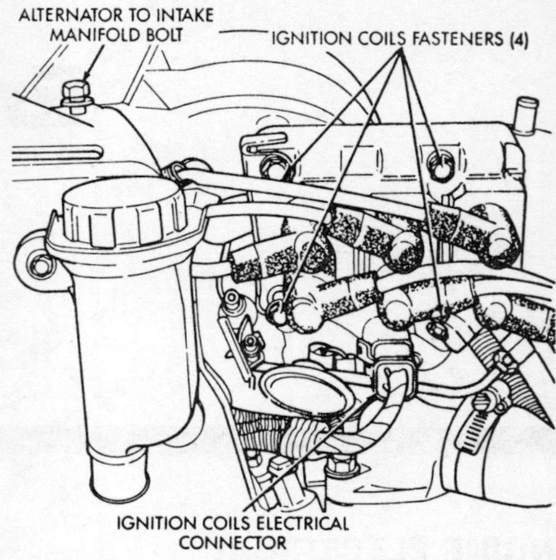

Ignition coil assembly removal – 3.3L engine

2. Remove the distributor cap.
3. Rotate the engine crankshaft (in the direction of normal rotation) until No. 1 cylinder is at TDC on compression stroke. make a mark on the block where the rotor points for installation reference.
4. Remove the distributor hold down bolt.
5. Carefully lift the distributor from the engine. The shaft will rotate slightly as the distributor is removed.
6. If the engine was not disturbed while the distributor was out, lower the distributor into

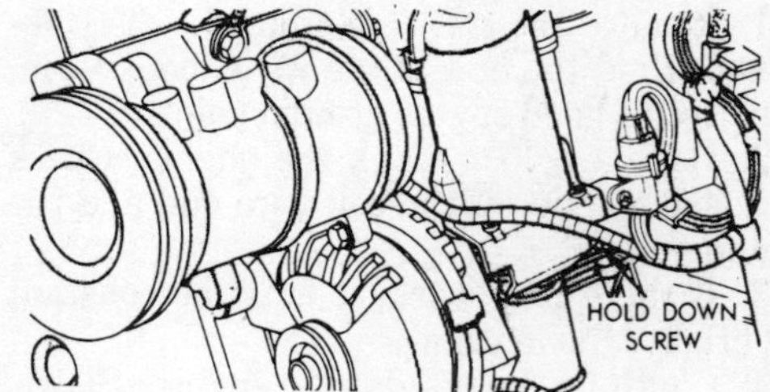

Distributor hold down – 2.2L engine

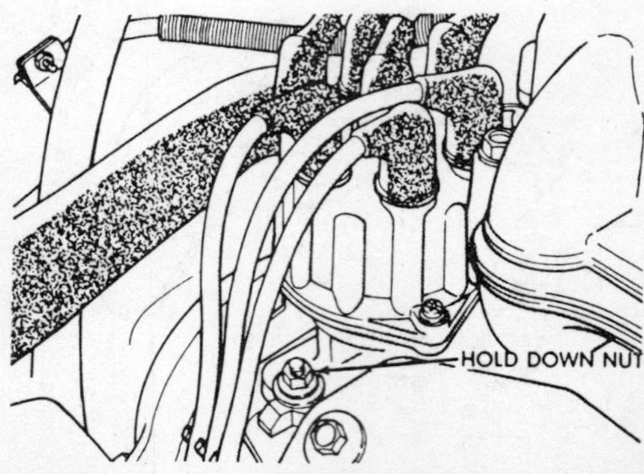

Distributor hold down nut location – 3.0L engine

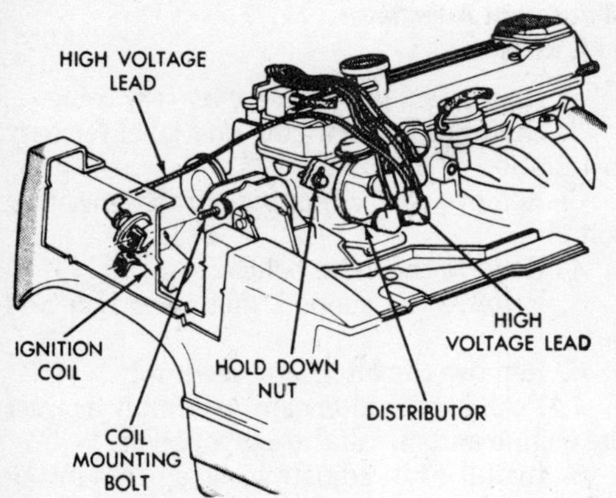

Distributor hold down – 2.6L engine

the engine, engaging the gears and making sure that the gasket is properly seated in the block. The rotor should line up with the mark made before removal.

7. Install the distributor cap.
8. Tighten the hold down bolt. Connect the wires and vacuum hose as necessary.
9. Check and, if necessary, adjust the ignition timing.

NOTE: *The following procedure is to be used if the engine was cranked with the distributor removed.*

10. If the engine has been cranked/turned while the distributor was removed, rotate the crankshaft until the number one piston is at TDC on the compression stroke. This will be indicated by the O mark on the flywheel (2.2L and 2.5L engines) aligned with the pointer on the clutch housing, or crank pulley (2.6L and 3.0L engines) aligned with the pointer on engine front cover.
11. Position the rotor just ahead of the No. 1 terminal of the cap and lower the distributor into the engine. With the distributor fully seated, the rotor should be directly under the No. 1 terminal.
12. Install the distributor cap.
13. Tighten the hold down bolt. Connect the wires and vacuum hose as necessary.
14. Check and, if necessary, adjust the ignition timing.

Alternator

ALTERNATOR PRECAUTIONS

Some precautions should be taken when working on this, or any other, AC charging system.

1. Never switch battery polarity.
2. When installing a battery, always connect the grounded terminal first.
3. Never disconnect the battery while the engine is running.
4. If the molded connector is disconnected from the alternator, never ground the hot wire.
5. Never run the alternator with the main output cable disconnected.
6. Never electric weld around the truck without disconnecting the alternator.
7. Never apply any voltage in excess of battery voltage while testing.
8. Never jump a battery for starting purposes with more than 12v.

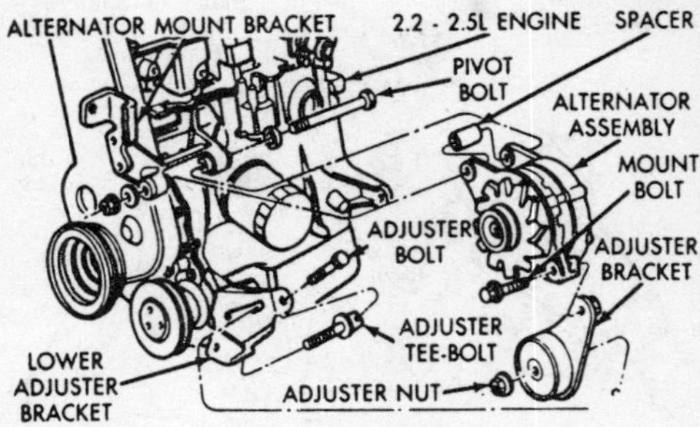

Alternator mounting – 2.2/2.5L engine

REMOVAL AND INSTALLATION

Chrysler Alternator
2.2L Engine

1. Disconnect the negative battery cable.
2. Disconnect the wiring and label for easy installation.
3. Remove the air conditioning compressor drive belt if equipped.
4. Loosen the alternator adjusting bracket bolt and adjusting bolt. Remove the alternator belt.
5. Remove the bracket bolt and the mounting bolt.
6. Remove the pivot bolt and nut.
7. Remove the alternator.
8. Position the alternator against the engine.
9. Install the pivot bolt and nut.
10. Install the mounting bracket bolts, and adjusting bolt.
11. Install drive belts and adjust to specification.
12. Tighten all the mounting bolts and nuts.
13. Connect all alternator terminals.
14. Connect the negative battery cable.

Bosch Alternator
2.2L Engine

1. Disconnect the negative battery cable.
2. Disconnect the wiring and label for easy installation.
3. Remove the air conditioning compressor drive belt.
4. Loosen the alternator adjusting bracket lock nut and adjusting screw. Remove the alternator belt.

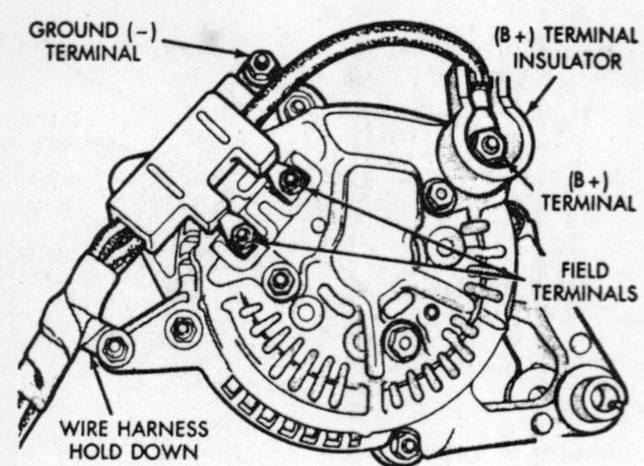

Disconnecting alternator wiring – 3.0L engine

5. Remove the bracket locknut and mounting bolt.
6. Remove the pivot bolt and nut.
7. Remove the alternator.
8. Position the alternator against the engine.
9. Install pivot bolt and nut.
10. Set the mounting bracket in place and install the bracket mounting bolt and locknut.
11. Install the drive belts and adjust to specification.
12. Tighten all the mounting bolts and nuts.
13. Connect all alternator terminals.
14. Connect the negative battery cable.

Bosch and Chrysler Alternators
2.5L Engine

1. Disconnect the negative battery cable.
2. Remove the drive belts.
3. Remove the adjusting bracket to engine mounting bolt.
4. Remove the adjusting locking bolt and nut, and remove the mounting bracket.
5. Position the alternator to gain access to the wiring.
6. Disconnect the wiring and label for easy installation.
7. Remove the pivot bolt, nut, and washers.
8. Remove the alternator assembly from the engine.
9. Position the alternator assembly against the engine.
10. Loosely install the pivot bolt, washers, and nut.
11. Install all wiring.
12. Position the mounting bracket and install engine mounting bolt.
13. Loosely install the adjusting locking bolt and nut.
14. Install the drive belts, and adjust to specification.
15. Tighten all mounting bolts and nuts.
16. Connect the negative battery cable.

Mitsubishi Alternator
2.6L Engine

1. Disconnect the negative battery cable.
2. Disconnect the wiring and label for easy installation.
3. Remove the adjusting strap mounting bolt.
4. Remove the drive belts.
5. Remove the support mounting bolt and nut.
6. Remove the alternator assembly.
7. Position the alternator assembly against the engine and install the support bolt.
8. Install the adjusting strap mounting bolt.
9. Install the alternator belts and adjust to specification.
10. Tighten all the support bolts and nuts.
11. Connect all alternator terminals.
12. Connect the negative battery cable.

Bosch and Nippondenso Alternator
3.0L Engine

1. Disconnect the negative battery cable.
2. Install a $1/2$ in. breaker bar in the tensioner slot. Rotate counterclockwise to release belt tension and remove poly-V belt.
3. Remove the alternator mounting bolts (2).

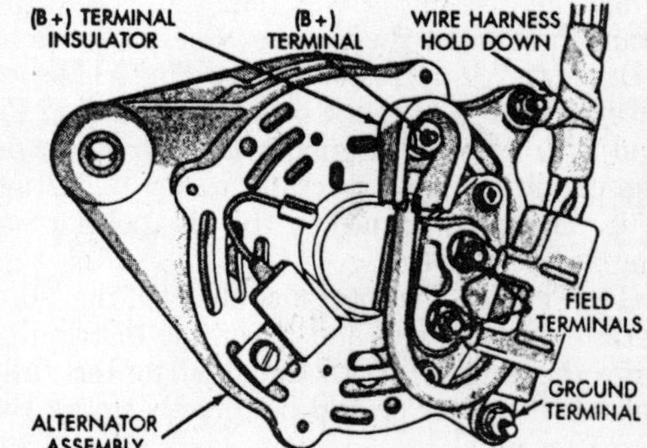

Disconnecting alternator wiring – 2.2/2.5L engines

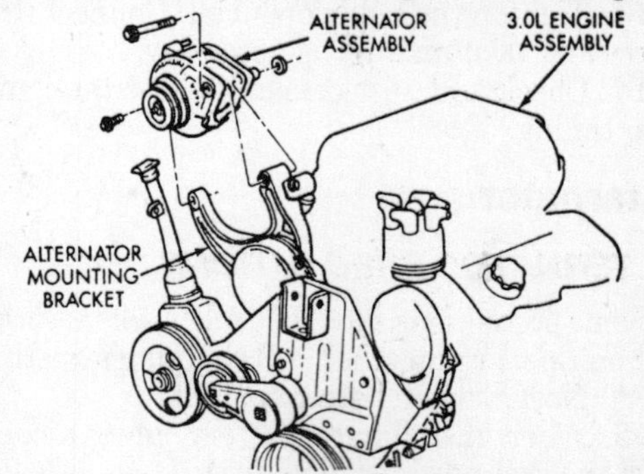

Alternator mounting – 3.0L engine

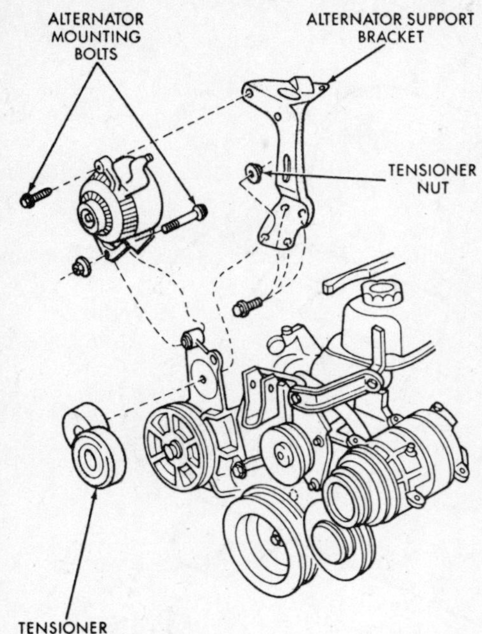

Alternator mounting – 3.3L engine

4. Remove the wiring and remove alternator.
5. To install, position the alternator and install wiring.
6. Set the alternator against the mounting bracket and install the mounting bolts.
7. Rotate the tensioner counterclockwise and install poly-V belt.
8. Connect the negative battery cable.

Nippondenso Alternator 3.3L Engine

1. Disconnect the negative battery cable.
2. Remove the alternator drive belt, by relieving the tension on the dynamic tensioner.
3. Loosen the nut on the support bracket at the exhaust manifold, do not remove it.
4. Remove the alternator tensioner/power steering bracket bolt.
5. Remove the tensioner stud nut and remove the tensioner.
6. Remove the alternator mounting bolts.
7. Remove the power steering reservoir from the mounting bracket, do not disconnect the hoses, and position it out of the way.
8. Remove the alternator support bracket bolts. Remove the intake plenum to alternator bracket bolt and remove the alternator support bracket from the engine.
9. Remove the alternator from the engine and disconnect the electrical leads.

To install:

10. Install the alternator in position on the engine and connect the electrical leads.
11. Install the alternator support bracket, tighten the retaining bolts to 40 ft. lbs. (54 Nm).
12. Install the power steering reservoir on the mounting bracket.
13. Install the alternator mounting bolts, tighten the bolts to 40 ft. lbs. (54 Nm).
14. Install the tensioner and tensioner mounting stud. Install the retaining nut on the exhaust manifold.
15. Install the alternator belt, insert a $1/2$ in. extension into the square hole in the tensioner and turn the tensioner. Tighten the tensioner bolt.
16. Connect the negative battery cable.

Regulator

REMOVAL AND INSTALLATION

Chrysler Alternator (Early Models)

1. Disconnect the negative battery cable.
2. Remove the electrical connection from voltage regulator assembly.
3. Remove the mounting bolts and remove the regulator.
4. This regulator is not adjustable and must be replaced as a unit if found to be defective.
5. Clean any dirt or corrosion from the regulator mounting surface, including mounting holes.
6. Install the replacement electronic voltage regulator.
7. Secured the mounting screws.
8. Connect the voltage regulator wiring connector. Connect the negative battery cable.

NOTE: *All Bosch, Nippondenso, Mitsubishi, and Chrysler (Late Models) alternators have an integral electronic voltage regulator. Voltage regulator replacement on these models requires removal and disassembly of the alternator.*

Starter

TEST PROCEDURES (ON VEHICLE)

NOTE: *The battery is the heart of the electrical system. If the battery is not up to specification it will not deliver the necessary amperage for proper starter operation.*

Starter Does Not Operate

CAUTION: *Before performing this test, disconnect the coil wire from the distributor cap center tower and secure to a good engine ground. This will prevent the engine from starting.*

1. Connect a voltmeter across the battery terminals and confirm that battery voltage

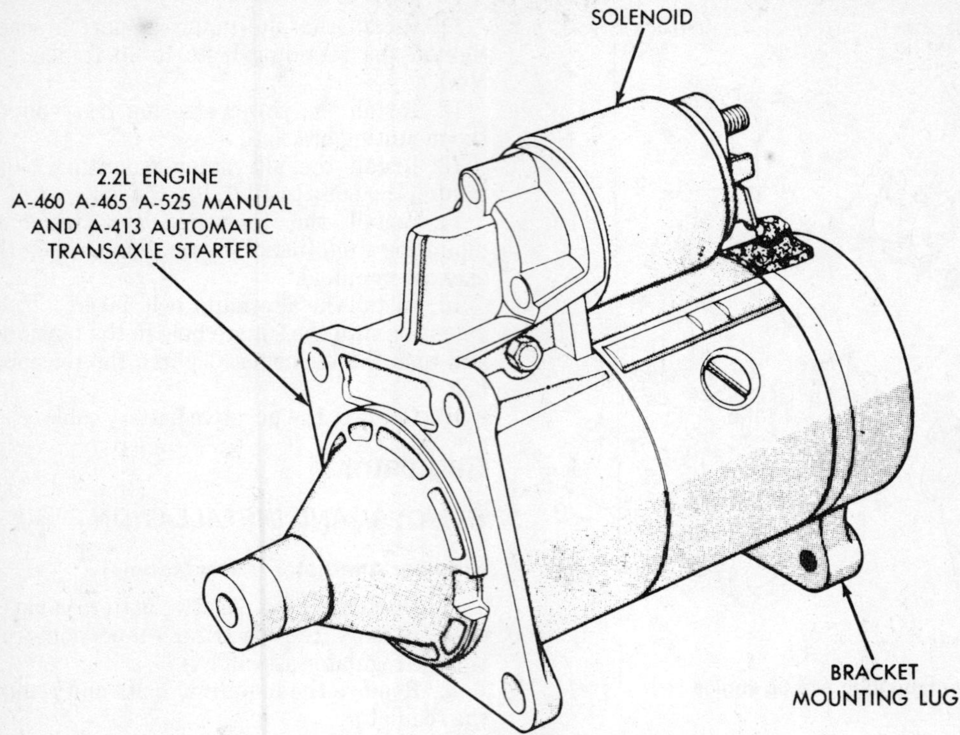

Bosch direct drive starter motor

(12.4 volts) is available for the ignition and cranking system.

2. Turn the headlights on.

3. If the headlights do not operate. Check the battery cables for loose or corroded connection.

4. If the headlights glow normally, have a helper operate the ignition switch. Headlights should remained reasonably bright when ignition switch is operated. If the headlights dim considerably or go out when the ignition switch is operated, the problem is battery related.

5. If headlights remain bright when the ignition switch is operated. The problem is at the starter relay, wiring, or starter motor.

6. Connect a test light to the battery feed terminal of the starter relay. The test light should go on. If the test light is off, check the battery feed wire to starter relay.

7. Connect the test light to the ignition switch terminal of starter relay and a known good engine ground. Have a helper operate the ignition switch. If the test light does not come on when the ignition switch is operated, check the wiring from the ignition switch to the relay. Test light should have came on.

8. Test light on.

9. Connect a heavy jumper wire, between the battery relay feed and the relay solenoid terminal. If the starter motor operates replace the starter relay. If the motor does not operate, remove the starter for repairs.

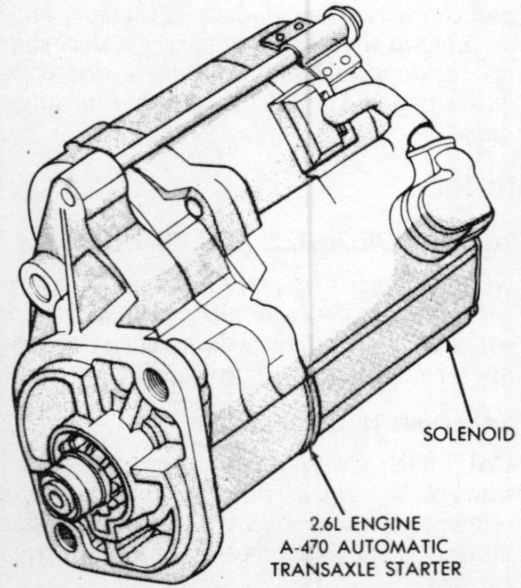

Nippondenso reduction gear starter motor

REMOVAL AND INSTALLATION

1. Disconnect the negative battery cable.

2. Remove the heat shield and its clamps if so equipped.

3. On the 2.2L and 2.5L engine loosen the air pump tube at the exhaust manifold and move the tube bracket away from the starter.

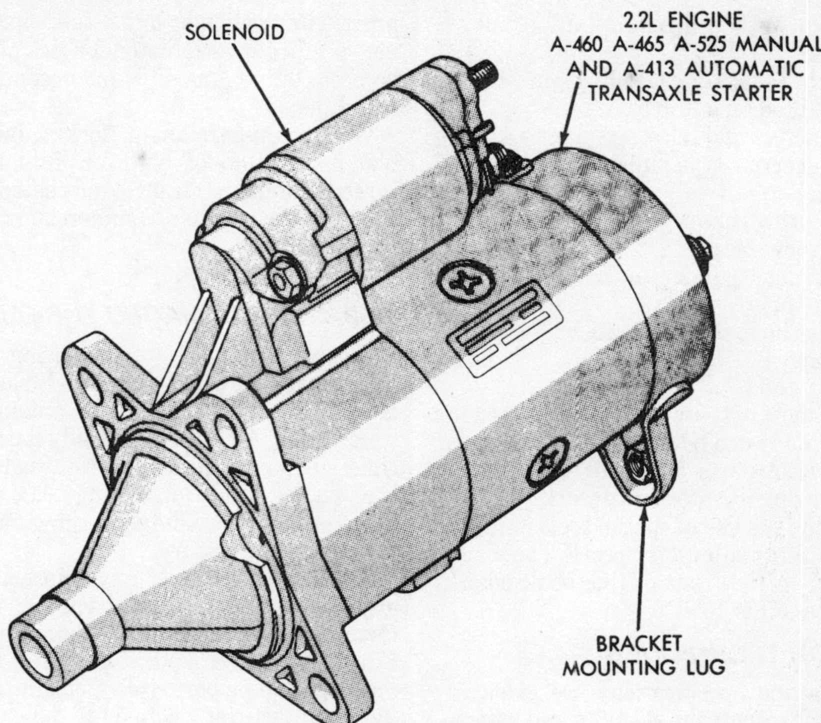

Nippondenso direct drive starter motor

4. Remove the electrical connections from the starter.
5. Remove the bolts attaching the starter to the flywheel housing and the rear bracket to the engine or transaxle.
6. Remove the starter.
7. Position the replacement starter against the mounting surface.
8. Install the mounting bolts.
9. Connect the starter wiring.
10. On 2.2L and 2.5L engines, position the air pump tube toward starter and connect tube bracket the to exhaust manifold.
11. Install the heat shield and clamp.
12. Connect the negative battery cable.

SOLENOID REPLACEMENT

1. Remove the starter as previously outlined.
2. Disconnect the field coil wire from the solenoid.
3. Remove the solenoid mounting screws.
4. Work the solenoid off of shift fork lever and remove the solenoid.
5. Install plunger on replacement solenoid.
6. Install plunger on shift fork lever.
7. Secure solenoid with mounting screws.

ENGINE MECHANICAL

Engine Overhaul Tips

Most engine overhaul procedures are fairly standard. In addition to specific parts replacement procedures and complete specifications for your individual engine, this section also is a guide to accept rebuilding procedures. Examples of standard rebuilding practice are shown and should be used along with specific details concerning your particular engine.

Competent and accurate machine shop services will ensure maximum performance, reliability and engine life.

In most instances it is more profitable for the do-it-yourself mechanic to remove, clean and inspect the component, buy the necessary parts and deliver these to a shop for actual machine work.

On the other hand, much of the rebuilding work (crankshaft, block, bearings, piston rods, and other components) is well within the scope of the do-it-yourself mechanic.

TOOLS

The tools required for an engine overhaul or parts replacement will depend on the depth of your involvement. With a few exceptions, they will be the tools found in a mechanic's tool kit (see "General Information and Maintenance").

More in-depth work will require any or all of the following:

- A dial indicator (reading in thousandths) mounted on a universal base
- Micrometers and telescope gauges
- Jaw and screw-type pullers
- Scraper
- Valve spring compressor
- Ring groove cleaner
- Piston ring expander and compressor
- Ridge reamer
- Cylinder hone or glaze breaker
- Plastigage®
- Engine stand

The use of most of these tools is illustrated in this section. Many can be rented for a one-time use from a local parts jobber or tool supply house specializing in automotive work.

Occasionally, the use of special tools is called for. See the information on Special Tools and Safety Notice in the front of this book before substituting another tool.

INSPECTION TECHNIQUES

Procedures and specifications are given in this section for inspecting, cleaning and assessing the wear limits of most major components. Other procedures such as Magnaflux® and Zyglo® can be used to locate material flaws and stress cracks. Magnaflux® is a magnetic process applicable only to ferrous materials. The Zyglo® process coats the material with a fluorescent dye penetrant and can be used on any material Check for suspected surface cracks can be more readily made using spot check dye. The dye is sprayed onto the suspected area, wiped off and the area sprayed with a developer. Cracks will show up brightly.

OVERHAUL TIPS

Aluminum has become extremely popular for use in engines, due to its low weight. Observe the following precautions when handling aluminum parts:

- Never hot tank aluminum parts (the caustic hot tank solution will eat the aluminum.
- Remove all aluminum parts (identification tag, etc.) from engine parts prior to the tanking.
- Always coat threads lightly with engine oil or anti-seize compounds before installation, to prevent seizure.
- Never over-torque bolts or spark plugs especially in aluminum threads.

Stripped threads in any component can be repaired using any of several commercial repair kits (Heli-Coil®, Microdot®, Keenserts®, etc.).

When assembling the engine, any parts that will be frictional contact must be prelubed to provide lubrication at initial start-up. Any product specifically formulated for this purpose can be used, but engine oil is not recommended as a prelube.

When semi-permanent (locked, but removable) installation of bolts or nuts is desired, threads should be cleaned and coated with Loctite® or other similar, commercial non-hardening sealant.

REPAIRING DAMAGED THREADS

Several methods of repairing damaged threads are available. Heli-Coil® (shown here), Keenserts® and Microdot® are among the most widely used. All involve basically the same principle – drilling out stripped threads, tapping the hole and installing a prewound insert – making welding, plugging and oversize fasteners unnecessary.

Two types of thread repair inserts are usually supplied: a standard type for most Inch Coarse, Inch Fine, Metric Course and Metric Fine thread sizes and a spark lug type to fit most spark plug port sizes. Consult the individual manufacturer's catalog to determine exact applications. Typical thread repair kits will contain a selection of prewound threaded inserts, a tap (corresponding to the outside diameter threads of the insert) and an installation tool. Spark plug inserts usually differ because they require a tap equipped with pilot threads and a combined reamer/tap section. Most manufacturers also supply blister-packed thread repair inserts separately in addition to a master kit containing a variety of taps and inserts plus installation tools.

Before effecting a repair to a threaded hole, remove any snapped, broken or damaged bolts or studs. Penetrating oil can be used to free frozen threads; the offending item can be removed with locking pliers or with a screw or stud extractor. After the hole is clear, the thread can be repaired, as follows:

Checking Engine Compression

A noticeable lack of engine power, excessive oil consumption and/or poor fuel mileage measured over an extended period are all indicators of internal engine war. Worn piston rings, scored or worn cylinder bores, blown head gaskets, sticking or burnt valves and worn valve seats are all possible culprits here. A check of each cylinder's compression will help you locate the problems.

As mentioned in the Tools and Equipment section, a screw-in type compression gauge is more accurate that the type you simply hold against the spark plug hole, although it takes slightly longer to use. It's worth it to obtain a more accurate reading. Follow the procedures below.

1. Warm up the engine to normal operating temperature.

2. Remove all spark plugs.

3. Disconnect the high tension lead from the ignition coil.

4. On fully open the throttle either by operating the carburetor throttle linkage by hand or by having an assistant floor the accelerator pedal.

5. Screw the compression gauge into the no.1 spark plug hole until the fitting is snug.

NOTE: *Be careful not to cross thread the plug hole. On aluminum cylinder heads use extra care, as the threads in these heads are easily ruined.*

6. Ask an assistant to depress the accelerator pedal fully on both carbureted and fuel injected trucks. Then, while you read the compression gauge, ask the assistant to crank the engine 2 or 3 times in short bursts using the ignition switch.

7. Read the compression gauge at the end of each series of cranks, and record the highest of these readings. Repeat this procedure for each of the engine's cylinders. Compare the highest reading of each cylinder to the compression pressure specification in the Tune-Up Specifications chart. The specs in this chart are maximum values.

A cylinder's compression pressure is usually acceptable if it is not less than 80% of maximum. The difference between each cylinder should be no more than 12-14 pounds.

8. If a cylinder is unusually low, pour a tablespoon of clean engine oil into the cylinder through the spark plug hole and repeat the compression test. If the compression comes up after adding the oil, it appears that the cylinder's piston rings or bore are damaged or worn. If the pressure remains low, the valves may not be seating properly (a valve job is needed), or the head gasket may be blown near that cylinder. If compression in any 2 adjacent cylinders is low, and if the addition of oil doesn't help the compression, there is leakage past the head gasket. Oil and coolant water in the combustion chamber can result from this problem. There may be evidence of water droplets on the engine dipstick when a head gasket has blown.

Engine

REMOVAL AND INSTALLATION

Engine Removal and Installation procedures are similar on all models.

1. Disconnect the negative battery cable.

2. Scribe the hood hinge outlines on the hood, and remove the hood.

3. Drain the cooling system. Remove the radiator hoses from the radiator and engine connections.

CAUTION: *When draining the coolant, keep in mind that cats and dogs are attracted by the ethylene glycol antifreeze, and are quite likely to drink any that is left in an uncov-*

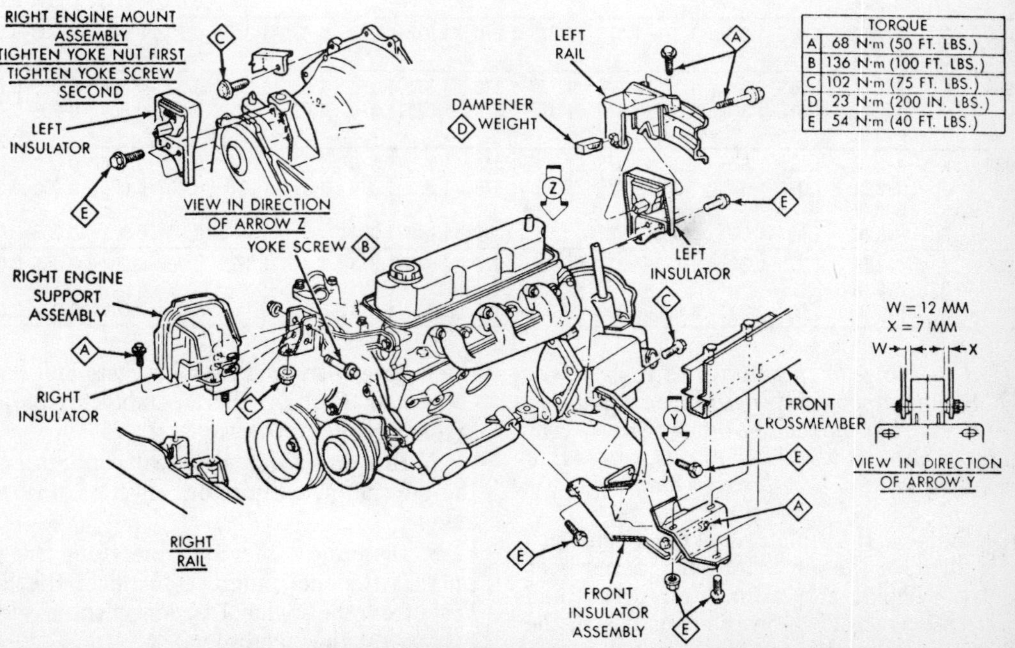

Engine assembly mounting — 3.3L engine

GENERAL ENGINE SPECIFICATIONS

Years	VIN	Engine No. Cyl. Liters	Fuel System Type	SAE Net Horsepower @ rpm	SAE Net Torque @ rpm (ft. lbs.)	Bore × Stroke (in.)	Com-pression Ratio	Oil Pressure @ rpm
1984	C	4-2.2L	2BBL	84 @ 4800	111 @ 2400	3.44 × 3.62	8.5:1	60–90 @ 2000
	G	4-2.6L	2BBL	92 @ 4500	131 @ 2500	3.59 × 3.86	8.2:1	56 @ 2000
1985	C	4-2.2L	2BBL	84 @ 4800	111 @ 2400	3.44 × 3.62	8.5:1	60–90 @ 2000
	G	4-2.6L	2BBL	92 @ 4500	131 @ 2500	3.59 × 3.86	8.2:1	56 @ 2000
1986	C	4-2.2L	2BBL	96 @ 5200	119 @ 3200	3.44 × 3.62	9.5:1	50 @ 2000
	G	4-2.6L	2BBL	101 @ 5600	140 @ 2800	3.59 × 3.86	8.7:1	85 @ 2500
1987	C	4-2.2L	2BBL	96 @ 5200	119 @ 3200	3.44 × 3.62	9.5:1	50 @ 2000
	K	4-2.5L	EFI	100 @ 4800	135 @ 2800	3.44 × 4.09	8.9:1	30–80 @ 3000
	G	4-2.6L	2BBL	101 @ 5600	140 @ 2800	3.59 × 3.86	8.7:1	85 @ 2500
1988	K	4-2.5L	EFI	100 @ 4800	135 @ 2800	3.44 × 4.09	8.9:1	30–80 @ 3000
	3	6-3.0L	EFI	142 @ 5000	173 @ 2800	3.59 × 2.99	8.9:1	30–80 @ 3000
1989	K	4-2.5L	EFI	100 @ 4800	135 @ 2800	3.44 × 4.09	8.9:1	30–80 @ 3000
	J	4-2.5L	TURBO	150 @ 4800	180 @ 2000	3.44 × 4.09	7.8:1	30–80 @ 3000
	3	6-3.0L	EFI	142 @ 5000	173 @ 2800	3.59 × 2.99	8.9:1	30–80 @ 3000
1990	K	4-2.5L	EFI	100 @ 4800	135 @ 2800	3.44 × 4.09	8.9:1	30–80 @ 3000
	J	4-2.5L	TURBO	150 @ 4800	180 @ 2000	3.44 × 4.09	7.8:1	30–80 @ 3000
	3	6-3.0L	EFI	142 @ 5000	173 @ 2800	3.59 × 2.99	8.9:1	30–80 @ 3000
	R	6-3.3L	EFI	150 @ 4000	185 @ 3600	3.66 × 3.19	8.9:1	30–80 @ 3000
1991	K	4-2.5L	EFI	100 @ 4800	135 @ 2800	3.44 × 4.09	8.9:1	30–80 @ 3000
	3	6-3.0L	EFI	142 @ 5000	173 @ 2800	3.59 × 2.99	8.9:1	30–80 @ 3000
	R	6-3.3L	EFI	150 @ 4000	185 @ 3600	3.66 × 3.19	8.9:1	30–80 @ 3000

CAMSHAFT SPECIFICATIONS

Years	Vin	Engine No. Cyl. Liters	Journal Diameter (in.)					Bearing Clearance (in.)	Camshaft Endplay (in.)
			1	2	3	4	5		
1984	C	4-2.2L	1.375–1.376	1.375–1.376	1.375–1.376	1.375–1.376	1.375–1.376	0.002–0.004	0.005–0.013
	G	4-2.6L	—	—	—	—	—	0.002–0.008	0.004–0.008
1985	C	4-2.2L	1.375–1.376	1.375–1.376	1.375–1.376	1.375–1.376	1.375–1.376	0.002–0.004	0.005–0.013
	G	4-2.6L	—	—	—	—	—	0.002–0.008	0.004–0.008
1986	C	4-2.2L	1.375–1.376	1.375–1.376	1.375–1.376	1.375–1.376	1.375–1.376	0.002–0.004	0.005–0.013
	G	4-2.6L	—	—	—	—	—	0.002–0.008	0.004–0.008
1987	C	4-2.2L	1.375–1.376	1.375–1.376	1.375–1.376	1.375–1.376	1.375–1.376	0.002–0.004	0.005–0.013
	K	4-2.5L	1.375–1.376	1.375–1.376	1.375–1.376	1.375–1.376	1.375–1.376	0.002–0.004	0.005–0.020
	G	4-2.6L	—	—	—	—	—	0.002–0.008	0.004–0.008
1988	K	4-2.5L	1.375–1.376	1.375–1.376	1.375–1.376	1.375–1.376	1.375–1.376	0.002–0.004	0.005–0.020
	3	6-3.0L	—	—	—	—	—	—	—
1989	K	4-2.5L	1.375–1.376	1.375–1.376	1.375–1.376	1.375–1.376	1.375–1.376	0.002–0.004	0.005–0.020
	J	4-2.5L	1.375–1.376	1.375–1.376	1.375–1.376	1.375–1.376	1.375–1.376	0.002–0.004	0.005–0.020
	3	6-3.0L	—	—	—	—	—	—	—
1990	K	4-2.5L	1.375–1.376	1.375–1.376	1.375–1.376	1.375–1.376	1.375–1.376	0.002–0.004	0.005–0.020
	J	4-2.5L	1.375–1.376	1.375–1.376	1.375–1.376	1.375–1.376	1.375–1.376	0.002–0.004	0.005–0.020
	3	6-3.0L	—	—	—	—	—	—	—
	R	6-3.3L	1.997–1.999	1.980–1.982	1.965–1.96	1.949–1.952	—	0.001–0.005	0.005–0.012
1991	K	4-2.5L	1.375–1.376	1.375–1.376	1.375–1.376	1.375–1.376	1.375–1.376	0.002–0.004	0.005–0.020
	3	6-3.0L	—	—	—	—	—	—	—
	R	6-3.3L	1.997–1.999	1.980–1.982	1.965–1.96	1.949–1.952	—	0.001–0.005	0.005–0.012

ered container or in puddles on the ground. This will prove fatal in sufficient quantity. Always drain the coolant into a sealable container. Coolant should be reused unless it is contaminated or several years old.

4. Remove the radiator and fan assembly.
5. Remove the air conditioner compressor from the engine and mounting brackets and hoses connected. Position the assembly to the side and secure out of the way.
6. Remove the power steering pump from the engine with mounting brackets and hoses connected. Position the assembly to the side and secure out of the way.
7. Disconnect all electrical connectors at the alternator, carburetor, injection unit and engine.
8. Disconnect the fuel line from the gas tank at the fuel pump. Disconnect the heat hoses from the engine. Disconnect the accelerator cable at the carburetor.
9. Remove the alternator. Disconnect the

clutch cable from the clutch lever, if equipped with a manual transaxle.

10. Remove the transaxle case lower cover.

11. Automatic transaxle, mark the flex plate to torque converter location.

12. Remove the bolts that mount the converter to the flex plate. Attach a small C-clamp to the front bottom of the converter housing to prevent the converter from falling off of the transaxle.

13. Disconnect the starter motor wiring and remove the starter motor.

VALVE SPECIFICATIONS CHART

Years	VIN	Engine No. Cyl. Liters	Seat Angle (Deg.)	Face Angle (Deg.)	Spring Test Pressure (lbs.)	Spring Installed Height (in.)	Stem-To-Guide Clearance In.		Stem Diameter (in.)	
							Intake	Exhaust	Intake	Exhaust
1984	C	4-2.2L	45	45	95	1.65	0.001-0.003	0.0030-0.0047	0.3124	0.3103
	G	4-2.6L	45	45	61	1.59	0.001-0.004	0.0020-0.0060	0.3150	0.3150
1985	C	4-2.2L	45	45	95	1.65	0.001-0.003	0.0030-0.0047	0.3124	0.3103
	G	4-2.6L	45	45	61	1.59	0.001-0.004	0.0020-0.0060	0.3150	0.3150
1986	C	4-2.2L	45	45	95	1.65	0.001-0.003	0.0030-0.0047	0.3124	0.3103
	G	4-2.6L	45	45	61	1.59	0.001-0.004	0.0020-0.0060	0.3150	0.3150
1987	C	4-2.2L	45	45	95	1.65	0.001-0.003	0.0030-0.0047	0.3124	0.3103
	K	4-2.5L	45	45	115	1.65	0.001-0.003	0.0030-0.0047	0.3124	0.3103
	G	4-2.6L	45	45	61	1.59	0.001-0.004	0.0020-0.0060	0.3150	0.3150
1988	K	4-2.5L	45	45	115	1.65	0.001-0.003	0.0030-0.0047	0.3124	0.3103
	3	6-3.0L	44.5	45.5	73	1.59	0.001-0.002	0.0020-0.0030	0.3130-0.3140	0.3120-0.3130
1989	K	4-2.5L	45	45	115	1.65	0.001-0.003	0.0030-0.0047	0.3124	0.3103
	J	4-2.5L	45	45	115	1.65	0.001-0.003	0.0030-0.0047	0.3124	0.3103
	3	6-3.0L	44.5	45.5	73	1.59	0.001-0.002	0.0020-0.0030	0.3130-0.3140	0.3120-0.3130
1990	K	4-2.5L	45	45	115	1.65	0.001-0.003	0.0030-0.0047	0.3124	0.3103
	J	4-2.5L	45	45	115	1.65	0.001-0.003	0.0030-0.0047	0.3124	0.3103
	3	6-3.0L	44.5	45.5	73	1.59	0.001-0.002	0.0020-0.0030	0.3130-0.3140	0.3120-0.3130
	R	6-3.3L	45	44.5	60	1.56				
1991	K	4-2.5L	45	45	115	1.65	0.001-0.003	0.0030-0.0047	0.3124	0.3103
	3	6-3.0L	44.5	45.5	73	1.59	0.001-0.002	0.0020-0.0030	0.3130-0.3140	0.3120-0.3130
	R	6-3.3L	45	44.5	60	1.56	0.002-0.016	0.0020-0.0160	0.3110-0.3120	0.3110-0.3120

CRANKSHAFT AND CONNECTING ROD SPECIFICATIONS

Years	VIN	Engine No. Cyl. Liters	Crankshaft				Connecting Rod		
			Main Brg. Journal Dia.	Main Brg. Oil Clearance	Shaft End-Play	Thrust On No.	Journal Diameter	Oil Clearance	Side Clearance
1984	C	4-2.2L	2.3630-2.3630	0.0003-0.0031	0.002-0.007	3	1.9680-1.9690	0.0008-0.0034	0.005-0.013
	G	4-2.6L	2.3622	0.0008-0.0028	0.002-0.007	3	2.0866	0.0008-0.0028	0.004-0.010
1985	C	4-2.2L	2.3630-2.3630	0.0003-0.0031	0.002-0.007	3	1.9680-1.9690	0.0008-0.0034	0.005-0.013
	G	4-2.6L	2.3622	0.0008-0.0028	0.002-0.007	3	2.0866	0.0008-0.0028	0.004-0.010
1986	C	4-2.2L	2.3630-2.3630	0.0003-0.0031	0.002-0.007	3	1.9680-1.9690	0.0008-0.0034	0.005-0.013
	G	4-2.6L	2.3622	0.0008-0.0028	0.002-0.007	3	2.0866	0.0008-0.0028	0.004-0.010
1987	C	4-2.2L	2.3630-2.3630	0.0003-0.0031	0.002-0.007	3	1.9680-1.9690	0.0008-0.0034	0.005-0.013
	K	4-2.5L	2.3630-2.3630	0.0003-0.0031	0.002-0.007	3	1.9680-1.9690	0.0008-0.0034	0.005-0.013
	G	4-2.6L	2.3622	0.0008-0.0028	0.002-0.007	3	2.0866	0.0008-0.0028	0.004-0.010
1988	K	4-2.5L	2.3630-2.3630	0.0003-0.0031	0.002-0.007	3	1.9680-1.9690	0.0008-0.0034	0.005-0.013
	3	6-3.0L	2.3610-2.3630	0.0006-0.0020	0.002-0.010	3	1.9680-1.9690	0.0008-0.0028	0.004-0.010
1989	K	4-2.5L	2.3630-2.3630	0.0003-0.0031	0.002-0.007	3	1.9680-1.9690	0.0008-0.0034	0.005-0.013
	J	4-2.5L	2.3630-2.3630	0.0003-0.0031	0.002-0.007	3	1.9680-1.9690	0.0008-0.0034	0.005-0.013
	3	6-3.0L	2.3610-2.3630	0.0006-0.0020	0.002-0.010	3	1.9680-1.9690	0.0008-0.0028	0.004-0.010
1990	K	4-2.5L	2.3630-2.3630	0.0003-0.0031	0.002-0.007	3	1.9680-1.9690	0.0008-0.0034	0.005-0.013
	J	4-2.5L	2.3630-2.3630	0.0003-0.0031	0.002-0.007	3	1.9680-1.9690	0.0008-0.0034	0.005-0.013
	3	6-3.0L	2.3610-2.3630	0.0006-0.0020	0.002-0.010	3	1.9680-1.9690	0.0008-0.0028	0.004-0.010
	R	6-3.3L	2.5190	0.0007-0.0022	0.001-0.007	2	2.283	0.0008-0.0030	0.005-0.015
1991	K	4-2.5L	2.3630-2.3630	0.0003-0.0031	0.002-0.007	3	1.9680-1.9690	0.0008-0.0034	0.005-0.013
	3	6-3.0L	2.3610-2.3630	0.0006-0.0020	0.002-0.010	3	1.9680-1.9690	0.0008-0.0028	0.004-0.010
	R	6-3.3L	2.5190	0.0007-0.0022	0.001-0.007	2	2.283	0.0008-0.0030	0.005-0.015

PISTON AND RING SPECIFICATIONS

				Ring Gap			Ring Side Clearance		
Years	VIN	Engine No. Cyl. Liters	Piston Clearance	Top Compression	Bottom Compression	Oil Control	Top Compression	Bottom Compression	Oil Control
1984	C	4-2.2L	0.0005–0.0015	0.0110–0.0120	0.0110–0.0120	0.0160–0.0550	0.0016–0.0028	0.0008–0.0020	0.0008–0.0020
	G	4-2.6L	0.0008–0.0016	0.0100–0.0180	0.0100–0.0180	0.0078–0.0350	0.0015–0.0031	0.0015–0.0037	—
1985	C	4-2.2L	0.0005–0.0015	0.0110–0.0120	0.0110–0.0120	0.0160–0.0550	0.0016–0.0028	0.0008–0.0020	0.0008–0.0020
	G	4-2.6L	0.0008–0.0016	0.0100–0.0180	0.0100–0.0180	0.0078–0.0350	0.0015–0.0031	0.0015–0.0037	—
1986	C	4-2.2L	0.0005–0.0015	0.0110–0.0120	0.0110–0.0120	0.0160–0.0550	0.0016–0.0028	0.0008–0.0020	0.0008–0.0020
	G	4-2.6L	0.0008–0.0016	0.0100–0.0180	0.0100–0.0180	0.0078–0.0350	0.0015–0.0031	0.0015–0.0037	—
1987	C	4-2.2L	0.0005–0.0015	0.0110–0.0120	0.0110–0.0120	0.0160–0.0550	0.0016–0.0028	0.0008–0.0020	0.0008–0.0020
	K	4-2.5L	0.0005–0.0015	0.0110–0.0120	0.0100–0.0120	0.0160–0.0550	0.0016–0.0028	0.0008–0.0020	0.0008–0.0020
	G	4-2.5L	0.0005–0.0015	0.0110–0.0120	0.0100–0.0120	0.0160–0.0550	0.0016–0.0028	0.0008–0.0020	0.0008–0.0020
1988	K	4-2.5L	0.0005–0.0015	0.0110–0.0120	0.0110–0.0120	0.0160–0.0550	0.0016–0.0028	0.0008–0.0020	0.0008–0.0020
	3	6-3.0L	0.0008–0.0015	0.0120–0.0180	0.0100–0.0160	0.0120–0.0350	0.0020–0.0035	0.0008–0.0020	—
1989	K	4-2.5L	0.0005–0.0015	0.0110–0.0120	0.0110–0.0120	0.0160–0.0550	0.0016–0.0028	0.0008–0.0020	0.0008–0.0020
	J	4-2.5L	0.0006–0.0018	0.0100–0.0200	0.0080–0.0190	0.0150–0.0550	0.0016–0.0030	0.0016–0.0030	0.0002–0.0080
	3	6-3.0L	0.0008–0.0015	0.0120–0.0180	0.0100–0.0160	0.0120–0.0350	0.0020–0.0035	0.0008–0.0020	—
1990	K	4-2.5L	0.0005–0.0015	0.0110–0.0120	0.0110–0.0120	0.0160–0.0550	0.0016–0.0028	0.0008–0.0020	0.0008–0.0020
	J	4-2.5L	0.0006–0.0018	0.0100–0.0200	0.0080–0.0190	0.0150–0.0550	0.0016–0.0030	0.0016–0.0030	0.0002–0.0080
	3	6-3.0L	0.0008–0.0015	0.0120–0.0180	0.0100–0.0160	0.0120–0.0350	0.0020–0.0035	0.0008–0.0020	—
	R	6-3.3L	0.0009–0.0022	0.0120–0.0220	0.0120–0.0220	0.0100–0.0400	0.0012–0.0037	0.0012–0.0037	0.0005–0.0089
1991	K	4-2.5L	0.0005–0.0015	0.0110–0.0120	0.0110–0.0120	0.0160–0.0550	0.0016–0.0028	0.0008–0.0020	0.0008–0.0020
	3	6-3.0L	0.0008–0.0015	0.0120–0.0180	0.0100–0.0160	0.0120–0.0350	0.0020–0.0035	0.0008–0.0020	—
	R	6-3.3L	0.0009–0.0022	0.0120–0.0220	0.0120–0.0220	0.0100–0.0400	0.0012–0.0037	0.0012–0.0037	0.0005–0.0089

14. Disconnect the exhaust pipe from the exhaust manifold.

15. Remove the right inner engine splash shield. Drain the engine oil and remove the oil filter. Disconnect the engine ground strap.

CAUTION: *The EPA warns that prolonged contact with used engine oil may cause a number of skin disorders, including cancer! You should make every effort to minimize your exposure to used engine oil. Protective gloves should be worn when changing the oil. Wash your hands and any other exposed skin areas as soon as possible after exposure to used engine oil. Soap and water, or waterless hand cleaner should be used.*

16. Attach hoist to the engine.

17. Support the transaxle. Apply slight upward pressure with the chain hoist and remove the through bolt from the right (timing case cover) engine mount.

NOTE: *If the complete engine mount is to be removed, mark the insulator position on the*

TORQUE SPECIFICATIONS

All readings in ft. lbs.

Years	VIN	Engine No. Cyl. Liters	Cylinder Head	Main Bearing	Rod Bearing	Crankshaft Damper	Flywheel	Manifold Intake	Manifold Exhaust
1984	C	4-2.2L	①	30②	40②	50	70	17	17
	G	4-2.6L	70	58	34	87	70	13	13
1985	C	4-2.2L	①	30②	40②	50	70	17	17
	G	4-2.6L	70	58	34	87	70	13	13
1986	C	4-2.2L	①	30②	40②	50	70	17	17
	G	4-2.6L	70	58	34	87	70	13	13
1987	C	4-2.2L	①	30②	40②	50	70	17	17
	K	4-2.5L	①	30②	40②	50	70	17	17
	G	4-2.6L	70	58	34	87	70	13	13
1988	K	4-2.5L	①	30②	40②	50	70	17	17
	3	6-3.0L	70	60	38	110	70	17	17
1989	K	4-2.5L	①	30②	40②	50	70	17	17
	J	4-2.5L	①	30②	40②	50	70	17	17
	3	6-3.0L	70	60	38	110	70	17	17
1990	K	4-2.5L	①	30②	40②	50	70	17	17
	J	4-2.5L	①	30②	40②	50	70	17	17
	3	6-3.0L	70	60	38	110	70	17	17
	R	6-3.3L	③	30②	40②	40	70	17	17
1991	K	4-2.5L	①	30②	40②	50	70	17	17
	3	6-3.0L	70	60	38	110	70	17	17
	R	6-3.3L	③	30②	40②	40	70	17	17

① Tighten in 3 steps:
1st Step: 45 ft. lbs.
2nd Step: 65 ft. lbs.
3rd Step: 65 ft. lbs. plus additional 90 degree turn

② Plus an additional 90 degree turn

③ Tighten in 3 steps:
1st Step: 45 ft. lbs.
2nd Step: 65 ft. lbs.
3rd Step: 65 ft. lbs. plus additional 90 degree turn
Last, torque the small bolt in the rear of the head to 25 ft. lbs.

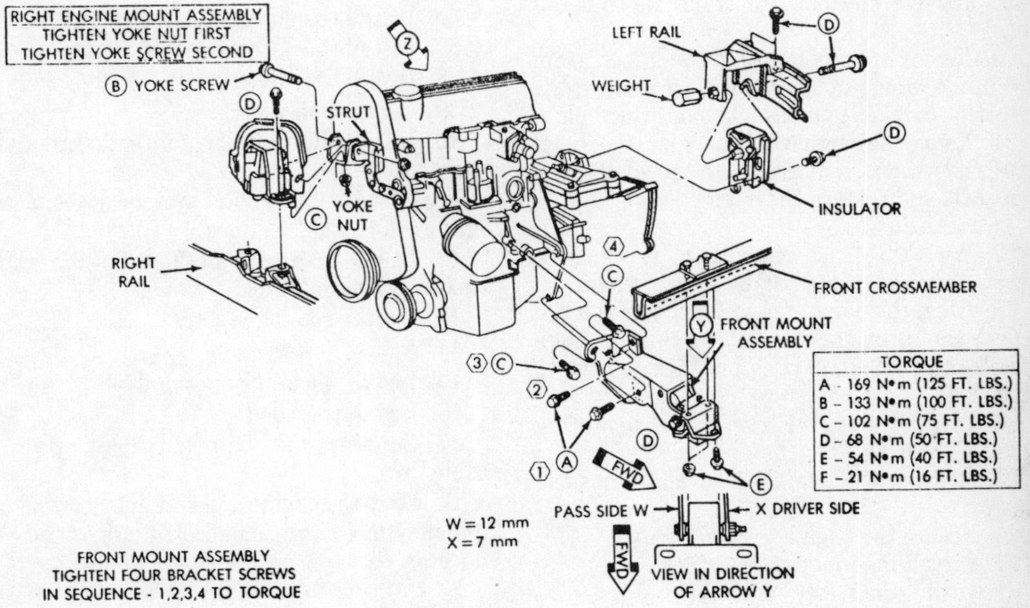

Engine assembly mounting — 2.2/2.5L engines

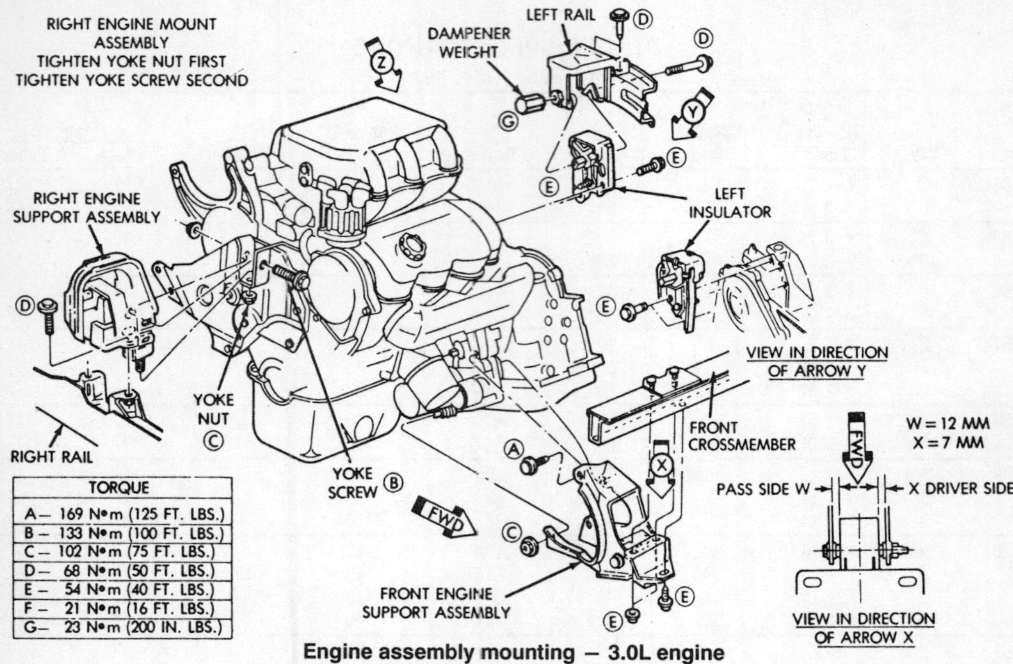

Engine assembly mounting – 3.0L engine

side rail to insure exact reinstallation location.

18. Remove the transaxle to cylinder block mounting bolts.
19. Remove the front engine mount through bolt. Remove the manual transaxle anti-roll strut.
20. Remove the insulator through bolt from the inside wheel house mount, or remove the insulator bracket to transaxle mounting bolt.
21. Raise the engine slowly with the hoist (transaxle supported). Separate the engine and transaxle and remove the engine.

To install:

22. With the hoist attached to the engine. Lower the engine into engine compartment.
23. Align the converter to flex plate and the engine mounts. Install all mounting bolts loosely until all are in position, then tighten to 40 ft. lbs.
24. Install the engine to transaxle mounting bolts. Tighten to 70 ft. lbs.
25. Remove the engine hoist and transaxle support.
26. Secure the engine ground strap.
27. Install the inner splash shield.
28. Install the starter assembly.
29. Install the exhaust system.
30. Install the transaxle case lower cover. (Manual Transaxle)
31. Remove the C-clamp from the torque converter housing, (Automatic Transaxle).
32. Align flex plate and torque converter with mark previously made. (Automatic Transaxle).
33. Install the convertor to flex plate mounting screws. Tighten to (40 ft. lbs.).
34. Install the case lower cover. (Automatic Transaxle).
35. Connect the clutch cable. (Manual Transaxle)
36. Install the power steering pump.
37. Install the air conditioning compressor.
38. Install the alternator.
39. Connect all wiring.
40. Install the radiator, fan and shroud assembly.
41. Connect all cooling system hoses, accelerator cable and fuel lines.
42. Install the engine oil filter. Fill the crankcase to proper oil level.
43. Fill the cooling system.
44. Adjust linkages.
45. Install the air cleaner and hoses.
46. Install the hood.
47. Connect the battery cables, positive cable first.
48. Start the engine and run until normal operation temperature is indicated. Adjust the carburetor.

ENGINE/TRANSAXLE POSITIONING

The insulator on the frame rail (right side) and on the transmission bracket (left side) are adjustable to allow right/left drive train adjustment in relation to the driveshaft distress, front end damage or insulator replacement.

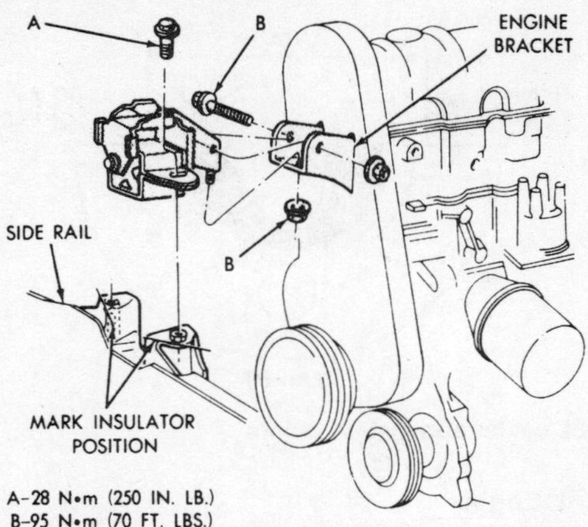

Right side engine mount — 4-cylinder engines

Adjustment

1. Remove the load on the engine mounts by carefully supporting the weight of the engine/transaxle assembly on a floor jack.
2. Loosen the right engine mount insulator vertical mounting bolts and the front engine mount bracket to cross member mounting nuts and bolts. The left insulator is sleeved to provide lateral movement.
3. Pry the engine/transaxle assembly to the left or right as required.
4. Tighten the right engine mount to 20 ft. lbs. and front engine mount to 40 ft. lbs.

Rocker (Valve) Cover

REMOVAL AND INSTALLATION

2.2L Engine

1. Disconnect the negative battery cable.
2. Remove the air cleaner assembly. Remove or relocate any hoses or cables that will interfere with rocker cover removal.

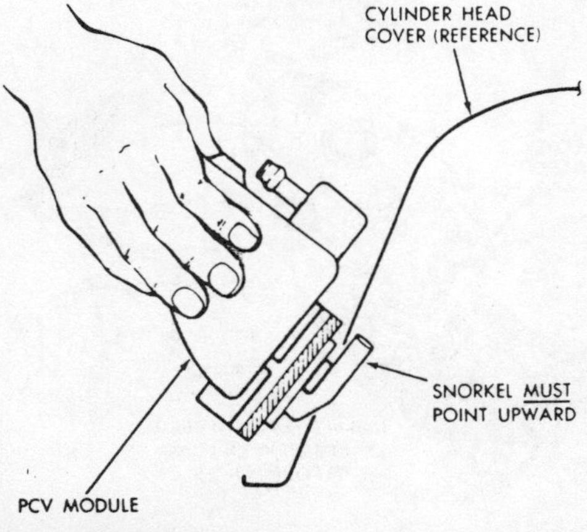

2.2L PCV module

Left side engine mount — 4-cylinder engines

3. Depress the retaining clip that holds the PCV module in the rocker cover and turn the module counterclockwise to remove the module.
4. Remove the cover mounting bolts and the rocker cover from the cylinder head.
5. Clean the cover and head mounting surfaces. Install the PCV module in rocker cover. Turn clockwise to install.

NOTE: *With PCV module installed, snorkel must point upward, toward top of valve cover. Snorkel should be free to rotate.*

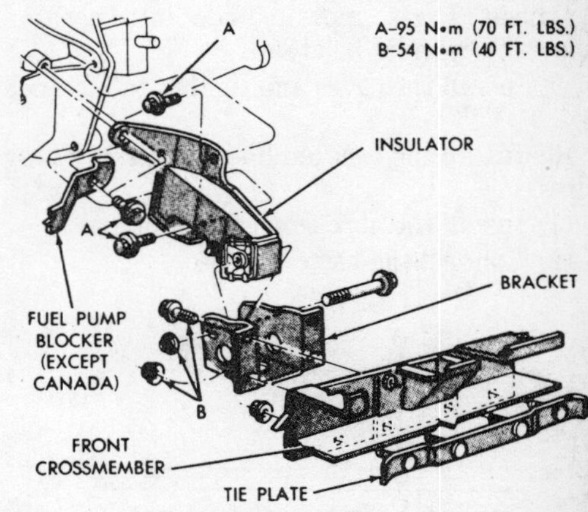

Front engine mount — 4-cylinder engines

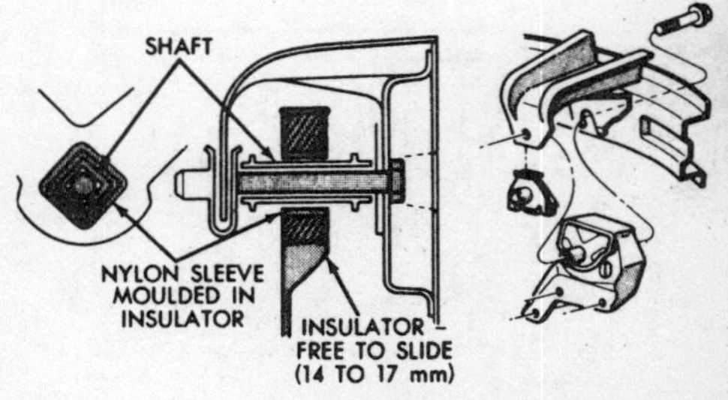

Left side engine mount movement

6. Apply RTV sealant to the rocker cover mounting rail, or install a new cover gasket if provided.

7. Install the rocker cover and tighten to 105 inch lbs.

8. Install the vacuum hoses and spark plug wires.

9. Install the air cleaner assembly.

10. Connect the battery cable.

2.5L Engine

A curtain aiding air/oil separation is located beneath the rocker cover on the cylinder head. The curtain is retained by rubber bumpers.

1. Disconnect the negative battery cable.

2. Remove the air cleaner assembly.

3. Remove any vacuum hoses necessary and relocate spark plug wires.

4. Remove the cover screws and remove the cover.

5. Remove the air/oil separation curtain.

6. Clean the cylinder head, curtain and cover mating surfaces before installation.

7. Install a gasket on the valve cover while pushing the tabs through slots in cover.

8. Install the curtain (manifold side first) with cutouts over cam towers and against cylinder head. Press opposite side into position below the cylinder head rail.

9. Install the cover and tighten to 105 inch lbs..

10. Install the vacuum hoses and spark plug wires.

11. Install the air cleaner assembly.

12. Connect the battery cable.

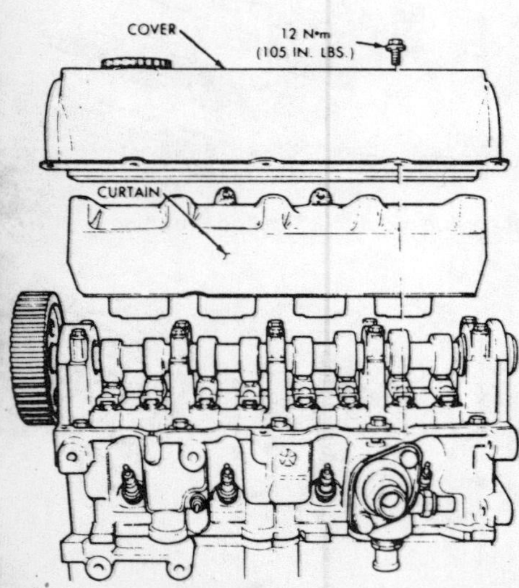

2.5L valve cover curtain

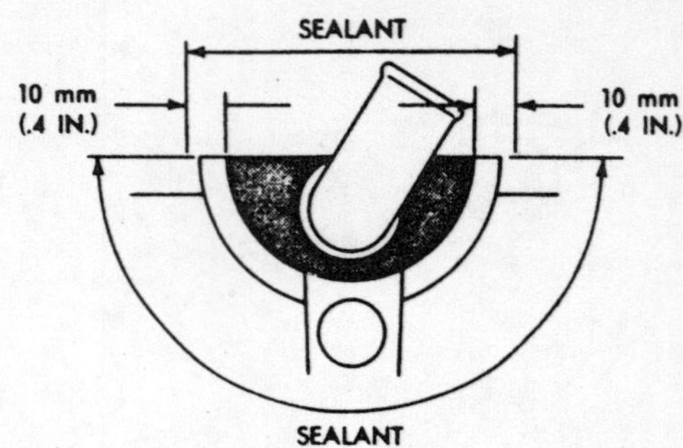

2.6L sealer application points

2.6L Engine

1. Disconnect the negative battery cable.

2. Remove the air cleaner assembly. Remove or relocate any hoses or cables that will interfere with rocker cover removal.

3. Disconnect the hoses to the PCV tube.

4. Remove the cover mounting bolts and remove the rocker cover from the cylinder head. The water pump pulley belt shield is attached at rear of rocker cover.

5. Clean the cover and head mounting surfaces.

6. Apply RTV sealant to the top of the rubber cam seal and install the rocker cover.

7. With rocker cover installed, apply RTV sealant to top of semi-circular packing.

8. Tighten screws to 55 inch lbs..

9. Install the vacuum hoses and spark plug wires.

10. Install the air cleaner assembly.

11. Connect the battery cable.

3.0L Engine

1. Disconnect the negative battery cable.

2. Remove the air cleaner assembly.

3. Remove any vacuum hoses necessary and relocate spark plug wires.

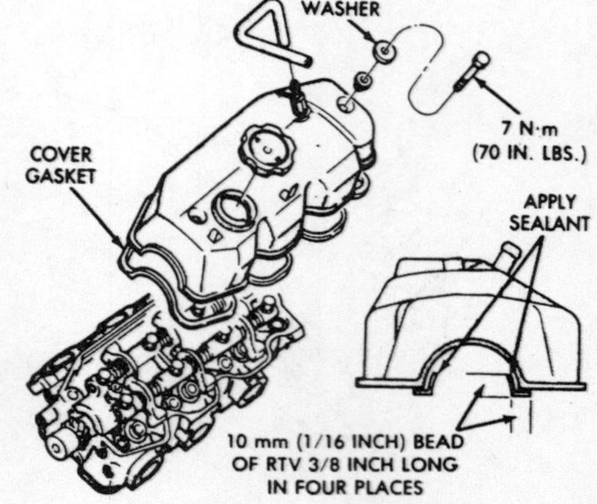

3.0L sealer application points

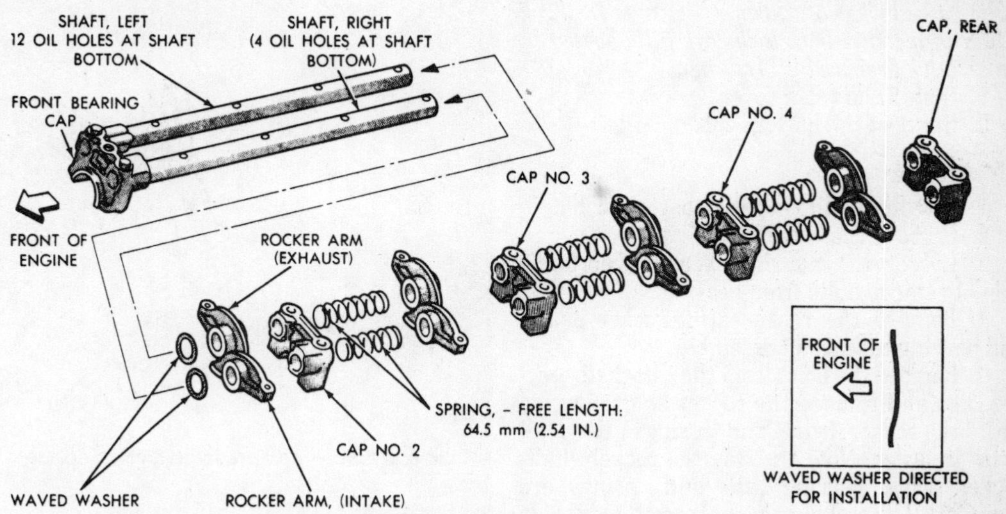

Rocker arm and shaft assemblies — 2.6L engines

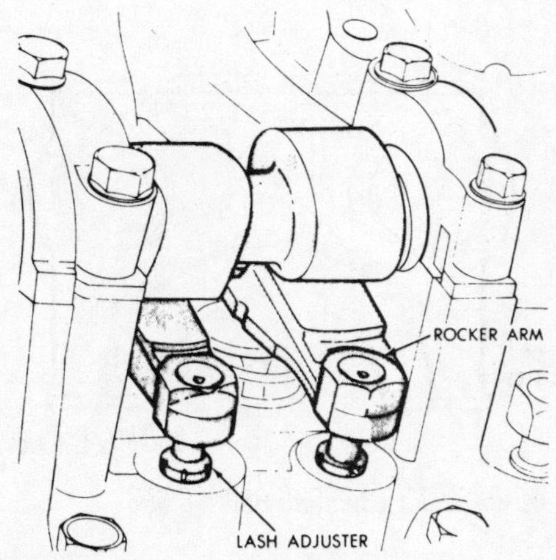

2.2L and 2.5L rocker arm and lash adjuster

4. Remove the cover screws and remove cover.
5. Clean the cylinder head and cover mating surfaces before installation.
6. Install a new gasket. Apply RTV sealant to cover ends.
7. Install the cover and tighten to 68 inch lbs.
8. Install the vacuum hoses and spark plug wires.
9. Install the air cleaner assembly.
10. Connect the battery cable.

3.3L Engine

1. Disconnect the negative battery cable.
2. Remove the air intake tube and disconnect it from the intake manifold.
3. Remove the upper intake manifold, disconnecting any hoses or wires.
4. Remove the spark plug wires. Disconnect the closed ventilation system and evaporation control from the valve cover.
5. Remove the cover and gasket.
6. Install a new gasket and the cover. Tighten the cover retaining bolts to 102 inch lbs.
7. Reinstall all ventilation control components and the upper intake manifold.
8. Reconnect the air intake tube to the intake manifold.
9. Connect the negative battery cable.

Rocker Arms and Shafts

REMOVAL AND INSTALLATION

2.2L and 2.5L Engines

1. Disconnect the negative battery cable.
2. Remove the valve cover.
3. Rotate the camshaft until the lobe base is on the rocker arm that is to be removed.
4. Slightly depress the valve spring using Chrysler tool-4682 or the equivalent. Slide the rocker off the lash adjuster and valve tip and remove. Label the rocker arms for position identification. Proceed to next rocker arm and repeat Steps 3 and 4.
5. Remove the lash adjuster if servicing is necessary.

To install:

6. If the lash adjuster was previously removed, partially fill with oil and install.
7. Rotate the camshaft until lobe base is in position with rocker arm. Slightly depress the valve spring using Chrysler tool 4682 or equivalent. Slide rocker arm in position.

NOTE: *When depressing the valve spring with Chrysler tool 4682, or the equivalent, the valve locks can become dislocated. Check and make sure both locks are fully seated in the valve grooves and retainer.*

8. Install the valve cover.
9. Connect the battery cable.

2.6L Engine

1. Disconnect the negative battery cable.
2. Remove the valve cover.
3. Loosen the camshaft bearing cap bolts. Do not remove bolts from bearing cap.
4. Remove the rocker arm, rocker shafts and bearing caps as an assembly.
5. Remove the bolts from the camshaft bearing caps and remove the rocker shafts, waved washers, rocker arms and springs. Keep all parts in order. Note the way the rocker shaft, rocker arms, bearing caps and springs are mounted. The rocker arm shaft on the Left side has 12 oil holes at shaft bottom, and the Right side shaft has 4 oil holes at shaft bottom.
6. Inspect the rocker arms mounting area and rockers for damage. Replace if worn or heavily damaged.

To install:

7. Position the camshaft bearing caps with arrows pointing toward the timing chain and in numerical order.
8. Insert both shafts into the front bearing cap and install bolts to hold shafts in position.
9. Install the wave washers, rocker arms, bearing caps, and springs. Install bolts in the rear cap to retain assembly.
10. Place the assembly into position.
11. Tighten the camshaft bearing cap bolts in sequence to 10 Nm (85 inch lbs.) as followed:
    a. No. 3 Cap
    b. No. 2 Cap
    c. No. 4 Cap
    d. Front Cap
    e. Rear Cap
12. Repeat Step 12 and increase torque to 175 inch lbs.
13. Install the distributor drive gear, timing chain/camshaft sprocket, and sprocket bolt. Torque sprocket bolt to 40 ft. lbs.

NOTE: *After servicing the rocker shaft assembly, Jet Valve Clearance (if used) and Intake/Exhaust Valve Clearance must be performed.*

14. Install the water pump (upper shield) and valve cover.
15. Connect the battery cable.

3.0L Engine

1. Disconnect the negative battery cable.
2. Remove the valve cover.
3. Loosen the camshaft bearing cap bolts. Do not remove bolts from bearing cap.
4. Remove the rocker arm, rocker shafts and bearing caps as an assembly.

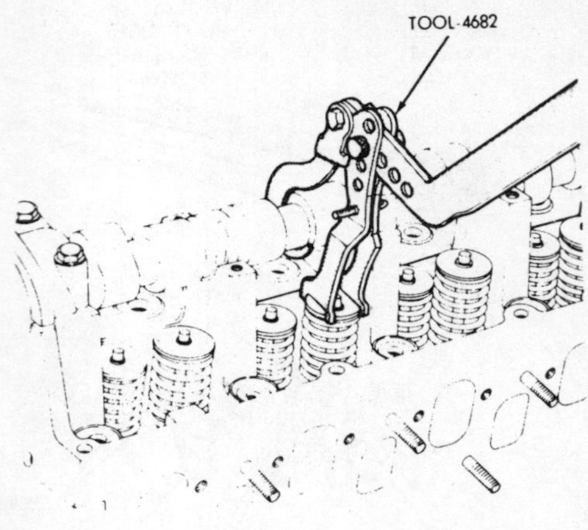

2.2L and 2.5L – compressing a valve spring

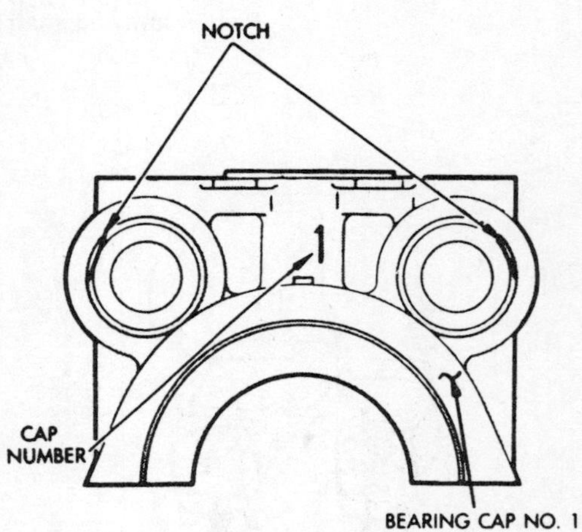

3.0L number 1 camshaft bearing cap

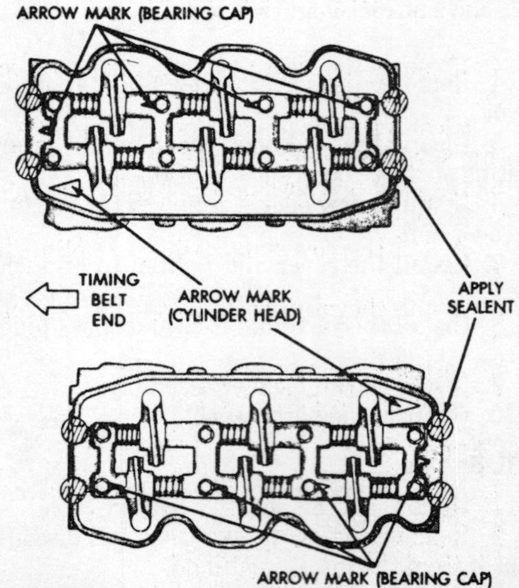

3.0L rocker arm and shaft assemblies

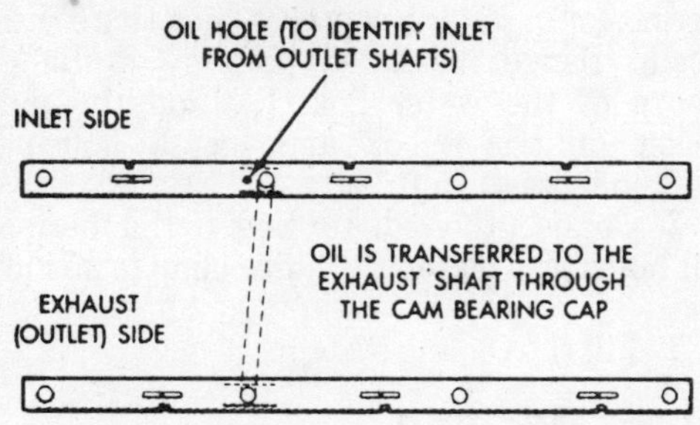

3.0L rocker shaft identification

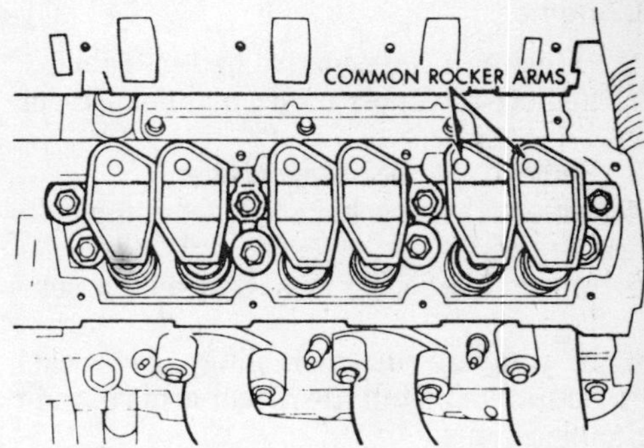

Rocker shaft assembly – 3.3L engine

5. Remove the bolts from the camshaft bearing caps and remove the rocker shafts and arms. Keep all parts in order. Note the way the rocker shaft, rocker arms, bearing caps and springs are mounted. The rocker arm shaft on the Intake side has a 3mm diameter oil passage hole from the cylinder head. The exhaust side does not have this oil passage.

6. Inspect the rocker arm mounting area and rocker for damage. Replace if worn or heavily damaged.

To install:

7. Identify No. 1 bearing cap, (No. 1 and No. 4 caps are similar). Install the rocker shafts into the bearing cap with notches in proper position. Insert the attaching bolts to retain assemble.

8. Install the rocker arms, springs and bearing caps on shafts in numerical sequence.

9. Align the camshaft bearing caps with arrows (depending on cylinder bank).

10. Install the bolts in number 4 cap to retain assembly.

11. Apply sealant at bearing cap ends.

12. Install the rocker arm shaft assembly.

NOTE: *Make sure the arrow mark on the bearing caps and the arrow mark on the cylinder heads are in the same direction. The direction of arrow marks on the front and rear assemblies are opposite to each other.*

13. Tighten the bearing caps bolts to 85 inch lbs. in the following manner:

   a. No. 3 Cap
   b. No. 2 Cap
   c. No. 1 Cap
   d. No. 4 Cap

14. Repeat Step 13 increasing torque to 180 inch lbs.

15. Install the valve cover.

16. Connect the battery cable.

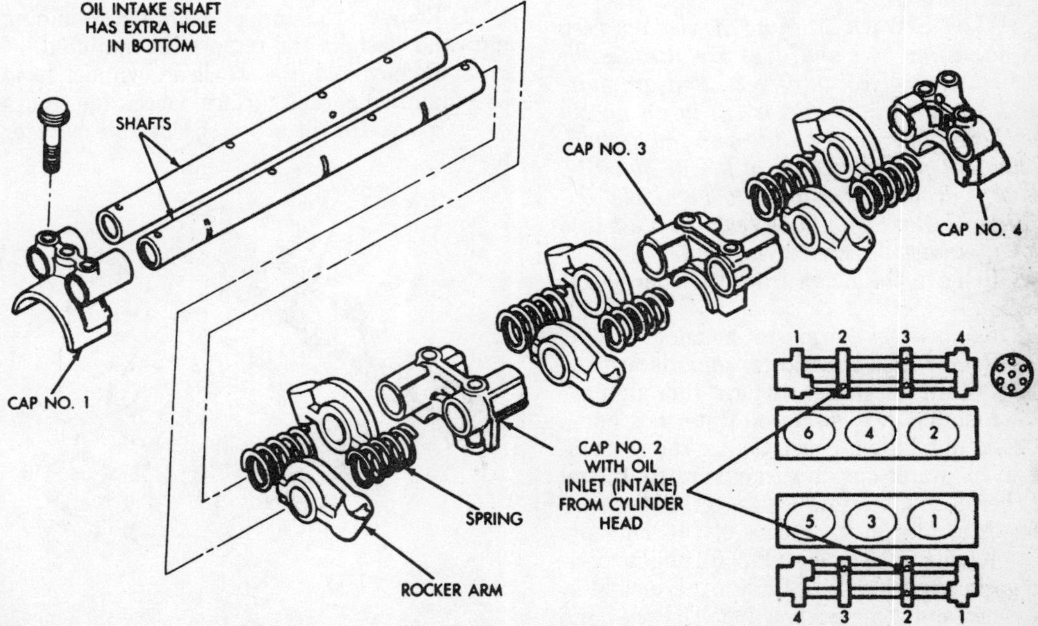

3.0L rocker shaft assembly installation

3.3L Engine

1. Disconnect the negative battery cable.
2. Remove the upper intake manifold assembly.
3. Remove the rocker arm cover.
4. remove the 4 rocker shaft retaining bolts and retainers.
5. remove the rocker arms and shaft assembly.
6. If you are disassembling the rocker shaft, be sure to install the rocker arms in their original locations.

To install:

7. Install the rocker arm and shaft assembly, using the 4 retainers. Tighten the retaining bolts to 250 inch lbs. (28 Nm).

NOTE: *The rocker arm shaft should be torqued down slowly, starting with the center bolts. Allow 20 minutes for tappet bleed down after installation, before engine operation.*

8. Install the rocker cover.
9. Install the crankcase ventilation components and connect the spark plug wires.
10. Install the upper intake manifold assembly. Connect the negative battery cable.

Thermostat

REMOVAL AND INSTALLATION

The thermostat is located in a water box at the side of the engine (facing grille) 2.2L and 2.5L engines. The thermostat on 2.6L, 3.0L and 3.3L engines is located in a water box at the timing belt end of the intake manifold.

1. Drain the cooling system to a level below the thermostat.

CAUTION: *When draining the coolant, keep in mind that cats and dogs are attracted by the ethylene glycol antifreeze, and are quite likely to drink any that is left in an uncovered container or in puddles on the ground. This will prove fatal in sufficient quantity. Always drain the coolant into a sealable container. Coolant should be reused unless it is contaminated or several years old.*

2. Remove the hoses from the thermostat housing.
3. Remove the thermostat housing.
4. Remove the thermostat and discard the gasket. Clean the gasket surfaces thoroughly.
5. Install a new gasket on water box housing 2.2L and 2.5L engines. Center the thermostat in the water box on gasket surface. Install the thermostat housing on gasket. Make sure thermostat sits in its recess of the housing. Tighten bolts to 15 ft. lbs. On 2.6L engine position gasket on water box. Center thermostat in water box and attached housing. Tighten bolts to 15 ft. lbs. On 3.0L and 3.3L engines position thermostat in water box pocket. Make sure thermostat flange in seated properly in flange groove of the water box. Position the new gasket on water box and install housing. Tighten bolts to 15 ft. lbs.
6. Connect the radiator hose to the thermostat housing. Tighten the hose clamp to 35 inch lbs.
7. Fill the cooling system.

Intake Manifold

REMOVAL AND INSTALLATION

2.6L Engine

1. Disconnect the negative battery cable.
2. Drain the cooling system and disconnect the hoses from the water pump to the intake manifold.

CAUTION: *When draining the coolant, keep in mind that cats and dogs are attracted by the ethylene glycol antifreeze, and are quite likely to drink any that is left in an uncovered container or in puddles on the ground. This will prove fatal in sufficient quantity. Always drain the coolant into a sealable container. Coolant should be reused unless it is contaminated or several years old.*

3. Disconnect the carburetor air horn adapter and move to one side.
4. Disconnect the vacuum hoses and throttle link,age from the carburetor.
5. Disconnect the fuel inlet line at the fuel filter.
6. Remove the fuel filter and fuel pump and move to one side.
7. Remove the intake manifold retaining nuts and washers and remove the manifold.
8. Remove old gasket. Clean cylinder head and manifold gasket surface. Check for cracks or warpage. Install a new gasket on cylinder head.

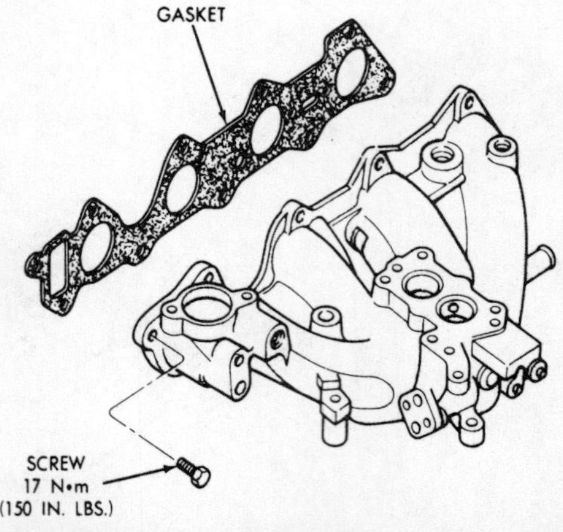

2.6L intake manifold assembly

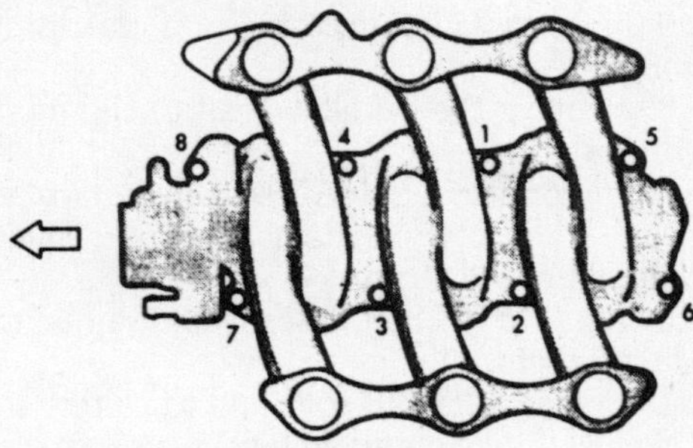

3.0L intake manifold torque sequence

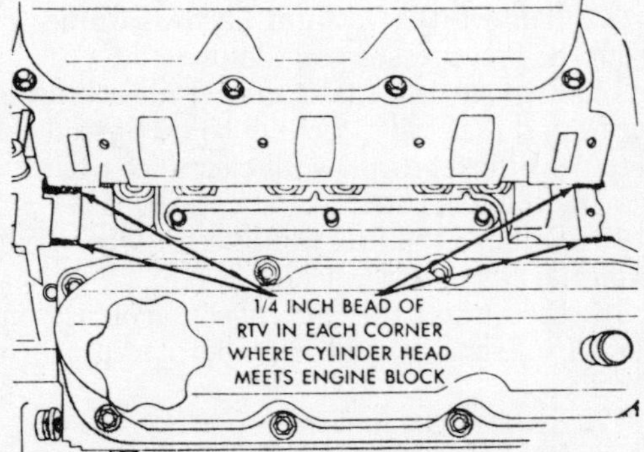

Intake manifold gasket retainers — 3.3L engine

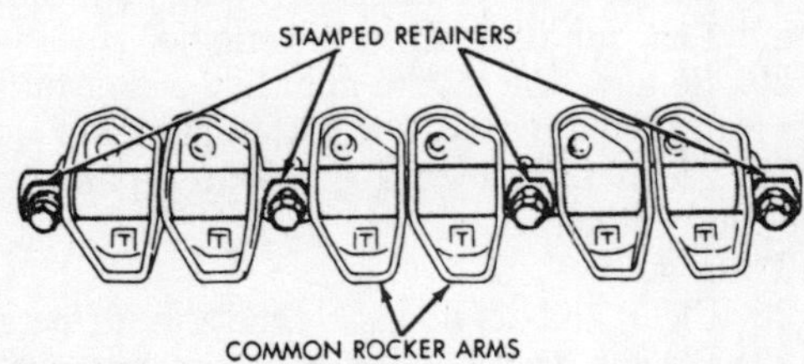

Intake manifold gasket sealing — 3.3L engine

9. Install manifold to cylinder head. Install washers and nuts. Refer to Torque Specification Chart.
10. Install the fuel pump and filter.
11. Install the carburetor air horn.
12. Install the throttle control cable.
13. Install the cooling system hose from water pump to manifold.
14. Install the vacuum hoses.
15. Connect the negative battery cable.

3.0L Engine

1. Release fuel system pressure.
2. Disconnect the negative battery cable.
3. Drain the cooling system.

CAUTION: *When draining the coolant, keep in mind that cats and dogs are attracted by the ethylene glycol antifreeze, and are quite likely to drink any that is left in an uncovered container or in puddles on the ground. This will prove fatal in sufficient quantity. Always drain the coolant into a sealable container. Coolant should be reused unless it is contaminated or several years old.*

4. Remove the air cleaner.
5. Remove the throttle cable and transaxle kickdown cable.
6. Remove the electrical and vacuum connections from throttle body.
7. Remove the air intake hose from air cleaner to throttle body.
8. Remove the EGR tube to intake plenum.
9. Remove the electrical connection from charge temperature and coolant temperature sensor.
10. Remove the vacuum connection from the pressure regulator and remove the air intake connection from the manifold.
11. Remove fuel hoses to fuel rail connection.
12. Remove the air intake plenum to manifold bolts (8) and remove air intake plenum and gasket.

WARNING: *Whenever the air intake plenum is removed, cover the intake manifold properly to avoid objects from entering cylinder head.*

13. Disconnect the fuel injector wiring harness from the engine wiring harness.
14. Remove the pressure regulator attaching bolts and remove pressure regulator from rail.
15. Remove the fuel rail attaching bolts and remove fuel rail.
16. Remove the radiator hose from thermostat housing and heater hose from pipe.
17. Remove the intake manifold attaching nuts and washers and remove intake manifold.
18. Clean the gasket material from cylinder head and manifold gasket surface. Check for cracks or damaged mounting surfaces.

To install:

19. Install a new gasket on the intake surface of the cylinder head and install the intake manifold.
20. Install the intake manifold washers and

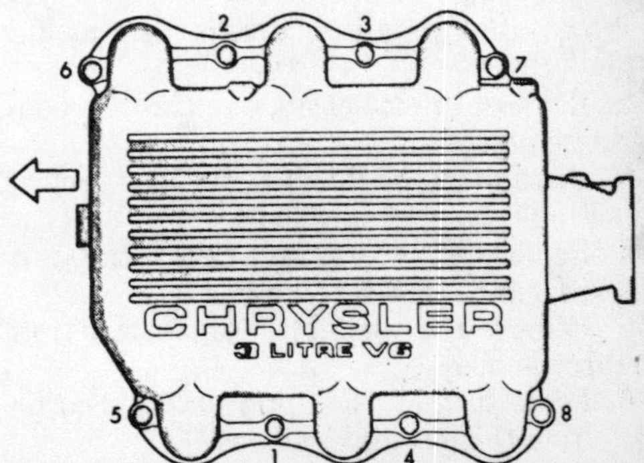

Intake plenum tightening sequence — 3.0L engine

nuts. Tighten in sequence shown. Refer to Torque Specification Chart.

21. Clean the injectors and lubricate the injector O-rings with a drop of clean engine oil.

22. Place the tip of each injector into their ports. Push assembly into place until the injectors are seated in their ports.

23. Install rail attaching bolts and tighten to 115 inch lbs.

24. Install pressure regulator to rail. Install pressure regulator mounting bolts and tighten to 95 inch lbs.

25. Install fuel supply and return tube holddown bolt and vacuum crossover tube holddown bolt. Torque to 95 inch lbs.

26. Torque fuel pressure regulator hose clamps to 10 inch lbs.

27. Connect injector wiring harness to engine wiring harness.

28. Connect vacuum harness to fuel rail and pressure regulator.

29. Remove covering from intake manifold.

30. Position the intake manifold gasket, beaded side up, on the intake manifold.

31. Put the air intake plenum in place. Install attaching bolts and tighten in sequence to 115 inch lbs.

32. Connect the fuel line to fuel rail. Tighten clamps to 10 inch lbs.

33. Connect the vacuum hoses to intake plenum.

34. Connect the electrical connection to coolant temperature sensor and charge temperature sensor.

35. Connect the EGR tube flange to intake plenum and torque to 15 ft. lbs.

36. Connect the throttle body vacuum hoses and electrical connections.

37. Install the throttle cable and transaxle kickdown linkage.

38. Install the radiator and heater hose. Fill the cooling system.

39. Connect the negative battery cable.

3.3L Engine

1. Disconnect the negative battery cable. Relieve the fuel pressure. Drain the cooling system.

2. Remove the air cleaner to throttle body hose assembly.

3. Disconnect the throttle cable and remove the wiring harness from the bracket.

4. Remove AIS motor and TPS wiring connectors from the throttle body.

5. Remove the vacuum hose harness from the throttle body.

6. Remove the PCV and brake booster hoses from the air intake plenum.

7. Disconnect the charge temperature sensor electrical connector. Remove the vacuum harness connectors from the intake plenum.

8. Remove the cylinder head to the intake plenum strut.

9. Disconnect the MAP sensor and oxygen sensor connectors. Remove the engine mounted ground strap.

10. Remove the fuel hoses from the fuel rail and plug them.

11. Remove the DIS coils and the alternator bracket to intake manifold bolt.

12. Remove the upper intake manifold attaching bolts and remove the upper manifold.

13. Remove the vacuum harness connector from the fuel pressure regulator.

14. Remove the fuel tube retainer bracket screw and fuel rail attaching bolts. Spread the retainer bracket to allow for clearance when removing the fuel tube.

15. Remove the fuel rail injector wiring clip from the alternator bracket.

16. Disconnect the cam sensor, coolant temperature sensor and engine temperature sensor.

17. Remove the fuel rail.

18. Remove the upper radiator hose, bypass hose and rear intake manifold hose.

19. Remove the intake manifold bolts and remove the manifold from the engine.

20. Remove the intake manifold seal retaining screws and remove the manifold gasket.

21. Clean out clogged end water passages and fuel runners.

To install:

22. Clean and dry all gasket mating surfaces.

23. Place a drop of silicone sealer onto each of the 4 manifold to cylinder head gasket corners.

24. Install the intake manifold gasket and torque the end retainers to 10 ft. lbs. (12 Nm).

25. Install the intake manifold and torque the bolts in sequence to 10 inch lbs. Repeat the sequence increasing the torque to 17 ft. lbs. (23 Nm) and recheck each bolt for 17 ft. lbs. of torque.

26. When the bolts are torqued, inspect the

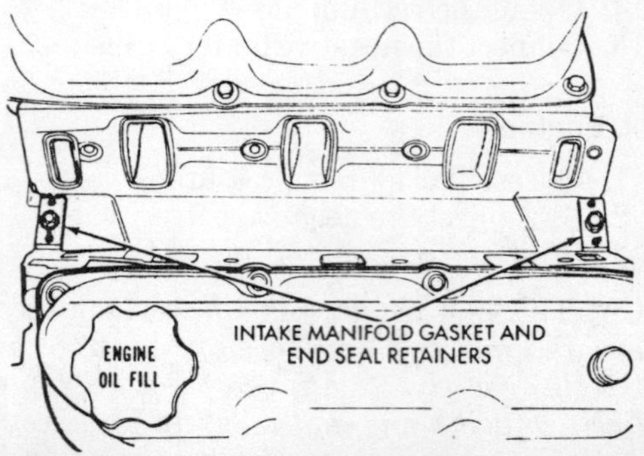

Intake manifold torque sequence — 3.3L engine

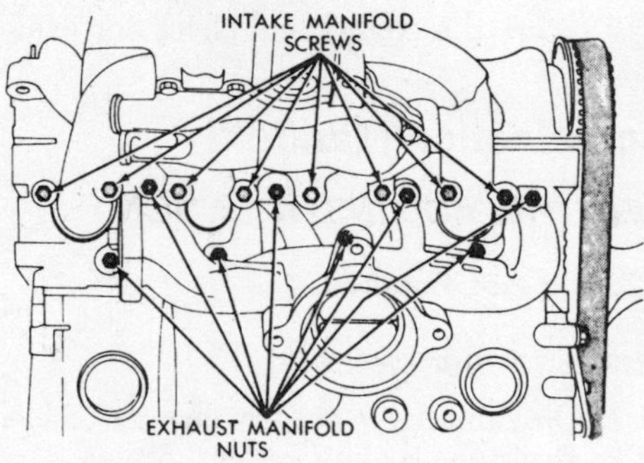

2.2L and 2.5L combination manifold bolt locations

seals to ensure that they have not become dislodged.

27. Lubricate the injector O-rings with clean oil and position the fuel rail in place. Install the rail mounting bolts.

28. Connect the cam sensor, coolant temperature sensor and engine temperature sensor.

29. Install the fuel rail injector wiring clip to the alternator bracket.

30. Install the fuel rail attaching bolts and fuel tube retainer bracket screw.

31. Install the vacuum harness to the pressure regulator.

32. Install the upper intake manifold with a new gasket. Install the bolts only finger tight. Install the alternator bracket to intake manifold bolt and the cylinder head to intake manifold strut and bolts. Torque the intake manifold mounting bolts to 21 ft. lbs. (28 Nm) starting from the middle and working outward. Torque the bracket and strut bolts to 40 ft. lbs. (54 Nm).

33. Install or connect all items that were removed or disconnected from the intake manifold and throttle body.

34. Connect the fuel hoses to the rail. Push the fittings in until they click in place.

35. Install the air cleaner assembly.

36. Connect the negative battery cable and check for leaks using the DRB I or II to activate the fuel pump.

Exhaust Manifold

REMOVAL AND INSTALLATION

2.6L Engine

1. Disconnect the negative battery cable.
2. Remove the air cleaner assembly.
3. Remove the belt from the power steering pump.
4. Raise the vehicle and make sure it is supported safely.
5. Remove the exhaust pipe from the manifold.
6. Disconnect the air injection tube assembly from the exhaust manifold and lower the vehicle.
7. Remove the power steering pump assembly and move to one side.
8. Remove the heat cowl from the exhaust manifold.
9. Remove the exhaust manifold retaining nuts and remove the assembly from the vehicle.
10. Remove the carburetor air heater from the manifold.
11. Separate the exhaust manifold from the catalytic converter by removing the retaining screws.
12. Clean gasket material from cylinder head and exhaust manifold gasket surfaces. Check mating surfaces for cracks or distortion.
13. Install a new gasket between the exhaust manifold an catalytic converter. Install mounting screws and tighten to 32 Nm (24 ft. lbs.).
14. Install the carburetor air heater on manifold and tighten to 80 inch lbs.
15. Lightly coat the new exhaust manifold gasket with sealant (P/N 3419115) or equivalent on cylinder head side.
16. Install the exhaust manifold and mounting nuts. Refer to Torque Specification Chart.
17. Install the heat cowl to manifold and tighten screws to 80 inch lbs.
18. Install the air cleaner support bracket.
19. Install the power steering pump assembly.
20. Install the air injection tube assembly to air pump.
21. Raise the vehicle and install air injection tube assembly to exhaust manifold.
22. Install the exhaust pipe to manifold.
23. Lower the vehicle and install power steering belt.
24. Fill the cooling system.
25. Install the air cleaner assembly.
26. Connect the negative battery cable.

3.0L Engine

1. Disconnect the negative battery cable.
2. Raise vehicle and support properly.

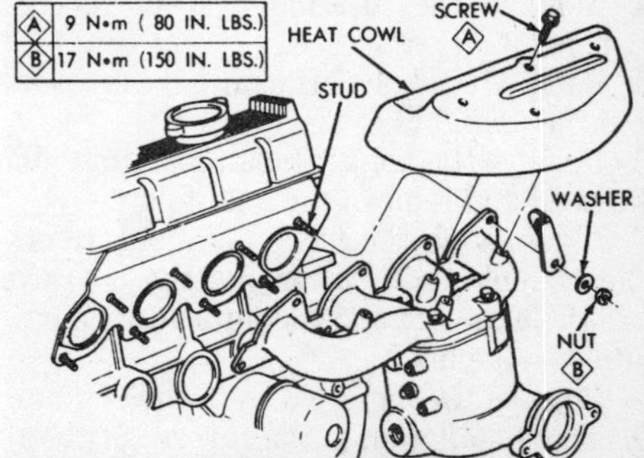

2.6L exhaust manifold assembly

3. Disconnect the exhaust pipe from rear (cowl side) exhaust manifold at articulated joint.

4. Remove the EGR tube from the rear manifold and disconnect oxygen sensor lead.

5. Remove the attaching bolts from crossover pipe to manifold.

6. Remove the attaching nuts which retained manifold to cylinder head and remove manifold.

7. Lower the vehicle and remove bolt securing front heat shield to front exhaust manifold.

8. Remove the bolts retaining crossover pipe to front exhaust manifold and nuts retaining manifold to cylinder head. Remove manifold assembly.

9. Clean all gasket material from cylinder the head and exhaust manifold gasket surfaces. Check mating surfaces for cracks or distortion.

10. Install the new gasket with the numbers 1-3-5 stamped on the top on the rear bank. The gasket with the numbers 2-4-6 must be installed on the front bank (radiator side).

11. Install rear exhaust manifold and tighten attaching nuts to 15 ft. lbs.

12. Install exhaust pipe to manifold and tighten shoulder bolts to 20 ft. lbs.

13. Install crossover pipe to manifold and tighten bolts to 69 Nm (51 ft. lbs.).

14. Install oxygen sensor lead and EGR tube.

15. Install front exhaust manifold and attach exhaust crossover.

16. Install front manifold heat shield and tighten bolts to 10 ft. lbs.

17. Connect the negative battery cable.

3.3L Engine

1. Disconnect the negative battery cable.

2. If removing the rear manifold, raise the vehicle and support safely. Disconnect the exhaust pipe at the articulated joint from the rear exhaust manifold.

3. Separate the EGR tube from the rear manifold and disconnect the oxygen sensor wire.

4. Remove the alternator/power steering support strut.

5. Remove the bolts attaching the crossover pipe to the manifold.

6. Remove the bolts attaching the manifold to the head and remove the manifold.

7. If removing the front manifold, remove the heat shield, bolts attaching the crossover pipe to the manifold and the nuts attaching the manifold to the head.

8. Remove the manifold from the engine.

9. The installation is the reverse of the removal procedure. Torque all exhaust manifold attaching bolts to 17 ft. lbs. (23 Nm).

10. Start the engine and check for exhaust leaks.

Combination Manifold

REMOVAL AND INSTALLATION

2.2L and 2.5L Engines

WITHOUT TURBOCHARGER

1. Disconnect the battery negative cable.

2. Drain the cooling system.

CAUTION: *When draining the coolant, keep in mind that cats and dogs are attracted by the ethylene glycol antifreeze, and are quite likely to drink any that is left in an uncovered container or in puddles on the ground. This will prove fatal in sufficient quantity. Always drain the coolant into a sealable container. Coolant should be reused unless it is contaminated or several years old.*

3. Remove the air cleaner, disconnect all vacuum lines, electrical wiring and fuel lines from carburetor and intake manifold.

4. Remove the throttle linkage.

5. Remove the water hoses from water crossover.

6. Raise the vehicle and remove exhaust pipe from manifold.

7. Remove power steering pump and set aside.

8. Remove intake manifold support bracket and EGR tube.

9. On Canadian cars remove (4) air injection tube bolts and injection tube assembly.

10. Remove the intake manifold retaining screws.

11. Lower vehicle and remove the intake manifold.

12. Remove exhaust manifold retaining nuts and remove exhaust manifold.

13. Clean gasket surface of both manifold and cylinder block surface.

14. Install a new gasket on exhaust and intake manifold. Coat manifold with Sealer (P/N 3419115) or equivalent on manifold side.

15. Position the exhaust manifold against cylinder block and install nuts. Tighten nuts from center while alternating outward in both direction. See Torque Specification Chart.

16. Position the intake manifold against cylinder head.

17. From beneath the vehicle tighten intake manifold screws. Start at the center while alternating outward in both direction. See Torque Specification Chart.

18. Install the exhaust pipe to exhaust manifold.

19. On Canadian cars install air injection tube assembly.

20. Install the intake manifold support bracket and EGR tube.

21. Install the power steering pump assembly and power steering belt.

22. Install the water hoses to water crossover.

23. Install the fuel lines, vacuum lines, and electrical wiring.

24. Fill the cooling system.

25. Connect the negative battery cable.

WITH TURBOCHARGER

NOTE: *On some vehicles, some of the manifold attaching bolts are not accessible or too heavily sealed from the factory and cannot be removed on the vehicle. Head removal would be necessary in these situations.*

1. Disconnect the negative battery cable. Drain the cooling system. Raise and safely support the vehicle.

2. Disconnect the exhaust pipe at the atriculated joint. Disconnect the oxygen sensor at the electrical connection.

3. Remove the turbocharger to engine support bracket.

4. Loosen the oil drain back tube connector hose clamps. Move the tube down on the engin block fitting.

5. Disconnect the turbocharger coolant inlet tube from the engine block and disconnect the tube support bracket.

6. Remove the air cleaner assembly, including the throttle body adapter, hose and air cleaner box with support bracket.

7. Disconnect the accelerator linkage, throttle body electrical connector and vacuum hoses.

8. Relocate the fuel rail assembly. Remove the bracket to intake manifold screws and the bracket to heat shield clips. Lift and secure the fuel rail (with injectors, wiring harness and fuel lines intact) up and out of the way.

9. Disconnect the turbocharger oil feed line at the oil sending unit Tee fitting.

10. Disconnect the upper radiator hose from the thermostat housing.

11. Remove the cylinder head, manifolds

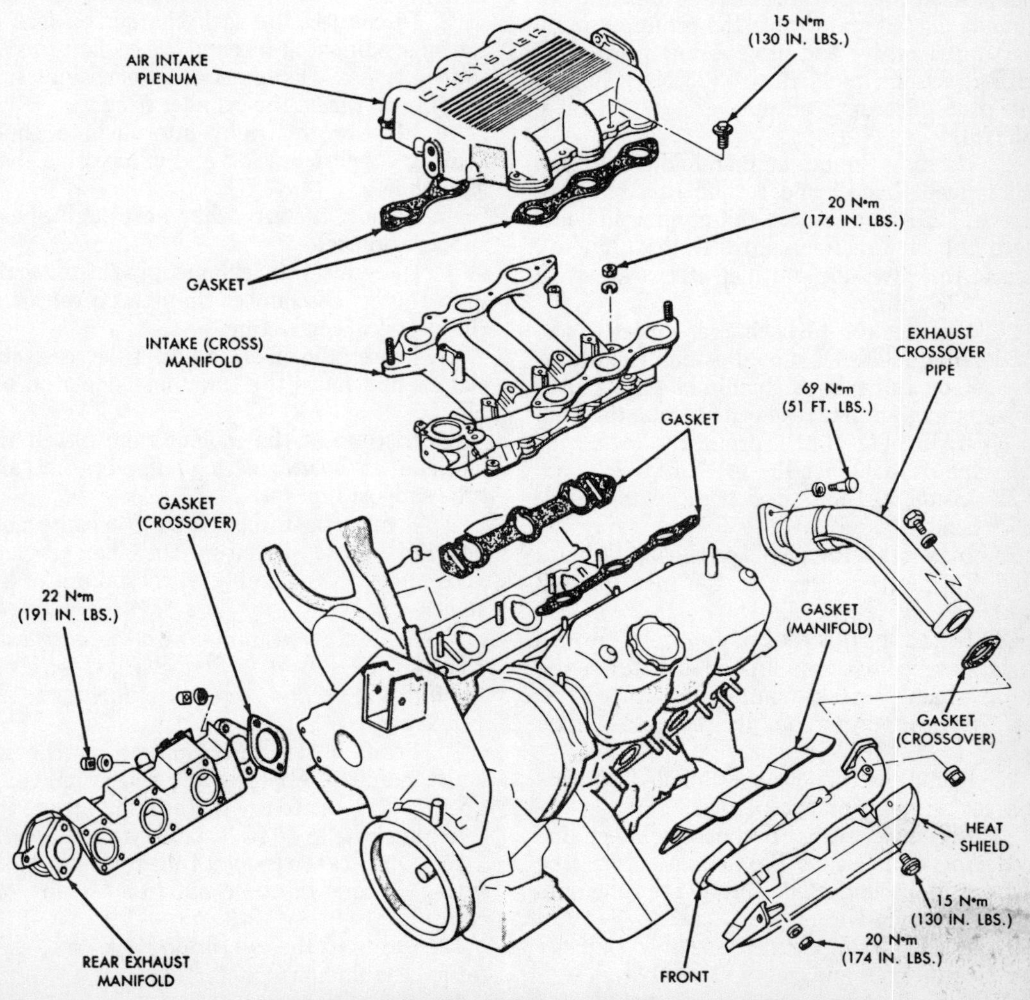

Manifold assemblies — 3.0L engine

and turbocharger as an assembly.

12. With the assembly on a workbench, loosen the upper turbocharger discharge hose end clamp.

NOTE: *Do not disturb the center deswirler retaining clamp.*

13. Remove the throttle body to intake manifold screws and throttle body assembly. Disconnect the turbocharger coolant return tube from the water box. Disconnect the retaining bracket on the cylinder head.

14. Remove the heat shield to intake manifold screws and the heat shield.

15. Remove the turbocharger to exhaust manifold nuts and the turbocharger assembly.

16. Remove the intake manifold bolts and the intake manifold.

17. Remove the exhaust manifold nuts and the exhaust manifold.

To install:

18. Place a new 2-sided Grafoil type intake/exhaust manifold gasket; do not use sealant.

19. Position the exhaust manifold on the cylinder head. Apply anti-seize compound to threads, install and torque the retaining nuts, starting at center and progressing outward in both directions, to 17 ft. lbs. (23 Nm). Repeat this procedure until all nuts are at 17 ft. lbs. (23 Nm).

20. Position the intake manifold on the cylinder head. Install and torque the retaining screws, starting at center and progressing outward in both directions, to 19 ft. lbs. (26 Nm). Repeat this procedure until all screws are at 19 ft. lbs. (26 Nm).

21. Connect the turbocharger outlet to the intake manifold inlet tube. Position the turbocharger on the exhaust manifold. Apply anti-seize compound to threads and torque the nuts to 30 ft. lbs. (41 Nm). Torque the connector tube clamps to 30 inch lbs. (41 Nm).

22. Install the tube support bracket to the cylinder head.

23. Install the heat shield on the intake manifold. Torque the screws to 105 inch lbs. (12 Nm).

24. Install the throttle body air horn into the turbocharger inlet tube. Install and torque the throttle body to intake manifold screws to 21 ft. lbs. (28 Nm). Torque the tube clamp to 30 inch lbs.

25. Install the cylinder head/manifolds/turbocharger assembly on the engine.

26. Reconnect the turbocharger oil feed line to the oil sending unit Tee fitting and bearing housing, if disconnected. Torque the tube nuts to 10 ft. lbs. (14 Nm).

27. Install the air cleaner assembly. Connect the vacuum lines and accelerator cables.

28. Reposition the fuel rail. Install and torque the bracket screws to 21 ft. lbs. (28 Nm). Install the air shield to bracket clips.

29. Connect the turbocharger inlet coolant tube to the engine block. Torque the tube nut to 30 ft. lbs. (41 Nm). Install the tube support bracket.

30. Install the turbocharger housing to engine block support bracket and the screws hand tight. Torque the block screw 1st to 40 ft. lbs. (54 Nm). Torque the screw to the turbocharger housing to 20 ft. lbs. (27 Nm).

31. Reposition the drain back hose connector and tighten the hose clamps. Reconnect the exhaust pipe at the EGR valve.

Turbocharger

REMOVAL AND INSTALLATION

2.5L Turbocharged Engine

1. Disconnect the negative battery cable. Drain the cooling system.

2. Disconnect the EGR valve tube at the EGR valve.

3. Disconnect the turbocharger oil feed at the oil sending unit hex and the coolant tube at the water box. Disconnect the oil/coolant support bracket from the cylinder head.

4. Remove the right intermediate shaft, bearing support bracket and outer drive shaft assemblies.

5. Remove the turbocharger to engine block support bracket.

6. Disconnect the exhaust pipe at the articulated joint. Disconnect the oxygen sensor at the electrical connection.

7. Loosen the oil drain-back tube connector clamps and move the tube hose down on the nipple.

8. Disconnect the coolant tube nut at the block outlet (below steering pump bracket) and tube support bracket.

9. Remove the turbocharger to exhaust manifold nuts. Carefully routing the oil and coolant lines, move the assembly down and out of the vehicle.

NOTE: *Before installing the turbocharger assembly, be sure it is first charged with oil. Failure to do this may cause damage to the assembly.*

10. Position the turbocharger on the exhaust manifold. Apply an anti-seize compound, Loctite® 771–64, to the threads and torque the retaining nuts to 40 ft. lbs. (54 Nm).

11. Connect the coolant tube to engine block fitting. Torque the tube nut to 30 ft. lbs. (41 Nm).

12. Position the oil drain-back hose and torque the clamps to 30 inch lbs.

13. Install and torque the:

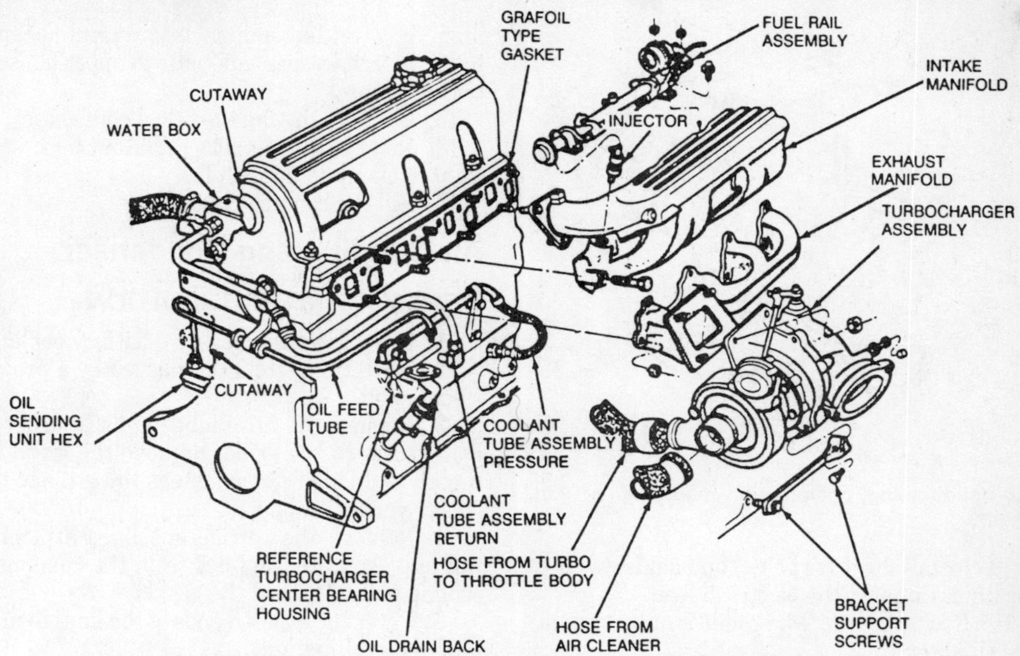

Manifolds, turbocharger and related components — 2.5L turbo charged engine

- Turbocharger to engine support bracket block screw to 40 ft. lbs. (54 Nm).
- Turbocharger housing screw to 20 ft. lbs. (27 Nm).
- Articulated joint shoulder bolts to 21 ft. lbs. (28 Nm).

14. Install the right drive shaft assembly, the starter and the oil feed line at the sending unit hex. Torque the oil feed tube nut to 10 ft. lbs. (14 Nm) and the EGR tube to EGR valve nut to 60 ft. lbs. (81 Nm).
15. Refill the cooling system. Connect the negative battery cable and check the turbocharger for proper operation.

Air Conditioning Compressor

REMOVAL AND INSTALLATION

1. Disconnect the negative battery cable.
2. Have the system discharged by a professional shop.
3. Remove the compressor drive belt(s). Disconnect the compressor lead.
4. Raise and safely support the vehicle, if necessary. Remove the refrigerant lines from the compressor and discard the gaskets. Cover the exposed ends of the lines to minimize contamination.
5. Remove the compressor mounting nuts and bolts.
6. Lift the compressor off of its mounting studs and remove from the engine compartment.

To install:

7. Install the compressor and tighten all mounting nuts and bolts.
8. Coat the new gaskets with wax-free refrigerant oil and install. Connect the refrigerant lines to the compressor and tighten the bolts.

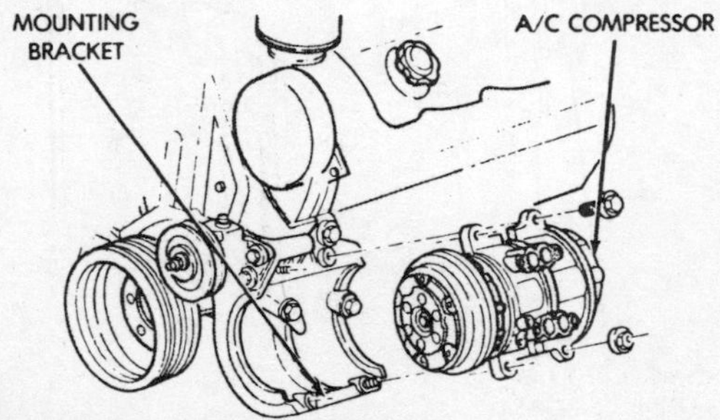

Air conditioning compressor mounting — 3.3L engine

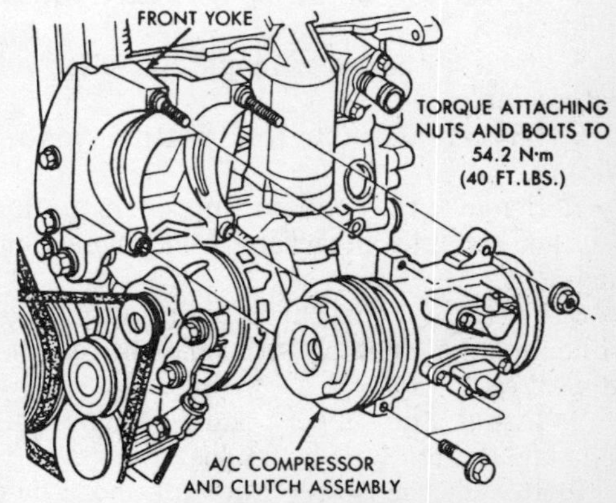

Air conditioning compressor mounting — 2.2/2.5L engines

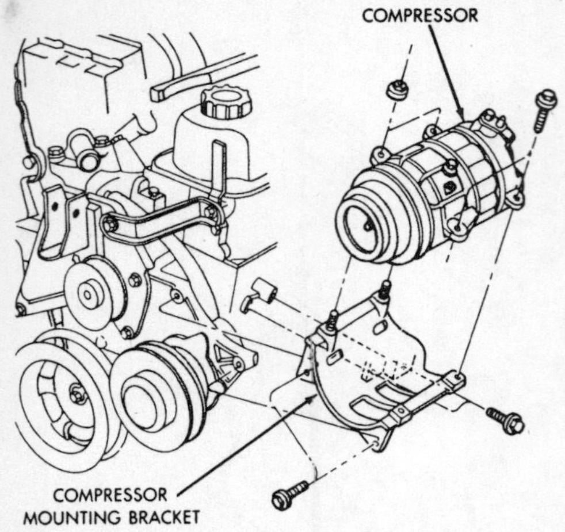

Air conditioning compressor mounting – 3.0L engine

9. Install the drive belt(s) and adjust to specification. Connect the electrical lead.

10. Recharge the air conditioning system. See Chapter 1.

11. Connect the negative battery cable and check the entire climate control system for proper operation and leaks.

Radiator

REMOVAL AND INSTALLATION

1. Disconnect the negative battery cable.

2. Drain the cooling system.

CAUTION: *When draining the coolant, keep in mind that cats and dogs are attracted by the ethylene glycol antifreeze, and are quite likely to drink any that is left in an uncovered container or in puddles on the ground. This will prove fatal in sufficient quantity. Always drain the coolant into a sealable container. Coolant should be reused unless it is contaminated or several years old.*

3. Remove the upper and lower hoses and coolant recovery tank tube to filler neck.

4. Disconnect the wiring harness from fan motor.

5. Remove the upper mounting bolts from fan assembly.

6. Lift fan assembly from bottom ring retaining clip.

7. Remove the radiator upper mounting bolts and carefully lift radiator from engine compartment.

8. Carefully slide the radiator into place while aligning radiator with holes in radiator support seat.

9. Install the upper radiator mounting bolts and tighten to 105 inch lbs.

10. Install the lower radiator hose and tighten to 35 inch lbs.

11. Carefully install the fan assembly while aligning lower fan support into retaining clip.

12. Attach washers and nuts to upper fan support.

13. Connect the fan electrical connector.

14. Install the upper radiator hose and tighten clamp to 35 inch lbs.

15. Fill the cooling system.

Air Conditioning Condenser

REMOVAL AND INSTALLATION

1. Disconnect the negative battery cable.

2. Have the system discharged by a professional shop.

3. Remove the headlight bezels in order to gain access to the grille. Remove the grille assembly. A hidden screw fastens the grille to the center vertical support.

4. Remove the refrigerant lines attaching nut and separate the lines from the condenser sealing plate. Discard the gasket.

5. Cover the exposed ends of the lines to minimize contamination.

6. Remove the bolts that attach the condenser to the radiator support.

7. Remove the condenser from the vehicle.

To install:

8. Position the condenser and install the bolts.

9. Coat the new gasket with wax-free refrigerant oil and install. Connect the lines to the condenser sealing plate and tighten the nut.

10. Install the grille assembly.

11. Evacuate and recharge the air conditioning system. Add 1 oz. of refrigerant oil during the recharge.

12. Connect the negative battery cable and check the entire climate control system for proper operation and leaks.

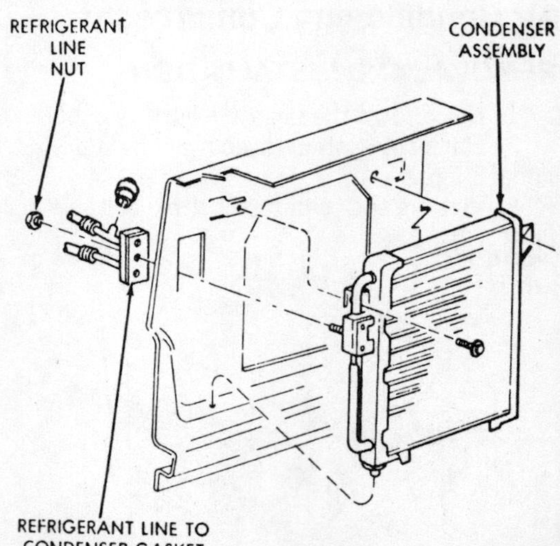

Air conditioning condenser mounting

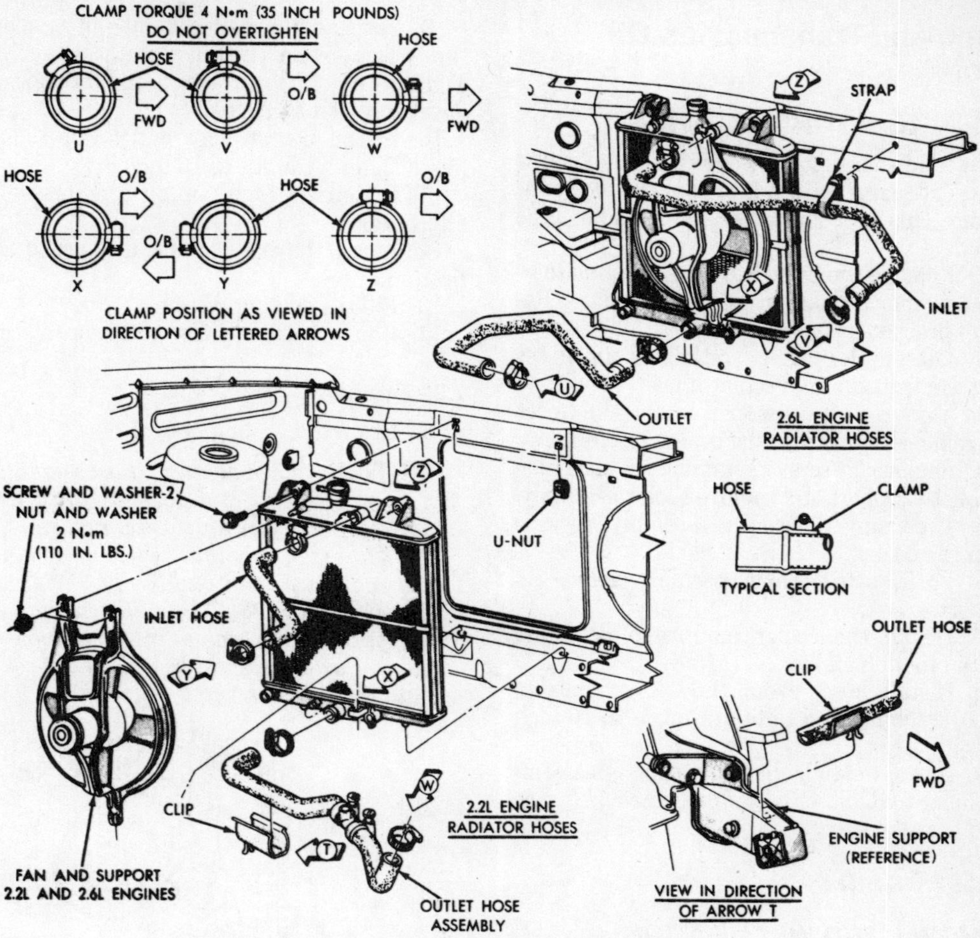

Radiator assembly mounting

Electric Cooling Fan

CAUTION: *Make sure the key is in the OFF position when checking the electric cooling fan. If not, the fan could turn ON at any time, causing serious personal injury.*

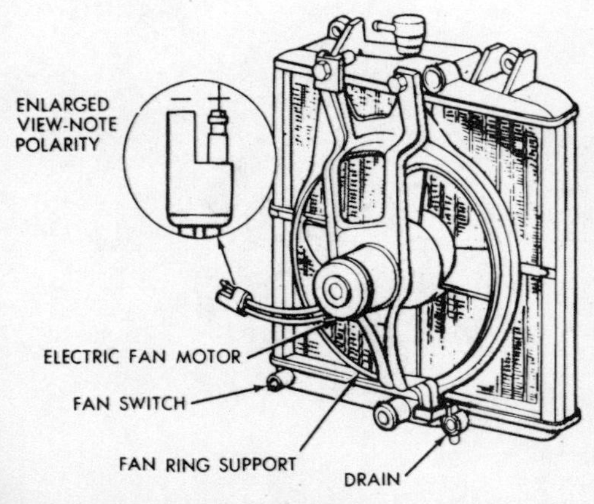

Electric cooling fan and motor

TESTING

1. Unplug the fan connector.
2. Using a jumper wire, connect the female terminal of the fan connector to the negative battery terminal.
3. The fan should turn on when the male terminal is connected to the positive battery terminal.
4. If not, the fan is defective and should be replaced.

REMOVAL AND INSTALLATION

1. Disconnect the negative battery cable.
2. Unplug the connector.
3. Remove the mounting screws.
4. Remove the fan assembly from the vehicle.
5. The installation is the reverse of the removal procedure.
6. Connect the negative battery cable and check the fan for proper operation.

Automatic Transmission Oil Cooler

REMOVAL AND INSTALLATION

The transmission oil cooler used on these models are externally mounted ahead of the radiator. This is considered an oil-to-air type system.

1. Remove the electrical cooling fan assembly and remove radiator. Refer to Radiator Removal procedures.
2. Loosen the clamps retaining the hoses from the transmission cooler lines.
3. Place an oil drain pan under the hoses and remove hoses from the cooler assembly.
4. Remove (2) screws retaining the cooler assembly to support and remove cooler assembly.
5. If reusing the cooler assembly, reverse flush the cooler.
6. Position the cooler assembly against its support.
7. Install the cooler mounting bolts and tighten to 35 inch lbs.
8. Install hoses from the cooler lines to cooler assembly and tighten clamps to 16 inch lbs.
9. Install the radiator and cooling fan assembly. Refer to Radiator procedures previously outlined.

Water Pump

REMOVAL AND INSTALLATION

2.2L and 2.5L Engine

1. Disconnect the negative battery cable.
2. Remove the drive belts.
3. Drain the cooling system.

CAUTION: *When draining the coolant, keep in mind that cats and dogs are attracted by the ethylene glycol antifreeze, and are quite likely to drink any that is left in an uncovered container or in puddles on the ground. This will prove fatal in sufficient quantity. Always drain the coolant into a sealable container. Coolant should be reused unless it is contaminated or several years old.*

4. Remove the upper radiator hose.
5. Without discharging the system, remove the air conditioning compressor from the engine brackets and set to one side.
6. Remove the alternator and move to one side.
7. Disconnect the lower radiator hose and heater hose.
8. Remove (3) upper screws and (1) lower screw retaining water pump to the engine and remove pump assembly.
9. Position the replacement pump against the engine and install mounting screws. Tighten the (3) upper screws to 20 ft. lbs. and lower screw to 50 ft. lbs.
10. Install heater hose and lower radiator hose. Tighten clamps to 16 inch lbs.
11. Install air conditioning compressor and alternator.
12. Install the drive belts and adjust to specification.
13. Fill the cooling system.
14. Connect the negative battery cable.

2.6L Engine

1. Drain the cooling system.

CAUTION: *When draining the coolant, keep in mind that cats and dogs are attracted by the ethylene glycol antifreeze, and are quite likely to drink any that is left in an uncovered container or in puddles on the ground. This will prove fatal in sufficient quantity. Always drain the coolant into a sealable container. Coolant should be reused unless it is contaminated or several years old.*

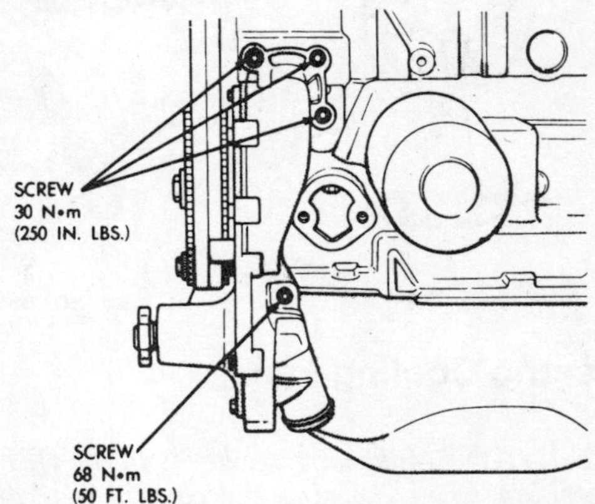

Water pump assembly – 2.2L and 2.5L engines

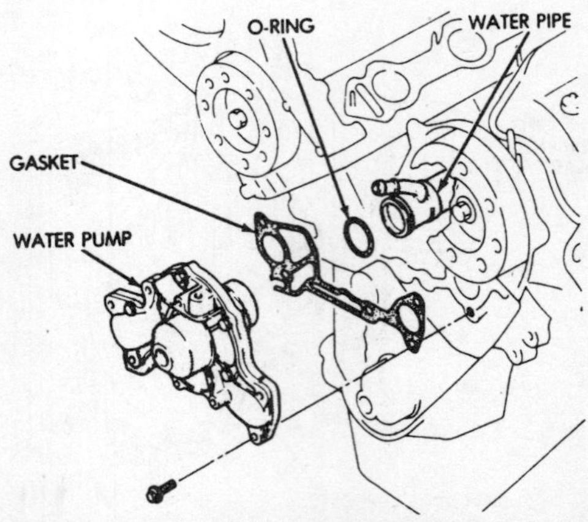

Water pump mounting – 3.0L engine

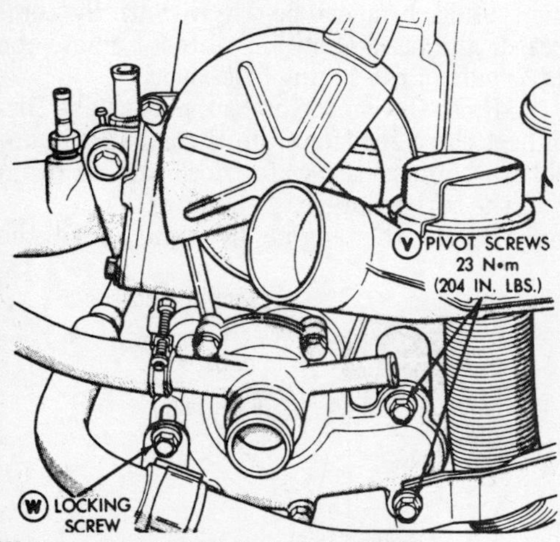

Water pump assembly – 2.6L engine

2. Remove the radiator hose, by-pass hose and heater hose from the water pump.
3. Remove the drive pulley shield.
4. Remove the locking screw and pivot screws.
5. Remove the drive belt and water pump from the engine.
6. Install a new O-ring gasket in O-ring groove of pump body assembly to cylinder block.
7. Position the water pump assembly against the engine and install pivot screws and locking screw finger tight.
8. Install the water pump drive belt and adjust to specification. New belt 8mm deflection, used belt 9mm deflection.
9. Install drive belt pulley cover.
10. Install the radiator hose, by-pass hose and heater hose.
11. Fill the cooling system.

3.0L Engine

1. Disconnect the negative battery cable.
2. Remove the drive belts.
3. Drain the cooling system.

CAUTION: *When draining the coolant, keep in mind that cats and dogs are attracted by the ethylene glycol antifreeze, and are quite likely to drink any that is left in an uncovered container or in puddles on the ground. This will prove fatal in sufficient quantity. Always drain the coolant into a sealable container. Coolant should be reused unless it is contaminated or several years old.*

4. Remove the timing case cover and timing belt. Refer to Timing Belt Covers and Timing Belt Removal procedures.
5. Remove the pump assembly mounting bolts.
6. Separate the pump assembly from water pipe and remove.
7. Clean gasket and O-ring mounting surfaces.
8. Install a new O-ring on water pipe and lubricate with water.
9. Install a new gasket on pump body.
10. Press the water pump assembly into water pipe.
11. Install pump mounting bolts and tighten to 27 Nm (20 ft. lbs.).
12. Install timing belt and cover. Refer to Timing Belt procedures.
13. Install drive belts.
14. Fill the cooling system.

3.3L Engine

1. Disconnect the negative battery cable.
2. Drain the cooling system.
3. Remove the serpentine belt.
4. Raise the vehicle and support safely. Remove the right front tire and wheel assembly and lower fender shield.
5. Remove the water pump pulley.
6. Remove the 5 mounting screws and remove the pump from the engine.
7. Discard the O-ring.

To install:

8. Using a new O-ring, install the pump to the engine. Torque the mounting bolts to 21 ft. lbs. (30 Nm).
9. Install the water pump pulley.
10. Install the fender shield and tire and wheel assembly. Lower the vehicle.
11. Install the serpentine belt.
12. Remove the engine temperature sending unit. Fill the radiator with coolant until the coolant comes out the sending unit hole. Install the sending unit and continue to fill the radiator.
13. Connect the negative battery cable, run the vehicle until the thermostat opens, fill the radiator completely and check for leaks.
14. Once the vehicle has cooled, recheck the coolant level.

Cylinder Head

REMOVAL AND INSTALLATION

2.2L and 2.5L Engines

1. Relieve the fuel pressure if equipped with fuel injection. Disconnect the negative battery cable and unbolt it from the head. Drain the cooling system. Remove the dipstick bracket nut from the thermostat housing.
2. Remove the air cleaner assembly. Remove the upper radiator hose and disconnect the heater hoses.
3. Disconnect and label the vacuum lines, hoses and wiring connectors from the manifold(s), carburetor or throttle body and from

the cylinder head. Remove the air pump, if equipped.

4. Disconnect the all linkages and the fuel line from the carburetor or throttle body. Unbolt the cable bracket. Remove the ground strap attaching screw from the fire wall.

5. If equipped with air conditioning, remove the upper compressor mounting bolts. The cylinder head can be remove with the compressor and bracket still mounted. Remove the upper part of the timing belt cover.

6. Raise the vehicle and support safely. Disconnect the converter from the exhaust manifold. Disconnect the water hose and oil drain from the turbocharger, if equipped.

7. Rotate the engine by hand, until the

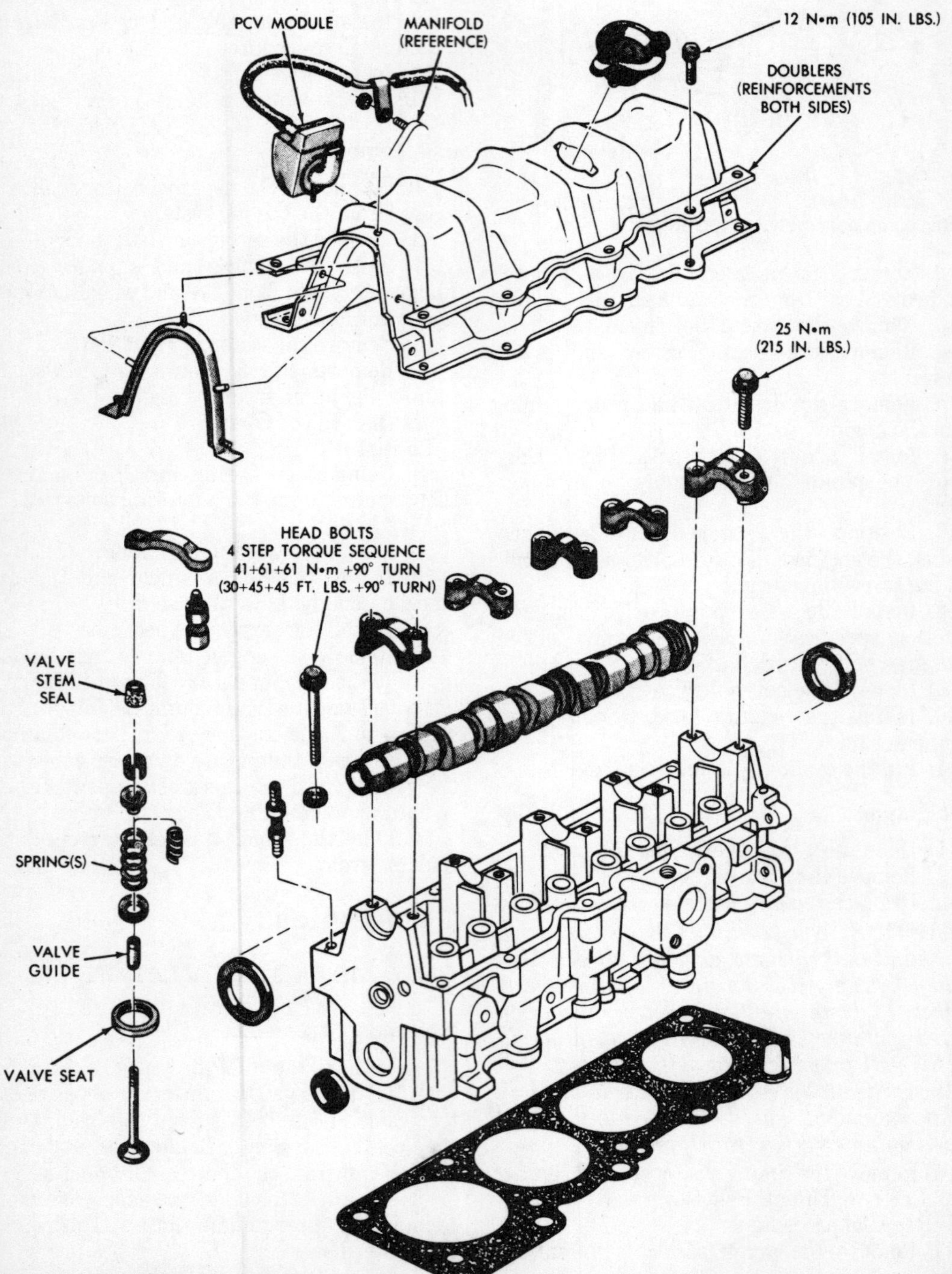

Cylinder head and related components — 2.2L engine

timing marks align (No. 1 piston at TDC). Lower the vehicle.

8. With the timing marks aligned, remove the camshaft sprocket. The camshaft sprocket can be suspended to keep the timing intact. Remove the spark plug wires from the spark plugs.

9. Remove the valve cover and curtain, if equipped. Remove the cylinder head bolts and washers, starting from the middle and working outward.

10. Remove the cylinder head from the engine.

NOTE: *Before disassembling or repairing any part of the cylinder head assembly, identify factory installed oversized components. To do so, look for the tops of the bearing caps pained green and O/SJ stamped rearward of the oil gallery plug on the rear of the head. In addition, the barrel of the camshaft is painted green and O/SJ is stamped onto the rear end of the camshaft. Installing standard sized parts in an head equipped with oversized parts—or visa versa—will cause severe engine damage.*

11. Clean the cylinder head gasket mating surfaces.

12. Using new gaskets and seals, install the head to the engine. Using new head bolts assembled with the old washers, torque the cylinder head bolts in sequence, to 45 ft. lbs. Repeating the sequence, torque the bolts to 65 ft. lbs. With the bolts at 65 ft. lbs., turn each bolt an additional 1/4 turn.

NOTE: *Head bolt diameter for 1986–91 vehicles is 11mm. These bolts are identified with the number 11 on the head of the bolt. The 10mm bolts used on previous vehicles will thread into an 11mm bolt hole, but will permanently damage the engine block. Make sure the correct bolts are being used.*

13. Install the timing belt.

14. Install or connect all items that were removed or disconnected during the removal procedures.

15. Refill the cooling system. Connect the negative battery cable. Start the engine and check for leaks.

2.6L Engine

1. Disconnect the negative battery cable and unbolt if from the head.

2. Drain the cooling system. Remove the upper radiator hose and disconnect the heater hoses. Remove the air cleaner assembly.

3. Remove the dipstick bracket bolt from the thermostat housing.

4. Remove the carburetor to valve cover bracket. Remove the valve cover. Remove and plug the fuel lines to the carburetor.

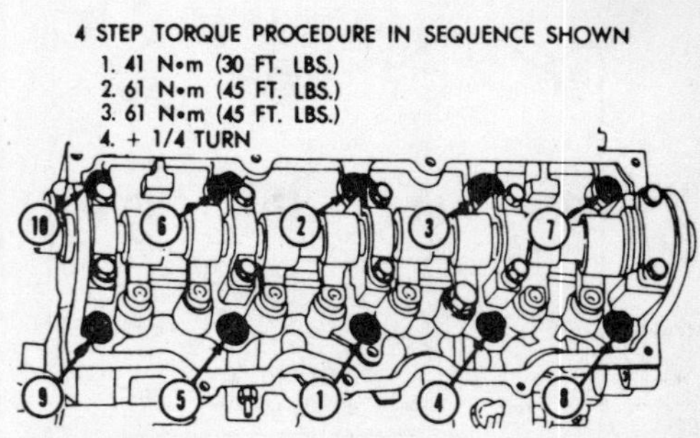

Cylinder head torque sequence — 2.2L and 2.5L engines

5. Matchmark the distributor gear to its drive gear and remove the distributor. Remove the camshaft bolt and remove the distributor drive gear. Remove the camshaft gear with the chain installed from the camshaft and allow to rest on the holder just below it. This will not upset the valve timing. Do not crank the engine until the distributor has been reinstalled or the timing will be lost and timing components could be damaged.

6. Remove the water pump drive pulley retaining bolt and remove the pulley from the camshaft.

7. Disconnect and label the vacuum lines, hoses and wiring connectors from the manifold(s), carburetor and cylinder head. Since some of the vacuum lines from the carburetor connect to a solenoid pack on the right side inner fender, unbolt the solenoids from the fender with the vacuum lines attached and fold the assembly over the carburetor.

8. Disconnect all the linkages and the fuel line from the carburetor. Remove the ground strap attaching screw from the fire wall. Unbolt the power steering pump from the bracket and position to the side.

9. Raise the vehicle and support safely. Disconnect the vacuum hoses from the source below the carburetor and disconnect the air feeder tubes.

10. Remove the exhaust pipe from the exhaust manifold. Lower the vehicle.

11. Remove the small end bolts from the head first, then remove the remaining head bolts, starting from the outside and working inward.

12. Remove the cylinder head from the engine.

13. Clean the cylinder head gasket mating surfaces.

To install:

14. Install a new head gasket to the block and install all head bolts and washers. Torque the bolts in sequence to 34 ft. lbs. (40 Nm). Repeat the sequence increasing the torque to 69 ft. lbs. (94 Nm). Tighten the small end bolts to 13 ft. lbs. (18 Nm).

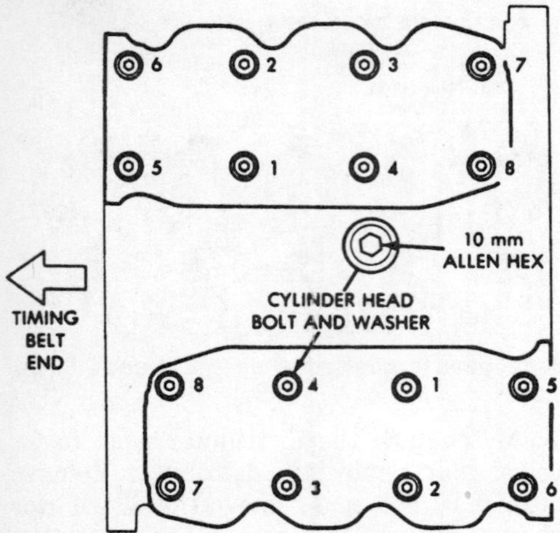

Cylinder head bolt tightening sequence – 3.0L engine

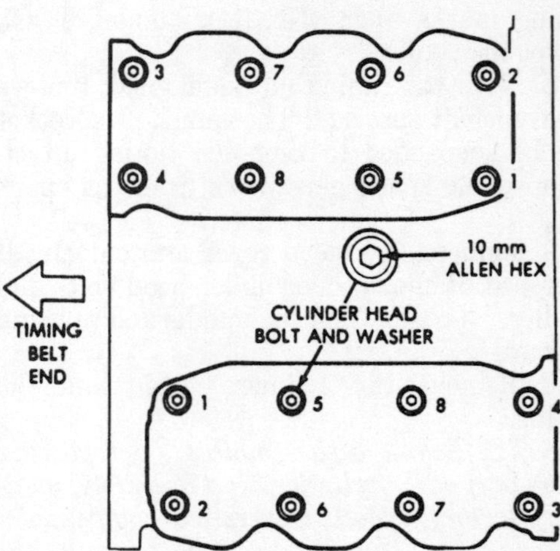

Cylinder head bolt loosening sequence – 3.0L engine

15. Install the camshaft gear with the timing chain. If the timing will not allow for gear installation, reach into the case with a long, thin tool and push the rubber foot into the oil pump to allow for more chain movement. Install the distributor drive gear, bolt and washer. Torque the bolt to 40 ft. lbs. (54 Nm). Install the distributor, aligning the match marks.

16. Install or connect all items that were removed or disconnected during the removal procedure.

17. Refill the cooling system. Connect the negative battery cable. Start the engine and check for leaks. Adjust the timing as required.

3.0L Engine

1. Relieve the fuel pressure. Disconnect the negative battery cable. Drain the cooling system.

2. Remove the drive belt and the air conditioning compressor from its mount and support it aside. Using a 1/2 in. drive breaker bar, insert it into the square hole of the serpentine drive belt tensioner, rotate it counterclockwise (to reduce the belt tension) and remove the belt. Remove the alternator and power steering pump from the brackets and move them aside.

3. Raise the vehicle and support safely. Remove the right front wheel assembly and the right inner splash shield.

4. Remove the crankshaft pulleys and the torsional damper.

5. Lower the vehicle. Using a floor jack and a block of wood positioned under the oil pan, raise the engine slightly. Remove the engine mount bracket from the timing cover end of the engine and the timing belt covers.

6. To remove the timing belt, perform the following procedures:

a. Rotate the crankshaft to position the No. 1 cylinder on the TDC of its compression stroke; the crankshaft sprocket timing mark should align with the oil pan timing indicator and the camshaft sprockets timing marks (triangles) should align with the rear timing belt covers timing marks.

b. Mark the timing belt in the direction of rotation for reinstallation purposes.

c. Loosen the timing belt tensioner and remove the timing belt.

NOTE: *When removing the timing belt from the camshaft sprocket, make sure the belt does not slip off of the other camshaft sprocket. Support extension.*

7. Remove the camshaft bearing assembly to cylinder head bolts (do not remove the bolts from the assembly). Remove the rocker arms, rocker shafts and bearing caps as an assembly, as required. Remove the camshafts from the cylinder head and inspect them for damage, if necessary.

8. Remove the intake manifold assembly.

9. Remove the exhaust manifold.

10. Remove the cylinder head bolts starting from the outside and working inward. Remove the cylinder head from the engine.

11. Clean the gasket mounting surfaces and check the heads for warpage; the maximum warpage allowed is 0.008 in. (0.20mm).

To install:

12. Install the new cylinder head gaskets over the dowels on the engine block.

13. Install the cylinder heads on the engine and torque the cylinder head bolts in sequence using 3 even steps, to 70 ft. lbs. (95 Nm).

14. Install or connect all items that were removed or disconnected during the removal procedure.

15. When installing the timing belt over the camshaft sprocket, use care not to allow the belt to slip off the opposite camshaft sprocket.

16. Make sure the timing belt is installed on the camshaft sprocket in the same position as when removed.

17. Refill the cooling system. Connect the negative battery cable. Start the engine and check for leaks using the DRB I or II to active the fuel pump. Adjust the timing as required.

3.3L Engine

1. Relieve the fuel pressure. Disconnect the negative battery cable. Drain cooling system.
2. Remove the intake manifold with throttle body.

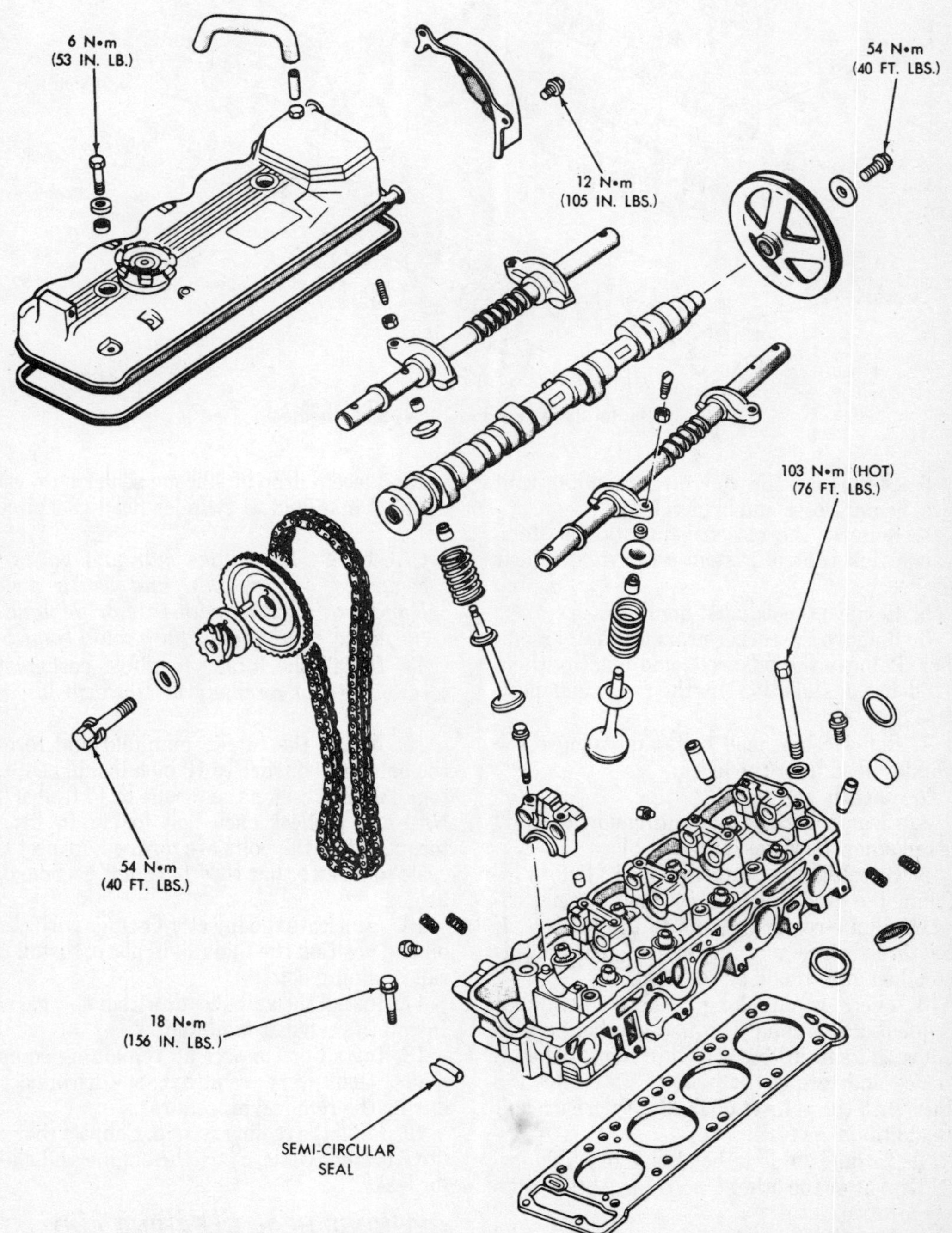

Cylinder head and related components — 2.6L engine

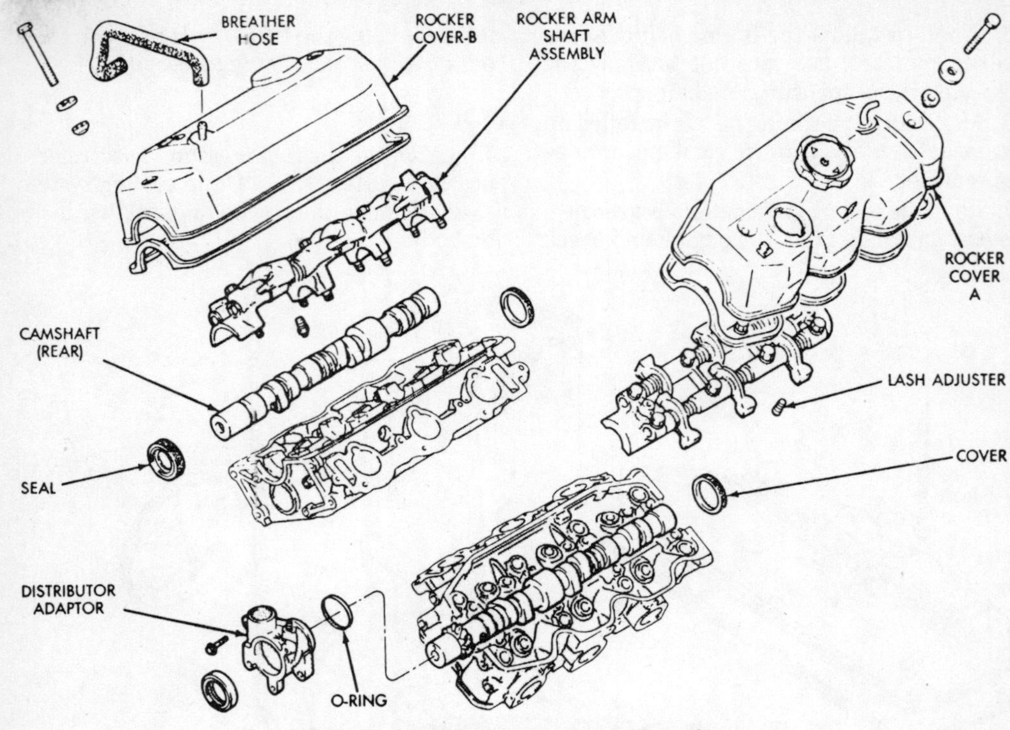

Cylinder head components — 3.0L engine

3. Disconnect the coil wires, sending unit wire, heater hoses and bypass hose.

4. Remove the closed ventilation system, evaporation control system and cylinder hear cover.

5. Remove the exhaust manifold.

6. Remove the rocker arm and shaft assemblies. Remove the pushrods and identify them in ensure installation in their original positions.

7. Remove the head bolts and remove the cylinder head from the block.

To install:

8. Clean the gasket mounting surfaces and install a new head gasket to the block.

9. Install the head to the block. Before installing the head bolts, inspect them for stretching. Hold a straight edge up to the threads. If the threads are not all on line, the bolt is stretched and should be replaced.

10. There is one long head bolt. Do not torque it at this time. Torque the other bolts in sequence to 45 ft. lbs. (61 Nm). Repeat the sequence and torque the bolts to 65 ft. lbs. (88 Nm). With the bolts at 65 ft. lbs., turn each bolt an additional $^{1}/_{4}$ turn.

11. Torque the long head bolt to 25 ft. lbs. (33 Nm) after the other 8 bolts have been properly torqued.

12. Install the pushrods, rocker arms and shafts and torque the bolts to 21 ft. lbs. (12 Nm).

13. Place a drop of silicone sealer onto each of the 4 manifold to cylinder head gasket corners.

CAUTION: *The intake manifold gasket is composed of very thin and sharp metal. Handle this gasket with care or damage to the gasket or personal injury could result.*

14. Install the intake manifold gasket and torque the end retainers to 105 inch lbs. (12 Nm).

15. Install the intake manifold and torque the bolts in sequence to 10 inch lbs. Repeat the sequence increasing the torque to 17 ft. lbs. (23 Nm) and recheck each bolt for 17 ft. lbs. of torque. After the bolts are torqued, inspect the seals to ensure that they have not become dislodged.

16. Lubricate the injector O-rings with clean oil and position the fuel rail in place. Install the rail retaining bolts.

17. Install the valve cover with a new gasket. Install the exhaust manifold.

18. Install or connect all remaining components that were removed or disconnected during the removal procedures.

19. Refill the cooling system. Connect the negative battery cable. Start the engine and check for leaks.

CYLINDER HEAD CLEANING AND INSPECTION

1. Turn the cylinder head over so that the

mounting surface is facing up and support evenly on wooden blocks.

2. Use a scraper and remove all of the gasket material and carbon stuck to the head mounting surface and engine block. Mount a wire carbon removal brush in an electric drill and clean away the carbon on the valve heads and head combustion chambers.

NOTE: *When scraping or decarbonizing the cylinder head, take care not to damage or nick the gasket mounting surface or combustion chamber.*

3. Clean cylinder head oil passages.

4. After cleaning check cylinder head for cracks or damage.

5. Check cylinder head flatness. Flatness must be within 0.1mm.

CYLINDER HEAD RESURFACING

If the cylinder head is warped, resurfacing by a automotive machine shop will be required. After cleaning the gasket surface, place a straight-edge across the mounting surface of the head, diagonally from one end to the other. Using a feeler gauge , determine the clearance at the center and alone the length between the head and straight-edge.

Valves

REMOVAL

The following procedures to be performed with cylinder head removed from engine.

1. Compress valve springs using Tool C-3422A or equivalent. Do not mix removed parts. Place the parts from each valve in a separate container, numbered and identified for the valve and cylinder.

2. Remove valve retaining locks, valve spring retainers, valve stem seal, valve springs and valve spring seats.

NOTE: *Before removing valve assembly remove any burrs from valve stem lock grooves to prevent damage to valve guides.*

3. Remove valve assembly.

INSPECTION

1. Clean valves thoroughly.

2. Check valve stem tip for pitting or depression.

3. Check for ridge wear on valve stem area.

4. Inspect valve (with Prussian blue) for even contact between valve face and cylinder head valve seat.

5. Gently remove valve stem seals with a pliers or screwdriver by prying side-to-side. Do not reused old seals.

6. Remove carbon and varnish deposits from inside of valve guides of cylinder head with a suitable guide cleaner.

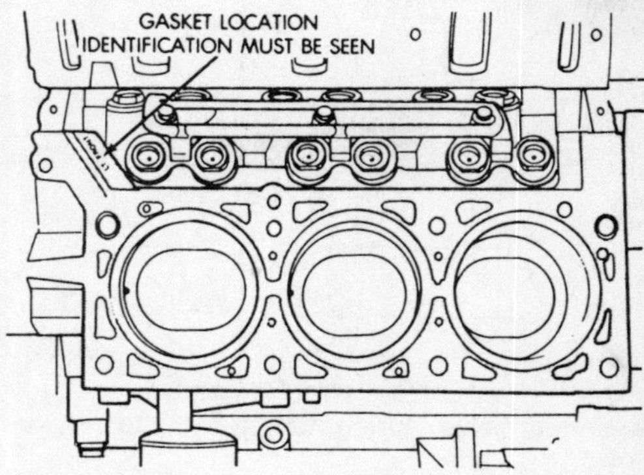

Cylinder head gasket installation – 3.3L engine

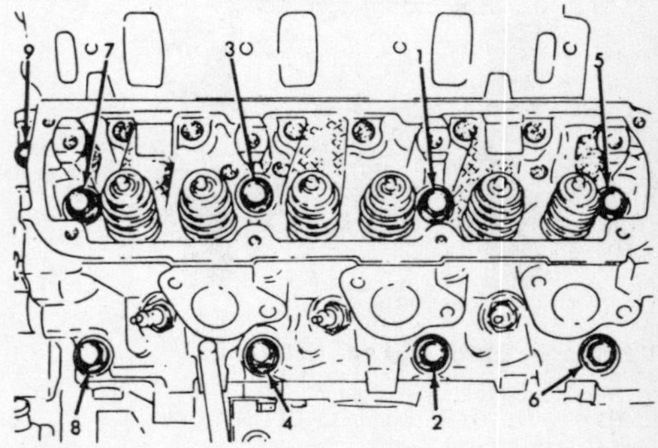

Cylinder head bolt tightening sequence – 3.3L engine

7. Use an electric drill and soft rotary wire brush to clean the intake and exhaust valve ports, combustion chamber and valve seats. In some cases, the carbon build-up will have to be chipped away. Use a blunt pointed drift for carbon chipping, be careful around valve seat areas.

NOTE: *When using a wire brush to clean carbon on the valve ports, valves, etc., be sure the deposits are actually removed, rather then burnished.*

8. Wash and clean all valve spring, locks, retainers etc., in safe solvent. Remember to keep parts from each valve separate.

NOTE: *If valve guide replacement is necessary, or valve or seat refacing is necessary, the job must be handled by a qualified machine shop. If a valve seat is damaged, burnt or loose, the seat may be resurfaced or replaced as necessary. The automotive machine shop can handle the job for you.*

CHECKING VALVE SPRINGS

Place the valve spring on a flat surface next to a carpenters square. Measure the height of the spring, and rotate the spring against the edge of the square to measure distortion. If the spring height varies (by comparison) by more

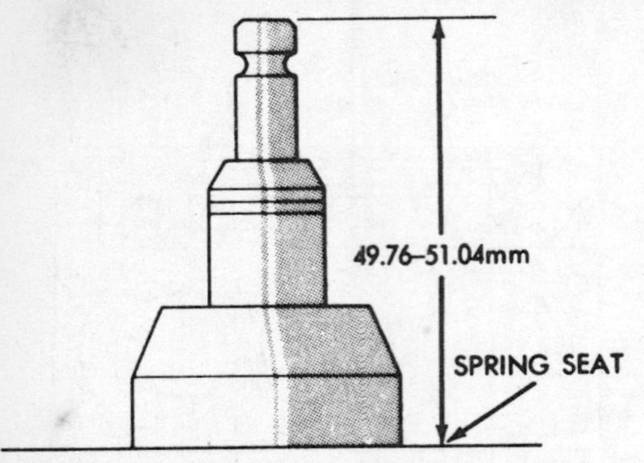

Measuring valve spring height – 2.2L engine shown

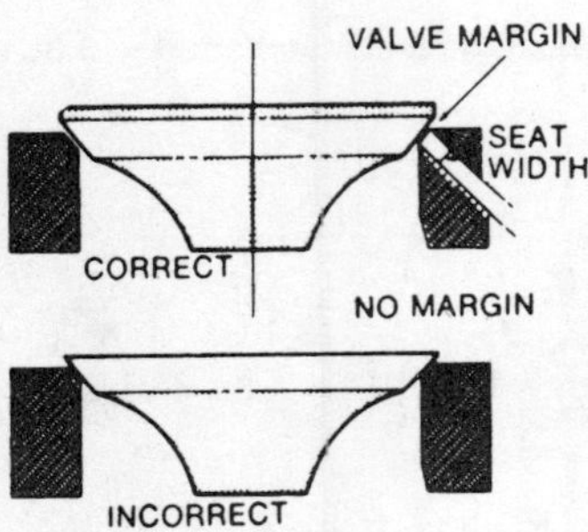

Valve seat width and centering

than $\frac{1}{16}$ in. or if the distortion exceeds $\frac{1}{16}$ in., replace the spring.

Have the valve springs tested for spring pressure at the installed and compressed (installed height minus valve lift) height using a valve spring tester. Springs should be within one pound, plug or minus each other. Replace springs as necessary.

INSTALLATION

1. Coat valve stems with lubrication oil and install in cylinder head.

2. Install a new valve stem seal on the valve. The valve stem seal should be install firmly and squarely over the valve guide. The lower edge of the seal should rest on the valve guide boss.

3. Install the valve spring seat, valve spring, and retainer.

4. Using Tool C-3422A or equivalent compress valve spring only enough to install retainer locks. Install retainer locks and make certain locks are in their correct location before removing valve compressor.

5. Repeat step 1 thru 4 on remaining valves.

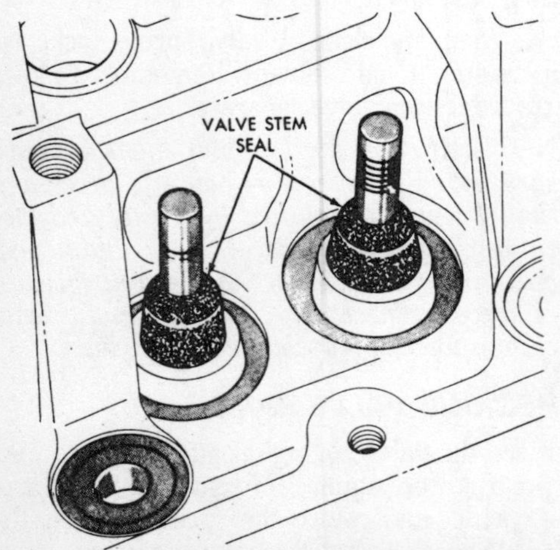

Valve stem oil seals – 2.2L engine shown

Oil Pan

REMOVAL AND INSTALLATION

2.2L Engine

1. Raise and safely support the vehicle on jackstands. Drain the oil pan.

CAUTION: *The EPA warns that prolonged contact with used engine oil may cause a number of skin disorders, including cancer! You should make every effort to minimize your exposure to used engine oil. Protective gloves should be worn when changing the oil. Wash your hands and any other exposed skin areas as soon as possible after exposure to used engine oil. Soap and water, or waterless hand cleaner should be used.*

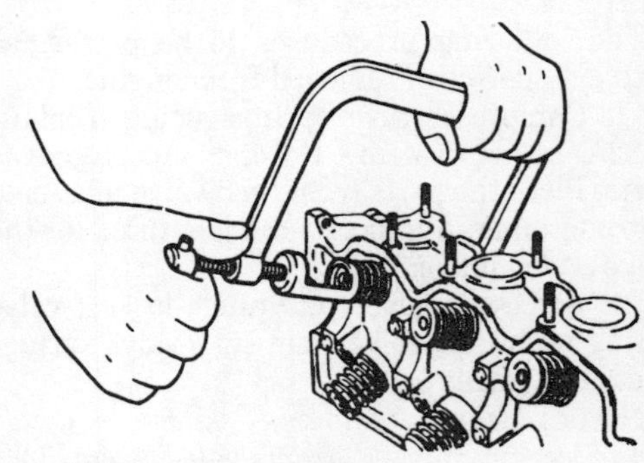

Removing the valve springs

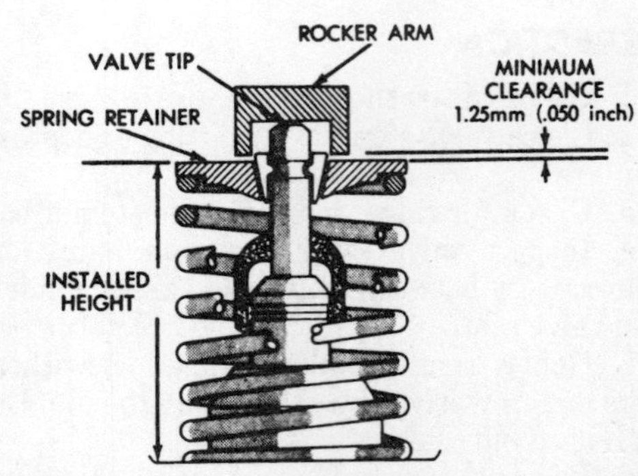

Checking the valve spring installed height – 2.2L engine shown

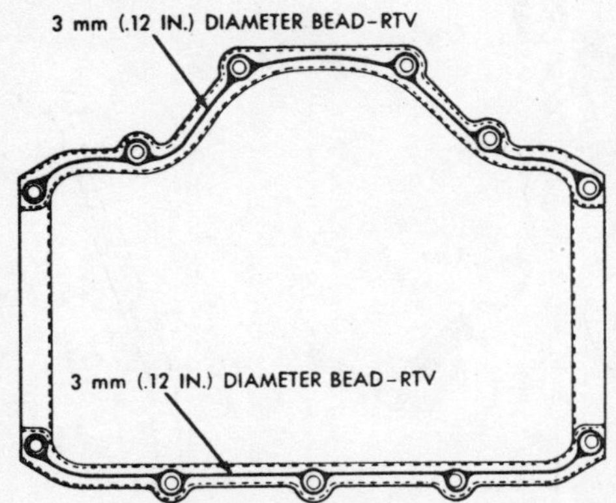

2.2L oil pan RTV sealer application

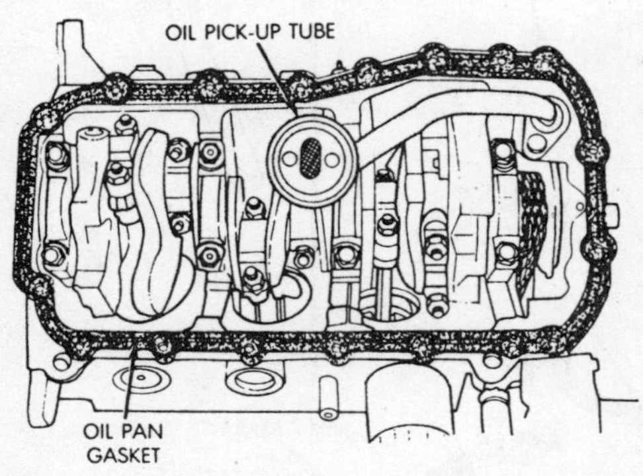

Oil pan gasket installation – 3.3L engine

2. Remove the oil pan attaching bolts and remove oil pan.

3. Clean the oil pan and engine block gasket surfaces thoroughly.

4. Apply RTV sealant to oil pan side rails.

5. Install new oil pan seals and install oil pan. Torque the pan screws to 15 ft. lbs.

6. Refill the crankcase, start the engine and check for leaks.

2.5L Engine

1. Raise and safely support the vehicle on jackstands. Drain the oil pan.

CAUTION: *The EPA warns that prolonged contact with used engine oil may cause a number of skin disorders, including cancer! You should make every effort to minimize your exposure to used engine oil. Protective gloves should be worn when changing the oil. Wash your hands and any other exposed skin areas as soon as possible after exposure to used engine oil. Soap and water, or waterless hand cleaner should be used.*

2. Remove the oil pan attaching bolts and remove oil pan.

3. Clean oil pan and engine block gasket surfaces thoroughly.

4. Apply RTV sealant to oil pan rail at the

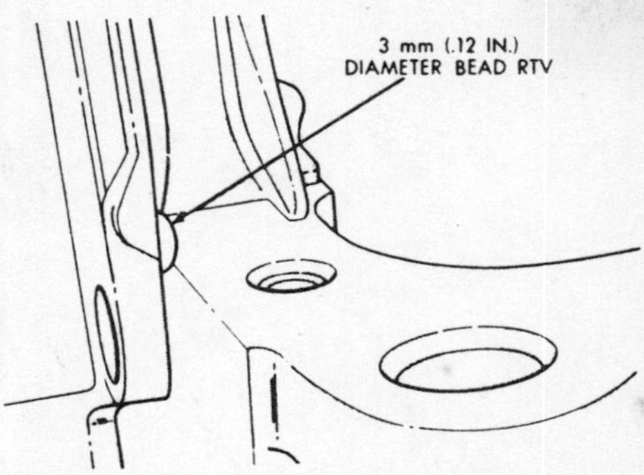

RTV application on the front and rear oil pan seals

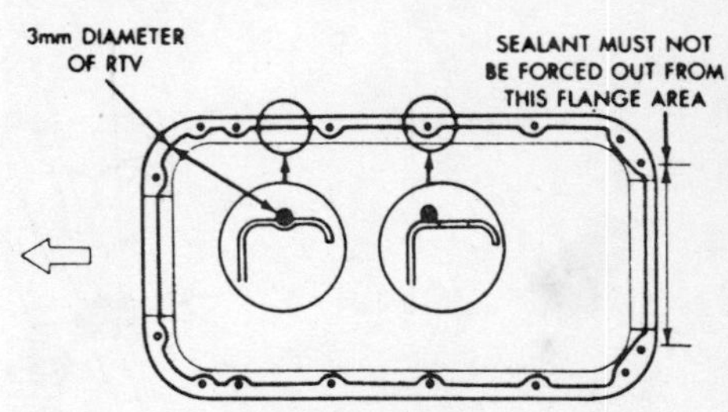

3.0L oil pan RTV sealer application

front seal retainer parting line.

5. Attach the oil pan side gaskets using heavy grease or RTV to hold the gasket in place.

6. Install the new oil pan seals and apply RTV sealant to the ends of the seals at junction where seals and gasket meets.

7. Install oil pan and tighten M8 screws to 15 ft. lbs., and M6 screws to 105 inch lbs.

2.6L Engine

1. Raise and safely support the vehicle on jackstands. Drain the oil pan.

CAUTION: *The EPA warns that prolonged contact with used engine oil may cause a number of skin disorders, including cancer! You should make every effort to minimize your exposure to used engine oil. Protective gloves should be worn when changing the oil. Wash your hands and any other exposed skin areas as soon as possible after exposure to used engine oil. Soap and water, or waterless hand cleaner should be used.*

2. Remove the oil pan attaching bolts and remove oil pan.

3. Clean oil pan and engine block gasket surfaces thoroughly.

4. Install a new pan gasket.

5. Install oil pan and tighten screws to 60 inch lbs.

3.0L Engine

1. Raise and safely support the vehicle on jackstands. Drain the oil pan.

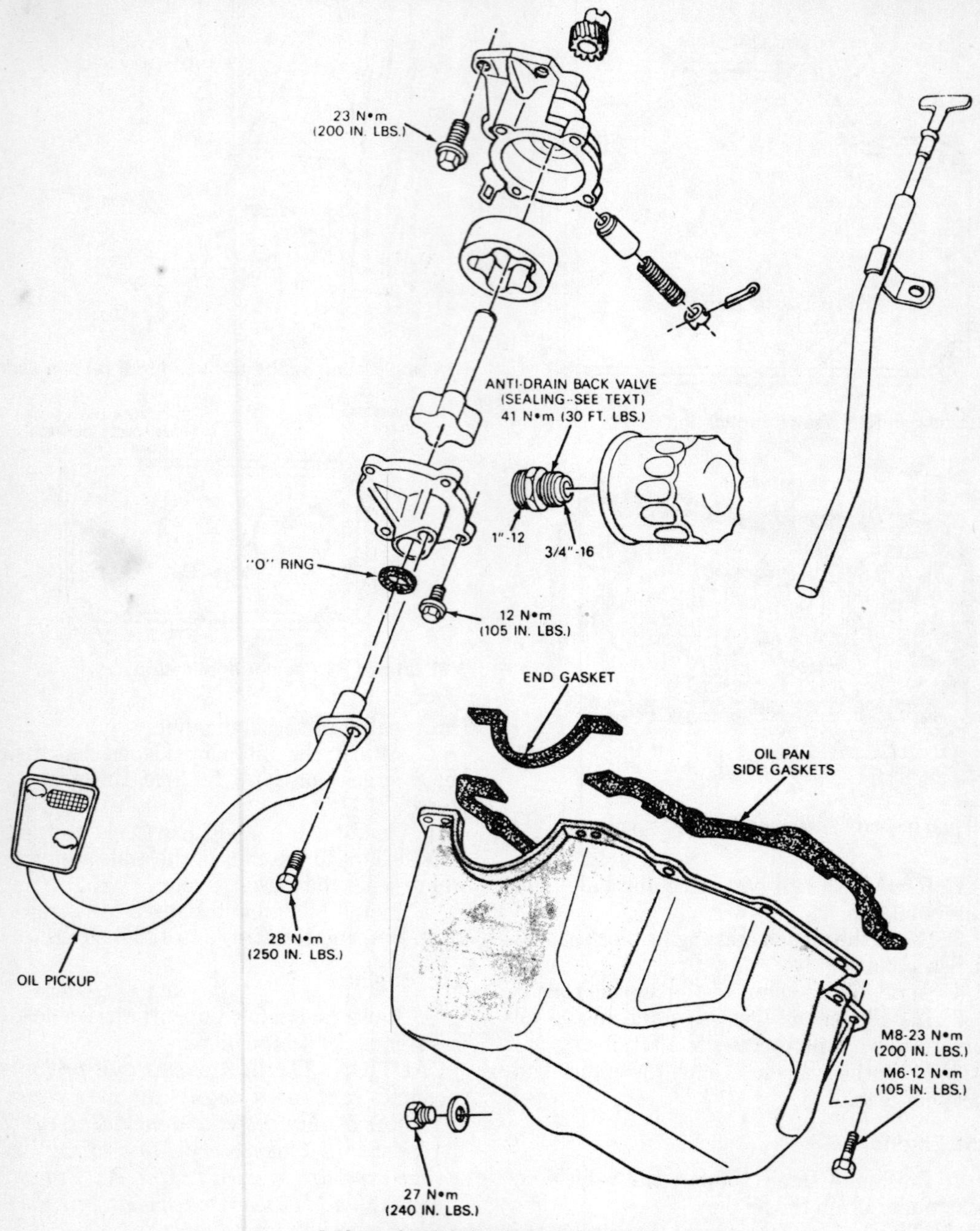

2.5L engine lubrication components

CAUTION: *The EPA warns that prolonged contact with used engine oil may cause a number of skin disorders, including cancer! You should make every effort to minimize your exposure to used engine oil. Protective gloves should be worn when changing the oil. Wash your hands and any other exposed skin areas as soon as possible after exposure to used engine oil. Soap and water, or waterless hand cleaner should be used.*

2. Remove the oil pan attaching bolts and remove oil pan.
3. Clean oil pan and engine block gasket surfaces thoroughly.
4. Apply RTV sealant to oil pan.
5. Install oil pan to engine and tighten screws in sequence, working from the center toward the ends, to 50 inch lbs.

3.3L Engine

1. Disconnect the negative battery cable.
2. Raise the vehicle and support safely.
3. Remove the torque converter bolt access cover, if equipped.

4. Drain the engine oil.
5. Remove the oil pan retaining screws and remove the oil pan and gasket.

To install:

6. Thoroughly clean and dry all sealing surfaces, bolts and bolt holes.
7. Apply silicone sealer to the chain cover to block mating seam and the rear main seal retainer to block seam, if equipped.
8. Install a new pan gasket or apply silicone sealer to the sealing surface of the pan and install to the engine.
9. Install the retaining screws and torque to 200 inch lbs. (23 Nm).
10. Install the torque converter bolt access cover, if equipped. Lower the vehicle.
11. Install the dipstick. Fill the engine with the proper amount of oil.
12. Connect the negative battery cable and check for leaks.

Oil Pump

REMOVAL AND INSTALLATION

2.2L and 2.5L Engine

1. Raise and safely support the vehicle.
2. Drain the oil and remove engine oil pan. See Oil Pan Removal.

CAUTION: *The EPA warns that prolonged contact with used engine oil may cause a number of skin disorders, including cancer! You should make every effort to minimize your exposure to used engine oil. Protective gloves should be worn when changing the oil. Wash your hands and any other exposed skin areas as soon as possible after exposure to used engine oil. Soap and water, or waterless hand cleaner should be used.*

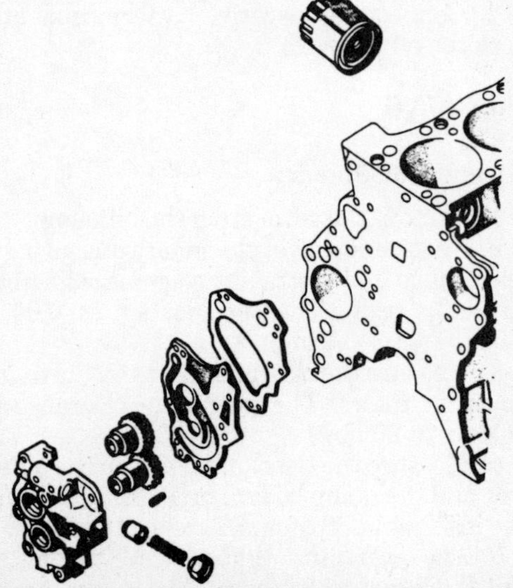

2.6L oil pump assembly

3. Remove the pump mounting bolts.
4. Pull the pump down and out of the engine.
5. Prime, by filling pump with fresh oil. Check crankshaft/intermediate shaft timing and oil pump drive alignment. Adjust if necessary.
6. Install pump and rotate back and forth slightly to ensure full surface contact of pump and block.
7. While holding pump in fully seated position, install pump mounting bolts. Torque to 15 ft. lbs.
8. Install engine oil pan. Refer to Oil Pan Installation procedures.

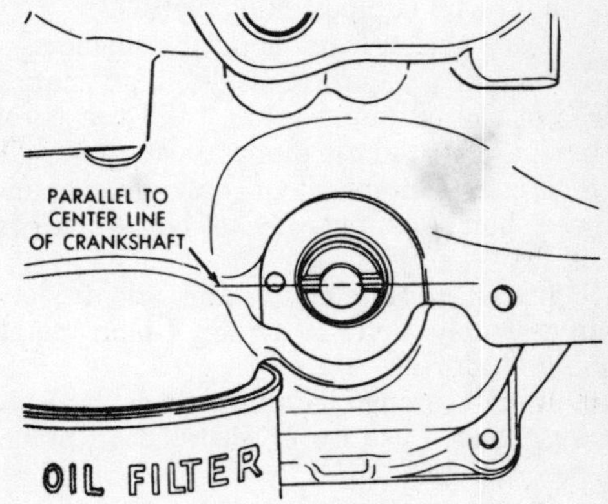

Oil pump shaft alignment — 2.2L engine

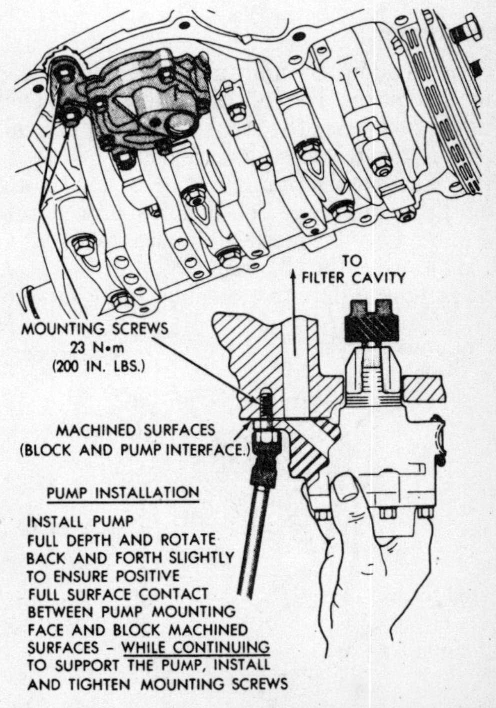

Oil pump application — 2.2L and 2.5L engine

9. Refill crankcase, start engine.
10. Check engine oil pressure.

2.6L Engine

1. Remove accessory drive belts.
2. Remove the timing chain case cover. Refer to Timing Chain Case Cover Removal procedures.
3. Remove the silent shaft chain assembly and timing chain assembly. Refer to Timing Chain Removal procedures.
4. Remove the silent shaft bolt (bolt directly above the silent chain sprocket).
5. Remove the oil pump bolts and pull the pump housing straight forward. Remove the gaskets and the oil pump backing plate.
6. Clean gasket from mounting surfaces.
7. Install new gaskets/seals, align mating marks of the oil pump gears, refill the pump with oil, and install the pump assembly.
8. Install oil pump silent shaft sprocket and sprocket bolt. Tighten sprocket bolt to 34 Nm (25 ft. lbs.).
9. Install timing chain and silent shaft chain assembly. Refer to Timing Chain Installation procedures.
10. Install timing chain case cover. Refer to Timing Chain Case Cover Installation procedures.
11. Install accessory drive belts.
12. Reconnect battery negative cable.
13. Start engine and check engine oil pressure.

3.0L Engine

The oil pump assembly used on this engine is mounted at the front of the crankshaft. The oil pump also retains the crankshaft front oil seal.

1. Remove accessory drive belts.
2. Remove the timing belt cover and timing belt. Refer to Timing Belt Removal procedures.
3. Remove the crankshaft sprocket.
4. Remove the oil pump mounting bolts (5), and remove oil pump assembly. Mark mounting bolts for proper installation during reassembly.
5. Clean the oil pump and engine block gasket surfaces thoroughly.
6. Position a new gasket on pump assembly and install on cylinder block. Make sure correct length bolts are in proper locations and torque all bolts to 10 ft. lbs.
7. Install the crankshaft sprocket and timing belt. Recheck engine timing marks. Refer to Timing Belt Installation procedures.
8. Install the timing belt covers. Refer to Timing Belt Cover Installation procedures.
9. Install accessory drive belts.
10. Refill the crankcase and start the engine.
11. Check engine oil pressure.

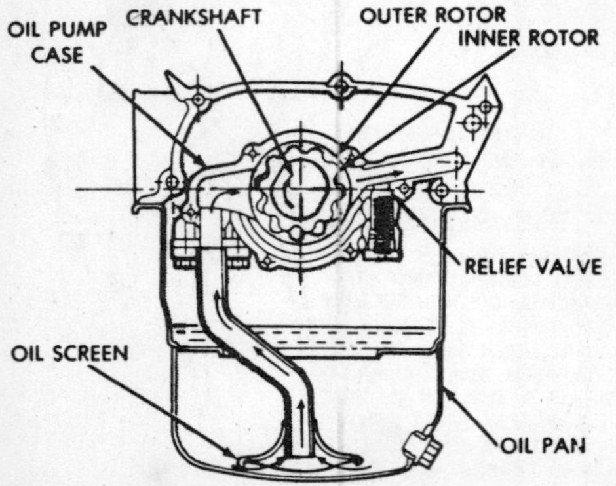

3.0L oil pump components

3.3L Engine

1. Disconnect the negative battery cable. Remove the dipstick.
2. Raise the vehicle and support safely. Drain the oil and remove the oil pan.
3. Remove the oil pickup.
4. Remove the chain case cover.
5. Disassemble the oil pump as required.

To install:

6. Assemble the pump. Torque the cover screws to 10 ft. lbs. (12 Nm).
7. Prime the oil pump by filling the rotor cavity with fresh oil and turning the rotors until oil comes out the pressure port. Repeat a few times until no air bubbles are present.
8. Install the chain case cover.
9. Clean out the oil pickup or replace as required. Replace the oil pickup O-ring and install the pickup to the pump.
10. Install the oil pan.
11. Install the dipstick. Fill the engine with the proper amount of oil.
12. Connect the negative battery cable and check the oil pressure.

CHECKING

2.2L and 2.5L Engines

1. Remove the cover from the oil pump.
2. Check endplay of the inner rotor using a feeler gauge and a straight edge placed across the pump body. The specification is 0.001–0.004 in. (0.03–0.09mm).
3. Measure the clearance between the inner and outer rotors. The maximum clearance is 0.008 in. (0.20mm).
4. Measure the clearance between the outer rotor and the pump body. The maximum clearance is 0.014 in. (0.35mm).
5. The minimum thickness of the outer rotor is 0.944 in. (23.96mm). The minimum diameter of the outer rotor is 2.77 in. (62.70mm).

The minimum thickness of the inner rotor is 0.943 in. (23.95mm).

6. Check the cover for warpage. The maximum allowable is 0.003 in. (0.076mm).

7. Check the pressure relief valve for damage. The spring's free length specification is 1.95 in. (49.50mm).

8. Assemble the outer rotor with the larger chamfered edge in the pump body. Torque the cover screws to 10 ft. lbs. (12 Nm).

2.6L Engine

1. Remove the cover from the oil pump.

2. Measure the clearance between the gears and their bearings. The specification for both is 0.0008–0.0020 in. (0.02–0.05mm).

3. Check the clearance between the gears and the housing. The specification for both gears is 0.004–0.006 in. (0.11–0.15mm).

4. Check endplay of the gears using a feeler gauge and a straight edge placed across the pump body. The specification for both is 0.002–0.004 in. (0.04–0.11mm).

5. Check the pressure relief valve for damage. The spring's free length specification is 1.85 in. (47.00mm).

6. If the gears were removed from the body, install them with the mating aligned. If they are not aligned properly, the silent shaft will be out of time.

7. Torque the cover screws to 13 ft. lbs. (18 Nm).

3.0L Engine

1. Remove the rear cover.

2. Remove the pump rotors and inspect the case for excessive wear.

3. Measure the diameter of the inner rotor hub that sits in the case. Measure the inside diameter of the inner rotor hub bore. Subtract the first measurement from the second; if the result is over 0.006 in. (0.15mm), replace the oil pump assembly.

4. Measure the clearance between the outer rotor and the case. The specification is 0.004–0.007 in. (0.10–0.18mm).

5. Check the side clearance of the rotors using a feeler gauge and a straight edge placed across the case. The specification is 0.0015–0.0035 in. (0.04–0.09mm).

6. Check the relief plunger and spring for damage and breakage.

7. Install the rear cover to the case.

3.3L Engine

1. Thoroughly clean and dry all parts. The mating surface of the chain case cover should be smooth. Replace the pump cover if it is scratched or grooved.

2. Lay a straight edge across the pump cover surface. If a 0.076mm feeler gauge can be inserted between the cover and the straight edge, the cover should be replaced.

3. The maximum thickness of the outer rotor is 0.301 in. (7.63mm). The minimum diameter of the outer rotor is 3.14 in. (79.78mm). The minimum thickness of the inner rotor is 0.301 in. (7.64m).

4. Install the outer rotor onto the chain case cover, press to one side and measure the clearance between the rotor and case. If the measurement exceeds 0.022 in. (56mm) and the rotor is good, replace the chain case cover.

5. Install the inner rotor to the chain case cover and measure the clearance between the rotors. If the clearance exceeds 0.008 in. (0.203mm), replace both rotors.

6. Place a straight edge over the chain case cover between bolt holes. If a 0.004 in. (0.102mm) thick feeler gauge can be inserted under the straight edge, replace the pump assembly.

7. Inspect the relief valve plunger for scoring and freedom of movement. Small marks may be removed with 400-grit wet or dry sandpaper.

8. The relief valve spring should have a free length of 1.95 in.

9. Assemble the pump using new parts where necessary.

Timing Gear/Belt/Chain Cover and Seal

REMOVAL AND INSTALLATION

2.2L and 2.5L Engine

1. Remove the accessory drive belts.

2. Remove the alternator.

3. Remove the air condition compressor belt idler bracket and disconnect air conditioning compressor and locate out of the way.

4. Remove the power steering pump lock screw. Remove the pivot bolt and nut. Remove the power steering pump and mounting bracket. The hoses need not be disconnected, locate the pump out of the way.

5. Loosen and remove the water pump pulley mounting screws and remove the pulley.

6. Support the vehicle on jackstands and remove the right inner splash shield.

7. Remove the crankshaft pulley.

8. Remove the nuts at upper portion of timing cover and screws from lower portion and remove both halves of cover.

9. Install the cover. Secure the upper section to cylinder head with nuts and lower section to cylinder block with screws.

10. Install the crankshaft pulley and tighten the bolt to 20 ft. lbs., lower vehicle.

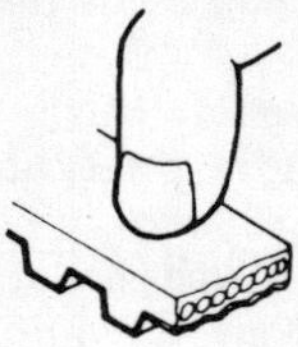

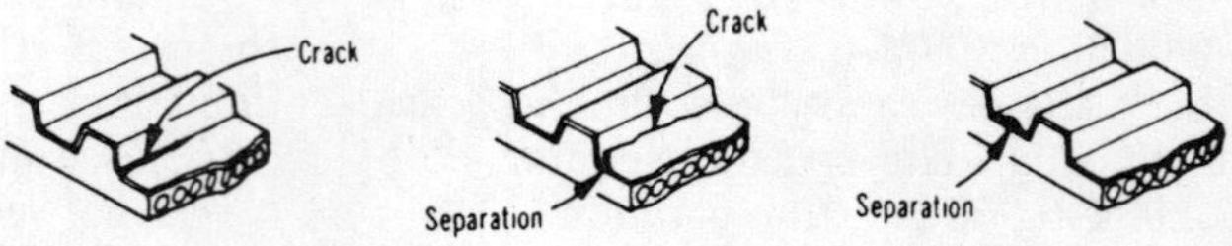

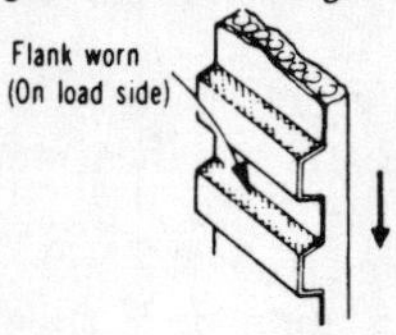

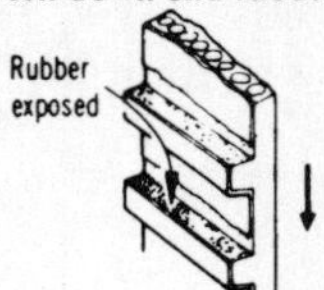

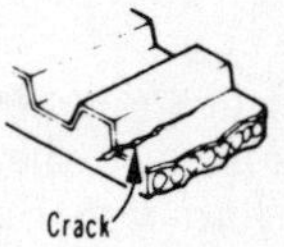

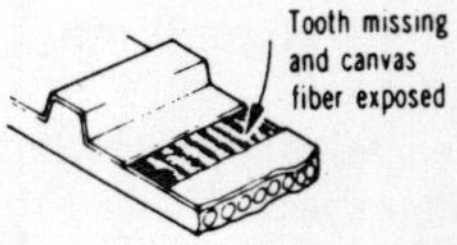

Description	Flaw conditions
1. Hardened back surface rubber	Back surface glossy. Non-elastic and so hard that even if a finger nail is forced into it, no mark is produced.
2. Cracked back surface rubber	
3. Cracked or exfoliated canvas	Crack Crack Separation Separation
4. Badly worn teeth (initial stage)	Canvas on load side tooth flank worn (Fluffy canvas fibers, rubber gone and color changed to white, and unclear canvas texture) Flank worn (On load side)
5. Badly worn teeth (last stage)	Canvas on load side tooth flank worn down and rubber exposed (tooth width reduced) Rubber exposed
6. Cracked tooth bottom	Crack
7. Missing tooth	Tooth missing and canvas fiber exposed
8. Side of belt badly worn	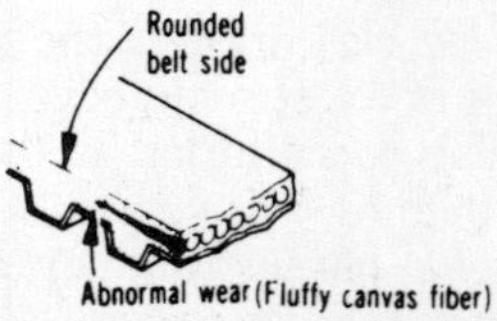 Rounded belt side Abnormal wear (Fluffy canvas fiber) Note: Normal belt should have clear-cut sides as if cut by a sharp knife.
9. Side of belt cracked	

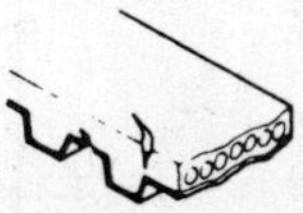

Checking the timing belt wear

11. Install the water pump pulley and tighten screws to 105 inch lbs.
12. Install the power steering pump assembly.
13. Install the air conditioning compressor assembly.
14. Install the alternator assembly.
15. Install the accessory drive belts.

2.6L Engine

1. Disconnect the negative battery cable.
2. Remove the air cleaner assembly.
3. Remove the accessory drive belts.
4. Remove the alternator mounting bolts and remove alternator.
5. Remove the power steering mounting bolts and set power steering pump aside.
6. Remove the air condition compressor mounting bolts and set compressor aside.
7. Support the vehicle on jackstands and remove right inner splash shield.
8. Drain the engine oil.

CAUTION: *The EPA warns that prolonged contact with used engine oil may cause a number of skin disorders, including cancer! You should make every effort to minimize your exposure to used engine oil. Protective gloves should be worn when changing the oil. Wash your hands and any other exposed skin areas as soon as possible after exposure to used engine oil. Soap and water, or waterless hand cleaner should be used.*

9. Remove the crankshaft pulley.
10. Lower the vehicle and place a jack under the engine with a piece of wood between jack and lifting point.

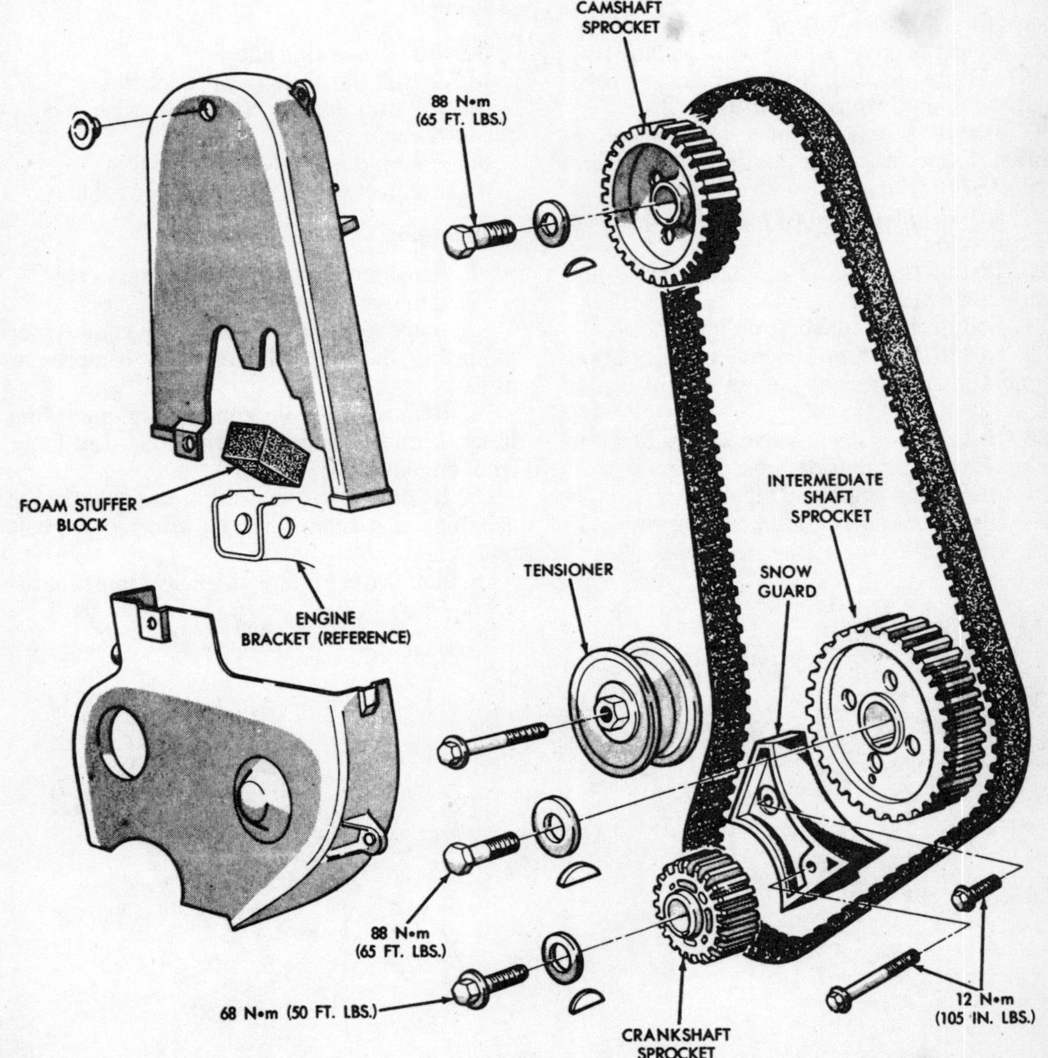

Timing belt and cover assembly — 2.2L and 2.5L engines

11. Raise the jack until contact is made with the engine. Relieve pressure by jacking slightly and remove the center bolt from the right engine mount. Remove right engine mount.
12. Remove the engine oil dipstick.
13. Remove the engine valve cover. Refer to Rocker Cover Removal procedures.
14. Remove the front (2) cylinder head to timing chain cover bolts. DO NOT LOOSEN ANY OTHER CYLINDER HEAD BOLTS.
15. Remove the oil pan retaining bolts and lower the oil pan.
16. Remove the screws holding the timing indicator and engine mounting plate.
17. Remove the bolts holding the timing chain case cover and remove cover.
18. Clean and inspect chain case cover for crack or other damage.
19. Position a new timing chain case cover gasket on case cover. Trim as required to assure fit at top and bottom.
20. Coat the cover gasket with sealant (P/N 3419115) or equivalent. Install chain case cover and tighten mounting bolts to 13 ft. lbs.
21. Install the (2) front cylinder head to timing chain case cover mounting bolts and tighten to 13 ft. lbs.
22. Install the engine oil pan tighten screws to 53 inch lbs.
23. Install the engine mounting plate and timing indicator.
24. Install the crankshaft pulley.
25. Install the right engine mount, lower engine and install right engine mount center bolt.
26. Install the engine valve cover. Refer to Rocker Cover Installation procedures.
27. Install the engine oil dipstick.
28. Install the air conditioner compressor.
29. Install the power steering pump.

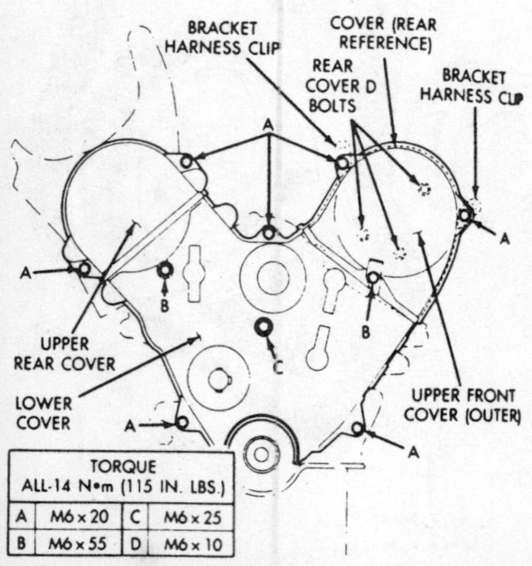

TORQUE ALL-14 N•m (115 IN. LBS.)			
A	M6×20	C	M6×25
B	M6×55	D	M6×10

Front timing cover mounting — 3.0L engine

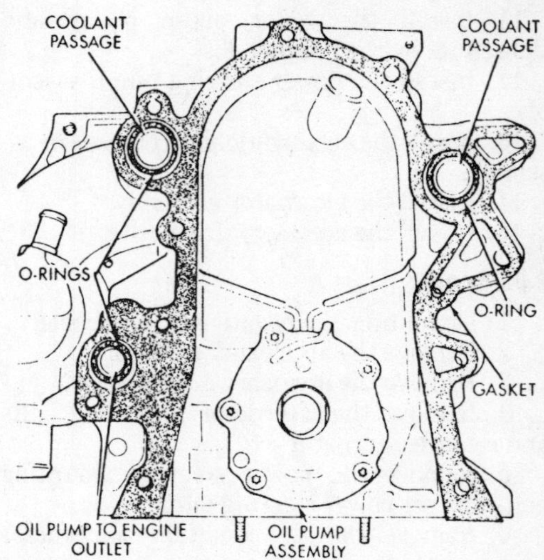

Timing chain case cover gaskets and O-rings — 3.3L engine

30. Install the alternator.
31. Install the accessory drive belts.
32. Fill the engine crankcase with recommended engine oil.
33. Install the air cleaner assembly.
34. Connect the negative battery cable.

3.0L Engine

1. Disconnect the negative battery cable.
2. Remove the accessory drive belts.
3. Remove the air conditioner compressor mounting bracket bolts and lay compressor aside.
4. Remove the air conditioner mounting bracket and adjustable drive belt tensioner from engine.
5. Remove the steering pump/alternator belt tensioner mounting bolt and remove belt tensioner.
6. Remove the power steering pump mount-

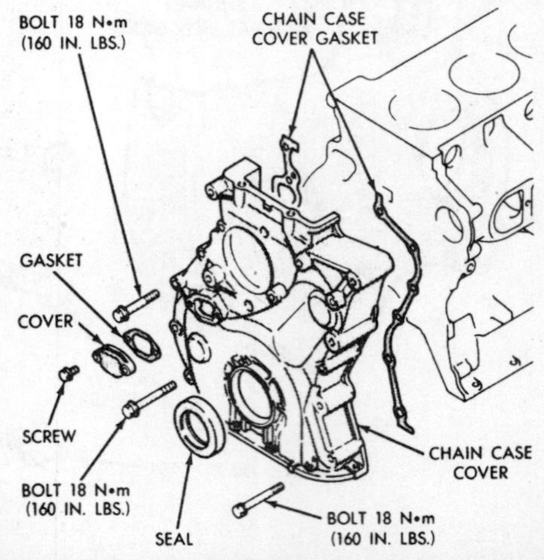

Timing case cover assembly — 2.6L engine

ing bracket bolts, rear support lock nut and set power steering pump aside.

7. Raise the vehicle and support on jackstands.

8. Remove the right inner splash shield.

9. Remove the crankshaft drive pulley bolt, drive pulley and torsional damper.

10. Lower the vehicle and place a floor jack under the engine. Separate engine mount insulator from engine mount bracket.

11. Raise the engine slightly and remove engine mount bracket.

12. Remove the timing belt covers.

13. Install the timing belt covers and tighten all screws to 10 ft. lbs.

14. Raise the engine slightly and install engine mount bracket.

15. Install the engine mount insulator into engine mount bracket.

16. Install the torsional damper, drive pulley and drive pulley bolt. Torque bolt to 110 Nm (150 ft. lbs.). Install the right inner splash shield.

17. Install the power steering mounting bracket and install the power steering pump.

18. Install the steering pump/alternator belt tensioner.

19. Install the air conditioner adjustable drive belt tensioner and mounting bracket.

20. Install the air conditioner compressor.

21. Install the accessory drive belts.

22. Connect the negative battery cable.

3.3L Engine

1. Disconnect the negative battery cable. Drain the cooling system.

2. Support the engine with a suitable engine support device and remove the right side motor mount.

3. Raise the vehicle and support safely. Drain the engine oil and remove the oil pan.

4. Remove the right wheel and tire assembly and the splash shield.

5. Remove the drive belt.

6. Unbolt the air conditioning compressor and position it to the side. Remove the compressor mounting bracket.

7. Remove the crankshaft pulley bolt and remove the pulley using a suitable puller.

8. Remove the idler pulley from the engine bracket and remove the bracket.

9. Remove the cam sensor from the timing chain cover.

10. Unbolt and remove the cover from the engine. Make sure the oil pump inner rotor does not fall out. Remove the 3 O-rings from the coolant passages and the oil pump outlet.

To install:

11. Thoroughly clean and dry the gasket mating surfaces. Install new O-rings to the block.

12. Remove the crankshaft oil seal from the cover. The seal must be removed from the cover when installing to ensure proper oil pump engagement.

13. Using a new gasket, install the chain case cover to the engine.

14. Make certain that the oil pump is engaged onto the crankshaft before proceeding, or severe engine damage will result. Install the attaching bolts and torque to 20 ft. lbs. (27 Nm).

15. Use tool C–4992 to install the crankshaft oil seal. Install the crankshaft pulley using a 5.9 in. suitable bolt and thrust bearing and washer plate L–4524. Make sure the pulley bottoms out on the crankshaft seal diameter. Install the bolt and torque to 40 ft. lbs. (54 Nm).

16. Install the engine bracket and torque the bolts to 40 ft. lbs. (54 Nm). Install the idler pulley to the engine bracket.

17. To install the cam sensor, first clean off

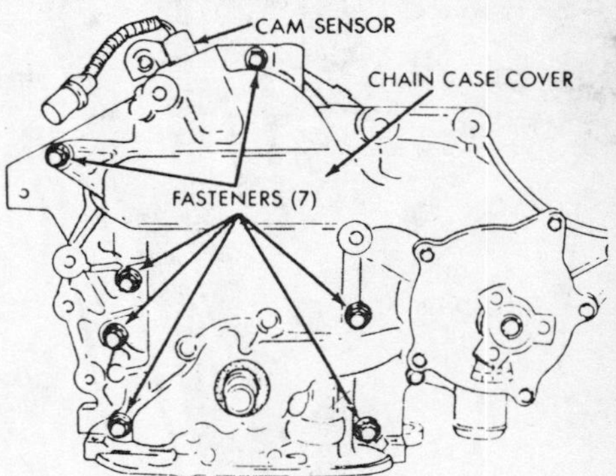

Timing chain case cover retaining bolts – 3.3L engine

the old spacer from the sensor face completely. Inspect the O-ring for damage and repalce if necessary. A new spacer must be attached to the cam sensor, prior to installation; if a new spacer is not used, engine performance will be affected. Oil the O-ring lightly and push the sensor in to its bore in the timing case cover until contact is made with the cam timing gear. Hold in this position and tighten it to 9 ft. lbs. (12 Nm).

18. Install the air conditioning compressor and bracket.

19. Install the drive belt.

20. Install the inner splash shield and the wheel and tire assembly.

21. Install the oil pan with a new gasket.

22. Install the motor mount.

23. Remove the engine temperature sensor and fill the cooling system until the level reaches the vacant sensor hole. Install the

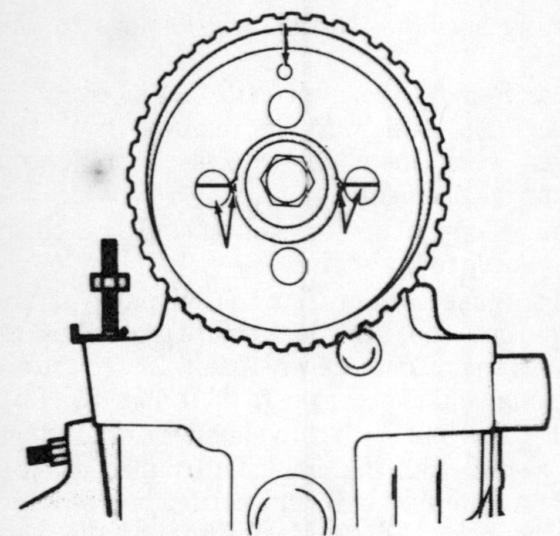

Camshaft sprocket timing alignment

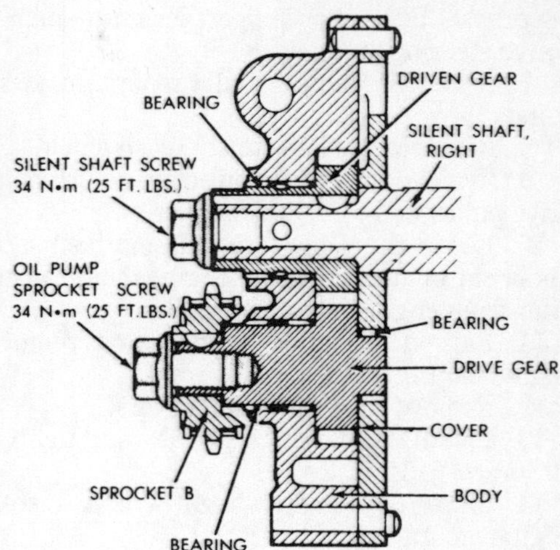

Oil pump and silent shaft installation – 2.6L engine

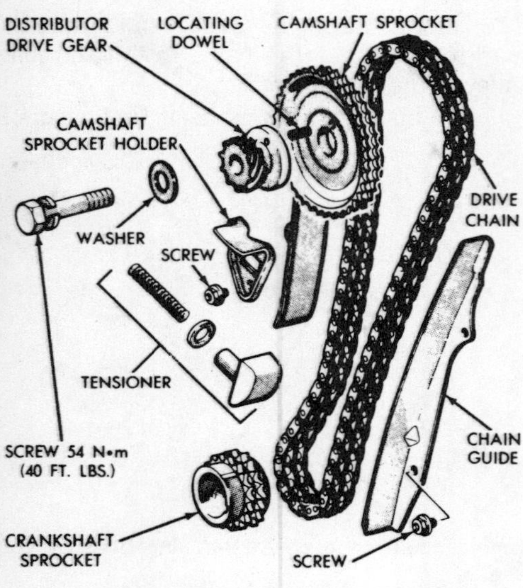

Timing chain components – 2.6L engine

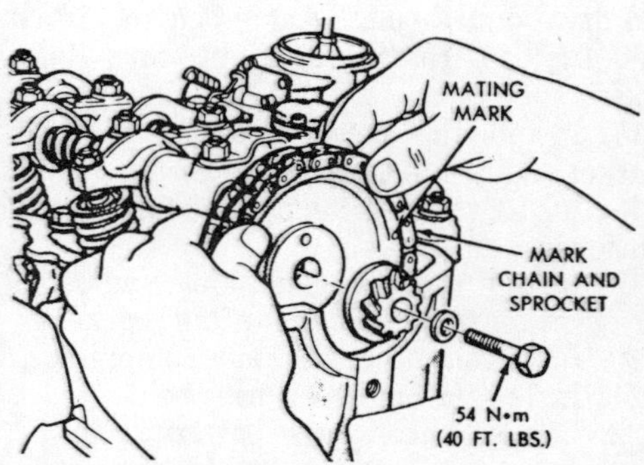

Mark the chain and sprockets and remove the bolt, washer, distributor drive gear and sprocket – 2.6L engine

sensor and continue to fill the radiator. Fill the engine with the proper amount of oil.

24. Connect the negative battery cable and check for leaks.

Timing Belt and/or Chain

REMOVAL AND INSTALLATION

2.2L and 2.5L Engine

1. Remove the accessory drive belts.
2. Remove the timing belt cover. Refer to Timing Belt Cover Removal procedures.
3. Loosen the timing belt tensioner screw, rotate the hex nut, and remove timing belt.
4. Turn the crankshaft and intermediate shaft until markings on both sprockets are aligned.
5. Rotate the camshaft so that the arrows on the hub are in line with No. 1 camshaft cap to cylinder head line. Small hole must be in vertical center line.
6. Install the timing belt over the drive sprockets and adjust.
7. Tighten the tensioner by turning the tensioner hex to the right. Tension should be correct when the belt can be twisted 90 degrees with the thumb and forefinger, midway between the camshaft and intermediate sprocket.
8. Turn the engine clockwise from TDC 2 revolutions with crankshaft bolt. Check the timing marks for correct alignment.

WARNING: *Do not used the camshaft or intermediate shaft to rotate the engine. Also, do not allow oil or solvent to contact timing belt as they will deteriorate the belt and cause slipping.*

9. Tighten lock nut on tensioner while holding weighted wrench in position to 61 Nm (45 ft. lbs.).
10. Install the timing belt cover. Refer to Timing Belt Cover Installation procedures.
11. Install the accessory drive belts.

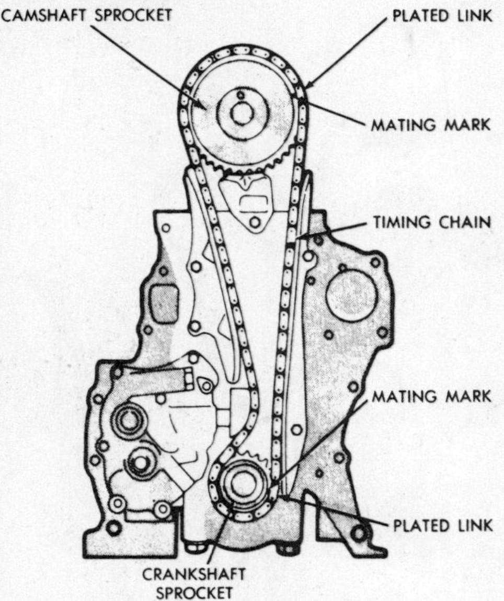

Timing chain installation — 2.6L engine

NOTE: *With timing belt cover installed and number one cylinder at TDC, the small hole in the cam sprocket should be centered in timing belt cover hole.*

2.6L Engine

1. Disconnect the negative battery cable.
2. Remove the accessory drive belts.
3. Remove the timing chain case cover. Refer to Timing Chain Case Cover Removal Procedures.
4. Remove the bolts securing the silent shaft chain guides. Mark all parts for proper location during assembly.

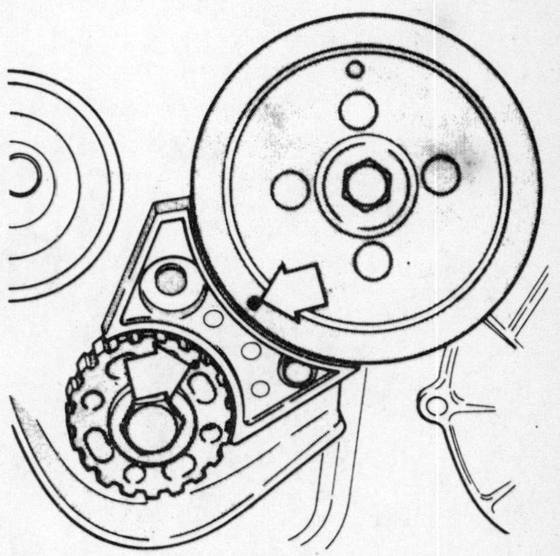

Crankshaft and intermediate shaft timing mark alignment — 2.2L and 2.5L engines

5. Remove the sprocket bolts, silent shaft drive chain, crankshaft/silent sprocket, silent shaft sprockets and spacer.
6. Remove the camshaft sprocket bolt and washer.
7. Remove the distributor drive gear.

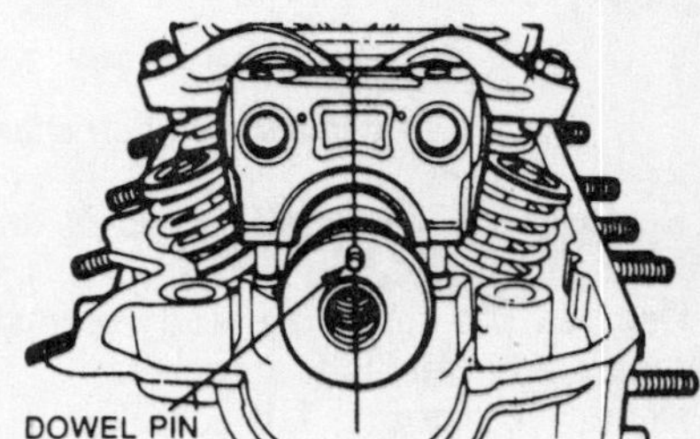

Dowel pin set at 12 o'clock — 2.6L engine

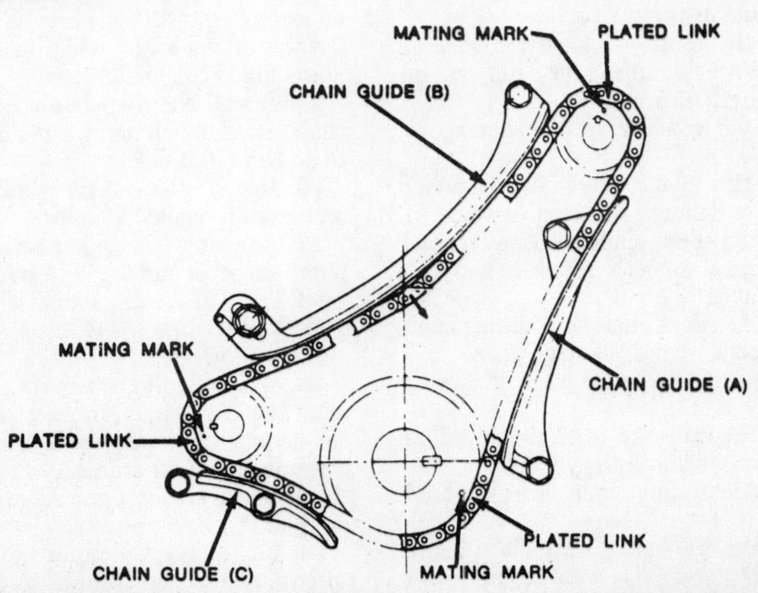

Timing mark alignment for silent shaft timing chain installation — 2.6L engine

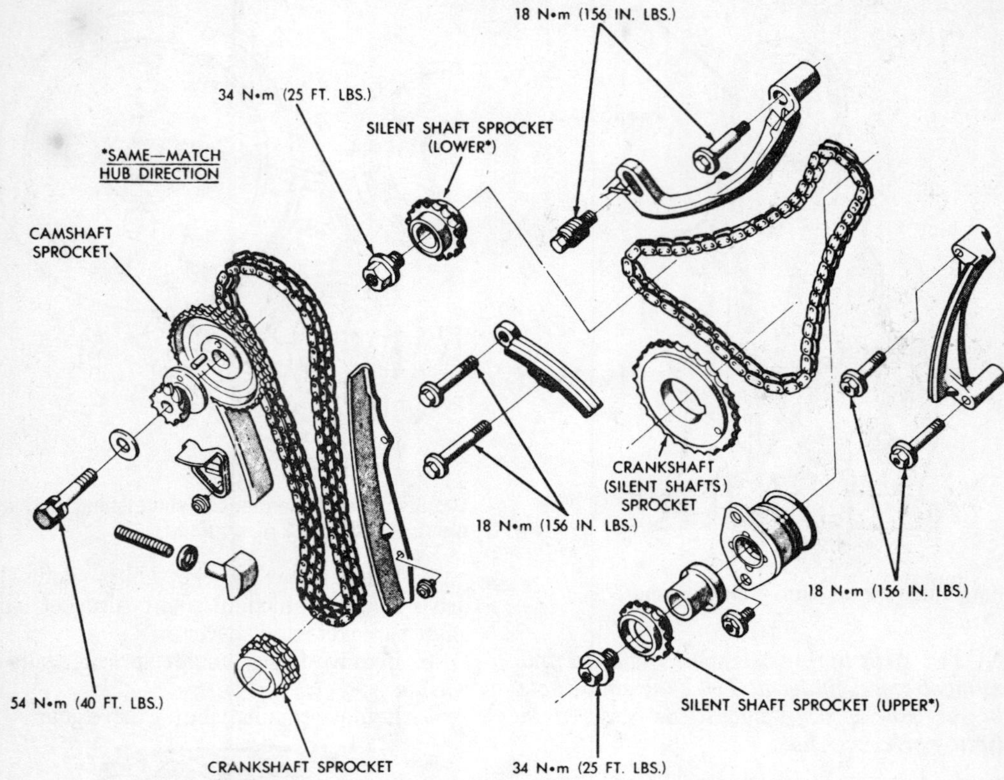

Timing/silent shaft chain and drive components – 2.6L engine

8. Remove the camshaft sprocket holder and timing chain guides.
9. Depress the tensioner and remove the timing chain and camshaft sprocket.
10. Remove the crankshaft sprocket.
11. Remove the tensioner shoe, washer and spring.
12. Clean and inspect all parts.
13. Check the tensioner shoe for wear or damage and tensioner spring for deterioration. Spring free length 65.7mm.
14. Check the chain cover for damage or cracks.
15. Check the silent shaft and camshaft chain guides for damage or excessive wear.
16. Check the silent shaft sprocket cushion ring for free and smooth rotation and ring guides for damage.
17. Check the silent chain and timing chain for excessive play, wear or damage links.
18. Check all sprockets for wear or damage teeth.
19. Rotate the camshaft until the dowel pin is at vertical center line with cylinder.
20. Install the timing chain sprocket holders.
21. Rotate the crankshaft until No. 1 piston is at Top Dead Center (TDC) of its compression stroke.
22. Install the timing chain tensioner spring, washer and shoe on oil pump body.
23. Assemble the timing chain on the camshaft and crankshaft sprockets.

NOTE: *The mating mark on the camshaft and crankshaft sprocket teeth must line up with plated links on timing chain.*

24. While holding the sprockets and chain as an assembly, install the crankshaft sprocket to key way of crankshaft and camshaft sprocket to dowel pin of camshaft.
25. Install the distributor drive gear, camshaft sprocket bolt and washer, and torque bolt to 54 Nm (40 ft. lbs.).
26. Install the silent shaft chain drive sprocket on crankshaft.
27. Assemble the silent shaft chain to oil pump sprocket and to silent shaft sprocket.

NOTE: *The timing marks on the sprockets teeth must line up with plated links on of silent shaft chain.*

28. While holding the parts as an assembly, align the crankshaft sprocket plated link with the punch mark on the sprocket. With the chain installed on crankshaft sprocket, install the oil pump sprocket and silent chain sprocket on their respective shafts.
29. Install the oil pump and silent shaft sprocket bolts and tighten to 34 Nm (25 ft. lbs.).
30. Loosely install the 3 silent shaft chain

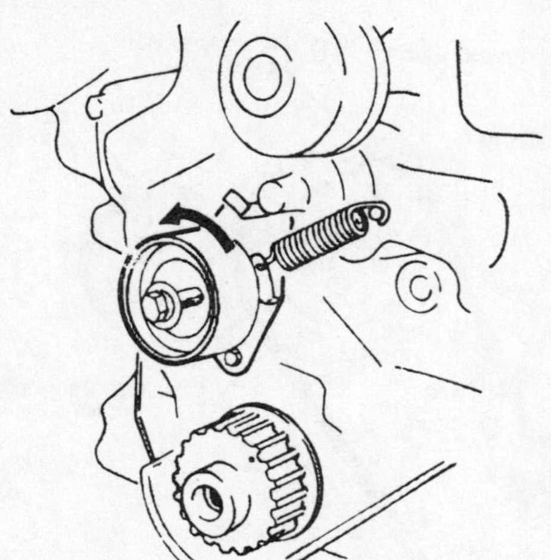

Positioning the tensioner — 3.0L engine

guides and adjust silent shaft chain tension as follows.

a. Tighten chain guide **A** mounting screws.

b. Tighten chain guide **C** mounting screws.

c. Slightly rotate the oil pump and silent shaft sprockets to remove any slack in the silent shaft chain.

d. Adjust the position of chain guide **B** so that when the chain is pulled inward, the clearance between chain guide **B** and the chain links will be 1.0-3.5mm. Tighten chain guide **B** mounting screws.

31. Install a new timing case cover gasket and install timing case cover.

SILENT SHAFT CHAIN ADJUSTMENT

If necessary silent shaft chain adjustment may be performed without removing timing chain case cover. Proceed as followed:

1. Remove the access cover from the timing case cover.
2. Through the access hole loosen special bolt **B**
3. Using your finger only push on boss to apply tension.
4. While applying tension tighten special bolt **B** to 13 ft. lbs.
5. Install access cover to timing chain case cover.

3.0L Engine

NOTE: *The timing belt can be inspected by removing the upper (front outer) timing cover.*

1. Disconnect the negative battery cable.
2. Remove the accessory drive belts.
3. Remove the timing belt covers. Refer to Timing Belt Cover Removal Procedures.
4. Identify the timing belt running direction to avoid reversal during installation.
5. Loosen timing belt tensioner bolt and remove timing belt.
6. Remove the crankshaft sprocket flange.
7. Rotate the crankshaft sprocket until timing mark on crankshaft sprocket is lined up with the oil pump timing mark at 1 o'clock position.
8. Rotate the (inner) camshaft sprocket until mark on (inner) camshaft sprocket is

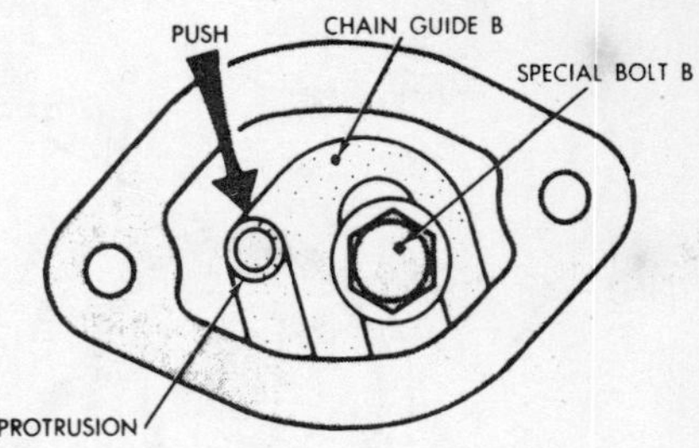

Silent shaft chain adjustment — 2.6L engine

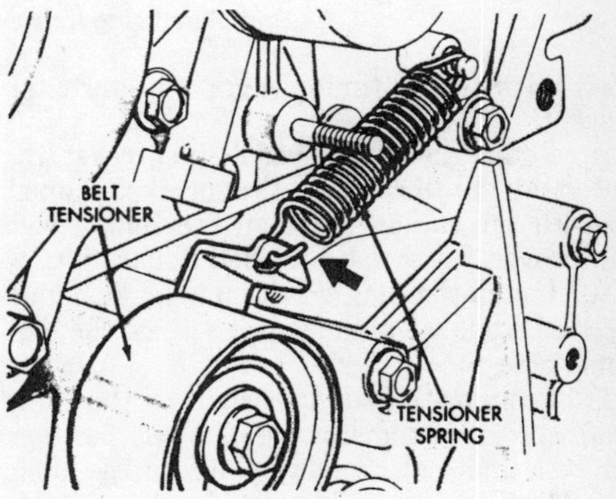

Timing belt tensioner — 3.0L engine

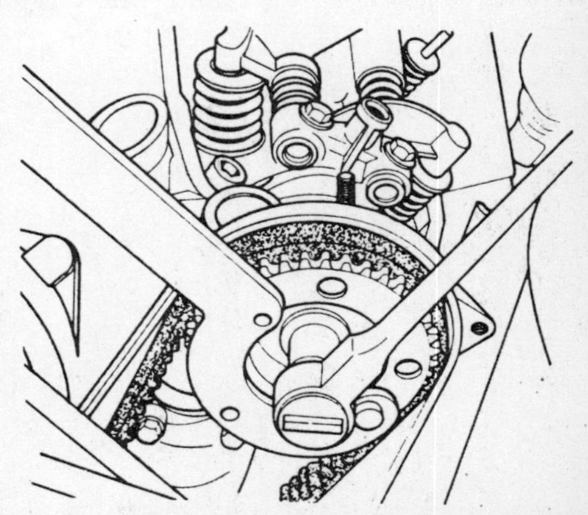

Secure the sprocket when removing or installing the nut

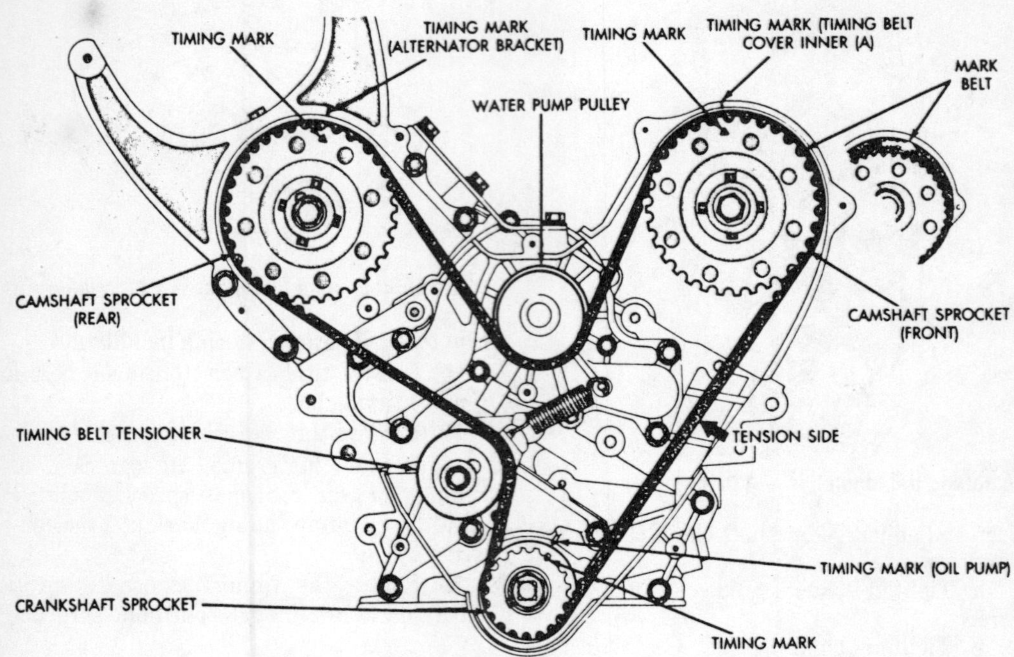

Sprocket timing for belt installation – 3.0L engine

lined up with the timing mark on alternator bracket.

9. Rotate the (outer) camshaft sprocket (radiator side) until mark on the sprocket is lined up with the timing mark on the timing belt inner cover. Refer to timing belt illustration.

10. Install the timing belt on the crankshaft sprocket while maintaining pressure on the tensioner side.

11. Position the timing belt over the camshaft sprocket (radiator side). Next, position the belt under the water pump pulley, then over the (inner) sprocket and finally over the tensioner.

12. Apply rotating force in the opposite direction to the camshaft sprocket (radiator side) to create tension on the timing belt tension side.

13. Rotate the crankshaft in a clockwise direction and recheck engine timing marks.

14. Install the crankshaft sprocket flange.

15. Loosen the tensioner bolt and allow tensioner spring to tension the belt.

16. Again rotate the crankshaft in a clockwise direction (2) full turns. Recheck the engine timing. Tighten the tensioner bolt to 31 Nm (23 ft. lbs.).

17. Install the timing covers.

18. Install the accessory drive belts.

19. Connect battery negative cable.

3.3L Engine

1. If possible, position the engine so that the No. 1 piston is at TDC on the compression

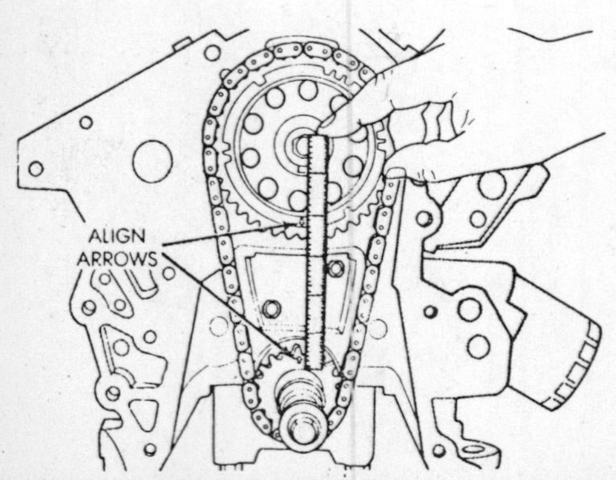

Timing mark alignment – 3.3L engine

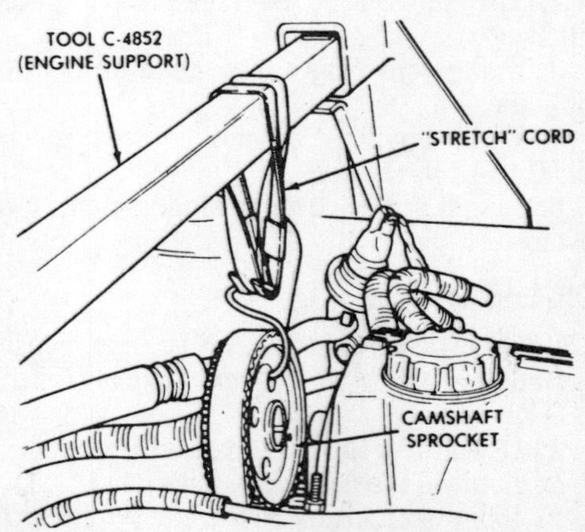

Suspending the sprocket to retain the engine timing

stroke. Disconnect the negative battery cable. Drain the coolant.

2. Remove the timing chain case cover.

3. Remove the camshaft gear attaching cup washer and remove the timing chain with both gears attached. Remove the timing chain snubber.

To install:

4. Assemble the timing chain and gears.

5. Turn the crankshaft and camshaft to line up with the key way locations of the gears.

6. Slide both gears over their respective shafts and use a straight edge to confirm alignment.

7. Install the cup washer and camshaft bolt. Torque the bolt to 35 ft. lbs. (47 Nm).

8. Check camshaft endplay. The specification with a new plate is 0.002–0.006 in. (0.051–0.052mm) and 0.002–0.010 in. (0.51–0.254mm) with a used plate. Replace the thrust plate if not within specifications.

9. Install the timing chain snubber.

10. Thoroughly clean and dry the gasket mating surfaces.

11. Install new O-rings to the block.

12. Remove the crankshaft oil seal from the cover. The seal must be removed from the cover when installing to ensure proper oil pump engagement.

13. Using a new gasket, install the chain case cover to the engine.

14. Make certain that the oil pump is engaged onto the crankshaft before proceeding, or severe engine damage will result. Install the attaching bolts and torque to 20 ft. lbs. (27 Nm).

15. Use tool C–4992 to install the crankshaft oil seal. Install the crankshaft pulley using a 5.9 in. suitable bolt and thrust bearing and washer plate L–4524. Make sure the pulley bottoms out on the crankshaft seal diameter. Install the bolt and torque to 40 ft. lbs. (54 Nm).

16. Install all other parts removed during the chain case cover removal procedure and fill the engine with oil.

19. Connect the negative battery cable, road test the vehicle and check for leaks.

Timing Sprockets/Gears

REMOVAL AND INSTALLATION

2.2L and 2.5L Engines

1. Remove the drive belts, timing belt cover and timing belt. See Timing Belt Cover and Timing Belt Removal Procedures as previously outlined.

2. Remove the crankshaft sprocket bolt.

3. Remove the crankshaft sprocket using Tool C-4685 and Tool L-4524 or an equivalent puller. If crankshaft seal removal is necessary, remove with Tool C-4679 (2.2L) or Tool C-4991 (2.5L), or an equivalent tool.

4. Clean the crankshaft seal surface with 400 grit paper.

5. Lightly coat the seal (Steel case seal) outer surface with Loctite Stud N' Bearing Mount (P/N 4057987) or equivalent. A soap and water solution is recommended to lubricate (Rubber Coated Case Seal) outer surface.

6. Lightly lubricate the seal lip with engine oil.

7. Install seal with Tool No. C-4680 (2.2L) or Tool No. C-4992 (2.5L).

8. Install the sprocket and install sprocket bolt.

9. Remove and install the camshaft and intermediate shaft sprockets with Tool C-4687 and Tool C-4687-1 in similar fashion.

10. Install the timing belt and timing belt cover. See Timing Belt and Timing Belt Cover Installation Procedures as previously outlined.

11. Install the accessory drive belts.

2.6L Engine

Refer to Timing Chain Case Cover Removalprocedures.

3.0L and 3.3L Engine

Refer to Timing Case Cover Removal procedures.

Camshaft and Bearings

REMOVAL AND INSTALLATION

2.2L and 2.5L Engines

The following procedure is preformed with the engine in the vehicle.

NOTE: *Removal of the camshaft requires removal of the camshaft sprocket. To maintain proper engine timing, the timing belt can be left indexed on the sprockets and suspended under light pressure. This will prevent the belt from coming off and maintain timing.*

1. Disconnect the negative battery cable. Relieve the fuel pressure, if equipped with fuel injection.

2. Turn the crankshaft so the No. 1 piston is at the TDC of the compression stroke. Remove the upper timing belt cover. Remove the air pump pulley, if equipped.

3. Remove the camshaft sprocket bolt and the sprocket and suspend tightly so the belt does not lose tension. If it does, the belt timing will have to be reset.

4. Remove the valve cover.

5. If the rocker arms are being reused, mark them for installation identification and

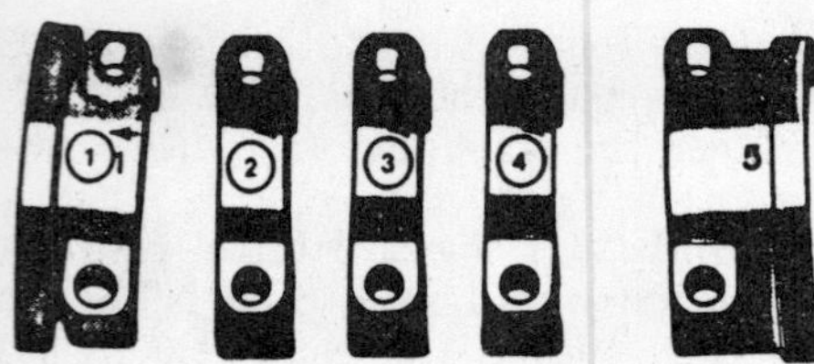

Camshaft bearing caps — 2.2L and 2.5L engines

loosen the camshaft bearing bolts, evenly and gradually.

6. Using a soft mallet, rap the rear of the camshaft a few times to break the bearing caps loose.

7. Remove the bolts, bearing caps and the camshaft with seals.

NOTE: *Before replacing the camshaft, identify factory installed oversized components. To do so, look for the tops of the bearing caps pained green and O/SJ stamped rearward of the oil gallery plug on the rear of the head. In addition, the barrel of the camshaft is painted green and O/SJ is stamped onto the rear end of the camshaft. Installing standard sized parts in an head equipped with oversized parts-or vice versa-will cause severe engine damage.*

8. Check the oil passages for blockage and the parts for damage. Clean all mating surfaces.

To Install:

9. Transfer the sprocket key to the new camshaft. New rocker arms and a new camshaft sprocket bolt are normally included with the camshaft package. Install the rocker arms, lubricate the camshaft and install with end seals installed.

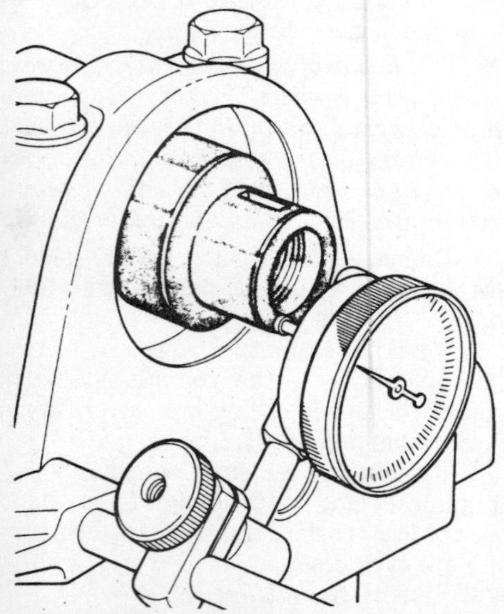

Measuring camshaft end play

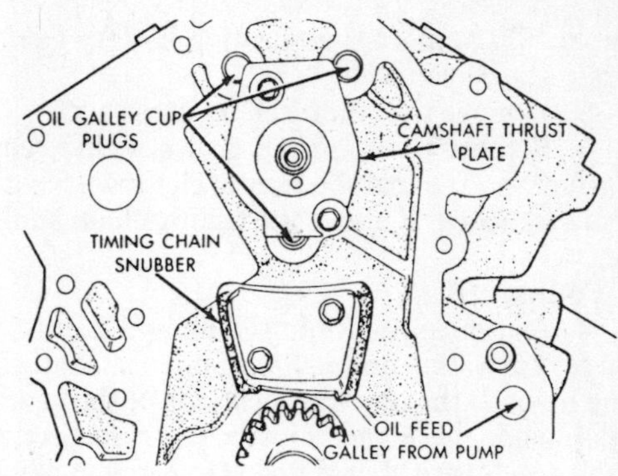

Camshaft thrust plate — 3.3L engine

10. Place the bearing caps with No. 1 at the timing belt end and No. 5 at the transaxle end. The camshaft bearing caps are numbered and have arrows facing forward. Torque the camshaft bearing bolts evenly and gradually to 18 ft. lbs. (24 Nm).

NOTE: *Apply RTV silicone gasket material to the No. 1 and 5 bearing caps. Install the bearing caps before the seals are installed.*

11. Mount a dial indicator to the front of the engine and check the camshaft endplay. Play should not exceed 0.006 in.

12. Install the camshaft sprocket and the new bolt. Install the air pump pulley, if equipped.

13. Install the valve cover with a new gasket.

14. Connect the negative battery cable and check for leaks.

2.6L Engine

1. Disconnect the negative battery cable.
2. Remove the valve cover.
3. Remove the camshaft gear retaining bolt and match mark the distributor gear to its drive gear. Remove the distributor. Pry the distributor drive gear off of the cam gear.
4. Remove the cam gear from the camshaft and allow it to rest on the holder below it.
5. Remove the water pump pulley.

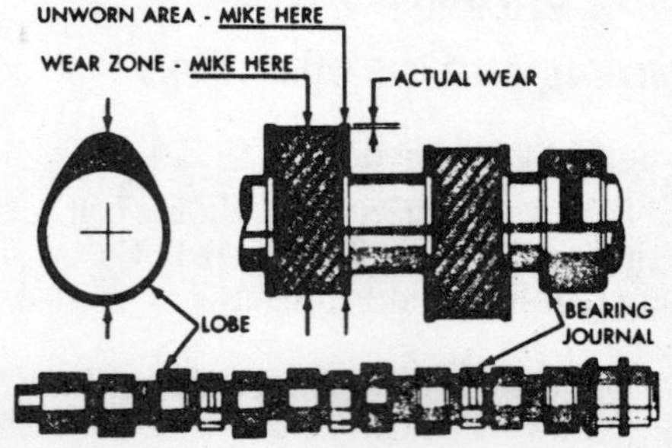

Checking camshaft lobe wear

6. Remove the camshaft cap bolts evenly and gradually.

7. Remove the caps, shafts, rocker arms and bolts together as an assembly.

8. Remove the camshaft with the rear seal from the engine.

To install:

9. Install a new roll pin to the camshaft. Lubricate the camshaft and install with the rear seal in place. Install the camshaft in position so the hole in the gear will line up with the roll pin.

10. Install the rocker caps, shafts and arms assembly. Tighten the camshaft bearing cap bolts in the following order to 85 inch lbs. (10 Nm): No. 3, No. 2, No. 4, front cap, rear cap. Repeat the sequence increasing the torque to 175 inch lbs. (19 Nm).

11. Install the gear to the camshaft engaging the roll pin. Install the distributor drive gear and install the bolt and washer. Torque the bolt to 40 ft. lbs. (54 Nm). Install the distributor.

12. Install the valve cover and all related parts.

3.0L Engine

1. Disconnect the negative battery cable. Remove the air cleaner assembly and valve covers.

2. Install auto lash adjuster retainers MD998443 or equivalent on the rocker arms.

3. If removing the right side (front) camshaft, remove the distributor extension.

4. Remove the camshaft bearing caps but do not remove the bolts from the caps.

5. Remove the rocker arms, rocker shafts and bearing caps, as an assembly.

6. Remove the camshaft from the cylinder head.

7. Inspect the bearing journals on the camshaft, cylinder head and bearing caps.

To Install:

8. Lubricate the camshaft journals and camshaft with clean engine oil and install the camshaft in the cylinder head.

9. Align the camshaft bearing caps with the arrow mark (depending on cylinder numbers) and in numerical order.

10. Apply sealer at the ends of the bearing caps and install the assembly.

11. Torque the bearing cap bolts, in the following sequence: No. 3, No. 2, No. 1 and No. 4 to 85 inch lbs. (10 Nm).

12. Repeat the sequence, increasing torque to 175 inch lbs. (18 Nm).

13. Install the distributor extension, if it was removed.

14. Install the valve cover and all related components.

3.3L Engine

1. Relieve the fuel system pressure. Disconnect the negative battery cable.

2. Remove the engine from the vehicle. Remove the intake manifold, cylinder heads, timing chain cover and timing chain from the engine.

3. Remove the rocker arm and shaft assemblies.

4. Label and remove the pushrod and lifters.

5. Remove the camshaft thrust plate.

6. Install a long bolt into the front of the camshaft to facilitate its removal. Remove the camshaft being careful not to damage the cam bearings with the cam lobes.

To install:

7. Install the camshaft to within 2 in. of its final installation position.

8. Install the camshaft thrust plate and 2 bolts and torque to 10 ft. lbs. (12 Nm).

9. Place both camshaft and crankshaft gears on the bench with the timing marks on the exact imaginary center line through both gear bores as they are installed on the engine. Place the timing chain around both sprockets.

10. Turn the crankshaft and camshaft so the keys line up with the key ways in the gears when the timing marks are in proper position.

11. Slide both gears over their respective shafts and use a straight edge to check timing mark alignment.

12. Measure camshaft endplay. If not within specifications, replace the thrust plate.

13. If the camshaft was not replaced, lubricate and install the lifters in their original loca-

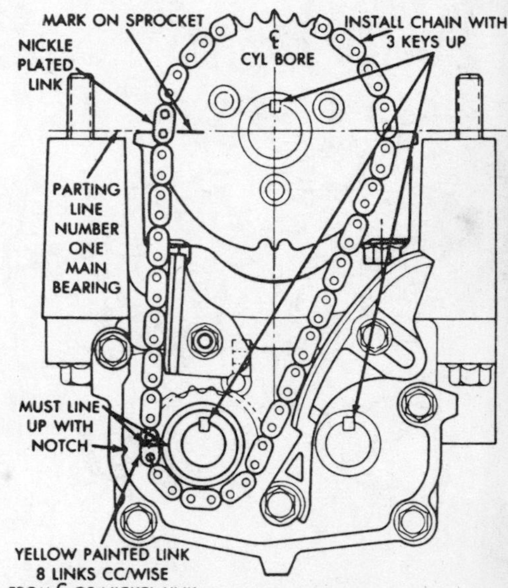

Balance shaft timing — 2.5L engine

tions. If the camshaft was replaced, new lifters must be used.

14. Install the pushrods and rocker shaft assemblies.

15. Install the timing chain cover, cylinder heads and intake manifold.

16. Install the engine in the vehicle.

17. When everything is bolted in place, change the engine oil and replace the oil filter.

NOTE: *If the camshaft or lifters have been replaced, add 1 pint of Mopar crankcase conditioner, or equivalent when replenishing the oil to aid in break in. This mixture should be left in the engine for a minimum of 500 miles and drained at the next normal oil change.*

18. Fill the radiator with coolant.

19. Connect the negative battery cable, set all adjustments to specifications and check for leaks.

CAMSHAFT INSPECTION

1. Inspect the camshaft bearing journals for wear or damage.

2. Inspect the cylinder head and check oil return holes.

3. Check the tooth surface of the distributor drive gear teeth of the right camshaft for wear or damage.

4. Check both camshaft surfaces for wear or damage.

5. Remove the distributor drive adaptor seal.

6. Check camshaft lobe height and replace if out of limit. Standard value is 41.00mm.

Auxiliary (Idler) Shaft

REMOVAL AND INSTALLATION

2.2L and 2.5L Engines

The following procedures to be performed with engine removed from vehicle.

1. Remove the distributor assembly.

2. Remove the fuel pump.

3. Remove timing case cover, and timing belt.

4. Remove the intermediate shaft sprocket. See Sprocket Removal Procedures.

5. Remove the intermediate shaft retainer screws and remove retainer.

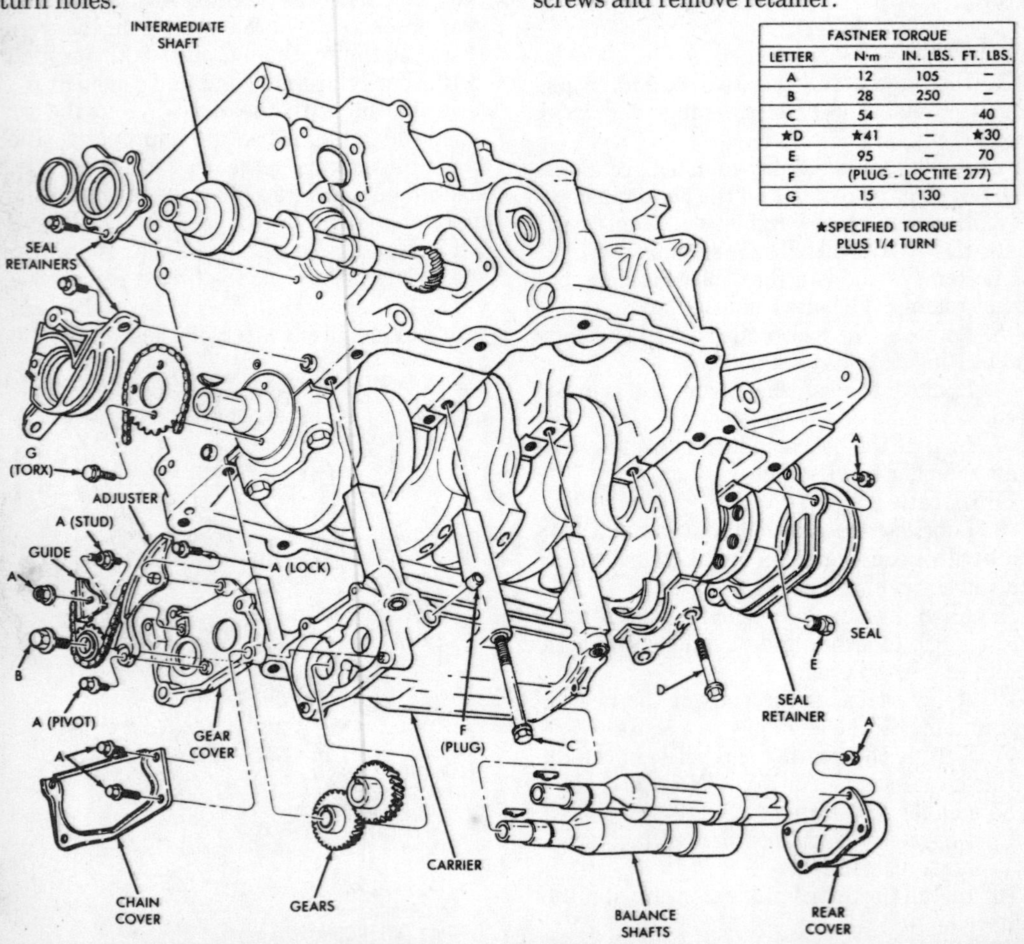

FASTNER TORQUE			
LETTER	N·m	IN. LBS.	FT. LBS.
A	12	105	–
B	28	250	–
C	54	–	40
★D	★41	–	★30
E	95	–	70
F	(PLUG - LOCTITE 277)		
G	15	130	–

★SPECIFIED TORQUE PLUS 1/4 TURN

Balance shaft assembly — 2.5L engine

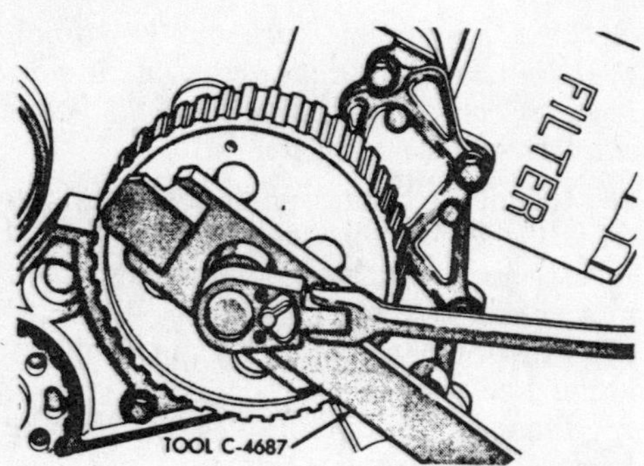

Removing the intermediate shaft sprocket

6. Remove the intermediate shaft and inspect journals and bushing.

7. When installing the shaft, lubricate the fuel pump eccentric and distributor drive gear. Install the intermediate shaft.

8. Inspect the shaft seal in retainer. Replace if necessary.

9. Lightly lubricate the seal lip with engine oil.

10. Install the intermediate shaft retainer assembly and retainer screws. Tighten screws to 105 inch lbs. On 2.5L engine apply anaerobic (Form-in-Place) gasket material to retainer sealing surface before installing.

11. Install the intermediate shaft sprocket.

12. Check engine timing. See Engine Timing Check Procedures.

13. Install the timing belt and adjust.

14. Install the timing belt cover.

15. Install the fuel pump.

16. Install the distributor. See Distributor Installation Procedures.

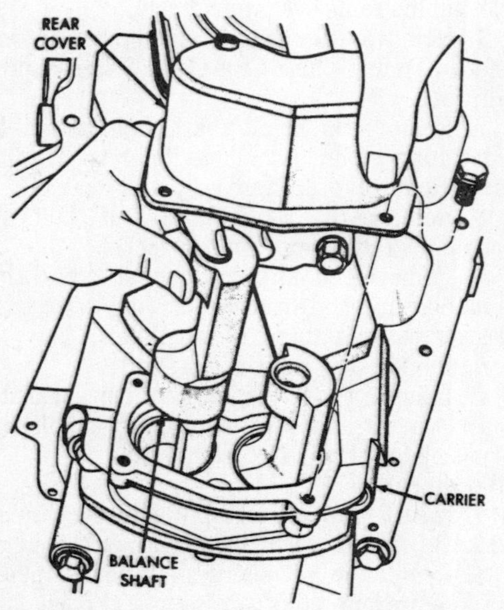

Balance shaft removal and installation — 2.5L engine

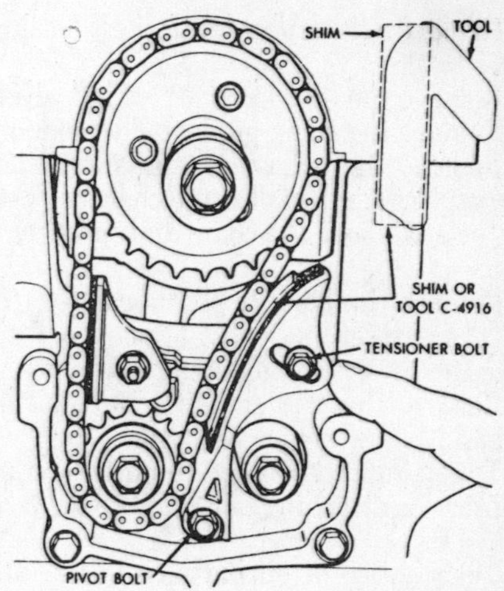

Balance shaft chain tensioner adjustment — 2.5L engine

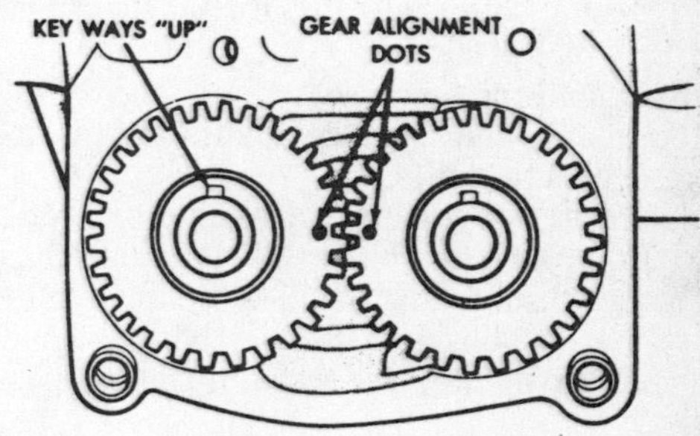

Balance shaft gear timing — 2.5L engine

Balance Shafts

The 2.5L engine is equipped with 2 balance shafts located in a housing attached to the lower crankcase. These shafts are driven by a chain and 2 gears from the crankshaft at 2 times crankshaft speed. This counterbalance certain engine reciprocating masses.

REMOVAL AND INSTALLATION

1. Remove the engine from vehicle.

2. Remove the timing case cover, timing belt and sprockets.

3. Remove the engine oil pan.

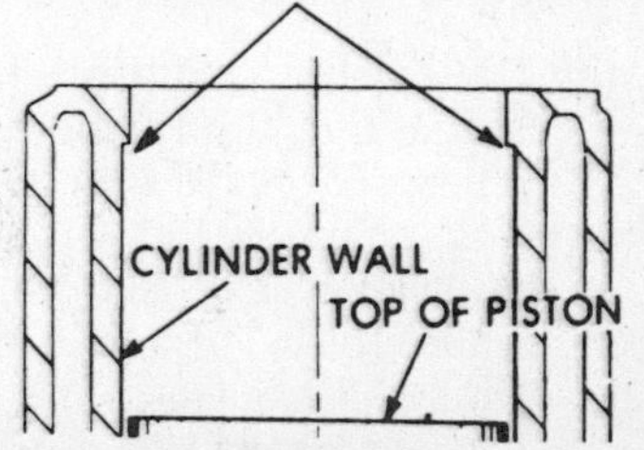

Cylinder bore ridge

4. Remove the front crankshaft seal retainer.

5. Remove the balance shafts chain cover.

6. Remove the chain guide and tensioner.

7. Remove the balance shafts sprocket retaining screws and crankshaft chain sprocket torx screws. Remove the chain and sprocket assembly.

8. Remove the balance shafts carrier front gear cover retaining double ended stud. Remove the cover and balance shafts gears.

9. Remove the carrier rear cover and balance shafts.

10. To separate the carrier, remove (6) crankcase to carrier attaching bolts and remove carrier.

11. Take notice of all parts to avoid interchanging.

To install:

12. Install both shafts into carrier the assembly from rear of carrier.

13. Install the rear cover.

14. Install the balance shafts drive and driven gears to shafts.

15. Position the carrier assembly on crankcase and tighten (6) bolts to 54 Nm (40 ft. lbs.).

16. Crankshaft to Balance Shaft Timing must be established. Rotate both balance shafts until the key ways are in the Up position.

17. Install the short hub drive gear on balance shaft driving shaft.

18. Install the long hub gear on the driven shaft.

19. With both gears on the balance shafts and key ways Up, the timing marks should be meshed.

20. Align the balance shaft carrier cover with the carrier housing dowel pin and install double ended stud. Tighten to 105 inch lbs.

21. Install the crankshaft sprocket and tighten sprocket torx screw to 11 ft. lbs.

22. Turn the crankshaft until number one cylinder is at TDC. The timing marks on the chain sprocket should line up with the parting line on the left side of number one main bearing cap.

23. Install the chain over the crankshaft sprocket so the nickel plated link of the chain is over the timing mark on the crankshaft sprocket.

24. Install the balance shaft sprocket into the timing chain so that the timing mark on the sprocket (yellow dot) mates with the yellow painted link on the chain.

25. With the balance shaft key way in 12 o'clock position slide the balance shaft sprocket on the nose of the balance shaft. The balance shaft may have to be pushed in slightly to allow for clearance.

NOTE: *The timing mark on the sprocket, the painted link, and the arrow on the side of the gear cover should line up if the balance shafts are timed correctly.*

26. Install the balance shaft bolt and tighten to 21 ft. lbs. Placed a wooden block between the crankcase and crankshaft counterbalance to prevent crankshaft from turning.

27. Proper balance shaft Timing Chain Tension must be established.

28. Place a shim 1.0mm thick by 70mm long between the chain and tensioner.

29. Apply firm hand pressure behind the adjustment slot and tighten adjustment bolt first, followed by the pivot screw to 105 inch lbs. Remove the shim.

30. Install the chain guide making sure the tab on the guide fits into slot on the gear cover. Install nut/washer and tighten to 105 inch lbs.

31. Install the chain cover and tighten screws to 105 inch lbs.

32. Apply a 1.5mm diameter bead of RTV gasket material to retainer sealing surface. Install retainer assembly.

33. Install the crankshaft sprocket and timing belt. See Timing Belt Adjustment and Engine Timing Procedures.

34. Install the timing cover.

Silent Shafts

The 2.6L engine uses 2 counter shafts (silent shafts) in the cylinder block to reduce engine noise and vibration.

REMOVAL AND INSTALLATION

The following procedures to be performed with engine removed from vehicle.

1. Remove the timing chain case cover. Refer to Timing Chain Case Cover Removal procedures.

2. Remove the silent shaft chain assembly and timing chain assembly. Refer to Timing Chain Removal procedures.

3. Remove the silent shaft bolt (bolt directly above the silent chain sprocket).

4. Remove the oil pump bolts and pull the pump housing straight forward. Remove the gaskets and the oil pump backing plate.

5. Remove the right silent shaft.

6. Remove the left silent shaft thrust plate by screwing 2 8mm screws into tapped holes in thrust plate. Remove left silent shaft.

To install:

7. Install both silent shafts into cylinder block. Be careful not to damage inner bearings.

8. Install the left silent shaft thrust plate on the left silent shaft using a new O-ring.

9. Install the oil pump. Refer to Oil Pump Installation procedures.

Use lengths of rubber tubing to protect the crankshaft journal and cylinder linings during piston and rod removal/installation

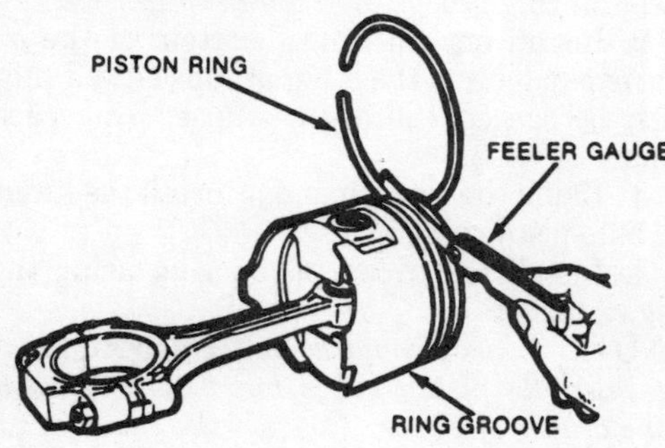

Check the piston ring side clearance

10. Install the timing chain and silent chain assembly. Refer to Timing Chain Installation procedures.
11. Install the timing chain case cover. See Timing Chain Case Cover Installation procedures.

SILENT SHAFT CLEARANCE

1. Outer diameter to outer bearing clearance: 0.02-0.06mm.
2. Inner diameter to inner bearing clearance: 0.05-0.09mm.

Pistons and Connecting Rods

REMOVAL

The following procedures are performed with the engine removed from vehicle.

1. Remove the engine from the vehicle.
2. Remove the timing case cover, timing belt or chain and sprockets.
3. Remove the intake manifold.
4. Remove the cylinder head from engine.
5. Remove the engine oil pan.

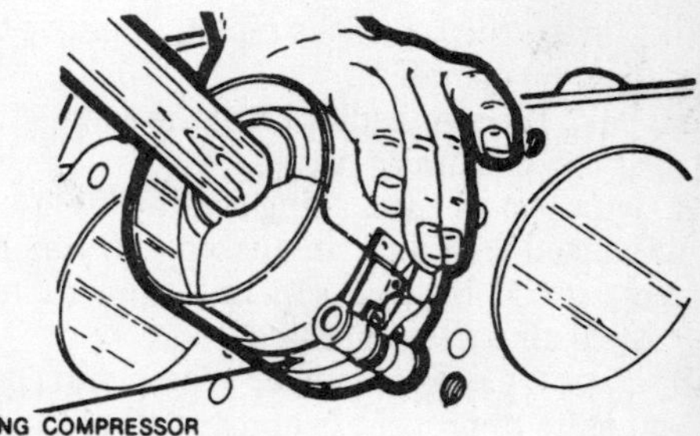

Piston installation

6. Remove the oil pump.
7. Remove the balance shaft carrier (2.5L engine).

NOTE: *Because the top piston ring does not travel to the very top of the cylinder bore, a ridge is built up between the end of the travel and the top of the cylinder walls. Pushing the piston and connecting rod assembly past the ridge is difficult and may cause damage to the piston. If new rings are installed and the ridge has not been removed, ring breakage and piston damage can occur.*

Turn the crankshaft to position the piston at the bottom of the cylinder bore. Cover the top of the piston with a rag. Install a ridge reamer in the bore and follow the manufacturer's instructions to remove the ridge. Use caution, avoid cutting too deeply. Remove the rag and

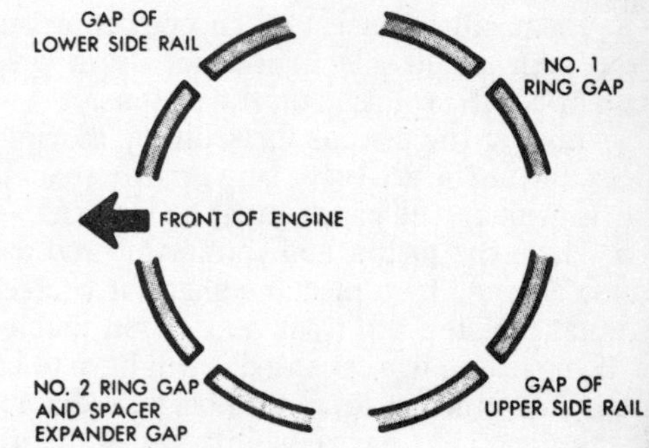

Piston ring positioning

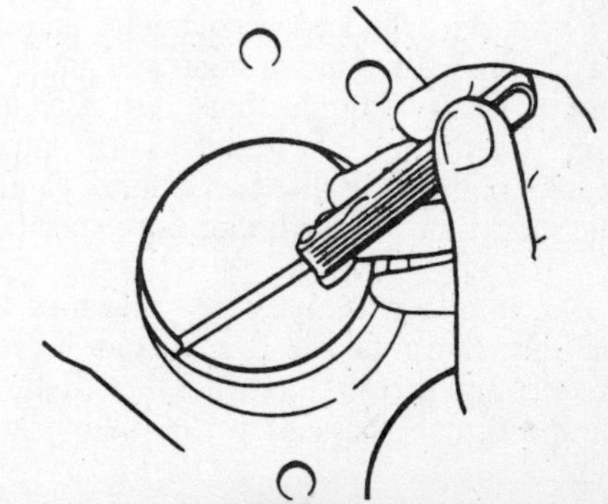

Check the piston ring end gap

cuttings from the top of the piston. Remove the ridge from all cylinders.

8. Turn the crankshaft until the connecting rod is at the bottom of travel.

9. Number all connecting rod caps if not already labeled to aid during assembly. Remove connecting rod bearing cap nuts and remove caps. Keep all parts separated.

10. Take 2 pieces of rubber tubing and cover the rod bolts to prevent cylinder wall scoring.

11. Before removing the piston assembly from cylinder bore scribe a mark indicating front position, or take notice of manufacturer identification mark. Using a wooden hammer handle, carefully tap piston assembly away from crankshaft and remove from cylinder block. Care should be taken not to damage crankshaft connecting rod journals or threads on connecting rod cap bolts.

12. Remove all the pistons from cylinder block in similar fashion.

NOTE: *It is not necessary to remove the crankshaft from cylinder block for piston service. If crankshaft service is necessary refer to Crankshaft Removal procedures.*

CLEANING AND INSPECTION

1. Use a piston ring expander and remove the rings from the piston.

2. Clean the ring grooves using an appropriate cleaning tool, exercise care to avoid cutting too deeply.

3. Clean all varnish and carbon from the piston with a safe solvent. Do not use a wire brush or caustic solution on the pistons.

4. Inspect the pistons for scuffing, scoring, cracks, pitting or excessive ring groove wear. If wear is evident, the piston must be replaced.

5. Have the piston and connecting rod assembly checked by a machine shop for correct alignment, piston pin wear and piston diameter. If the piston has collapsed it will have to be replaced or knurled to restore original diameter. Connecting rod bushing replacement, piston pin fitting and piston changing can be handled by the machine shop.

6. Check the cylinder bore diameter and cylinder bore for wear using a telescope gauge at 3 different levels. Cylinder bore out of round: 0.05mm maximum. Cylinder bore taper: 0.13mm maximum. Refer to General Engine Specification Chart for cylinder bore specification.

7. Check piston dimensions. Measure approximately 2mm above the bottom of the piston skirt and across the thrust face. Refer to Piston and Ring Specification Chart for piston diameter.

8. After recording cylinder bore measurement and piston diameter, subtract the low reading. The difference is Piston to Cylinder Wall Clearance: 0.02-0.04mm.

9. Check piston ring gap using a piston to position the ring at least 16mm from the bottom of cylinder bore. Measure clearance using a feeler gauge. Refer to Piston and Rings Specification Chart.

10. Check the piston ring to piston ring groove clearance using a feeler gauge.

11. Check the ring groove by rolling the new piston ring around the groove to check for burrs or carbon deposits. If any are found, remove with a fine file.

12. If all clearances and measurements are within specifications, honing or glaze breaking the cylinder bore is all that is required.

INSTALLATION

1. Start with the oil ring expander in the lower oil ring groove.

2. Install one oil rail at bottom of the oil ring expander and the other at top. The oil rails must be spaced 180 degrees apart from each other.

3. Using the ring expander install the intermediate piston ring.

4. Install the upper piston ring using the ring expander.

NOTE: *Generally marks on the upper and intermediate piston rings must point toward the crown of piston. Consult the illustration with piston ring set instruction sheet for ring positioning.*

5. Install a ring compressor and insert the piston and rod assembly into the engine with mark previously made or labeled mark on piston head toward timing chain end of cylinder block.

6. Rotate the crankshaft so that the connecting rod journal is on center of cylinder bore. Install a new connecting rod bearing in connecting rod and cap. Check the connecting rod bearing oil clearance using Plastigage. Follow the manufacturer procedures. Refer to Crankshaft and Connecting Rod Specification Chart.

7. Tighten the connecting rod cap nuts to specification. Refer to Torque Specification Chart.

8. Install the remaining piston and rod assemblies.

9. Using a feeler gauge, check connecting rod side clearance.

10. On 2.5L engine install the balance shaft carrier.

11. Install the oil pump and pick-up.

12. Install the cylinder head.

13. Install the intake manifold.

14. Install the timing chain or belt and sprockets.

15. Install the timing case cover.

16. Install the engine oil pan. Refer to Oil Pan Installation procedures.

Freeze Plugs

REMOVAL AND INSTALLATION

Freeze plugs can be removed with the engine in or out of the vehicle.

Using a blunt tool, such as a drift and hammer, strike the bottom edge of the plug. With the plug rotated, grasp it firmly with pliers and remove it. Do not drive the plug into the block as coolant flow restriction would occur.

When installing the replacement plug, thoroughly clean the plug bore, removing any old sealant. Coat the new plug with Loctite® Stud Mount, or equivalent. Position the plug on the block and drive it into the block so that the sharp edge is at least 0.020 in. (0.5mm) inside the chamfer. Check the plug for leaks after cooling system refilling.

Engine Block Heater

REMOVAL AND INSTALLATION

1. Disconnect the negative battery cable.
2. Drain the cooling system, including the engine block.
3. Detach the power cord plug from the block heater assembly.
4. Loosen the screw in the center of the heater and pull the heater from the block.

To install:

5. Clean the heater hole in the block and the heater seat.
6. Insert the heater with the element loop facing upward.
7. Tighten the heater retaining screw securely.
8. Refill the cooling system and pressurize the cooling system with a radiator pressure tool. Check for leaks before operating block heater.
9. Connect the negative battery cable.

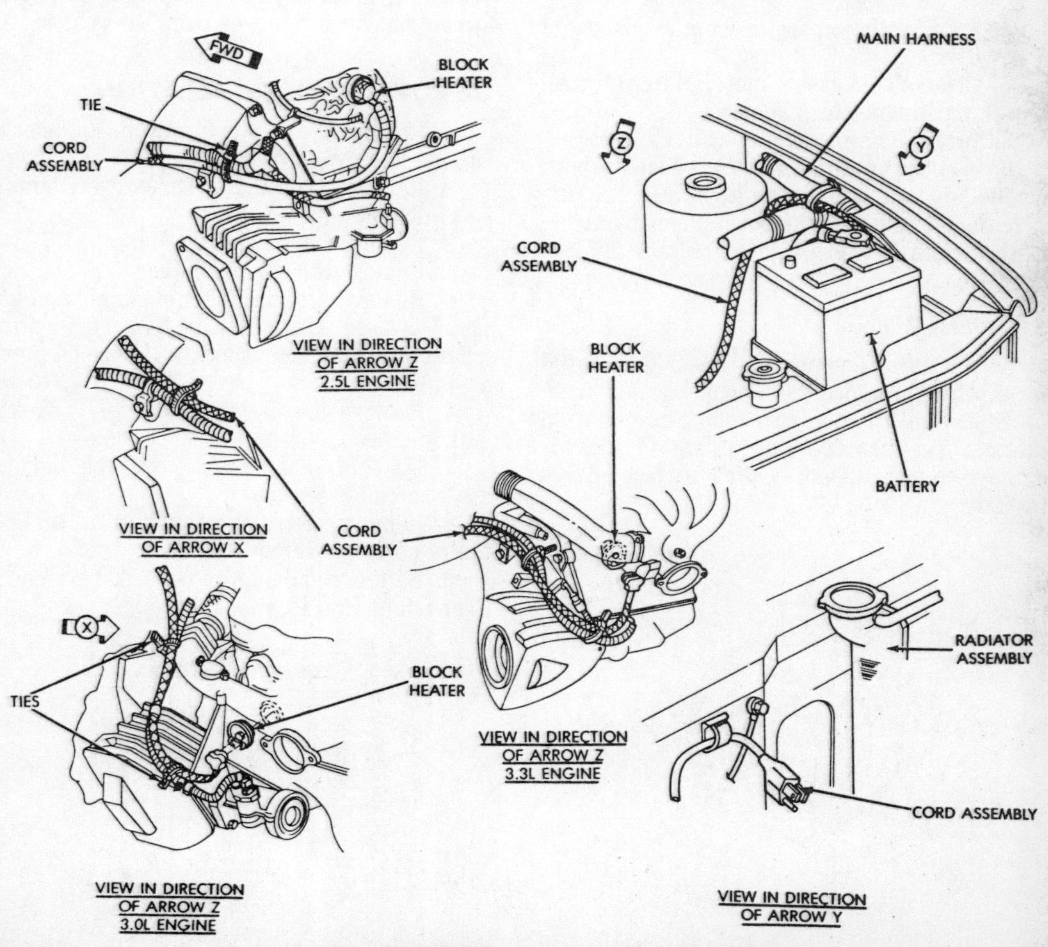

Engine block heater system components

Rear Main Seal

REMOVAL AND INSTALLATION

2.2L and 2.5L Engines

1. With the engine or transaxle removed from vehicle, remove the flywheel or flexplate.
2. Pry out rear crankshaft oil seal from seal retainer. Be careful not to nick of damage crankshaft sealing surface or seal retainer.
3. Place Tool C-4681 or equivalent on the crankshaft.
4. Lubricate outer diameter with Loctite Stud N' Bearing Mount (PN. 4057987) or equivalent.
5. Lightly lubricate the seal lip with engine oil and tap in place with a plastic hammer.
6. Install the flywheel/flex plate and tighten bolts to 95 Nm (70 ft. lbs.).

2.6L Engine

1. With the engine or transaxle removed from vehicle, remove the flywheel or flex plate.
2. Remove the rear crankshaft seal retainer.
3. Remove the separator from retainer and remove seal.
4. Clean all old gasket material from the retainer and engine block surface.
5. Install a new gasket on the retainer.
6. Lightly lubricate the new seal lip with engine oil and install the separator making sure the oil hole is at the bottom of separator.
7. Install flywheel tighten bolts to 95 Nm (70 ft. lbs.).

3.0L and 3.3L Engine

1. With the engine or transaxle removed from vehicle, remove the flywheel or flex plate.
2. Pry out the rear crankshaft oil seal from the seal retainer. Be careful not to nick or damage the crankshaft sealing surface or seal retainer.

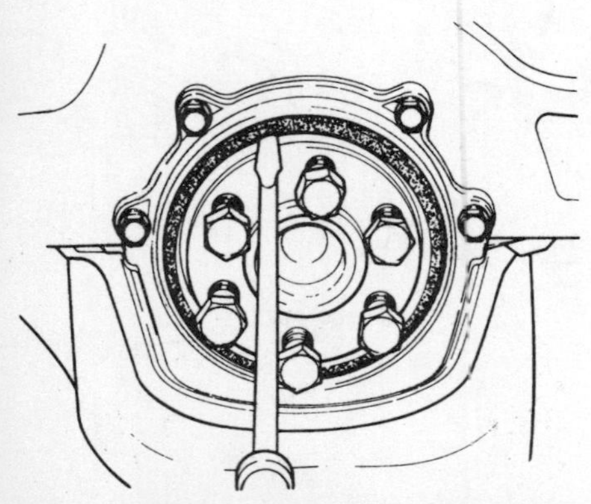

Removing the rear main oil seal – 2.2L engine

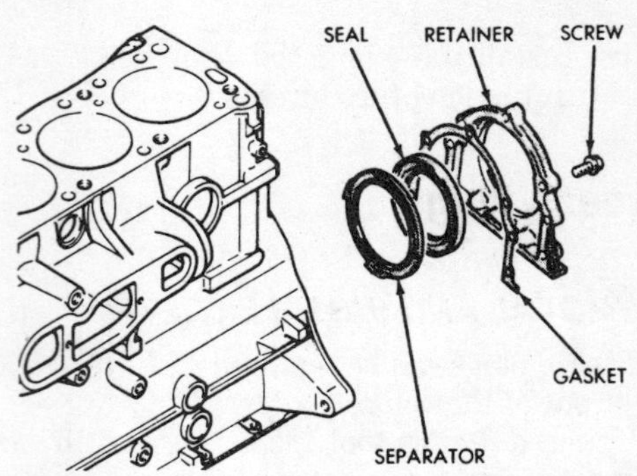

Rear main oil seal installation – 2.6L engine

3. Lightly lubricate the new seal lip with engine oil and install seal in retainer housing using Tool MD998718 or equivalent.
4. Install flywheel and tighten the bolts to 95 Nm (70 ft. lbs.).

Crankshaft and Main Bearings

Although, crankshaft service can be performed without removing the engine from the vehicle, it is far easier to work on the engine after it has been removed from the vehicle.

REMOVAL AND INSTALLATION

1. Remove the engine from vehicle. Refer to Engine Removal procedures.
2. Remove the timing case cover, timing belt or chain and sprockets.
3. Remove the flywheel.
4. Remove the engine oil pan.
5. Remove the front crankshaft seal retainer if used. On 3.0L and 3.3L engines the front crankshaft seal is located in the oil pump assembly.
6. Remove the oil pump assembly 3.0L and 3.3L engines.
7. On 2.5L engines, remove the balance shaft carrier assembly.
8. Remove the rear crankshaft oil seal retainer bolts and remove retainer.
9. Before removing the crankshaft check Crankshaft End Play. as follows:

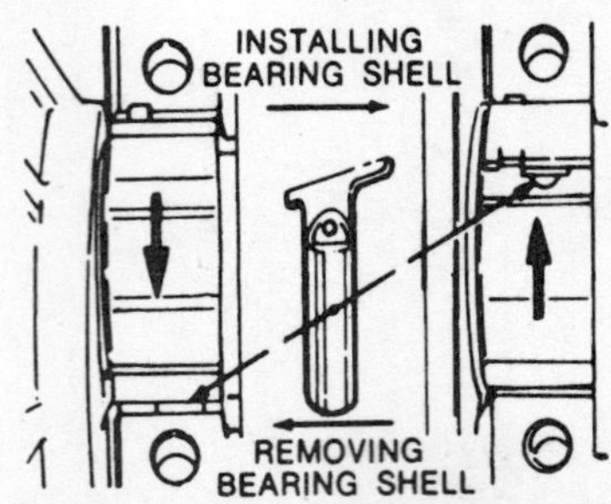

Remove the upper main bearing insert, using a roll out pin

a. Position a screwdriver between a main bearing cap and crankshaft. Move the crankshaft all the way to the rear of its travel.

b. Position a feeler gauge between the thrust bearing and crankshaft machined surface to determine end play. Refer to Crankshaft and Connecting Rod Specification Chart.

Use the following procedure if only crankshaft removal is necessary. If other engine repairs are being perform complete engine disassembly will be required.

10. Number all connecting rod caps if not already labeled to aid during assembly. Remove the connecting rod bearing caps nuts and remove caps.

11. Take 2 pieces of rubber tubing and cover the rod bolts to prevent crankshaft scoring.

12. Tap the piston assembly lightly away from crankshaft. Care should be taken not to damage crankshaft connecting rod journals or threads on connecting rod cap bolts.

13. Remove the main bearing cap bolts and remove caps. Remove crankshaft.

To install:

14. Install the main bearing shells with the lubrication groove in the cylinder block. Make certain the oil holes are in alignment, and bearing tabs seat in block.

15. Install the thrust bearing in journal No.3. 16. Oil the bearings and journals and install crankshaft.

17. Install the lower main bearing shells (without oil grooves) in lower bearing caps.

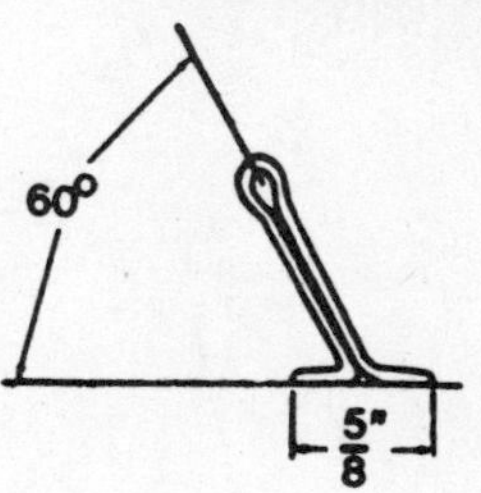

Home made roll out pin

18. Check the main or connecting bearing oil clearance as followed:

a. Wipe oil from bearing shells.

b. Cut a piece of Plastigage to the same length as width of the bearing and place it in parallel with the journal.

c. Install the bearing cap and torque to specification.

NOTE: *Do not rotate crankshaft or the Plastigage will be smeared.*

d. Carefully remove the bearing cap and measure the width of the Plastigage at the widest part using the scale printed on the Plastigage package. Refer to Crankshaft and Connecting Rod Specification Chart.

19. Install all main bearing caps with arrows toward the timing chain end of cylinder block. Dip bolts in engine oil and install bolts finger tight then alternately torque each bolt. Refer to Torque Specification Chart.

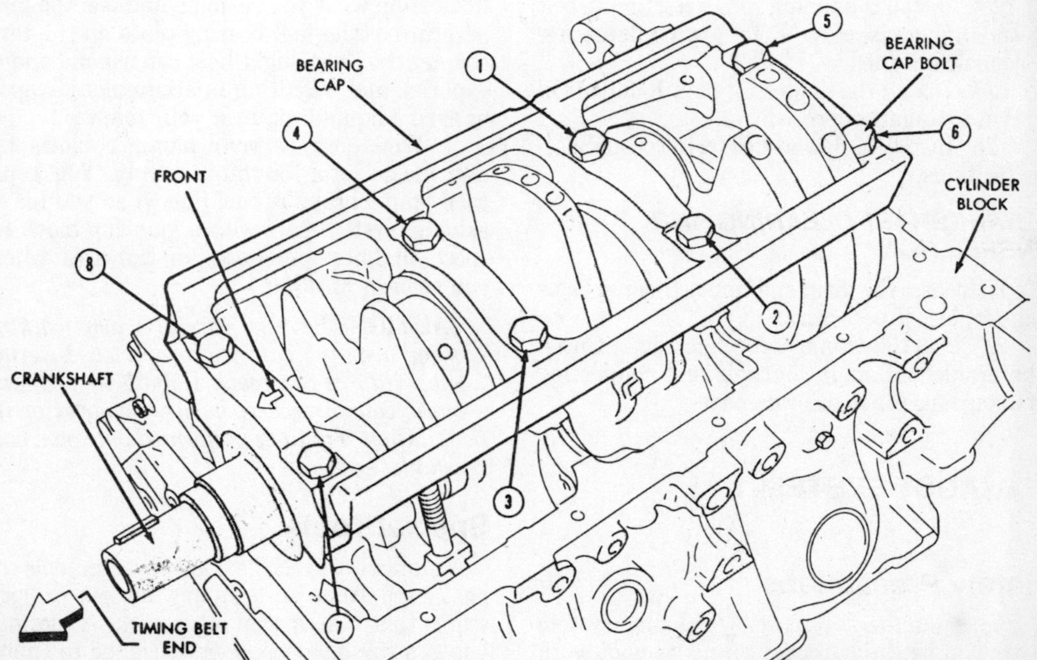

Installing the crankshaft mono-block main bearing — 3.0L engine. Tighten the bolts in the sequence shown

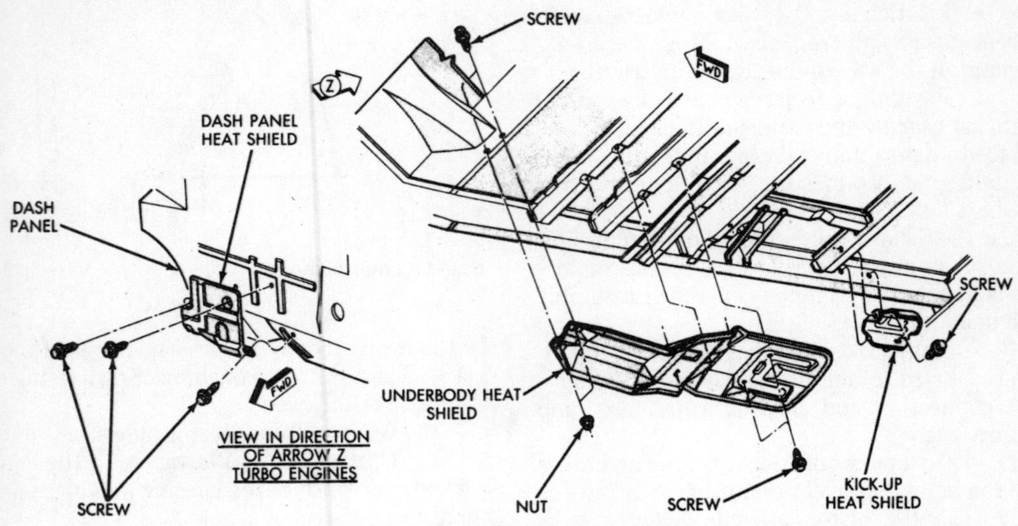

Exhaust system heat shield mounting

20. Position the connecting rods with new bearing shells against crankshaft. Install lower caps.
21. Before installing the nuts oil the threads. Install the nut on each bolt finger tight, then alternately torque each nut to specification. Refer to Torque Specification Chart.
22. On 2.5L engine install balance shaft carrier assembly.
23. Install the front and rear crankshaft oil seal retainer assembly. Apply a 1.5mm diameter bead of RTV gasket material to retainers sealing surface.
24. Install the timing sprockets, timing belt and timing case cover. Refer to procedures previously outlined.
25. Install the engine oil pan. Refer to Oil Pan Installation procedures.
26. Install the flywheel. Refer to Torque Specifications.

CRANKSHAFT CLEANING AND INSPECTION

1. Inspect the main and connecting rod bearings replace if necessary.
2. Clean the crankshaft oil passages. Check the crankshaft main journals and connecting rod journals for wear or damage.

EXHAUST SYSTEM

Safety Precautions

For a number of reasons, exhaust system work can be the most dangerous type of work you can do on your car. Always observe the following precautions:

- Support the car extra securely. Not only will you often be working directly under it, but you'll frequently be using a lot of force, say, heavy hammer blows, to dislodge rusted parts. This can cause a car that's improperly supported to shift and possibly fall.
- Wear goggles. Exhaust system parts are always rusty. Metal chips can be dislodged, even when you're only turning rusted bolts. Attempting to pry pipes apart with a chisel makes the chips fly even more frequently.
- If you're using a cutting torch, keep it a great distance from either the fuel tank or lines. Stop what you're doing and feel the temperature of the fuel bearing pipes on the tank frequently. Even slight heat can expand and/or vaporize fuel, resulting in accumulated vapor, or even a liquid leak, near your torch.
- Watch where your hammer blows fall and make sure you hit squarely. You could easily tap a brake or fuel line when you hit an exhaust system part with a glancing blow. Inspect all lines and hoses in the area where you've been working.

CAUTION: *Be very careful when working on or near the catalytic converter. External temperatures can reach 1,500°F (816°C) and more, causing severe burns. Removal or installation should be performed only on a cold exhaust system.*

Special Tools

A number of special exhaust system tools can be rented from auto supply houses or local stores that rent special equipment. A common one is a tail pipe expander, designed to enable you to join pipes of identical diameter.

It may also be quite helpful to use solvents

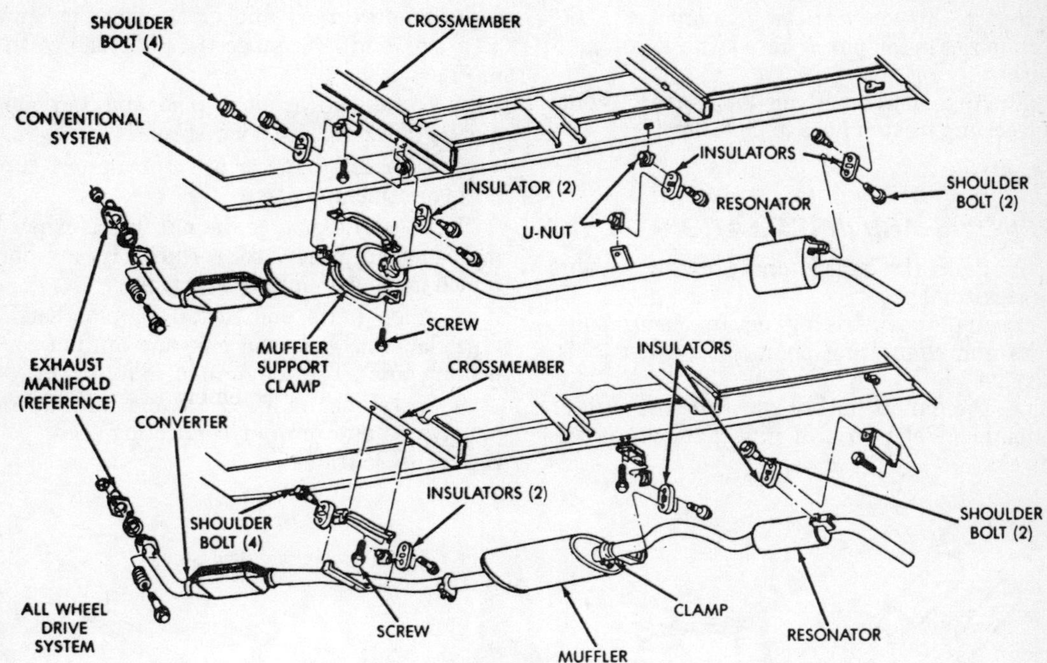

Exhaust system $components

designed to loosen rusted bolts or flanges. Soaking rusted parts the night before you do the job can speed the work of freeing rusted parts considerably. Remember that these solvents are often flammable. Apply only to parts after they are cool!

Exhaust (Converter/Resonator) Pipe

REMOVAL AND INSTALLATION

1. Raise the vehicle and properly support on jackstands.

CAUTION: *Be very careful when working on or near the catalytic converter! External temperatures can reach 1,500°F (816°C) and more, causing severe burns! Removal or installation should be performed only on a cold exhaust system.*

2. Apply penetrating oil to clamp bolts, nuts and connecting points of system to be remove.
3. Remove the nuts and clamp assembly from exhaust pipe to muffler connecting point.
4. Remove the shoulder bolts, springs and nuts attaching exhaust pipe to exhaust manifold.
5. Remove the exhaust pipe/converter assembly from muffler.
6. Clean the exhaust manifold to exhaust pipe/converter assembly gasket mating surfaces and the end of muffler with a wire brush.
7. Install the exhaust pipe/converter assembly or resonator into muffler. Make certain the key on the converter or resonator pipe bottomed in slot of muffler.
8. Install a new gasket on the exhaust pipe and position exhaust pipe into exhaust manifold. Install springs, shoulder bolts and nuts. Tighten nuts to 21 ft. lbs.
9. Align parts and install a new clamp assembly at exhaust pipe and muffler connecting point tighten clamps nuts to 23 ft. lbs.

Tailpipe

REMOVAL AND INSTALLATION

1. Raise the vehicle and properly support on jackstands.
2. Apply penetrating oil to clamp bolts, nuts and connecting points of system to be remove.
3. Remove the support saddle type clamp assembly from the tail pipe to muffler connecting point.
4. Remove the U-nut and shoulder bolts from tail pipe mid-point and rear tail pipe bracket.
5. When removing the tail pipe, raise the rear of vehicle enough to provide clearance between pipe and rear axle parts.
6. Remove the tailpipe from muffler.
7. Clean the muffler mating surface with a wire brush.
8. Replace broken or worn insulators, supports or attaching parts.
9. Loosely assemble the tail pipe to muffler,

mid-point support and tail pipe bracket. Make certain slot in tail pipe is keyed with key in muffler.

10. Align parts and install support saddle type clamp tighten nuts to 28 ft. lbs.

Muffler

REMOVAL AND INSTALLATION

1. Raise the vehicle and properly support on jackstands.
2. Apply penetrating oil to clamp bolts, nuts and connecting points of system to be remove.
3. Disconnect the tail pipe from the muffler assembly. Refer to Tail Pipe Removal procedures.
4. Remove nuts and clamp from exhaust pipe and muffler connection and remove the muffler.
5. Clean the exhaust pipe and tail pipe mating surfaces with a wire brush.
6. Replace broken or worn insulators, supports or attaching parts.
7. Loosely assemble the muffler to exhaust pipe and tail pipe. Make certain keys are bottomed in slots of muffler and pipes.
8. Align parts and install support saddle type clamp between tail pipe and muffler connecting point. Tighten nuts to 28 ft. lbs.
9. Install clamp assembly and nuts at exhaust pipe and muffler connecting point and tighten to 25 ft. lbs.

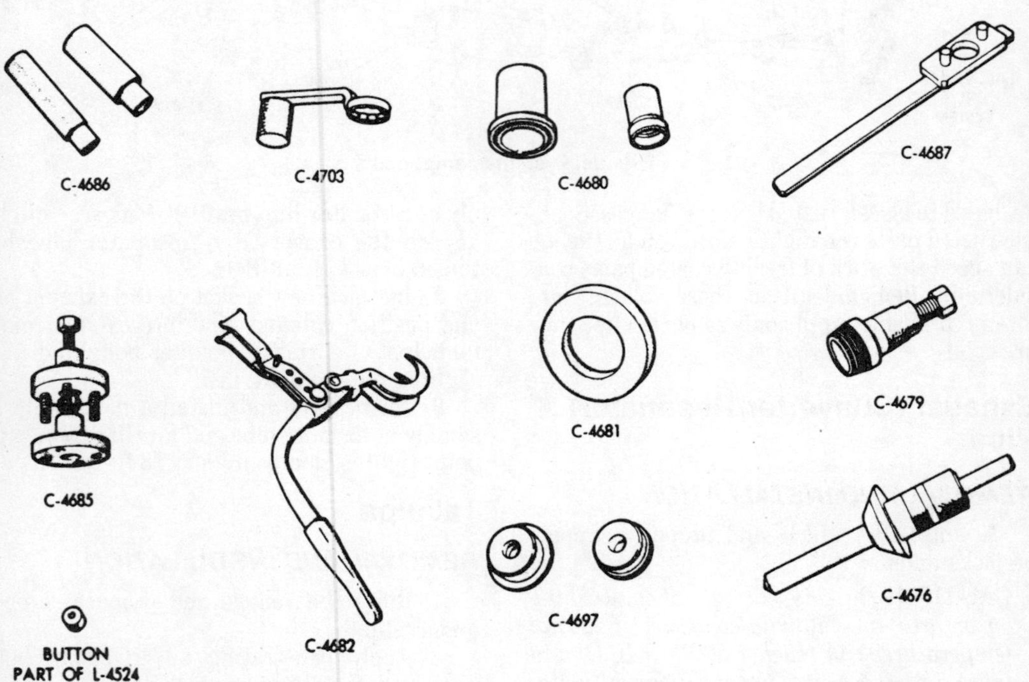

Special tools for exhaust system work

Emission Controls

4

EMISSION CONTROLS

Vehicle Emission Control Information Label

All vehicles described in this Repair and Tune-Up Guide are equipped with a Vehicle Emission Control Information Label (VECI). The VECI label is located in the engine compartment and is permanently attached. No attempt should be made to remove the VECI label. The VECI label contains specific information for the vehicle to which it is attached. If the specifications on the VECI label differ from the information contain in this manual, those shown on the label should be followed.

Crankcase Ventilation System

The Positive Crankcase Ventilation System is described, and servicing procedures are detailed in the"General Information and Maintenance" section of this book.

Evaporative Emission Controls

The Evaporative Emission Control System prevents gasoline vapor emissions from the fuel system, from entering the atmosphere.

Evaporating fuel from the gas tank or carburetor, passes through vent hoses and tubes to a charcoal canister where they are temporarily stored until they can be drawn into the intake manifold and burned when the engine is running.

CHARCOAL CANISTER

The charcoal canister is a sealed, maintenance free unit which stores fuel vapors from the fuel tank and carburetor bowl. Although all carburetor bowls are vented internally, some models do not required venting to the canister. In cases where the carburetor is not vented to

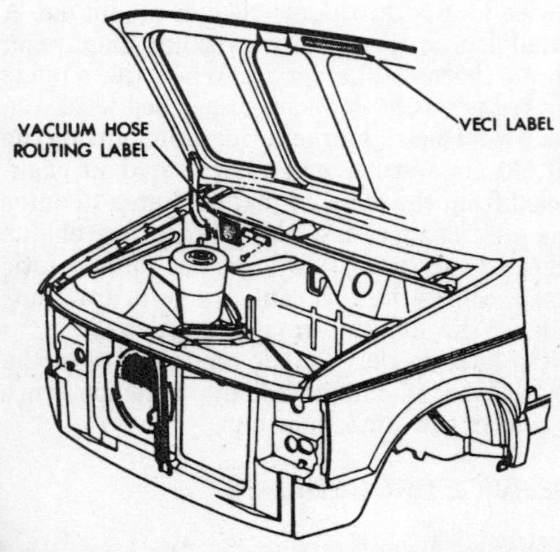

1984-86 underhood label identification

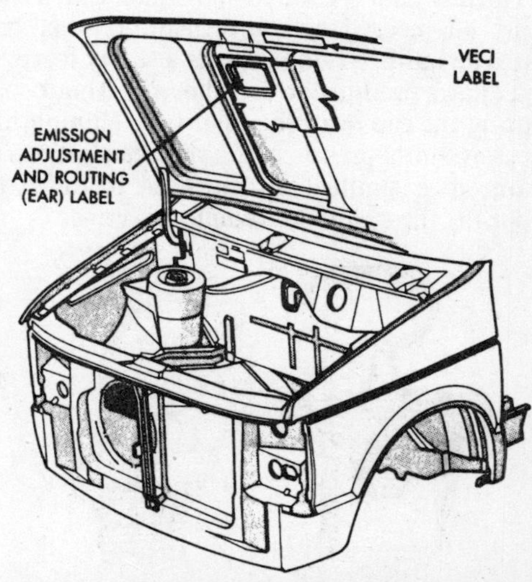

1997-91 underhood label identification

the canister, the bowl vent port on the canister will be capped. If the canister becomes damaged, replacement with a new unit is required. The hoses connecting the canister are of fuel resistant construction. Use only fuel resistant hoses if replacement is necessary.

DAMPING CANISTER

Some models are equipped with a damping canister that is connected in series with the charcoal canister. The damping canister cushions the effect of a sudden release of fuel rich vapors when the purge valve is signaled to open. The rich vapors are held momentarily and then gradually fed into the intake manifold to be burned.

CANISTER PURGE SOLENOID

All engines are equipped with a canister purge solenoid which is connected in series with the charcoal canister. The canister purge solenoid is electrically operated by the Single Module Engine Controller (SMEC) which grounds the solenoid if engine temperature is below 66°C. This prevents vacuum from reaching the charcoal canister. When the engine reaches operating temperature the SMEC de-energizes the solenoid and allows purge vapors from the canister to pass through the throttle body.

ROLLOVER VALVE

All vehicles pass a full 360° rollover without allowing fuel leakage. To accomplish this, fuel and vapor flow controls are needed for all fuel tank connections. A rollover valve is mounted in the top of the fuel tank to prevent leakage if the vehicle is involved in a rollover.

GAS TANK FILLER CAP

The fuel tank is covered and sealed with a specially engineered pressure/vacuum relief gas cap. The built-in relief valve is a safety feature, and allows pressure to be relieved without separating the cap from the filler tube eliminating excessive tank pressure. If a replacement cap is required, a similar cap must be installed in order for the system to remain effective.

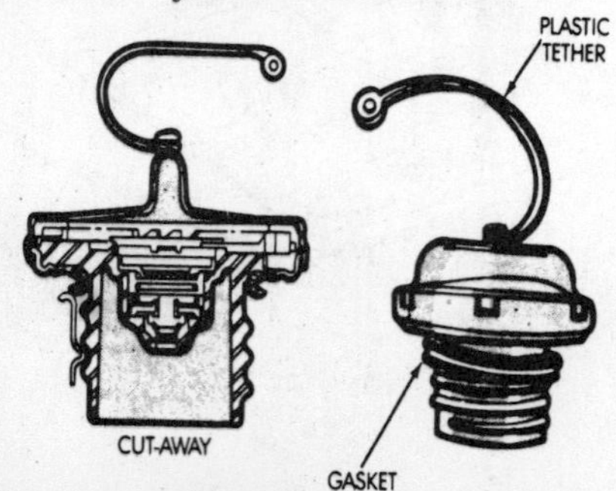

Pressure vacuum gas filler cap

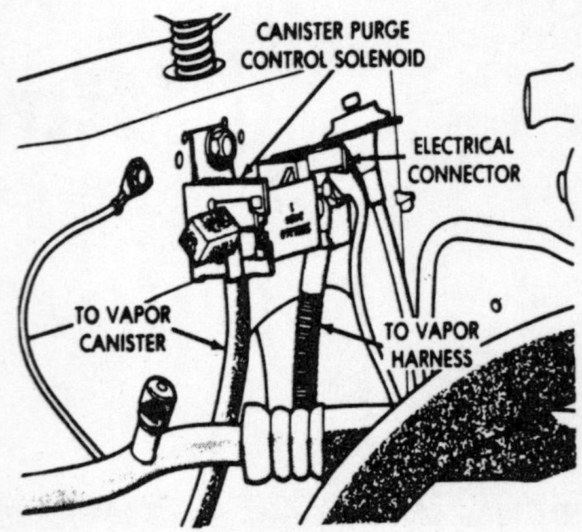

Canister purge solenoid

NOTE: *Always remove the gas tank cap to release pressure whenever the fuel system requires servicing.*

BOWL VENT VALVE

The bowl vent valve (carburetor equipped models) is connected to the carburetor fuel bowl, the charcoal canister, and the air pump discharge. When the engine is not running and no air pump pressure is applied, a direct connection between the carburetor and canister exists. When the engine is running, air pump pressure closes the connection between the canister and the fuel bowl. When the engine is shut off, air pressure in the valve bleeds down and the fuel bowl is allow to vent vapors into the canister.

Exhaust Emission Controls

HEATED INLET AIR SYSTEM

All TBI engines are equipped with a vacuum device located in the air cleaner air intake. A small door is operated by a vacuum diaphragm and a thermostatic spring. When the outside air temperature is below a specified level, the door will block off air entering from outside the air cleaner snorkel, and allow heated air channeled from the exhaust manifold area to enter the air cleaner assembly. With the engine warmed up and running the thermostatic spring allows the heat control door to draw outside air through the air cleaner snorkel.

On later models the air temperature in the air intake is monitored by a temperature sensor in the intake housing.

SERVICE PROCEDURES

NOTE: *A malfunction in the heated air system will affect driveability and the emissions output of the vehicle.*

2.2L Engine

1. Verify all vacuum hoses and the flexible heat pipe between the air cleaner and heat stove are properly attached and in good condition.

2. On a cold engine with an ambient temperature less than 19°C (65°F) the heat door valve plate in the snorkel should be in the up position (Heat On).

3. With the engine running at normal operating temperature, the heat door should be in the down position (Heat Off).

4. If the heat door valve plate does not respond to hot and cold temperatures, the door diaphragm or the sensor may need replacing.

5. To test the diaphragm, remove the air cleaner from the engine and allow it to cool down to 19°C (65°F).

6. Connect a hand operated vacuum pump to the vacuum diaphragm and apply 20 inches of vacuum. The diaphragm should not leak down more than 10 inches in 5 minutes. The control door should not lift from the bottom of the snorkel at less than 2 inches of vacuum and be in the full up position with no more than 4 inches of vacuum. If the vacuum test proves the diaphragm defective, replace the air cleaner.

7. If the vacuum test shows the diaphragm in proper working condition, replace the sensor.

8. Label the vacuum hoses at the sensor to aid during reassemble. Disconnect the vacuum hoses, remove the retaining clips with a screwdriver and discard. Remove the sensor and mounting gasket.

9. Position the new gasket on the sensor and install sensor. Support the sensor on the outer diameter, and install the retaining clips.

10. Reconnect vacuum hoses.

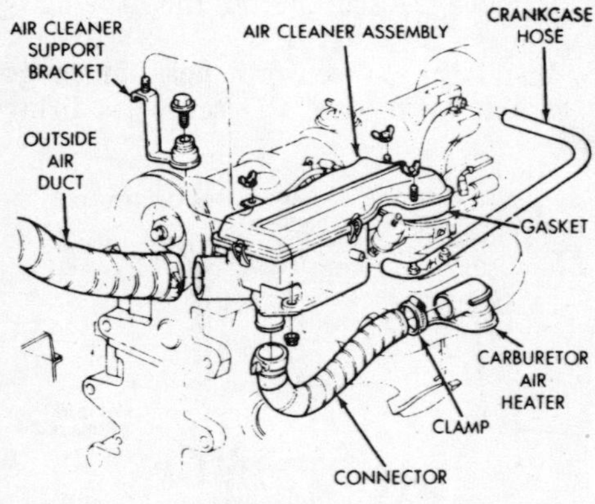

Heated air intake system on 2.2L engine

2.5L Engine

1. Verify all vacuum hoses and the flexible heat pipe between the air cleaner and heat stove are properly attached and in good condition.

2. On a cold engine with an ambient temperature less than 46°C (115°F) the heat door valve plate in the snorkel should be in the up position (Heat On).

3. With the engine running at normal operating temperature, the heat door should be in the down position (Heat Off).

4. If the heat door valve plate does not respond to hot and cold temperatures, the door diaphragm or the sensor may need replacing.

5. To test the diaphragm, remove the air cleaner from the engine and allow it to cool down to 46°C (115°F).

6. Connect a hand operated vacuum pump to the sensor and apply 20 inches of vacuum. The door valve should be in the up position (Heat On).

7. If the door does not raise to "Heat On" position, test the vacuum diaphragm for proper operation.

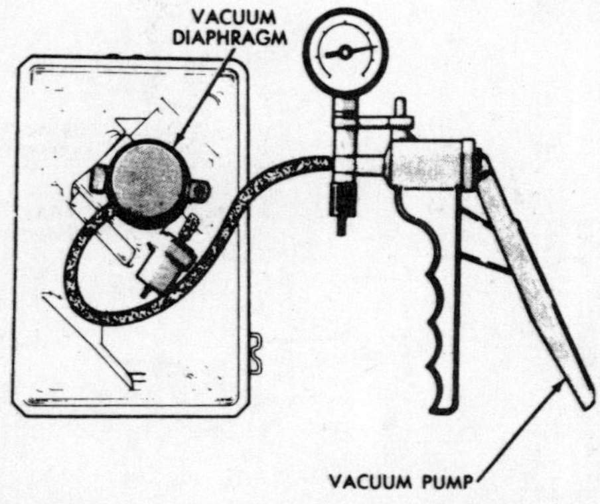

Testing the vacuum diaphragm

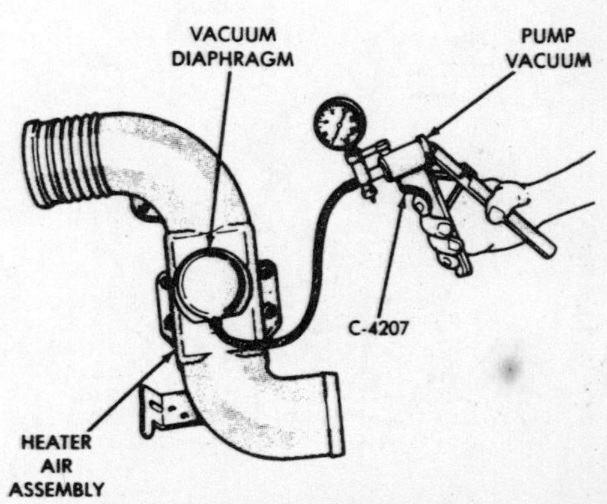

Testing the heated air inlet diaphragm

8. Apply 20 inches of vacuum with a hand operated vacuum pump to the vacuum diaphragm. The diaphragm should not leak down more than 10 inches in 5 minutes. The control door should not lift from the bottom of the snorkel at less than 2 inches of vacuum and be in the full up position with no more than 4 inches of vacuum. If the vacuum test proves the diaphragm defective, replace the air cleaner.

9. If the vacuum test shows the diaphragm in proper working condition, replace the sensor.

10. Label the vacuum hoses at the sensor to aid during assembly. Disconnect the vacuum hoses, remove the retaining clips with a screwdriver and discard. Remove the sensor and mounting gasket.

11. Position the new gasket on the sensor and install sensor. Support the sensor on the outer diameter, and install the retaining clips.

12. Connect the vacuum hoses.

2.6L Engine

1. Verify all vacuum hoses and the flexible heat pipe between the air cleaner and heat stove are properly attached and in good condition.

2. On a cold engine with an ambient temperature less than 30°C (84°F) the heat door valve plate in the snorkel should be in the up position (Heat On).

3. With the engine running at normal operating temperature, the heat door should be in the down position (Heat Off).

4. If the heat door valve plate does not respond to hot and cold temperatures, the door diaphragm or the sensor may need replacing.

5. To test the diaphragm, remove the air cleaner from the engine and allow it to cool down to 30°C (84°F).

6. Connect a hand operated vacuum pump to the sensor and apply 15 inches of vacuum. The valve should be in the up position (Heat On).

7. If the door does not raise to Heat On position, test the vacuum motor for proper operation.

8. Apply 10 inches of vacuum to the vacuum motor with a hand operated vacuum pump, if the valve does not remain in the full up position replace the air cleaner body assembly.

9. If the door perform adequately with vacuum applied to the motor, replace the sensor.

HEATED AIR TEMPERATURE SENSOR REPLACEMENT

The heated air temperature sensor is located in the air cleaner housing and can be removed with the air filter removed from the housing.

1. Remove the top of the air cleaner housing, this can be done by releasing the clips.

2. Remove the air filter.

3. Disconnect the vacuum lines from the sensor.

4. Remove the sensor from the housing by prying it carefully out.

5. Install the new sensor in position using a new gasket. Make sure the sensor is firmly seated.

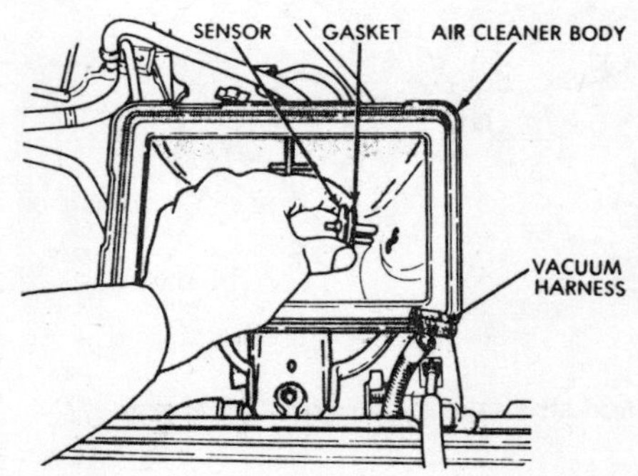

Installing the heated air temperature sensor – TBI engines

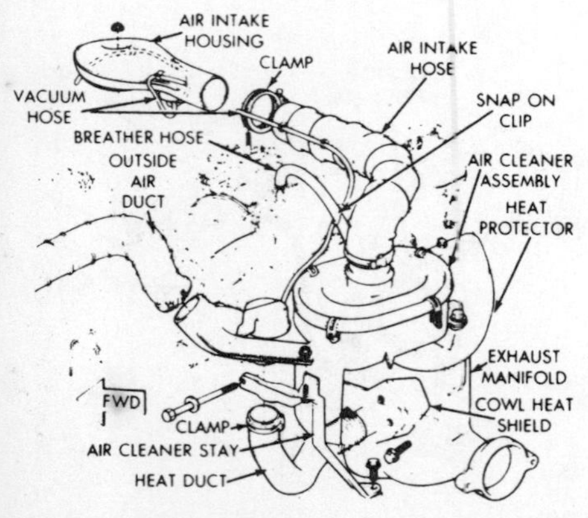

Heated air intake system on the 2.6L engine

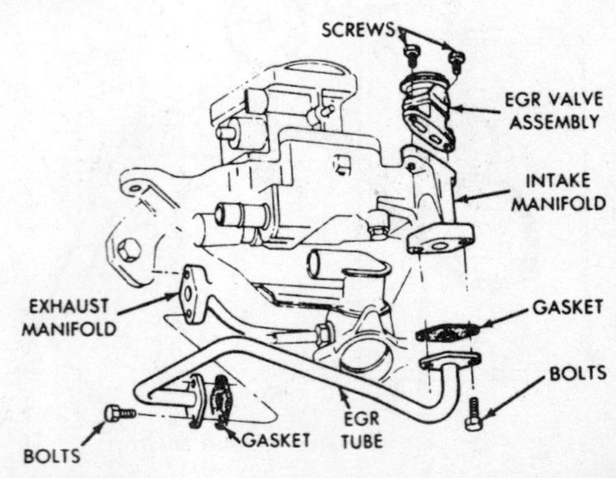

EGR system – late model 2.5L engines

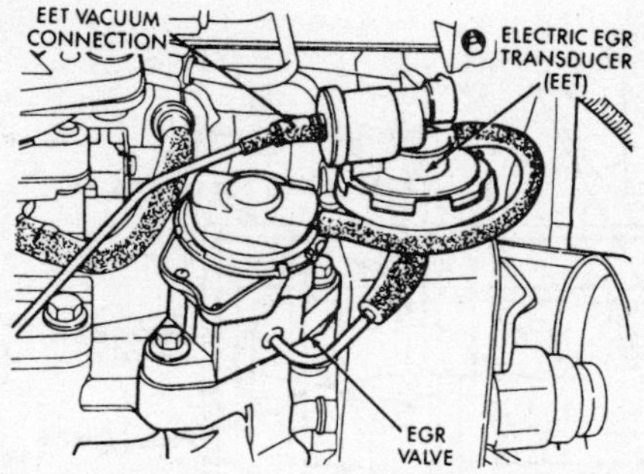

EGR valve and Electric Transducer mounting – late model 2.5L engines

6. Reconnect the vacuum lines to the sensor and reinstall the air filter.

Exhaust Gas Recirculation (EGR) System

The EGR system reduces the oxides of nitrogen in the engine exhaust. The reduction of NOx is accomplished by allowing a predetermined amount of the hot exhaust gas to recirculate and dilute the incoming fuel and air mixture. This dilution reduces peak flame temperature during combustion.

SERVICE

2.2L Engine

The components of the EGR system on the 2.2L engine are; a Coolant Controlled Exhaust Gas Recirculation/Coolant Vacuum Switch Cold Closed (CVSCC) unit mounted in the thermostat housing, an EGR valve, and a EGR tube.

The CVSCC prevents vacuum from being supplied to the EGR system or other systems until the coolant temperature reaches a certain level. When a certain temperature is reached the CVSCC opens and vacuum is supplied as necessary.

To assure proper operation test the system as follows:

1. Inspect all passages and moving parts for free movement.
2. Inspect all hoses. If any are hardened, cracked or have faulty connection, replacement is necessary.
3. Allow the engine to reach normal operating temperature. Locate the EGR valve at the end of the intake manifold. Allow the engine to idle for about a minute, then abruptly accelerate to about 2000 rpm, but not over 3000 rpm. Visible movement of the EGR valve stem should be noticed. Movement of the stem indicates the valve is operating normally. If no movement is noticed. Remove the EGR valve and inspect it for deposits and wear.
4. If deposits around the poppet and seat are more than a film, apply some heat control solvent to the area to help soften the deposits. Apply vacuum to the valve with a hand operated vacuum pump. When the valve opens, scrap away the deposits from the poppet and seat. If the valve poppet does not open when vacuum is applied, replace the valve. If the stem or seat is worn replace the valve.
5. If the EGR valve is functioning properly, check the CVSCC.
6. Check condition of vacuum hoses at the CVSCC and properly routed (see vacuum hose under hood sticker).
7. Check engine coolant level.
8. Disconnect the vacuum hoses and remove the valve from the thermostat housing. Place the valve in an ice bath below 4.4°C (40°F) so that the threaded portion is covered. Attach a vacuum pump to the lower connection on the valve (the one connected to the vacuum hose showing a yellow stripe). Apply 10 inches of vacuum. Pressure should drop no more than one inch in one minute. If the vacuum drops more, replace the CVSCC.

2.6L Engine

With this system exhaust gases are partially recirculated from an exhaust port in the cylinder head into a port at the intake manifold below the carburetor. EGR flow is controlled by thermo valves, and a combination of a Dual EGR valve and Sub EGR valve.

The dual EGR valve consists of a primary and secondary valve which are controlled by a different carburetor vacuums in response to the throttle opening. EGR flow is halted at idle and wide open throttle operation. The primary valve controls the EGR flow at narrow throttle openings, while the secondary valve allows flow into the intake mixture at wider throttle openings. Vacuum to the dual EGR valve is controlled by thermo valves.

A carburetor mounted Sub EGR valve is directly opened and closed by the throttle linkage

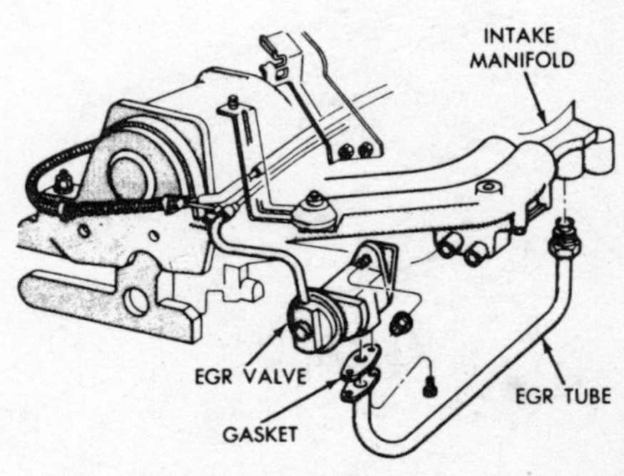

EGR system on the 2.2L engine

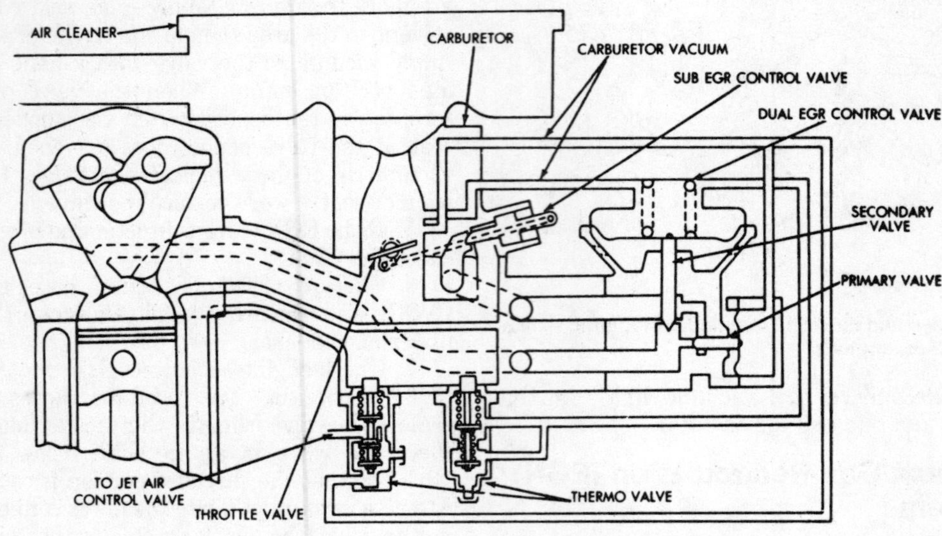

EGR system on the 2.6L engine

in order to closely modulate the EGR flow controlled by the EGR control valve, in response to the throttle opening.

Two thermo valves connected to the EGR system, sense coolant temperature changes and open and close accordingly to control the vacuum flow to the EGR system.

Test the system as follows:

1. Check the vacuum hose for good condition and proper routing (see vacuum hose under hood sticker).

2. Engine must be cold. Cold start the engine and allow to idle.

3. Check to make sure that the fast idle does not cause the secondary EGR valve to operate. If the secondary EGR valve operates at cold start fast idle, replace the secondary EGR valve thermo valve.

4. Run the engine until the operating temperature exceeds 65°C (149°F). The secondary EGR valve should now be in operation. If if it does not operate, inspect the EGR valve or thermo valve.

5. Disconnect the green stripped vacuum hose from the carburetor. Connect a hand vacuum pump to the hose and apply 6 inches of vacuum while opening the sub EGR valve by hand. If the idle speed becomes unstable, the secondary valve is operating properly. If the idle speed remains the same, replace the secondary EGR valve and thermo valve.

6. Connect the green stripped hose to the carburetor. Disconnect the yellow stripped hose from the carburetor and connect it to the hand vacuum pump. Hold the sub EGR valve opened and apply 6 inches of vacuum.

7. If the idle speed becomes unstable, the primary EGR valve is operating properly. If the idle speed remains unchanged, replace the primary EGR valve and thermo valve.

2.5L and 3.0L Engines

The EGR system for late model vehicles equipped with the 2.5L engines, is a back pressure type. A back pressure transducer meas-

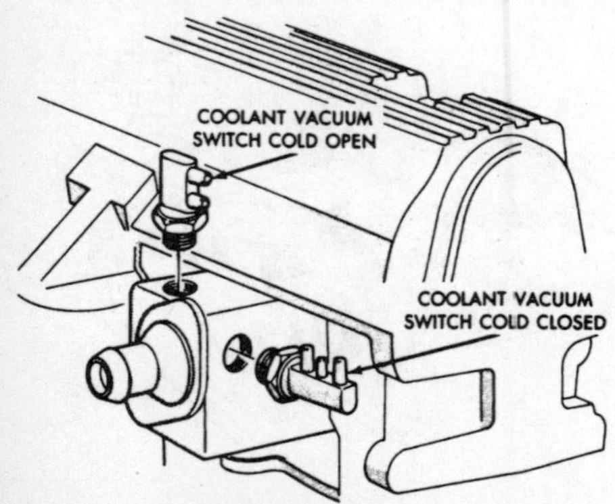

Coolant vacuum switch

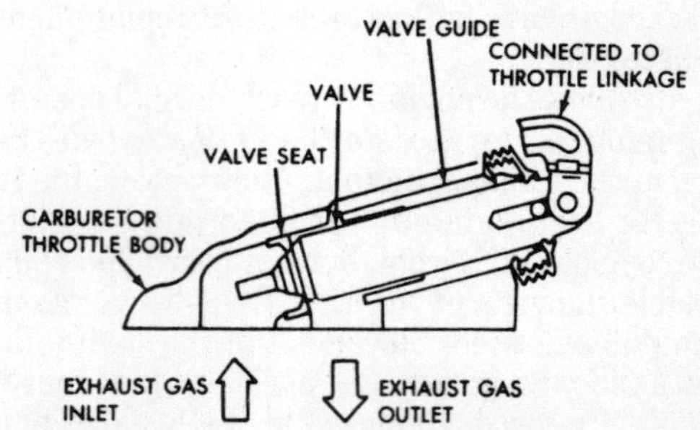

Sub EGR valve assembly

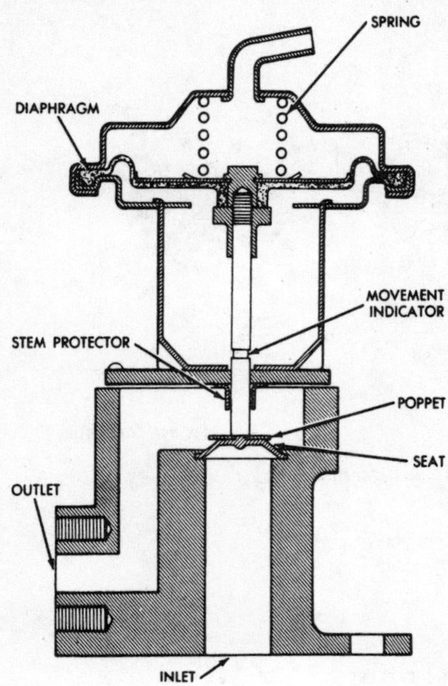

EGR valve – cut away view

ures the amount of exhaust gas back pressure on the exhaust side of the EGR valve and varies the strength of the vacuum signal applied to the EGR valve. The transducer uses this back pressure signal to provide the correct amount of exhaust gas recirculation under all conditions.

This utilizes an intake manifold mounted EGR valve and Electric EGR Transducer (EET). An EGR tube carries the exhaust gases from the intake manifold to the exhaust manifold. The EGR systems are solenoid controlled, using a manifold vacuum signal from the throttle body. The EGR solenoid is part of the EET. These systems do not allow EGR at idle. EGR systems operate at all temperatures above 60°F (16°C).

California vehicles with EGR have an onboard diagnostic system and a solenoid in series with the vacuum line to the EGR valve. The engine controller monitors EGR system performance and energized or de-energized the solenoid base on engine/driving conditions. If the system malfunction the engine controller will turn on the Check Engine light and a fault code will be stored in the diagnostic system.

Test the system as follows:

1. Inspect all passages and moving parts for free movement.
2. Inspect all hoses. If any are hardened, cracked or have faulty connection, replacement is necessary.
3. Warm the engine to normal operating temperature. Allow the engine to idle for about a minute, then abruptly accelerate to about 2000 rpm, but not over 3000 rpm. Visible movement of the groove on EGR valve stem should be noticed. Movement of the stem indicates the valve is operating normally. If no movement is noticed.
4. Disconnect the vacuum hoses from the EGR vacuum transducer, and attach a hand operated vacuum pump. Raise the engine to 2000 rpm and apply 10 inches of vacuum, while checking valve movement. If no valve movement occurs, replace the valve/transducer assembly.

NOTE: *If the back-pressure EGR valve does not function satisfactory. Replace the entire Valve/Transducer assembly. No attempt should be made to clean the valve.*

5. If movement occurs, check the diaphragm for leaks. Valve should remain open at least 30 seconds.
6. If the valve is functioning satisfactory, remove the throttle body and inspect port in throttle bore and associated passages. Apply some heat control solvent to the area to help soften any deposit.
7. Install the throttle body and recheck EGR operation.

Air Injection System

2.2L engines are equipped with an air injection system. This system is designed to supply a controlled amount of air to the exhaust gases, through exhaust ports, aiding in the oxidation of the gases and reduction of carbon monoxide and hydrocarbons to an appreciable level.

During engine warm-up air is injected into the base of the exhaust manifold. After the engine warms up, the air flow is switched (by a Coolant Vacuum Switch Cold Open or by a vacuum solenoid) to the 3-way catalyst where it further aids in the reduction of carbon monoxide and hydrocarbons in the exhaust system.

The system consists of a belt driven air pump, hoses, a switch/relief valve and a check valve to prevent the components within the system from high temperature exhaust gases.

NOTE: *No repairs are possible on any of the air injection system components. All replacement parts must be serviced as a unit.*

Coolant Vacuum Switch Cold Open

1. Locate the switch on the thermostat housing.
2. Label the hoses before removing. Remove hoses.
3. Remove the vacuum switch from housing.
4. Install a new vacuum switch and connect

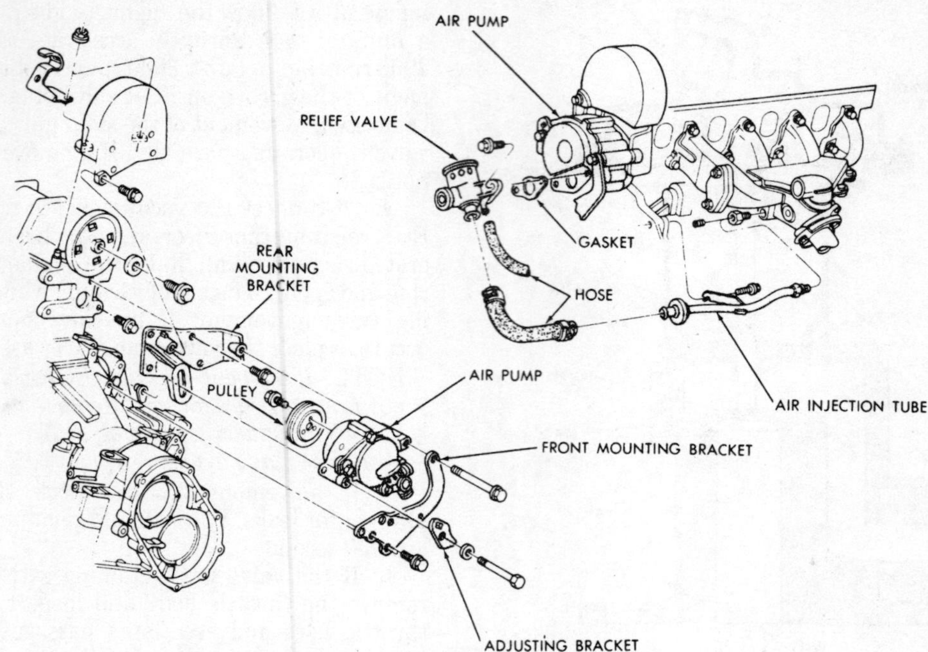

Air injection system on the 2.2L engine — Federal/Canadian shown

the vacuum hoses. (See under hood vacuum hose routing label).

Air Pump

NOTE: *The air injection system is not completely noiseless. Do not assume the air pump is defective because it squeals. If the system creates excessive noise, remove the drive belt and operate the engine. If the noise ceases, check all hoses connection for proper tightening. Replace pump if necessary.*

1. Remove all hoses and vacuum lines from the air pump and diverter valve or switch/relief valve (depending on how equipped).
2. Remove the air pump drive pulley shield.
3. Remove the air pump pivot bolt and remove air pump belt.
4. Remove the remaining mounting bolts and remove pump.
5. Remove the diverter valve or switch/relief valve from pump.
6. Clean all gasket material from valve and pump mounting surface.
7. Install the diverter valve or switch/relief valve using a new gasket, to the new pump.
8. Install the pump on the engine and loosely install pivot bolt.
9. Install drive belt and tighten pivot bolt.
10. Install air pump drive pulley shield.
11. Install all hoses and vacuum lines.

Switch/Relief Valve

If vacuum is apply to the valve and air injection is not upstream, or if air injection is in both upstream and downstream, the valve is faulty and must be replaced.

1. Remove all air hoses and vacuum hoses.
2. Remove the valve to pump mounting bolts, and remove valve.
3. Clean all gasket material from mounting surfaces.
4. Install the new valve to the pump with a new gasket.
5. Secure the valve with mounting bolts, tighten bolts to 14Nm (125 inch lbs.).
6. Reinstall all air hoses and vacuum hoses.

Relief Valve

The purpose of this valve is to control air pump pressure during high engine speeds. If the pump discharge pressure exceeds 9 PSI the valve will open and vent the excess pressure to the atmosphere.

1. Remove the air hoses from the valve.
2. Remove the valve mounting screws and remove valve.
3. Clean all gasket material from mounting surfaces.
4. Install a new gasket on valve and secure with mounting screws.
5. Reconnect air hoses.

Check Valve

The check valve is located in the injection tube which lead to the exhaust manifold and converter assembly. The valve has a one-way diaphragm to protect the pump and hoses from high exhaust system pressure if the belt or pump failed.

Remove the air hose from check valve inlet tube. If exhaust gas escapes from the inlet tube, the valve have failed and must be replaced.

1. Loosen clamp and remove inlet hose from the valve.
2. Remove the tube nut retaining the tube to the exhaust manifold or catalyst.
3. Loosen the starter motor mounting bolt and remove injection tube from engine.
4. Remove the catalyst injection tube mounting screws from catalyst flange and remove injection tube.
5. Position the injection tube to catalyst flange and secured with mounting screws.
6. Install the injection tube into fitting in exhaust manifold and bracket at starter motor.
7. Connect hoses to the check valve.

Pulse Air Feeder System

2.6L engines use a pulse air feeder system to promote oxidation of exhaust emissions in the rear catalytic converter. The system consists of a main reed valve and sub-reed valve. The main reed valve is controlled by a diaphragm which is activated by pressure pulses from the crankcase. The sub-reed valve is activated by pulsation in the exhaust system between the front and rear converters.

1. Remove the air duct from the right side of the radiator.
2. Remove the carburetor protector shield.
3. Remove the engine oil dipstick and tube.
4. Remove the pulse air feeder mounting bolts.
5. Raise and support the front of the vehicle on jackstands. Disconnect the pulse air feeder hoses and remove the feeder.
6. Install hoses on pulse air feeder.
7. Lower the vehicle and tighten feeder mounting bolts.
8. Check O-ring on lower end of the dipstick tube. Replace if damaged.
9. Install carburetor protector shield.
10. Install the air deflector on radiator.

Dual Air Aspirator System

2.6L engines use an air aspirator system which aids in reducing carbon monoxide (CO) and hydrocarbon emissions. The system uses pulsating exhaust pressure to draw fresh air from the air cleaner assembly. Failure of the aspirator valve will result in excess noise.

SYSTEM TEST

1. Check the aspirator tube/exhaust manifold assembly joint and hoses. If aspirator tube/exhaust manifold joint is leaking, retighten to 68 Nm (50 ft. lbs.). If hoses are harden, replace as necessary.
2. Disconnect the inlet hose from aspirator valve.
3. With engine at idle, the negative (vacuum) exhaust pulses should be felt at the valve inlet.
4. If hot exhaust gases escaped from the aspirator inlet, replace the valve.

REMOVAL AND INSTALLATION

1. Remove the air inlet hose from aspirator valve.
2. Remove screws from aspirator bracket, and remove tube assembly from engine.
3. Install tube and tighten nuts to 54 Nm (40 ft. lbs.).
4. Install tube bracket assembly and torque to 28 Nm (250 in.lbs.).
5. Connect the air hose to valve and air cleaner nipple, install clamps.

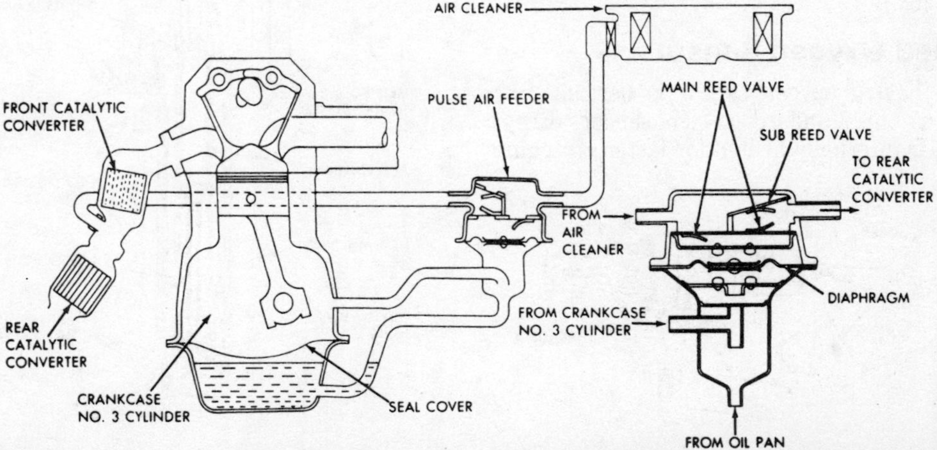

Pulse air feed system on the 2.6L engine

Electronic Feedback Carburetor (EFC) System

Some models are equipped with an Electronic Feedback Carburetor (EFC) System which is designed to convert Hydrocarbons(HC), Carbon Monoxide (CO) and Oxides of Nitrogen (NOx) into harmless substances. An exhaust gas oxygen sensor generates an electronic signal which is used by the Spark Control Computer to precisely control the air-fuel mixture ratio to the carburetor.

There are two operating modes in the EFC system:

1. OPEN LOOP-During cold engine operation the air-fuel ratio will be fixed to a richer mixture programmed into the computer by the manufacture.
2. CLOSED LOOP-The computer varies the air-fuel ratio based on information supplied by the oxygen sensor.

Oxygen Sensor

The oxygen sensor is a galvanic battery which produces electrical voltage after being heated by exhaust gases. The sensor monitors the oxygen content in the exhaust stream, convert it to an electrical voltage and transmit this voltage to the Spark Control Computer.

WARNING: *Use care when working around the oxygen sensor as the exhaust manifold may be extremely hot. The sensor must be remove using Tool C-4907.*

When the sensor is removed, the exhaust manifold threads must be cleaned with an 18mm x 1.5 x 6E tap.

If the sensor is to be reinstalled, the sensor threads must be coated with an anti-seize compound such as Loctite 771-64 or equivalent. New sensors are coated with compound on the threads and no additional compound is required. The sensor should be torque to 27 Nm (20 ft. lbs.).

Heated Oxygen Sensor

The heated oxygen sensor is basically the same as the standard oxygen sensor, except that it is internally heated for faster switching during engine operation. Replacement of the heated oxygen sensor is the same as the standard sensor.

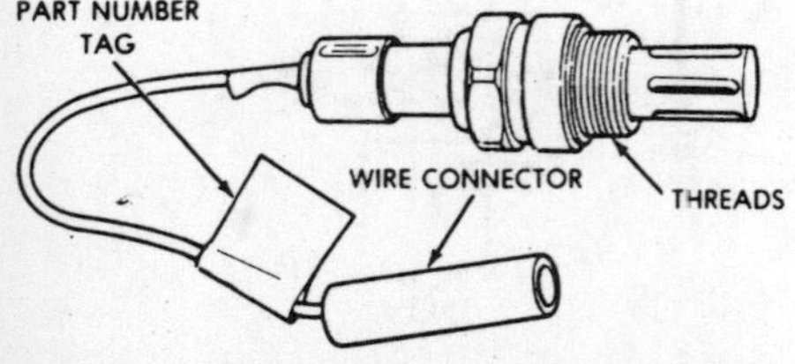

Oxygen sensor assembly

Oxygen Feedback Solenoid

In addition to the oxygen sensor, EFC uses an Oxygen Feedback Solenoid. It purpose is to regulate the fuel-air ratio of the feedback carburetor, along with a conventional fixed main metering jet, in response to the electrical signal generated by the Spark Control Computer.

With the feedback solenoid de-energized, the main metering orifice is fully uncovered and the richest condition exists within the carburetor.

With the feedback solenoid energized, the solenoid push rod seals the main metering orifice. This position offers the leanest condition within the carburetor.

Electric Choke Assembly

The electric choke system is a heater and switch assembly sealed within the choke housing. When the engine is running and the engine oil pressure is 2.7 kPa (4 psi) or above, the contacts in the oil pressure switch closes and feed current to the automatic choke system to open the choke and keep it open.

NOTE: *The choke assembly must never be immersed in fluid as damage to the internal switch and heater assembly will result.*

TESTING

1. Disconnect the electrical lead from choke heater assembly.
2. Connect direct battery voltage to choke heater connection.

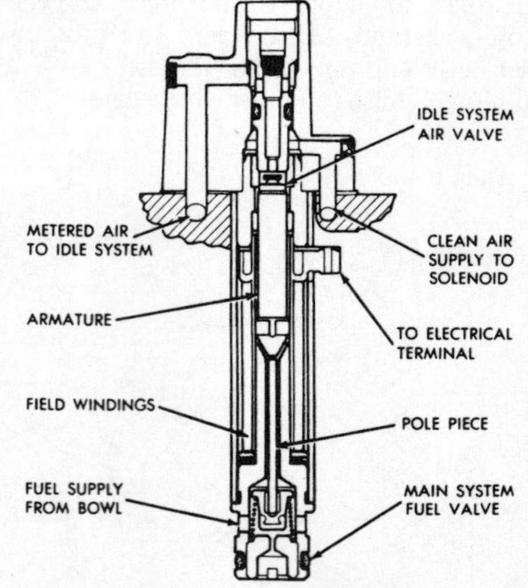

Oxygen feedback solenoid — cut away

3. The choke valve should reach the open position within five minutes.

WARNING: *Operation of any type should be avoided if there is a loss of choke power. This condition cause a very rich mixture to burn and result in abnormally high exhaust system temperatures, which may cause damage to the catalyst or other underbody parts of the vehicle.*

Emission Maintenance Light

All models have an Emission Maintenance Reminder (EMR) lamp, this lamp is illuminated when the ignition key is turned **ON**. The lamp is connected with the engine controller, which records the vehicle mileage and stores it into memory every 8 miles. At the time the mileage is stored, the controller checks for the 60,000, 82,500 and 120,000 mile trip points. When the current mileage matches one of these mileages, the EMR lamp is illuminated.

When the EMR lamp is illuminated some of the emission components are supposed to be changed. These components are: EGR valve, EGR tube and PCV valve at 60,000 miles and 120,000 miles. At 82,500 miles the oxygen sensor must also be replaced. The EMR lamp can then be reset using an appropriate DRB tester or equivalent.

VACUUM DIAGRAMS

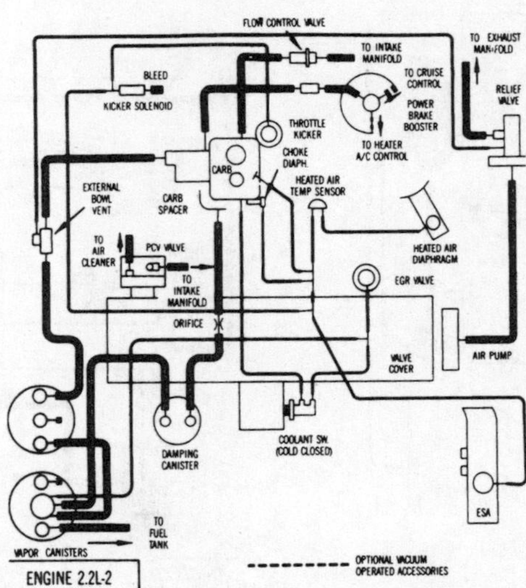

1984 Federal 2.2L vacuum hose routing

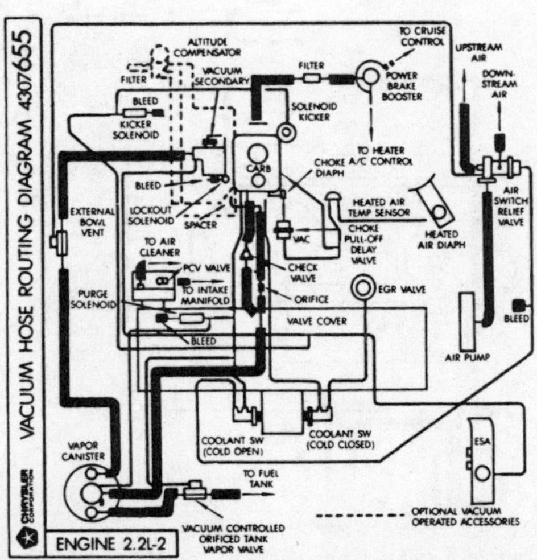

1986 California 2.2L vacuum hose routing

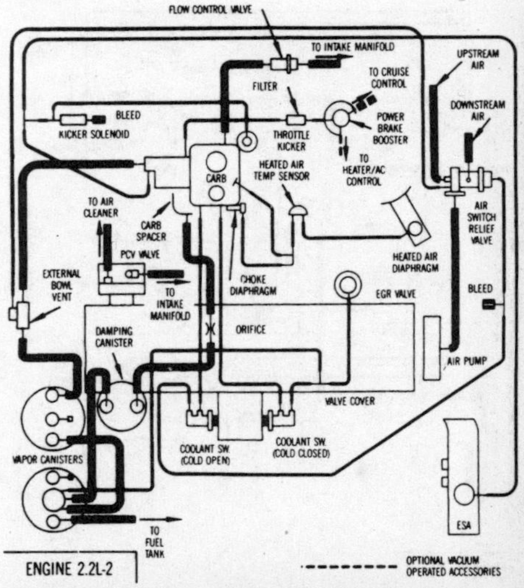

1984 California 2.2L vacuum hose routing

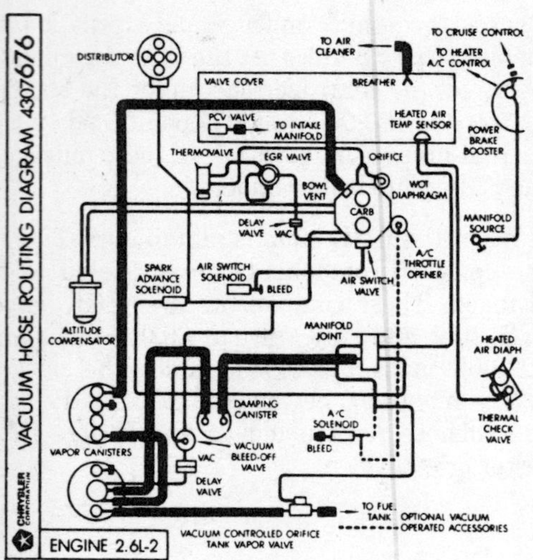
1986 Altitude 2.6L vacuum hose routing

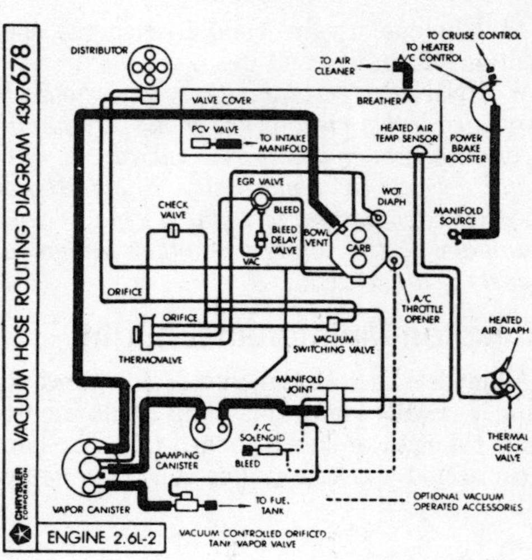
1986 Federal 2.6L vacuum hose routing

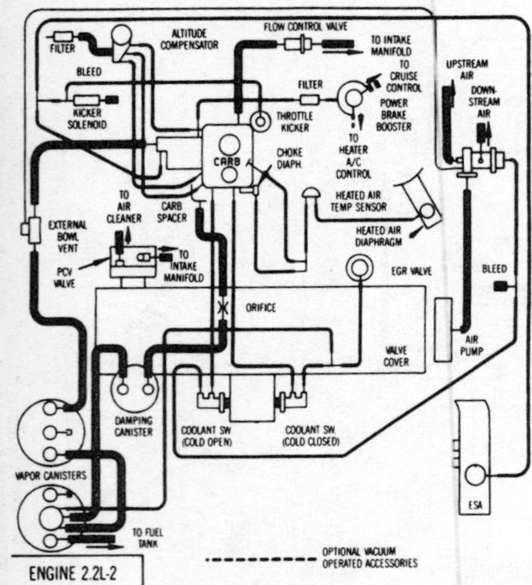
1984 Altitude 2.2L vacuum hose routing

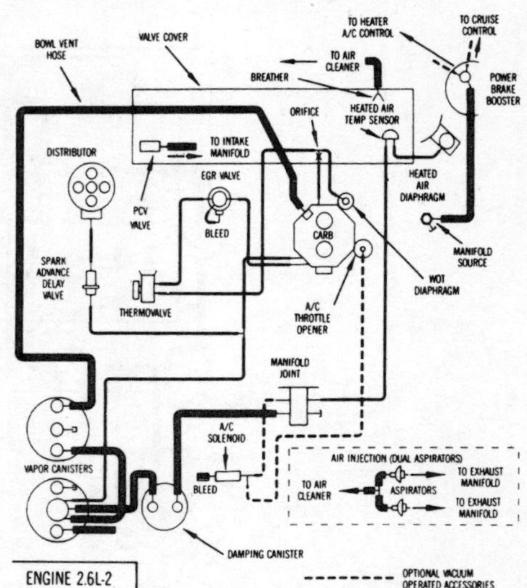
1984 Federal 2.6L vacuum hose routing

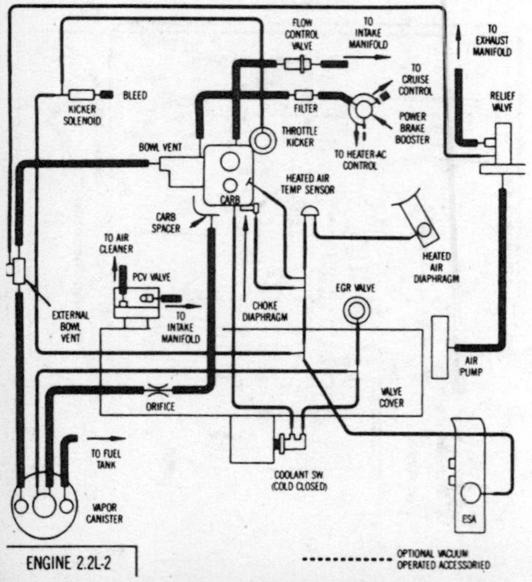
1984 Canadian 2.2L vacuum hose routing

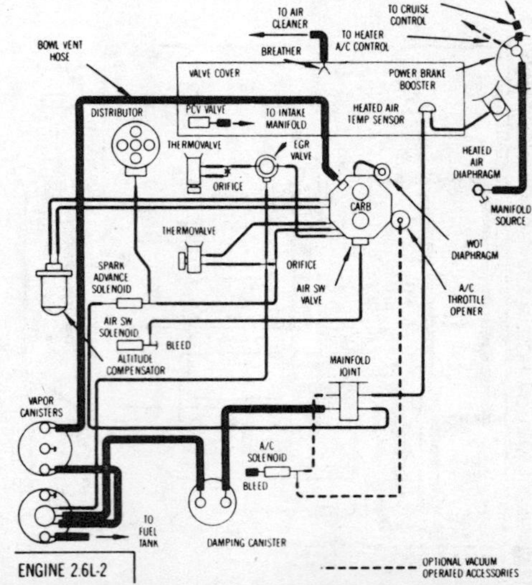
1984 California 2.6L vacuum hose routing

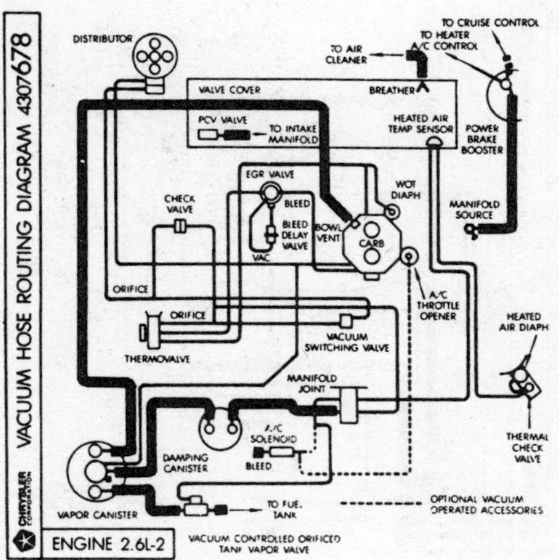

1984 Canadian 2.6L vacuum hose routing

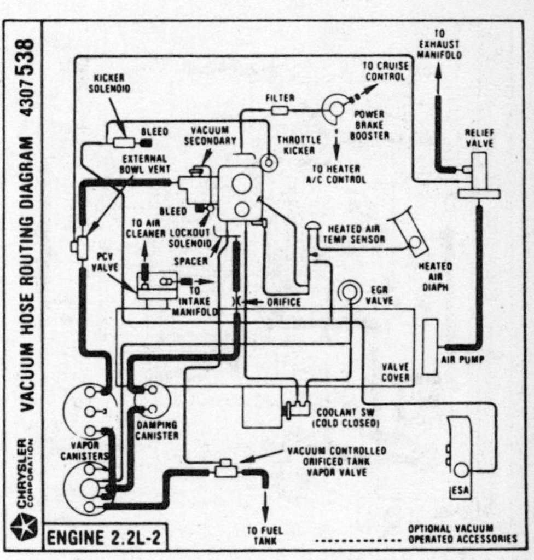

1985 Federal 2.2L vacuum hose routing

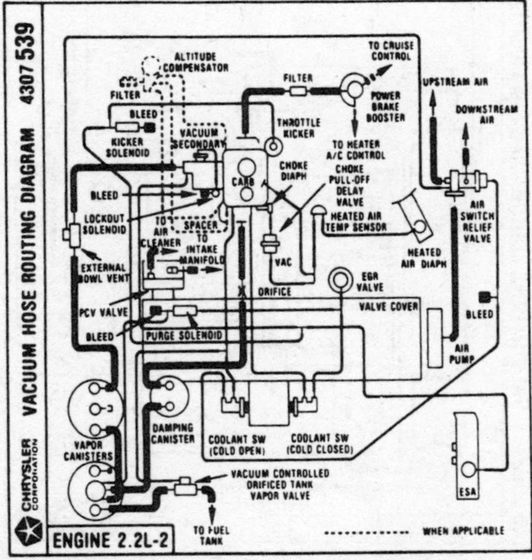

1985 California 2.2L vacuum hose routing

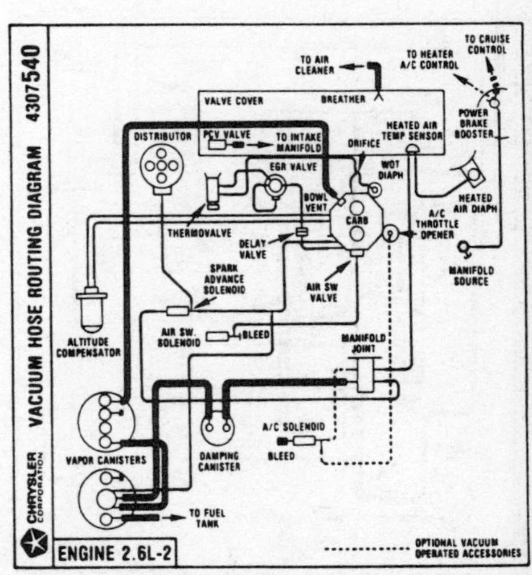

1985 Altitude 2.6L vacuum hose routing

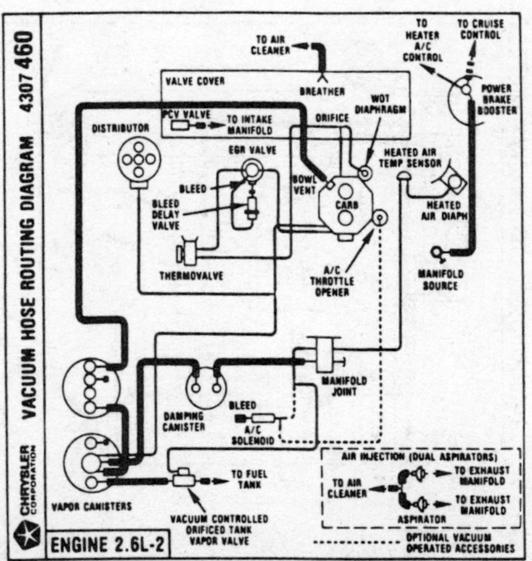

1985 Federal 2.6L vacuum hose routing

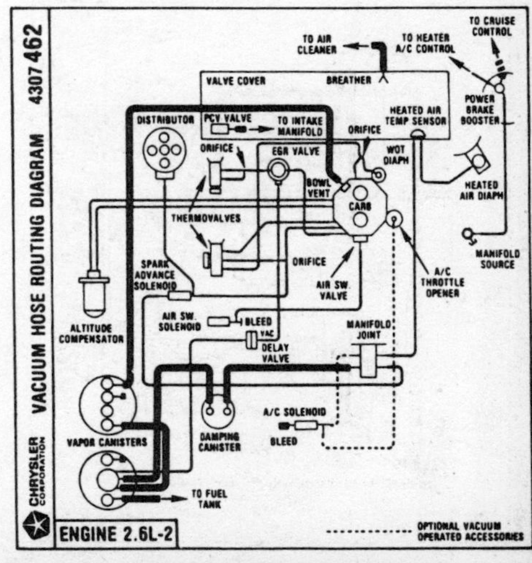

1985 California 2.6L vacuum hose routing

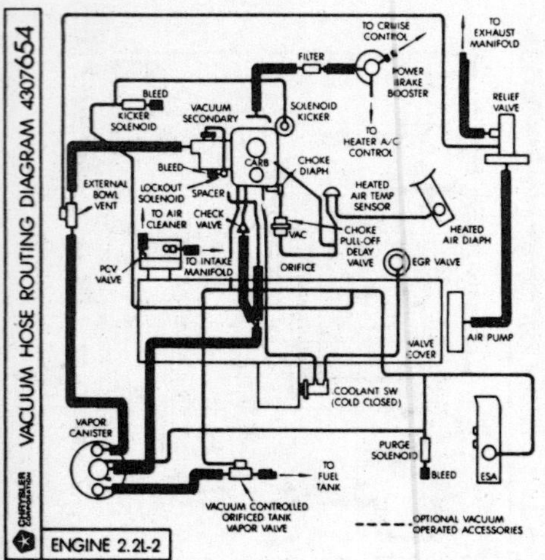

1986 Federal 2.2L vacuum hose routing

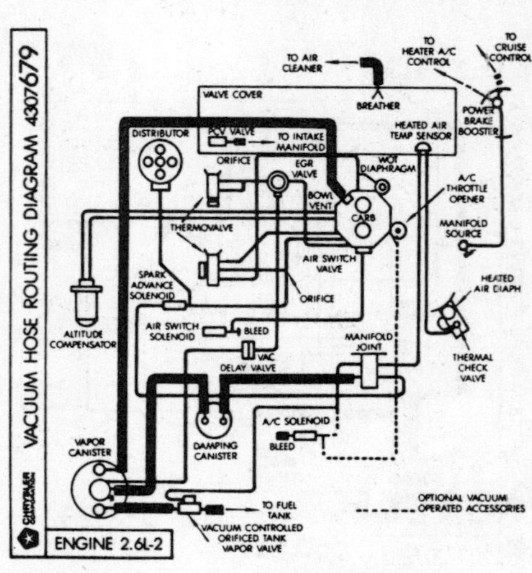

1986 California 2.6L vacuum hose routing

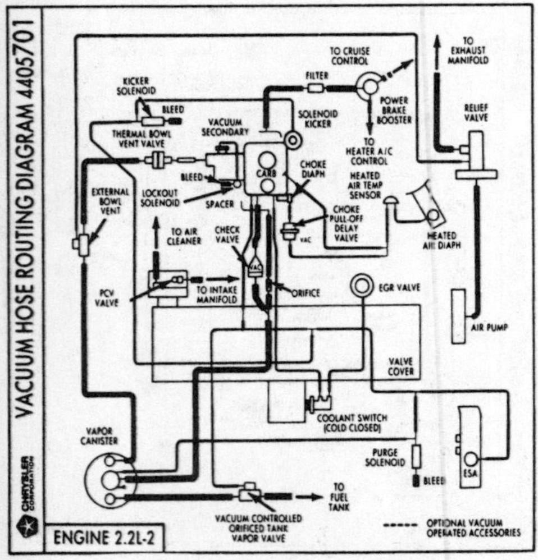

1987 Federal 2.2L vacuum hose routing

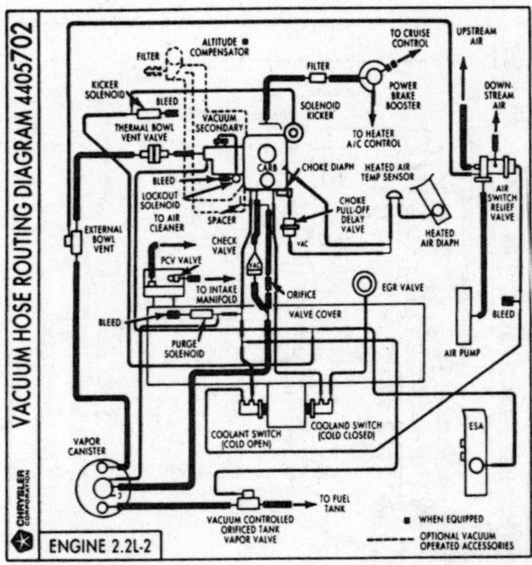

1987 California 2.2L vacuum hose routing

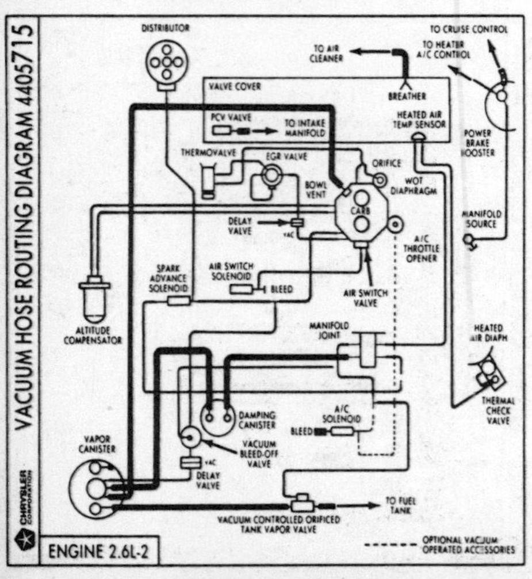

1987 Federal 2.6L vacuum hose routing

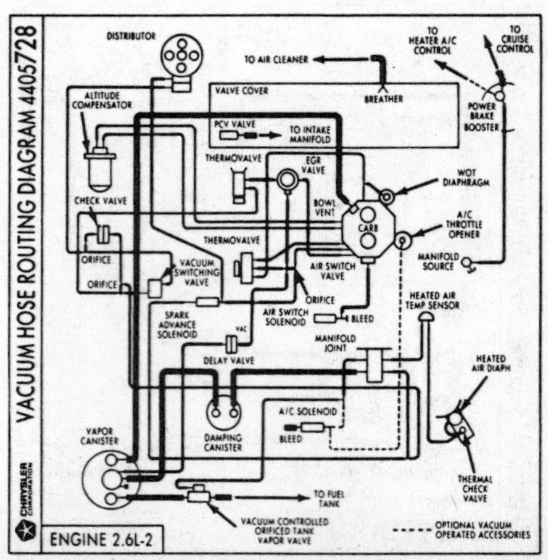

1987 California 2.6L vacuum hose routing

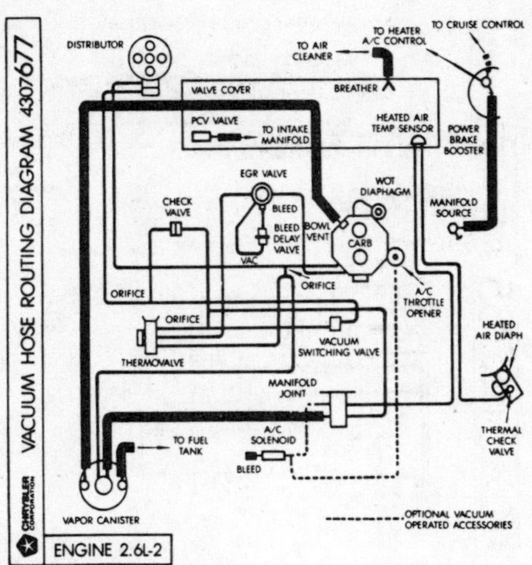

1987 Canadian 2.6L vacuum hose routing

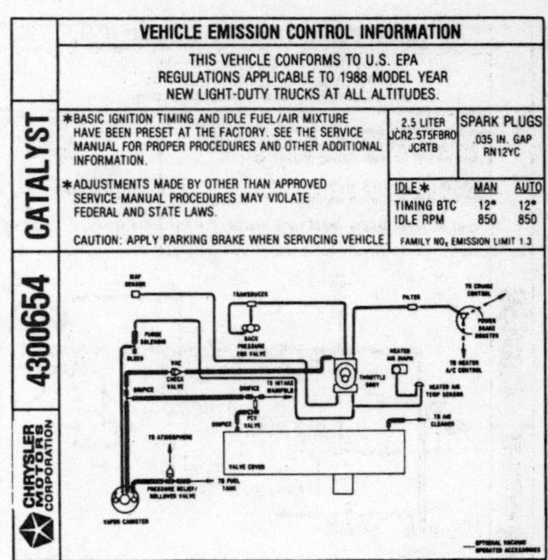

1988 Federal and Altitude 2.5L vacuum hose routing

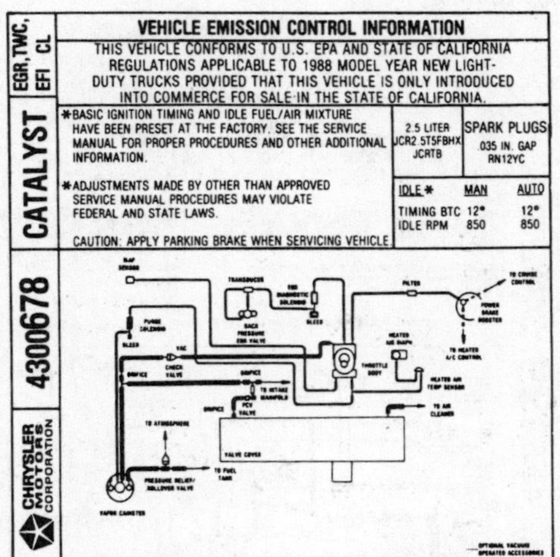

1988 California 2.5L vacuum hose routing

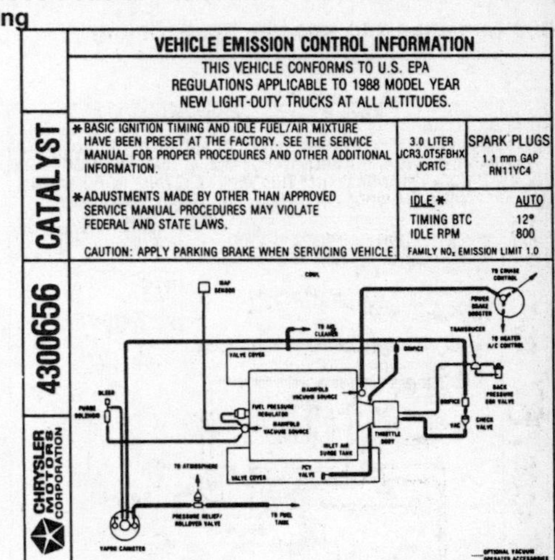

1988 Federal and Altitude 3.0L vacuum hose routing

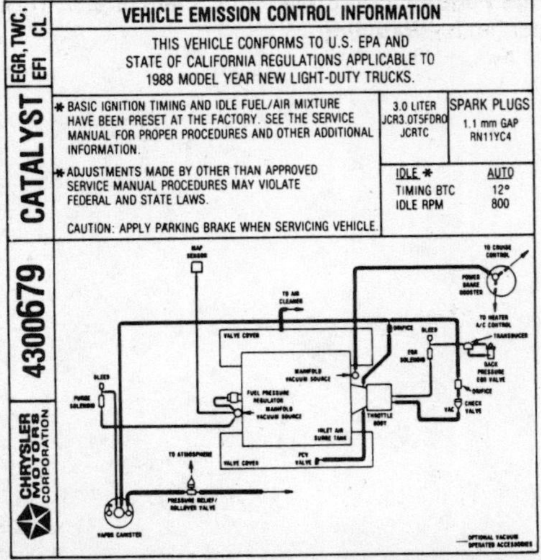

1988 California 3.0L vacuum hose routing

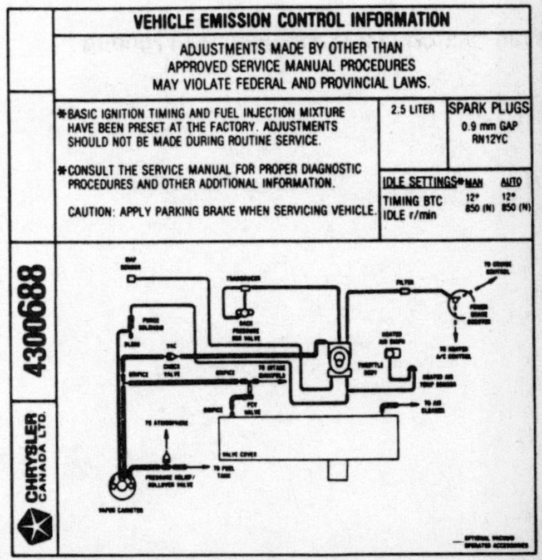

1988 Canadian 2.5L vacuum hose routing

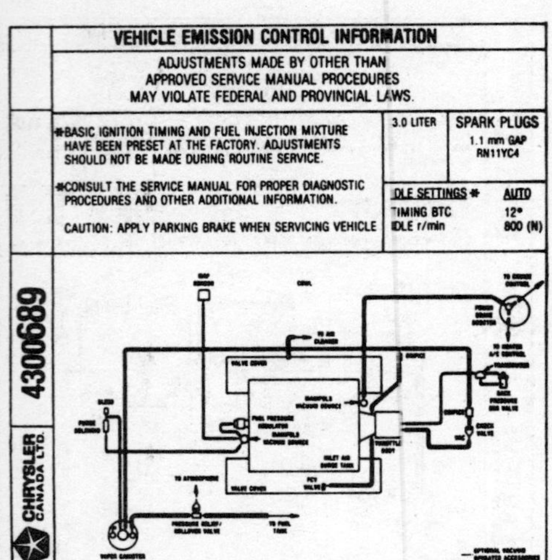

1988 Canadian 3.0L vacuum hose routing

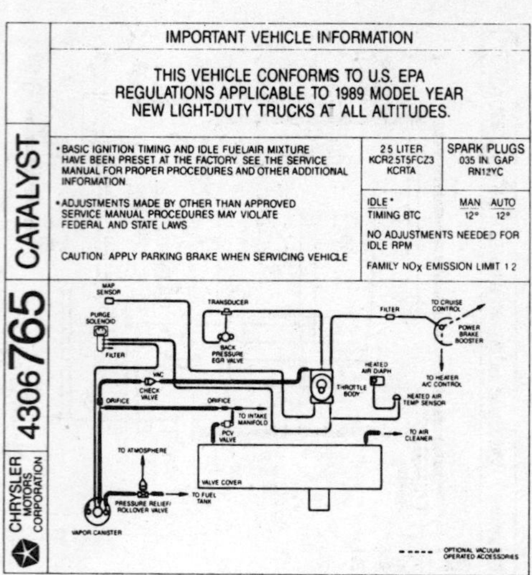

1989 Federal, Altitude and Canadian 2.5L vacuum hose routing

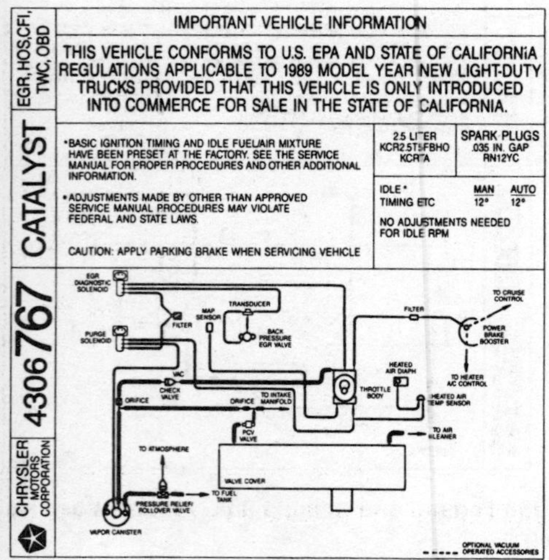

1989 California 2.5L vacuum hose routing

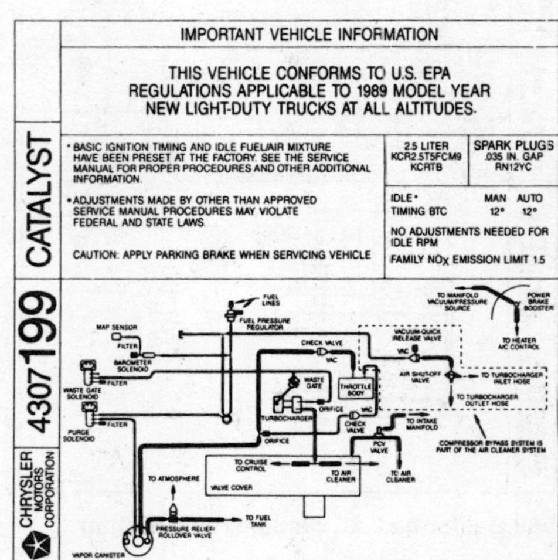

1989 Federal, California and Canadian 2.5L Turbo vacuum hose routing

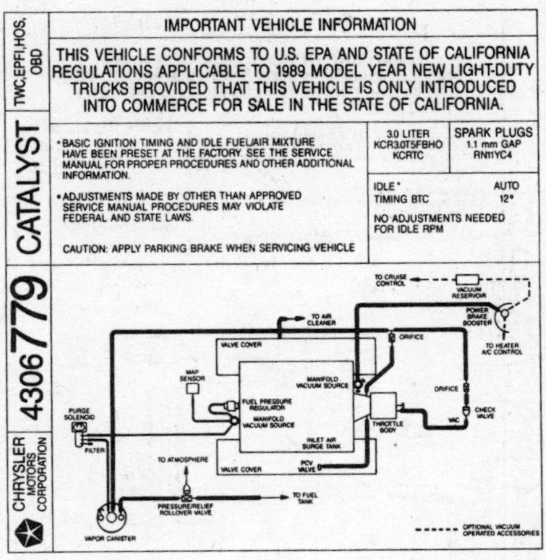

1989 California, Federal and Canadian 3.0L vacuum hose routing

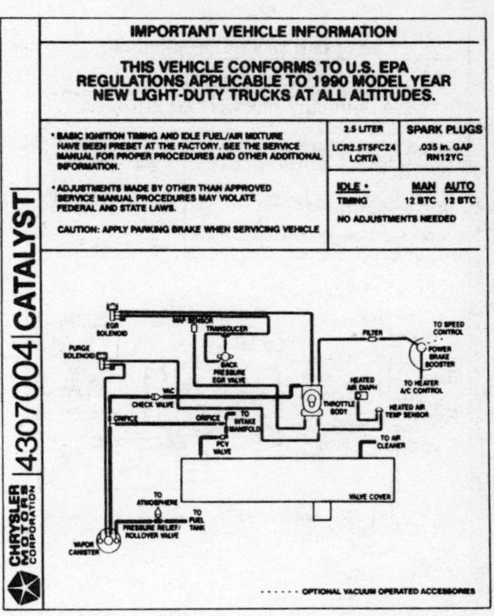

1990 Federal, Altitude and Canadian 2.5L vacuum hose routing

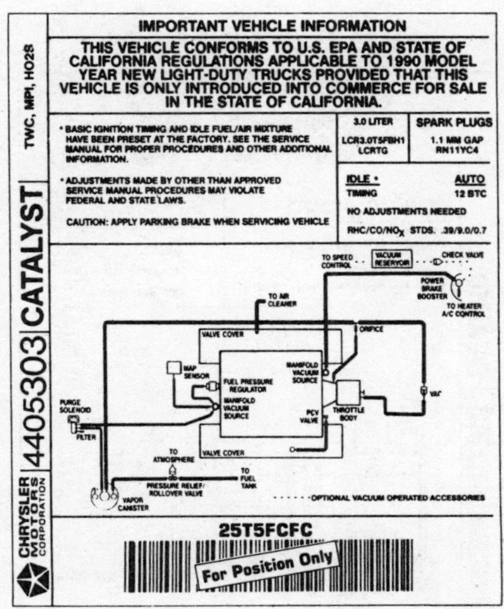

1990 Federal, Altitude and Canadian 3.0L vacuum hose routing

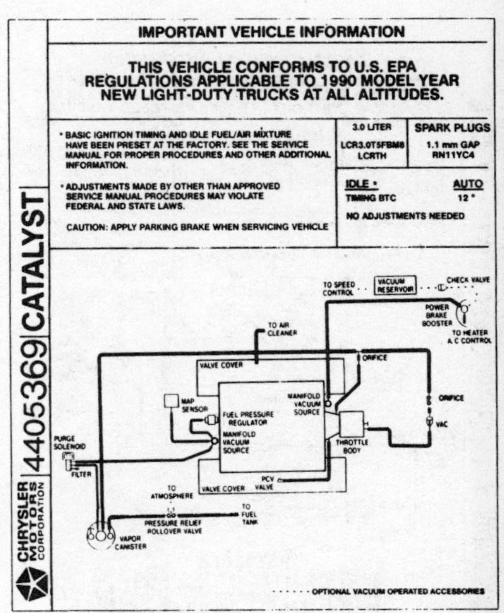

1990 Federal, Altitude and Canadian 3.0L vacuum hose routing – Town & Country

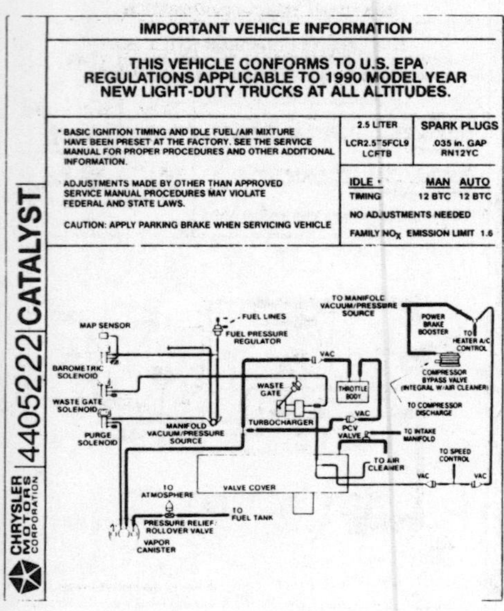

1990 Federal, California, Canadian and Altitude 2.5L Turbo vacuum hose routing

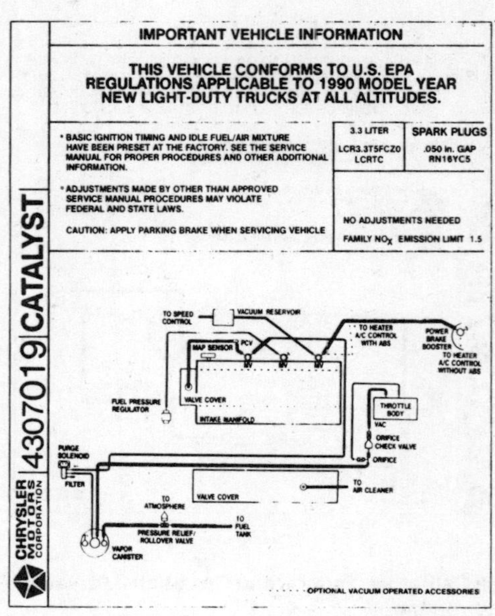

1990 Federal, Altitude and Canadian 3.3L vacuum hose routing

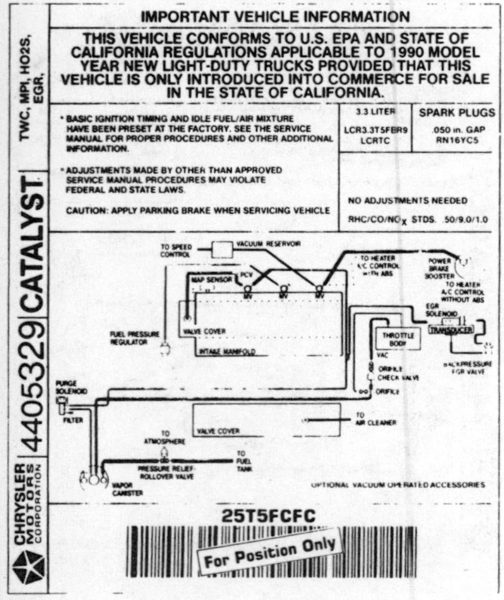

1990 California 3.3L vacuum hose routing

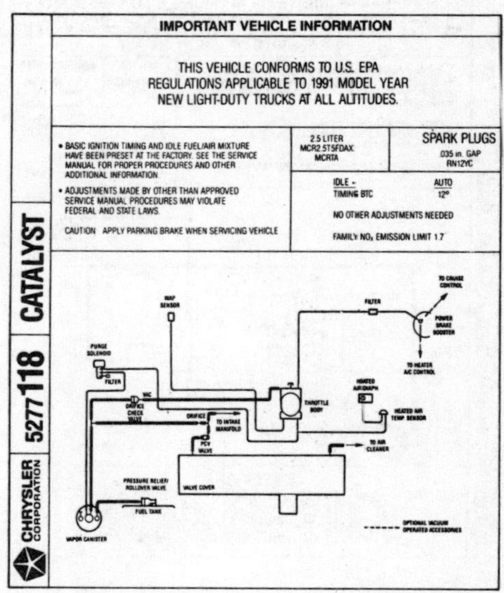

1991 Federal and Canadian 2.5L vacuum hose routing

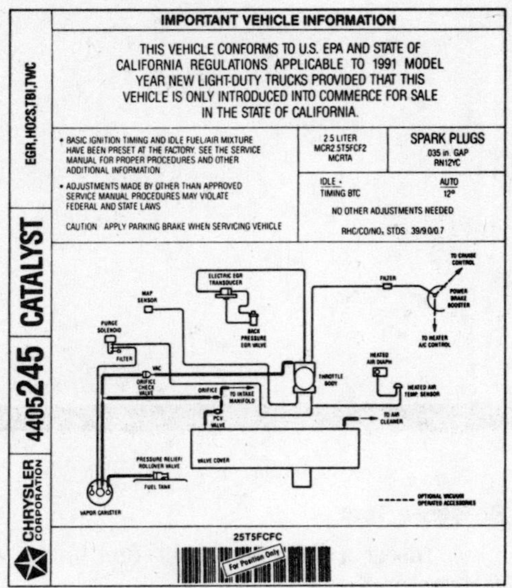

1991 California 2.5L vacuum hose routing

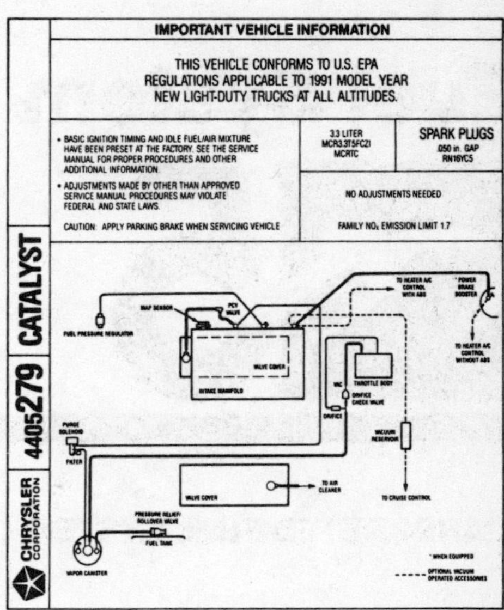

1991 Federal, California and Canadian 3.3L vacuum hose routing — front wheel drive

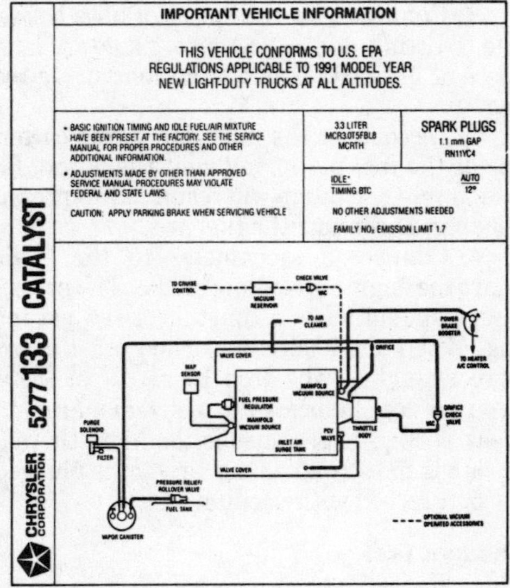

1991 Federal, California and Canadian 3.0L vacuum hose routing

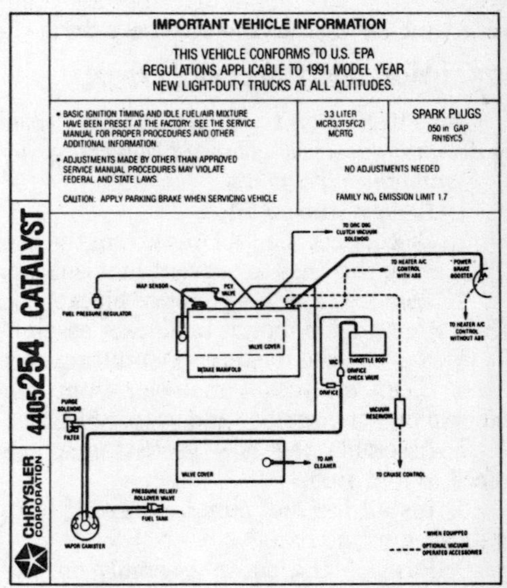

1991 Federal, California and Canadian 3.3L vacuum hose routing — all wheel drive

Fuel System

5

CARBURETED FUEL SYSTEM

Mechanical Fuel Pump

The 2.2L and 2.6L engine use a mechanical type fuel pump located on the side of the engine. The fuel pump is driven by an eccentric cam which is cast on the accessory drive shaft.

REMOVAL AND INSTALLATION

CAUTION: *Don't smoke when working around gasoline, cleaning solvent or other flammable substances.*

1. Remove the oil filter.
2. Disconnect the fuel lines from the pump.
3. Plug the lines to prevent fuel leakage.
4. Remove the fuel pump blocker strut from front engine mount to blocker assembly.
5. Remove the fuel pump mounting bolts.
6. Clean all gasket material from engine block mounting surface and spacer block.
7. Assemble the new gaskets and spacer block to fuel pump.
8. Install the fuel pump mounting bolts in pump mounting flange.
9. Position the pump assembly on engine block and torque bolts alternately to 250 inch lbs.
10. Connect the fuel lines to the pump.
11. Position the fuel pump blocker strut on blocker assembly and front engine mount. Tighten assembly.
12. Install the oil filter. Check and adjust oil level.
13. Start the engine and check fuel fittings for leaks.

TESTING

Volume Test

The fuel pump should supply 1 qt. of fuel in 1 minute or less at idle.

Pressure Test

1. Insert a T-fitting in the fuel line at the carburetor.

CAUTION: *Never smoke when working around gasoline! Avoid all sources of sparks or ignition. Gasoline vapors are EXTREMELY volatile!*

2. Connect a six inch piece of hose between the T-fitting and a pressure gauge. A longer piece of hose will result in an inaccurate reading.
3. Disconnect the inlet line to the carburetor at the fuel pump and vent the pump. Failure to vent the pump will result in low pressure reading. Reconnect the fuel line.
4. Connect a tachometer to the engine. Start the engine and allow to idle. The pressure gauge should show a constant $4^1/_2$-6 psi reading. When the engine is turned off, the pressure should slowly drop to zero. An instant drop to zero indicates a leaky diaphragm or weak spring. If pressure is too high, the main spring is too strong or the air vent is plugged.
5. Proceed with vacuum test.

Vacuum Test

1. Remove the inlet and outlet fuel lines from the pump.

CAUTION: *Never smoke when working around gasoline! Avoid all sources of sparks or ignition. Gasoline vapors are EXTREMELY volatile!*

2. Plug the fuel line to the carburetor to prevent fuel leakage.
3. Connect a vacuum gauge to the fuel pump inlet fitting.
4. Using the starter motor, turn the engine over several times and observe the vacuum gauge. The fuel pump should develop a minimum of 11 inches of vacuum.
5. If the vacuum readings are below specification, replace the pump.

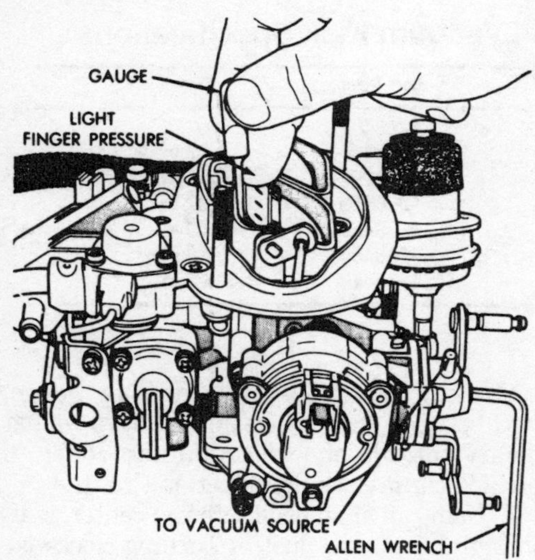

Choke vacuum kick adjustment on 2.2L enigne

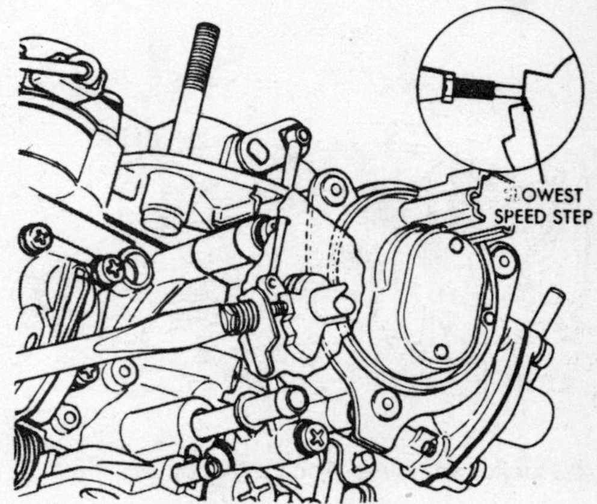

Fast idle adjustment on 2.2L engine

Carburetor

ADJUSTMENTS

Idle Speed/Solenoid Kicker Check – Holley

2.2L air conditioned vehicles are equipped with a solenoid kicker.

1. Start engine and run until operating temperature is reached.
2. Turn air conditioning switch on and set temperature control lever to the coldest position.
3. Notice the kicker solenoid for in and out movement as the compressor cycles on and off. If no movement occurred, check the kicker system for vacuum leaks. Check the operation of the vacuum solenoid. If no problems are found, replace the kicker.
4. If the kicker solenoid functions properly, turn off the air conditioning switch and shut engine off.

Solenoid Kicker Adjustment – Holley

1. Check ignition timing and adjust if necessary.
2. Disconnect and plug vacuum connector at the CVSCC.
3. Unplug connector at cooling fan and jumper harness so fan will run continuously.
4. Remove the PCV valve and allow it to draw underhood air.
5. Connect a tachometer to the engine.
6. Ground the carburetor switch with a jumper wire.
7. Disconnect the oxygen system test lead located on the left fender shield on vehicles equipped with 6520 carburetors.
8. Start the engine and run until normal operating temperature is reached.
9. Adjust idle speed screw to specification given in under hood label.
10. Reconnect PCV valve, oxygen connector and CVSCC vacuum connector.
11. Remove the jumper from carburetor switch.
12. Remove the jumper from radiator fan and reconnect harness.

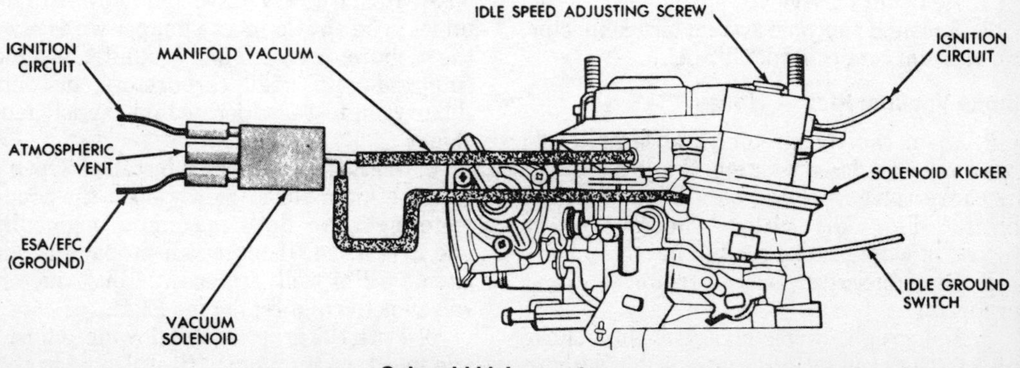

Solenoid kicker system

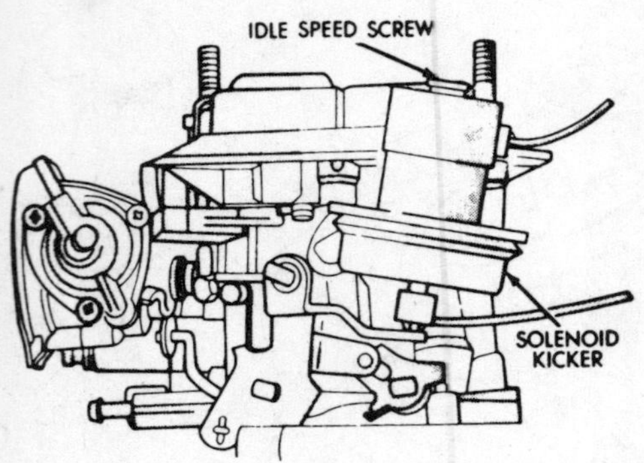

A/C kicker adjustment on 2.2L engine

NOTE: *After Steps 10, 11 and 12 are completed, the idle speed may change slightly. This is normal and engine speed should not be readjusted.*

Fast Idle – Holley

Before adjusting fast idle, check and adjust ignition timing.

1. Disconnect the electrical harness at the radiator fan and install a jumper wire so the fan will run continuously.
2. Remove the PCV valve and allow it to draw under hood air.
3. Disconnect and plug the vacuum connector at the CVSCC.
4. Install a tachometer.
5. Jumper the carburetor switch.
6. Disconnect oxygen system test connector located on the left fender shield by shock tower.
7. Start engine and allow to reach normal operating temperature.
8. Open throttle slightly and place adjustment screw on the lowest step of fast idle cam.
9. Adjust the fast idle screw to specification shown on under hood VECI label. Return engine to idle and repeat Step 8, readjust if necessary.
10. Stop engine, remove jumper wire from radiator fan harness and reconnect connector.
11. Reinstall PCV valve.
12. Reconnect oxygen system test connector, and vacuum connector at CVSCC.

Choke Vacuum Kick – Holley

1. Open the carburetor throttle and hold choke valve in closed position. While maintaining choke valve in closed position, release the throttle. Fast idle system should now be trapped at closed choke condition.
2. Disconnect carburetor vacuum source at carburetor.
3. Using light finger pressure, close choke valve to the smallest opening possible without disturbing linkage system.

Vacuum Kick Specifications

Carb Number	Setting
4288460	.07 in.
4288461	.07 in.
4288262	.07 in.
4288263	.07 in.
4288456	.08 in.
4288458	.08 in.
4288459	.08 in.

4. Using the proper size drill or gauge, insert between choke valve and air horn wall at primary throttle end of carburetor. Refer to Choke Vacuum Kick Specification Chart.
5. Using an allen head screw in center of diaphragm housing, adjust by turning clockwise or counterclockwise to obtain correct setting.
6. Reconnect vacuum hose to carburetor vacuum source.

Mixture Adjustment (Propane Assisted)

NOTE: *The following procedures require the use of a propane cylinder, vacuum hose and a special control valve to provide proper enrichment. Any adjustments made other than those in the following procedures, may violate Federal and State Laws.*

1. Remove the concealment plug. Refer to Steps 18 through 20 under carburetor disassembling procedure.
2. Set the parking brake and place the transaxle in neutral position. Turn off all accessories. Start engine and allow to idle on second highest step of fast idle cam until normal operating temperature is reached. Return engine to idle.
3. Disconnect vacuum connector at CVSCC and plug. Disconnect the vacuum hose to the heated air door sensor at the three way connector, and in its place, install the supply hose from the propane bottle.
4. Unplug the radiator fan connector and jumper harness so the fan will run continuously. Remove PCV valve and allow it to draw under hood air. Connect a jumper wire between the carburetor switch and ground. On vehicles equipped with 6520 carburetors, disconnect the oxygen test lead located on the left fender shield.
5. With the air cleaner installed. Open the propane main valve. Slowly open the propane metering valve until maximum engine RPM idle is reached. If too much propane is added engine RPM will decrease. Adjust metering valve for the highest engine RPM.
6. With the propane still flowing, adjust the idle speed screw on top of the solenoid to obtain specified RPM on under hood label. Again

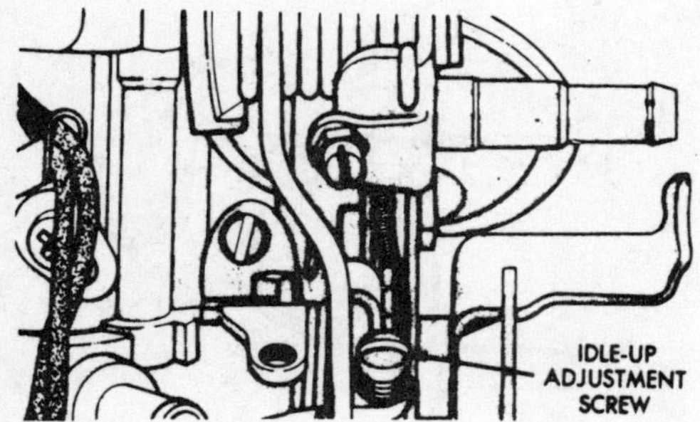

Idle up adjustment on the Mikuni carburetor

adjust the propane metering valve to get the highest engine RPM. If the maximum RPM changes, readjust the idle speed screw to the specified propane RPM.

7. Shut off the propane main valve and allow the engine to stabilize. With the air cleaner still in place, slowly adjust the mixture screws to obtain the specified set RPM. Pause for a few seconds after each adjustment to allow engine speed to stabilized.

8. Again turn on the propane main valve and adjust the metering valve to obtain the highest engine RPM. If the maximum speed differs more than 25 RPM, repeat Steps 5 through 8.

9. Shut off both valves on propane cylinder. Disconnect the propane vacuum supply hose and connect the vacuum hose to the heated air door sensor at the three way connector.

10. Install concealment plug. Proceed with fast idle adjustment starting at Step 7.

Anti-Dieseling Adjustment – Holley

NOTE: *Always check and adjust ignition timing before any idle speed adjustment is performed.*

1. Warm engine to normal operating temperature. Place transaxle in neutral position and set parking brake.

2. Turn off all accessories. Jumper wire between carburetor switch and ground.

3. Remove the RED wire from the 6-Way connector (carburetor side).

4. Adjust the throttle stop speed screw to obtain 700 rpm.

5. Reconnect RED wire and remove jumper from carburetor switch.

Idle RPM – Mikuni Carburetor

1. Check and adjust ignition timing.

2. Set the parking brake and place transaxle in neutral. Turn off all accessories.

3. Disconnect the radiator fan.

4. Connect a tachometer to the engine.

5. Start engine and run until operating temperature is reached.

6. Disconnect cooling fan. Run engine at 2500 RPM for 10 seconds and return to idle.

7. Wait 2 minutes and record RPM. If RPM differs from VECI under hood specification label, turn idle speed adjusting screw until specification is obtained.

8. On air condition models, set the temperature lever to the coldest position and turn air conditioning switch on. With the air condition running, set the engine speed to 900 RPM using the idle-up adjustment screw.

9. Shut engine off. Connect the cooling fan and remove tachometer.

Fast Idle – Mikuni Carburetor

1. Connect a tachometer to the engine. Check and adjust ignition timing.

2. Set the parking brake and place transaxle in neutral. Turn off all accessories.

3. Start engine and run until operating temperature is reached.

4. Disconnect radiator fan. Remove and plug vacuum advance hose at distributor.

5. Open the throttle slightly and install Tool 4812-2C on cam follower pin.

6. Release throttle lever and adjust fast idle adjusting screw to specification shown on VECI under hood label.

7. Remove tool and shut engine off. Reconnect fan, unplug and reconnect vacuum hose, and remove tachometer.

Idle Mixture (Propane Assist) Mikuni Carburetor

NOTE: *The following procedures require the use of a propane cylinder, vacuum hose and a special control valve to provide proper enrichment. Any adjustments made other than those in the following procedures, may violate Federal and State Laws.*

1. Remove concealment plug. Refer to Concealment Plug Removal procedure. Check and adjust ignition timing.

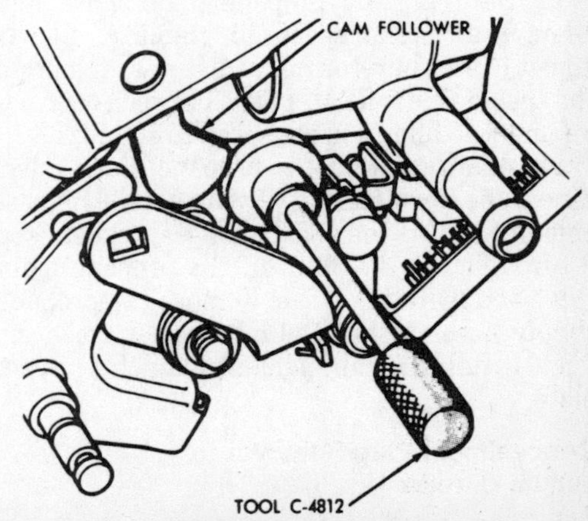

Installing tool C4812 on the Mikuni carburetor

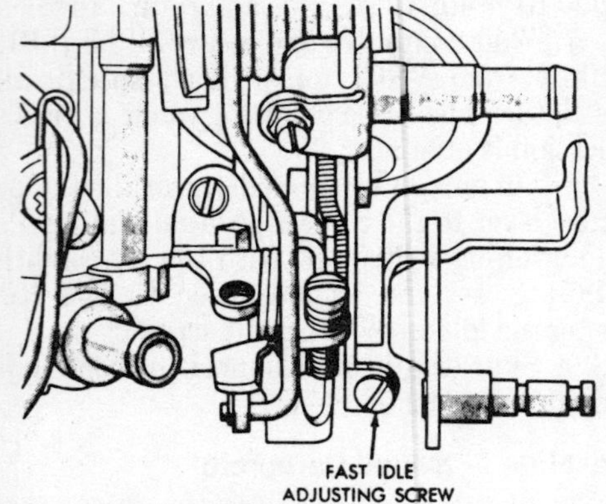

Fast idle adjustment on the Mikuni carburetor

2. Set the parking brake and place transaxle in neutral. Turn off all accessories.
3. Disconnect the cooling fan.
4. Connect a tachometer to the engine.
5. Start engine and run until operating temperature is reached.
6. Disconnect cooling fan. Run engine at 2500 RPM for 10 seconds and return to idle. Allow engine to idle for 2 minutes.
7. Remove the air cleaner fresh air duct. Place the propane bottle in a safe location and in an upright position. Insert the propane supply hose approximately 4 inches into the air cleaner snorkel.
8. Open the propane bottle main valve. Slowly open the metering valve until the highest engine RPM is reached. If too much propane is added, the engine RPM will decrease. Fine Tune the propane metering valve to obtain the highest engine RPM.
9. With the propane still flowing, adjust the idle speed screw to the specified RPM shown on VECI under hood label. Again Fine Tune the propane metering valve to get the highest engine RPM. If the RPM increases, readjust the idle speed screw to specification.
10. Shut off the propane main valve and allow the engine speed to stabilize. Slowly adjust the carburetor mixture screws to obtain the specified idle RPM. Pause between each adjustment to allow engine speed to stabilize.
11. Again turn on the propane main valve, Fine Tune the metering valve to get the highest engine RPM. If the RPM changes, repeat Step 8 through 10. 12. Shut off the propane main valve and metering valve. Remove the propane supply hose. Install the air cleaner fresh air duct. Install the concealment plug and impact plate.

Concealment Plug Removal
Mikuni Carburetor

1. Remove the impact plate, if used.

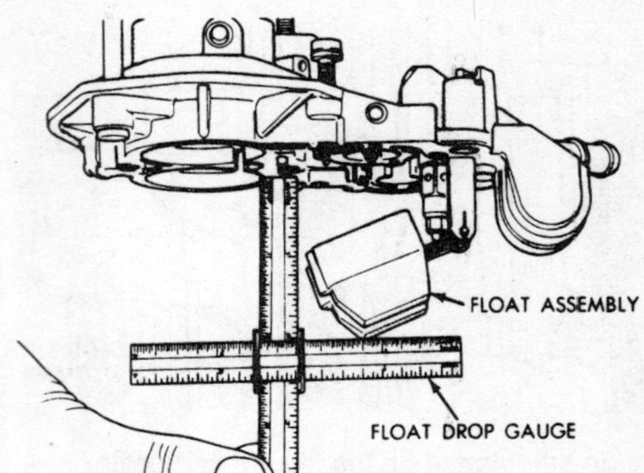

Measuring the float drop on the 2.2L carburetor

2. Remove the vacuum connector from high altitude compensator (HAC) fitting on carburetor, if used.
3. With an eight inch long 1/4″ diameter drill bit, drill out concealment plug at location show.
4. Remove concealment plug.

Float Level

MIKUNI CARBURETOR

1. Remove air horn from carburetor main body.
2. Remove air horn gasket and invert air horn.
3. Using a gauge measure the distance from bottom of float to air horn surface. The distance should be 20mm ± 1mm. If distance is not within specification, the shim under the needle and seat must be changed. Shim pack MD606952 or equivalent has three shims: 0.3mm, 0.4mm, or 0.5mm. Adding or removing one shim will change the float level three its thickness.

REMOVAL AND INSTALLATION

2.2L Engine

CAUTION: *Never remove a carburetor from an engine that has just been road tested.*

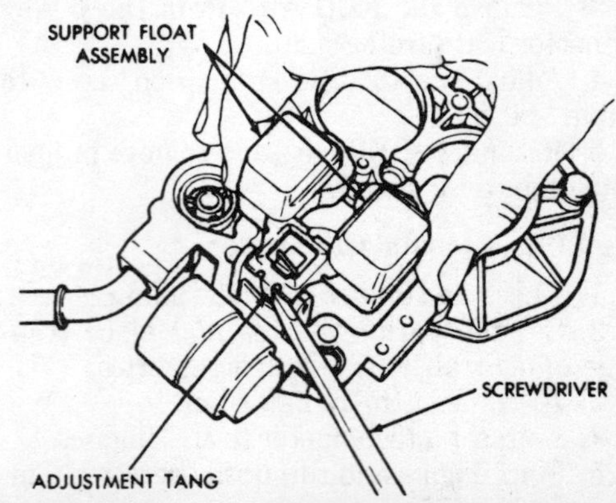

Float drop adjustment on the 2.2L carburetor

Allow the engine to cool down to prevent accidental fuel ignition or personal injury.

1. Disconnect the negative battery cable.
2. Remove the air cleaner.
3. Remove the fuel tank filler cap to relieve fuel system pressure.
4. Disconnect all carburetor electrical wiring.

CAUTION: *Never smoke when working around gasoline! Avoid all sources of sparks or ignition. Gasoline vapors are EXTREMELY volatile!*

5. Disconnect the carburetor inlet line and block off line to prevent fuel leakage.
6. Disconnect the throttle linkage. Label and remove all vacuum hoses.
7. Remove the carburetor mounting nuts and remove carburetor.
8. Inspect the mating surfaces of the carburetor and isolator for nicks, burrs, dirt or other damage. It is not necessary to disturb the isolator to intake manifold mounting screws, unless the isolator is damage.
9. Carefully install carburetor on engine. Install nuts evenly and torque to 200 inch lbs. Make certain throttle plates and choke plate opens and closes properly when operated.
10. Connect the throttle linkage and fuel inlet line.
11. Connect the vacuum hoses.
12. Connect the negative battery cable.
13. Install the air cleaner and adjust the carburetor.

2.6L Engine

CAUTION: *Never remove a carburetor from an engine that has just been road tested. Allow the engine to cool down to prevent accidental fuel ignition or personal injury.*

1. Disconnect the negative battery cable.
2. Remove the air cleaner.
3. Remove the fuel tank filler cap.to relieve fuel system pressure.
4. Disconnect the carburetor protector and all carburetor electrical wiring.
5. Drain the cooling system. Label and remove the vacuum hoses and coolant hoses at carburetor.

CAUTION: *When draining the coolant, keep in mind that cats and dogs are attracted by the ethylene glycol antifreeze, and are quite likely to drink any that is left in an uncovered container or in puddles on the ground. This will prove fatal in sufficient quantity. Always drain the coolant into a sealable container. Coolant should be reused unless it is contaminated or several years old.*

6. Disconnect the carburetor inlet line and block off line to prevent fuel leakage.

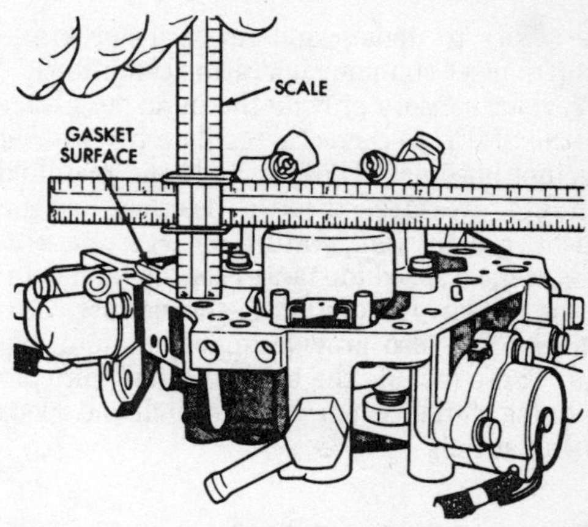

Measuring the float level on the Mikuni carburetor

CAUTION: *Never smoke when working around gasoline! Avoid all sources of sparks or ignition. Gasoline vapors are EXTREMELY volatile!*

7. Disconnect the throttle linkage.
8. Remove the carburetor mounting bolts and nuts and remove carburetor.
9. Inspect the mating surfaces of the carburetor and intake manifold for nicks, burrs, dirt or other damage.
10. Install a new gasket on intake manifold.
11. Carefully install the carburetor on the engine. Install mounting bolts and nuts. Tighten evenly and torque to 150 inch lbs. Make certain throttle plates and choke plate opens and closes properly when operated.
12. Connect the throttle linkage, fuel line and electrical connectors.
13. Install and tighten carburetor protector.
14. Fill the cooling system.
15. Connect the negative battery cable.
16. Install the air cleaner and adjust the carburetor.

CHRYSLER MULTI-POINT ELECTRONIC FUEL INJECTION

General Information

The turbocharged and non-turbocharged Multi-Point Electronic Fuel Injection (MPI) system combines an electronic fuel and spark advance control system with a turbocharged intake system or cross type intake system. At the center of this system is a digital computer containing a microprocessor known as a Single Module Engine Controller (SMEC) that regulates ignition timing, air/fuel ratio, emission control devices, idle speed, cooling fan, charging system, turbocharger waste gate (on turbo models) and speed control. This component has the ability to update and revise its programming to meet changing operating conditions.

Various sensors provide the input necessary for the SMEC to correctly regulate fuel flow at the fuel injectors. These include the manifold absolute pressure, throttle position, oxygen sensor, coolant temperature, charge temperature, vehicle speed (distance) sensors and detonation sensor. In addition to the sensors, various switches also provide important information. These include the neutral-safety, air conditioning clutch switch, brake switch and speed control switch.

SERVICE PRECAUTIONS

- When working around any part of the fuel system, take precautionary steps to prevent fire and/or explosion.
- Disconnect negative terminal from battery (except when testing with battery voltage is required).
- When ever possible, use a flashlight instead of a drop light.
- Keep all open flame and smoking material out of the work area.
- Use a shop cloth or similar to catch fuel when opening a fuel system.
- Always relieve fuel system pressure before servicing any part of the fuel system.
- Always use eye protection.
- Always keep a dry chemical (class B) fire extinguisher near the area.

FUEL PRESSURE RELEASE

All Engines

CAUTION: *The fuel injection system is under a constant pressure. Before servicing any part of the fuel system, the system pressure must be relieved.*

1. Loosen the fuel filler cap to release the pressure.
2. Remove the wiring harness connector from the injector.
3. Connect a jumper wire to the No. 1 terminal of the injector harness connector and to engine ground.
4. Connect a jumper wire to the positive terminal No. 2 of the injector harness and touch battery positive post for no longer than 5 seconds. This releases system pressure.
5. Remove test equipment and continue fuel system service.

FUEL PRESSURE

Testing

2.5L TURBO ENGINES

1. Release fuel system pressure.
2. Remove the protective cover from the service valve on the fuel rail.
3. Connect a suitable fuel pressure gauge to fuel rail service valve.
4. Using the DRBII tester, with the key in the **RUN** position, use "Actuate Outputs Test-Auto Shutdown Relay" this will activate the fuel pump for 1.5 seconds to pressurize the system.
5. If the gauge reads 53–57 psi fuel pressure is correct and no further testing is necessary. Remove all test equipment.
6. If pressure is not correct, record the pressure and continue with the test procedure.
7. If the fuel pressure is below specifications, install the fuel pressure gauge in the fuel supply line, between the fuel tank and fuel filter at the rear of the vehicle.
8. Repeat test. If pressure is 5 psi higher than recorded pressure replace the fuel filter. If no change in pressure is observed, gently squeeze the return hose. If the pressure increases replace the pressure regulator. If no change is observed check for a defective fuel pump or plugged filter sock.

NOTE: *The test (Step 9) should be performed when fuel tank is a least 1/2–3/4 full.*

9. If the fuel pressure is above specifications, remove the fuel return line hose from the chassis line at fuel tank and connect a 3 foot piece of fuel hose to the return line. Position the other end in suitable container (2 gallons or more). Repeat test and, if pressure is now correct, check in-tank return hose for kinking.
10. Replace the fuel tank assembly if the in-tank reservoir check valve or the aspirator jet is blocked.
11. If the pressure is still above specifications, remove fuel return hose from fuel pressure regulator. Connect a suitable hose to the fuel pressure regulator nipple and place the other in a suitable container. Repeat test. If pressure is now correct, check for restricted fuel line. If no change is observed, replace fuel pressure regulator.

3.0L AND 3.3L ENGINE

1. Release fuel system pressure.
2. Disconnect the fuel supply hose from the engine fuel line assembly. Connect a suitable fuel pressure gauge between fuel supply hose and engine fuel line assembly.

3. Using the DRBII tester, with the key in the **RUN** position, use "Actuate Outputs Test-Auto Shutdown Relay" this will activate the fuel pump for 1.5 seconds to pressurize the system.

4. If the gauge reads 46–50 psi fuel pressure is correct and no further testing is necessary. Remove all test equipment.

5. If pressure is not correct, record the pressure and continue with the test procedure.

6. If the fuel pressure is below specifications, install the fuel pressure gauge in the fuel supply line, between the fuel tank and fuel filter at the rear of the vehicle.

7. Repeat test. If pressure is 5 psi higher than recorded pressure replace the fuel filter. If no change in pressure is observed, gently squeeze the return hose. If the pressure increases replace the pressure regulator. If no change is observed check for a defective fuel pump or plugged filter sock.

NOTE: *The test (Step 8) should be performed when fuel tank is a least $^1/_2$–$^3/_4$ full.*

8. If the fuel pressure is above specifications, remove the fuel return line hose from the chassis line at fuel tank and connect a 3 foot piece of fuel hose to the return line. Position the other end in suitable container (2 gallons or more). Repeat test and, if pressure is now correct, check in-tank return hose for kinking.

9. Replace the fuel tank assembly if the in-tank reservoir check valve or the aspirator jet is blocked.

10. If the pressure is still above specifications, remove fuel return hose from fuel pressure regulator. Connect a suitable hose to the fuel return line and place the other end in a suitable container. Repeat the test. If the pressure is now correct, check for restricted fuel line. If no change has occured, replace the fuel pressure regulator.

WASTEGATE CALIBRATION

Check

2.5L Turbo Engines

1. Disconnect the vacuum hose from the wategate diaphragm.

2. Connect a cooling system pressure tester or equivalent to the wastegate diaphragm.

3. Slowly apply pressure while watching the actuator rod.

4. If the wastegate actuator rod moves more than 0.015 inch before 2–4 psi (4 psi on Turbo II) or does not move after 5 psi is applied the wastegate is faulty.

5. Service faulty component as necessary.

Component Replacement

THROTTLE BODY

Removal and Installation

When servicing the fuel portion of the throttle body, it will be necessary to bleed fuel pressure before opening any hoses refer to Fuel Pressure Release procedure. Always reassemble throttle body components with new O-rings and seals where applicable. Use care when removing fuel hoses to prevent damage to hose or hose nipple. Always use new hose clamps of the correct type when reassembling and torque hose clamps to 10 inch lbs. (1 Nm).

1. Drain engine coolant, if necessary, and release fuel pressure. Disconnect negative battery cable.

2. Remove air cleaner to throttle body screws (or nuts), loosen hose clamp and remove air cleaner adaptor.

NOTE: *When removing accelerator cable, note position or adjustment for correct installation.*

3. Remove accelerator, speed control and transaxle kick-down cables and return spring.

4. Remove throttle cable bracket from throttle body.

5. Disconnect all necessary electrical connector(s).

6. Disconnect vacuum hoses from throttle body.

7. Loosen throttle body-to-turbocharger hose clamp if so equipped.

8. Remove throttle body-to-intake manifold or adapter screws (or nuts). Always note position of retaining bolts as some may be different in length.

9. Remove throttle body and gasket.

10. Reverse the above procedure for installation.

NOTE: *If fuel system hoses are to be replaced, only hoses marked EFI/EFM may be used.*

THROTTLE POSITION SENSOR

Removal and Installation

1. Disconnect negative battery cable and 3-way throttle position sensor wiring connector.

2. Remove 2 screws, mounting throttle position sensor to throttle body.

3. Lift throttle position sensor off throttle shaft.

4. To install, reverse removal procedure and torque screws to 17 inch lbs. (2 Nm).

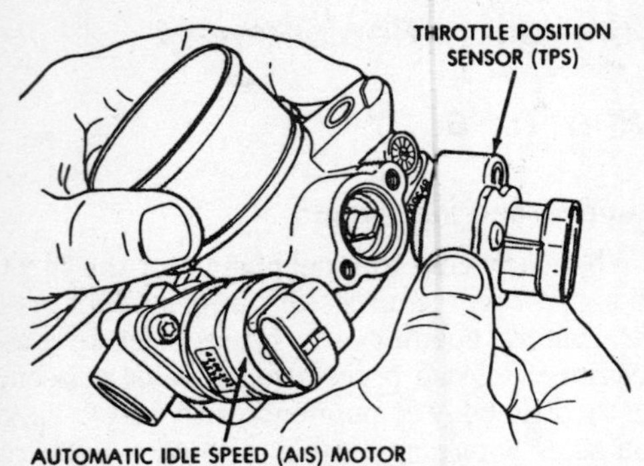

Throttle position sensor servicing – 3.0L/3.3L engines

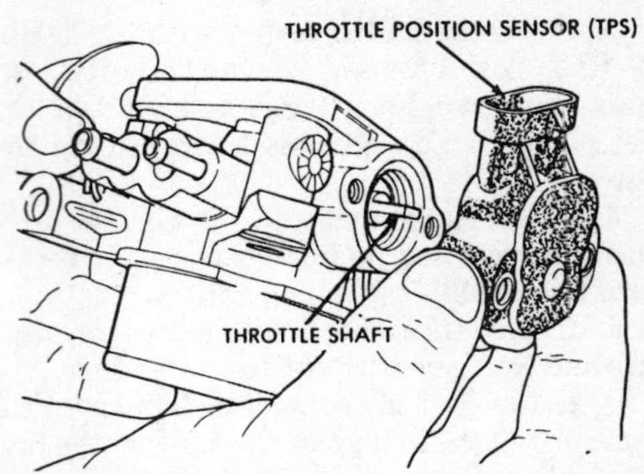

Throttle position sensor servicing – 2.5L turbo engine

AUTOMATIC IDLE SPEED (AIS) MOTOR

Removal and Installation

1. Disconnect negative battery cable and 4-way AIS motor wiring connector.
2. Remove 2 screws that mount AIS motor to throttle body.
3. Remove AIS motor from throttle body. Make certain that the O-ring is on the AIS motor.
4. To install, place new O-ring on AIS motor. If pintle measures more than 1 inch, it must be retracted by using the AIS Motor Test in the Actuate Outputs mode of the DRBII. (Battery must be reconnected for this operation.)
5. Carefully place AIS motor into throttle body.
6. Install 2 mounting screws and torque to 17 inch lbs. (2 Nm).
7. Connect 4 way wiring connector to AIS motor and reconnect negative battery cable.

FUEL INJECTOR RAIL ASSEMBLY

Removal and Installation

2.5L TURBO ENGINES

1. Perform fuel system pressure release procedure.
2. Disconnect negative battery cable.
3. Remove air cleaner assembly.
4. Disconnect detonation (knock) sensor and fuel injector wiring connectors.
5. Loosen fuel supply hose clamp at fuel rail inlet and remove hose. Wrap a shop towel around hose to absorb any fuel spillage which may occur when removing.
6. Loosen fuel return hose clamp at the fuel pressure regulator and remove the hose. Wrap a shop towel around the hose to absorb any fuel spillage, which may occur when removing the hose.
7. Disconnect the vacuum hose from the fuel pressure regulator.
8. Remove the fuel pressure regulator mounting bolts from the fuel rail.
9. Remove the fuel pressure regulator from the fuel rail.
10. Remove the PCV vacuum harness and vacuum vapor harness from the intake manifold.
11. Remove the fuel rail to the valve cover bracket screw. Remove the knock sensor connector from the sensor.
12. Remove the fuel rail to intake manifold mounting bolts.
13. Remove fuel rail and injector assembly by pulling rail so that injectors come straight out of there ports.
14. Be careful not to damage rubber injector

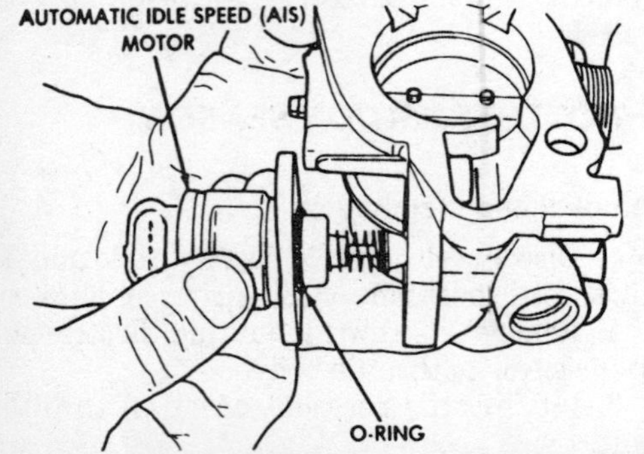

Automatic Idle Speed (AIS) motor servicing – 2.5L turbo engine

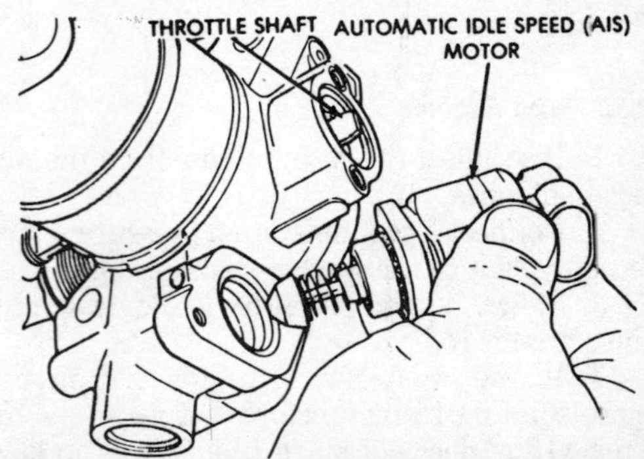

Automatic Idle Speed (AIS) motor servicing – 3.0L/3.3L engine

O-ring upon removal from ports.

15. Remove fuel rail assembly from vehicle.

16. Do not remove fuel injectors until fuel rail assembly has been completely removed from vehicle.

To install:

17. To install, be sure injectors are seated into receiver cup, with lock ring in place.

18. Install injector wiring harness to injectors and fasten into wiring clips.

19. Make sure injector holes are clean and all plugs have been removed.

20. Lube injector O-ring with a drop of clean engine oil to ease installation.

21. Put tip of each injector into respective ports. Push assembly into place until injectors are seated in ports.

22. Install attaching bolts and ground eyelet. Torque bolts to 250 inch lbs. (28 Nm).

23. Connect detonation (knock) sensor wire connector to sensor. Install fuel rail to valve cover bracket screw.

24. Lube fuel pressure O-ring with a drop of clean engine oil and install into receiver cup on fuel rail.

25. Install attaching nuts and torque to 65 inch lbs. (7 Nm).

26. Install the PCV system hose harness and vacuum hose harness.

27. Reconnect vacuum hose from fuel pressure regulator.

28. Connect fuel return hose to fuel pressure regulator tighten hose clamp.

29. Connect fuel supply hose to fuel rail inlet and tighten hose clamp.

30. Connect fuel injector and detonation (knock) sensor wiring connector.

31. Install air cleaner assembly.

32. Connect negative battery cable.

33. Use ATM tester to test for leaks.

3.0L ENGINE

1. Perform fuel system pressure release procedure.

2. Disconnect negative battery cable.

3. Remove air cleaner to throttle body hose.

4. Remove throttle cable and transaxle kickdown linkage.

5. Remove Automatic Idle Speed (AIS) motor and Throttle Position Sensor (TPS) wiring connectors from throttle body.

6. Remove vacuum hose harness from throttle body.

7. Remove PCV and brake booster hoses from air intake plenum.

8. If equipped, remove EGR tube flange from intake plenum.

9. Remove wiring connectors from charge temperature sensor and coolant temperature sensor.

10. Remove vacuum connections from air intake plenum vacuum connector.

11. Remove fuel hoses from fuel rail. Wrap a shop towel around hose to absorb any fuel spillage which may occur when removing.

12. Remove fasteners from air intake plenum to intake manifold.

13. Remove air intake plenum.

14. Cover intake manifold with suitable cover when servicing.

15. Remove vacuum hoses from fuel rail and fuel pressure regulator.

16. Disconnect fuel injector wiring harness from engine wiring harness.

17. Remove the fuel pressure regulator attaching bolts. Loosen the hose clamps and remove the fuel pressure regulator from the fuel rail.

18. Remove the fuel rail attaching bolts and lift the fuel rail from the intake manifold.

19. Be careful not to damage the injector ports when removing.

20. Remove the fuel rail assembly from the vehicle.

21. Do not remove the injectors until the fuel rail has been completely removed from the vehicle.

To install:

22. Make sure the injectors are completely seated with the lockring in place.

23. Make sure the injector holes are clean and that all plugs have been removed.

24. Lube injector O-ring with a drop of clean engine oil to ease installation.

25. Put tip of each injector into respective ports. Push assembly into place until injectors are seated in ports.

26. Install fuel rail attaching bolts. Torque bolts to 115 inch lbs. (13 Nm).

27. Install fuel pressure regulator and hose assembly onto fuel rail. Install attaching bolts to intake manifold. Torque to 77 inch lbs. (8.7 Nm).

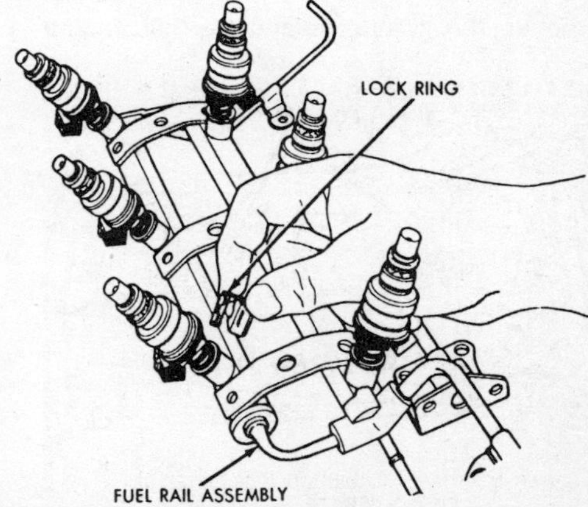

Fuel rail assembly — 3.0L engine

28. Install fuel supply and return tube hold-down bolt and vacuum crossover tube hold-down bolt. Torque to 95 inch lbs. (10 Nm).

29. Tighten fuel pressure regulator hose clamps.

30. Connect fuel injector wiring harness to engine wiring harness.

31. Connect vacuum harness to fuel pressure regulator and fuel rail assembly.

32. Remove covering from lower intake manifold and clean surface.

33. Place intake manifold gaskets, with beaded sealer up, on lower manifold. Put air intake in place. Install attaching fasteners and torque to 115 inch lbs. (13 Nm).

34. Connect fuel line to fuel rail and tighten.

35. Connect vacuum harness to air intake plenum.

36. Connect charge temperature sensor and coolant temperature sensor electrical connectors to sensors.

37. If equipped, connect EGR tube flange to intake plenum and torque to 200 inch lbs. (22 Nm).

38. Connect PCV and brake booster supply hose to intake plenum.

39. Connect Automatic Idle Speed (AIS) motor and Throttle Position Sensor (TPS) electrical connectors.

40. Connect vacuum vapor harness to throttle body.

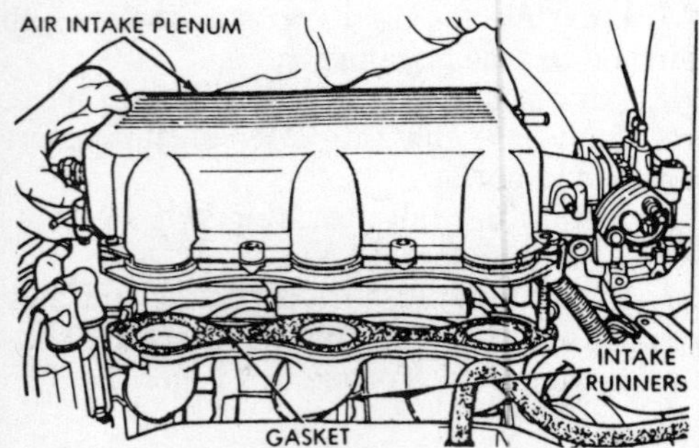

Removing the air intake plenum — 3.0L engine

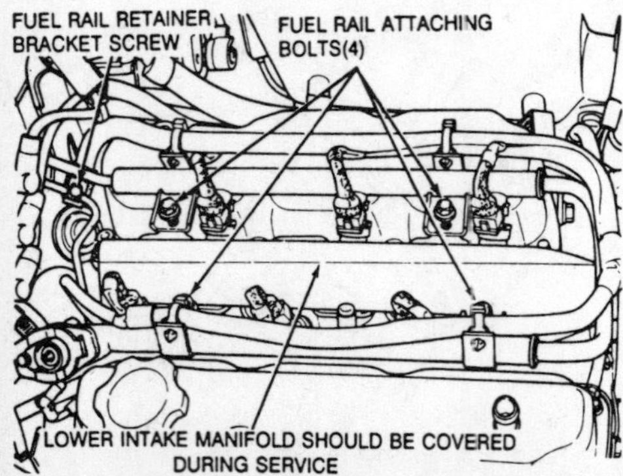

Fuel rail assembly — 3.3L engine

41. Install throttle cable and transaxle kick-down linkage.

42. Install air inlet hose assembly.

43. Connect negative battery cable.

44. Use ATM tester to test for leaks.

3.3L ENGINE

1. Relieve the fuel pressure.

2. Disconnect the negative battery cable.

3. Remove the air cleaner and hose assembly.

4. Disconnect the throttle cable. Remove the wiring harness from the throttle cable bracket and intake manifold water tube.

5. Remove the vacuum hose harness from the throttle body.

6. Remove the PCV and brake booster hoses from the air intake plenum.

7. Remove the EGR tube flange from the intake plenum, if equipped.

8. Unplug the charge temperature sensor and unplug all vacuum hoses from the intake plenum.

9. Remove the cylinder head to intake plenum strut.

10. Disconnect the MAP sensor and oxygen sensor connector. Remove the engine mounted ground strap.

11. Release the fuel hose quick disconnect fittings and remove the hoses from the fuel rail. Plug the hoses.

12. Remove the Direct Ignition System (DIS) coils and the alternator bracket to intake manifold bolt.

13. Remove the intake manifold bolts and rotate the manifold back over the rear valve cover. Cover the intake manifold.

14. Remove the vacuum harness from the pressure regulator.

15. Remove the fuel tube retainer bracket screw and the fuel rail attaching bolts. Spread the retainer bracket to allow for clearance when removing the fuel tube.

16. Remove the fuel rail injector wiring clip from the alternator bracket.

17. Disconnect the camshaft sensor, coolant temperature sensor and engine temperature sensor.

18. Remove the fuel rail.

19. Position the fuel rail on a work bench, so that the injectors are easy to get at.

20. Remove the small connector retaining clip and unplug the injector. Remove the injector clip from the fuel rail and injector. Pull the injector straight off of the rail.

To install:

21. Lubricate the rubber O-ring with clean oil and install to the rail receiver cap. Install the injector clip to the slot in the injector, plug in the connector and install the connector clip.

22. Install the fuel rail.
23. Connect the cam sensor, coolant temperature sensor and engine temperature sensor.
24. Install the fuel rail injector wiring clip to the alternator bracket.
25. Install the fuel rail attaching bolts and fuel tube retainer bracket screw.
26. Install the vacuum harness to the pressure regulator.
27. Install the intake manifold with a new gasket. Install the bolts only fingertight. Install the alternator bracket to intake manifold bolt and the cylinder head to intake manifold strut and bolts. Torque the intake manifold mounting bolts to 21 ft. lbs. (28 Nm) starting from the middle and working outward. Torque the bracket and strut bolts to 40 ft. lbs. (54 Nm).
28. Install or connect all items that were removed or disconnected from the intake manifold and throttle body.
29. Connect the fuel hoses to the rail. Push the fittings in until they click in place.
30. Install the air cleaner assembly.
31. Connect the negative battery cable and check for leaks using the DRB I or II to activate the fuel pump.

FUEL INJECTOR

Removal and Installation

1. Remove fuel rail.
2. Disconnect injector wiring connector from injector.
3. Position fuel rail assembly so that fuel injectors are easily accessible.
4. Remove injector clip off fuel rail and injector. Pull injector straight out of fuel rail receiver cup.
5. Check injector O-ring for damage. If O-ring is damaged, it must be replaced. If injector is to be reused, a protective cap must be installed on injector tip to prevent damage while injector is out for service.
6. Repeat for remaining injectors.
7. Before installing an injector, the rubber O-ring must be lubricated with a drop of clean engine oil to aid in installation.
8. Install injector top end into fuel rail receiver cup. Be careful not to damage O-ring during installation.
9. Install injector clip by sliding open end into top slot of injector and onto receiver cup ridge into side slots of clip.
10. Repeat steps for remaining injectors.

FUEL PRESSURE REGULATOR

Removal and Installation

1. Perform fuel system pressure release procedure.
2. Disconnect negative battery cable.
3. Remove vacuum hose from fuel pressure regulator.
4. Loosen fuel supply hose clamp at fuel rail inlet and remove hose. Wrap a shop towel around hose to absorb any fuel spillage which may occur when removing hose.
5. Loosen fuel return hose clamp at fuel pressure regulator and remove hose. Wrap a shop towel around hose to absorb any fuel spillage which may occur when removing hose.
6. Remove the fuel pressure regulator attaching nuts. Remove the fuel pressure regulator from the fuel rail.

To install:

7. Lubricate the O-ring for the fuel pressure regulator with a drop of clean engine oil and install it into the receiver cup, on the fuel rail.
8. Install the attaching nuts and torque to 65 inch lbs. (7 Nm).
9. Connect the fuel return hose to the pressure regulator.
10. Connect the fuel supply hose to the fuel rail.
11. Install the vacuum hose to the pressure regulator.
12. Connect the negative battery cable. Using the DRBII tester or equivalent, use the Actuate Outputs Test-Auto Shutdown Relay to pressurize the system and check for leaks.

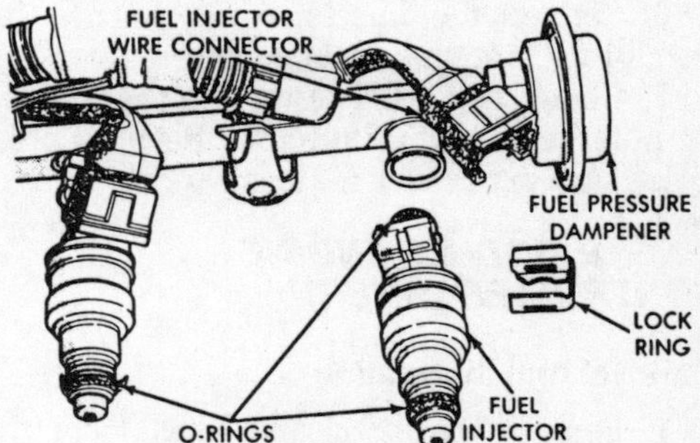

Fuel injector installation — 2.5L turbo engine

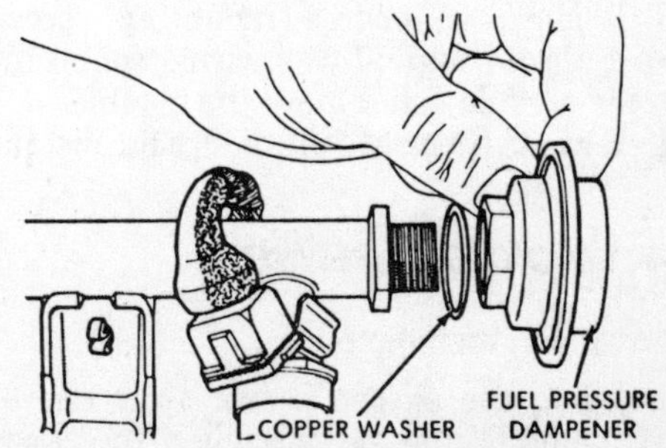

Fuel injector dampener — servicing

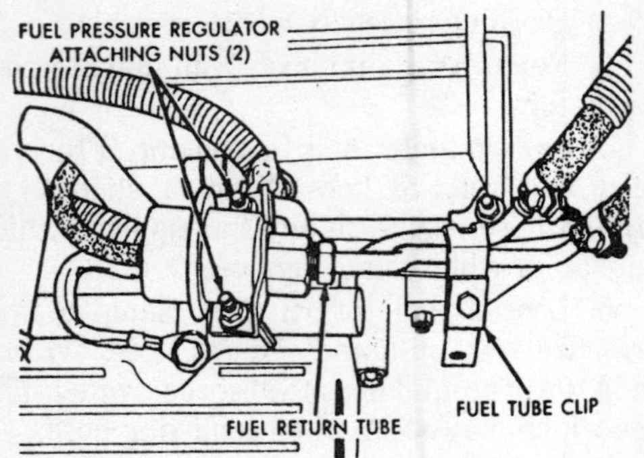

Fuel pressure regulator installation – 2.5L turbo engine

FUEL PRESSURE DAMPER

Removal and Installation

1. Perform fuel system pressure release procedure.
2. Remove PCV system hose assembly from intake manifold and valve cover.
3. Place a shop towel under fuel pressure damper to absorb any fuel spillage.
4. Using 2 open end wrenches, 1 on the flats of fuel rail and the other on fuel pressure damper. Remove fuel pressure damper and copper washer.
5. To install, place a new copper washer on fuel rail and install fuel pressure damper torque to 30 ft. lbs. (41 Nm) using a wrench to hold fuel rail while tightening fuel pressure damper.
6. Connect fuel injector wiring harness reinstall PCV system hose assembly.
7. Using the DRBII tester use the Actuate Outputs Test–Auto Shutdown Relay to pressurize system to check for leaks.

SINGLE MODULE ENGINE CONTROLLER (SMEC)

Removal And Installation

1. Remove the air cleaner duct from the SMEC.
2. Remove the battery.
3. Remove 2 module mounting screws. Remove the 14 and 60 way wiring connectors from the module and remove the module.
4. Reverse the above procedure for installation.

HEATED OXYGEN SENSOR

Removal and Installation

Removing the oxygen sensor from the exhaust manifold may be difficult if the sensor was overtorqued during installation. Use tool C–4907 or equivalent, to remove the sensor. The threads in the exhaust manifold must be cleaned with an 18mm × 1.5 × 6E tap. If the same sensor is to be reinstalled, the threads must be coated with an anti-seize compound such as Loctite® 771–64 or equivalent. New sensors are packaged with anti-seize compound on the threads and no additional compound is required. Sensors must be torqued to 20 ft. lbs. (27 Nm).

CHRYSLER SINGLE POINT FUEL INJECTION SYSTEM

General Information

The electronic fuel injection system is a computer regulated single point fuel injection system that provides precise air/fuel ratio for all driving conditions. At the center of this system is a digital pre-programmed computer known as a Single Module Engine Controller (SMEC) that regulates ignition timing, air/fuel ratio, emission control devices, idle speed and cooling fan and charging system. This component has the ability to update and revise its programming to meet changing operating conditions.

Various sensors provide the input necessary for the SMEC to correctly regulate the fuel flow at the fuel injector. These include the manifold absolute pressure, throttle position, oxygen sensor, coolant temperature, vehicle speed (distance) sensors and throttle body temperature. In addition to the sensors, various switches also provide important information. These include the neutral-safety switch, air conditioning clutch relay, and auto shut-down relay.

All inputs to the SMEC are converted into signals which are used by the computer. Based on these inputs, air-fuel ratio, ignition timing or other controlled outputs are adjusted accordingly.

The SMEC tests many of its own input and output circuits. If a fault is found in a major system this information is stored in the memory. Information on this fault can be displayed to a technician by means of the instrument panel check engine light or by connecting a diagnostic read out and reading a numbered display code which directly relates to a specific fault.

SERVICE PRECAUTIONS

When working around any part of the fuel system, take precautionary steps to prevent possible fire and/or explosion:

- Disconnect the negative battery termi-

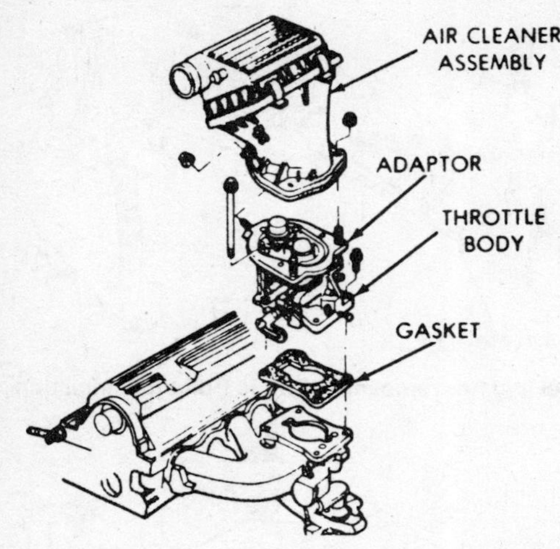

Throttle body mounting – 4 cylinder engines

nal, except when testing with battery voltage is required.

- Whenever possible, use a flashlight instead of a drop light to inspect fuel system components or connections.
- Keep all open flames and smoking material out of the area and make sure there is adequate ventilation to remove fuel vapors.
- Use a clean shop cloth to catch fuel when opening a fuel system. Dispose of gasoline-soaked rags properly.
- Relieve the fuel system pressure before any service procedures are attempted that require disconnecting a fuel line.
- Use eye protection.
- Always keep a dry chemical (class B) fire extinguisher near the area.

Fuel System Pressure Release

1. Loosen gas cap to release tank pressure.
2. Remove wiring harness connector from injector.
3. Ground 1 terminal of injector.
4. Connect jumper wire to second terminal and touch battery positive post for no longer than 10 seconds. This releases system pressure.
5. Remove jumper wire and continue fuel system service.

THROTTLE BODY

Removal and Installation

1. Remove air cleaner.
2. Perform fuel system pressure release.
3. Disconnect negative battery cable.
4. Disconnect vacuum hoses and electrical connectors.
5. Remove throttle cable and, if so

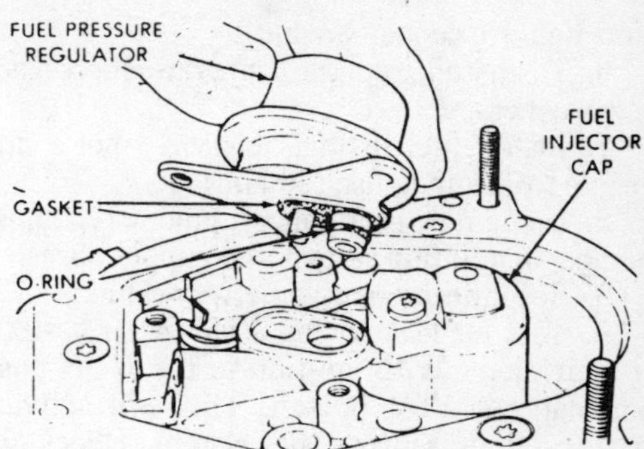

Fuel pressure regulator servicing – Single Point fuel injection

equipped, speed control and transaxle (or transmission) kickdown cables.

6. Remove return spring.
7. Remove fuel intake and return hoses.
8. Remove throttle body mounting screws and lift throttle body from vehicle.
9. When installing throttle body, use a new gasket. Install throttle body and torque mounting screws to 175 inch lbs. (20 Nm).
10. Install fuel intake and return hoses using new original equipment type clamps.
11. Install return spring.
12. Install throttle cable and, if so equipped, install kickdown and speed control cables.
13. Install wiring connectors and vacuum hoses.
14. Install air cleaner.
15. Reconnect negative battery cable.

FUEL FITTINGS

Removal and Installation

1. Remove air cleaner assembly.
2. Perform fuel system pressure release.
3. Disconnect negative battery cable.
4. Loosen fuel intake and return hose clamps. Wrap a shop towel around each hose, twist and pull off each hose.
5. Remove each fitting and note inlet diam-

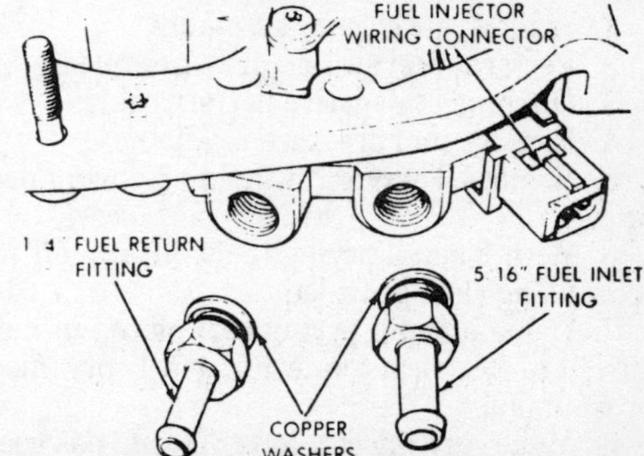

Fuel fitting service – Single Point fuel injection

eter. Remove copper washers.

6. To install, replace copper washers with new washers.

7. Install fuel fittings in proper ports and torque to 175 inch lbs. (20 Nm).

8. Using new original equipment type hose clamps, install fuel return and supply hoses.

9. Reconnect negative battery cable.

10. Test for leaks using ATM tester C–4805 or equivalent. With ignition in the **RUN** position depress ATM button. This will activate pump and pressurize the system. Check for leaks.

11. Reinstall air cleaner assembly.

FUEL PRESSURE REGULATOR

Removal and Installation

1. Remove air cleaner assembly.
2. Perform fuel system pressure release.
3. Disconnect negative battery cable.
4. Remove 3 screws attaching pressure regulator to throttle body. Place a shop towel around inlet chamber to contain any fuel remaining in the system.
5. Pull pressure regulator from throttle body.
6. Carefully remove O-ring from pressure regulator and remove gasket.
7. To install, place new gasket on pressure regulator and carefully install new O-ring.
8. Position pressure regulator on throttle body press into place.
9. Install 3 screws and torque to 40 inch lbs. (5 Nm).
10. Connect negative battery cable.
11. Test for leaks using ATM tester C–4805 or equivalent. With ignition in the **RUN** position depress ATM button. This will activate pump and pressurize the system. Check for leaks.
12. Reinstall air cleaner assembly.

FUEL INJECTOR

Removal and Installation

1. Remove air cleaner assembly.
2. Perform fuel system pressure release.
3. Disconnect negative battery cable.
4. Remove fuel pressure regulator.
5. Remove Torx® screw holding down injector cap.
6. With 2 small prying tools, lift cap off injector using slots provided.
7. Using a small prying tool placed in hole in front of electrical connector, gently pry injector from pod.
8. Make sure injector lower O-ring has been removed from pod.
9. To install, place a new lower O-ring on injector and a new O-ring on injector cap. The injector will have upper O-ring already installed.
10. Put injector cap on injector. (Injector and cap are keyed). Cap should sit on injector without interference. Apply a light coating of castor oil or petroleum jelly on O-rings. Place assembly in pod.
11. Rotate cap and injector to line up attachment hole.
12. Push down on cap until it contacts injector pod.
13. Install Torx® screw and torque to 35–45 inch lbs. (4–5 Nm).
14. Install fuel pressure regulator.
15. Connect negative battery cable.
16. Test for leaks using ATM tester C–4805 or equivalent. With ignition in the **RUN** posi-

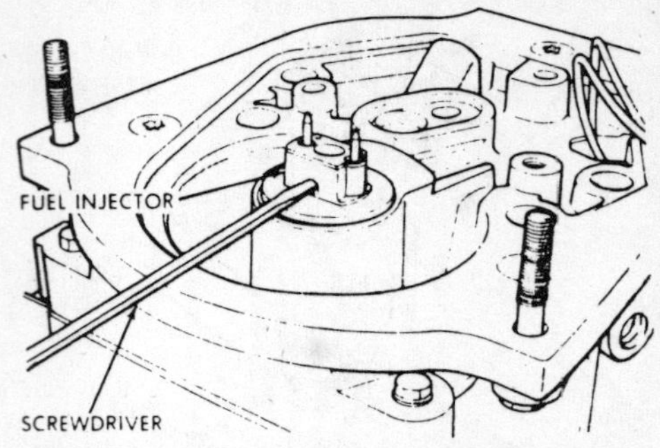

Fuel injector removal – Single Point fuel injection

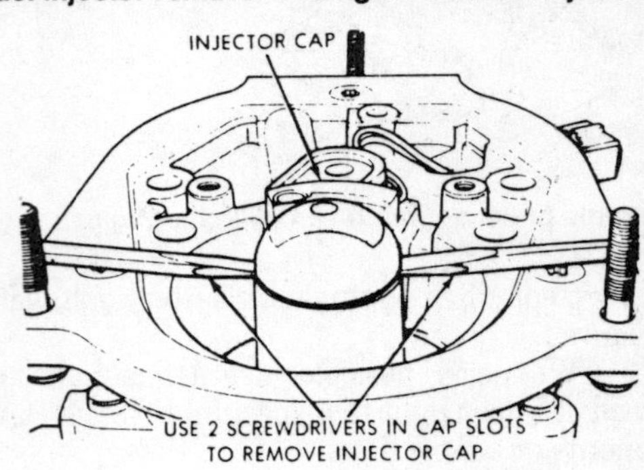

Injector cap removal – Single Point fuel injection

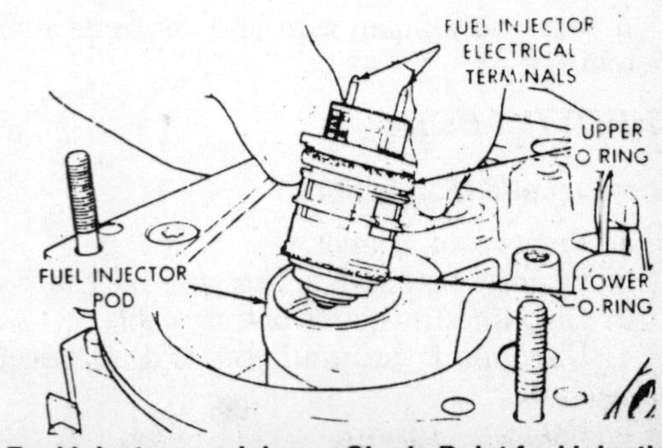

Fuel injector servicing – Single Point fuel injection

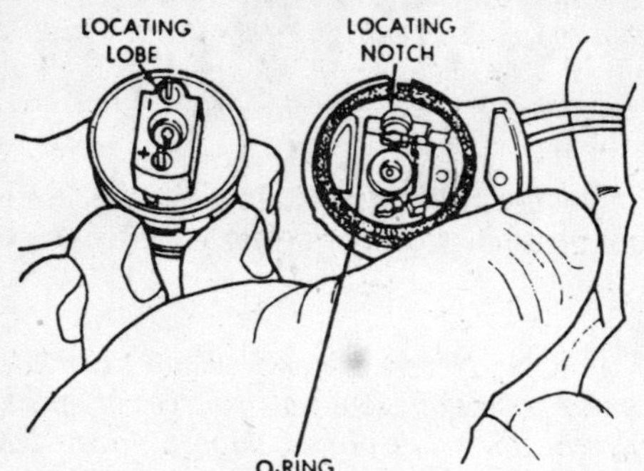

Fuel injector terminal identification – Single Point fuel injection

tion depress ATM button. This will activate pump and pressurize the system. Check for leaks.

17. Reinstall air cleaner.

THROTTLE POSITION SENSOR

Removal and Installation

1. Disconnect negative battery cable.
2. Remove air cleaner.
3. Disconnect 3 way connector at throttle position sensor.
4. Remove 2 screws mounting throttle position sensor to throttle body.
5. Lift throttle position sensor off throttle shaft.
6. To install, install throttle position sensor to throttle body, position connector toward rear of vehicle.
7. Connect 3 way connector at throttle position sensor.
8. Install air cleaner.
9. Connect negative battery cable.

THROTTLE BODY TEMPERATURE SENSOR

Removal and Installation

1. Remove air cleaner.
2. Disconnect throttle cables from throttle body linkage.
3. Remove 2 screws from throttle cable bracket and lay bracket aside.
4. Disconnect wiring connector.
5. Unscrew sensor.
6. To install, apply heat transfer compound to tip portion of new sensor.
7. Install and torque to 100 inch lbs. (11 Nm).
8. Connect wiring connector.
9. Install throttle cable bracket with 2 screws.
10. Connect throttle cables to throttle body linkage and install clips.
11. Install air cleaner.

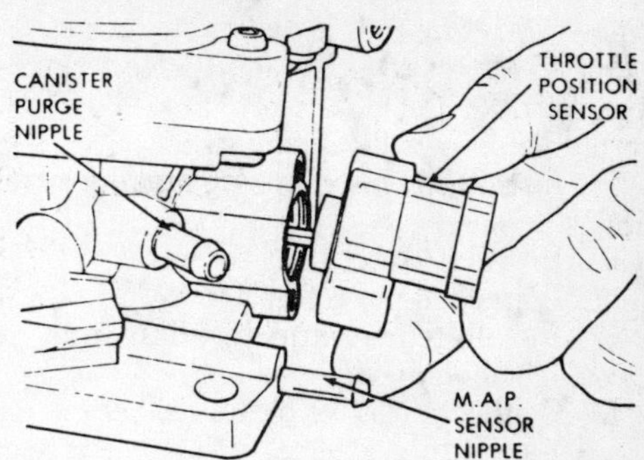

Throttle position sensor servicing – Single Point fuel injection

AUTOMATIC IDLE SPEED (AIS) MOTOR ASSEMBLY

Removal and Installation

1. Remove air cleaner.
2. Disconnect negative battery cable.
3. Disconnect 4 pin connector on AIS.
4. Remove temperature sensor from throttle body housing.
5. Remove 2 Torx® head screws.
6. Remove AIS from throttle body housing, making sure that O-ring is with AIS.
7. To install, be sure that pintle is in the retracted position. If pintle measures more

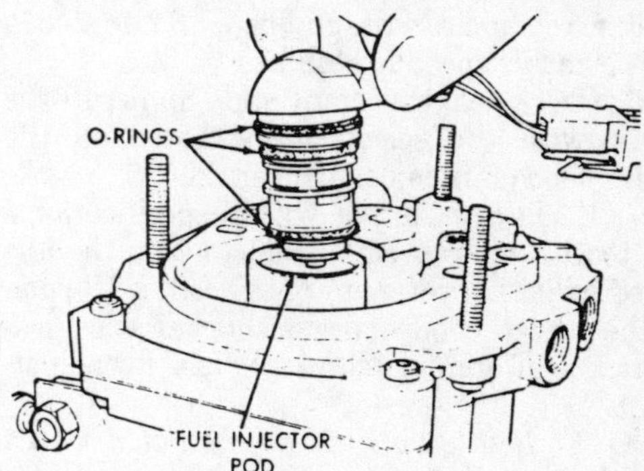

Fuel injector installation – Single Point fuel injection

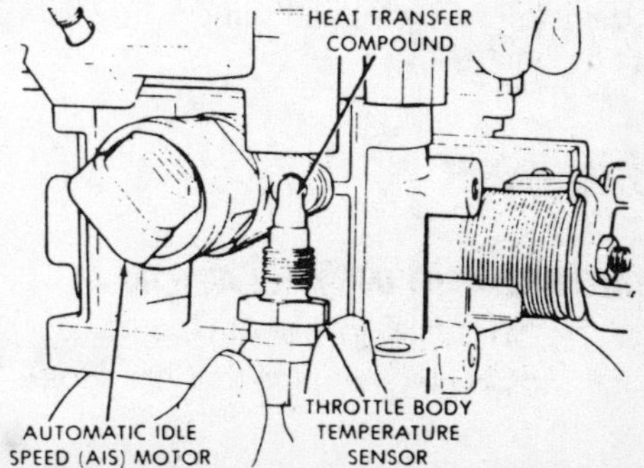

Throttle body temperature sensor servicing – Single Point fuel injection

than 1 in. (25mm), it must be retracted by using ATM test code No. 03. (Battery must be connected for this operation.)

8. Install new O-ring on AIS.
9. Install AIS into housing making sure O-ring is in place.
10. Install 2 Torx® head screws.
11. Connect 4 pin connector to AIS.
12. Install temperature sending unit into throttle body housing.
13. Connect negative battery cable.

MINIMUM IDLE SPEED

Adjustment

1. Before adjusting the idle on fuel injected vehicles, the following items must be checked:
   a. AIS motor has been checked for operation.
   b. Engine has been checked for vacuum or EGR leaks.
   c. Engine timing has been checked and set to specifications.
   d. Coolant temperature sensor has been checked for operation.
2. Connect a tachometer and timing light to engine.
3. Close AIS by using ATM tester C–4805 or equivalent, ATM test code No. 03.
4. Connect a jumper to radiator fan so that it will run continuously.
5. Start and run the engine for 3 minutes to allow the idle speed to stabilize.
6. Check engine rpm and compare the result with the specifications listed on the under hood emission control sticker.
7. If idle rpm is not within specifications, use tool C–4804 or equivalent to turn the idle speed adjusting screw to obtain 800 ± 10 rpm. If the under hood emission sticker specifications are different, use those values for adjustment.

NOTE: *If idle will not adjust down, check for binding linkage, speed control servo cable adjustment or throttle shaft binding.*

8. Turn off the engine, disconnect tachometer, reinstall AIS wire and remove jumper wire from fan motor.

FUEL TANK

REMOVAL AND INSTALLATION

NOTE: *All Wheel Drive vehicles, have a fuel tank that is made of plastic. Care should be taken to avoid damaging this tank. The fuel tank in AWD vehicles is mounted at the side of the vehicle instead of the rear.*

1. Release the fuel system pressure. Refer to fuel system pressure release procedure in this Chapter.

CAUTION: *Never smoke when working around gasoline! Avoid all sources of sparks or ignition. Gasoline vapors are EXTREMELY volatile!*

2. Disconnect battery negative cable.
3. Raise the vehicle and support properly.
4. Remove drain tube rubber cap on left rail and connect a siphon hose to drain tube. Drain fuel into a safe gasoline container.
5. Remove screws supporting filler tube to inner and outer quarter panel.
6. Disconnect wiring and lines from the tank.
7. Position a transmission jack to support the fuel tank and remove the bolts from fuel tank straps.
8. Lower tank slightly, and carefully work filler tube from tank.
9. Lower tank, disconnect vapor separator rollover valve hose and remove the fuel tank and insulator pad from vehicle.

To install:

10. Support the fuel tank with a transmission jack. Connect the vapor separator rollover valve hose and position insulator pad on fuel tank.

NOTE: *Be certain vapor vent hose is clipped to the tank and not pinch between tank and floor pan during installation.*

11. Raise tank into position and carefully work filler tube into tank.
12. Install straps and tighten bolts to 54.2 Nm (40 ft. lbs.). Remove transmission jack.
13. Connect lines, drain tube cap and wiring connector, use new hose clamps.
14. Install and tighten filler tube to inner and outer quarter panel. On some models be sure to install the gasket between the filler tube and the inner quarter panel, before installing the mounting screws.
15. Replace cap on drain tube using a new hose clamp.
16. Fill the fuel tank, install the cap, connect battery cable and check operation.

55 WAYS TO IMPROVE FUEL ECONOMY

CHILTON'S

FUEL ECONOMY & TUNE-UP TIPS

Tune-up • Spark Plug Diagnosis • Emission Controls

Fuel System • Cooling System • Tires and Wheels

General Maintenance

CHILTON'S FUEL ECONOMY & TUNE-UP TIPS

Fuel economy is important to everyone, no matter what kind of vehicle you drive. The maintenance-minded motorist can save both money and fuel using these tips and the periodic maintenance and tune-up procedures in this Repair and Tune-Up Guide.

There are more than 130,000,000 cars and trucks registered for private use in the United States. Each travels an average of 10-12,000 miles per year, and, and in total they consume close to 70 billion gallons of fuel each year. This represents nearly ⅔ of the oil imported by the United States each year. The Federal government's goal is to reduce consumption 10% by 1985. A variety of methods are either already in use or under serious consideration, and they all affect you driving and the cars you will drive. In addition to "down-sizing", the auto industry is using or investigating the use of electronic fuel delivery, electronic engine controls and alternative engines for use in smaller and lighter vehicles, among other alternatives to meet the federally mandated Corporate Average Fuel Economy (CAFE) of 27.5 mpg by 1985. The government, for its part, is considering rationing, mandatory driving curtailments and tax increases on motor vehicle fuel in an effort to reduce consumption. The government's goal of a 10% reduction could be realized — and further government regulation avoided — if every private vehicle could use just 1 less gallon of fuel per week.

How Much Can You Save?

Tests have proven that almost anyone can make at least a 10% reduction in fuel consumption through regular maintenance and tune-ups. When a major manufacturer of spark plugs sur-

---

TUNE-UP

1. Check the cylinder compression to be sure the engine will really benefit from a tune-up and that it is capable of producing good fuel economy. A tune-up will be wasted on an engine in poor mechanical condition.

2. Replace spark plugs regularly. New spark plugs alone can increase fuel economy 3%.

3. Be sure the spark plugs are the correct type (heat range) for your vehicle. See the Tune-Up Specifications.

Heat range refers to the spark plug's ability to conduct heat away from the firing end. It must conduct the heat away in an even pattern to avoid becoming a source of pre-ignition, yet it must also operate hot enough to burn off conductive deposits that could cause misfiring.

The heat range is usually indicated by a number on the spark plug, part of the manufacturer's designation for each individual spark plug. The numbers in bold-face indicate the heat range in each manufacturer's identification system.

Manufacturer	**Typical Designation**
AC	R **45** TS
Bosch (old)	WA **145** T30
Bosch (new)	HR **8** Y
Champion	RBL **15** Y
Fram/Autolite	41**5**
Mopar	P-**62** PR
Motorcraft	BRF-**42**
NGK	BP **5** ES-15
Nippondenso	W **16** EP
Prestolite	14GR **5** 2A

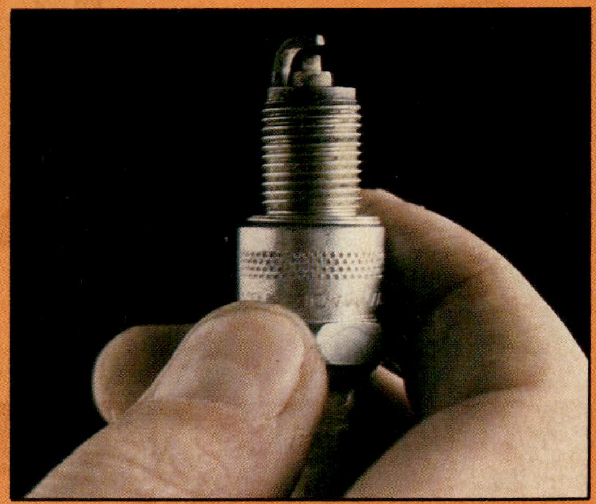

Periodically, check the spark plugs to be sure they are firing efficiently. They are excellent indicators of the internal condition of your engine.

On AC, Bosch (new), Champion, Fram/Autolite, Mopar, Motorcraft and Prestolite, a higher number indicates a hotter plug. On Bosch (old), NGK and Nippondenso, a higher number indicates a colder plug.

4. Make sure the spark plugs are properly gapped. See the Tune-Up Specifications in this book.

5. Be sure the spark plugs are firing efficiently. The illustrations on the next 2 pages show you how to "read" the firing end of the spark plug.

6. Check the ignition timing and set it to specifications. Tests show that almost all cars have incorrect ignition timing by more than 2°.

veyed over 6,000 cars nationwide, they found that a tune-up, on cars that needed one, increased fuel economy over 11%. Replacing worn plugs alone, accounted for a 3% increase. The same test also revealed that 8 out of every 10 vehicles will have some maintenance deficiency that will directly affect fuel economy, emissions or performance. Most of this mileage-robbing neglect could be prevented with regular maintenance.

Modern engines require that all of the functioning systems operate properly for maximum efficiency. A malfunction anywhere wastes fuel. You can keep your vehicle running as efficiently and economically as possible, by being aware of your vehicle's operating and performance characteristics. If your vehicle suddenly develops performance or fuel economy problems it could be due to one or more of the following:

PROBLEM	POSSIBLE CAUSE
Engine Idles Rough	Ignition timing, idle mixture, vacuum leak or something amiss in the emission control system.
Hesitates on Acceleration	Dirty carburetor or fuel filter, improper accelerator pump setting, ignition timing or fouled spark plugs.
Starts Hard or Fails to Start	Worn spark plugs, improperly set automatic choke, ice (or water) in fuel system.
Stalls Frequently	Automatic choke improperly adjusted and possible dirty air filter or fuel filter.
Performs Sluggishly	Worn spark plugs, dirty fuel or air filter, ignition timing or automatic choke out of adjustment.

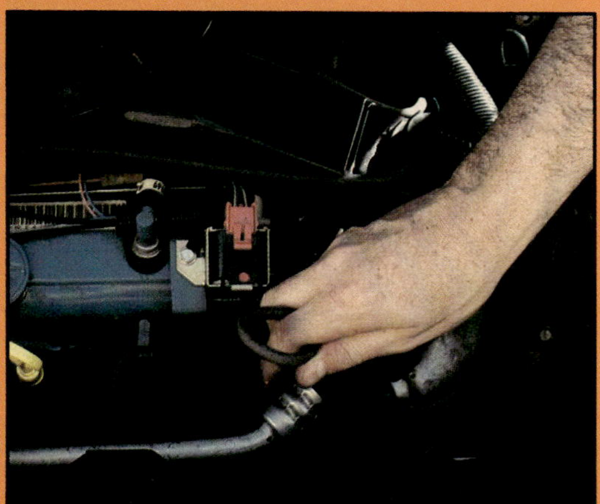

Check spark plug wires on conventional point type ignition for cracks by bending them in a loop around your finger.

Be sure that spark plug wires leading to adjacent cylinders do not run too close together. (Photo courtesy Champion Spark Plug Co.)

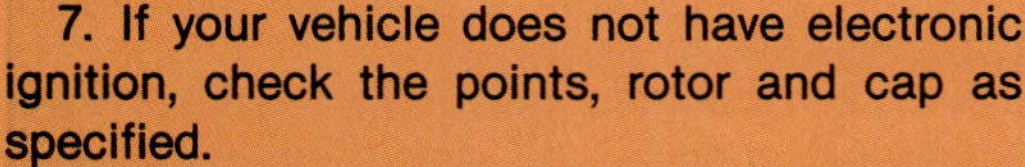

7. If your vehicle does not have electronic ignition, check the points, rotor and cap as specified.

8. Check the spark plug wires (used with conventional point-type ignitions) for cracks and burned or broken insulation by bending them in a loop around your finger. Cracked wires decrease fuel efficiency by failing to deliver full voltage to the spark plugs. One misfiring spark plug can cost you as much as 2 mpg.

9. Check the routing of the plug wires. Misfiring can be the result of spark plug leads to adjacent cylinders running parallel to each other and too close together. One wire tends to pick up voltage from the other causing it to fire "out of time".

10. Check all electrical and ignition circuits for voltage drop and resistance.

11. Check the distributor mechanical and/or vacuum advance mechanisms for proper functioning. The vacuum advance can be checked by twisting the distributor plate in the opposite direction of rotation. It should spring back when released.

12. Check and adjust the valve clearance on engines with mechanical lifters. The clearance should be slightly loose rather than too tight.

SPARK PLUG DIAGNOSIS

Normal

APPEARANCE: This plug is typical of one operating normally. The insulator nose varies from a light tan to grayish color with slight electrode wear. The presence of slight deposits is normal on used plugs and will have no adverse effect on engine performance. The spark plug heat range is correct for the engine and the engine is running normally.
CAUSE: Properly running engine.
RECOMMENDATION: Before reinstalling this plug, the electrodes should be cleaned and filed square. Set the gap to specifications. If the plug has been in service for more than 10-12,000 miles, the entire set should probably be replaced with a fresh set of the same heat range.

Oil Deposits

APPEARANCE: The firing end of the plug is covered with a wet, oily coating.
CAUSE: The problem is poor oil control. On high mileage engines, oil is leaking past the rings or valve guides into the combustion chamber. A common cause is also a plugged PCV valve, and a ruptured fuel pump diaphragm can also cause this condition. Oil fouled plugs such as these are often found in new or recently overhauled engines, before normal oil control is achieved, and can be cleaned and reinstalled.
RECOMMENDATION: A hotter spark plug may temporarily relieve the problem, but the engine is probably in need of work.

Incorrect Heat Range

APPEARANCE: The effects of high temperature on a spark plug are indicated by clean white, often blistered insulator. This can also be accompanied by excessive wear of the electrode, and the absence of deposits.
CAUSE: Check for the correct spark plug heat range. A plug which is too hot for the engine can result in overheating. A car operated mostly at high speeds can require a colder plug. Also check ignition timing, cooling system level, fuel mixture and leaking intake manifold.
RECOMMENDATION: If all ignition and engine adjustments are known to be correct, and no other malfunction exists, install spark plugs one heat range colder.

Carbon Deposits

APPEARANCE: Carbon fouling is easily identified by the presence of dry, soft, black, sooty deposits.
CAUSE: Changing the heat range can often lead to carbon fouling, as can prolonged slow, stop-and-start driving. If the heat range is correct, carbon fouling can be attributed to a rich fuel mixture, sticking choke, clogged air cleaner, worn breaker points, retarded timing or low compression. If only one or two plugs are carbon fouled, check for corroded or cracked wires on the affected plugs. Also look for cracks in the distributor cap between the towers of affected cylinders.
RECOMMENDATION: After the problem is corrected, these plugs can be cleaned and reinstalled if not worn severely.

Photos Courtesy Fram Corporation

MMT Fouled

APPEARANCE: Spark plugs fouled by MMT (Methycyclopentadienyl Maganese Tricarbonyl) have reddish, rusty appearance on the insulator and side electrode.
CAUSE: MMT is an anti-knock additive in gasoline used to replace lead. During the combustion process, the MMT leaves a reddish deposit on the insulator and side electrode.
RECOMMENDATION: No engine malfunction is indicated and the deposits will not affect plug performance any more than lead deposits (see Ash Deposits). MMT fouled plugs can be cleaned, regapped and reinstalled.

High Speed Glazing

APPEARANCE: Glazing appears as shiny coating on the plug, either yellow or tan in color.
CAUSE: During hard, fast acceleration, plug temperatures rise suddenly. Deposits from normal combustion have no chance to fluff-off; instead, they melt on the insulator forming an electrically conductive coating which causes misfiring.
RECOMMENDATION: Glazed plugs are not easily cleaned. They should be replaced with a fresh set of plugs of the correct heat range. If the condition recurs, using plugs with a heat range one step colder may cure the problem.

Ash (Lead) Deposits

APPEARANCE: Ash deposits are characterized by light brown or white colored deposits crusted on the side or center electrodes. In some cases it may give the plug a rusty appearance.
CAUSE: Ash deposits are normally derived from oil or fuel additives burned during normal combustion. Normally they are harmless, though excessive amounts can cause misfiring. If deposits are excessive in short mileage, the valve guides may be worn.
RECOMMENDATION: Ash-fouled plugs can be cleaned, gapped and reinstalled.

Detonation

APPEARANCE: Detonation is usually characterized by a broken plug insulator.
CAUSE: A portion of the fuel charge will begin to burn spontaneously, from the increased heat following ignition. The explosion that results applies extreme pressure to engine components, frequently damaging spark plugs and pistons.

Detonation can result by over-advanced ignition timing, inferior gasoline (low octane) lean air/fuel mixture, poor carburetion, engine lugging or an increase in compression ratio due to combustion chamber deposits or engine modification.
RECOMMENDATION: Replace the plugs after correcting the problem.

Photos Courtesy Champion Spark Plug Co.

EMISSION CONTROLS

13. Be aware of the general condition of the emission control system. It contributes to reduced pollution and should be serviced regularly to maintain efficient engine operation.

14. Check all vacuum lines for dried, cracked or brittle conditions. Something as simple as a leaking vacuum hose can cause poor performance and loss of economy.

15. Avoid tampering with the emission control system. Attempting to improve fuel econ-

FUEL SYSTEM

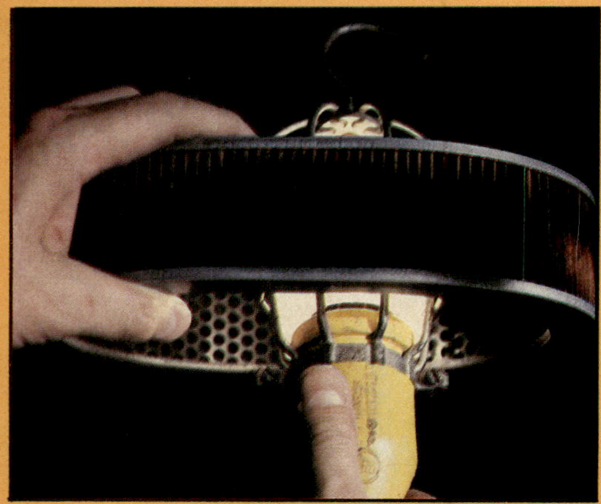

Check the air filter with a light behind it. If you can see light through the filter it can be reused.

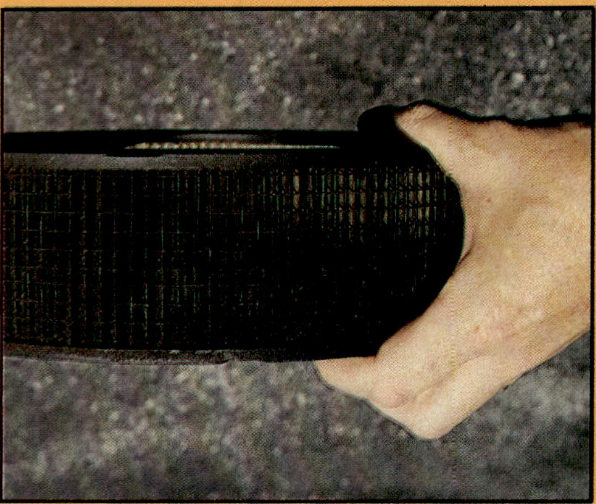

Extremely clogged filters should be discarded and replaced with a new one.

18. Replace the air filter regularly. A dirty air filter richens the air/fuel mixture and can increase fuel consumption as much as 10%. Tests show that ⅓ of all vehicles have air filters in need of replacement.

19. Replace the fuel filter at least as often as recommended.

20. Set the idle speed and carburetor mixture to specifications.

21. Check the automatic choke. A sticking or malfunctioning choke wastes gas.

22. During the summer months, adjust the automatic choke for a leaner mixture which will produce faster engine warm-ups.

COOLING SYSTEM

29. Be sure all accessory drive belts are in good condition. Check for cracks or wear.

30. Adjust all accessory drive belts to proper tension.

31. Check all hoses for swollen areas, worn spots, or loose clamps.

32. Check coolant level in the radiator or expansion tank.

33. Be sure the thermostat is operating properly. A stuck thermostat delays engine warm-up and a cold engine uses nearly twice as much fuel as a warm engine.

34. Drain and replace the engine coolant at least as often as recommended. Rust and scale

TIRES & WHEELS

38. Check the tire pressure often with a pencil type gauge. Tests by a major tire manufacturer show that 90% of all vehicles have at least 1 tire improperly inflated. Better mileage can be achieved by over-inflating tires, but never exceed the maximum inflation pressure on the side of the tire.

39. If possible, install radial tires. Radial tires deliver as much as ½ mpg more than bias belted tires.

40. Avoid installing super-wide tires. They only create extra rolling resistance and decrease fuel mileage. Stick to the manufacturer's recommendations.

41. Have the wheels properly balanced.

omy by tampering with emission controls is more likely to worsen fuel economy than improve it. Emission control changes on modern engines are not readily reversible.

16. Clean (or replace) the EGR valve and lines as recommended.

17. Be sure that all vacuum lines and hoses are reconnected properly after working under the hood. An unconnected or misrouted vacuum line can wreak havoc with engine performance.

23. Check for fuel leaks at the carburetor, fuel pump, fuel lines and fuel tank. Be sure all lines and connections are tight.

24. Periodically check the tightness of the carburetor and intake manifold attaching nuts and bolts. These are a common place for vacuum leaks to occur.

25. Clean the carburetor periodically and lubricate the linkage.

26. The condition of the tailpipe can be an excellent indicator of proper engine combustion. After a long drive at highway speeds, the inside of the tailpipe should be a light grey in color. Black or soot on the insides indicates an overly rich mixture.

27. Check the fuel pump pressure. The fuel pump may be supplying more fuel than the engine needs.

28. Use the proper grade of gasoline for your engine. Don't try to compensate for knocking or "pinging" by advancing the ignition timing. This practice will only increase plug temperature and the chances of detonation or pre-ignition with relatively little performance gain.

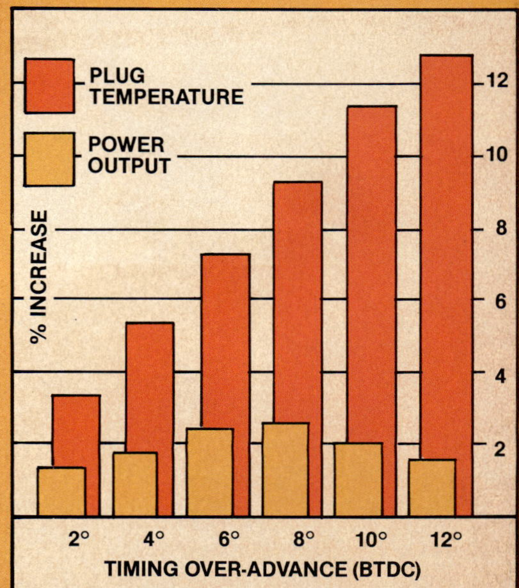

Increasing ignition timing past the specified setting results in a drastic increase in spark plug temperature with increased chance of detonation or preignition. Performance increase is considerably less. (Photo courtesy Champion Spark Plug Co.)

that form in the engine should be flushed out to allow the engine to operate at peak efficiency.

35. Clean the radiator of debris that can decrease cooling efficiency.

36. Install a flex-type or electric cooling fan, if you don't have a clutch type fan. Flex fans use curved plastic blades to push more air at low speeds when more cooling is needed; at high speeds the blades flatten out for less resistance. Electric fans only run when the engine temperature reaches a predetermined level.

37. Check the radiator cap for a worn or cracked gasket. If the cap does not seal properly, the cooling system will not function properly.

42. Be sure the front end is correctly aligned. A misaligned front end actually has wheels going in differed directions. The increased drag can reduce fuel economy by .3 mpg.

43. Correctly adjust the wheel bearings. Wheel bearings that are adjusted too tight increase rolling resistance.

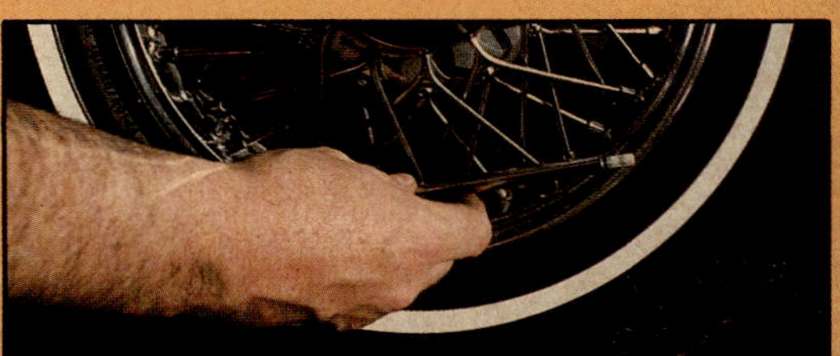

Check tire pressures regularly with a reliable pocket type gauge. Be sure to check the pressure on a cold tire.

GENERAL MAINTENANCE

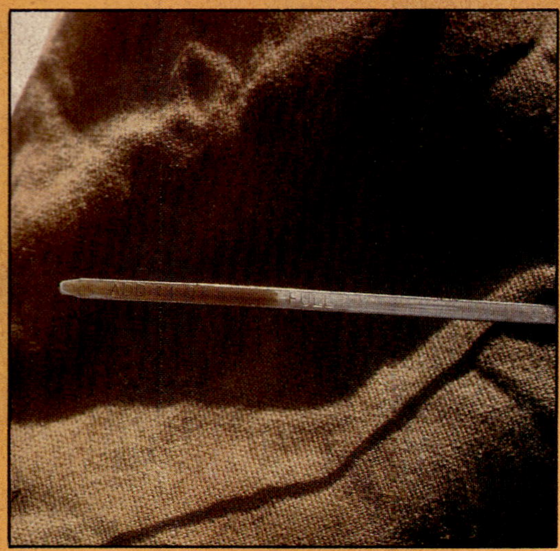

Check the fluid levels (particularly engine oil) on a regular basis. Be sure to check the oil for grit, water or other contamination.

A vacuum gauge is another excellent indicator of internal engine condition and can also be installed in the dash as a mileage indicator.

44. Periodically check the fluid levels in the engine, power steering pump, master cylinder, automatic transmission and drive axle.

45. Change the oil at the recommended interval and change the filter at every oil change. Dirty oil is thick and causes extra friction between moving parts, cutting efficiency and increasing wear. A worn engine requires more frequent tune-ups and gets progressively worse fuel economy. In general, use the lightest viscosity oil for the driving conditions you will encounter.

46. Use the recommended viscosity fluids in the transmission and axle.

47. Be sure the battery is fully charged for fast starts. A slow starting engine wastes fuel.

48. Be sure battery terminals are clean and tight.

49. Check the battery electrolyte level and add distilled water if necessary.

50. Check the exhaust system for crushed pipes, blockages and leaks.

51. Adjust the brakes. Dragging brakes or brakes that are not releasing create increased drag on the engine.

52. Install a vacuum gauge or miles-per-gallon gauge. These gauges visually indicate engine vacuum in the intake manifold. High vacuum = good mileage and low vacuum = poorer mileage. The gauge can also be an excellent indicator of internal engine conditions.

53. Be sure the clutch is properly adjusted. A slipping clutch wastes fuel.

54. Check and periodically lubricate the heat control valve in the exhaust manifold. A sticking or inoperative valve prevents engine warm-up and wastes gas.

55. Keep accurate records to check fuel economy over a period of time. A sudden drop in fuel economy may signal a need for tune-up or other maintenance.

Chassis Electrical 6

HEATING AND AIR CONDITIONING

Service such as blower motor and heater core replacement on 1984–87 models, requires the removal of the Heater/Evaporator unit from the vehicle. Two persons will be required for the operation.

NOTE: *The refrigerant system should be discharged by a professional shop before any work requiring the disconnecting of the refrigerant lines.*

Heater/Evaporator Unit

REMOVAL AND INSTALLATION

1984-87 Models

CAUTION: *The air conditioning system contains refrigerant under high pressure. Severe personal injury may result from improper service procedures. The system should be discharged by a qualified service person.*

1. Have the system discharged. See the CAUTION notice above.
2. Block the vehicle wheels and apply the parking brake.
3. Disconnect the negative battery cable. Drain the cooling system.

CAUTION: *When draining the coolant, keep in mind that cats and dogs are attracted by the ethylene glycol antifreeze, and are quite likely to drink any that is left in an uncovered container or in puddles on the ground. This will prove fatal in sufficient quantity. Always drain the coolant into a sealable container. Coolant should be reused unless it is contaminated or several years old.*

4. Remove the passenger side lower instrument panel.
5. Remove the steering column lower cover.
6. Remove the right side cowl and sill trim.
7. Remove the mounting bolt from the right side instrument panel to the right cowl.
8. Loosen the (2) brackets supporting the lower edge to air conditioning and heater unit housing.
9. Remove the mid-reinforcement instrument panel trim molding.

Heater/evaporator assembly components

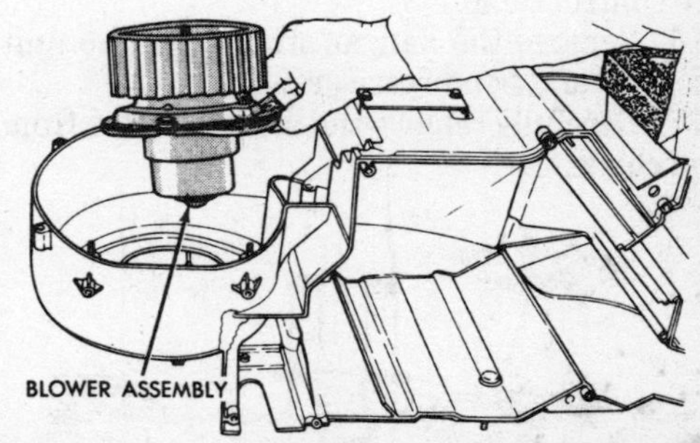

Blower motor removal and installation – 1984-90 models

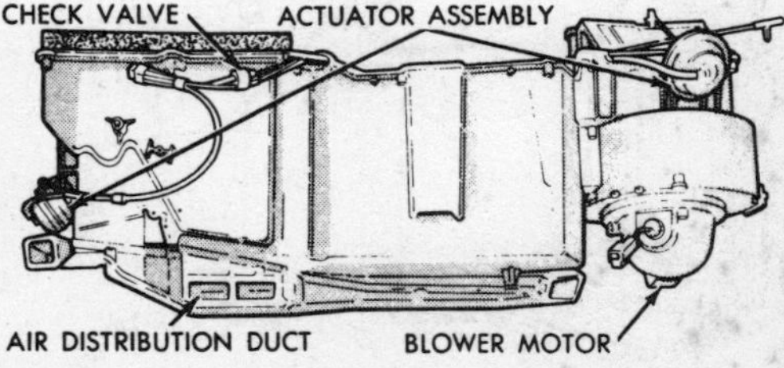

Evaporator/Heater assembly

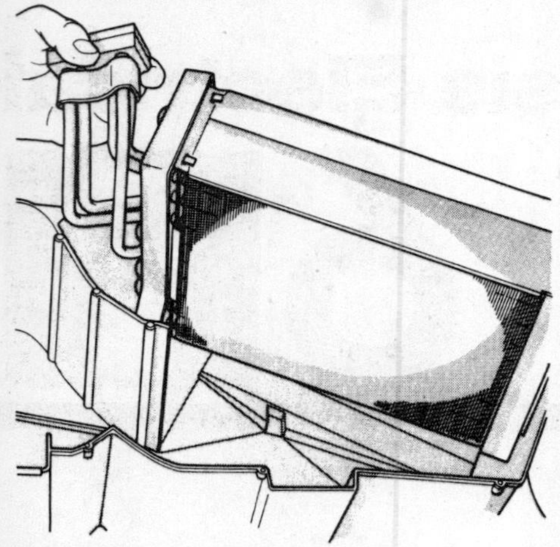

Removing or installing the evaporator

10. Remove the attaching screws from the right side to center of the steering column.

11. From the engine compartment; disconnect the vacuum line at brake booster and water valve.

12. Remove the hoses from the heater core. Plug the heater tubes.

13. Disconnect the air conditioning plumbing at the H-valve.

14. Remove the (4) nuts from engine compartment package mounting studs.

15. From the passenger compartment, pull the right side of lower instrument panel rearward until it reaches the passenger seat. Disconnect the electrical connectors and temperature control cable.

16. Remove the hangar strap from the unit assembly and bend rearward.

17. Carefully remove the unit assembly from the vehicle.

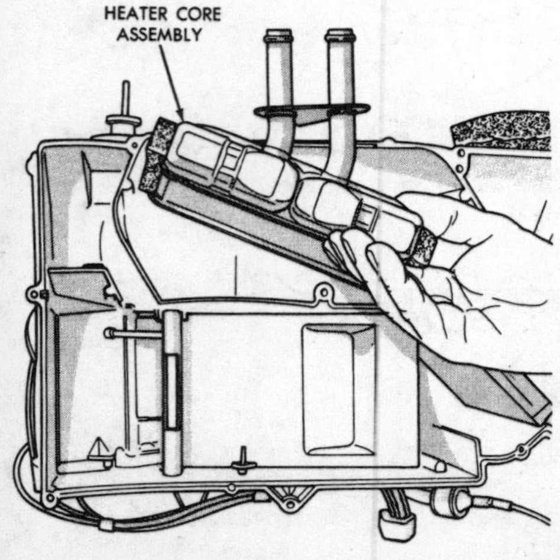

Removing and installing the heater core assembly

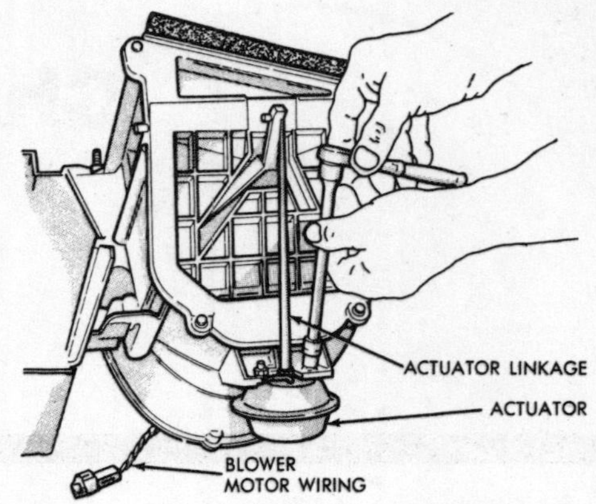

Removing and installing actuator and linkage on the blower housing

18. Place the heater/evaporator unit assembly on a work bench.

19. Remove the vacuum harness attaching screw and remove the harness through the access hole in the cover.

20. Remove the (13) attaching screws from the cover and remove the cover. The temperature control door will come out with the cover.

21. Remove the retaining bracket screws and the remove heater core assembly.

22. Remove the evaporator core assembly.

23. Disconnect the actuator linkage from the recirculation door and remove the vacuum line. Remove the actuator retaining screws and remove the actuator.

24. Remove the (4) attaching screws from the recirculation door cover to evaporator/ heater assembly. Lift the cover from the unit and remove the recirculation door from its housing.

25. Remove the (5) attaching screws from the blower assembly sound helmet.

26. Remove the retaining clamp from the blower wheel hub and slide the blower wheel from the blower motor shaft.

27. Remove the blower motor (3) mounting screws from the helmet and remove the blower motor assembly.

To install:

28. Install the blower wheel to the blower motor shaft and secure it with the retaining clamp.

29. Feed the blower motor electrical wires through the access hole in the sound helmet and lower the blower motor into helmet.

30. Secure the blower motor with the (3) mounting screws.

31. Install the blower assembly and helmet into the fan scroll and secure it with (5) retaining screws.

32. Install the recirculation door into its hous-

ing. Place the recirculation door cover onto the unit and secure with the (4) retaining screws.

33. Install the actuator shaft onto the recirculation door and slide the actuator into its bracket. Secure the actuator assembly with (2) nuts.

34. Install the evaporator core into the unit.

35. Install the heater core into the unit and secure the core tube retaining bracket with attaching screws.

36. Install the unit cover and secure with (13) attaching screws.

37. Install the vacuum harness through the access hole in the cover and secure the vacuum harness.

38. Place the heater/evaporator assembly into the vehicle and position it against the dash panel.

39. Install the hangar strap.

40. Connect the temperature control cable,

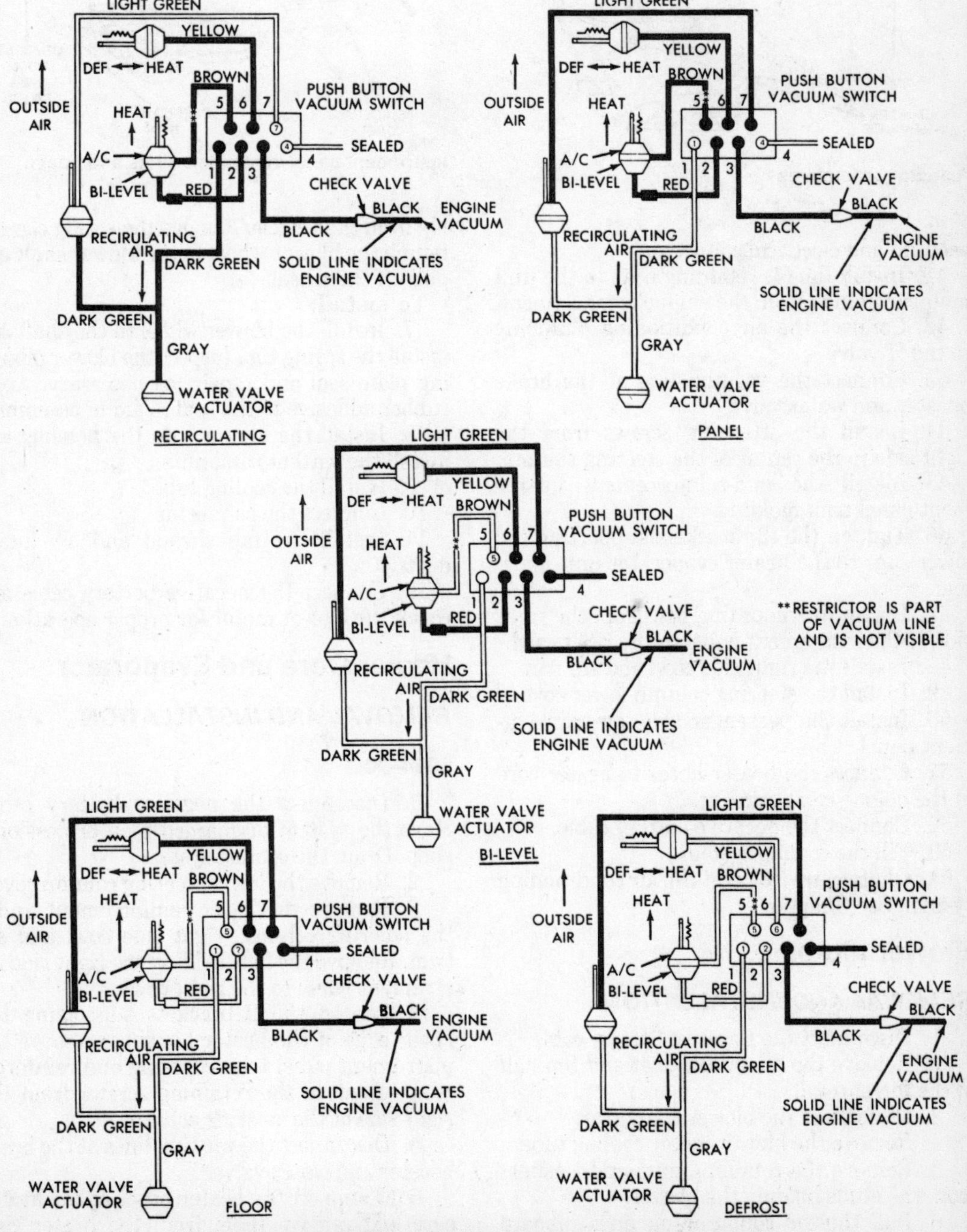

Air conditioning and heating system — vacuum circuits

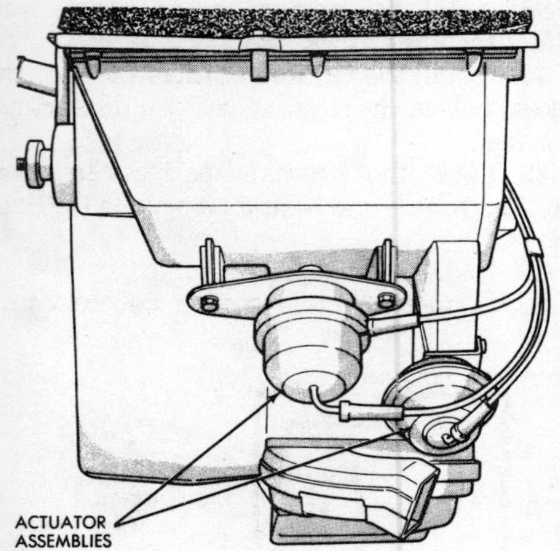

Actuator assemblies

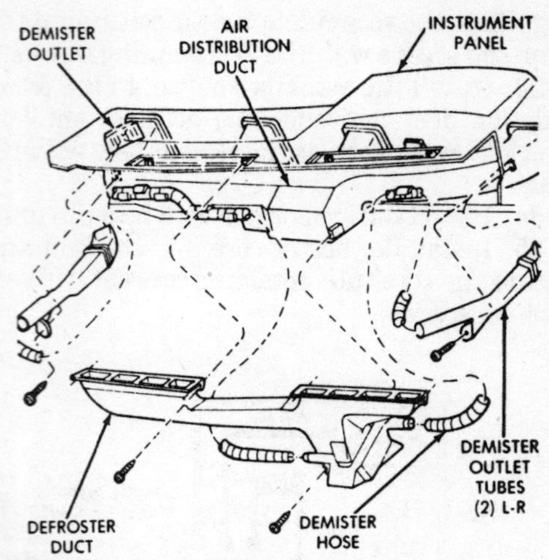

Instrument panel ventilation ducts and hoses

vacuum and electrical connectors.

41. Install the (4) retaining nuts to the unit mounting studs from the engine compartment.
42. Connect the air conditioning plumbing to the H-valve.
43. Connect the vacuum line at the brake booster and water valve.
44. Install the attaching screws from the right side to the center of the steering column.
45. Install the mid-reinforcement instrument panel trim molding.
46. Tighten the (2) brackets supporting the lower edge to the heater/evaporator unit housing.
47. Install the mounting bolt from the right side of the instrument panel to the right cowl.
48. Install the right side cowl and sill trim.
49. Install the steering column lower cover.
50. Install the passenger side lower instrument panel
51. Connect the heater hoses to heater core in the engine compartment.
52. Connect the negative battery cable.
53. Fill the cooling system.
54. Charge and leak test the air conditioning system. See Chapter 1.

Blower Motor

REMOVAL AND INSTALLATION

1. Disconnect the negative battery cable.
2. Remove the air intake duct and top half of the fan shroud.
3. Disconnect the blower connector.
4. Remove the blower motor cooling tube.
5. Remove the retaining nuts and washers from the studs holding the blower.
6. Pull the air conditioning lines inboard and upward while removing the blower assembly from the vehicle. Remove the spring clip fastening the blower wheel to the blower shaft and pull off the wheel.

To install:

7. Install the blower wheel to the shaft and install the spring clip. Inspect the blower mounting plate seal and repair, as necessary. Apply rubber adhesive to the seal to aid in assembly.
8. Install the blower into the housing and install the washers and nuts.
9. Install the cooling tube.
10. Connect the connector.
11. Install the fan shroud and air intake duct.
12. Connect the negative battery cable and check the blower motor for proper operation.

Heater Core and Evaporator

REMOVAL AND INSTALLATION

1984–90

1. Disconnect the negative battery cable. Have the system discharged by a professional shop. Drain the cooling system.
2. Remove the lower steering column cover.
3. Remove the lower reinforcement under the steering column, right side cowl and sill trim. Remove the bolt holding the right side instrument panel to the right cowl.
4. Loosen the 2 brackets supporting the lower edge of the heater housing. Remove the instrument panel trim covering and reinforcement. Remove the retaining screws from the right side of the steering column.
5. Disconnect the vacuum lines at the brake booster and water valve.
6. Clamp off the heater hoses at the heater core and remove them from the heater core tubes. Plug the ends to prevent leakage.

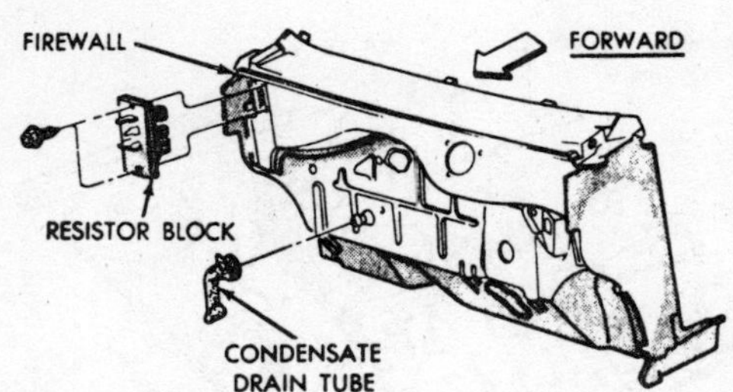

Resistor block removal or installation

7. Disconnect the H-valve at the water valve and remove it. Remove the retaining nuts at the package tray mounting studs. Remove the drain tube.

8. Disconnect the blower motor wiring and temperature control cable. Disconnect the vacuum harness at the top of the heater unit.

9. Remove the retaining nuts from the package mounting studs at the firewall. Disconnect the hanger strap from the package and rotate it aside.

10. Pull the right side of the instrument panel out as far as possible. Fold the carpeting and insulation back to provide a little more working room and to prevent spillage from staining the carpeting.

11. Remove the entire housing assembly from the dash panel and remove it from the vehicle.

12. To disassemble the housing assembly, remove the vacuum diaphragm and retaining screws from the cover and remove the cover.

13. Remove the retaining screw from the heater core and/or evaporator and remove from the housing assembly.

To install:

14. Remove the temperature control door from the unit and clean the unit out with solvent. Lubricate the lower pivot rod and its well and install. Wrap the heater core and/or evaporator with foam tape and place in position. Secure with the screws.

15. Assemble the unit, making sure all vacuum tubes are properly routed.

16. Install the assembly to the vehicle and connect the vacuum harness. Install the nuts to the firewall and install the condensation tube. Fold the carpeting back into position.

17. Connect the hanger strap from the package and rotate it aside. Install the 2 brackets supporting the lower edge of the heater housing. Connect the blower motor wiring, resistor wiring and the temperature control cable.

18. Install the retaining screws from the right side to the steering column. Install the instrument panel trim covering and reinforcement.

19. Install the bolt holding the right side instrument panel to the right cowl. Install the lower reinforcement under the steering column, right side cowl and sill trim.

20. Connect the vacuum lines at the brake booster and water valve.

21. Connect the heater hoses to the core tubes.

22. Using new gaskets, install the H-valve and connect the refrigerant lines. Install the condensation tube.

23. Charge the air conditioning system, if equipped. See Chapter 1. Add 2 oz. of refrigerant oil during the recharge. Fill the cooling system.

24. Connect the negative battery cable and check the entire climate control system for proper operation and leaks.

25. Connect the negative battery cable and check the entire climate control system for proper operation and leakage.

1991

1. Disconnect the negative battery cable. Have the system discharged by a professional service person, if equipped. Drain the cooling system.

2. Remove the steering column cover and left and right side under panel silencers.

3. Remove the center bezel by unclipping it from the instrument panel.

4. Remove the accessory switch carrier and the heater/air conditioning control head.

5. Remove storage bin and lower right instrument panel.

6. Disconnect the blower motor lead under the right side of the instrument panel.

7. Remove the right side 40-way connector wiring bracket.

8. Remove the lower right reinforcement, body computer bracket and mid-to-lower reinforcement as an assembly.

9. Disconnect the vacuum lines at the brake booster and water valve.

10. Clamp off the heater hoses near the heater core and remove the hoses from the core tubes. Plug the hose ends and the core tubes to prevent spillage of coolant.

11. If equipped with air conditioning, remove the H-valve and condensation tube.

12. Disconnect the temperature control cable and vacuum harness at the connection at the top of the unit.

13. Remove the retaining nuts from the package mounting studs at the firewall. Disconnect the hanger strap from the package and rotate it aside.

To install:

14. Remove the temperature control door from the unit and clean the unit out with solvent. Lubricate the lower pivot rod and its well

and install. Wrap the heater core and/or evaporator with foam tape and place in position. Secure with the screws.

15. Assemble the unit, making sure all vacuum tubes are properly routed.

16. Install the assembly to the vehicle and connect the vacuum harness. Install the nuts to the firewall and install the condensation tube. Fold the carpeting back into position.

17. Connect the hanger strap from the package and rotate it aside. Install the 2 brackets supporting the lower edge of the heater housing. Connect the blower motor wiring, resistor wiring and the temperature control cable.

18. Install the retaining screws from the right side to the steering column. Install the instrument panel trim covering and reinforcement.

19. Assemble the unit, making sure all vacuum tubes are properly routed.

20. Install the assembly to the vehicle and connect the vacuum harness. Install the nuts to the firewall and install the condensation tube. Fold the carpeting back into position.

22. Connect the hanger strap from the package and rotate it aside. Connect the blower motor wiring and temperature control cable.

23. Install the lower right reinforcement, body computer bracket and mid-to-lower reinforcement as an assembly.

24. Install the right side 40-way connector wiring bracket.

25. Install the lower right instrument panel and storage bin.

26. Install the heater/air conditioning control head and accessory switch carrier.

27. Install the center bezel to the instrument panel.

28. Install the under panel silencers and steering column cover.

29. Install the vacuum lines at the brake booster and water valve.

30. Connect the heater hoses to the core tubes.

31. Using new gaskets, install the H-valve and connect the refrigerant lines. Install the condensation tube.

32. Charge the air conditioning system, if equipped. See Chapter 1. Add 2 oz. of refrigerant oil during the recharge. Fill the cooling system.

33. Connect the negative battery cable and check the entire climate control system for proper operation and leaks.

34. Connect the negative battery cable and check the entire climate control system for proper operation and leakage.

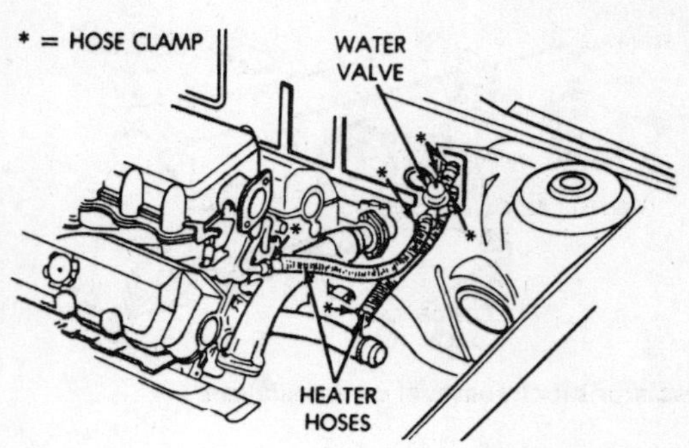

Heater hose routing – V6 engines

Climate Control Head

REMOVAL AND INSTALLATION

1. Disconnect the negative battery cable.
2. Remove the necessary bezel(s) in order to gain access to the control head.
3. Remove the screws that fasten the control head to the instrument panel.
4. Pull the unit out and unplug the electrical and vacuum connectors. Disconnect the temperature control cable by pushing the flag in and pulling the end from its seat.
5. Remove the control head from the instrument panel.
6. The installation is the reverse of the removal proceed that fasten the control head to the instrument panel.

AUXILIARY HEATER/AIR CONDITIONER

Blower Motor

REMOVAL AND INSTALLATION

1. Disconnect the negative battery cable.
2. Remove the middle bench, if equipped. Remove the left lower quarter trim panel.
3. Remove 1 blower scroll cover to floor screw and 7 scroll to unit screws.
4. Remove the blower relay.
5. Rotate the blower scroll cover from under the unit.
6. Remove the fan from the blower motor, remove the 3 motor attaching screws and remove the motor from the unit.
7. The installation is the reverse of the removal procedure.
8. Connect the negative battery cable and check the blower motor for proper operation.

Heater Core

REMOVAL AND INSTALLATION

1. Disconnect the negative battery cable. Pinch off the hoses to the rear heater core.
2. Raise the vehicle and support safely. Disconnect the underbody heater hoses from the rear heater core tubes.
3. Remove the middle bench, if equipped. Remove the interior left lower quarter trim panel.
4. Remove the 7 screws that attach the air distribution duct to the floor and unit. Pull the distribution duct straight up to remove.
5. Remove the 6 screws from the top surface of the unit and remove the unit cover.
6. Pull the heater core straight up and out of the unit.
7. The installation is the reverse of the removal procedure.
8. Connect the negative battery cable and check for leaks.

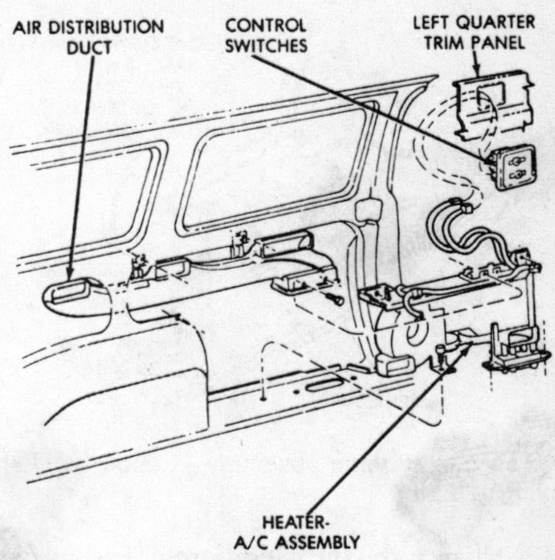

Rear air conditioning/heater assembly components

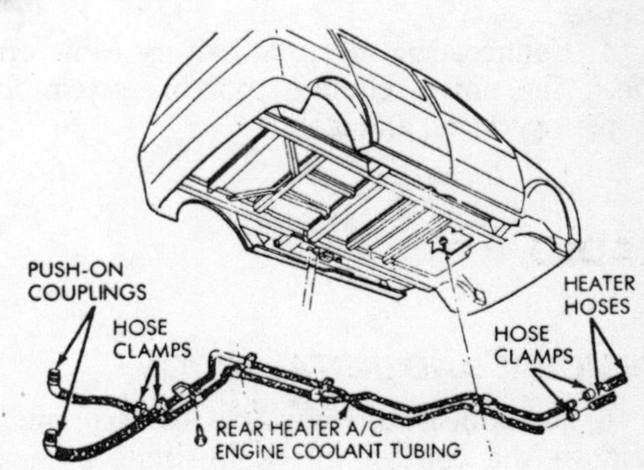

Rear heater assembly — underbody hose routing

Evaporator

REMOVAL AND INSTALLATION

1. Disconnect the negative battery cable.
2. Have the system discharged by a professional service person.
3. Remove the unit cover and duct.
4. Remove the middle bench, if equipped. Remove the interior left lower quarter trim panel.
5. Remove the 7 screws that attach the air distribution duct to the floor and unit. Pull the distribution duct straight up to remove.
6. Remove the 6 screws from the top surface of the unit and remove the unit cover.
7. Pull the evaporator and expansion valve straight up in order to clear the extension tube pilots and remove from the vehicle. Cover the exposed ends of the lines to minimize contamination.
8. Remove the Torx® screws and remove the expansion valve from the evaporator. Discard the gasket.

To install:

9. Lubricate the gasket with wax-free refrigerant oil and assemble the expansion valve and evaporator.
10. Lubricate the gasket with wax-free refrigerant oil and install the evaporator and expansion valve assembly to the refrigerant lines and install the bolt.
11. Install the unit cover and air distribution duct.
12. Install the interior trim cover and middle bench.

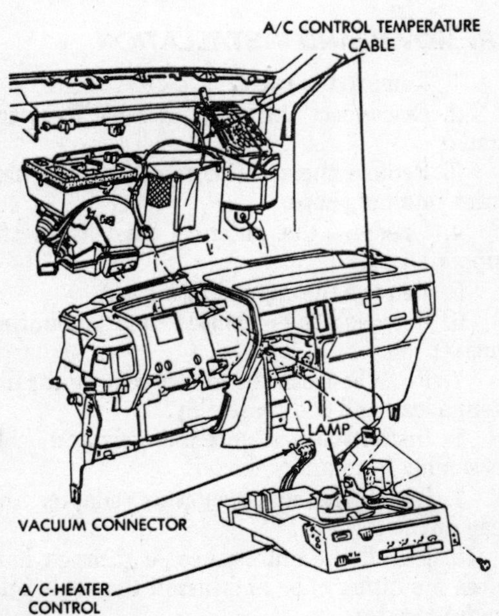

Air conditioning and heater control head removal

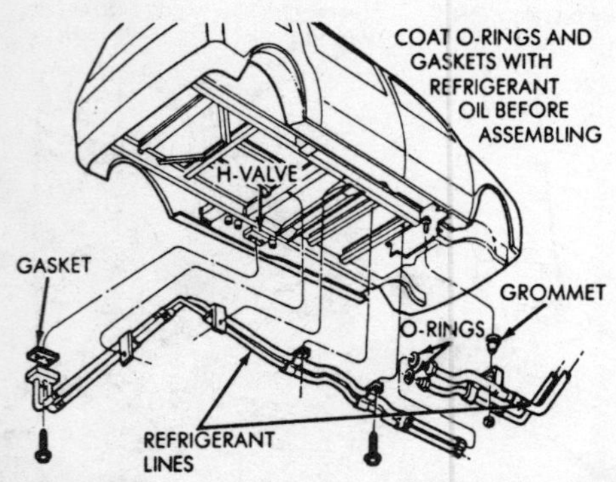

Rear air conditioning assembly – underbody line routing

13. Charge the air conditioning system. See Chapter 1. If the evaporator was replaced, measure the amount of oil that was in the original evaporator and add that amount during the recharge.

14. Connect the negative battery cable and check the entire climate control system for proper operation and leaks.

RADIO

REMOVAL AND INSTALLATION

1. Disconnect the negative battery cable. Remove the control knobs by pulling them from the mounting stalks. Remove the three (3) screws from the top of the radio trim bezel.
2. Remove the ash tray to gain access to the trim bezel lower screws.
3. Remove the two (2) screws from the lower portion of the trim bezel.
4. Pull outward on the left side of bezel to unsnap the mounting clips. Remove the bezel.

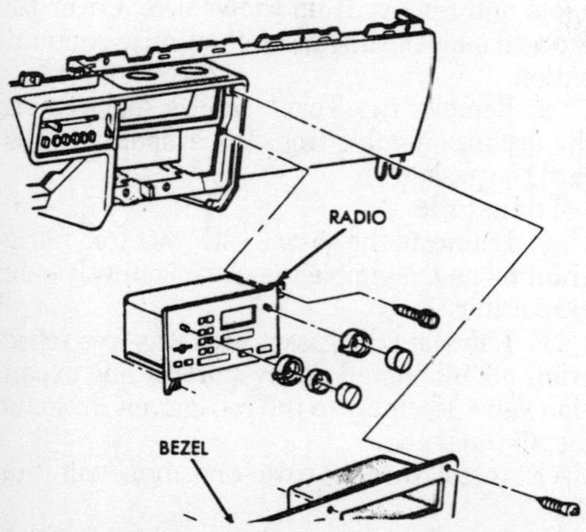

Radio assembly removal

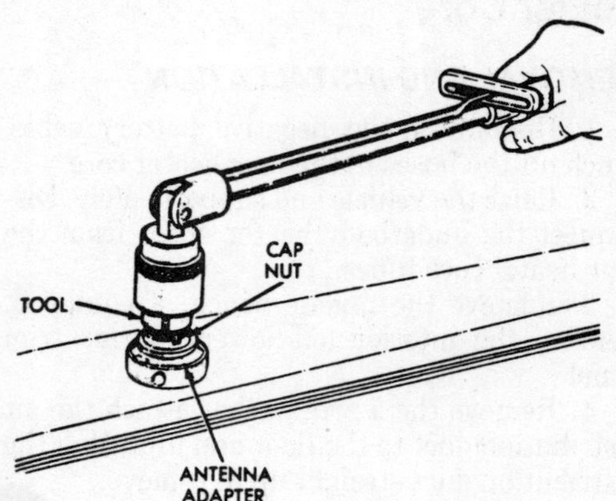

Antenna removal

5. Remove the radio to instrument panel retaining screws.
6. Pull the radio through the front of the instrument panel and unplug the wiring harness, ground strap and antenna plug.
7. Connect the radio wiring harness, ground strap and antenna lead.
8. Position the radio into the instrument panel and install the retaining screws.
9. Install the trim bezel and secure it with the lower and upper retaining screws. Install the ash tray.

Antenna

REMOVAL AND INSTALLATION

1. Remove the radio.
2. Disconnect the antenna cable from the radio.
3. Remove the antenna cable from the harness retaining clips.
4. Unscrew the antenna mast from the upper adapter.
5. Remove the cap mounting nut.
6. Remove the adapter and mounting gasket.
7. From beneath the fender remove the antenna lead and body assembly.
8. Install the new antenna body and cable assembly from under fender.
9. Install the adapter gasket, adapter and cap nut.
10. Install the antenna cable through harness mounting clips and install the cable into radio receiver.
11. Install the radio into the instrument panel.

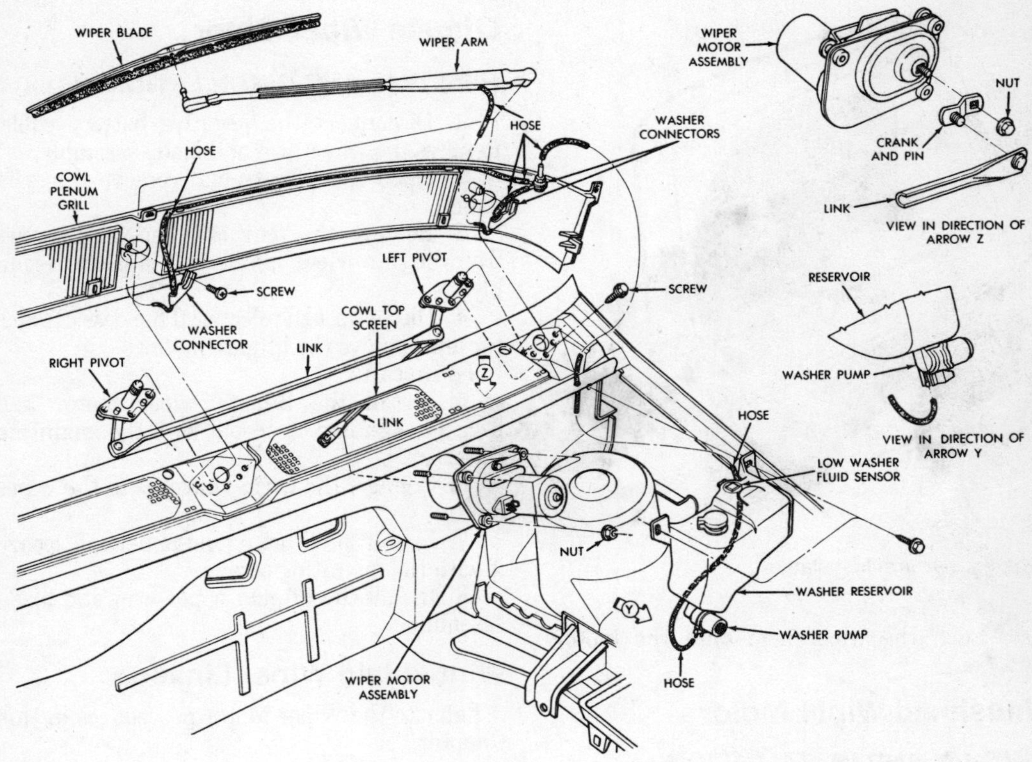

Windshield wiper motor and linkage assemblies

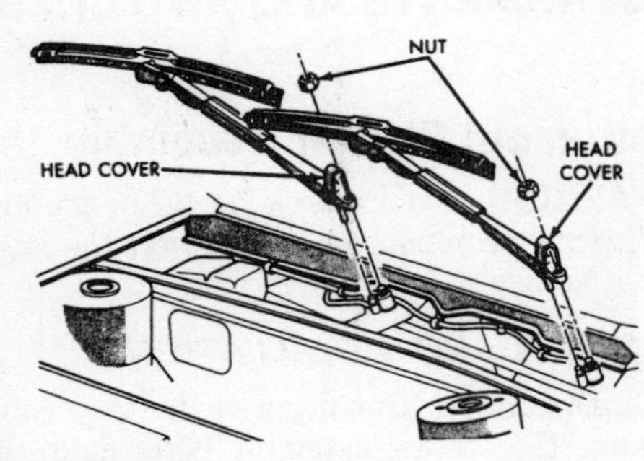

Wiper arm servicing

WINDSHIELD WIPERS

Wiper Blade

Refer to "General Information and Maintenance" for removal and installation procedure.

Wiper Arm (Windshield)

REMOVAL AND INSTALLATION

1. Remove the head cover from the wiper arm base.
2. Remove the arm to pivot attaching nut.
3. Remove the wiper arm from pivot using a rocking motion.
4. With the wiper motor in Park position, position the arm on the pivot shaft. Choose a point where the tip of the left wiper arm is approximately 2 to 3 inches above the windshield cowl top, and the right arm 1 to 1.5 inches above the windshield cowl top.
5. Install the attaching nut and torque to 120 in. lbs.
6. Install the pivot head cover on the wiper arm.

Wiper Arm (Liftgate)

REMOVAL AND INSTALLATION

1. Insert Tool C-3982 or the equivalent between the wiper arm and wiper motor output shaft.

NOTE: *The use of screwdrivers or other prying tool may damaged the spring clip in the base of the arm, while trying to release the arm. Damage of the spring clip will result in the arm coming off the shaft regardless of how carefully it is installed.*

2. Lift the arm and remove it from motor output shaft.
3. With motor in the Park position, position the arm on the motor output shaft. Choose a point where the tip of blade is about 38mm parallel with the bottom lower edge of liftgate

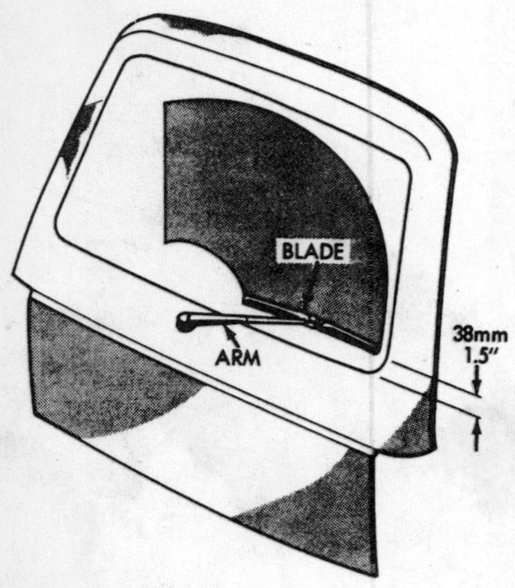

Liftgate wiper arm installation

glass. Push the wiper arm onto the motor shaft.

Windshield Wiper Motor

REMOVAL AND INSTALLATION

1. The motor and wiper linkage are serviced as a unit. Disconnect the negative battery cable. Remove the wiper arm and blade assemblies. Refer to the windshield wiper arm removal and installation procedure in this Chapter.
2. Open the hood and remove the cowl plenum grille and plastic screen.
3. Remove the hoses from the turret connector. Remove the pivot mounting screws.
4. Disconnect the motor wiring connector from the motor.
5. Remove the retaining nut from the wiper motor shaft to linkage drive crank, and remove the drive crank from the wiper motor shaft.
6. Remove the wiper motor assembly mounting screws and nuts, and remove the wiper motor.

To install:

7. Position the wiper motor against it's mounting surface and secure in position with the mounting screws and nuts Connect the wiring harness.
8. Install the linkage drive crank onto the wiper motor shaft and secure it with the retaining nut. Torque the nut to 95 in. lbs.
9. Install cowl plenum grille plastic screen.
10. Connect hoses to turret connector.
11. Install the cowl plenum grille. Connect the negative battery cable. Close the hood.
12. Install the windshield wiper arm and blade assemblies.

Liftgate Wiper Motor

REMOVAL AND INSTALLATION

1. Disconnect the negative battery cable. Remove the wiper arm and blade assembly.
2. Open the liftgate and remove the trim panel.
3. Remove the four (4) mounting screws from liftgate wiper motor and bracket assembly.
4. Disconnect the electrical harness connector and remove the liftgate motor.

To install:

5. Install the liftgate wiper motor and bracket assembly. Secure it with the mounting screws.
6. Connect the wiring harness to the wiper motor.
7. Install the liftgate trim panel and secure it with the mounting screws.
8. Install the liftgate wiper arm and blade assembly.

Windshield Wiper Linkage

Refer to the Wiper Motor procedures in this Chapter.

INSTRUMENTS AND SWITCHES

Instrument Cluster Assembly

WARNING: *Before servicing the instrument cluster or components, disconnect the negative battery.*

REMOVAL AND INSTALLATION

1. Disconnect the negative battery cable. Remove the cluster assembly bezel mounting (7) screws and remove the cluster bezel.
2. On vehicles equipped with an automatic transaxle, remove the steering column lower cover. Disconnect the shift indicator wire.
3. Remove the cluster assembly retaining screws.

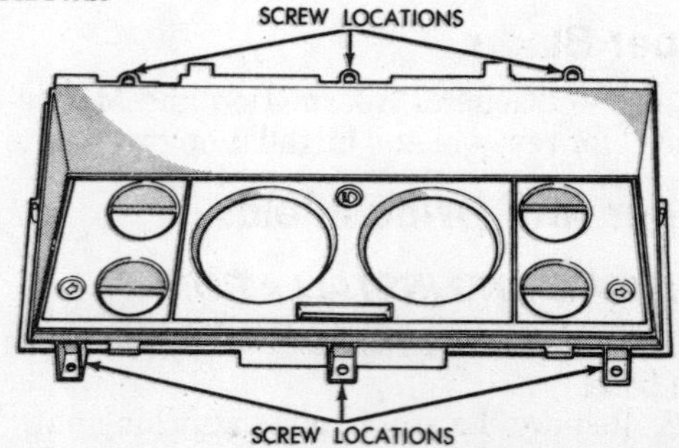

Instrument cluster mask/lens — 1984-90 models

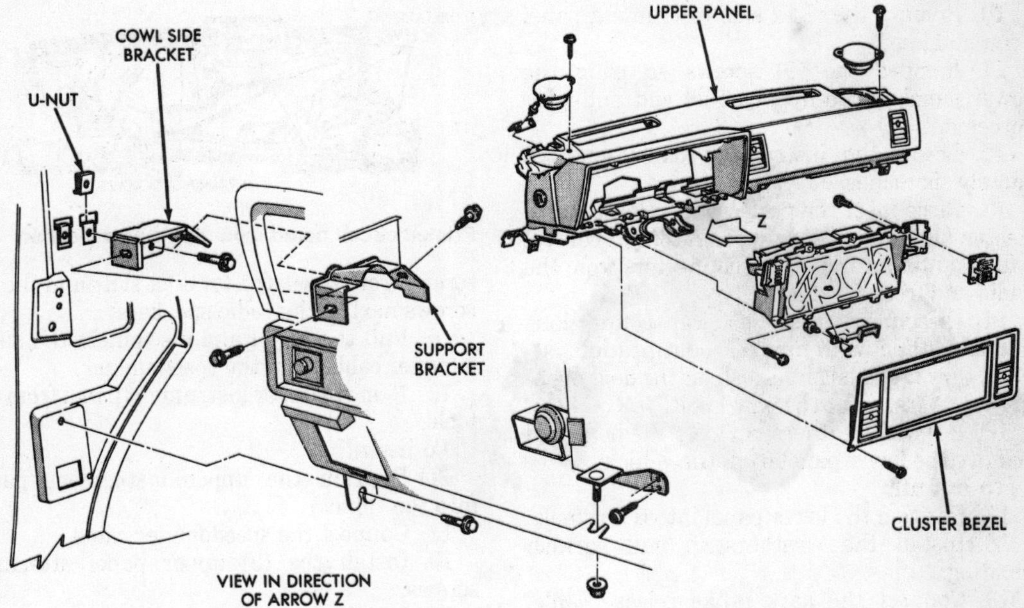

Upper instrument panel and cluster mounting – 1984-90 models, 1991 models similar

4. Carefully pull the cluster assembly from the panel and disconnect the speedometer cable.
5. Remove the cluster assembly wiring harness.
6. Remove the cluster assembly past the right side of the steering column.

To install:

7. Position the cluster assembly to the dash from the right side of the steering column.
8. Connect the cluster wiring.
9. Connect the speedometer cable.
10. Install the cluster assembly and retaining screws.
11. On models equipped with an automatic transaxle, place the selector lever in (D) Drive position.
12. Connect the shift indicator wire to the steering column shift housing. Route the wire on the outside of slotted flange.
13. Place the shift lever in (P) Park position to make the indicator self-adjust.
14. Connect the shift indicator wire.
15. Install the steering column lower cover.
16. Install the cluster assembly bezel. Secure the bezel with the retaining screws.

NOTE: *The following instruments can be serviced after removing the instrument cluster mask/lens. Do not completely remove the cluster assembly if only instrument service or cluster bulb replacement is necessary.*

Instrument Panel (Lower)

REMOVAL AND INSTALLATION

CAUTION: *Before servicing the lower instrument panel, chock the wheels. Servicing the steering column may cause an automatic transaxle to come out of the (P) Park position. Always release the parking brake before the release cable is disconnected. Disconnecting the parking brake cable without releasing the parking brake may cause personal injury.*

1. Block the vehicle wheels and release the parking brake. Disconnect the negative battery cable.
2. Remove the steering column lower left cover.
3. Remove the side cowl and the sill molding.
4. Remove the instrument panel silencer and reinforcement.
5. Loosen the bolt in the side cowl, but do not remove the bolt.
6. Place the gear selector into the (N) Neutral position and disconnect the shift indicator cable.
7. Remove the steering wheel.
8. Remove the (5) nuts securing the steering column to the support bracket.
9. Lower the steering column. Use a cover to protect the steering column and the front seat.

10. Remove the right side instrument panel trim molding.

11. Remove the (9) screws securing the lower panel to the upper panel and mid-reinforcement.

12. Lower the instrument panel approximately six inches.

13. Disconnect the park brake release cable, heater attachment or air conditioning control cables, antenna and wiring connectors from the radio and fresh air ducts.

14. Disconnect the electrical connections and label them with tape for identification.

15. Pry the A-pillar garnish off the door opening weatherstrip at the panel bolt.

16. Pull the weatherstrip from the body and remove the lower panel from the vehicle.

To install:

17. Position the lower panel into the vehicle.

18. Install the weatherstrip and garnish molding.

19. Connect the park brake release cable, heater attachment or air conditioning control cables, antenna and wiring connectors to the radio and fresh air ducts.

20. Connect all electrical connections.

21. Secure the lower instrument panel to upper panel and mid-reinforcement with (9) retaining screws.

22. Install the right side instrument panel trim molding.

23. Raise the steering column and install the (5) nuts securing steering column to the support bracket.

24. Install the steering wheel.

25. Connect the shift indicator cable.

26. Install the lower reinforcement, silencer and the lower left steering column cover. Connect the negative battery cable.

Instrument Panel (Upper)

REMOVAL AND INSTALLATION

1. Disconnect the negative battery cable. Separate the lower instrument panel from the upper half (see Steps 1 through 12 of the Lower Instrument Panel procedure).

2. Disconnect the speedometer cable from the engine compartment.

3. Remove (2) nuts at the steering column floating bracket.

4. Disconnect the gear shift selector indicator wire.

5. Disconnect the electrical connector at the radio speakers.

6. Remove the radio speaker and defroster grilles.

7. Remove the (2) mounting screws from each side cowl bracket.

8. Remove the (4) upper panel attaching screws from the defroster duct slots and the (2) screws next to the radio speakers.

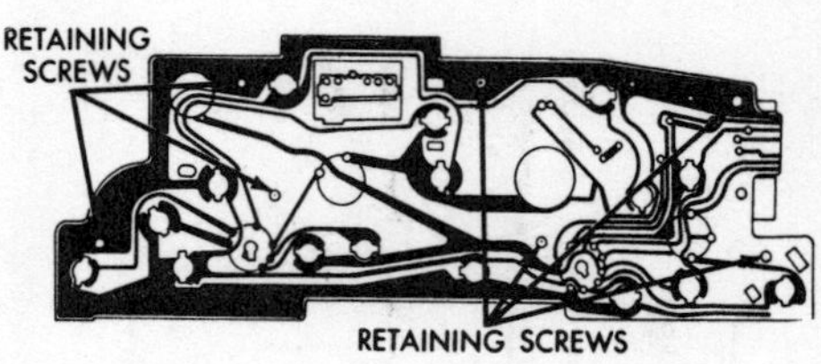

Printed circuit board mounting screw location

9. Pull the panel and disconnect the speedometer cable from the speedometer.

10. Remove upper instrument panel from vehicle.

To install:

11. Position the upper instrument panel into the vehicle.

12. Connect the speedometer cable.

13. Install the (6) upper panel attaching screws.

14. Install the cowl bracket retaining screws.

15. Install the radio speaker and defroster grilles.

16. Connect the radio speaker wiring.

17. Connect the gear shift selector indicator wire.

18. Install the retaining nuts at the steering column floating bracket.

19. Connect the speedometer cable in the engine compartment.

20. Install the lower panel to the upper.

Windshield Wiper Switch

The windshield wiper switch on all 1984-90 models is an stalk mounted control. On 1991 models, the wiper switch is mounted on the instrument cluster pod.

REMOVAL AND INSTALLATION

1984-90 Models With Standard Steering Column

1. Disconnect negative battery cable.

2. Remove the steering wheel horn pad assembly.

3. Remove the lower steering column cover, silencer and reinforcement.

4. Remove the wiper switch wiring harness from the steering column retainer.

5. Remove the wash/wipe switch cover. Rotate the cover upward.

6. Disconnect the wipe/wash seven terminal electrical connector. Disconnect intermittent the wipe switch electrical connector or speed control electrical connector, if equipped.

7. Unlock the steering column and turn the wheel so that the access hole provided in the wheel base is in the 9 o'clock position.

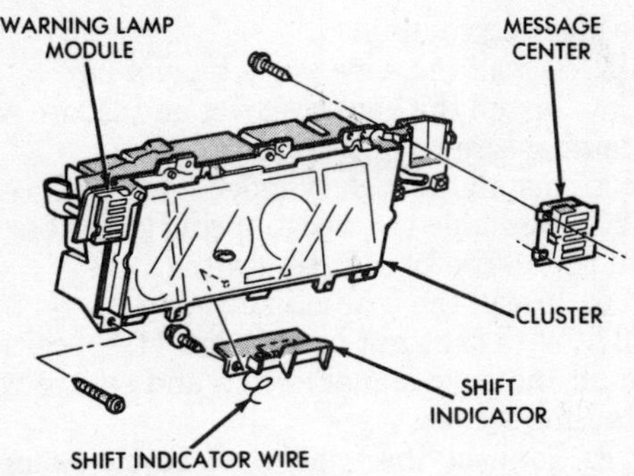

Shift indicator and message center mounting on the instrument cluster

8. Reach through the access hole using a small screwdriver and loosen the turn signal lever mounting screw.
9. Remove the wipe/wash switch assembly the from steering column.
10. Slide the circular hider up the control stalk and remove the (2) screws that attach the control stalk sleeve to wipe/wash switch.
11. Remove the wipe/wash switch control knob from the multifunction control stalk. Rotate the control stalk to full clockwise position and pull the shaft from the switch.

To install:

12. Install the stalk shaft into the wash/wipe switch and rotate full counterclockwise.
13. Install the wash/wipe switch control knob onto the end of the multifunction control stalk.
14. Install (2) retaining screws that secure the wipe/wash switch to the control stalk sleeve.
15. Install the wipe/wash switch assembly to the steering column.
16. Install and tighten the turn signal lever screw (through the access hole).
17. Connect the wipe/wash seven terminal electrical connector. Connect the intermittent wipe switch electrical connector or speed control electrical connector, if equipped.
18. Install the wash/wipe switch cover.
19. Secure the wiring harness into the steering column retainer.
20. Install the reinforcement, silencer and lower steering column cover.
21. Install the steering wheel horn pad assembly.
21. Connect the negative batter cable.

1984-90 Models With Tilt Steering Column

1. Disconnect the negative battery cable.
2. Remove the horn cover pad from the steering wheel. Remove steering column cover. Remove the steering wheel nut.
3. Remove the steering wheel using puller C-3428B or equivalent.

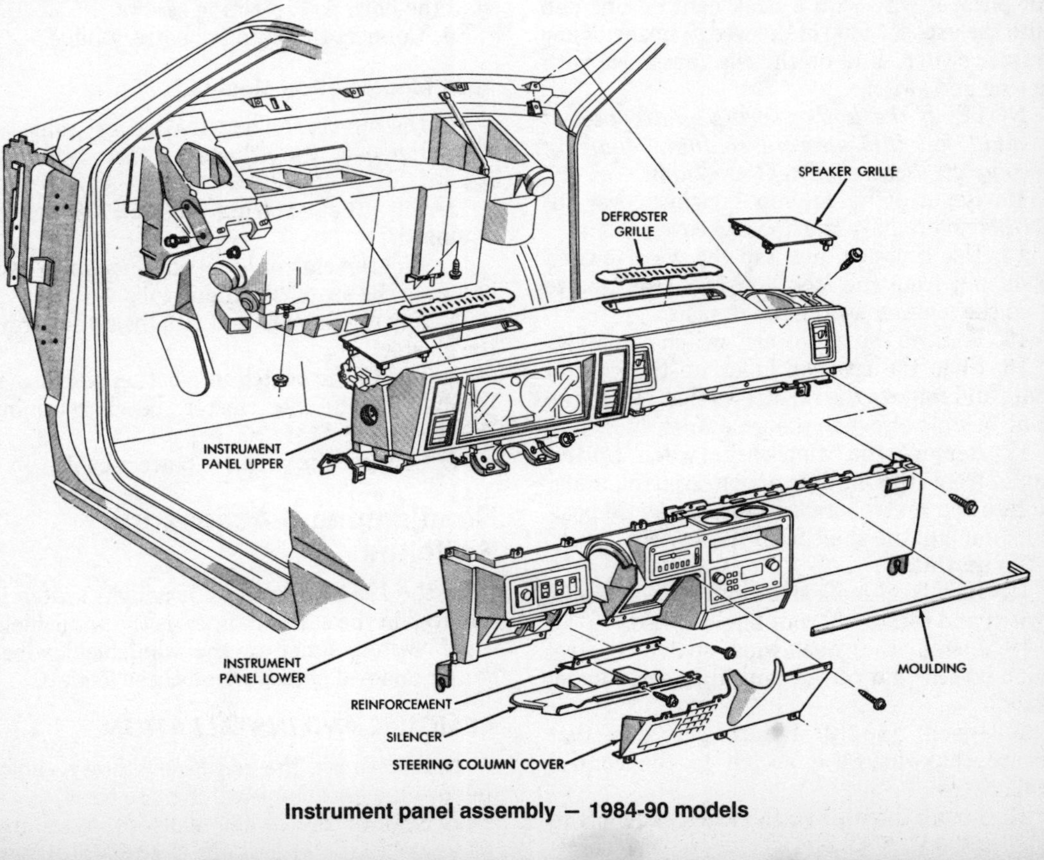

Instrument panel assembly — 1984-90 models

4. Carefully remove the plastic cover from the locking plate. Install locking plate depressing tool C-4156 or equivalent onto the steering shaft. Depress the locking plate and remove the retaining ring from the mounting groove using a small screwdriver. To avoid difficulty when removing the retaining ring, the full load of the upper bearing spring should not be relieved. Remove the locking plate, canceling cam, and upper bearing spring.

5. Remove the switch stalk actuator screw and arm.

6. Remove the hazard warning knob.

7. Disconnect the wipe/wash seven terminal electrical connector. Disconnect the intermittent wipe switch electrical connector or speed control electrical connector, if equipped.

8. Remove the turn signal switch (3) retaining screws.

9. Tape the connectors at end of the wiring to prevent snagging when removing. Place the shift bowl in low (1st) position. Remove the switch and wiring.

10. Remove the ignition key lamp located next to the hazard warning knob.

11. Insert a thin screwdriver into the lock release slot next to the lock cylinder mounting and depress the spring latch at the bottom of the slot. Remove the lock cylinder.

12. Insert a straightened paper clip or similar piece of wire with a hook bent on one end into the exposed loop of the wedge spring of key buzzer switch. Pull on the clip to remove both spring and switch.

NOTE: *If the wedge spring is dropped, it could fall into steering column, requiring complete disassembly of the column.*

13. Remove the column housing cover (3) screws and remove the housing cover.

14. Use a punch, and tap the wiper switch pivot pin from the lock housing. Use tape to hold the dimmer switch rod in place.

15. Remove the wipe/wash switch assembly.

16. Slide the circular hider up the control stalk and remove the (2) screws that attach the control stalk sleeve to the wipe/wash switch.

17. Remove the wipe/wash switch control knob from the multifunction control stalk. Rotate the control stalk to full clockwise position and pull the shaft from the switch.

To install:

18. Install the stalk shaft into the wash/wipe switch and rotate full counterclockwise.

19. Install the wash/wipe switch control knob on the end of the multifunction control stalk.

20. Install the (2) retaining screws that secure the wipe/wash switch to the control stalk sleeve.

21. Install the wipe/wash switch assembly to the steering column.

22. Install the wiper switch pivot pin.

23. Install the housing cover and secure with retaining screws.

24. Install the lock cylinder.

25. Assemble the wedge spring to key buzzer and install the key buzzer switch.

26. Install the ignition key lamp.

27. With the shift bowl in low (1st) position, install the turn signal switch and secure with retaining screws.

28. Connect the wipe/wash seven terminal electrical connector. Connect the intermittent wipe switch electrical connector or speed control electrical connector, if equipped.

29. Secure the wiring harness in retainer.

30. Install the hazard warning knob.

31. Install the switch stalk actuator screw and arm.

32. Install the locking plate, canceling cam, and upper bearing spring. Install the locking plate. Depress the locking plate with tool C-4156 or equivalent and install the retaining ring in groove of steering shaft. Install the plastic cover on locking plate.

33. Install the reinforcement, silencer and lower steering column cover.

34. Install the steering wheel and steering shaft nut.

35. Install the horn contact, horn pad and install the horn pad retaining screws.

36. Connect the negative battery cable.

1991 Models – Pod Mounted

1. Disconnect the negative battery cable.
2. Remove the cluster bezel retaining screws.
3. Tilt the steering column down, if equipped.
4. Pull the cluster bezel out enough to gain access to the switch retaining tabs.
5. Release the tabs and pull the switch from the cluster.
6. Install the switch in position and seat it firmly. Install the cluster bezel retaining screws.
7. Connect the negative battery cable.

Headlamp and Accessory Switches

On the 1991 models, the headlight switch is removed in the same manner as the windshield wiper switch. Refer to the windshield wiper switch removal procedure on these models.

REMOVAL AND INSTALLATION

1. Disconnect the negative battery cable. Remove the headlamp switch plate bezel.
2. Remove the switch plate (4) retaining

screws and pull the switch plate rearward.

3. Disconnect the electrical connectors. Remove the headlamp switch knob and shaft by depressing button on the switch body. Pull the knob and shaft out of the switch.

4. Remove the (2) screws retaining the headlamp switch to switch plate assembly.

5. Remove the headlamp switch retainer.

To install:

6. Install the replacement switch into the headlamp switch plate with retainer.

7. Install the headlamp switch retaining screws to the switch plate assembly.

8. Install the headlamp switch knob and shaft.

9. Connect the electrical connectors.

10. Secure the headlamp switch plate with (4) attaching screws.

11. Install the headlamp switch plate bezel.

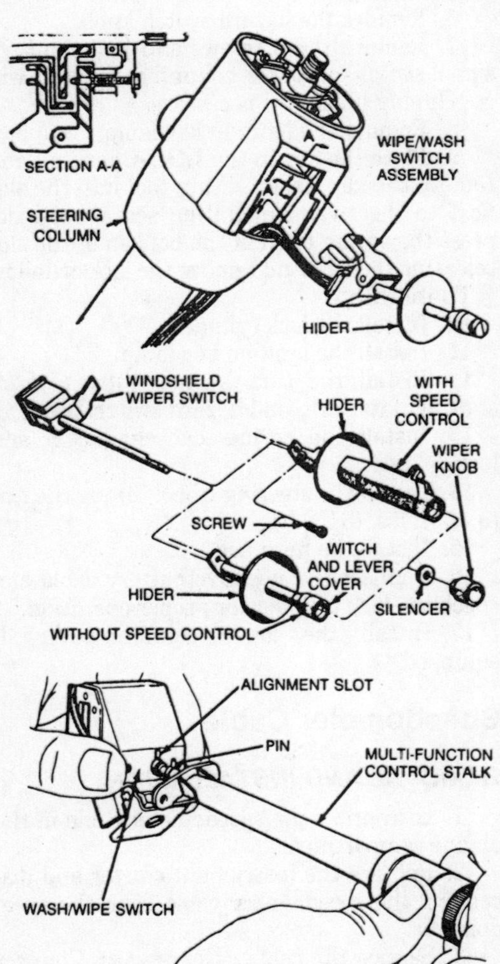

Removing the wiper switch – standard steering column

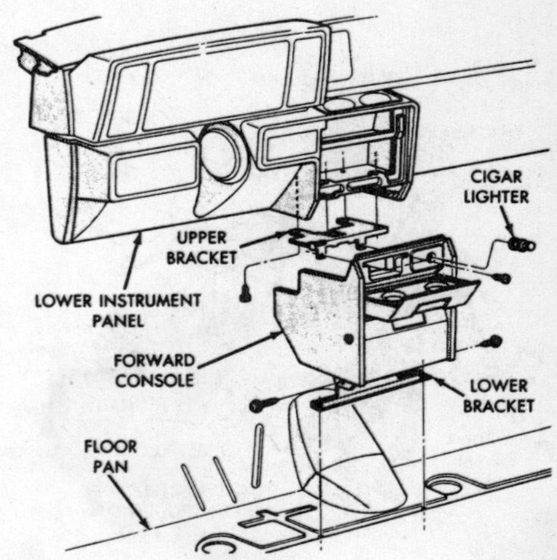

Forward console mounting

Ignition Lock/Switch

REMOVAL AND INSTALLATION

Except Tilt Column

1. Disconnect the negative battery cable.

2. Remove the horn pad mounting screws from behind the steering wheel and remove the horn pad.

3. Remove the steering wheel nut, matchmark the steering wheel to the shaft and remove the steering wheel with a suitable puller.

4. Remove the hazard switch knob. Remove the slotted hex-head screw that attaches the wiper switch to the turn signal switch.

5. Remove the 3 screws and pull the turn signal switch out of the column as far as it will go. Unplug it below if necessary.

6. Remove the ignition switch key lamp.

7. Place the key in the **LOCK** position and remove the key.

8. Insert 2 suitable small diameter tools into both release holes and push inward to release the spring loaded lock retainers while si-

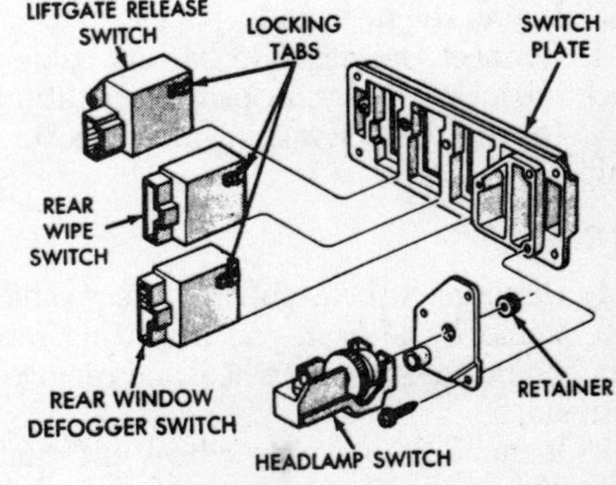

Headlight and accessory switches – 1984-90 models

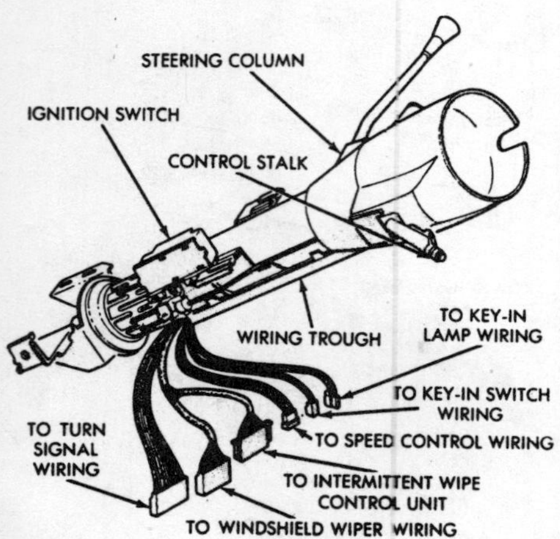

Steering column wiring connector identification

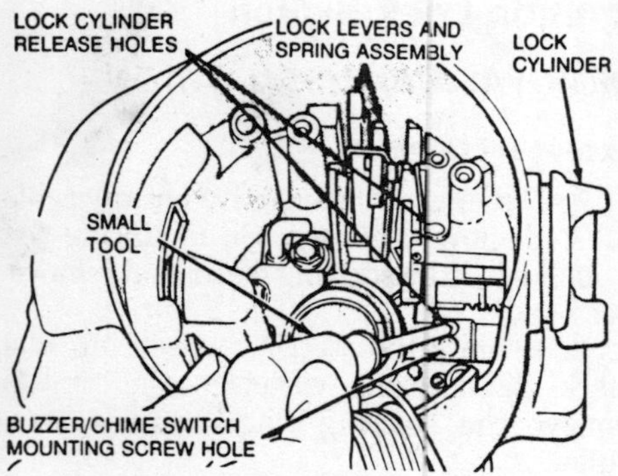

Removing the key lock cylinder – except on tilt wheel

multaneously pulling the key lock cylinder out of its bore.

To install:

9. Install the key cylinder.
10. Install the ignition switch key lamp.
11. Install the turn signal switch and hazard switch knob. Connect the wires if they were disconnected.
12. Install the steering wheel torque the nut to 45 ft. lbs. (61 Nm).
13. Install the horn pad.
14. Connect the negative battery cable and check the lock cylinder for proper operation.
15. Install the lower column cover, if equipped.

Tilt Column

1. Disconnect the negative battery cable.
2. Remove the horn pad mounting screws from behind the steering wheel and remove the horn pad.
3. Remove the steering wheel nut, matchmark the steering wheel to the shaft and remove the steering wheel with a suitable puller.

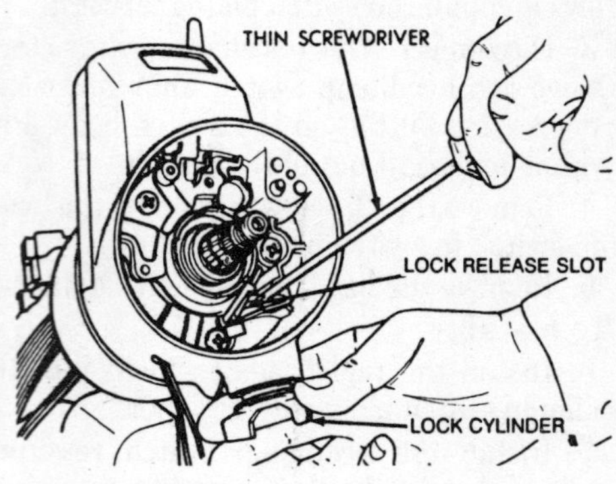

Removing the key lock cylinder – tilt wheel

4. Depress the lock plate with the proper depressing tool, remove the retaining ring from its groove and remove the tool, ring, lock plate, canceling cam and spring.
5. Remove the stalk actuator screw and arm.
6. Remove the hazard switch knob.
7. Remove the 3 screws and pull the turn signal switch out of the column as far as it will go. Unplug it below if necessary.
8. Remove the ignition key lamp.
9. Place the key in the **LOCK** position and remove the key. Insert a thin tool into the slot next to the switch mounting screw boss, depress the spring latch at the bottom of the slot releasing the lock and remove the lock cylinder.

To install:

10. Install the lock cylinder.
11. Install the ignition key lamp.
12. Install the turn signal switch, switch stalk actuator arm and hazard switch knob.
13. Install the spring, canceling cam and lock cylinder.
14. Install the steering wheel torque the nut to 45 ft. lbs. (61 Nm).
15. Install the horn pad.
16. Connect the negative battery cable and check the lock cylinder for proper operation.
17. Install the lower column cover, if equipped.

Speedometer Cable

REMOVAL AND INSTALLATION

1. Disconnect the speedometer cable in the engine compartment.
2. Remove the instrument cluster and disconnect the speedometer cable from the speedometer.
3. Service the cable as necessary. Connect the cable to the speedometer.
4. Install the instrument cluster. Connect the speedometer cable in the engine compartment.

LIGHTING

Headlights

REMOVAL AND INSTALLATION

Sealed Beam

1. Remove the headlight bezel retaining screws and remove the bezel.
2. Remove the headlamp retaining ring screws and remove the retaining ring. Do not disturb the headlamp adjusting crews.
3. Pull the sealed beam forward and disconnect the electrical connector.
4. Install the replacement beam and connect the electrical connector.
5. Install the retaining ring.
6. Install the headlight bezel.

Aerodynamic Headlamp

1. From the engine compartment, remove the three wire connector behind the headlamp assembly.
2. Rotate the bulb retaining ring counterclockwise and remove the retaining ring and lamp bulb.
3. Install the replacement bulb and retaining ring assembly. Rotate the ring clockwise.
4. Connect the three wire connector.

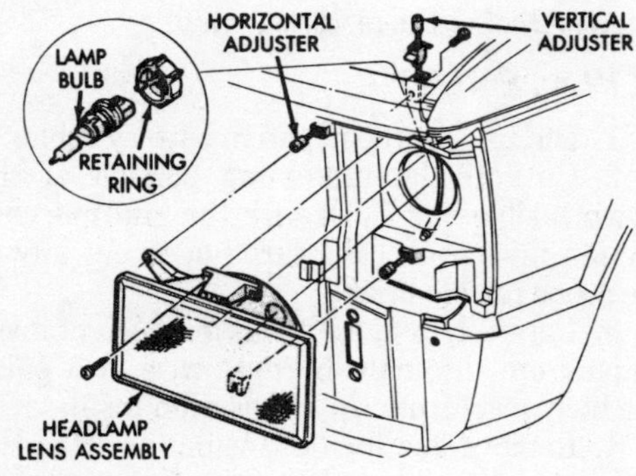

Aero headlamp replacement

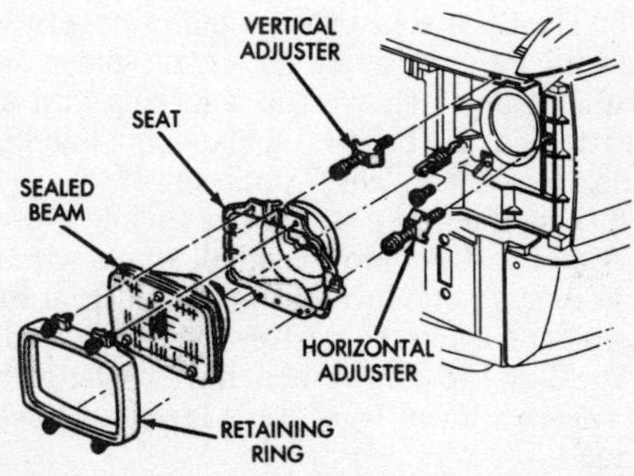

Sealed beam headlamp replacement

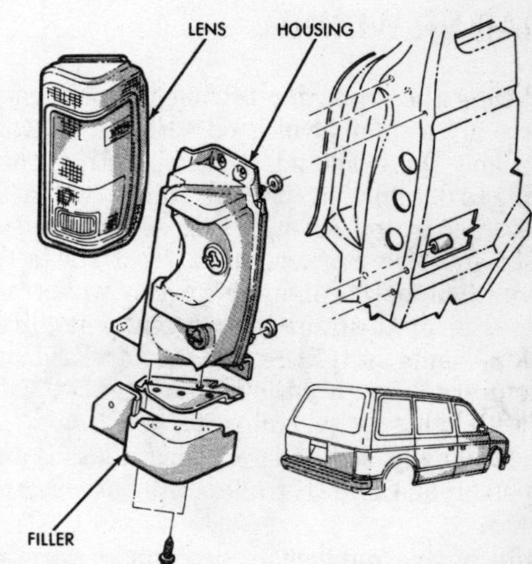

Tail, stop, turn signal, back-up and side marker lamp replacement

Signal and Marker Lights

REMOVAL AND INSTALLATION

Front Park, Turn Signal and Side Marker

1. Remove the headlamp bezel retaining screws and remove the bezel.
2. Twist the bulb from the lamp socket.
3. Install the replacement bulb and twist into position.
4. Install the headlamp bezel and retaining screws.

Rear Tail, Stop, Turn Signal, Back Up, Side Marker and License Lamp

1. To replace the bulb, remove (4) attaching screws.
2. Pull out the lamp assembly. Twist the socket from the lamp and replace the bulb.
3. Install the replacement bulb and twist the socket into the lamp assembly.
4. Position the lamp assembly in place and secure with (4) attaching screws.

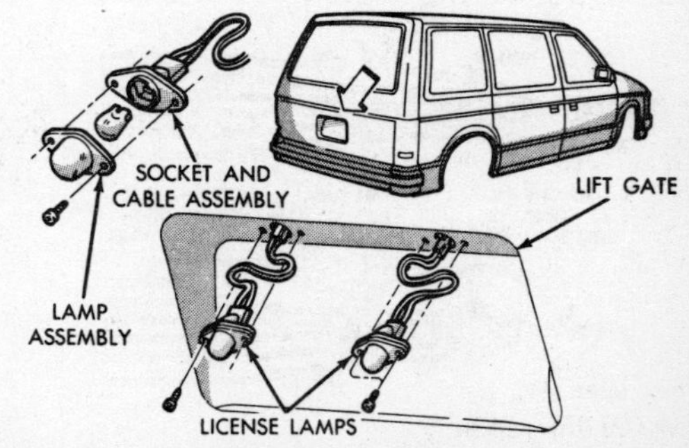

License lamp assembly replacement

TRAILER WIRING

Wiring the truck for towing is fairly easy. There are a number of good wiring kits available and these should be used, rather than trying to design your own. All trailers will need brake lights and turn signals as well as tail lights and side marker lights. Most states require extra marker lights for overly wide trailers. Also, most states have recently required back-up lights for trailers, and most trailer manufacturers have been building trailers with back-up lights for several years.

Additionally, some Class I, most Class II and just about all Class III trailers will have electric brakes.

Add to this number an accessories wire, to operate trailer internal equipment or to charge the trailer's battery, and you can have as many as seven wires in the harness.

Determine the equipment on your trailer and buy the wiring kit necessary. The kit will contain all the wires needed, plus a plug adapter set which included the female plug, mounted on the bumper or hitch, and the male plug, wired into, or plugged into the trailer harness.

When installing the kit, follow the manufacturer's instructions. The color coding of the wires is standard throughout the industry.

One point to note, some domestic vehicles, and most imported vehicles, have separate turn signals. On most domestic vehicles, the brake lights and rear turn signals operate with the same bulb. For those vehicles with separate turn signals, you can purchase an isolation unit so that the brake lights won't blink whenever the turn signals are operated, or, you can go to your local electronics supply house and buy four diodes to wire in series with the brake and turn signal bulbs. Diodes will isolate the brake and turn signals. The choice is yours. The isolation units are simple and quick to install, but far more expensive than the diodes. The diodes, however, require more work to install properly, since they require the cutting of each bulb's wire and soldering in place of the diode.

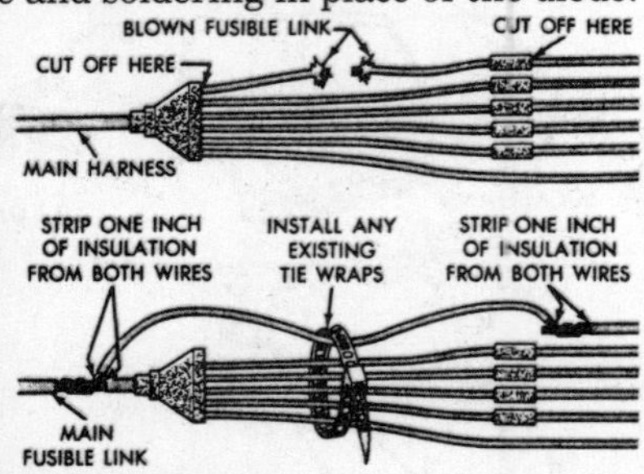

Fusible link repair

One final point, the best kits are those with a spring loaded cover on the vehicle mounted socket. This cover prevents dirt and moisture from corroding the terminals. Never let the vehicle socket hang loosely. Always mount it securely to the bumper or hitch.

CIRCUIT PROTECTION

Fuse Block

The fuse block and relay bank is located on the driver's side under the lower instrument panel. The fuse block contains fuses for various circuits as well as circuit breakers, horn relay, ignition lamp thermal time delay, and the turn signal flasher. The hazard warning flasher is mounted into a bracket below the fuse block.

Fusible Links

The main wiring harnesses are equipped with fusible links to protect against harness damage should a short circuit develop.

Never replace a fusible link with standard wire. Only fusible link wire of the correct gauge with hypalon insulation should be used.

When a fusible link blows, it is very important to locate and repair the short. Do not just replace the link to correct the problem.

Always disconnect battery negative cable when servicing the electrical system.

REPLACEMENT

1. Disconnect the negative battery cable.
2. Cut off the remaining portion of the blown fusible link flush with the multiple connection insulator. Take care not to cut any of the other fusible links.
3. Carefully remove about one inch of insulation from the main harness wire at a point one inch away from the connection insulator.
4. Remove one inch of insulation from the replacement fusible link wire and wrap the exposed area around the main harness wire at the point where the insulation was removed.
5. Heat the splice with a high temperature soldering gun and apply resin type solder until it runs freely. Remove the soldering gun and confirm that a "bright" solder joint has been made. Resolder if "cold" (dull) joint.
6. Cut the other end of the fusible link off at a point just behind the small single wire insulator. Strip one inch of insulation from fusible link and connection wires. Wrap and solder.
7. After the connections have cooled, wrap the splices with at least three layers of electrical tape.

Drive Train 7

MANUAL TRANSAXLE

Identification

Seven manual transaxles, built by Chrysler, are used; a 4-speed, A-460 and six 5-speeds; A-465, A-520, A-523, A-525, A-555 and A-568. All of these transaxles are based on the same design and components, therefore servicing each is almost identical. The transmission and differential are contained together in a single die-cast aluminum case. All of the transmissions are fully synchronized in all gears. Dexron®II automatic transmission type fluid (models through 1986) or 5W-30 motor oil (1987 and later models) is used for lubrication. The transaxle model, build date and final drive ratio are stamped on a tag that is attached to the top of the transaxle. Always give the tag information when ordering parts for the unit.

Adjustments

SHIFT LINKAGE

NOTE: *If a hard shifting situation is experienced, determine if the cables are binding and need replacement, or if a linkage adjustment is necessary. Disconnect both cables at the transaxle and move the selector through the various positions. If the selector moves freely an adjustment may be all that is necessary; if not, cable replacement might be indicated.*

1. Working over the left front fender, unscrew the lock pin, from the transaxle selector shaft housing.

2. Reverse the lock pin so that the long end faces down and insert into the same threaded hole it was removed from. Push the selector shaft into the selector housing while inserting the pin. A hole in the selector shaft will align with the lock pin, allowing the pin to be threaded into the housing. This will lock the selector shaft into the neutral position.

3. From inside the vehicle, remove the gearshift knob by pulling straight up. Remove the reverse pull up ring by first removing the retaining nut and then pull the ring up and off of the lever.

4. Remove the shift lever boot. Remove the console.

5. For models built through 1987: Fabricate two adjusting lock pins out of $^{3}/_{16}$ in. rod. Total length of the pins should be 5 inches with a hook shaped on one end.

6. Loosen the selector and cross-over cable end adjusting/retainer bolts. Be sure the transaxle end of the cables are connected.

7. Install one adjusting lock pin on the side of the lever bracket in hole provided while moving lever slightly to help alignment. Install the other lock pin at the rear of the lever bracket (cross-over cable). Be sure that both cable end pieces are free to move.

8. After pins are inserted, the cable ends will be positioned to the correct adjustment

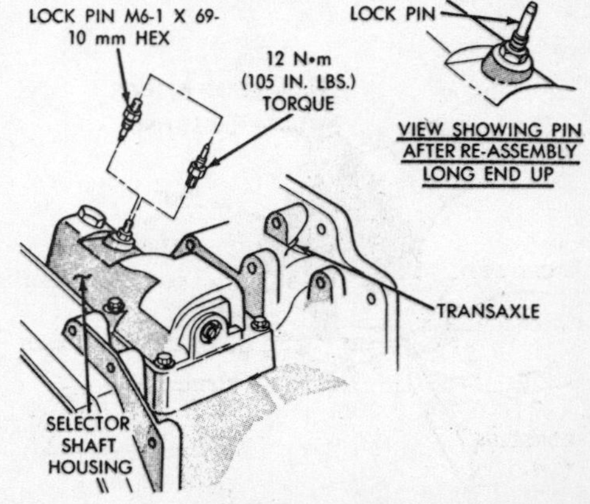

Transaxle pinned in the neutral position to adjust gearshift linkage

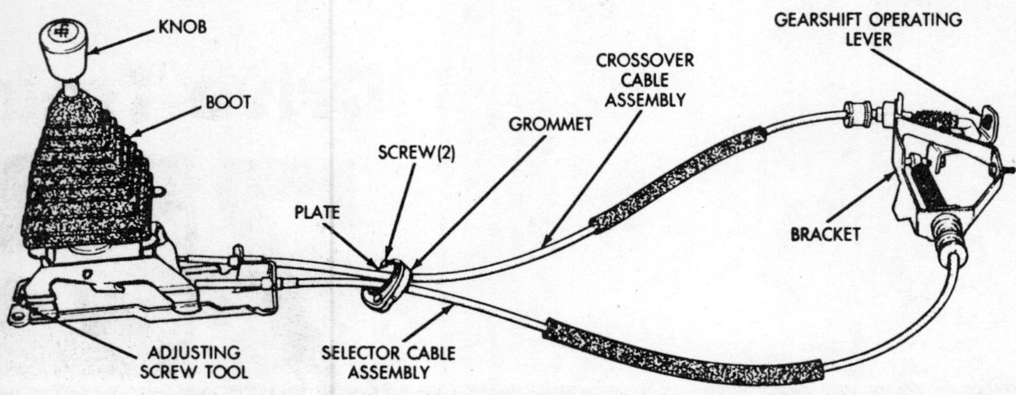

Cable operated gearshift linkage

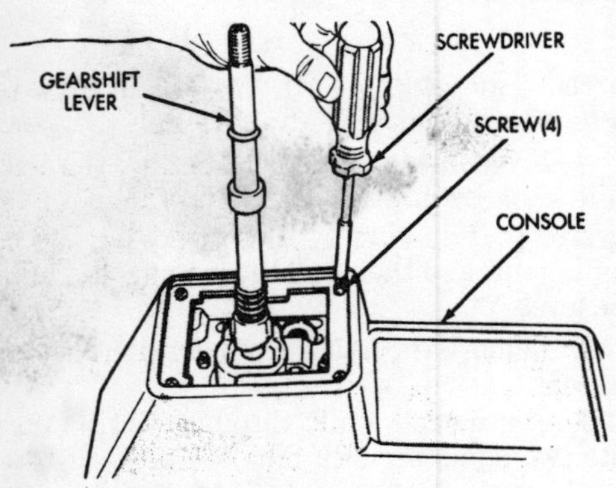

Remove the center console

point. Tighten the adjustment/retainer bolts to 55 inch lbs.

9. On model built in late 1986 and later: Loosen the selector and crossover cable adjusting screws.Remove the adjusting screw tool and attached spacer block from the shifter support.

10. Install the adjusting screw tool through the attached spacer, and screw the tool into the base of the shifter tower base.

11. Tighten the adjusting screw tool to 20 in. lbs.

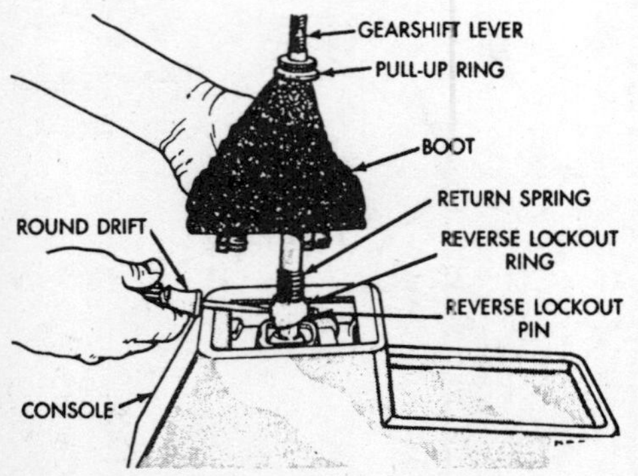

Remove the pull up ring and boot

12. Tighten the selector/crossover cable retaining screws to 70 in. lbs. Proper torque on the selector/crossover cable bracket is very important for proper operation.

13. Remove the adjusting screw tool and attach it to the bracket.

14. Check the gearshift cables for proper connection to the transaxle.

15. Install console and remainder of the removed parts.

16. Remove the selector housing lock pin at the transaxle and install it in the reversed posi-

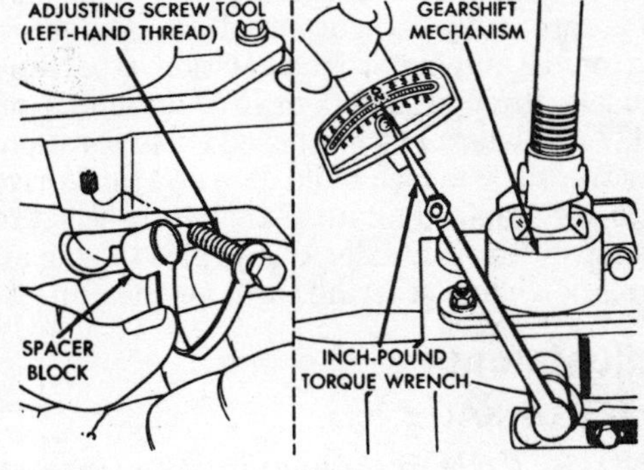

Install the adjusting screw tool as shown

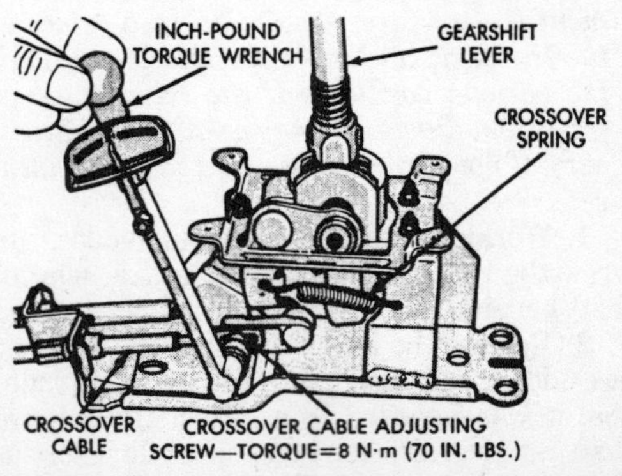

Adjusting the crossover cable

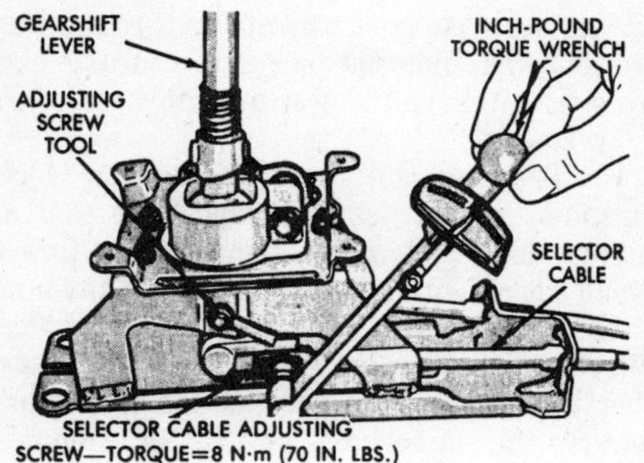

Adjusting the selector cable

Engine support fixture installed

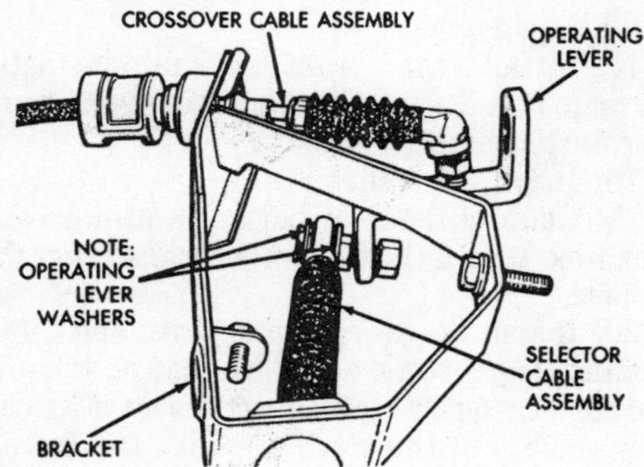

Gearshift cable connections at the transaxle

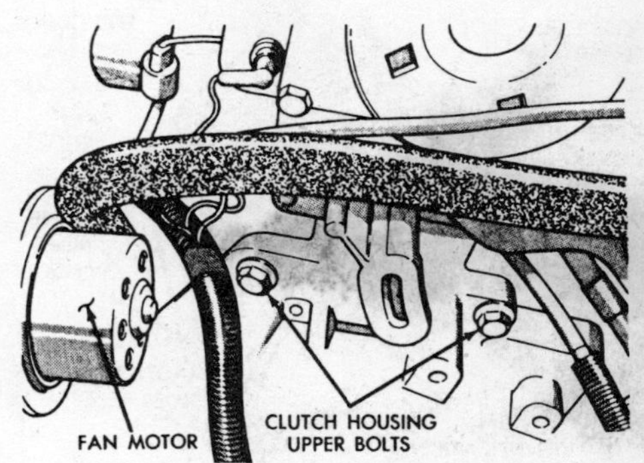

Remove the clutch housing bolts

tion (see Step 1). Tighten the lock pin to 105 inch lbs. check gear shift operation.

Back-up Light Switch

The back-up light switch is located at the upper left side of the transaxle case. The switch is screwed into the transaxle and serviced by replacement. No adjustment is possible.

Manual Transaxle

REMOVAL AND INSTALLATION

NOTE: *Transaxle removal does not require engine removal.*

1. Disconnect the negative battery cable from the battery.

2. Install a sling or lifting bracket to the No. 4 cylinder exhaust manifold mounting bolt (through 1987), or the battery ground strap bolt (1988 and later). Place an engine support device across the engine compartment and connect to the sling. Tighten until slight upward pressure is applied to the engine.

3. Disconnect the gearshift operating control from the transaxle selector lever.

4. Loosen the wheel lug nuts slightly. Raise and support the front of the vehicle.

5. Remove both front wheel and tire assemblies. Remove the left front engine splash shield. Drain the fluid from the transaxle.

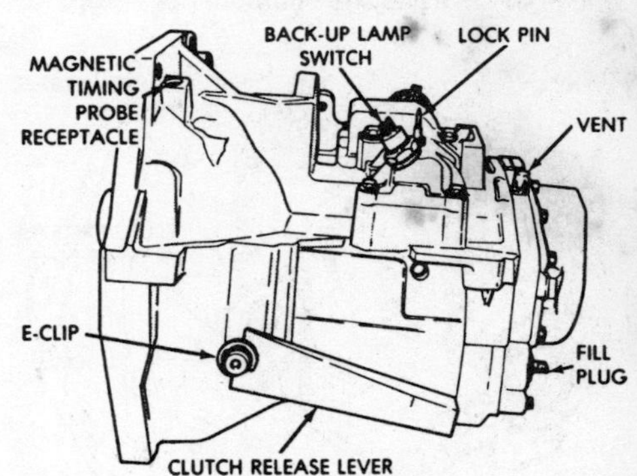

4- and 5-speed transaxle components – left side

6. Remove the left front mount from the transaxle. Remove the speedometer cable adapter and pinion from the transaxle.

7. Disconnect the front sway bar. Disconnect the anti-rotational link (anti-hop damper) from the cross member bracket, do not remove the bracket from the transaxle. Remove both lower ball joint-to-steering knuckle mounting bolts. Pry the ball joint from the steering knuckle. Remove the halfshaft from the drive wheel hub.

8. Remove the halfshafts from the differential.

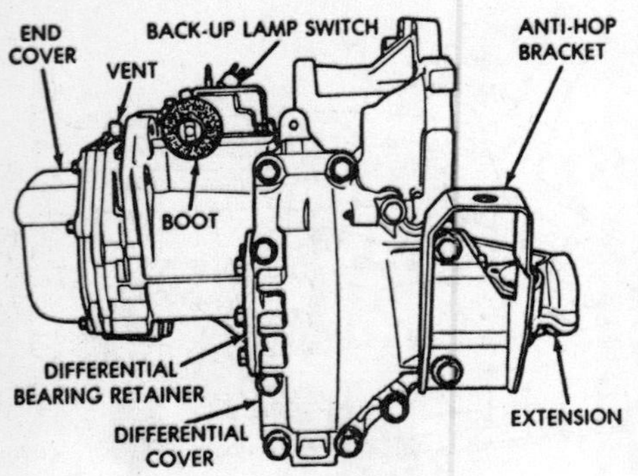

4- and 5-speed transaxle components — right side

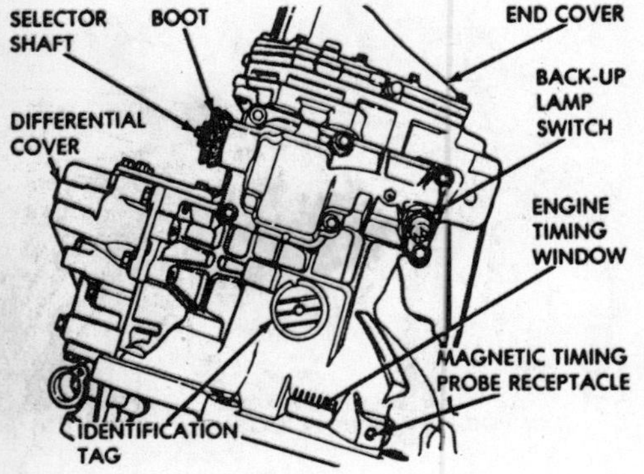

4- and 5-speed transaxle components — top

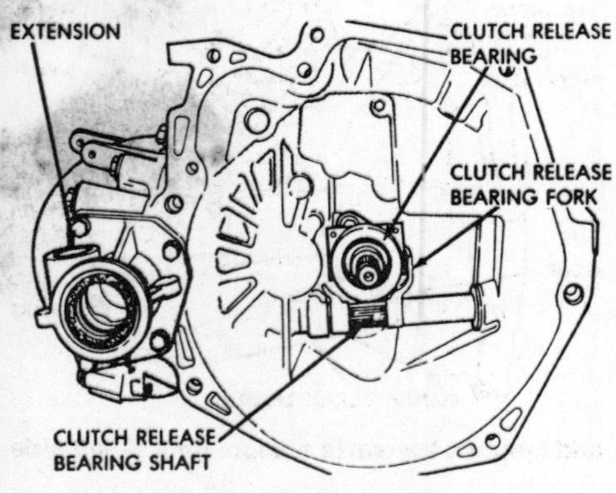

4- and 5-speed transaxle components — front

9. Remove the back-up light switch connector.

10. Remove the engine mount bracket from the front crossover.

11. Remove the front mount insulator through bolt. Place a suitable floor jack or transmission jack under the transaxle and raise to gently support.

12. Remove the top bell housing bolts.

13. Remove the left engine mount at rear cover plate. Remove the starter motor.

14. Secure the transaxle to the jack and remove the lower bell housing bolts. Check that all transaxle support mounts or through bolts are removed. Slide the jack and transaxle away from the engine and lower assembly.

To install:

15. To install the transaxle; make two locating pins for extra same thread bolts that are slightly longer than the mounting bolts. Cut the heads off with a hacksaw, remove any burrs or sharp edges with a file. Install the bolts into the rear of the engine and guide the transaxle over them. After the transaxle is in position, remove the guide bolts and install mounting bolts.

16. Raise the transaxle into position and slide it over the locating pins. Install the top bell housing bolts.

17. Install the front mount insulator through bolt. Install the left engine mount and the starter motor.

18. Install the halfshafts.

19. Connect the sway bar and anti-hop/rotation link. Install the front wheels and lower the vehicle.

20. Install the speedometer drive and cable. Connect the throttle and shift linkage. Remove the engine support and connect the negative battery cable. Fill the transaxle with the correct lubrication fluid.

Halfshafts

The halfshafts used on your vehicle are of three piece construction, and are unequal in length and material composition. A short solid interconnecting shaft is used on the left side and a longer tubular interconnecting shaft is installed on the right side.

The halfshaft assemblies are three piece units. Each shaft has a Tripod joint on the transaxle side, an interconnecting shaft and a Rzeppa joint on the wheel side. The Rzeppa joint mounts a splined stub shaft that connects with the wheel hub. The inner Tripod joint mounts a spring that maintains constant spline engagement with the transaxle. The design en-

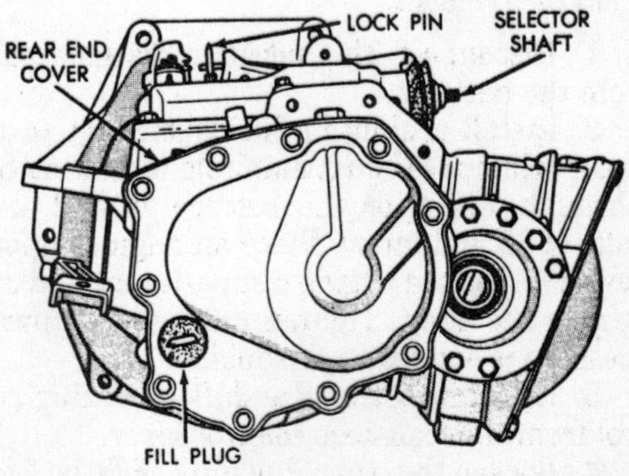

4- and 5-speed transaxle components — rear

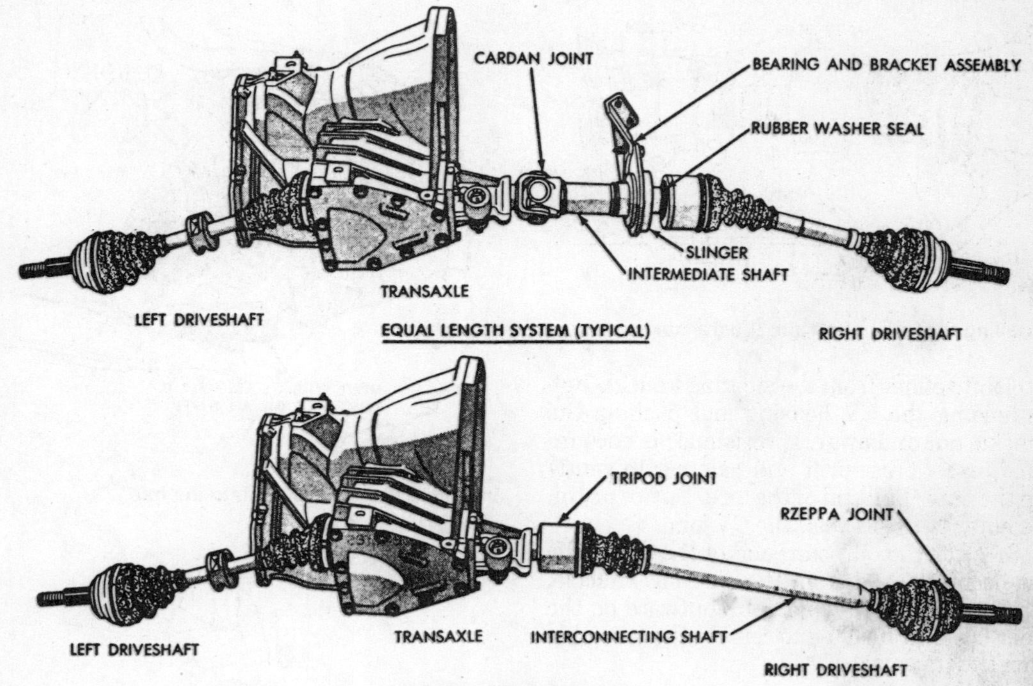

Halfshaft type and identification

ables the halfshaft to be removed without dismantling the transaxle.

Models equipped with a turbo charged engine incorporate an equal length halfshaft system. This system includes and extra, intermediate shaft installed on the right side. This helps to prevent torque steer induced by the power of the engine. The halfshaft removal procedure for all vehicles is the same.

REMOVAL AND INSTALLATION

1. Remove the cotter pin, lock and spring washer from the front axle ends.
2. Have a helper apply the service brakes and loosen the front axle hub retaining nut.
3. Raise and support the front of the vehicle on jackstands.
4. Remove the hub nut, washer and wheel assembly. Drain transaxle fluid.

NOTE: *The speedometer drive pinion must be removed from the transaxle housing before the right side drive axle can be removed. Remove the retaining bolts and lift the pinion with cable connected from the housing.*

5. Remove the clamp bolt that secures the ball joint stud with the steering knuckle.
6. Separate the ball joint from the knuckle by prying downward against the knuckle connecting point and the control arm. Take care not to damage the rubber boot.
7. Separate the outer CV (constant veloc-

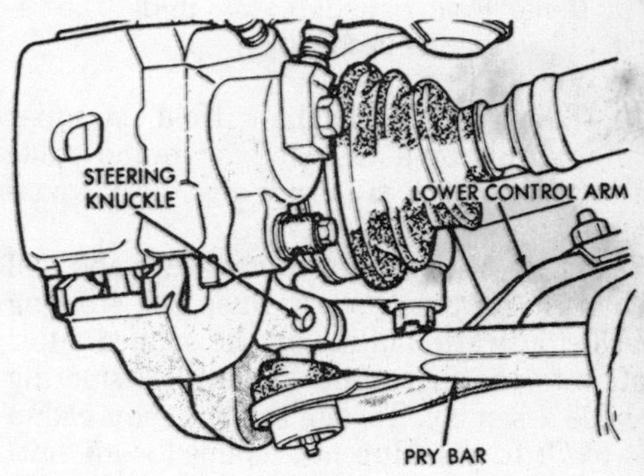

Separating ball joint from the knuckle

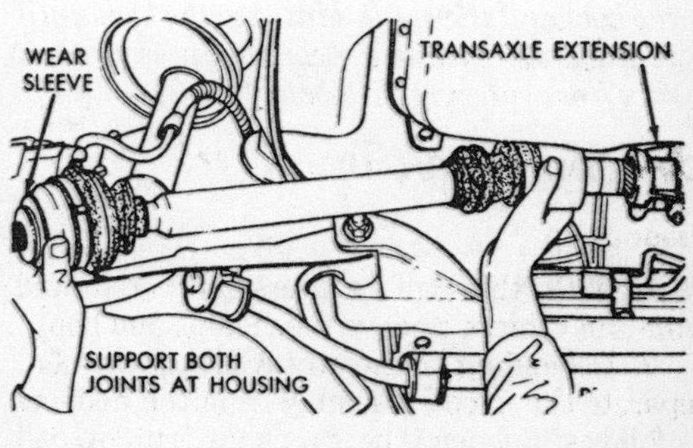

Removing the driveshaft assembly

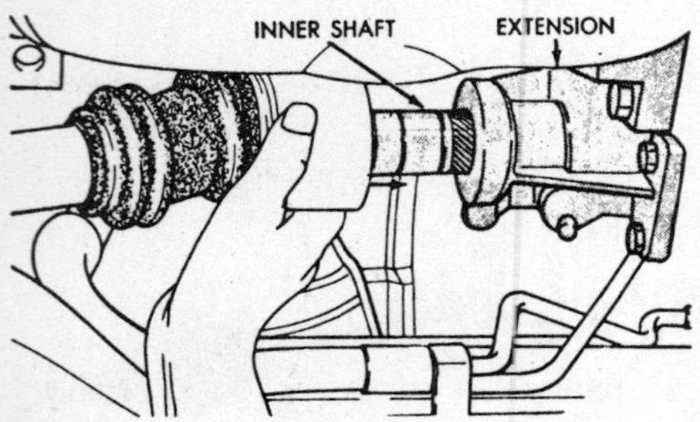

Installing the inner shaft into the transaxle

ity) joint splines from the steering knuckle hub by holding the CV housing and pushing the knuckle out and away. If resistance is encountered, use a brass drift and hammer to gently tap the outer hub end of the axle. Do not pry on the outer wear sleeve of the CV joint.

8. After the outboard end of the drive axle has been removed from the steering knuckle, support the assembly and pull outward on the inner CV joint housing to remove the assembly from the transaxle.

WARNING: *Do not pull on the shaft or the assembly will disconnect. Pull only on the inner CV joint housing.*

9. Remove the halfshaft from under the vehicle and service as necessary.

To install:

10. To install the halfshaft; Hold the inner joint assembly by its housing, align and guide the shaft into the transaxle or intermediate shaft assembly.

11. Lubricate the outer wear sleeve and seal with multi-purpose grease. Push the steering knuckle outward and install the splined outer shaft into the drive hub. Install the steering knuckle assembly. Torque the ball joint clamp bolt to 70 ft. lbs. Hub nut (splined shaft nut) torque to 180 ft. lbs. Refill the transaxle with the proper lubrication fluid.

NOTE: *If after installing the axle assembly, the inboard boot appears collapsed, vent the boot by inserting a thin round rod between the boot and the shaft. Massage the boot until is expands. Install a new clamp to prevent dirt from entering the boot.*

CV-JOINT OVERHAUL

Inner Joint

1. With the halfshaft assembly removed from the vehicle, remove the clamps and boot.

2. Depending on the unit (GKN or Citroen) separate the tripod assembly from the housing as follows: Citroen type: Since the trunion ball rollers are not retained on bearing studs a retaining ring is used to prevent accidental tripod/

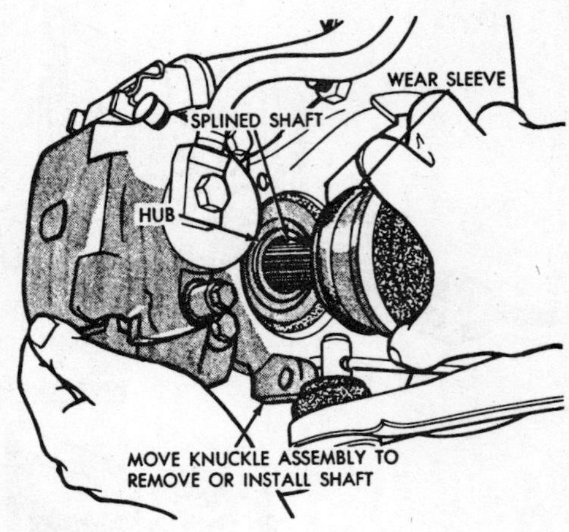

Installing the outer shaft into the hub

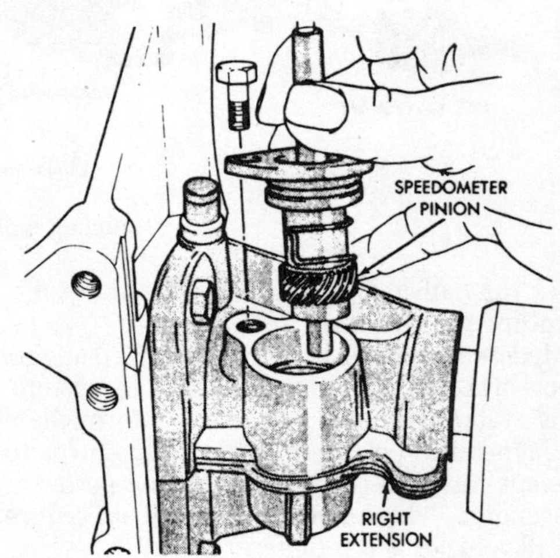

Speedometer pinion removal and installation

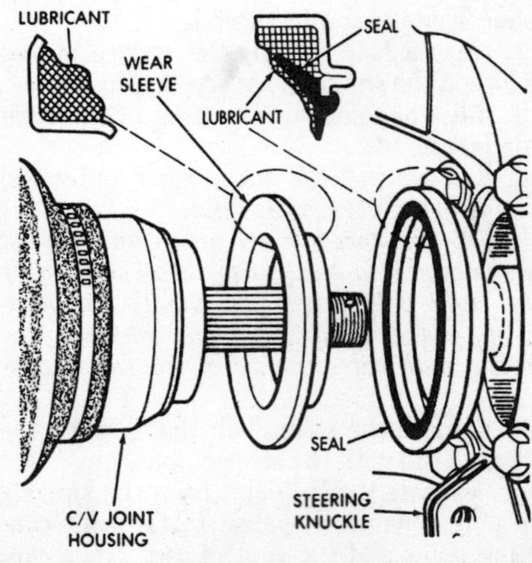

Seal and wear sleeve lubrication points

housing separation, which would allow roller and needle bearings to fall away.

In the case of the spring loaded inner CV-joints, if it weren't for the retaining ring, the spring would automatically force the tripod out of the housing whenever the shaft was not installed in the vehicle.

Separate the tripod from the housing by slightly deforming the retaining ring in 3 places, with a suitable tool.

WARNING: *Secure the rollers to the studs during separation. With the tripod out of the housing secure the assembly with tape.*

3. GKN type: Spring loaded GKN inboard CV-joints have tabs on the can cover that prevent the spring from forcing the tripod out of the housing. These tabs must be bent back with a pair of pliers before the tripod can be removed. Under normal conditions it is not necessary to secure the GKN rollers to their studs during separation due to the presence of a retainer ring on the end of each stud. This retention force can easily be overcome if the rollers are pulled or impacted. It is also possible to pull the rollers off by removing or installing the tripod with the connecting shaft at too high an angle, relative to the housing.

4. Remove the snapring from the shaft end groove, then remove the tripod with a brass punch.

To install:

5. Remove as much grease as possible from the assembly. Look at the ball housing races, and the components for excessive wear.

NOTE: *DO NOT CLEAN THE INNER HOUSING WITH MINERAL SPIRITS OR SOLVENT. Solvents will destroy the rubber seals that are hidden in the housing and permit grease leakage. If wear is excessive, replace as necessary.*

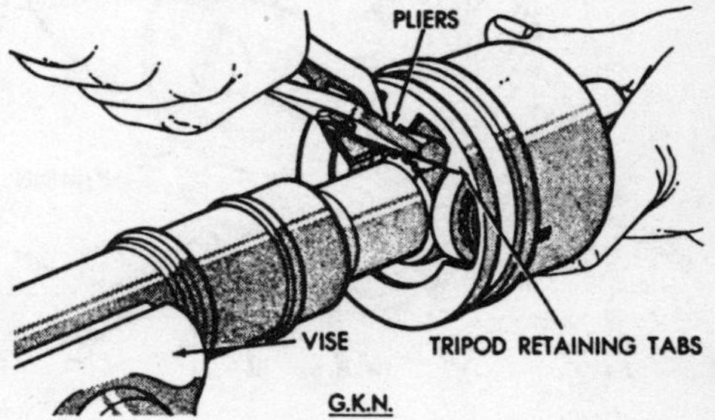

Separating the tripod from the housing

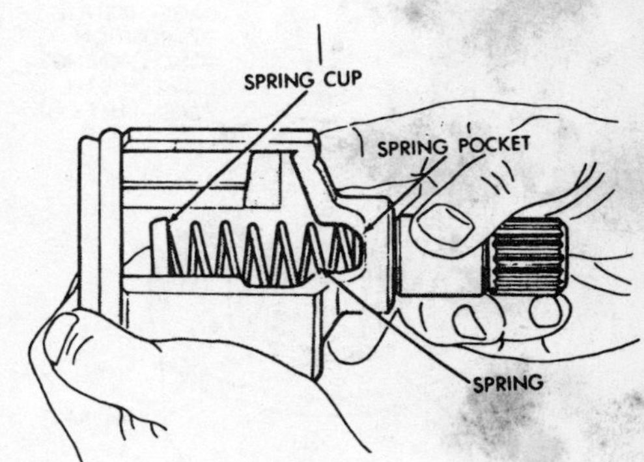

Spring and cup installation

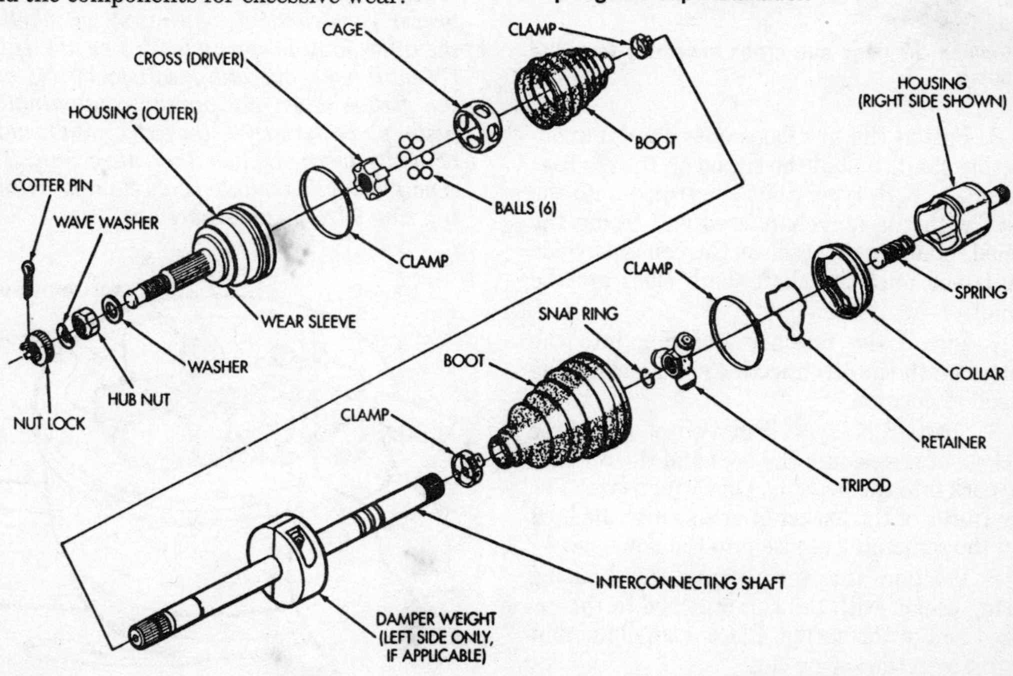

Halfshaft assembly — exploded view

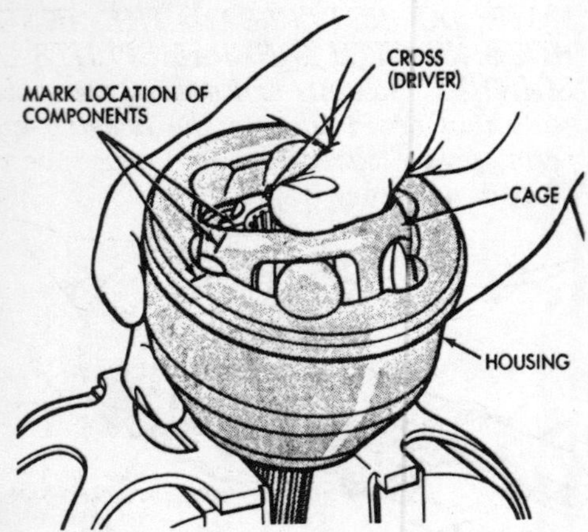

Rotate the cage and cross to remove the balls

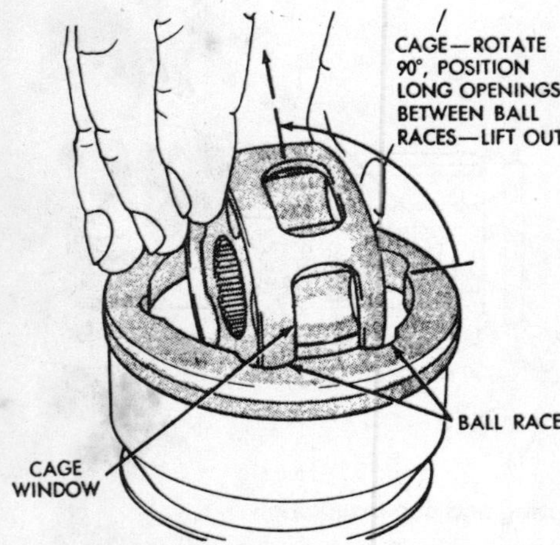

Removing the cage and cross assembly form the housing

6. Fasten the new boot onto the interconnecting shaft. Install the tripod on the shaft as follows: G.K.N. type: Slide the tripod onto the shaft with the non-chamfered end facing the tripod retaining ring groove. Citroen type: Slide the tripod onto the shaft (both sides are the same).

7. Install the retainer snapring into the groove on the interconnecting shaft locking the tripod in position.

8. On G.K.N. type: Put two of the three packets of grease into the boot and the remaining pack into the housing. On Citroen type: Put two thirds of the packet of grease into the boot and the remaining grease into the housing.

9. Position the spring into the housing spring pocket with the cup attached to the exposed end of the spring. Place a small amount of grease in the spring cup.

10. On G.K.N type: Slip the tripod into the housing and bend down the retaining tabs. Make sure the tabs are holding the housing firmly. On Citroen type: Remove the tape holding the rollers and needle bearings in place. Hold the rollers and needles in place and install the housing. Install the retaining ring into the machined groove in the housing with a punch and plastic hammer. Hold the retaining collar in position with two C-clamps while installing the retainer ring.

WARNING: *When installing the tripod, the spring must be centered in the housing to insure proper positioning.*

11. Position the boot over the retaining groove in the housing and clamp in position.

Outer Joint

1. Remove the boot clamps and discard them.

2. Wipe away the grease to expose the joint.

3. Support the shaft in a vise (Cushion the vise jaws to prevent shaft damage). Hold the outer joint, and using a plastic hammer, give a sharp tap to the top of the joint body to dislodge it from the internal circlip.

4. If the shaft is bent carefully pry the wear sleeve from the CV-joint machined ledge.

5. Remove the circlip from the shaft and discard it.

NOTE: *Replacement boot kits will contain this circlip.*

6. Unless the shaft is damaged do not remove the heavy spacer ring from the shaft.

NOTE: *If the shaft must be replaced, care must be taken that the new shaft is of the proper construction, depending on whether the inner joint is spring loaded or not. If the CV-joint was operating satisfactorily, and the grease down not appear contaminated, just replace the boot. If the outer joint is noisy or badly worn, replace the entire unit. The repair kit will include boot, clamps, retaining ring (circlip) and lubricant.*

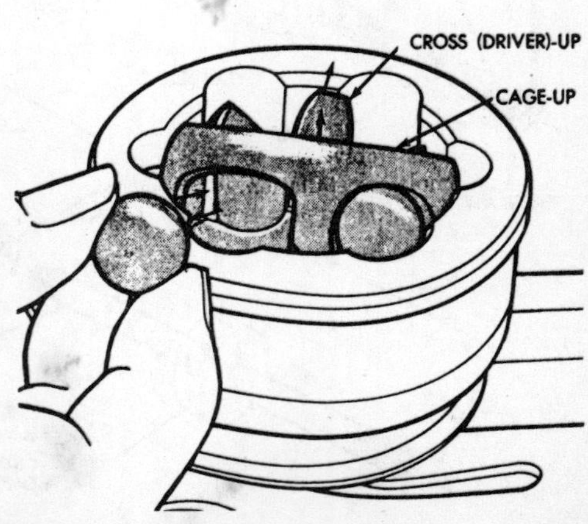

Removing the balls from the joint

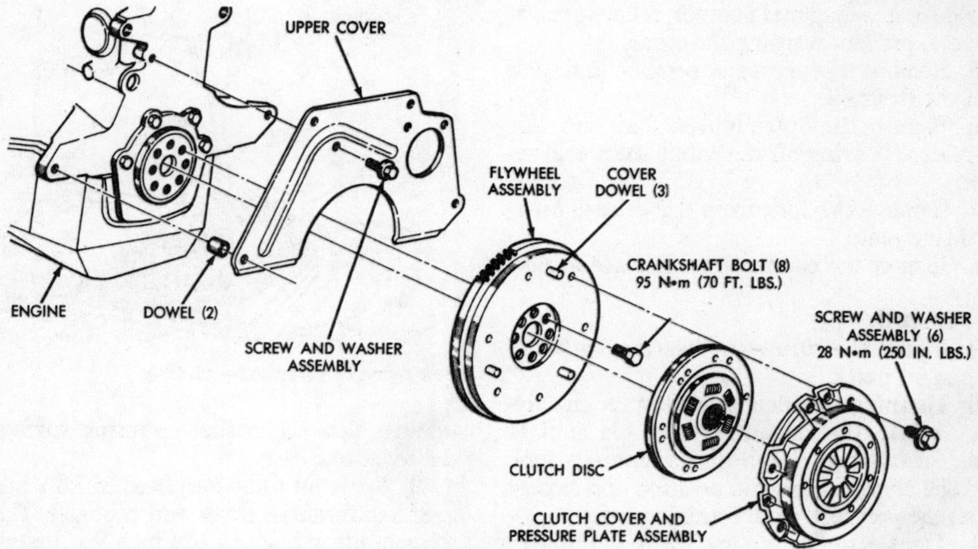

Clutch components

7. Wipe off the grease and mark the position of the inner cross, cage and housing with a dab of paint.

8. Hold the joint vertically in a vise. Do not crush the splines on the shaft.

9. Press down on one side of the inner race to tilt the cage and remove the balls from the opposite side.

10. If the joint is tight, use a hammer and brass drift pin to tap the inner race. Repeat this step until all balls have been removed. DO NOT hit the cage.

11. Tilt the cage and inner race assembly vertically and position the two opposing, elongated cage windows in the area between the ball grooves. Pull the cage out of the housing.

12. Turn the inner cross 90° and align the race lands with an elongated hole in the cage. Remove the inner race.

To install:

13. Position a new wear sleeve on the joint housing and install it using a suitable driver. Lubricate all of the components before assembly.

14. Align the parts according to paint markings.

15. Install one of the inner race lands into the cage window and feed the race into the cage.

16. Turn the cross 90° and align the opposing cage windows with the land, pivot another 90° and complete land installation.

17. When properly installed, the cross counter bore should be facing outward from the joint on G.K.N. type. The cross and cage chamfers will be facing out on Citroen type.

18. Apply the grease to the ball races. Install the balls into the raceway by tilting the cage and inner race assembly.

19. Fasten the boot to the shaft. Install the new retainer circlip provided. Position the outer joint on the splined end of the stub shaft, engage the splines and tap sharply to engage the circlip. Attempt to pull the shafts apart to see if the circlip is properly seated.

20. Position the large end of the boot and secure with a clamp. Install the halfshaft.

CLUTCH

CAUTION: *The clutch driven disc contains asbestos, which has been determined to be a cancer causing agent. Never clean clutch surfaces with compressed air! Avoid inhaling any dust from any clutch surface! When cleaning clutch surfaces, use a commercially available brake cleaning fluid.*

Adjustments

All models are equipped with a self-adjusting clutch. No free-play adjustment is possible.

Driven Disc and Pressure Plate

NOTE: *Chrysler recommends the use of special tool #C4676 for disc alignment.*

REMOVAL AND INSTALLATION

1. Remove the transaxle.

2. Matchmark the clutch cover and flywheel for easy reinstallation.

3. Insert special tool C4676 or its equivalent to hold the clutch disc in place.

4. Loosen the cover attaching bolts. Do this

procedure in a diagonal manner, a few turns at a time to prevent warping the cover.

5. Remove the cover assembly and disc from the flywheel.

6. Remove the clutch release shaft and slide the release bearing off the input shaft seal retainer.

7. Remove the fork from the release bearing thrust plate.

8. Inspect the components. Replace as necessary.

To install:

9. Install the throw out bearing, fork and component parts.

10. Mount the clutch assembly on the flywheel (Mate the matchmarks if old unit is used). Install the clutch disc alignment tool. Hold the alignment tool in position and loosely install the pressure plate retaining bolts.

11. Tighten the bolts a few turns at a time in rotation. Tighten to 250 in. lbs.

RELEASE CABLE ADJUSTMENT

The clutch release cable cannot be adjusted. When the cable is properly installed, a spring in the clutch pedal adjusts the cable to the proper position, regardless of clutch disc wear.

AUTOMATIC TRANSAXLE

Fluid Pan and Filter

REMOVAL AND INSTALLATION

1. Raise and support the front of the vehicle on jackstands.

2. Remove the splash shield if it will interfere with the fluid pan removal.

3. Place a suitable container that will hold at least four quarts of fluid under the oil pan. Loosen all of the pan bolts slightly until the fluid stats to drain. Loosen the bolts around the point where the fluid is draining to increase the flow.

4. When the bulk of the fluid has drained, remove the oil pan. Clean the dirt from the pan and magnet. Remove RTV sealant or gasket material from the pan and case mounting surfaces.

5. Remove the filter from the bottom of the valve body.

To install:

6. Install a new filter and gasket. Tighten the mounting screw to 40 inch lbs.

7. Apply a unbroken bead of RTV sealant to the oil pan and install on case. Tighten the mounting bolts to 165 inch lbs.

8. Remove the differential cover. Use a clean cloth and wipe the cover and magnet to remove dirt. Clean the mounting surfaces of the cover and case.

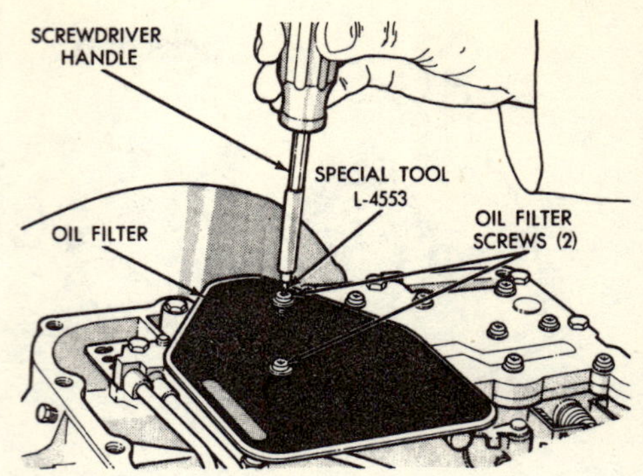

Removing the transaxle oil filter

9. Apply an unbroken bead of RTV sealant to the differential cover and reinstall. Tighten the mounting bolts to 165 inch lbs. Install the splash shield, etc. and lower the vehicle.

10. Pour four quarts of Dexron II type fluid through the dipstick fill tube. Start the engine, with the parking and service brakes applied, move the gear selector through the various positions ending up in Park.

11. Add sufficient fluid, if necessary, to bring the level to $^1/_8$ in. below the Add mark.

12. Check the fluid level after engine and transaxle have reached the normal operating temperature. The level should be within the Hot range on the dipstick.

NOTE: *Always make sure that the dipstick is fully seated in its tube to prevent dirt from entering the transaxle.*

Adjustments

KICKDOWN CABLE

1. Run the engine until the normal operating temperature is reached. Be sure the choke is fully opened.

2. Loosen the adjustment bracket lock bolt mounted on transaxle to engine flange.

3. Be sure that the adjustment bracket can slide freely. Clean as necessary.

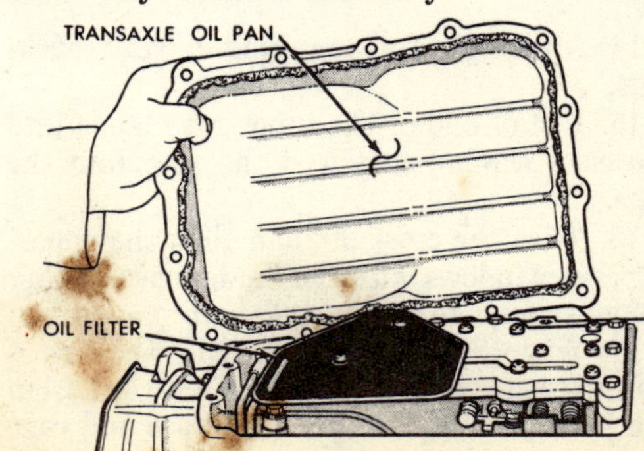

Transaxle pan removal — out of vehicle view

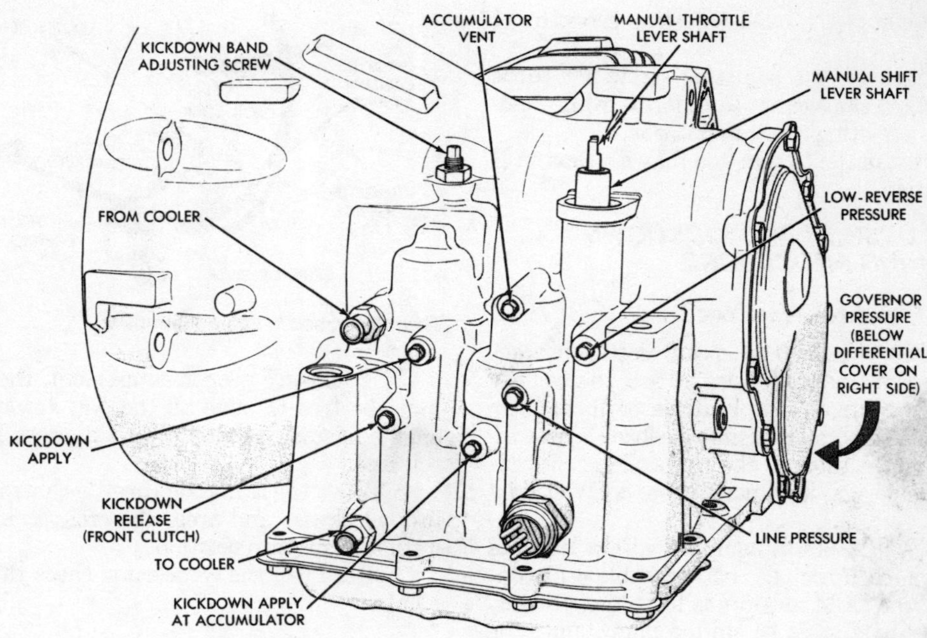

Transaxle adjustment and maintenance points

4. Slide the bracket toward the engine as far as possible. Release the bracket and move the throttle lever to the right as far as it will go. tighten the adjustment lock bolt to 105 inch lbs.

KICKDOWN BAND (FRONT)

The kickdown band adjusting screw is located on left top front side of the transaxle case.

1. Clean the locknut, adjusting screw and area around with safe solvent and brush. Loosen the locknut and back it off about five turns.

2. Tighten the band adjusting screw to 72 inch lbs. Back the adjustment screw off $2^1/_2$ turns. Hold the adjustment screw in position and tighten the locknut to 35 ft. lbs.

LOW/REVERSE BAND (REAR)

1. Drain the fluid and remove the oil pan from the transaxle.

2. Loosen and back off the locknut about five turns.

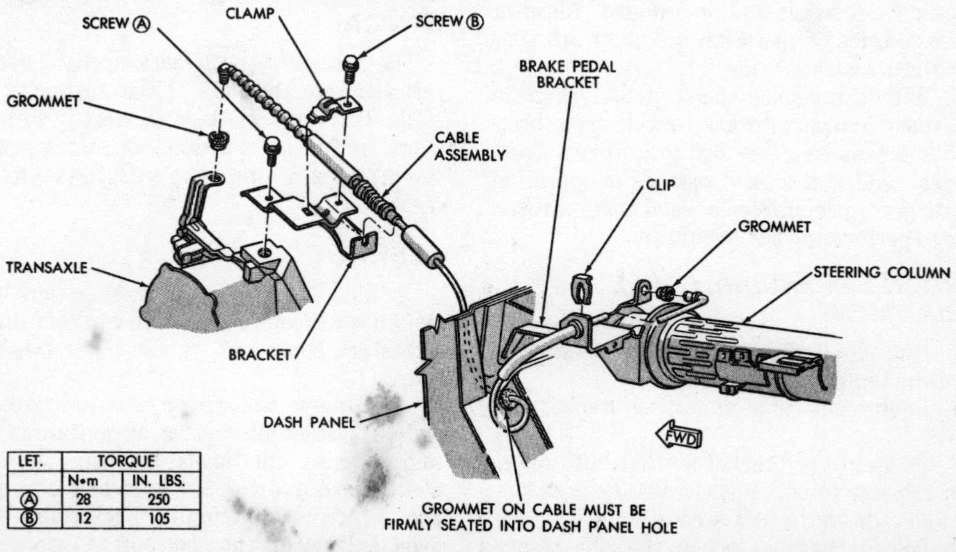

LET.	TORQUE	
	N•m	IN. LBS.
Ⓐ	28	250
Ⓑ	12	105

Gearshift linkage routing and mounting

3. Tighten the band adjusting screw to 41 inch lbs.

4. Back off the adjusting screw $3^1/_2$ turns and tighten the locknut to 10 ft. lbs. while holding the adjusting screw in position.

5. Install the oil pan and fill with Dexron II type fluid.

A-604 UPSHIFT AND KICKDOWN LEARNING PROCEDURE

A–604 Ultradrive Transaxle

In 1989, the A–604 4 speed, electronic transaxle was introduced; it is the first to use fully adaptive controls. The controls perform their functions based on real time feedback sensor information. Although, the transaxle is conventional in design, its functions are controlled by the ECM.

Since the A–604 is equipped with a learning function, each time the battery cable is disconnected, the ECM memory is lost. In operation, the transaxle must be shifted many times for the learned memory to be reinputed in the ECM; during this period, the vehicle will experience rough operation. The transaxle must be at normal operating temperature when learning occurs.

1. Maintain constant throttle opening during shifts. Do not move the accelerator pedal during upshifts.

2. Accelerate the vehicle with the throttle $^1/_8$–$^1/_2$ open.

3. Make 15 to 20 1/2, 2/3 and 3/4 upshifts. Accelerating from a full stop to 50 mph each time at the aforementioned throttle opening is sufficient.

4. With the vehicle speed below 25 mph, make 5 to 8 wide open throttle kick downs to 1st gear from either 2nd or 3rd gear. Allow at least 5 seconds of operation in 2nd or 3rd gear prior to each kickdown.

5. With the vehicle speed greater than 25 mph, make 5 to part throttle to wide open throttle kick downs to either 3rd or 2nd gear from 4th gear. Allow at least 5 seconds of operation in 4th gear, preferably at road load throttle prior to performing the kickdown.

THROTTLE PRESSURE CABLE ADJUSTMENT

1. Run the engine until it reaches normal operating temperature.

2. Loosen the cable mounting bracket lock screw.

3. Position the bracket so that both alignment tabs are touching the transaxle case surface and tighten the lock screws.

4. Release the cross lock on the cable assembly by pulling the cross lock up.

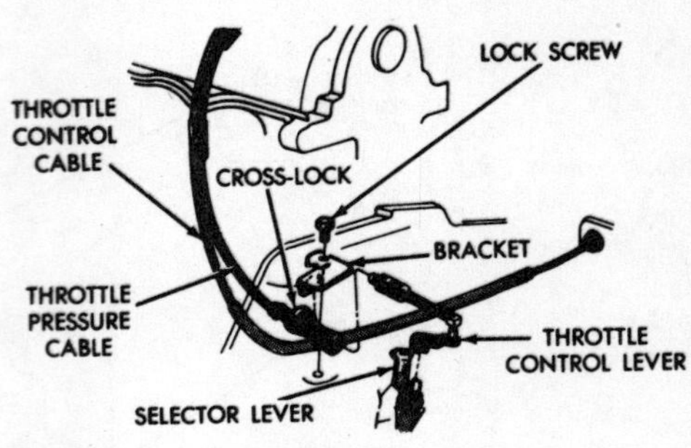

Throttle pressure cable mounting

5. To ensure proper adjustment, the cable must be free to slide all the way toward the engine against its stop after the cross lock is released.

6. Move the transaxle throttle control lever fully clockwise and press the cross lock down until it snaps into position.

7. Road test the vehicle and check the shift points.

THROTTLE PRESSURE ROD ADJUSTMENT

1. Run the engine until it reaches normal operating temperature.

2. Loosen the adjustment swivel lock screw.

3. To ensure proper adjustment, the swivel must be free to slide along the flat end of the throttle rod. Disassembly, clean and lubricate as required.

4. Hold the transaxle throttle control lever firmly toward the engine and tighten the swivel screw.

5. Road test the vehicle and check the shift points.

Neutral Starting/Back-up Light Switch

The neutral starting/back-up light switch is screwed into the side of the automatic transaxle. If the vehicle fails to start in either the Park or Neutral positions, or starts in any of the drive gears a problem with the switch is indicated.

TESTING

1. The Neutral/Park sensing part of the switch is the center terminal, while the back-up lights are controlled by the outer two terminals.

2. Remove the wiring connector from the switch. Use an ohmmeter or continuity tester and connect the leads between the center switch terminal and the transaxle case to test the Neutral/Park circuit. Continuity should exist only when the gearshift is either in the Park or Neutral positions. Check the gearshift

cable adjustment first before replacing the switch.

3. Connect an ohmmeter or continuity tester connected between the outer two terminals of the switch to check the back-up light. Continuity should be present when the gearshift selector is in the Reverse position.

REMOVAL AND INSTALLATION

1. Remove the wiring connector. Place a container under the switch to catch transaxle fluid and unscrew the switch.

2. Move the gearshift selector to the Park and Neutral positions and check to see that the switch operating fingers center in the case opening.

3. Screw the new switch and new mounting seal into the transaxle case. Tighten to 24 ft. lbs. Retest switch operation. Add transaxle fluid if needed.

Automatic Transaxle

REMOVAL AND INSTALLATION

NOTE: *If the vehicle is going to be rolled while the transaxle is out of the vehicle, obtain 2 outer CV joints to install to the hubs. If the vehicle is rolled without the proper torque applied to the front wheel bearings, the bearings will be destroyed.*

1. Disconnect the negative battery cable. If equipped with 3.0L or 3.3L engine, drain the coolant. Remove the dipstick.

2. Remove the air cleaner assembly if it is preventing access to the upper bell housing bolts. Remove the upper bell housing bolts and water tube, where applicable. Unplug all electrical connectors from the transaxle.

3. If equipped with a 2.2L or 2.5L engine, remove the starter attaching nut and bolt at the top of the bell housing.

4. Raise the vehicle and support safely. Remove the tire and wheel assemblies. Remove the axle end cotter pins, nut locks, spring washers and axle nuts.

5. Remove the ball joint retaining bolts and pry the control arm from the steering knuckle. Position a drain pan under the transaxle where the axles enter the differential or extension housing. Remove the axles from the transaxle or center bearing. Unbolt the center bearing and remove the intermediate axle from the transaxle, if equipped.

6. Drain the transaxle. Disconnect and plug the fluid cooler hoses. Disconnect the shifter and kickdown linkage from the transaxle, if equipped.

7. Remove the speedometer cable adaptor bolt and remove the adaptor from the transaxle.

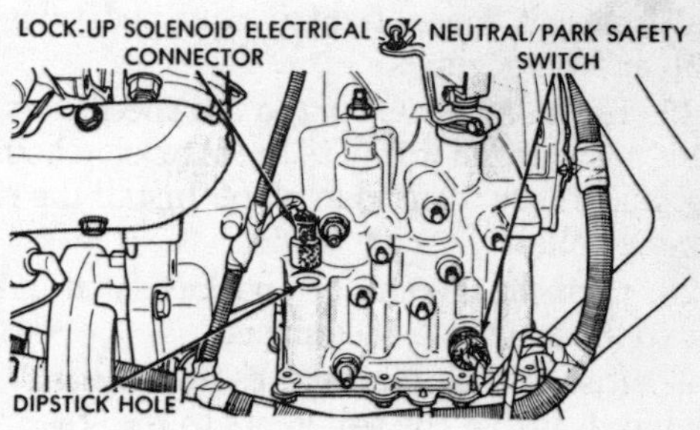

Lock-up solenoid and neutral safety switch location

8. Remove the starter. Remove the torque converter inspection cover, matchmark the torque converter to the flex plate and remove the torque converter bolts.

9. Using the proper equipment, support the weight of the engine.

10. Remove the front motor mount and bracket.

11. Position a suitable jack under the transaxle.

12. Remove the lower bell housing bolts.

13. Remove the left side splash shield. Remove the transaxle mount bolts.

14. Carefully pry the engine from the transaxle.

15. Slide the transaxle rearward until the locating dowels disengage from the mating holes in the transaxle.

16. Pull the transaxle completely away from the engine and remove it from the vehicle.

17. To prepare the vehicle for rolling, support the engine with a suitable support or reinstall the front motor mount to the engine. Then reinstall the ball joints to the steering knuckle and install the retaining bolt. Install the obtained outer CV joints to the hubs, install the washers and torque the axle nuts to 180 ft. lbs. (244 Nm). The vehicle may now be safely rolled.

To install:

18. Install the transmission securely on the transmission jack. Rotate the converter so it will align with the positioning of the flex plate.

19. Apply a coating of high temperature grease to the torque converter pilot hub.

20. Raise the transaxle into place and push it forward until the dowels engage and the bell housing is flush with the block.

21. Install the transaxle to bell housing bolts.

22. Jack the transaxle up and install the left side mount bolts. Install the torque converter bolts and torque to 55 ft. lbs. (74 Nm).

23. Install the front motor mount and bracket. Remove the engine and transaxle support fixtures.

24. Install the starter to the transaxle. In-

stall the bolt finger tight if equipped with a 2.2L or 2.5L engine.

25. Install a new O-ring to the speedometer cable adaptor and install to the extension housing; make sure it snaps in place. Install the retaining bolt.

26. Connect the shifter and kickdown linkage to the transaxle, if equipped.

27. Install the axles and center bearing, if equipped. Install the ball joints to the steering knuckles. Torque the axle nuts to 180 ft. lbs. (244 Nm) and install new cotter pins. Install the splash shield and install the wheels. Lower the vehicle. Install the dipstick.

28. Install the upper bell housing bolts and water pipe, if removed.

29. If equipped with 2.2L or 2.5L engine, install the starter attaching nut and bolt at the top of the bell housing. Raise the vehicle again and tighten the starter bolt from underneath the vehicle. Lower the vehicle.

30. Connect all electrical wiring to the transaxle.

31. Install the air cleaner assembly, if it was removed. Fill the transaxle with the proper amount of Dexron®II.

32. Connect the negative battery cable and check the transaxle for proper operation. On the A-604 transaxle perform the upshift and kickdown learn procedure found earlier in this section.

POWER TRANSFER UNIT

Identification

For 1991 Chrysler introduced an All Wheel Drive (AWD) version of the Caravan/Voyager. The AWD equipped vehicles use the same basic drivetrain layout as the front wheel drive versions, with the exception of the rear driveline module. To transfer the power from the engine and transaxle, to the rear driveline module, these vehicles use an Power Transfer Unit (PTU). The PTU is connected to the transaxle where the right halfshaft extension housing would be.

The PTU is a separate unit from the transaxle. It uses a standard hypoid type ring and pinion. The PTU is sealed from the transaxle and has its own oil sump. The unit uses SAE 85W-90 gear lube and holds 1.22 qts.

The PTU is not a repairable unit and can only be replaced. If you suspect the PTU has failed, take the vehicle to an authorized service center.

REAR DRIVE LINE MODULE

Identification

As an option in 1991, Chrysler offered All Wheel Drive (AWD) on Caravan/Voyager models. These models are basically the same as

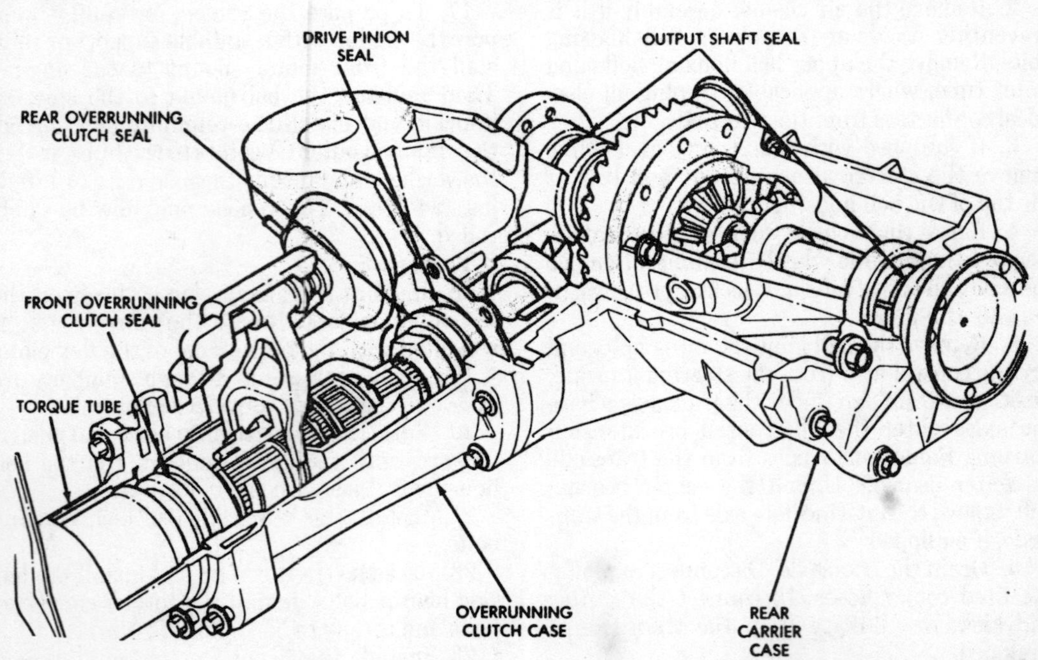

Rear driveline module — seal locations

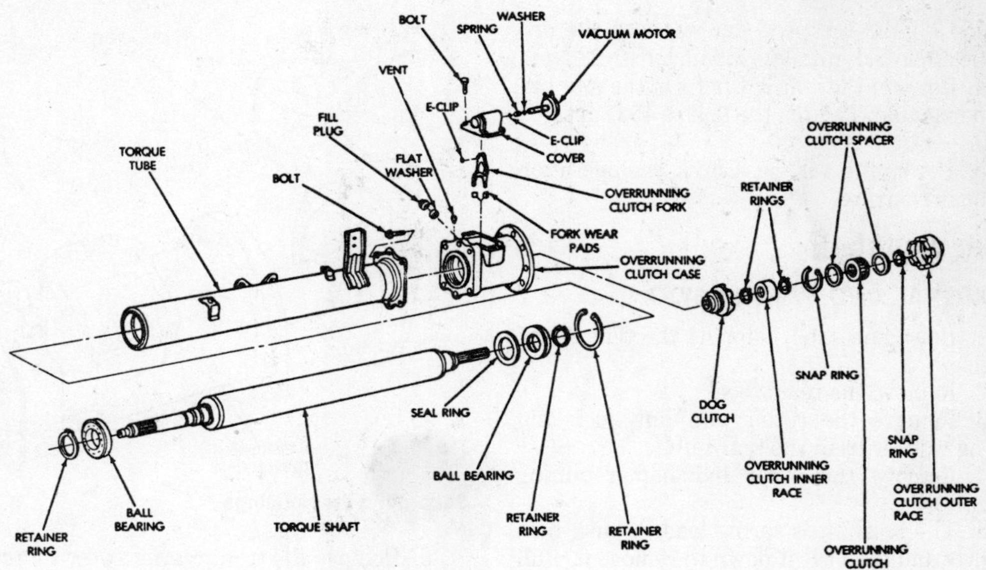

Torque tube and overrunning clutch assemblies — exploded view

the front wheel drive versions, with the exception of the components needed for driving the rear wheels as well.

The power is transferred to the rear wheels through the Power Transfer Unit (PTU) attached to the transaxle. The power travels through the PTU to a torque tube that contains the center driveshaft. The power then enters an overrunning clutch assembly, attached to the front of the rear differential carrier.

The overrunning clutch assembly is separate from the rear carrier. The overrunning clutch assembly has an vacuum operated dog clutch, it is lubricated with Mopar ATF type 7176. The rear carrier is lubricated with SAE 85W-90 gear lube.

Rear Drive Line Assembly Module

REMOVAL AND INSTALLATION

1. Raise and safely support the rear of the vehicle.
2. Remove the right and left inner halfshaft joint mounting bolts.
3. Support the inner side of the halfshafft, by hanging it from the frame using a piece of wire. Do not allow the shafts to hang freely or the joints will be damaged.
4. Remove the mounting bolts from the rear side of the propeller shaft at, the rear carrier.
5. Support the propeller shaft.
6. Remove the viscous coupling retaining nut and slide the viscous coupling off the rear driveline assembly.
7. Disconnect the vacuum line at the driveline module. Also disconnect the electrical lead from the assembly.
8. Support the rear of the driveline module with a jack.
9. Remove the rear driveline module front mounting bolts. Partially lower the unit from the vehicle.
10. Remove the rear driveline module from the vehicle.

To install:

11. Position the driveline module in the vehicle. Install the front mounting bolts and tighten to 40 ft. lbs. (54 Nm).
12. Reconnect the vacuum line and electrical lead. Install the viscous coupling and nut. Tighten the nut to 120 ft. lbs. (162 Nm).

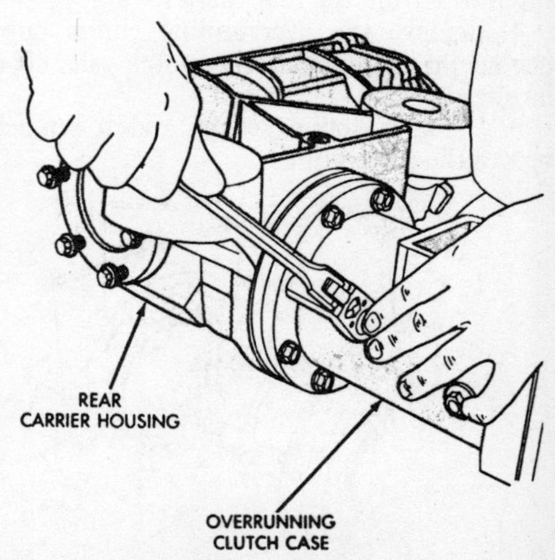

Overrunning clutch case to rear carrier bolts

13. Connect the propeller shaft to the driveline module, tighten to 250 inch lbs. (28 Nm).

14. Connect the rear halshafts to the rear driveline module. Tighten the bolt to 45 ft. lbs. (61 Nm).

15. Lower the vehicle. Check the operation of the drive train.

Rear Halfshaft

REMOVAL AND INSTALLATION

1. Raise and safely support the rear of the vehicle.
2. Remove the rear wheel.
3. Remove the cotter pin, nut, lock and spring washer from the rear hub.
4. Remove the inner halfshaft retaining bolts.
5. The halshaft is spring loaded, push it in slightly and then tilt it down to remove it. Pull it out from under the vehicle.

To install:

6. Insert the end of the halshaft into the rear hub assembly.
7. Position it on the rear carrier unit and install the retaining bolts.
8. Tighten the retaining bolts to 45 ft. lbs. (61 Nm).
9. Install the hub nut, spring and lock washers, and cotter pin.
10. Install the wheel and tire assembly.

Drive Pinion

REMOVAL AND INSTALLATION

1. Raise and safely support the vehicle.
2. Remove the rear driveline module from the vehicle.
3. Remove the overrunning clutch case-to-rear carrier bolts. Separate the overrunning clutch case from the rear carrier.
4. Remove the overrunning clutch outer race snapring and slide the clutch race off of the shaft.
5. Using a spline socket and a wrench, remove the pinion nut.

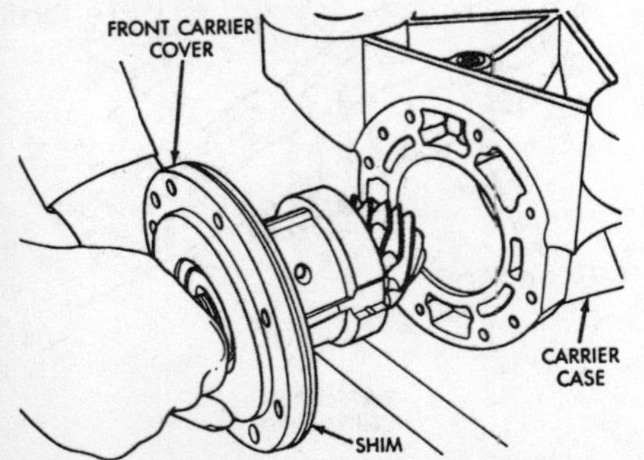

Removing the front carrier cover and pinion

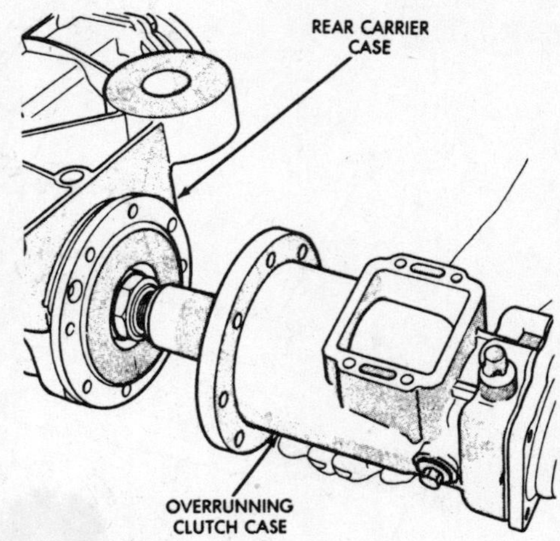

Separating the housings

6. Remove the front carrier cover retaining bolts and remove the carrier cover.
7. Place a block of wood under the end of the pinion shaft. Tap the end of the pinion against the wood to remove the spacer from the shaft.

To install:

8. Install the front carrier onto the case and tighten the retaining nuts to 105 inch lbs. (12 Nm).
9. Clean and inspect the seal area, apply a light coat of oil to the drive pinion seal. Install the seal using a seal installer. The seal must be installed with the spring towards the rear of the case.
10. Apply a light coat of oil onto the drive pinion spacer and slide it onto the pinion shaft with the tapered side facing out.
11. Apply a light coat of oil to the overrunning clutch seal and install with a seal installer,

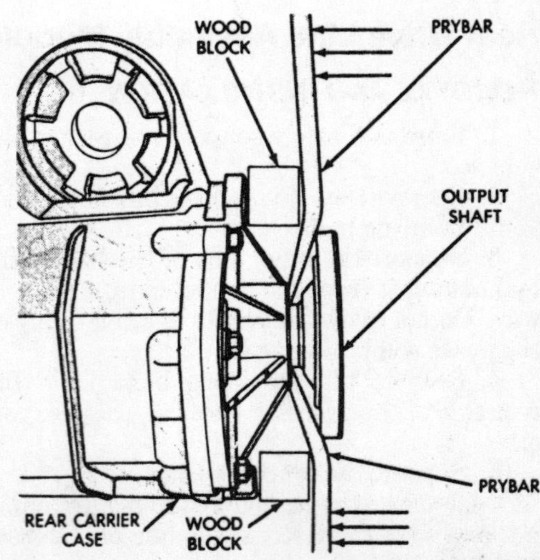

Removing the output flange, using 2 pry bars

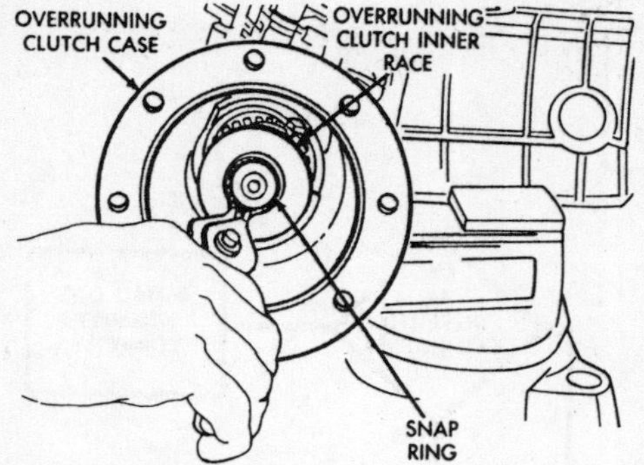

Inner snapring removal – overrunning clutch case

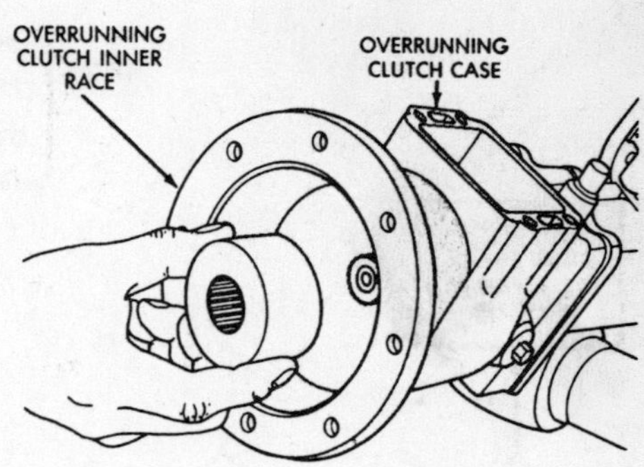

Removing overrunning clutch inner race

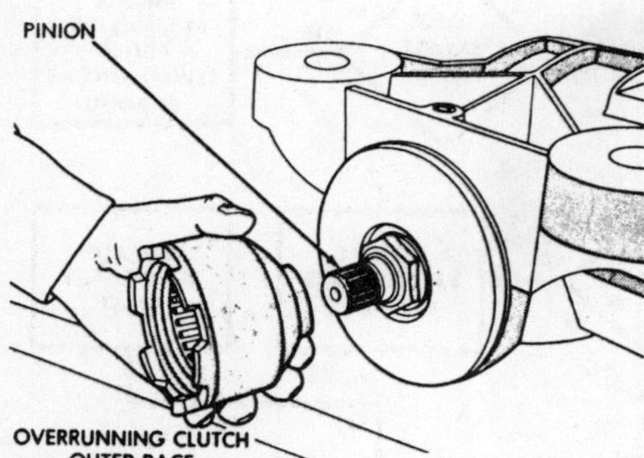

Overrunning clutch – outer race removal

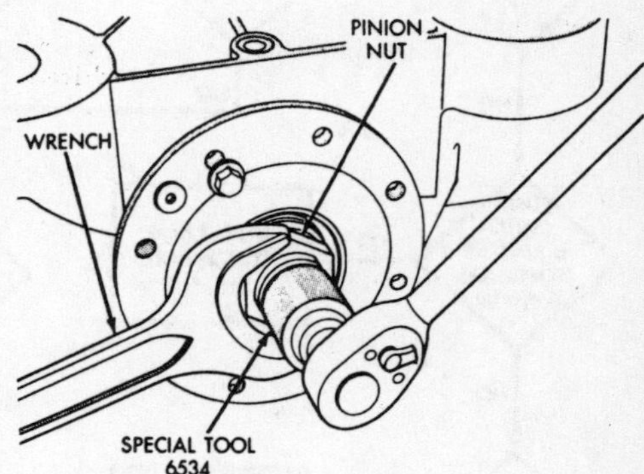

Removing the pinion nut

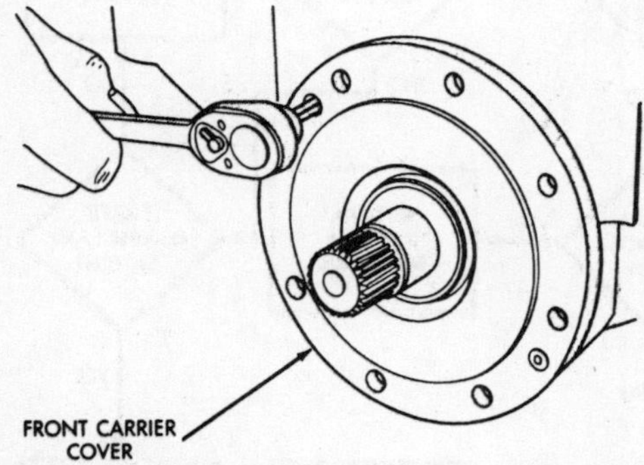

Removing the front carrier cover retaining bolts

the seal must be installed with the spring facing outward.

12. Install the pinion nut and tighten to 150 ft. lbs. (203 Nm).

13. Install the overrunning clutch outer race and snapring. Apply Loctite® sealer to the overrunning clutch sealing surface and install the clutch case to the rear carrier. Tighten to 250 inch lbs. (28 Nm).

14. Install the rear driveline module into the vehicle. Check and fill the fluid as required.

Torque Tube

REMOVAL AND INSTALLATION

1. Raise and safely support the vehicle.
2. Remove the rear driveline module assembly from the vehicle.
3. Remove the viscous coupling, snapring and torque tube bearing shield.
4. Remove torque tube to overrunning clutch case bolts.
5. Slide the torque tube off of the torque shaft.
6. Install the torque tube onto the torque shaft. Install the Torque tube to overrunning clutch case bolts, tightening to 250 inch lbs. (28 Nm).
7. Install the bearing shield and snapring. Install the viscous coupling.
8. Install the driveline module into the vehicle. Lower The vehicle.

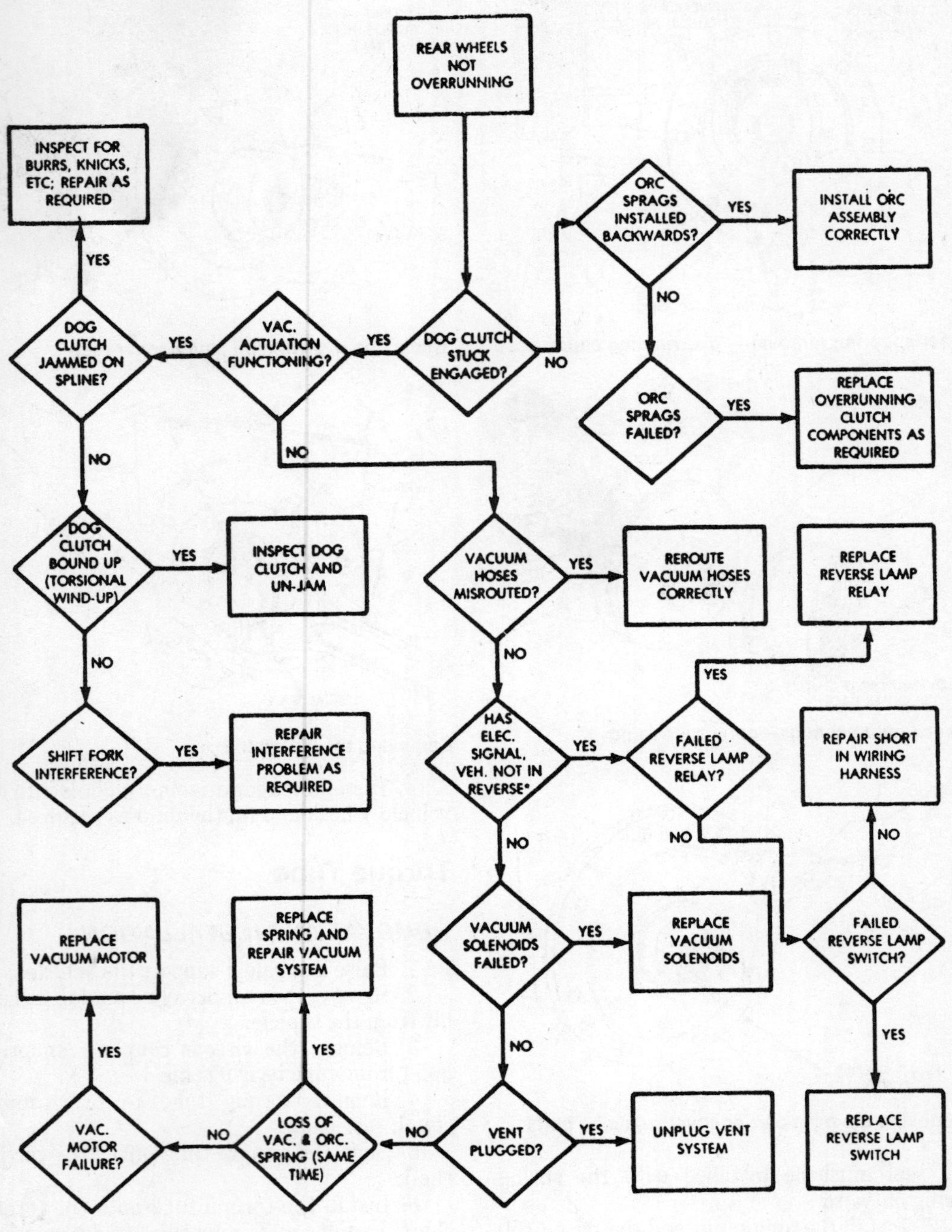

Rear driveline vacuum shift motor diagnosis

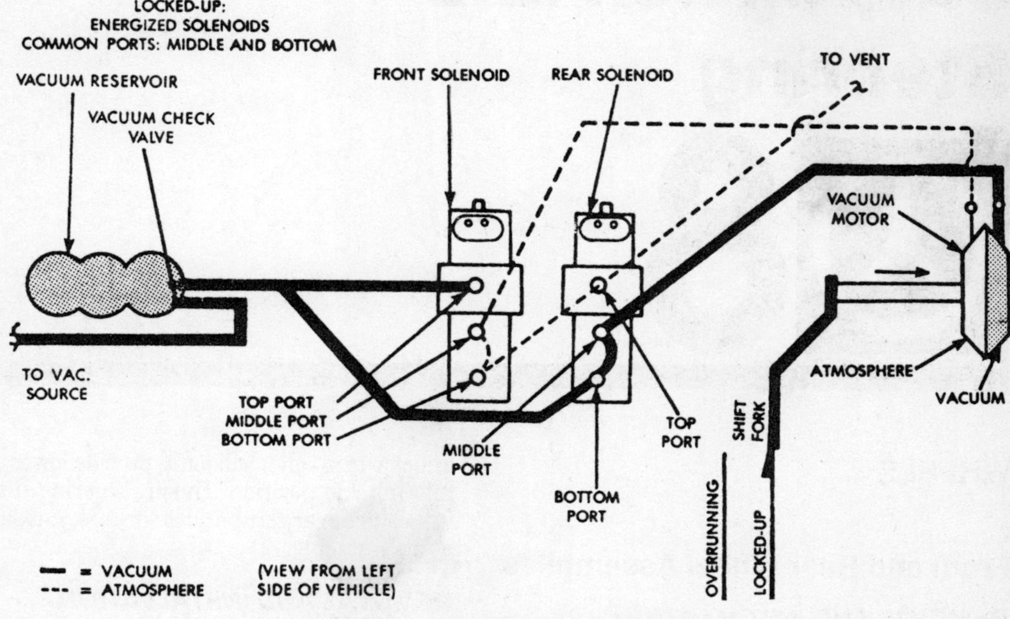

Vacuum actuation schematic — solenoids energized

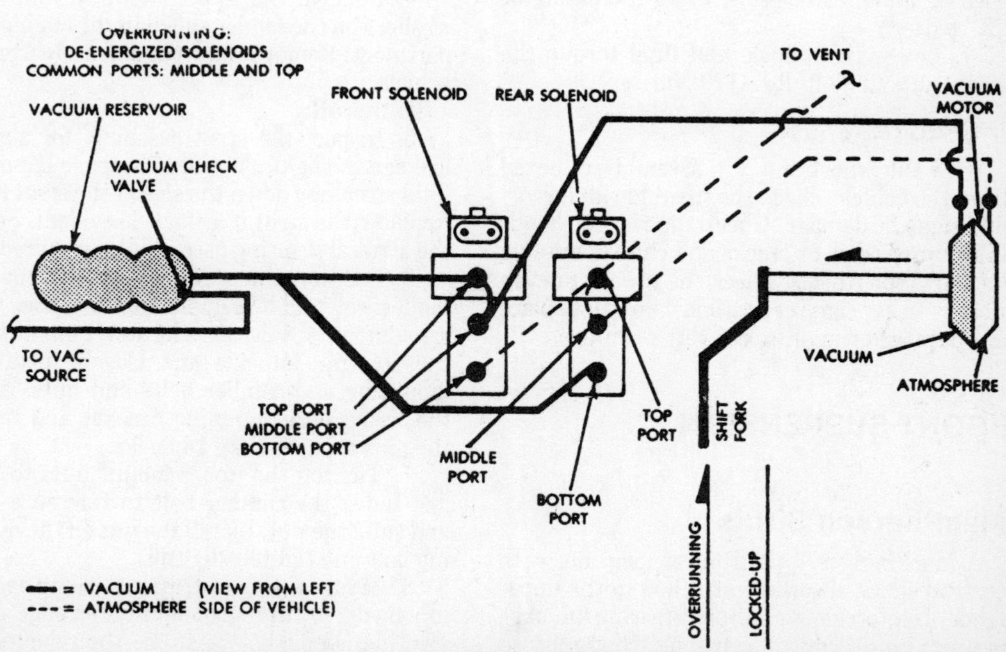

Vacuum actuation schematic — solenoids de-energized

Suspension and Steering

WHEELS

Front and Rear Wheel Assemblies

REMOVAL AND INSTALLATION

1. Place the vehicle transmission in PARK.
2. Block the wheel diagonally from the wheel being removed.
3. Remove the hub cap and loosen the lug nuts.
4. Raise the vehicle and place a jackstand underneath it on the side being raised.
5. Remove the lug nuts and the tire and wheel assembly.
6. Install the wheel on the vehicle and install the lug nuts. The lug nuts should be tightened as much as possible, using a crossing or "X" pattern.
7. Lower the vehicle and final torque the wheel nuts to 95 ft. lbs. (129 Nm).

INSPECTION

With the wheel and tire assembly removed from the vehicle, check the tire and rim for visible signs of damage. Check the rim for bends in its outer edge, or cracks and chunks missing on alloy type wheels. Check the tire for uneven wear or other signs of possible damage. Replace any damaged rim or excessively worn tire.

FRONT SUSPENSION

MacPherson Struts

A MacPherson Type front suspension, with vertical shock absorbers attached to the upper fender reinforcement and the steering knuckle, is used. Lower control arms, attached inboard to a crossmember and outboard to the steering knuckle through a ball joint, provide lower steering knuckle position. During steering maneuvers, the upper strut and steering knuckle turn as an assembly.

REMOVAL AND INSTALLATION

1. Loosen the front wheel lug nuts slightly. Raise and support the front of the vehicle on jackstands.
2. Remove the wheel and tire assemblies.

NOTE: *If the original strut assemblies are to be installed, mark the camber eccentric bolt and strut for installment in same position.*

3. Remove the lower camber bolt and nut(at the steering knuckle), and the knuckle bolt and nut. Remove the brake hose to strut bracket mounting bolt.
4. Remove the upper mounting nuts and washers on the fender shield in the engine compartment. Remove the strut assembly from the vehicle.

To install:

5. Inspect the strut assembly for signs of leakage. A slight amount of seepage is normal, fluid streaking down the side of the strut is not. Replacer the strut if leakage is evident. Service the strut and spring assembly as required.
6. Position the strut assembly under the fender well and loosely install the upper washers and nuts. Position the lower mount over the steering knuckle and loosely install the mounting and camber bolts and nuts. Attach the brake hose retaining bracket and tighten the mounting bolts to 10 ft. lbs.
7. Tighten the upper mount nuts to 20 ft. lbs. Index the camber bolt to reference mark and snug the nut. Install the nut on the mounting bolt and tighten slightly.
8. Mount a 4 in. (102mm) C-clamp over the inner edge of the strut and outer edge of the steering knuckle. Tighten the clamp just enough to eliminate any looseness between the

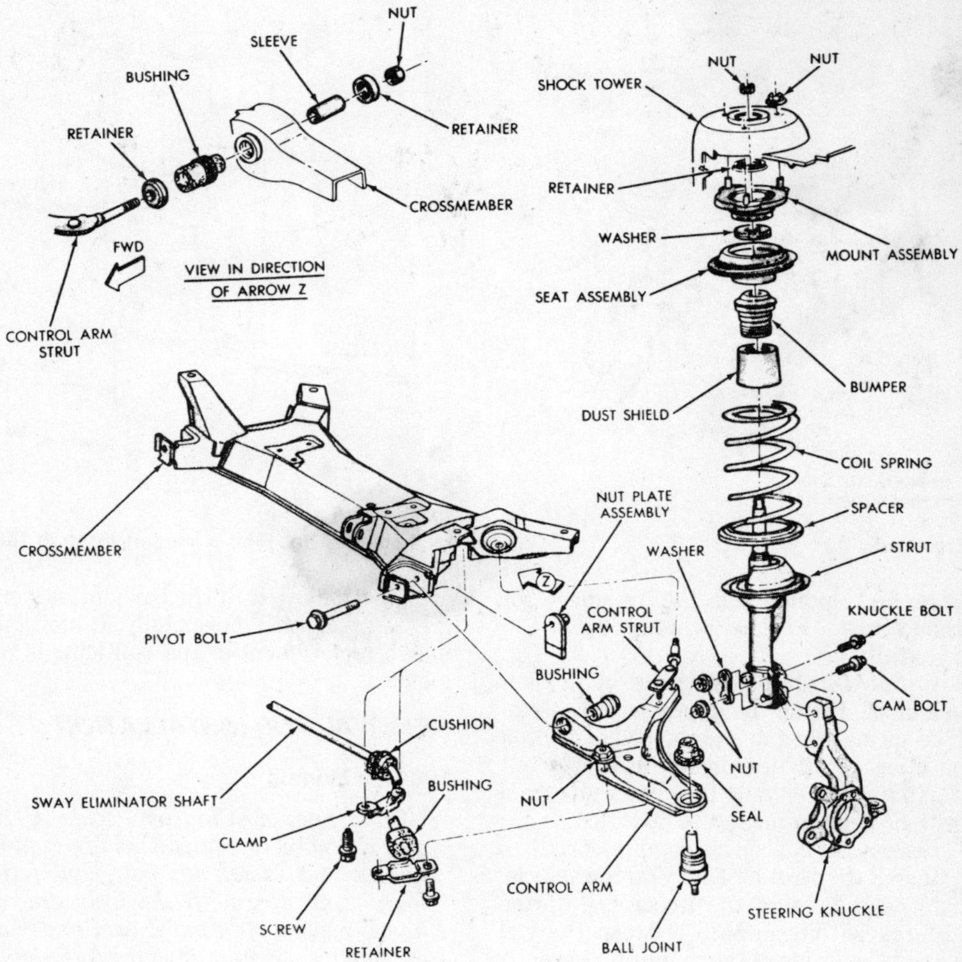

Front suspension components – exploded view

knuckle and the strut. check the alignment of the camber bolt and strut reference marks. Tighten the mounting and camber nuts to 75 ft. lbs. plug 1/4 turn more. Remove the C-clamp.

9. Install the wheel and tire assembly and lower the vehicle.

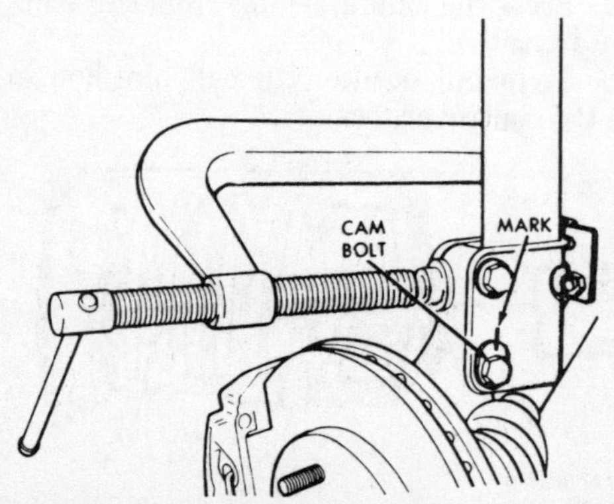

Clamp positioning for strut installation

Strut Spring

REMOVAL AND INSTALLATION

NOTE: *A coil spring compressor Chrysler Tool C-4838 or equivalent is required.*

1. Remove the strut and spring assembly from the vehicle.

2. Compress the coil spring with Chrysler Tool C-4838 or equivalent. Make sure the compressor is mounted correctly and tighten jaws evenly. If the spring slips from the compressor, bodily injury could occur.

3. Hold the strut center rod from turning and remove the assembly nut.

NOTE: *The coil springs on each are rated differently. Be sure to mark the spring for side identification.*

4. Remove the mount assembly and the coil spring. Inspect the assembly for rubber isolator deterioration, distortion, cracks and bonding failure. Replace as necessary. Check the mount

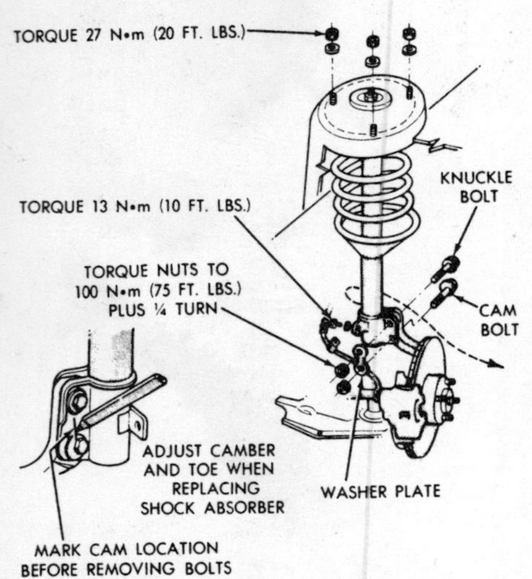

Strut removal

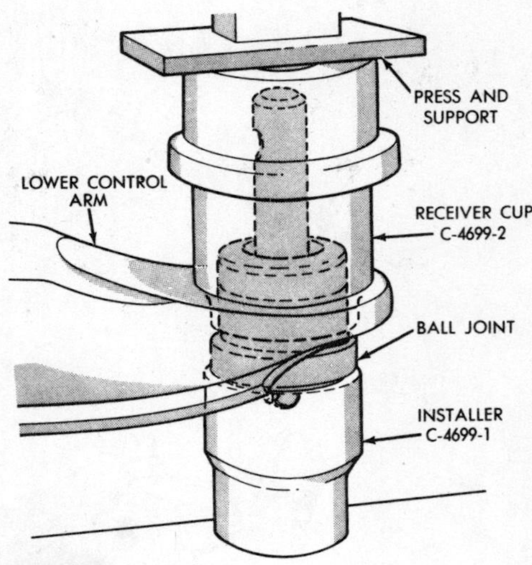

Installing the ball joint – models through 1989

bearings for binding and the retainers for bends and cracks. Replace as necessary.

To install:

5. Install the spring on the strut in compressed mode. Install the upper mount assembly. The spring seat tab and the end of the coil spring must be aligned. install assembly nut and tighten while holding the center strut rod in position. Tighten the nut to 60 ft. lbs.

6. Release the coil spring compressor.

7. Install the strut assembly on the vehicle.

8. Misalignment of the upper coil spring seat can cause interference between the coil spring and the inside of the mounting tower. A scraping noise on turns will be an indication if the problem. To correct, raise and support the vehicle to take the weight off of the front wheels. Use two wrenches, one on the top of the center strut rod and one on the assembly nut. Turn both the strut rod and nut in the same direction. The spring will wind up and snap into position. Check the torque on the assembly nut (60 ft. lbs.).

Lower Ball Joint

The lower front suspension ball joints operate with no free play. The ball joint housing is pressed into the lower control arm with the joint stud retained in the steering knuckle with a (clamp) bolt.

On models from 1990, the lower ball joint is welded to the lower control arm. This requires the replacement of the complete lower control arm in the case of ball joint failure,

INSPECTION

With the weight of the vehicle resting on the ground, grasp the ball joint grease fitting, and attempt to move it. If the ball joint is worn the grease fitting will move easily. If movement is noted, replacement of the ball joint is recommended.

REMOVAL AND INSTALLATION

1984–89 Models

NOTE: *Special Chrysler Tools C-4699-1 and C-4699-2 or equivalents are required to remove and install the ball joint form the lower control arm. If the tools are not on hand, remove the control arm and have an automotive machine shop press the ball joint out and in. Refer to the Lower Control Arm Section.*

1. Remove the lower control arm. Pry off the seal from the ball joint.

2. Position a receiving cup, special tool C-4699-2 or its equivalent to support the lower control arm.

3. Install a $1^1/8$ in. deep socket over the stud and against the joint upper housing.

4. Press the joint assembly from the arm.

To install:

5. To install, position the ball joint housing into the control arm cavity.

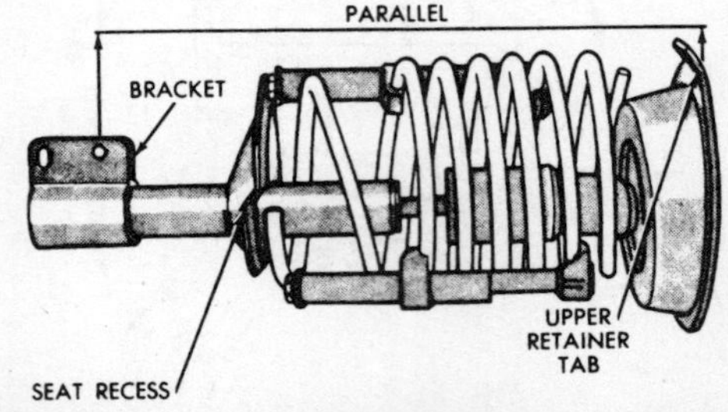

Spring compressor installed position

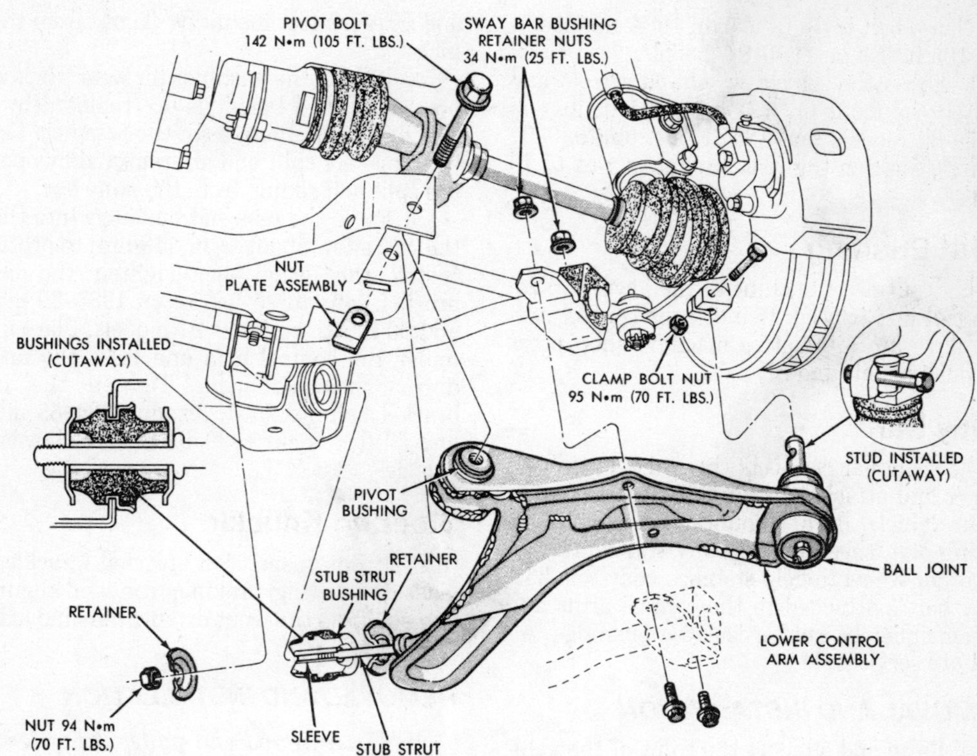

Lower control arm assembly removal and installation

6. Position the assembly in a press with special tool C-4699-1 or its equivalent, supporting the control arm.

7. Align the ball joint assembly, then press it until the housing ledge stops against the control arm cavity down flange.

8. To install a new seal, support the ball joint housing with tool #C-4699-2 and place a new seal over the stud, against the housing.

9. With a $1^1/2$ in. socket, press the seal onto the joint housing with the seat against the control arm. Install control arm.

1990–91 Models

Refer to the lower control arm removal procedure for ball joint replacement on these models.

Lower Control Arm

REMOVAL AND INSTALLATION

1. Jack up the vehicle and support it with jackstands.

2. Remove the front inner pivot through bolt, the rear stub strut nut, retainer and bushing, and the ball joint-to-steering knuckle clamp bolts.

3. Separate the ball joint stud from the steering knuckle by prying between the ball stud retainer on the knuckle and the lower control arm.

WARNING: *Pulling the steering knuckle out from the vehicle after releasing it from the ball joint can separate the inner CV joint.*

4. Remove the sway bar-to-control arm nut and reinforcement and rotate the control arm over the sway bar. Remove the rear stub strut bushing, sleeve and retainer. Remove the control arm.

To install:

NOTE: *The substitution of fasteners other than those of the grade originally used is not recommended.*

5. Install the retainer, bushing and sleeve on the stub strut.

6. Position the control arm over the sway bar and install the rear stub strut and front pivot into the crossmember.

7. Install the front pivot bolt and loosely install the nut.

8. Install the stub strut bushing and retainer and loosely assembly the nut.

9. Position the sway bar bracket and stud through the control arm and install the retainer nut. Tighten the nuts to 25 ft. lbs. on 1984–1989 models and 50 ft. lbs. On 1990–91 models.

10. Install the ball joint stud into the steering knuckle and install the clamp bolt. Torque

the clamp bolt to 70 ft. lbs. on 1984–89 models and 105 ft. lbs. on 1990–91 models.

11. Lower the vehicle, weight on wheels, and tighten the front pivot bolt to 105 ft. lbs. on 1984--89 models and 125 ft. lbs. on 1990–91 models. Tighten the rear stub strut nut to 70 ft. lbs.

Pivot Bushing

The front pivot bushing of the lower control arm can be replaced. Remove the control arm and have an automotive machine shop press the bushing out and in.

Sway Bar

The sway bar connects the control arms together and attaches to the front crossmember of the vehicle, Bumps, jounce and rebound affecting one wheel are partially transmitted to the other wheel to help stabilize body roll. The sway bar is attached to the control arms and crossmember by rubber-isolated bushings. All part are serviceable.

REMOVAL AND INSTALLATION

1. Raise and support the front of the vehicle on jackstands.
2. Remove the nuts, bolts and retainer connecting the sway bar to the control arms.
3. Remove the bolt that mount the sway bar to the crossmember. Remove the sway bar and crossmember mounting clamps from the vehicle.
4. Inspect the bushings for wear. Replace as necessary. End bushings are replaced by cutting or driving them from the retainer. Center bushings are split and are removed by opening the split and sliding from the sway bar.
5. Force the new end bushings into the retainers, allow about 1/2 in. (13mm) to protrude. Install the sway bar. Tighten the center bracket bolts to 25 ft. lbs. on 1984–89 models and 50 ft. lbs. on 1990–91 models. Place a jack under the control arm and raise the arm to normal design height. Tighten the outer bracket bolts to 25 ft. lbs. on 1984–89 models and 50 ft. lbs. on 1990–91 models. Lower the vehicle.

Steering Knuckle

The front suspension steering knuckle provides for steering, braking, front end alignment and supports the front driving hub and axle assembly.

REMOVAL AND INSTALLATION

NOTE: *A tie rod end puller (Chrysler Tool C-3894A or equivalent) is necessary.*

1. Remove the wheel cover, center hub cover, cotter pin, nut lock and spring washer from the front wheel.
2. Loosen the front hub nut and wheel lug

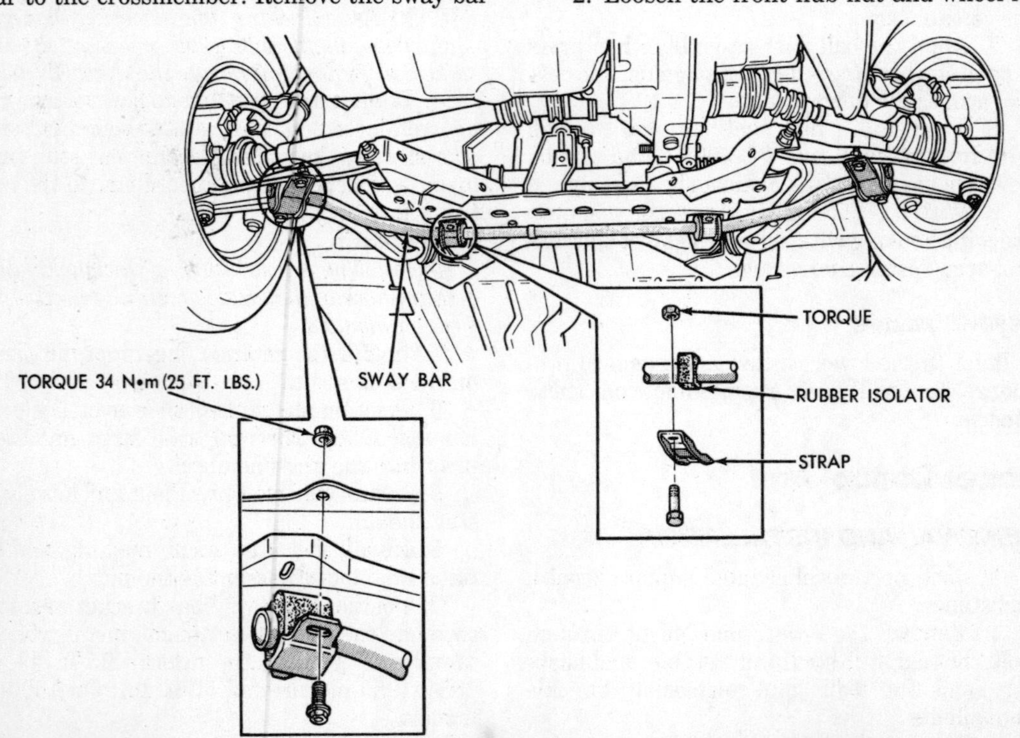

Sway bar assembly mounting

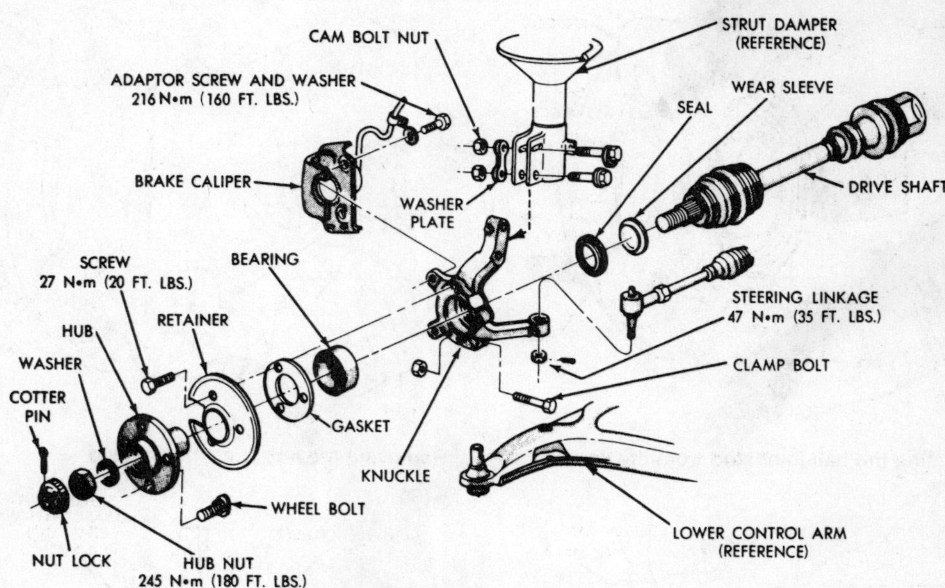

Steering knuckle installation

nuts. Raise the front of the vehicle and support on jackstands.

3. Remove the wheel and tire assembly. Remove the center hub nut.

4. Disconnect the tie rod end from the steering knuckle arm with Tool C-3894A or equivalent. Disconnect the front brake hose bracket from the strut.

5. Remove the caliper assembly and support it with a piece of wire. Do not permit the caliper to hang from the brake hose. Remove the disc brake rotor, inner pad and caliper mounting adapter.

6. Remove the clamp bolt that secures the ball joint and steering knuckle together.

7. Insure that the splined halfshaft is loose in the hub by tapping lightly with a brass drift and hammer. Separate the ball joint and steering knuckle. Pull the knuckle assembly out and away from the halfshaft. Remove the steering knuckle from the strut assembly.

To install:

8. Service hub, bearing, seal and steering knuckle as necessary.

9. Install the steering knuckle to the strut assembly. Install the halfshaft through the hub and steering knuckle. Connect the ball joint to the knuckle and tighten the clamp bolt to 70 ft. lbs. on 1984–89 models and 105 ft. lbs (145 Nm) on 1990–91 models.

10. Install the tie rod end and tighten the retaining nut to 35 ft. lbs. Install and bend the cotter pin.

11. Install the brake adapter, pads, rotor and caliper. Connect the brake hose bracket to the strut.

12. Install the center hub washer and retaining nut. Apply the brakes and tighten the nut to 180 ft. lbs. Install the spring washer, nut and new cotter pin. Install the wheel and tire assembly. Tighten the lug nuts to 95 ft. lbs. Lower the vehicle.

Front Hub and Bearing

REMOVAL AND INSTALLATION

Press In Type

NOTE: *A special set of tools, C-4811 or the equivalent, is required to remove and install the hub and bearing. If the special tool is not on hand, remove the steering knuckle and take it to an automotive machine shop for bearing replacement.*

1. Remove the cotter pin, nut lock and spring from the front halfshaft hub nut.

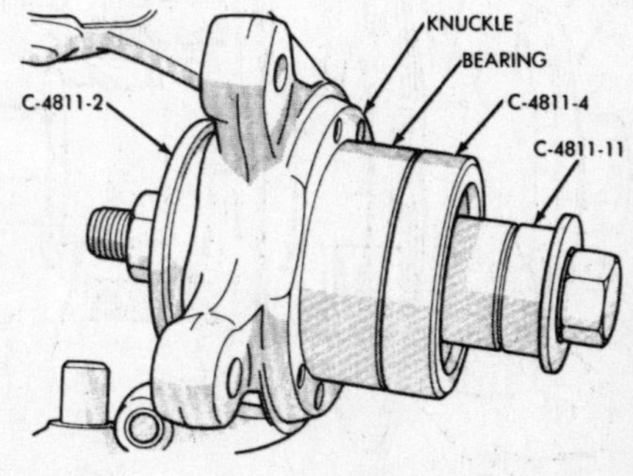

Installing the bearing in the knuckle

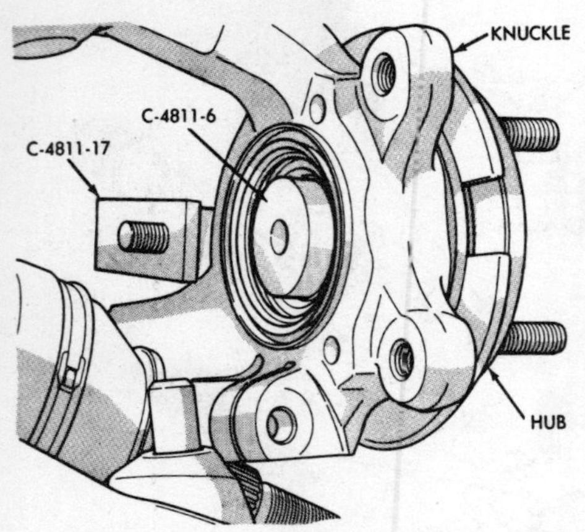

Separating the ball joint stud from the knuckle assembly

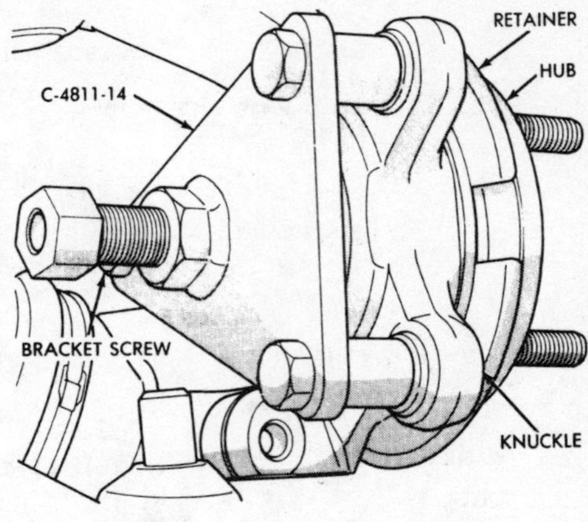

Removing the hub from the knuckle

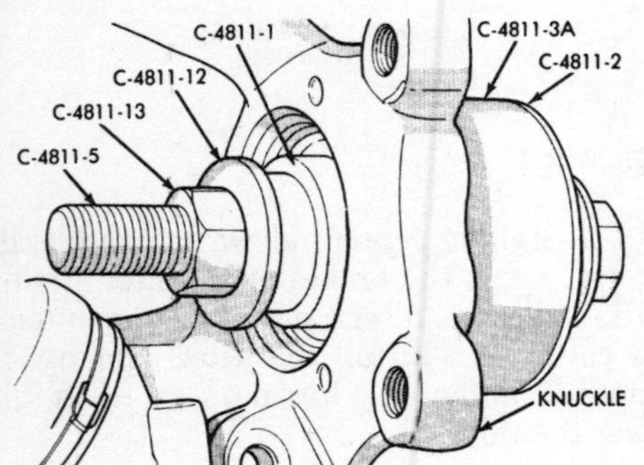

Removing the bearing from the knuckle

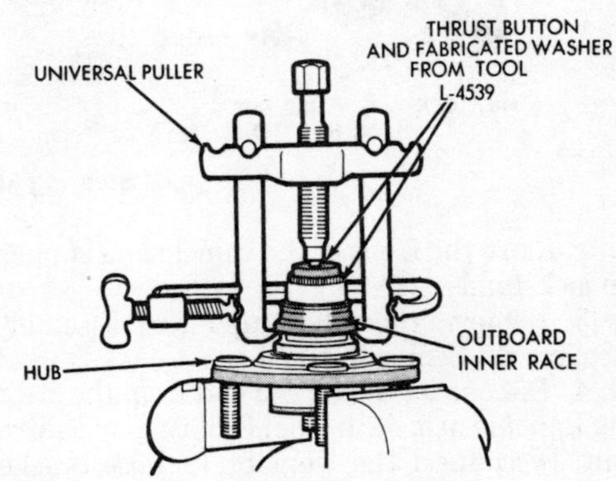

Removing the outer bearing race

Loosen the hub nut. Loosen the wheel lug nuts slightly.

2. Raise and safely support the vehicle on jackstands.

3. Remove the wheel assembly. Remove the center hub nut.

4. Disconnect the tie rod end from the steering arm. Disconnect the brake hose from the strut retainer. Remove the ball joint clamp nut.

5. Remove the brake caliper, suspend it with wire so that no strain is put on the brake hose. Remove the disc rotor.

6. Separate the knuckle from the control arm ball joint.

7. Pull the knuckle from the halfshaft. Tap the halfshaft with a brass hammer to loosen it if necessary. Use care so that the inner CV joint does not separate. Support the halfshaft.

8. Using tool C-4811, or equivalent. Back out one of the bearing and install the tool adapter bolt into the retainer threads.

9. Position the tool at the back of the knuckle and install two mounting bolts in the brake caliper mounting holes. Center the tool and tighten the caliper adapter mounting bolts and the retainer bolt.

10. Tighten the center threaded driver on the tool and push the hub from the knuckle.

11. Remove the tool from the front side of the knuckle. Carefully pry the grease seal from the knuckle. Press the bearing from the knuckle using tool C-48ll.

To install:

12. Install a new bearing by using the puller

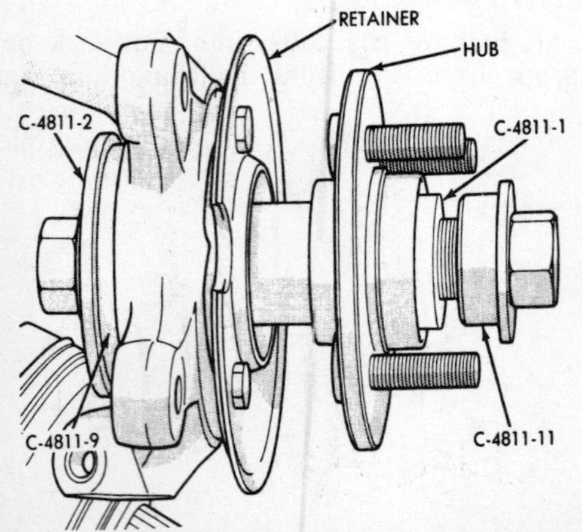

Installing the hub assembly

adapter of tool C-4811. Install a new seal and lubricate. Install the bearing retainer and bolts, torque the bolts to 20 ft. lbs.

13. Press the hub into the bearing. Install a new wear/wipe seal. Install the halfshaft. Attach the ball joint and tie rod end. Install the brake rotor and caliper. Secure the brake hose. Tighten the clamp bolt to 70 ft. lbs. Tighten the tie rod end nut to 35 ft. lbs.

14. Install the washer and hub nut. Tighten the nut firmly. Install the wheel assemblies and tighten the lug nuts firmly.

15. Lower the vehicle. Tighten the center hub nut to 180 ft. lbs. Tighten the wheel lugs to 95 ft. lbs.

Bolt-In Type

Starting with 1989 eight-passenger model vehicles, a bolt in knuckle bearing is used. The bearing unit is serviced as a complete assembly. and is attached to the steering knuckle by four mounting bolts that are removed through a provided access hole in the hub flange.

1. Loosen the center splined retaining hub nut while the vehicle is on the ground. Loosen the wheel lug nuts slightly.
2. Raise and safely support the vehicle on jackstands.
3. Remove the wheel assembly. Remove the hub nut and washer.
4. Disconnect the tie rod end from the steering arm and the clamp bolt that retains the ball joint to the knuckle.
5. Remove the disc brake caliper and suspend it with wire so that there is no strain on the brake hose. Remove the rotor.
6. Separate the knuckle from the ball joint. Pull the knuckle assembly away from the halfshaft. Take care not separate the halfshaft inner CV joint. Support the halfshaft.

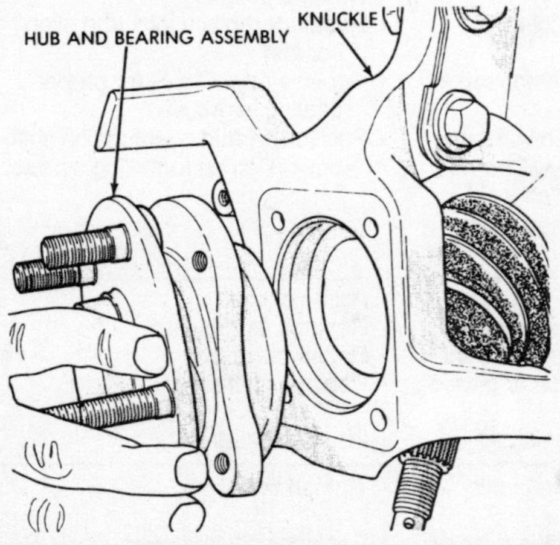

Removing the hub and bearing assembly from the knuckle – bolt on type

7. Remove the four hub and bearing retaining bolts. Remove the assembly.

To install:

8. Install the new bearing assembly and tighten the mounting bolts in a criss-cross manner to 45 ft. lbs.
9. Install a new wear sleeve seal. Lubricate the sealing surfaces with multi-purpose grease. Install the halfshaft through the hub.
10. Install the steering knuckle onto the lower control arm. Torque the clamp bolt to 70 ft. lbs. on 1984–89 models and 105 ft. lbs. on 1990–91 models.
11. Install the tie rod end. Tighten the nut to 35 ft. lbs. Install the brake disc rotor and caliper assembly.
12. Install and tighten the hub nut reasonably tight. Install the wheel assembly, tighten the lug nuts fairly tight. Lower the vehicle and tighten the hub nut to 180 ft. lbs. and the wheel lugs to 85 ft. lbs.

FRONT END ALIGNMENT

Front wheel alignment is the proper adjustment of all the interrelated suspension angles affecting the running and steering of the front wheels.

There are six basic factors which are the foundation of front wheel alignment, height, caster, camber, toe-in, steering axis inclination, and toe-out turns. of these basic factors, only camber and toe are mechanically adjustable. Any checks and required adjustments should be made to the camber first, then to the toe.

CAMBER

Camber is the number of degrees or inches the top of the wheel is tilted inward or outward from true vertical. Outward tilt is positive camber, inward-negative camber. Excessive camber (inward or outward) can cause poor handling, pulling and excessive tire wear.

TOE

Toe is measured in degrees or inches and is the distance that the front edges of the tires are closer or further apart then the rear edges. Front wheel drive vehicles usually have toe out which means that the outer edges are further apart than the inner. Incorrect toe adjustment will also cause poor handling and excessive tire wear.

Troubleshooting the Steering Column

Problem	Cause	Solution
Will not lock	• Lockbolt spring broken or defective	• Replace lock bolt spring
High effort (required to turn ignition key and lock cylinder)	• Lock cylinder defective • Ignition switch defective • Rack preload spring broken or deformed • Burr on lock sector, lock rack, housing, support or remote rod coupling • Bent sector shaft • Defective lock rack • Remote rod bent, deformed • Ignition switch mounting bracket bent • Distorted coupling slot in lock rack (tilt column)	• Replace lock cylinder • Replace ignition switch • Replace preload spring • Remove burr • Replace shaft • Replace lock rack • Replace rod • Straighten or replace • Replace lock rack
Will stick in "start"	• Remote rod deformed • Ignition switch mounting bracket bent	• Straighten or replace • Straighten or replace
Key cannot be removed in "off-lock"	• Ignition switch is not adjusted correctly • Defective lock cylinder	• Adjust switch • Replace lock cylinder
Lock cylinder can be removed without depressing retainer	• Lock cylinder with defective retainer • Burr over retainer slot in housing cover or on cylinder retainer	• Replace lock cylinder • Remove burr
High effort on lock cylinder between "off" and "off-lock"	• Distorted lock rack • Burr on tang of shift gate (automatic column) • Gearshift linkage not adjusted	• Replace lock rack • Remove burr • Adjust linkage
Noise in column	• One click when in "off-lock" position and the steering wheel is moved (all except automatic column) • Coupling bolts not tightened • Lack of grease on bearings or bearing surfaces • Upper shaft bearing worn or broken • Lower shaft bearing worn or broken • Column not correctly aligned • Coupling pulled apart • Broken coupling lower joint • Steering shaft snap ring not seated • Shroud loose on shift bowl. Housing loose on jacket—will be noticed with ignition in "off-lock" and when torque is applied to steering wheel.	• Normal—lock bolt is seating • Tighten pinch bolts • Lubricate with chassis grease • Replace bearing assembly • Replace bearing. Check shaft and replace if scored. • Align column • Replace coupling • Repair or replace joint and align column • Replace ring. Check for proper seating in groove. • Position shroud over lugs on shift bowl. Tighten mounting screws.
High steering shaft effort	• Column misaligned • Defective upper or lower bearing • Tight steering shaft universal joint • Flash on I.D. of shift tube at plastic joint (tilt column only) • Upper or lower bearing seized	• Align column • Replace as required • Repair or replace • Replace shift tube • Replace bearings
Lash in mounted column assembly	• Column mounting bracket bolts loose • Broken weld nuts on column jacket • Column capsule bracket sheared	• Tighten bolts • Replace column jacket • Replace bracket assembly

Troubleshooting the Steering Column (cont.)

Problem	Cause	Solution
Lash in mounted column assembly (cont.)	• Column bracket to column jacket mounting bolts loose • Loose lock shoes in housing (tilt column only) • Loose pivot pins (tilt column only) • Loose lock shoe pin (tilt column only) • Loose support screws (tilt column only)	• Tighten to specified torque • Replace shoes • Replace pivot pins and support • Replace pin and housing • Tighten screws
Housing loose (tilt column only)	• Excessive clearance between holes in support or housing and pivot pin diameters • Housing support-screws loose	• Replace pivot pins and support • Tighten screws
Steering wheel loose—every other tilt position (tilt column only)	• Loose fit between lock shoe and lock shoe pivot pin	• Replace lock shoes and pivot pin
Steering column not locking in any tilt position (tilt column only)	• Lock shoe seized on pivot pin • Lock shoe grooves have burrs or are filled with foreign material • Lock shoe springs weak or broken	• Replace lock shoes and pin • Clean or replace lock shoes • Replace springs
Noise when tilting column (tilt column only)	• Upper tilt bumpers worn • Tilt spring rubbing in housing	• Replace tilt bumper • Lubricate with chassis grease
One click when in "off-lock" position and the steering wheel is moved	• Seating of lock bolt	• None. Click is normal characteristic sound produced by lock bolt as it seats.
High shift effort (automatic and tilt column only)	• Column not correctly aligned • Lower bearing not aligned correctly • Lack of grease on seal or lower bearing areas	• Align column • Assemble correctly • Lubricate with chassis grease
Improper transmission shifting—automatic and tilt column only	• Sheared shift tube joint • Improper transmission gearshift linkage adjustment • Loose lower shift lever	• Replace shift tube • Adjust linkage • Replace shift tube

Troubleshooting the Ignition Switch

Problem	Cause	Solution
Ignition switch electrically inoperative	• Loose or defective switch connector • Feed wire open (fusible link) • Defective ignition switch	• Tighten or replace connector • Repair or replace • Replace ignition switch
Engine will not crank	• Ignition switch not adjusted properly	• Adjust switch
Ignition switch wil not actuate mechanically	• Defective ignition switch • Defective lock sector • Defective remote rod	• Replace switch • Replace lock sector • Replace remote rod
Ignition switch cannot be adjusted correctly	• Remote rod deformed	• Repair, straighten or replace

Troubleshooting the Power Steering Pump

Problem	Cause	Solution
Chirp noise in steering pump	• Loose belt	• Adjust belt tension to specification
Belt squeal (particularly noticeable at full wheel travel and stand still parking)	• Loose belt	• Adjust belt tension to specification
Growl noise in steering pump	• Excessive back pressure in hoses or steering gear caused by restriction	• Locate restriction and correct. Replace part if necessary.
Growl noise in steering pump (particularly noticeable at stand still parking)	• Scored pressure plates, thrust plate or rotor • Extreme wear of cam ring	• Replace parts and flush system • Replace parts
Groan noise in steering pump	• Low oil level • Air in the oil. Poor pressure hose connection.	• Fill reservoir to proper level • Tighten connector to specified torque. Bleed system by operating steering from right to left—full turn.
Rattle noise in steering pump	• Vanes not installed properly • Vanes sticking in rotor slots	• Install properly • Free up by removing burrs, varnish, or dirt
Swish noise in steering pump	• Defective flow control valve	• Replace part
Whine noise in steering pump	• Pump shaft bearing scored	• Replace housing and shaft. Flush system.
Hard steering or lack of assist	• Loose pump belt • Low oil level in reservoir **NOTE:** Low oil level will also result in excessive pump noise • Steering gear to column misalignment • Lower coupling flange rubbing against steering gear adjuster plug • Tires not properly inflated	• Adjust belt tension to specification • Fill to proper level. If excessively low, check all lines and joints for evidence of external leakage. Tighten loose connectors. • Align steering column • Loosen pinch bolt and assemble properly • Inflate to recommended pressure
Foaming milky power steering fluid, low fluid level and possible low pressure	• Air in the fluid, and loss of fluid due to internal pump leakage causing overflow	• Check for leaks and correct. Bleed system. Extremely cold temperatures will cause system aeriation should the oil level be low. If oil level is correct and pump still foams, remove pump from vehicle and separate reservoir from body. Check welsh plug and body for cracks. If plug is loose or body is cracked, replace body.
Low pump pressure	• Flow control valve stuck or inoperative • Pressure plate not flat against cam ring	• Remove burrs or dirt or replace. Flush system. • Correct
Momentary increase in effort when turning wheel fast to right or left	• Low oil level in pump • Pump belt slipping • High internal leakage	• Add power steering fluid as required • Tighten or replace belt • Check pump pressure. (See pressure test)
Steering wheel surges or jerks when turning with engine running especially during parking	• Low oil level • Loose pump belt • Steering linkage hitting engine oil pan at full turn • Insufficient pump pressure	• Fill as required • Adjust tension to specification • Correct clearance • Check pump pressure. (See pressure test). Replace flow control valve if defective.

WHEEL ALIGNMENT SPECIFICATIONS

Years	Model		Caster (Deg.) Range	Caster (Deg.) Preferred Setting	Camber (Deg.) Range	Camber (Deg.) Preferred Setting	Toe-In (in.)
1984	Caravan/Voyager	Front	①	②	0.25N–0.75P	0.30P	0.06
		Rear	—	—	1.00N–0.050P	0.25N	0
1985	Caravan/Voyager	Front	①	②	0.25N–0.75P	0.30P	0.06
		Rear	—	—	1.00N–0.050P	0.25N	0
1986	Caravan/Voyager	Front	①	②	0.25N–0.75P	0.30P	0.06
		Rear	—	—	1.00N–0.050P	0.25N	0
1987	Caravan/Voyager	Front	①	②	0.25N–0.75P	0.30P	0.06
		Rear	—	—	1.00N–0.050P	0.25N	0
1988	Caravan/Voyager	Front	①	②	0.25N–0.75P	0.30P	0.06
		Rear	—	—	1.00N–0.050P	0.25N	0
1989	Caravan/Voyager	Front	①	②	0.25N–0.75P	0.30P	0.06
		Rear	—	—	1.00N–0.050P	0.25N	0
1990	Caravan/Voyager	Front	①	②	0.25N–0.75P	0.30P	0.06
		Rear	—	—	1.00N–0.050P	0.25N	0
1991	Caravan/Voyager, Town & Country	Front	①	②	0.25N–0.75P	0.30P	0.06
		Rear	—	—	1.00N–0.050P	0.25N	0

N-Negative
P-Positive

① Not adjustable; maximum variation between sides should not exceed 1.5 degrees

② Van: 0.040P
Wagon: 0.70P

REAR SUSPENSION

The rear suspension consists of a tube and casting axle, shock absorbers and leaf springs. Stub axles are mounted to the axle and spring by U-bolts. It is possible to align both the camber and toe of the rear wheels.

The rear leaf springs are mounted by shackles and a fixed end bushing. the shackle angles have been selected to provide increasing suspension rates as the vehicle is loaded. These angles provide a comfortable unloaded ride and ample suspension travel when the vehicle is loaded.

The rear shock absorbers are mounted at an angle, forward at the top and parallel to the springs. Greater stability and ride control are provided by this design.

WARNING: *Do not install after market load leveling devices, air shocks or helper springs on your vehicle. These devices will cause the rear brake height sensing valve to adjust for a lighter lead than actually is contained.*

Rear Springs

REMOVAL AND INSTALLATION

Front Wheel Drive Models

1. Raise and support the rear of the vehicle on jackstands. Locate the jackstands under the frame contact points just ahead of the rear spring fixed ends.
2. Raise the rear axle just enough to relieve the weight on the springs and support on jackstands.
3. Disconnect the rear brake proportioning valve spring. Disconnect the lower ends of the shock absorbers at the rear axle bracket.
4. Loosen and remove the nuts from the U-bolts. Remove the washer and U-bolts.
5. Lower the rear axle assembly to permit the rear springs to hang free. Support the spring and remove the four bolts that mount the fixed end spring bracket. Remove the rear spring shackle nuts and plate. Remove the shackle from the spring.
6. Remove the spring. Remove the fixed end mounting bolts from the bracket and remove the bracket. Remove the front pivot bolt from the front spring hanger.

To install:

7. Install the spring on the rear shackle and hanger. Start the shackle nuts but do not tighten completely.
8. Assembly the front spring hanger on the spring. Raise the front of the spring and install the four mounting bolts. Tighten the mounting bolts to 45 ft. lbs.
9. Raise the axle assembly and align the spring center bolts in correct position. Install

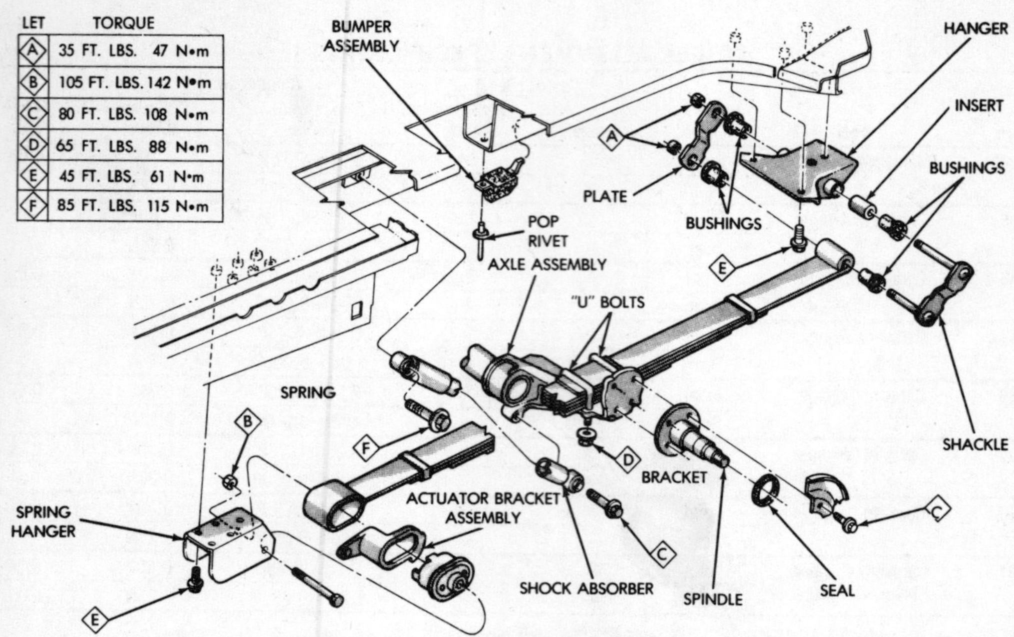

Rear suspension components — 1989–91 models

the mounting U-bolts. Tighten the nuts to 60 ft. lbs.

10. Install the rear shock absorber to the lower brackets.

11. Lower the vehicle to the ground so that the full weight is on the springs. Tighten the mounting components as follows: Front fixed end bolt; 95 ft. lbs. Shackle nuts; 35 ft. lbs. Shock absorber bolts; 50 ft. lbs.

12. Raise and support the vehicle. Connect the brake valve spring and adjust the valve.

All Wheel Drive Models

1. Raise and support the rear of the vehicle on jackstands. Locate the jackstands under the chassis, ahead of the springs.

2. Raise the rear axle just enough to relieve the weight on the springs and support on jackstands.

3. Disconnect the rear brake proportioning valve spring. Disconnect the lower ends of the shock absorbers at the rear axle bracket.

4. Loosen and remove the nuts from the U-

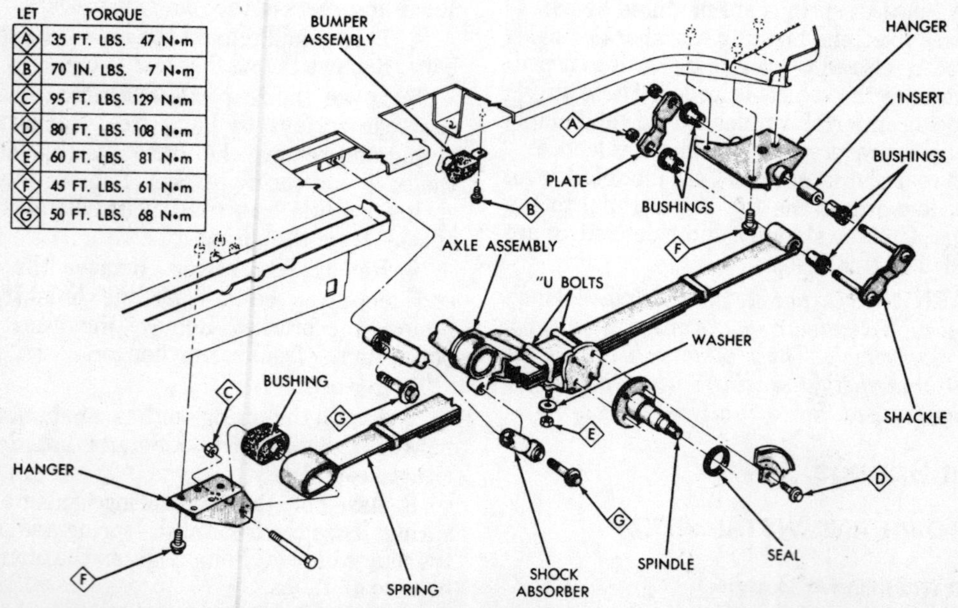

Rear suspension components — 1984–88 models

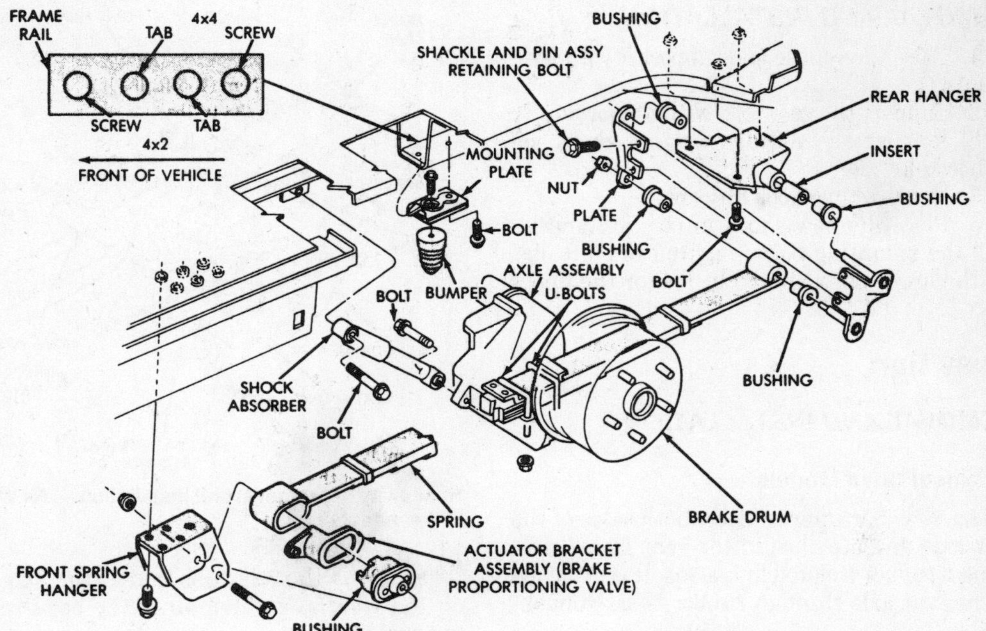

Rear suspension components – 1991 All Wheel Drive models

bolts. Remove the washer and U-bolts.

5. Lower the rear axle assembly to permit the rear springs to hang free. Support the spring and remove the four bolts that mount the fixed end spring bracket. Remove the rear spring shackle nuts and plate. Remove the shackle from the spring.

6. Remove the spring. Remove the fixed end mounting bolts from the bracket and remove the bracket. Remove the front pivot bolt from the front spring hanger.

7. Separate the rear shackle plate from the shackle and pin assembly. Remove the shackle and pin assembly from the spring.

8. Assemble the shackle and pin assembly, bushing and shackle plate on rear of spring and spring hanger. Start the shackle and pin assembly through bolts, do not tighten.

9. Assemble the front spring hanger to the front of the spring eye and install pivot bolt and nut. Do not tighten.

NOTE: *Pivot bolt must inboard to prevent structural damage during spring installation.*

10. Raise the front of the spring into position and install the 4 hanger bolts, tighten them to 45 ft. lbs. (61 Nm). Connect the actuator assembly for the proportioning valve.

11. Raise the axle assembly into position, centered under the spring center bolt.

12. Install the U-bolts, nuts and washers. Tighten the U-bolt nuts to 65 ft. lbs. (88 Nm).

13. Install the shock absorbers and start the bolts.

14. Lower the vehicle to the ground, with the full weight of the vehicle on the wheels. Tighten all of the fasteners in the following sequence and to the listed torques:

a. Front pivot bolts – 105 ft. lbs. (142 Nm)

b. Shackle and pin assembly through bolt nuts – 35 ft. lbs. (47 Nm)

c. Shackle and pin assembly retaining bolts – 35 ft. lbs. (47 Nm)

d. Shock absorber upper bolts – 85 ft. lbs. (115 Nm)

e. Shock absorber lower bolts – 80 ft. lbs. (108 Nm)

15. Raise the vehicle and connect the proportioning valve.

Shock Absorbers

TESTING

Shock absorbers require replacement if the car fails to recover quickly after hitting a large bump or if it sways excessively following a directional change.

A good way to test the shock absorbers is to intermittently apply downward pressure to the side of the vehicle until it is moving up and down for almost its full suspension travel. Release it and observe its recovery. If the vehicle bounces once or twice after having been released and then comes to a rest, the shocks are alright. If the vehicle continues to bounce, the shock will probably require replacement.

REMOVAL AND INSTALLATION

1. Raise the vehicle and support it with jackstands.
2. Support the rear axle with a floor jack.
3. Remove the top and bottom shock absorber bolts.
4. Remove the shock absorbers.
5. Place the new shock in position and install the mounting bolts. Tighten to 80 ft. lbs. for the lower bolts and 85 ft. lbs for the upper bolts.

Sway Bar

REMOVAL AND INSTALLATION

All Wheel Drive Models

The sway bar interconnects both sides of the rear axle and attaches to the rear frame rails using 2 rubber isolated link arms. It is attached to the rear axle through rubber isolated bushings.

1. Raise and support the vehicle.
2. Remove the 2 lower bolts which hold the sway bar to the link arm on each side of the vehicle.
3. Loosen the bolts that attach the sway bar bushings to the rear axle housing.
4. While holding the sway bar in place, remove the 4 bushing retaining bolts and remove the sway bar from the axle.

To install:

5. Inspect the bushings and replace any that appear damaged.
6. Install the sway bar to the rear axle. The slits in the bushing should face up in the installed position. Do not tighten the bolts.
7. Install the 2 lower link bolts, do not tighten these.

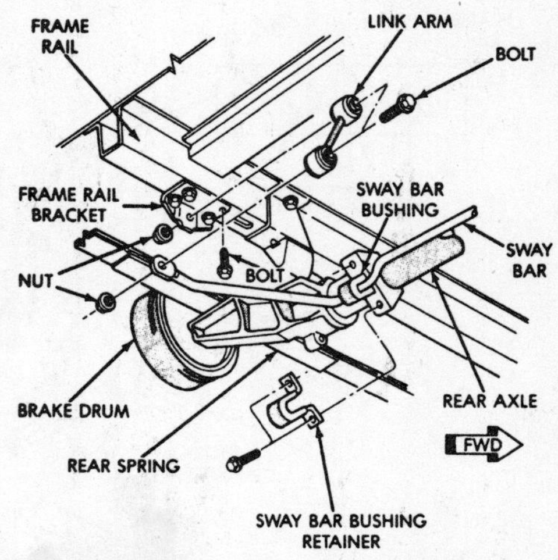

Rear sway bar removal and installation – All Wheel Drive models

8. Lower the vehicle so that all the weight is on the wheels. Tighten all of the bolts to the following torques:
   a. Bushing-to-axle bracket – 45 ft. lbs. (61 Nm)
   b. Link arm-to-frame rail – 45 ft. lbs. (61 Nm)
   c. Sway bar-to-link arm – 45 ft. lbs. (61 Nm)
   d. Link arm bracket-to-frame rail 290 inch lbs. (33 Nm)

Rear Wheel Bearings

SERVICING

Front Wheel Drive Models

NOTE: *Sodium-based grease is not compatible with lithium-based grease. Read the package labels and be careful not to mix the two*

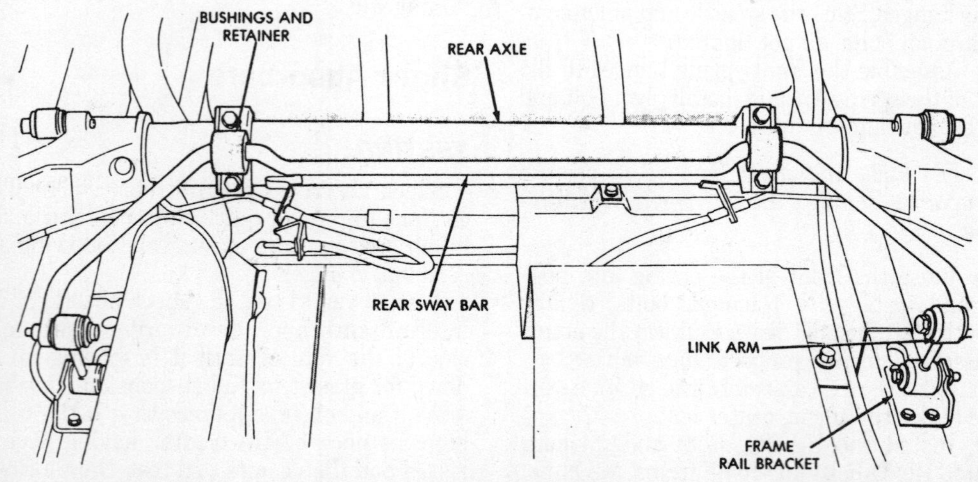

Rear sway bar mounting – All Wheel Drive models

types. If there is any doubt as to the type of grease used, completely clean the old grease from the bearing and hub before replacing.

Before handling the bearings, there are a few things that you should remember to do and not to do.

Remember to DO the following:

- Remove all outside dirt from the housing before exposing the bearing.
- Treat a used bearing as gently as you would a new one.
- Work with clean tools in clean surroundings.
- Use clean, dry canvas gloves, or at least clean, dry hands.
- Clean solvents and flushing fluids are a must.
- Use clean paper when laying out the bearings to dry.
- Protect disassembled bearings from rust and dirt. Cover them up.
- Use clean rags to wipe bearings.
- Keep the bearings in oil-proof paper when they are to be stored or are not in use.
- Clean the inside of the housing before replacing the bearing.

Do NOT do the following:

- Don't work in dirty surroundings.
- Don't use dirty, chipped or damaged tools.
- Try not to work on wooden work benches or use wooden mallets.
- Don't handle bearings with dirty or moist hands.
- Do not use gasoline for cleaning; use a safe solvent.
- Do not spin-dry bearings with compressed air. They will be damaged.
- Do not spin dirty bearings.
- Avoid using cotton waste or dirty cloths to wipe bearings.
- Try not to scratch or nick bearing surfaces.
- Do not allow the bearing to come in contact with dirt or rust at any time.

The rear wheel bearings should be inspected and relubricated whenever the rear brakes are serviced or at least every 30,000 miles. Repack the bearings with high temperature multi-purpose grease.

Check the lubricant to see if it is contaminated. If it contains dirt or has a milky appearance indicating the presence of water, the bearings should be cleaned and repacked.

Clean the bearings in kerosene, mineral spirits or other suitable cleaning fluid. Do not dry them by spinning the bearings. Allow them to air dry.

1. Raise and support the vehicle with the rear wheels off the floor.
2. Remove the wheel grease cap, cotter pin, nut-lock and bearing adjusting nut.
3. Remove the thrust washer and bearing.
4. Remove the drum from the spindle.
5. Thoroughly clean the old lubricant from the bearings and hub cavity. Inspect the bearing rollers for pitting or other signs of wear. Light discoloration is normal.

To install:

6. Repack the bearings with high temperature multi-purpose EP grease and add a small amount of new grease to the hub cavity. Be sure to force the lubricant between all rollers in the bearing.
7. Install the drum on the spindle after coating the polished spindle surfaces with wheel bearing lubricant.
8. Install the outer bearing cone, thrust washer and adjusting nut.
9. Tighten the adjusting nut to 20-25 ft. lbs. while rotating the wheel.
10. Back off the adjusting nut to completely release the preload from the bearing.
11. Tighten the adjusting nut finger-tight.
12. Position the nut-lock with one pair of slots in line with the cotter pin hole. Install the cotter pin.
13. Clean and install the grease cap and wheel.
14. Lower the vehicle.

All Wheel Drive Vehicles

The rear wheel bearings used on these models is a bolt in type unit, this is the same unit that is used on the front knuckle assembly.

1. Raise and support the vehicle.
2. Remove the wheel and tire assembly.
3. Remove the halfshaft flange retaining bolts and remove the halfshaft assembly.
4. Remove the wheel bearing mounting bolts and remove the wheel bearing and hub assembly.

To install:

5. Install the hub and bearing assembly, tighten the bolts to 96 ft. lbs (130 Nm) in a criss-cross pattern.

NOTE: *Thoroughly clean the seal and wear sleeve, lubricate both before installation.*

6. Install the halfshaft.
7. Install the washer and hub nut, with the brakes applied tighten the nut to 180 ft. lbs. (244 Nm).
8. Install the spring washer, nut lock and new cotter pin.
9. Install the wheel and tire assembly.

Rear Axle Alignment

Camber and Toe adjustment are possible through the use of shims. Shims are added or subtracted between the spindle mounting surface and the axle mounting plate. Each shim equals a wheel angle change of 0.3 degrees.

STEERING

Steering Wheel

REMOVAL AND INSTALLATION

NOTE: *A steering wheel puller (Chrysler tool C3428B or the equivalent) is required.*

1. Disconnect the negative battery cable at the battery.
2. Remove the center horn pad assembly. On standard steering wheels the horn pad is retained by two screws which are removed from underneath the wheel. Premium steering wheels require that the horn pad be pried from internal retainers. Pry the horn pad up from the bottom edges of the steering wheel.
3. Disconnect the horn wires from the center pad. Remove the pad.
4. Mark the column shaft and wheel for reinstallation reference and remove the steering wheel retaining nut.
5. Remove the steering wheel using a steering wheel puller (Chrysler Tool C3428B or the equivalent).

To install:

6. Line up the reference marks on the steering wheel and column shaft. Push wheel on to the shaft and draw into position with the mounting nut. Tighten the nut to 45 ft. lbs. Install the center horn pad after connecting the horn connectors. Connect the negative battery cable.

Turn Signal Switch

REMOVAL AND INSTALLATION

1. Disconnect the negative battery cable at the battery.
2. Remove the steering wheel. Remove the lower steering column cover, silencer panel and reinforcement.
3. The wiring harness is contained by a trough that is mounted on the side of the steering column. Remove the trough by prying the connectors from the column. New connectors may be required for installation.
4. Disconnect the turn signal wiring harness connector at the bottom of the steering column.
5. Disassemble the steering column for switch removal as follows:

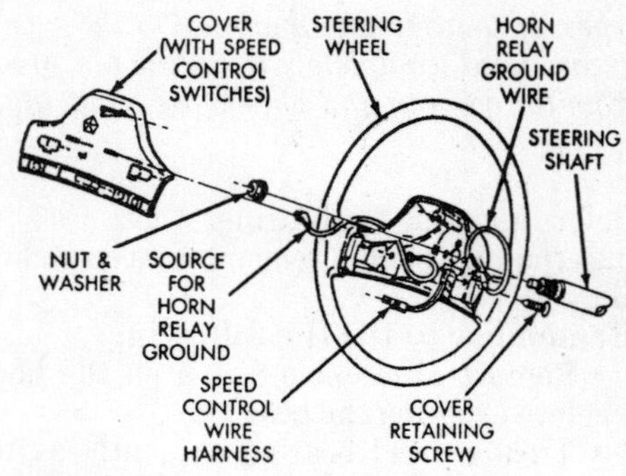

Steering wheel horn pad and wiring

6. On standard columns; remove the screw holding the wiper-washer switch to the turn signal switch. Allow the control stalk and switch to remain in position. Remove the three screws that attach the bearing retainer and turn signal switch to the upper bearing housing. Remove the turn signal and hazard warning switch assembly by gently pulling the switch up from the column while straightening the wires and guiding them up through the column opening. Be sure to disconnect the ground connector.
7. On models with tilt wheel; remove the plastic cover (if equipped) from the lock plate. Depress the lock plate and pry the retaining ring form mounting groove. (Chrysler Tool C4156 or equivalent is used to compress the lock plate). Remove the lock plate, canceling cam and upper bearing spring. Place the turn signal switch in right turn position. Remove the screw that attaches the link between the turn signal and wiper-washer switches. Remove the screw that attaches the hazard warning switch knob. Remove the three screws attaching the turn signal switch to the steering column. Remove the turn signal and hazard warning switch assembly by gently pulling the switch up from the column while straightening and guiding the wires up through the column opening.

To install:

8. On models with the standard column; lubricate the turn signal switch pivot hole with a white lube (such as Lubriplate). Thread the connector and wires through the column hole carefully. Position the turn signal switch and bearing retainer in place on the upper bearing housing and install the three mounting screws. Position the turn signal lever to turn signal pivot and secure with the mounting screws. Be sure the dimmer switch rod is in mounting pocket.
9. On models with tilt wheel; thread connector and wire harness through column hole. Position the turn signal switch in the upper

column housing. Place the switch in the right turn position. Install the three mounting screws. Install the link between the turn signal switch and the wiper-washer switch pivot and secure mounting screw. Install the lock plate bearing spring, canceling cam and new retainer clip using Tool C4156 or equivalent. Install the hazard warning knob, screw.

10. Connect the wiring harness plug. Install the cover through wiring cover to the steering column.

11. Install the steering wheel and retaining nut. Connect battery cable and test the switch for operation.

Ignition Lock

REMOVAL AND INSTALLATION

For removal of the ignition switch refer to Chapter 6 of this manual.

1. Follow the turn signal switch removal procedure previously described.
2. Unclip the horn and key light ground wires.
3. Remove the retaining screw and move the ignition key lamp assembly out of the way.
4. Remove the four screws that hold the bearing housing to the lock housing.
5. Remove the snap ring from the upper end of the steering shaft.
6. Remove the bearing housing from the shaft.
7. Remove the lock plate spring and lock plate from the steering shaft.
8. Remove the ignition key, then remove the screw and lift out the buzzer/chime switch.
9. Remove the two screws attaching the ignition switch to the column jacket.
10. Remove the ignition switch by rotating the switch 90 degrees on the rod then sliding off the rod.
11. Remove the two mounting screws from the dimmer switch and disengage the switch from the actuator rod.
12. Remove the two screws that mount the bellcrank and slide the bellcrank up in the lock housing until it can be disconnect from the ignition switch actuator rod.
13. To remove the lock cylinder and lock levers place the cylinder in the lock position and remove the key.
14. Insert a small diameter screwdriver or similar tool into the lock cylinder release holes and push into the release spring loaded lock retainers. At the same time pull the lock cylinder out of the housing bore.
15. Grasp the lock lever and spring assembly and pull straight out of the housing.
16. If necessary the lock housing may be removed from the column jacket by removing the hex head retaining screws.

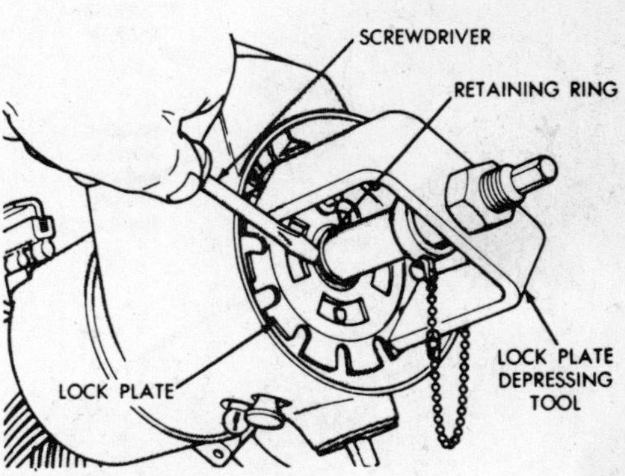

Depressing the lock plate

17. Installation is the reverse of removal. If the lock housing was removed tighten the lock housing screws to 90 inch pounds.
18. To install the dimmer switch, firmly seat the push rod into the switch. Compress the switch until two $^{1}/_{8}$ in. (3mm) drill shanks can be inserted into the alignment holes. Reposition the upper end of the push rod in the pocket of the wash/wipe switch. With a light rearward pressure on the switch, install the two screws.
19. Grease and assemble the two lock levers, lock lever spring and pin.
20. Install the lock lever assembly in the lock housing. Seat the pin firmly into the bottom of the slots and make sure the lock lever spring leg is firmly in place in the lock casting notch.
21. Install the ignition switch actuator rod from the bottom through the oblong hole in the lock housing and attach it to the bellcrank onto its mounting surface. The gearshift lever should be in the park position.
22. Place the ignition switch on the ignition switch actuator rod and rotate it 90 degrees to lock the rod into position.
23. To install the ignition lock, turn the key to the lock position and remove the key. Insert the cylinder far enough into the housing to contact the switch actuator. Insert the key and press inward and rotate the cylinder.

Steering Linkage

REMOVAL AND INSTALLATION

Tie Rod Ends

1. Jack up the front of the vehicle and support on jackstands.
2. Loosen the jam nut which connects the tie rod end to the rack.
3. Mark the tie rod position on the threads.
4. Remove the tie rod cotter pin and nut.
5. Using a puller, remove the tie rod from the steering knuckle.

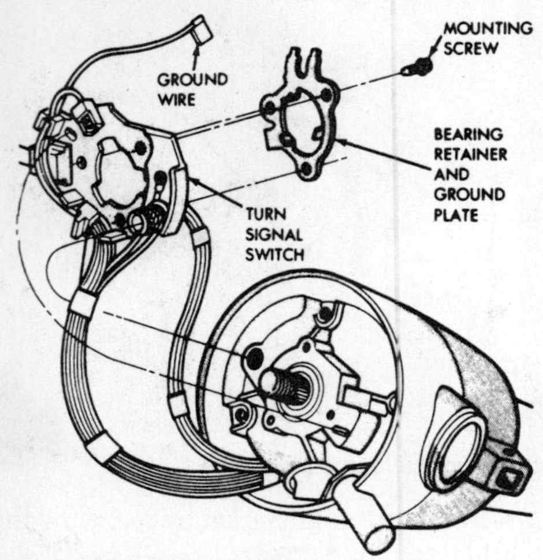

Turn signal switch removal

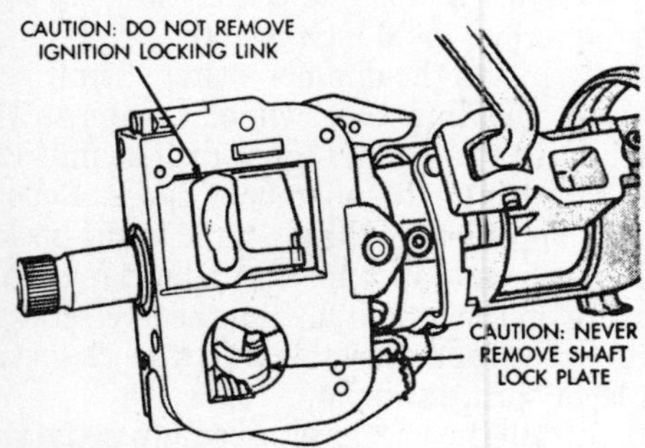

Ignition lock mounting

NOTE: *Count the number of turns when removing tie rod end. Install the new end the same amount of turns.*

6. Unscrew the tie rod end from the rack.

To install:

7. Install a new tie rod end, screw in the same number of turns as removal. Tighten the jam nut to 55 ft. lbs..

8. Check the wheel alignment.

Steering Gear

The steering system (either manual or power) used on these vehicles is of the rack and pinion design.

The manual steering gear assembly consists of a tube which contains a toothed rack and a housing containing a straddle mounted, helical-cut pinion gear. Tie rods are connected to each end of the rack and an adjustable end (on each side) connects to the steering knuckles. A double universal joint attaches the pinion to the steering column shaft. Steering wheel movement is transmitted by the column shaft and the rack and pinion converts the rotational movement of the pinion to transverse movement of the rack. The manual steering gear is permanently lubricated at the factory and periodic lubrication is not necessary. The manual steering gear cannot be adjusted or serviced. If a malfunction occurs, the entire assembly must be replaced.

The power steering gear is similar to appearance, except for a rotary valve assembly and two fluid hose assemblies. The rotary valve assembly directs fluid from the power steering pump, through hoses, to either side of an internal rack piston. As steering wheel effort is applied, an internal torsion bar twists causing the rotary valve to direct the fluid behind an internal rack piston, which in turn builds up hydraulic pressure and assists in the turning effort.

Rubber boots seal the tie rods and rack assembly. Inspect the boots periodically for cuts, tears or leakage. Replace the boots as necessary.

REMOVAL AND INSTALLATION

Front Wheel Drive Models

1. Loosen the wheel lugs slightly. Raise and support the front of the vehicle at the frame point below the front doors, not on the front crossmember. Use jackstands for supporting.

2. Remove the front wheels and tire assemblies.

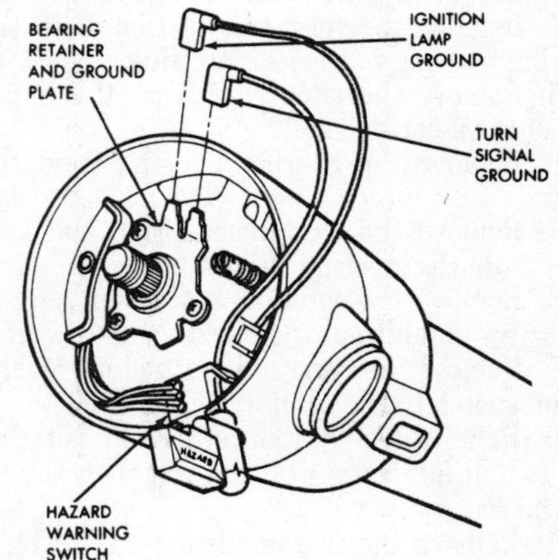

Hazard warning switch removal

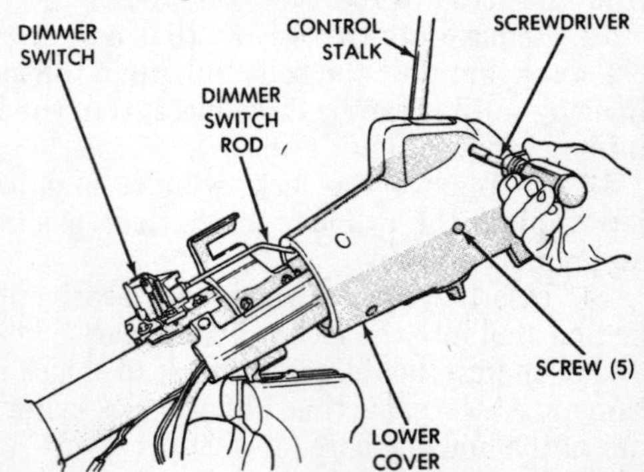

Removing upper and lower column covers

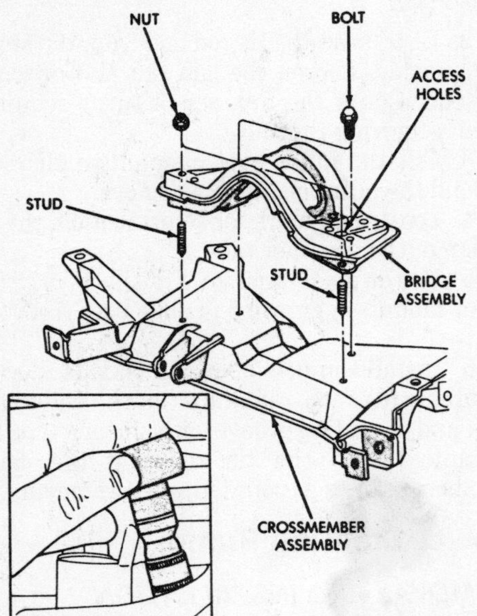

Bridge assembly removal – All Wheel Drive vehicles

3. Remove the tie rod ends from the steering knuckles.

4. Lower and disconnect the steering column from the steering gear pinion shaft.

5. If equipped, remove the anti-rotation link from the crossmember and the air diverter valve from the left side of the crossmember.

6. Place a transmission jack, or floor jack with a wide lifting flange, under the front suspension K-crossmember. Support the crossmember and remove the four crossmember to frame attaching bolts. Slowly lower the crossmember until enough room is gained to remove the steering gear assembly. Place stands under the crossmember, if available.

7. Remove the splash and boot shields. If equipped with power steering, disconnect the power steering hoses.

8. Remove the bolts that attach the steering gear assembly to the crossmember. Remove the assembly from the left side of the vehicle.

To install:

9. Line up the gear pinion with the column. Installation is in the reverse order of removal. On models with manual steering, be sure the master serration of the steering gear aligns with the steering column connector. the right rear crossmember bolt is the alignment pilot for reinstallation. Install first and tighten.

10. Attach the gear to the K-frame and secure the K-frame. Secure the anti-rotation link. Secure the K-frame. Torque all crossmember attaching bolts to 90 ft. lbs. Steering gear mounting bolts are tightened to 250 inch lbs.

11. Connect the tie rod ends. Fill power steering reservoir (if equipped), start engine, turn the steering wheel from lock to lock and check for fluid leaks.

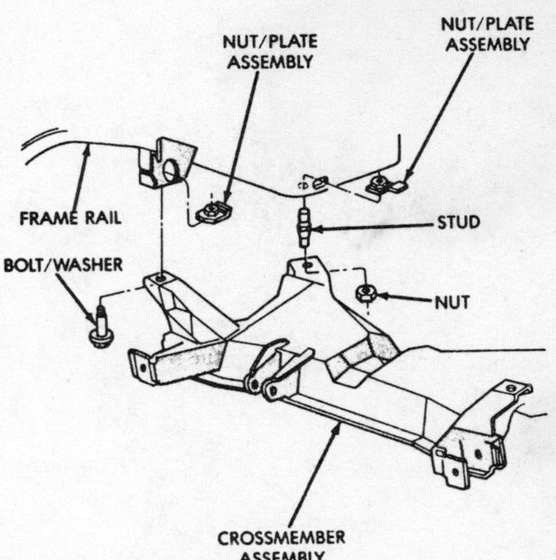

Crossmember assembly mounting

12. Check toe adjustment.

All Wheel Drive (AWD) Models

Before removing the steering gear on AWD models, the steering column must be removed to provide clearance for steering rack removal.

1. Raise and support the vehicle. Remove the wheel and tire assemblies.

2. Remove the steering column assembly from the vehicle.

3. Remove the tie rod ends from the steering knuckle using a suitable puller.

4. Remove the 2 bolts and the 2 nuts that attach the bridge assembly to the crossmember. The bolts and nuts can be reached through the access holes in the top of the bridge assembly.

5. Remove the crossmember to frame rail attaching bolts. Use a jack to lower the crossmember so that it is suspended from the lower control arms. It is necessary to remove the crossmember completely from the vehicle.

6. Disconnect and plug the power steering lines from the steering gear. Remove the hose retaining bracket from the crossmember.

7. Remove the 4 bolts that retain the steering gear to the bridge assembly.

NOTE: *Note the position of each bolt as it is removed, there are different bolts for the left and right sides.*

8. Remove the lower steering column coupler from the steering gear. Drive the roll pin from the coupler using a punch. If this is not done, there will not be enough clearance for rack removal.

9. Remove the steering gear from the vehicle by pulling it out through the drivers side wheel well. Rotate the gear to clear the frame rail.

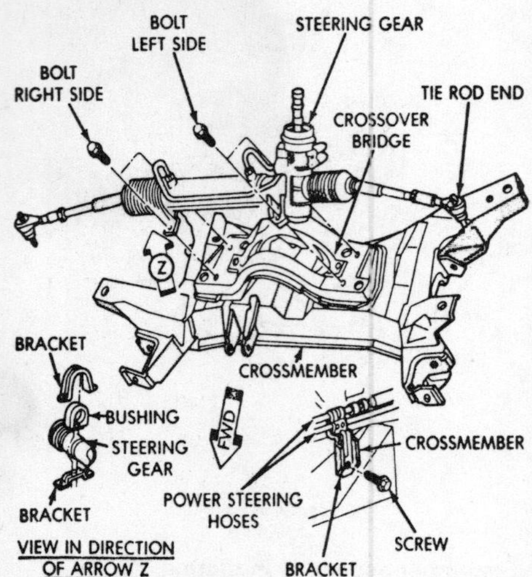

Steering gear removal and installation

To install:

10. Install the steering gear into the vehicle. Work it in through the left wheel opening, rotating it as needed.

11. Install the steering column coupler, make sure to fully seat the roll pin.

12. Install the steering gear mounting bolts. Do not torque them at this time, be sure to install them in the proper locations.

13. Install the steering hose bracket in position, tighten to 70 inch lbs. (8 Nm). Install the hoses on the steering rack and tighten them to 275 inch lbs. (31 Nm).

14. Raise the crossmember into position and install the bolts to the following torques:

a. Crossmember-to-frame rail screw and washer – 90 ft. lbs. (122 Nm)

b. Crossmember-to-frame rail stud nut – 90 ft. lbs. (122 Nm)

15. Install the bridge assembly onto the crossmember and tighten the mounting nuts to 50 ft. lbs. (68 Nm).

16. Install the outer tie rod ends on the steering knuckle and tighten the nuts, tighten to 38 ft. lbs. (52 Nm). Be sure to install a new cotter pin.

17. Install the wheel and tire assemblies. Lower the vehicle.

18. Connect the negative battery cable. Start the vehicle and check the power steering lines for leaks. Check the fluid level.

Boot Seals

REMOVAL AND INSTALLATION

1. Raise and support the front of the vehicle on jackstands.

2. Disconnect the tie rod end from the steering knuckle. Loosen the jam nut and unscrew the end. Count the number of turns required when removing the end.

3. Cut the inner boot clamp, use pliers to expand the outer clamp and remove.

4. Locate and mark for reinstallation, the location of the breather tube.

5. Use a small tool to lift the boot from inner mounting groove and slide boot from the shaft.

6. Install the new boot and clamps. Locate breather tube to reference mark. Lubricate boot and mounting groove with silicone type lubricant. Install the tie rod end the same number of turns as counted when removing.

Power Steering Pump

REMOVAL AND INSTALLATION

1. Disconnect the negative battery cable from the battery. Disconnect the vapor hose (canister) from the carburetor. Disconnect the A/C compressor clutch wire harness connector at the compressor.

2. Remove the power steering pump adjustment bolt. Remove the power steering hose bracket from mounting.

3. Raise and support the front of the vehicle on jackstands.

4. Disconnect the return hose from the steering gear and drain the fluid into a container.

5. Remove the right side splash shield if it interferes with pump removal. After the fluid has drained from the pump, disconnect and plug the hoses from the pump.

6. Remove the lower pivot bolt and nut from the pump mounting.

7. Remove the drive belt. Move the pump to the rear and remove the adjusting bracket.

8. Rotate the pump clockwise so that the drive pulley faces the rear of the vehicle. Remove the power steering pump.

To install:

9. Place the pump in position and install it in reverse order of removal. Install new O-ring seal on the pump hoses before installation. Tighten the tube nuts to 25 ft. lbs. Refer to belt adjustments in "General Information and Maintenance".

10. Lower the vehicle and connect the vapor hose and A/C compressor clutch switch harness.

11. Fill the power steering pump reservoir with fluid. Start the engine and turn the steering wheel from stop to stop, several times, to bleed the system. check the fluid level.

Brakes 9

STANDARD BRAKE SYSTEM

Adjustments

Periodic brake adjustment is not necessary as the front calipers are inherently self-adjusting, and the rear brakes are equipped with self-adjusters. In the event of a brake reline or component service requiring brake shoe removal, initial manual adjustment of the rear brake shoes will speed up servicing time. Front brake pads adjust themselves as the brake pedal is applied. After installing new front brake pads pump the brake pedal several times until a firm feeling is obtained. The pads will be incorrect adjustment.

DRUM BRAKES

1. To make an initial rear brake shoe adjustment, raise and support the rear of the vehicle on jackstands, so that both wheels are off the ground and can turn freely.
2. Remove the adjusting hole cover at the back of the brake mounting plates.
3. Be sure the parking brake is fully released and that there is slack in the brake cables.
4. Insert a brake adjusting tool through the hole in the backing plate until the adjuster star wheel is engaged. move the adjusting tool upward to turn the star wheel. Continue until a slight drag is felt when the wheel is rotated.
5. Insert a thin screwdriver or piece of stiff rod through the backing plate slot and push the adjuster lock tab away from the star wheel. Move the adjusting tool down while holding the locking tab out of the way. Back off the star wheel until the wheel turns freely without any brake drag. Install the adjusting slot cover.
6. Repeat the procedure for the other rear wheel. Adjust the parking brake after initial rear brake adjustment is finished. Check parking brake adjustment after applying several times, insure freedom from brake drag.

Brake Light Switch

The brake light switch is a self adjusting unit installed on the brake pedal shaft pivot pin.

REMOVAL AND INSTALLATION

1. Remove the old switch from the retaining bracket.
2. Install the new brake light switch into the bracket and push the switch as far forward as it will go.
3. The brake pedal will move forward slightly when the switch is pushed forward.
4. Pull back on the brake pedal gently. As the brake pedal is pulled back, the switch striker will move toward the switch. When the brake pedal can not be pull back any further, the switch will ratchet to the correct position. Very little movement is required, and no further adjustment is required.

Master Cylinder

The master cylinder is of tandem design, having an anodized aluminum body and a glass reinforced nylon reservoir. If the cylinder bore is pitted or scratched, the body must be replaced as honing will remove the anodized surface. The reservoir is indexed to prevent incorrect installation and the cap diaphragms are slotted to allow internal pressure to equalize. A secondary outlet tube leading from the master cylinder is connected to the differential valve mounted underneath the master cylinder. The front part of the valve supplied the right rear and left front brakes. The rear portion supplied the right rear and left front. The rear portion of the valve is connect to the primary outlet tube of the master cylinder.

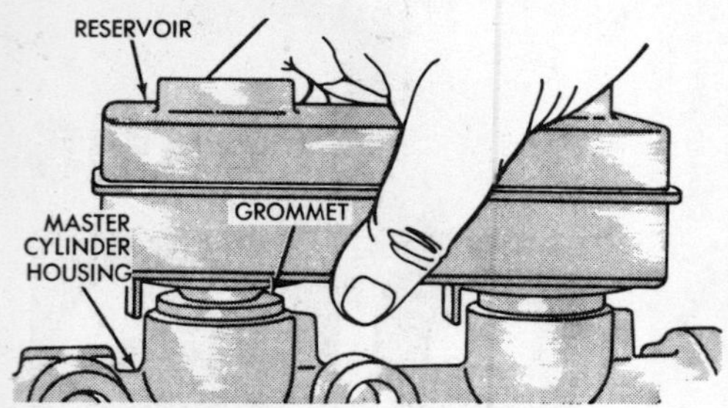

Removing the reservoir

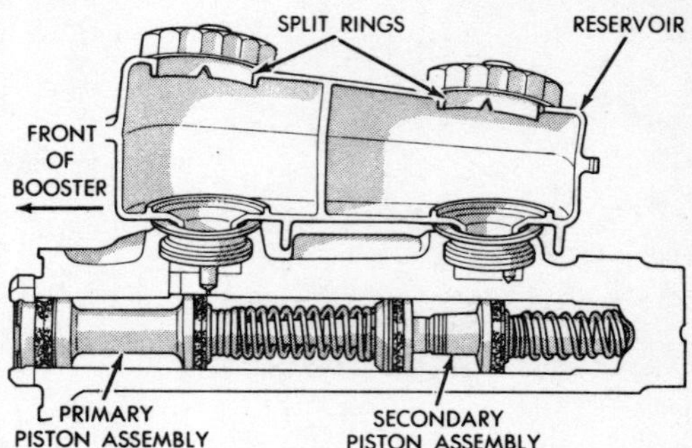

Master cylinder – cutaway view

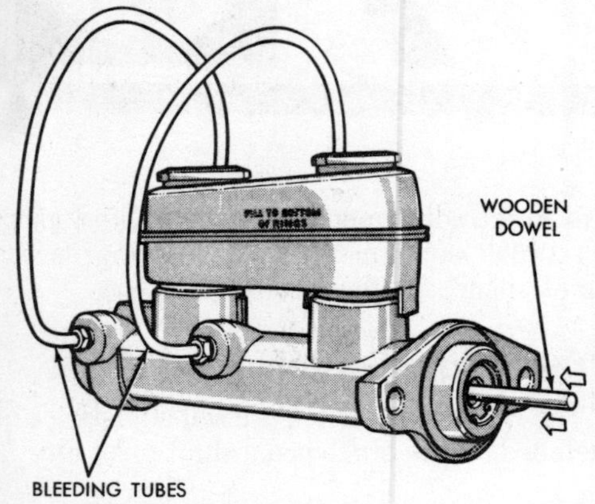

Bleeding the master cylinder

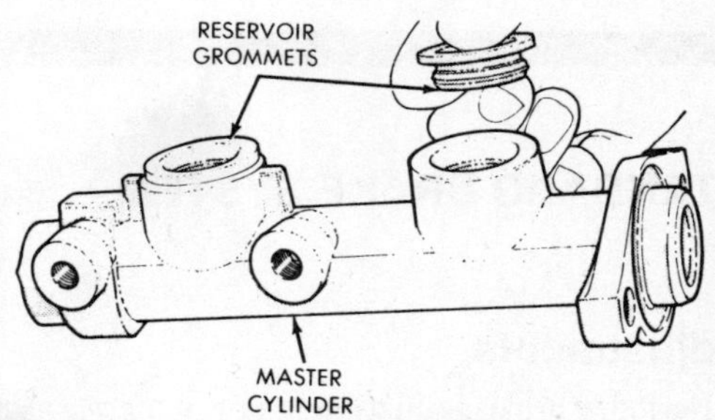

Removing reservoir mounting grommets

REMOVAL AND INSTALLATION

1. Disconnect the primary and secondary brake lines at the master cylinder. Tape or plug the ends of the lines.
2. Remove the nuts attaching the master cylinder to the power brake booster.
3. Wrap a rag around the brake line tilting holes, slide the master straight away from the booster and remove from the vehicle. Take care not to spill any brake fluid on the finish. Flush off with water if any fluid is spilled.

To install:

4. Bench bleed the master cylinder. (See the Bleeding section). Install the master cylinder over the mounting studs. After aligning the master cylinder pushrod and mounting studs, hold the cylinder in position and start the attaching nuts but do not tighten completely. Install the brake lines but do not tighten completely.
5. After the brake lines are installed, tighten the cylinder mounting nuts fully and then the brake lines.
6. Finish bleeding the brake system.

OVERHAUL

The aluminum master cylinder cannot be rebuilt; service is limited to replacement.

Fluid Reservoir

REMOVAL AND INSTALLATION

1. Remove the master cylinder from the vehicle. Clean the outside of the reservoir and cylinder.
2. Remove the reservoir caps and empty the brake fluid. Do not reuse the old fluid.
3. Position the master cylinder in a vise. Pad the vise jaws and do not over tighten.
4. Rock the reservoir from side to side to loosen and lift up to remove from the master cylinder. Do not pry the reservoir with an tools. Damage to the reservoir will result.
5. Remove the old housing to reservoir mounting grommets. Clean the cylinder and reservoir grommet mounting surfaces.

To install:

6. Install new mounting grommets in the master cylinder housing.
7. Lubricate the mounting surfaces of the grommets with brake fluid.
8. Place the reservoir in position over the grommets and seat it into the grommets using a rocking motion.
9. Be sure that the reservoir is fully seated on the master cylinder and the bottom of the reservoir touches the top of the grommets.
10. Fill the reservoir with fresh brake fluid and bench bleed the master cylinder.

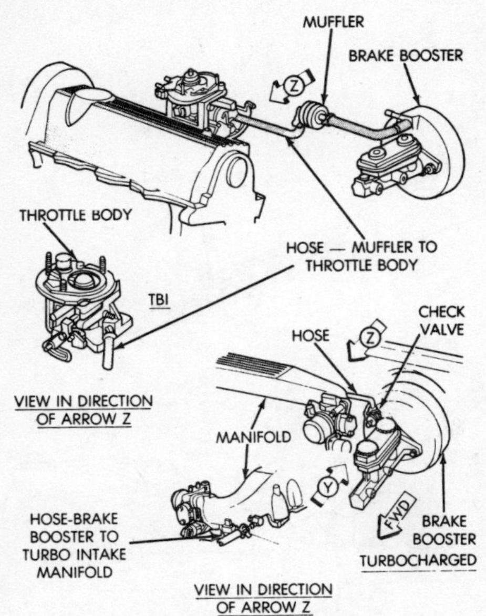

Power brake unit/vacuum hose connections — 2.2L and 2.5L engines

Power Brake Booster

REMOVAL AND INSTALLATION

1. Remove the nuts that attach the master cylinder to the power brake booster. Slowly and carefully slide the master cylinder away from the booster, off the mounting studs. Allow the cylinder to rest against the fender shield.
2. Disconnect the vacuum hose from the brake booster.
3. From the inside of the vehicle under the instrument panel, locate the point where the booster linkage connects to the brake pedal. Use a small tool and position between the center tang of the booster linkage to brake pedal retaining clip. Rotate the tool and pull the retainer from the pin. disconnect the brake pedal.
4. Remove the brake booster mounting nuts and unfasten the brackets mounting the steel water line at the firewall and left frame rail. On models equipped with a manual transmission, unfasten the clutch cable bracket at the shock tower and move it to the side.
5. The booster mounting bracket holes are

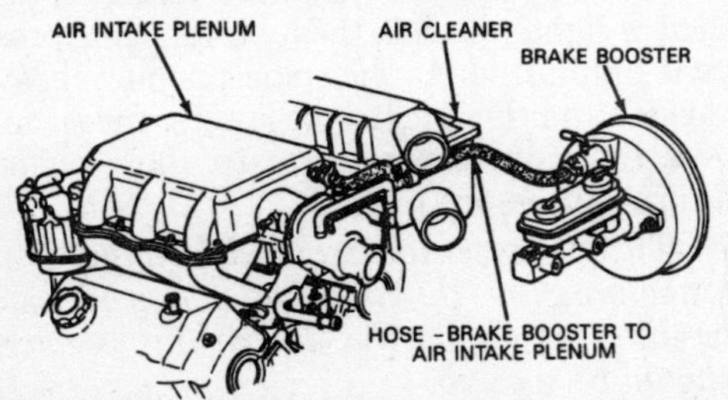

Power brake unit/vacuum hose connections — 3.0L engine

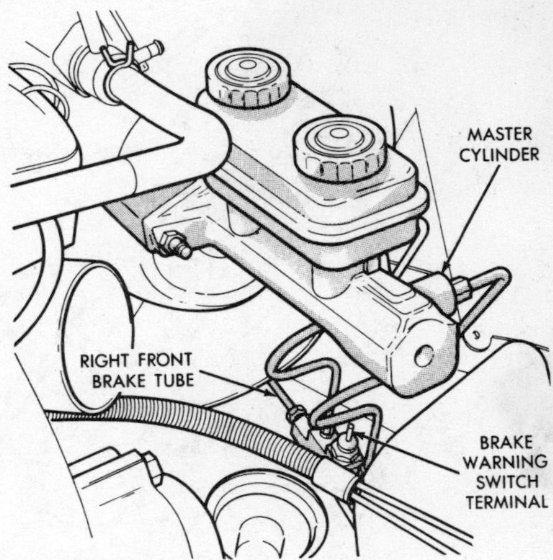

Brake warning switch location

slotted, slide the booster up and to the left. Tilt the booster inboard and up to remove from the engine compartment.

6. Position the power booster over the firewall mounting studs. Install the mounting nuts and tighten to 200-300 inch lbs.
7. install the steel heater line bracket and clutch cable bracket, if equipped.
8. Carefully install the master cylinder and tighten the mounting bolts to 200-300 inch lbs.
9. Connect the vacuum line to the power brake booster.
10. Connect the pedal linkage to the booster push rod after lubricating the pivot point with white grease. Install a new retainer clip. Check brake and stoplight operation.

Pressure Differential Switch/ Warning Light

As mentioned before, the hydraulic brake system on your vehicle is diagonally split; the

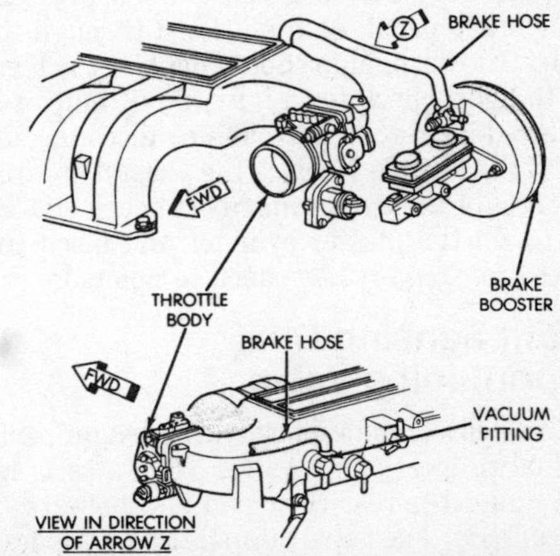

Power brake unit/vacuum hose connections — 3.3L engine

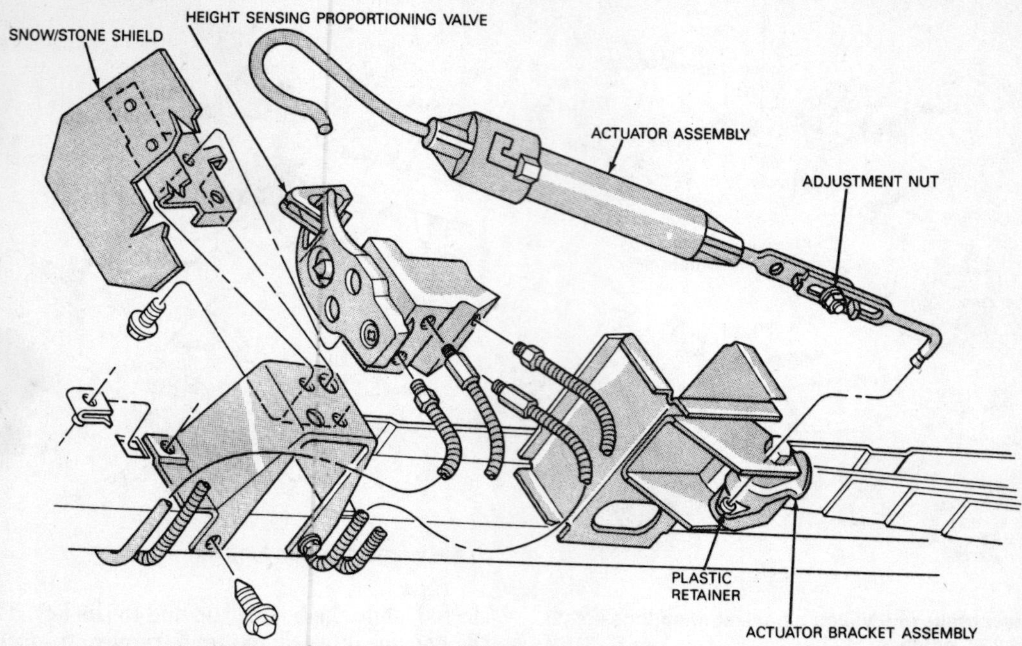

Height sensing proportioning valve assembly — late model, non-ABS equipped vehicles

left front and right rear are part of one system and the right front and left rear part of the other. Both systems are routed through a pressure differential switch (located under the master cylinder) which is designed to warn the driver should a failure occur. If hydraulic pressure is lost in one side of the split system the switch will activate a warning light on the instrument panel, indicating that the brake system should be checked and repaired, if necessary. After repairs to the system have been made, the switch will automatically recenter itself and the light will go out.

TESTING

To test the warning switch system, raise the front or rear of the vehicle and safely support with jackstands. Open a caliper or wheel cylinder bleeder valve while a helper holds pressure on the brake pedal. As fluid is lost through the bleeder, the dash lamp should light. If the lamp fails to light, check for a burned out bulb, disconnected socket, or a broken or disconnected wire at the switch. Replace the warning switch if the rest of the circuit members check out. Be sure to fill the master cylinder and bleed the brakes after repairs have been completed.

Height Sensing Dual Proportioning Valve

All vehicles are equipped with a height sensing dual proportioning valve. The valve is located under the rear floor pan just forward of the rear axle. The valve automatically provides the proper brake balance between the front and rear brakes regardless of the vehicle load condi-

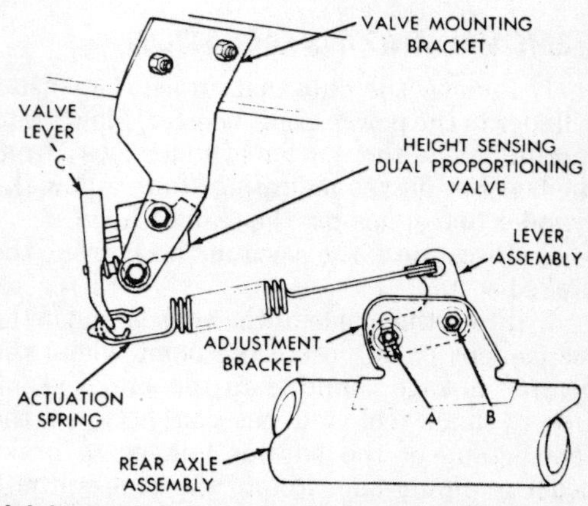

Height sensing dual proportioning valve and adjustment points — early models

tion. the valve modulates the rear brakes sensing the loading condition of the vehicle through relative height movement between the rear axle and load floor.

The valve is mounted on a crossmember and connected to an adjustable lever on the rear axle by a large spring. When the vehicle is unloaded or lightly leaded, the hydraulic line pressure is minimized. As the vehicle is more heavily loaded and the ride height lowers, the spring moves the valve control arm to allow higher rear brake pressure.

NOTE: *Because ride height determines rear brake pressure, the use of after market load leveling or capacity increasing devices should be avoided.*

The proportioning section of the valve transmits full input pressure up to a certain point, called the split point. Beyond the split point the valve reduces the amount of pressure increase to the rear brakes according to a certain ratio. This means that on light brake pedal application equal pressure will be transmitted to the front and rear brakes. On harder pedal application, pressure transmitted to the rear brakes will be lower to prevent rear wheel lock-up and skid.

TESTING

NOTE: *Two pressure gauges and adapter fittings (tool set C4007A or equivalent) are required of the following test.*

If premature rear wheel lock-up and skid is experienced frequently, it could be an indication that the fluid pressure to the rear brakes is excessive and that a malfunction has occurred in the proportioning valve or an adjustment is necessary.

1. If a pressure gauge and adapter fittings are on hand, proceed with the following test.
2. Disconnect the external spring at the valve lever.
3. Install one pressure gauge and T-fitting in line from either master cylinder port to the brake valve assembly.
4. Install the second gauge to either rear brake outlet port between the valve assembly and the rear brake line. Bleed the rear brakes.
5. Have a helper apply and hold pedal pressure to get a reading on the valve inlet gauge and outlet gauge. The inlet pressure should be 500 psi and the outlet pressure should be 100-200 psi. If the required pressures are not present, replace the valve. If the test pressures are all right, adjust the external spring and arm.

VALVE REMOVAL, INSTALLATION AND ADJUSTMENT

1. Raise and support the rear of the vehicle. Position jackstands at the rear contact pads so that the rear axle will hang free with the tires off the ground.
2. Loosen the rear axle mounted adjustable lever assembly and remove the actuating spring. Remove the brake lines from the proportioning valve and remove the valve.
3. Install the brake lines loosely in the proportioning valve and mount valve in position.
4. Tighten the brake lines, fill the master cylinder to the correct fluid level and bleed the brakes.
5. Confirm that the axle is hanging free and at full rebound position with the wheels and tires mounted.
6. Confirm that the actuating spring is connected between the proportioning valve and axle adjusting lever. the axle adjusting lever mounting bolts should be loose so that the bracket can be moved.
7. Push the control lever on the proportioning valve towards the valve until it is against the body and hold it in that position.
8. Move the axle lever up and away to apply tension to the spring. When all free play is taken out of the spring, but the spring is not stretched, tighten the mounting bolt that goes through the slotted side of the adjustment bracket. Tighten the anchor bolt. Both mounting bolts should be tightened to 150 inch lbs.

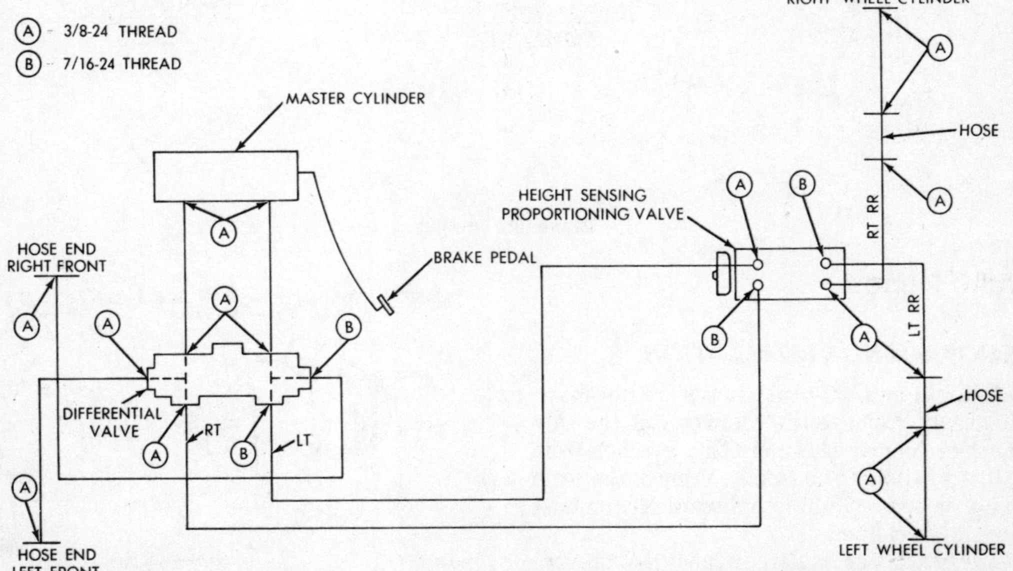

Proper nut thread size and tube routing — non-ABS models

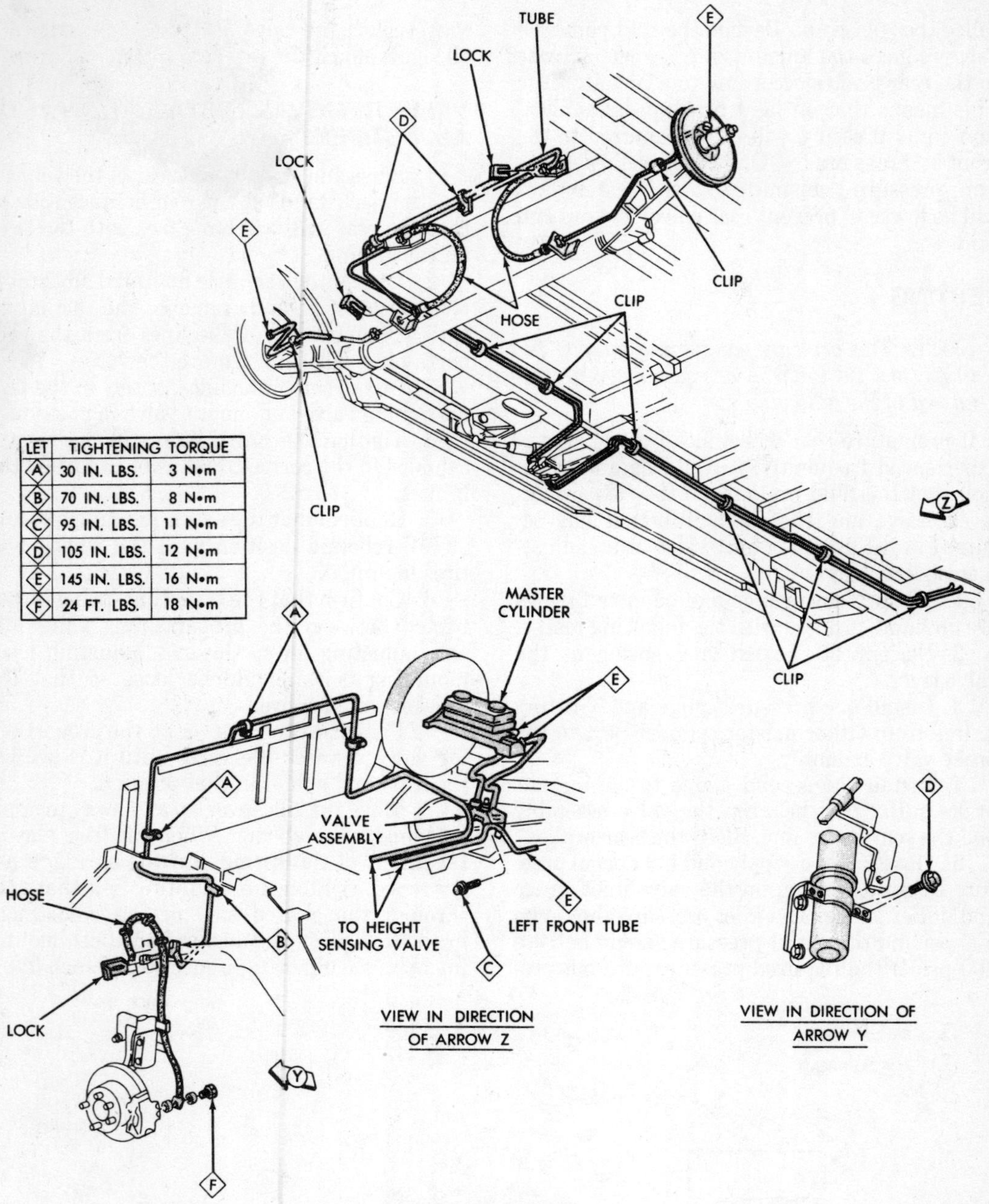

LET	TIGHTENING TORQUE	
A	30 IN. LBS.	3 N•m
B	70 IN. LBS.	8 N•m
C	95 IN. LBS.	11 N•m
D	105 IN. LBS.	12 N•m
E	145 IN. LBS.	16 N•m
F	24 FT. LBS.	18 N•m

Brake line routing

Brake Hoses

REMOVAL AND INSTALLATION

1. Right and left brake hoses are not interchangeable. Remove the connecter at the caliper, then remove the mounting bracket from the strut support and finally, remove the from the upper body mount and disconnect the hose from the steel line.
2. Always use a flare wrench to prevent rounding of the line fittings.
3. Install the new hose to the caliper first.

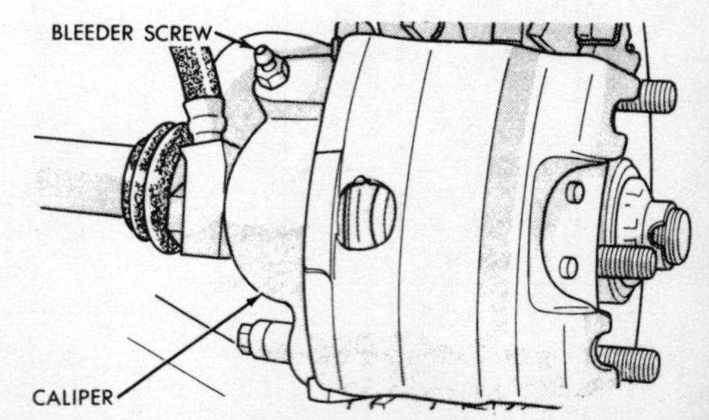

Open the bleeder screw at least one full turn

Always use a new copper washer after making sure the mounting surfaces are clean. Tighten the caliper hose fitting. Install the strut bracket next, then attach the steel line fitting. Position the upper keyed end of the hose to the body bracket and secure it.

4. Rear brake hoses should be attached first to the trailing arm bracket and the to the floor pan tubes.

5. Keep the hose as straight as possible, avoid twisting.

6. Bleed the brake system.

Bleeding the Brake System

The purpose of bleeding the brakes is to expel air trapped in the hydraulic system. The system must be bled whenever the pedal feels spongy, indicating that compressible air has entered the system. It must also be bled whenever the system has been opened or repaired. You will need a helper to help bleed the system. Always use fresh brake fluid.

BENCH BLEEDING

Always bench bleed the master cylinder before installing it on the vehicle.

1. Place the master cylinder in a vise.

2. Connect two lines to the fluid outlet orifices, bend the lines upwards and insert the opened ends into the reservoir.

3. Fill the reservoir with brake fluid.

4. Using a wooden dowel, depress the pushrod slowly, allowing the pistons to return. do this several times until the air bubbles are all expelled.

5. Remove the bleeding tubes from the master cylinder, plug the outlets and install the caps.

NOTE: *It is not necessary to bleed the entire system after replacing the master cylinder, provided that master cylinder has been bled and filled upon installation. However, if a soft pedal is experienced, bleed the entire system.*

SYSTEM BLEEDING

CAUTION: *Do not allow brake fluid to spill on the vehicle's finish; it will remove the paint. In case of a spill, flush the area with water.*

1. The sequence for bleeding is right rear, left front, left rear and right front. If the vehicle is equipped with power brakes, remove the vacuum by applying the brakes several times. Do not run the engine while bleeding the brakes.

2. Clean all the bleeder screws. You may want to give each one a shot of penetrating solvent to help loosen the fitting. Seizure is a common problem with bleeder screws, which then brake off, sometimes requiring replacement of the part to which they are attached.

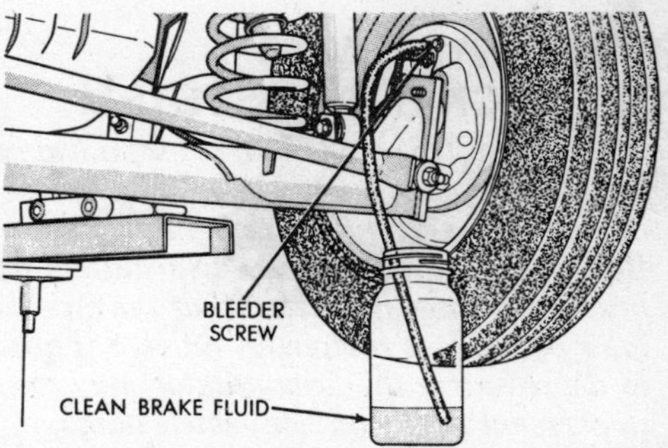

Proper method for bleeding the brake system

3. Check the fluid level in the master cylinder and fill with DOT 3 brake fluid, if necessary.

NOTE: *Brake fluid absorbs moisture from the air. Don't leave the master cylinder or the fluid container uncovered any longer than necessary. Be careful handling the brake fluid,it is a great paint remover. If any brake fluid spills on the vehicle's finish, flush off with water immediately. Check the level of the fluid often when bleeding, and refill the reservoirs as necessary. Don't let them run dry, or you will have to repeat the process.*

4. Attach a length of clear vinyl tubing to the bleeder screw at the wheel cylinder or caliper. Insert the other end of the tube into a clear, clean jar half filled with brake fluid. Start at a rear cylinder first, then bleed the opposite side front cylinder.

5. Have your assistant slowly depress the brake pedal. As this is done, open the bleeder screw $^1/_3$-$^1/_2$ of a turn on wheel cylinders and at least one turn on calipers, and allow the fluid to run through the tube. Then close the bleeder screw before the pedal reaches the end of its travel. Have your assistant slowly release the pedal after the bleeder screw is closed. Repeat this process until no air bubbles appear in the expelled fluid.

6. Repeat the procedure on the other calipers and cylinders, checking the level of fluid in the master cylinder reservoir often. After you're done, there should be no sponginess in the brake pedal feel. If there is, either there is still air in the line, in which case the process should be repeated, or there is a leak somewhere, which of course must be corrected before moving the vehicle.

BENDIX SYSTEM 10 ANTI-LOCK BRAKE SYSTEM

CAUTION: *This brake system uses a hydraulic accumulator which, when fully charged, contains brake fluid at very high pressure. Before disconnecting any hydraulic lines, hoses or fittings be certain that the accumulator pressure is completely relieved. Failure to depressurize the accumulator may result in personal injury and/or vehicle damage.*

FILLING THE SYSTEM

1. Turn the ignition **OFF** and leave it **OFF** during inspection.
2. Depressurize the system.
3. Thoroughly clean the reservoir cap and the surrounding area.
4. Carefully remove reservoir cap, keeping all dirt out of the reservoir. Inspect the fluid level; fill to the top of the white screen in the front strainer if required. Do not overfill. Use only fresh DOT 3 brake fluid from unopened containers. Do not use any fluid containing a petroleum base. Do not use any fluid which has been exposed to water or moisture. Failure to use the correct fluid will affect system function and component life.
5. Replace the reservoir cap.

BLEEDING THE SYSTEM

The brake system must be bled any time air is permitted to enter the system, through loosened or disconnected lines.It is important to realize that air in the system, will cause a primary pressure fault to be set in the controller.

The system must be bled any time a hose or line is disconnected. Bleeding is also required after replacement of the hydraulic unit, caliper or wheel cylinder.

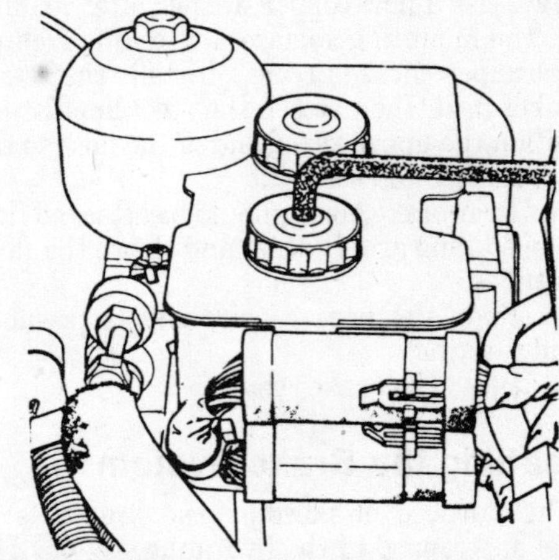

The dummy cap must be installed, when using pressure bleeding equipment

When bleeding any part of the system, the reservoir must remain close to FULL at all times. Check the level frequently and top off the fluid as needed. Do not allow the pump to run continuously for more than 60 seconds. If it becomes necessary to run the pump extensively, allow several minutes of cooling time between each 60 second operation period. Severe damage will occur to the pump if it is not allowed to cool. Never operate the pump with no fluid in the system.

Pressure Bleeding the Brake Lines

Only diaphragm pressure bleeding equipment should be used. The diaphragm prevents the entry of dirt and moisture into the fluid.

1. Depressurize the system. The ignition

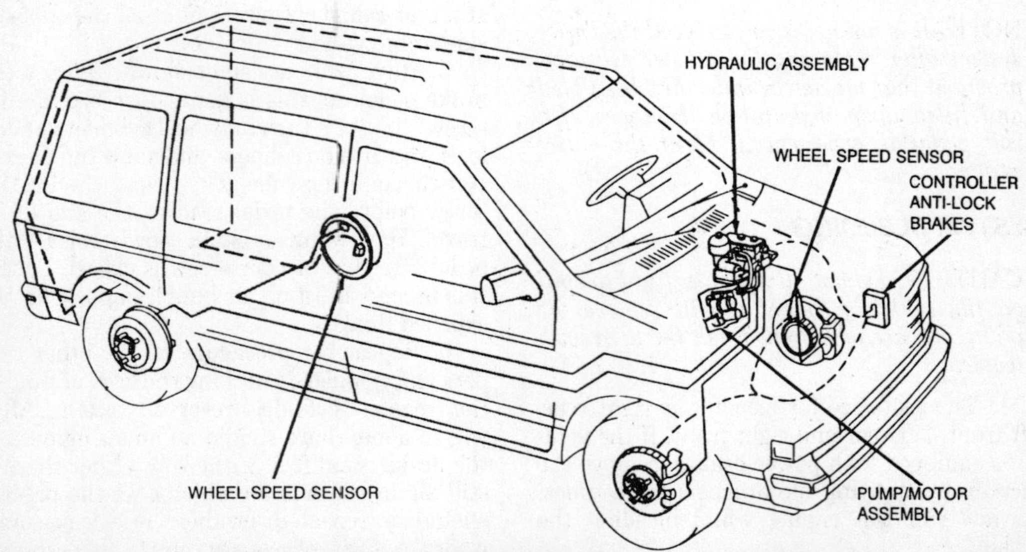

Bendix System 10 Anti-lock brake system – component layout

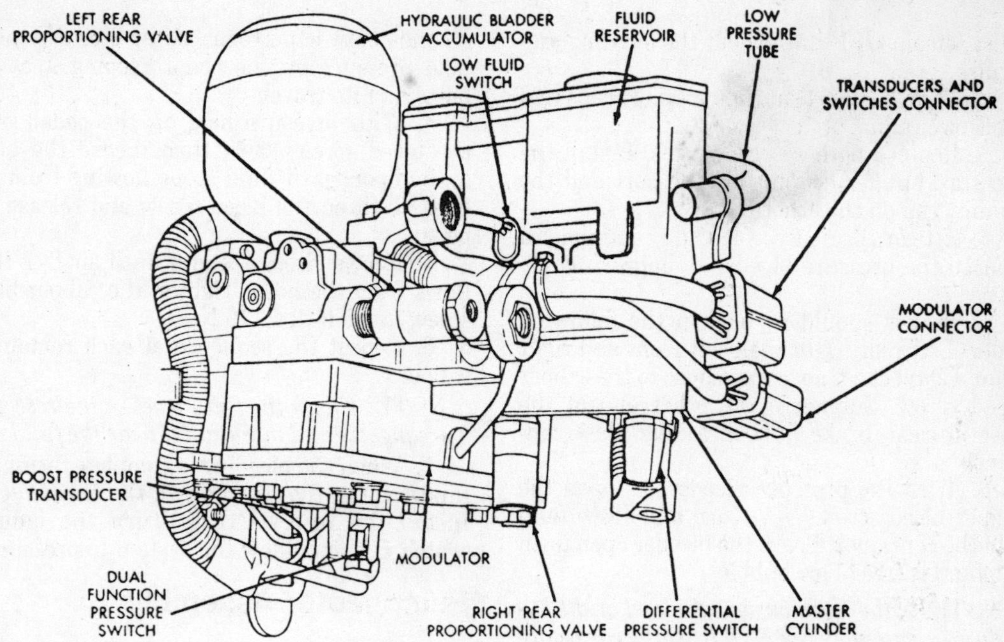

Hydraulic assembly component location – ABS equipped models

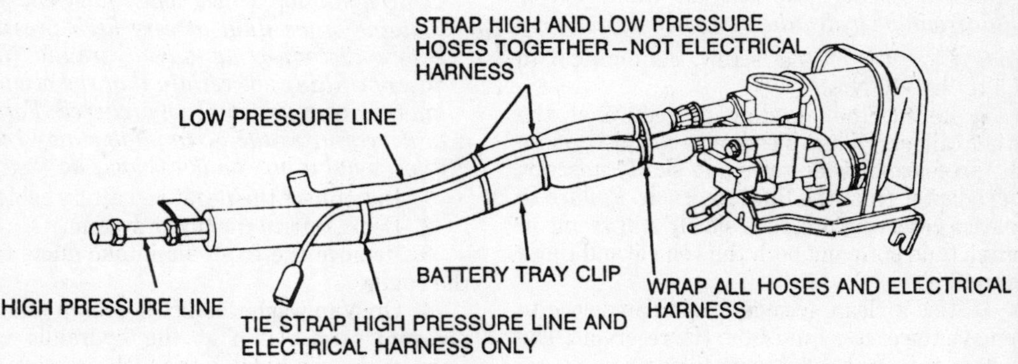

Correct position of tie straps – ABS equipped models

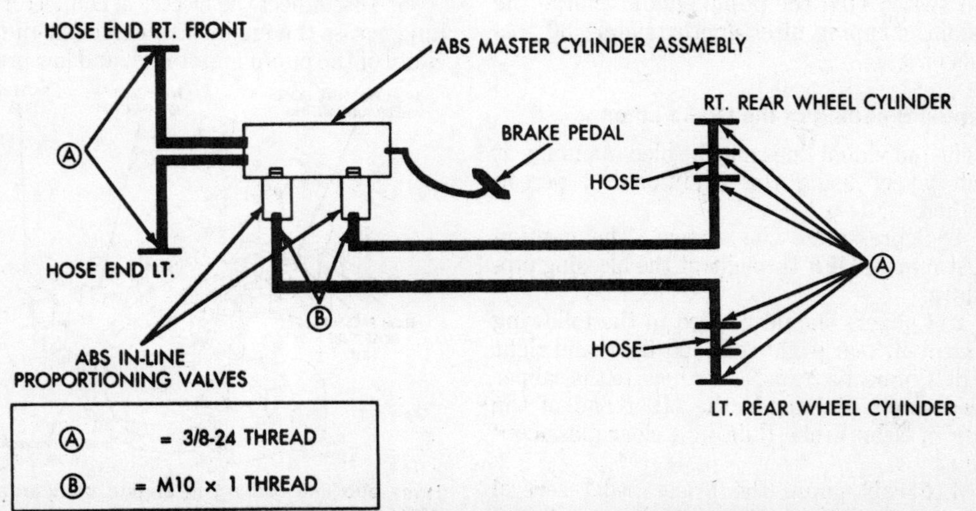

Proper nut thread size and tube routing – ABS equipped models

must remain **OFF** throughout the bleeding procedure.

2. Thoroughly clean the reservoir caps and the surrounding area.

3. Remove both reservoir caps. Install the pressure bleeder adapter on one port and the dummy cap on the other port.

4. Attach pressure bleeding equipment. Charge the pressure bleeder to approximately 20 psi.

5. Brakes should be bled in the following order: Left rear, right rear, left front and right front. Connect a transparent hose to the caliper bleed screw. Submerge the other end of the hose in clean brake fluid in a clear glass container.

6. Turn the pressure bleeder on; open the caliper bleed screw $^1/_2$–$^3/_4$ turn and allow fluid into the container. Leave the bleeder open until the fluid is free of air bubbles.

NOTE: *If the reservoir was drained or the hydraulic assembly removed from the car before bleeding, pump the brake pedal slowly once or twice while the bleed screw is open and fluid is flowing. This will aid the escape of air from the hydraulic assembly.*

7. Close the bleeder screw, tightening it to 7.5 ft. lbs. (10 Nm).

8. Repeat the bleeding procedure at the other calipers. When bleeding is complete, close the pressure bleeder valve and slowly unscrew the adapter from the fluid reservoir. Failure to release reservoir pressure slowly will result in brake fluid spraying both the vehicle and those around it.

9. Use a clean syringe or similar device to remove the excess fluid from the reservoir. The system must not be left over filled.

10. Install the reservoir caps. Turn the ignition switch **ON**; the pump should charge the system, stopping after approximately 30 seconds or less.

Manual Bleeding of the Brake Lines

The individual lines may be bled manually at each wheel using the traditional 2 person method.

1. Depressurize the system. The ignition must remain **OFF** throughout the bleeding procedure.

2. Calipers should be bled in the following order: Left rear, right rear, left front and right front. Connect a transparent hose to the caliper bleed screw. Submerge the other end of the hose in clean brake fluid in a clear glass container.

3. Slowly pump the brake pedal several times. Use full strokes of the pedal and allow 5 seconds between strokes. After 2 or 3 strokes, hold pressure on the pedal keeping it at the bottom of its travel.

4. With pressure held on the pedal, open the bleed screw $^1/_2$–$^3/_4$ turn. Leave the bleed screw open until fluid stops flowing from the hose. Tighten the bleed screw and release the pedal.

5. Repeat Steps 3 and 4 until air-free fluid flows from the hose. Tighten the caliper bleed screw to 7.5 ft. lbs. (10 Nm).

6. Repeat the sequence at each remaining caliper.

NOTE: *Check the fluid level in the reservoir frequently and maintain it near the full level.*

7. When the bleeding is complete, bring the fluid level in the reservoir to the correct level. Install the reservoir cap. Turn the ignition switch **ON** and allow the system to pressurize.

Pump/Motor Assembly

REMOVAL AND INSTALLATION

CAUTION: *This brake system uses a hydraulic accumulator which, when fully charged, contains brake fluid at very high pressure. Before disconnecting any hydraulic lines, hoses or fittings be certain that the accumulator pressure is completely relieved. Failure to depressurize the accumulator may result in personal injury and/or vehicle damage.*

1. Disconnect the negative battery cable.

2. Depressurize the brake system.

3. Remove the fresh air intake ducts from the engine.

4. On Van/wagon vehicles, loosen the low pressure hose clamp at the hydraulic unit. Remove the clip holding the high pressure line to the battery tray.

5. Disconnect the electrical connectors running across the engine compartment in the vicinity of the pump/motor high and low pressure

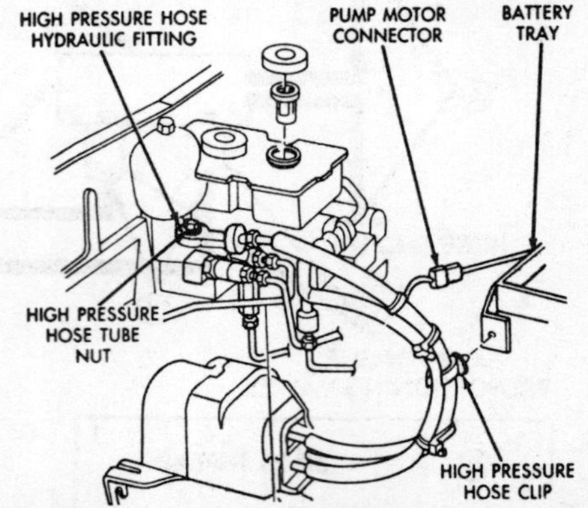

Hose and line routing in engine compartment – ABS equipped models

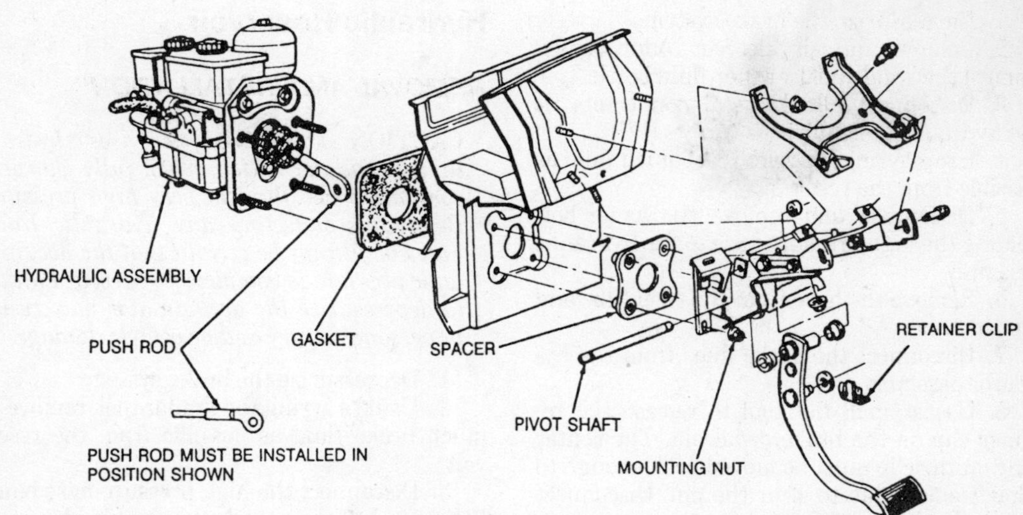

Hydraulic assembly mounting and under dash connections – ABS equipped models

hoses. One of these connectors is the one for the pump/motor assembly.

6. Disconnect the high and low pressure hoses from the hydraulic assembly. Cap or plug the reservoir fitting.

7. Disconnect the pump/motor electrical connector from the engine mount.

8. Remove the heat shield bolt from the front of the pump bracket. Remove the heat shield.

9. Lift the pump/motor assembly from the bracket and out of the vehicle.

To install:

10. Fit the pump motor assembly onto the bracket; install the heat shield and its retaining bolt.

11. Install the pump/motor electrical connector to the engine mount.

12. Connect the high and low pressure hose to the hydraulic assembly. Tighten the high pressure line to 145 inch lbs. (16 Nm). Tighten the hose clamp on the low pressure hose to 10 inch lbs (1 Nm).

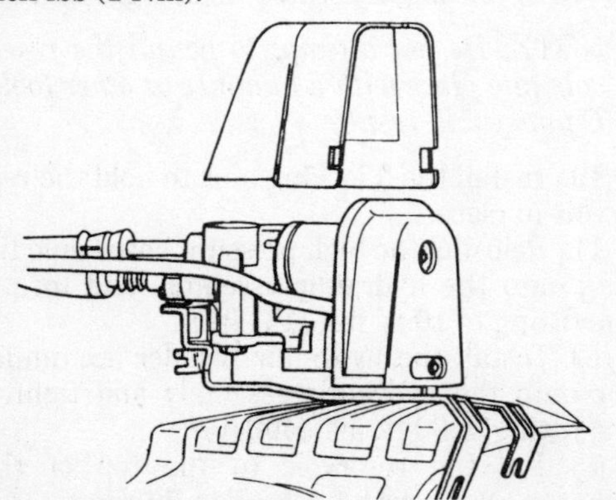

Integrated pump and motor assembly – ABS equipped models

13. Connect the electrical connectors which were removed for access.

14. Install the high pressure line retaining clip to the battery tray if it was removed.

15. Install the fresh air intake ducts.

16. Bleed the brake system.

High Pressure and Return Hoses

REMOVAL AND INSTALLATION

1. Remove the pump/motor assembly.

2. Carefully cut the wire ties (Van/wagons, 4 ties; others, 2 ties)) holding the hoses and wiring harnesses.

3. Remove the banjo bolt from the pump/motor assembly and remove the hoses.

4. When installing, lubricate the rubber O-ring for the high and low pressure hoses with clean brake fluid before installation.

5. Place the hoses in position and install the banjo bolt.

6. Use care when routing the wiring along the hoses; install new wire ties in the proper locations. Noted that the wiring harness is not held within all the wire ties.

7. Install the pump/motor assembly.

Hydraulic Assembly

REMOVAL AND INSTALLATION

CAUTION: *This brake system uses a hydraulic accumulator which, when fully charged, contains brake fluid at very high pressure. Before disconnecting any hydraulic lines, hoses or fittings be certain that the accumulator pressure is completely relieved. Failure to depressurize the accumulator may result in personal injury and/or vehicle damage.*

1. Depressurize the brake system.
2. Remove the air cleaner. Additionally, remove the windshield washer fluid bottle.
3. Disconnect all electrical connectors at the hydraulic assembly.
4. Use a syringe to remove as much fluid as possible from the reservoir.
5. Disconnect and remove the banjo bolt holding the high pressure hose to the hydraulic assembly.
6. Remove the hose from the steel tube and cap the tube.
7. Disconnect the brake lines from the hydraulic assembly.
8. Use a small flat tool to release the retainer clip on the brake pedal pin. The center tang on the clip must be moved back enough to allow the lock tab to clear the pin. Disconnect the pushrod from the pedal pin.
9. Under the dash at the firewall, remove the 4 bolts holding the hydraulic assembly.
10. Remove the hydraulic assembly from the engine compartment.

To install:

11. Position the hydraulic assembly and install the retaining nuts. Tighten the nuts to 21 ft. lbs. (28 Nm).
12. Coat the contact surface of the pedal pin with all-purpose grease. Connect the pushrod to the pedal pin and install a new retainer clip. Make certain the lock tab on the retainer is firmly engaged.

WARNING: *The hydraulic assembly pushrod must be in the correct position before assembly.*
13. Install the brake lines and tighten them to 12 ft. lbs. (16 Nm). If the proportioning valves were removed, reinstall and tighten them to 30 ft. lbs. (40 Nm).

NOTE: *Be certain the brake tubes are connected to the proper location.*

14. Install the return hose to the reservoir or the steel tube.
15. Before connecting the pressure hose to the hydraulic assembly, make certain the washers are in their correct positions. Install the hose and tighten the banjo bolt to 13. ft. lbs. (17 Nm).
16. Fill the reservoir to the top of the strainer screen.
17. Connect all the electrical connectors to the hydraulic assembly.
18. Bleed the entire brake system.
19. Install the air cleaner and washer bottle (Van/wagon) and the fresh air intake duct and clamps.

Hydraulic Reservoir

REMOVAL AND INSTALLATION

CAUTION: *This brake system uses a hydraulic accumulator which, when fully charged, contains brake fluid at very high pressure. Before disconnecting any hydraulic lines, hoses or fittings be certain that the accumulator pressure is completely relieved. Failure to depressurize the accumulator may result in personal injury and/or vehicle damage.*

1. Depressurize the brake system.
2. Using a syringe or similar tool, remove as much brake fluid as possible from the reservoir.
3. Disconnect the high pressure hose banjo fitting and remove the hydraulic bladder accumulator from the hydraulic assembly.
4. Remove the 3 retaining pins holding the reservoir to the hydraulic assembly.
5. Use a blunt prying tool carefully installed between the reservoir and hydraulic assembly body to lift the reservoir. Use a rocking motion to gently lift the reservoir free of the grommets.

NOTE: *Be extremely careful to avoid damaging or puncturing the reservoir.*

6. Remove the fluid level sensor switch from the reservoir.
7. Use fingers only to remove the grommets from the hydraulic assembly. Discard the grommets.

To install:

8. Lubricate new grommets with clean brake fluid and install them onto the hydraulic assembly. Always use new grommets.
9. Install the fluid level switch into the reservoir. Position the reservoir on the grommets and press it into place using hand pressure only. A rocking motion is helpful; make certain the reservoir is fully seated in all 3 grommets.

NOTE: *Do not attempt to pound the reservoir into place with a hammer or other tools. Damage will result.*

10. Install the 3 locking pins to hold the reservoir in place.
11. Reinstall the high pressure hose banjo fitting onto the hydraulic assembly and torque the fitting to 10 ft. lbs. (13 Nm).
12. Install the hydraulic bladder accumulator onto the hydraulic assembly and tighten the fitting to 30 ft. lbs. (40 Nm).
13. Fill the reservoir to the top of the strainer screen with fresh clean fluid.
14. Bleed the entire brake system including the booster.

Proportioning Valves

REMOVAL AND INSTALLATION

CAUTION: *This brake system uses a hydraulic accumulator which, when fully charged, contains brake fluid at very high pressure. Before disconnecting any hydraulic lines, hoses or fittings be certain that the accumulator pressure is completely relieved. Failure to depressurize the accumulator may result in personal injury and/or vehicle damage.*

1. Depressurize the brake system.
2. Remove the air cleaner and intake duct.
3. Disconnect the high pressure and return hoses from the hydraulic unit.
4. Remove the brake tube and fitting from the proportioning valve.
5. Remove the proportioning valve from the hydraulic assembly.

To install:

6. Install the valve to the hydraulic assembly and tighten it to 30 ft. lbs. (40 Nm).
7. Install the brake line and tighten to 12 ft. lbs. (16 Nm).
8. Install the high pressure and return hoses. Tighten the high pressure hose fitting to 145 inch lbs (16 Nm.).
9. Install the air cleaner and the ductwork.
10. Only the affected brake circuit needs bleeding.

Bladder Accumulator

REMOVAL AND INSTALLATION

CAUTION: *This brake system uses a hydraulic accumulator which, when fully charged, contains brake fluid at very high pressure. Before disconnecting any hydraulic lines, hoses or fittings be certain that the accumulator pressure is completely relieved. Failure to depressurize the accumulator may result in personal injury and/or vehicle damage.*

1. Depressurize the brake system.
2. Loosen the accumulator fitting at the hydraulic assembly and remove the accumulator assembly.
3. Reinstall the accumulator and tighten the to 30 ft. lbs. (40 Nm).
4. Turn the ignition switch **ON**. Allow the pump to pressurize the system. Inspect the accumulator area carefully for any sign of leakage.
5. If any seepage or leaking is noted, turn the ignition **OFF** and fully depressurize the system before beginning any repairs.

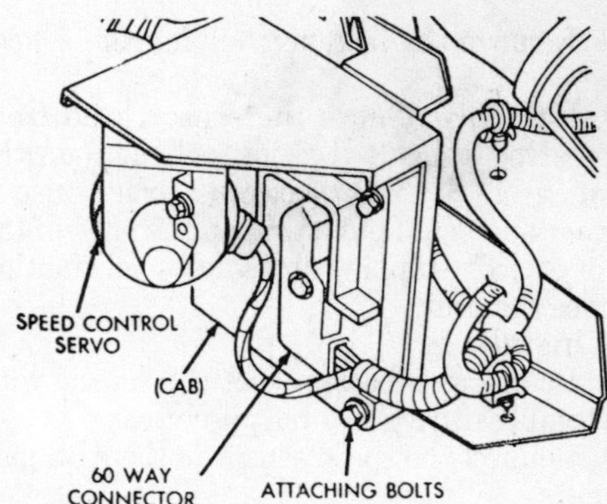

Controller Anti-lock Brake (CAB) mounting location

Controller Anti-Lock Brakes (CAB)

REMOVAL AND INSTALLATION

1. Turn the ignition switch to the **OFF** position or disconnect the negative battery cable.
2. Remove the speed control servo (cruise control).
3. Double check that the ignition switch is **OFF** or that the battery cable is disconnected.
4. Disconnect the 60-pin wiring connector at the CAB.
5. Remove the 3 CAB mounting bolts and remove the controller from the vehicle.

To install:

6. Install the CAB and tighten the mounting bolts.
7. After checking that the ignition is **OFF** or the battery disconnected, connect the 60-pin harness to the controller. Make certain that the connector is properly seated and locked in place. Do not force the connector into place.
8. Reinstall the speed control servo.
9. If the vehicle is elevated, lower it to the ground. Connect the negative battery cable if it was removed.

Wheel Speed Sensors

REMOVAL AND INSTALLATION

Front Wheel

1. Elevate and safely support the vehicle. Remove the wheel and tire.
2. Remove the screw from the sensor retaining clip.
3. Carefully remove the sensor wiring grommet from the fender shield.
4. Disconnect the sensor wiring from the ABS harness.
5. Remove the screws holding the sensor wiring tube to the fender well.
6. Remove the retainer grommets from the bracket on the strut.

7. Remove the fastener holding the sensor head.

8. Carefully remove the sensor head from the steering knuckle. Do not use pliers on the sensor head; if it is seized in place, use a hammer and small punch to tap the edge of the sensor ear. The tapping and side-to-side motion will free the unit.

To install:

9. Before installation, coat the sensor with high temperature multi-purpose grease.

10. Connect the speed sensor to the ABS harness.

11. Push the sensor assembly grommet into the hole in the fender shield. Install the retainer clip and screw.

12. Install the sensor grommets into the brackets on the fender shield and strut. Install the retainer clip at the strut.

13. On Van/wagons, install the sensor wiring tube and tighten the retaining bolts to 35 inch lbs. (4 Nm).

14. Install the sensor to the knuckle. Install the retaining screw and tighten it to 60 inch lbs. (7 Nm).

NOTE: *Proper installation of the sensor and its wiring is critical to system function. Make certain that wiring is installed in all retainers and clips. Wiring must be protected from moving parts and not be stretched during suspension movements.*

15. Install the tire and wheel. Lower the vehicle to the ground.

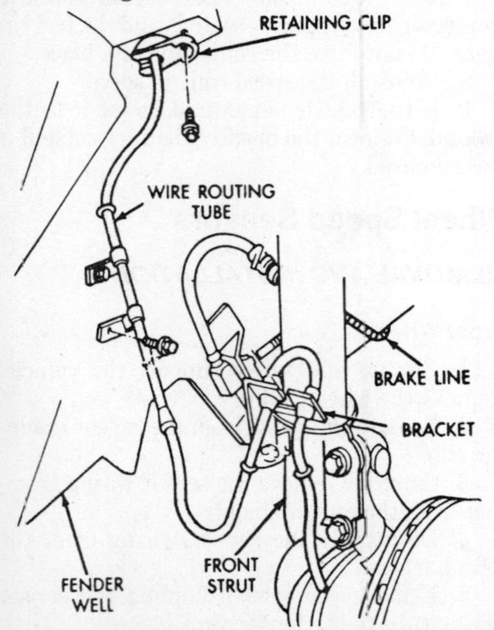

Front wheel speed sensor cable routing — ABS equipped models

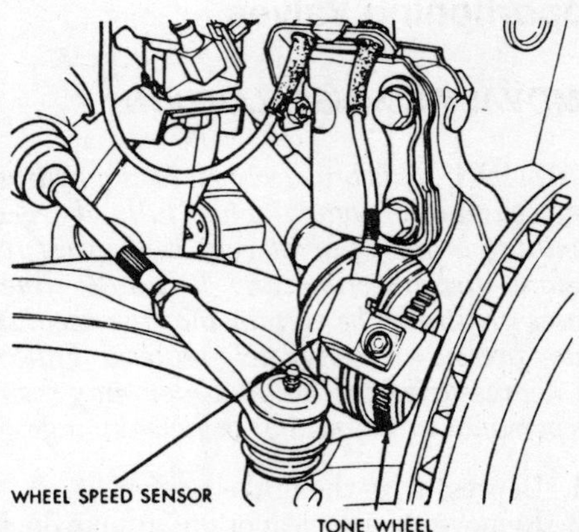

Front wheel speed sensor and tone wheel — ABS equipped models

Rear Wheel

1. Elevate and safely support the vehicle. Remove the wheel and tire.

2. Remove the sensor assembly grommet from the underbody and pull the harness through the hole in the body.

3. Disconnect the sensor wiring from the ABS harness.

4. Remove the 4 clips holding the sensor wiring along the underside.

5. Remove the attaching bracket holding the wiring to the frame rail.

6. On FWD Van/wagons, remove the nuts from the rear axle U-bolts. Remove the sensor mounting bracket.

7. Remove the fastener holding the sensor head.

8. Carefully remove the sensor head from the adapter assembly. Do not use pliers on the sensor head; if it is seized in place, use a hammer and small punch to tap the edge of the sensor ear. The tapping and side-to-side motion will free the unit.

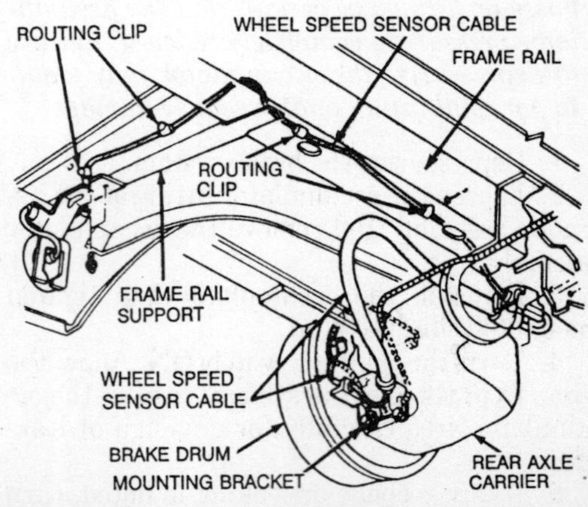

Rear wheel speed sensor cable routing — All Wheel Drive (AWD) ABS equipped models

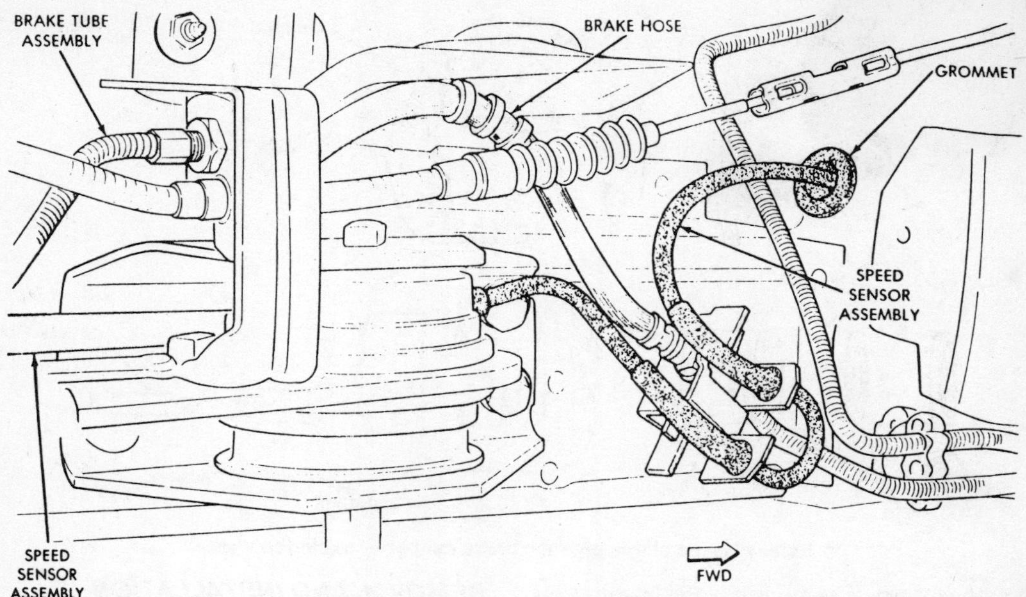

Rear wheel speed sensor cable routing – Front Wheel Drive (FWD) ABS equipped models

To install:

9. Position the sensor bracket under the brake tube and start the outer attaching bolt by hand.
10. Align the brake tube clip and the bracket; install the retaining bolt.
11. Tighten both retaining bolts to 145 inch lbs. (17 Nm).
12. Before installation coat the sensor with high temperature, multi-purpose grease.
13. Install the sensor head into the rear axle and install the bolt. Tighten the bolt to 60 inch lbs. (7 Nm).
14. Carefully bend the rubber hose section of the sensor assembly toward the rear of the vehicle. Position the anti-rotation tab correctly and install the frame rail bracket. Tighten the bolt to 50 inch lbs. (5 Nm).
15. Connect the sensor wiring to the rear harness. Push the sensor assembly wiring grommet back into the hole.
15. Install the rear sensor grommet retaining bracket and tighten the 2 retaining bolts to 50 inch lbs. (5 Nm). Make certain the bracket does not pinch the sensor wiring.
16. Route the sensor wiring along the vehicle frame rail and install the 4 retaining clips.
17. install the rear wheel and tire; lower the vehicle to the ground.

Tone Rings

REMOVAL AND INSTALLATION

The front toothed wheel or tone ring is an integral part of the outer Constant Velocity (CV) joint. Should the ring become unusable, the CV-joint must be replaced. Likewise, the rear tone ring is an integral part of the hub assembly and cannot be replaced individually.

The tone rings may be inspected in place on the vehicle. After gaining access, inspect for any evidence of contact between the speed sensor and the ring. If any contact occurred, the cause must be found and corrected before new parts are installed.

Teeth on the wheels should be unbroken and uncracked. The teeth and the valleys on the ring should be reasonably clean. Excessive run out of the tone ring can cause an erratic wheel speed signal. Replace the ring if run out exceeds 0.010 in. (0.25mm).

The air gap between the tone ring and the sensor is not adjustable. It is established by the correct installation of the wheel speed sensor.

FRONT DISC BRAKES

CAUTION: *Brake shoes contain asbestos, which has been determined to be a cancer causing agent. Never clean the brake surfaces with compressed air! Avoid inhaling any dust from any brake surface! When cleaning brake surfaces, use a commercially available brake cleaning fluid.*

The front disc brakes are of the single position, floating caliper type. The caliper "floats" through a rubber bushing, inserted into the inboard portion of the caliper, via a guide pin that is threaded into the mounting adapter. the mounting adapter for the caliper if fitted with two machined abutments that position and

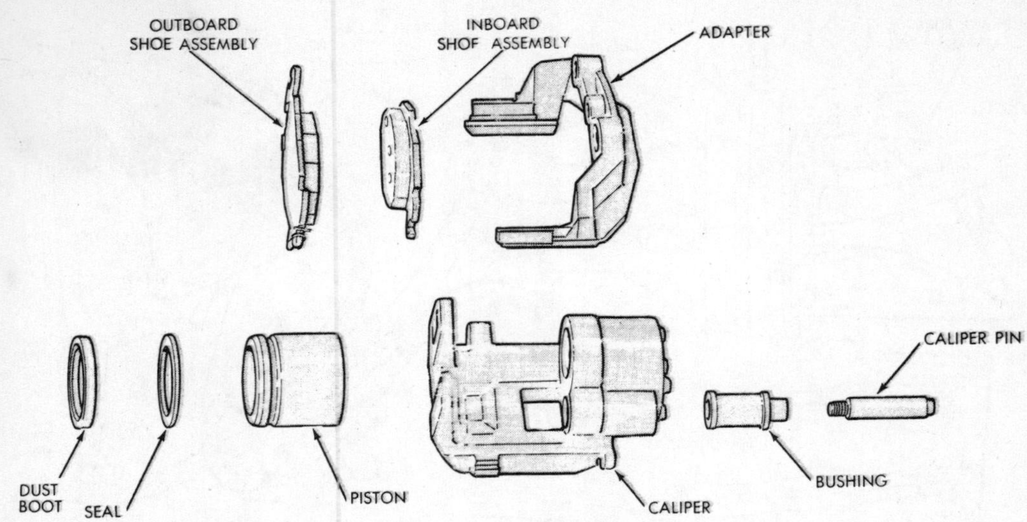

Kelsey Hayes single pin disc brake caliper — exploded view

align the caliper. The guide pin and bushing, on the Kelsey-Hayes type caliper, control the movement of the caliper when the brakes are applied, providing a clamping force. The A.T.E. type caliper, uses two steel guide pins and mounting bushings to control the movement of the caliper upon brake application.

Disc Brake Pads

INSPECTION

1. Loosen the front wheel lug nuts slightly. Raise and support the front of the vehicle safely on jackstands. Remove the front wheel.

2. When the front wheels are off, the cutout built into the caliper housing will be exposed. Look through the opening and check the lining thickness of the inner and outer pads.

3. If a visual inspection does not give a clear picture of lining wear, a physical check will be necessary.

4. Refer to the following section covering pad removal and installation for instructions.

REMOVAL AND INSTALLATION

Kelsey-Hayes Type

NOTE: *Three anti-rattle clips are provided on each brake caliper, take note of locations for installation purposes.*

1. The Kelsey Hayes caliper uses one mounting pin. Loosen the wheel lug nuts slightly. Raise and safely support the front of the vehicle on jackstands. Remove the front wheel and tire assemblies.

CAUTION: *On models equipped with ABS, the system pressure must be released before disconnecting any of the hydraulic lines. Failure to do so, can cause personal injury.*

2. Siphon about one quarter of the brake fluid from the master cylinder and replace the cover caps.

3. Use the proper size socket wrench and remove the threaded caliper guide pin.

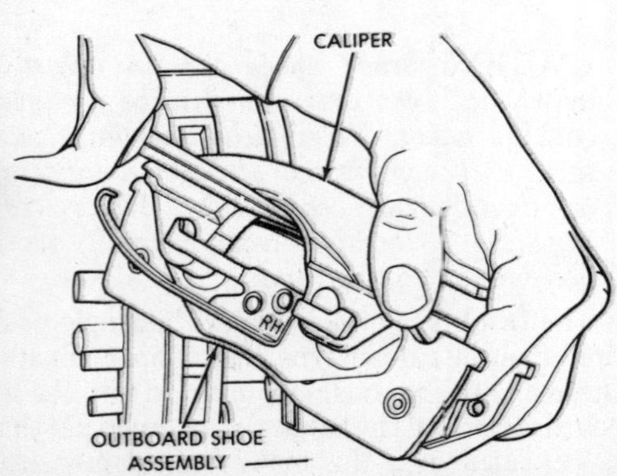

Prying the outboard shoe assembly from the caliper

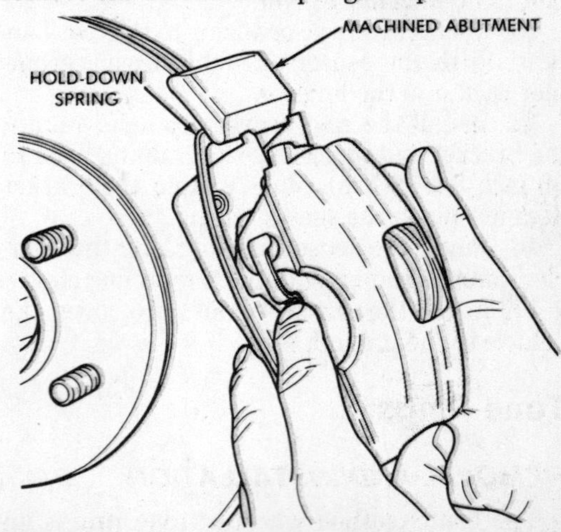

Removing the caliper and brake shoes as an assembly

4. Insert a small prybar between the front edge of the caliper and the adapter rail. Apply steady upward pressure to loosen the adhesive seals. Remove the caliper by slowly sliding it up and off the adapter and disc rotor.

5. Support the caliper by hanging it out of the way on wire. Do not allow the caliper to be supported by the brake hose.

6. Observe the location of the anti-rattle clips. One clip is on the top of the inboard (closes to axle) brake pad. Another clip is on the bottom of the outboard brake pad, and the third is installed on the top finger of the caliper.

7. Slide the outboard brake pad from the adapter. Remove the brake disc rotor and remove the inboard pad.

8. Measure the brake lining and pad thickness. If the combined thickness at the thinnest point of the is $^1/_8$ in. (3mm) or less replace both front wheel brake pad assemblies.

To install:

9. Check around the caliper piston and boot for signs of brake fluid leakage. Inspect the dust boot around the caliper piston for cuts and breaks. If the boot is damaged or fluid leakage is visible, the caliper should be serviced. Check the adapter and caliper mounting surfaces for rust and dirt, clean them with a wire brush.

10. Remove the protective paper from the gaskets mounted on the metal part of the brake pads. Install the anti-rattle clips in position. Install inner brake pad on the adapter.

11. Install the brake disc rotor and outer brake pad.

12. Press the caliper back into the caliper until it bottoms. If may be necessary to place a small piece of wood on the piston and use a C-clamp to retract the piston. If so, tighten the clamp with slow steady pressure. Stop when resistance is felt.

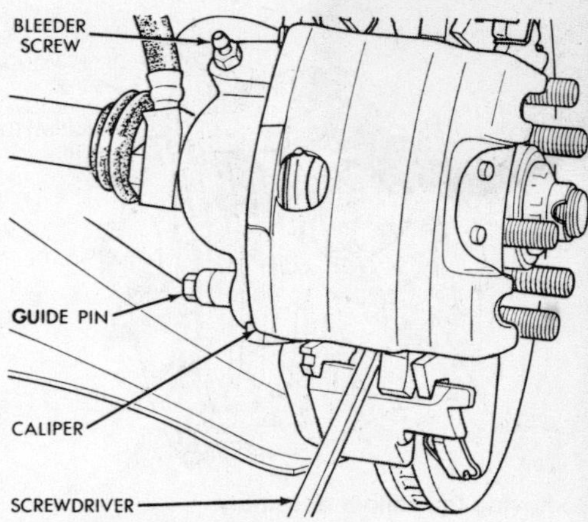

Loosening the caliper assembly

13. Lower the caliper over the brake pads and disc rotor. Install the caliper guide pin and tighten to 25-35 ft. lbs. Take care not to cross thread the guide pin.

14. After both calipers have been installed, fill the master cylinder and bleed the brakes if the caliper were rebuilt. If the calipers were not serviced, pump the brakes until a firm brake pedal is obtained.

15. Install the front wheels and lower the vehicle. After the vehicle is lowered, check the lug nut torque and tighten to required specification to 95 ft. lbs. Road test the vehicle and make several firm but not hard stops to wear off any dirt from the pads or rotor.

A.T.E. Type

NOTE: *The caliper is equipped with one holddown spring running across the outboard fingers of the caliper, and is also equipped with an inner shoe to piston mounting clip.*

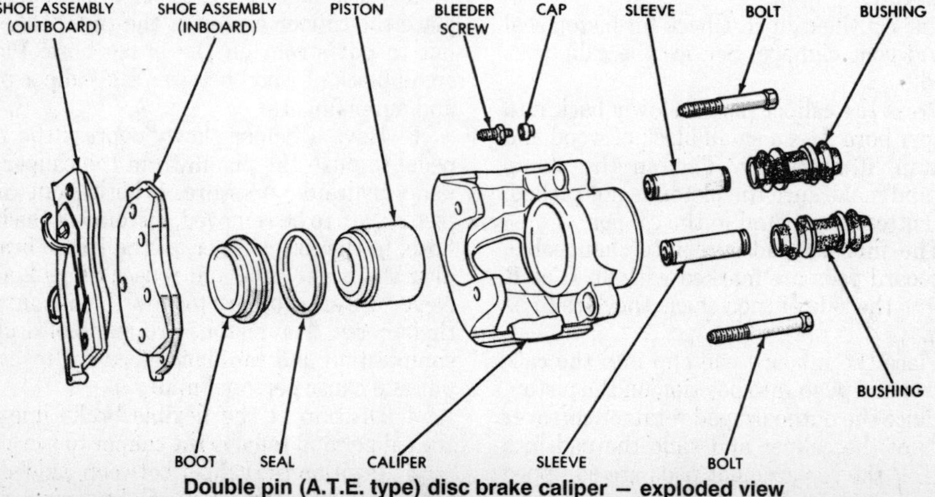

Double pin (A.T.E. type) disc brake caliper — exploded view

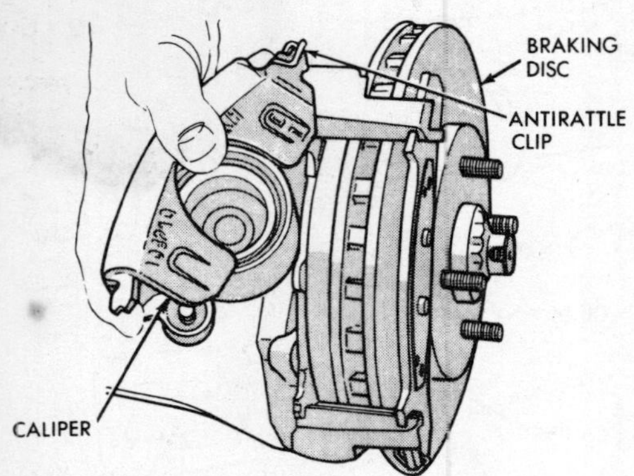

Removing the caliper assembly

1. The A.T.E. caliper uses two mounting pins. Loosen the wheel lugs slightly. Raise and safely support the front of the vehicle.

2. Remove the wheel and tire assembly.

CAUTION: *On models equipped with ABS, the system pressure must be released before disconnecting any of the hydraulic lines. Failure to do so, can cause personal injury.*

3. Loosen, but do not remove the two steel caliper guide pins. Back the pins out until the caliper can be moved freely.

4. Pull the lower end of the caliper out from the steering knuckle support. Roll the caliper up and away from the disc rotor. The disc brake pads will remain located in their caliper positions.

5. Take care, while servicing the pads, that strain is not put on the brake hose.

6. Pry the outboard pad toward the bottom opened end of the caliper. The pad is retained by a captured clip. Remove the pad.

7. Remove the inboard pad by pulling it outward from the caliper piston. It is retained by a captive clip.

To install:

8. Inspect the caliper. Check for piston seal leaks and boot damage. Service the caliper as required.

9. Press the caliper piston slowly back into the caliper bore. Use a small block of wood and a C-clamp, if necessary. Tighten the clamp slowly, and make sure the piston is not cocked. Gently bottom the piston in the caliper.

10. The inboard pads are interchangeable, the outboard pads are marked with an **L** or **R** relating to the side of the vehicle they are to be used on.

11. Place the inboard pad clip into the caliper piston and push into position on the piston.

12. Place the outboard pad retainer clip over the ears of the caliper and slide the pad into position. If the replacement pads are equipped with a noise suppression gasket, remove the protective paper from the gasket before installation.

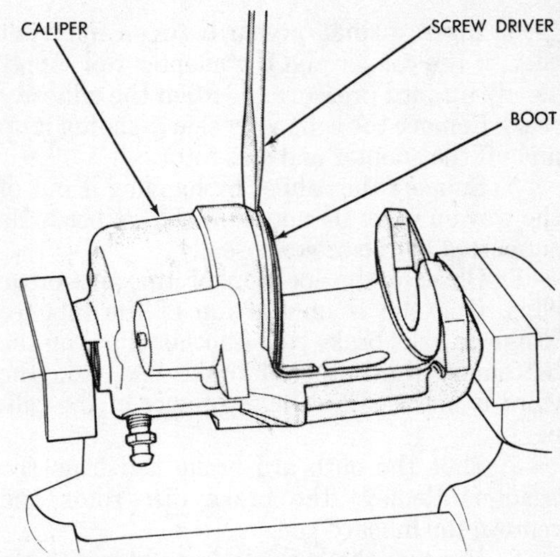

Removing the caliper piston dust boot

13. Lower the caliper over the disc rotor and align the holddown spring under the machined surface of the steering knuckle. Install the caliper mounting pins, take care not to cross thread and tighten the pins to 18-26 ft. lbs. Pump the brake pedal several times to move the pads against the rotor. If the caliper has been rebuilt, or other system service completed, bleed the brake system.

14. Install the wheel and tire assembly. Lower the vehicle. Do not move the vehicle until a firm brake pedal is verified.

Caliper

OVERHAUL

1. Remove the caliper as described in the previous section.

2. Place rags on the upper control arm and place the caliper on top of the rags. Take care not to put strain on the brake hose. Place a small block of wood between the caliper piston and outer fingers.

3. Have a helper slowly depress the brake pedal to push the piston from the caliper bore using hydraulic pressure. If both front caliper pistons are to be removed, disconnect the brake hose, to the first caliper, at the frame bracket; plug the brake tube and repeat Steps 2 and 3. Never use air pressure to blow the pistons from their bores. The pistons are made of a plastic composition and can damage easily, or can fly out and cause personal injury.

4. Disconnect the flexible brake line from the caliper and remove the caliper to work area.

5. Position the caliper between padded jaws of a bench vise. Do not overtighten since exces-

sive pressure can distort the caliper bore. Remove the dust boot.

6. Use a plastic tool and work the piston seal from the mounting groove. Do not use a metal tool; damage can result to the bore or burrs can be created on the edges of the machined seal groove.

7. Remove the guide pin bushing from the caliper. A wooden dowel makes a good tool for this purpose.

To install:

8. Clean all parts using a safe solvent or alcohol and blow dry if compressed air is on hand.

9. Inspect the piston bore for pitting or scores. Light scratches or pitting can be cleaned with crocus cloth and brake fluid. Deep scratches or pitting require honing.

10. Caliper hones are available from an auto parts supplier. Do not remove more than 0.001 in. (0.025mm) of material from the bore. Deep scratches or pitting require caliper replacement.

11. After cleaning up the caliper bore with crocus cloth or hone, remove all the dirt and grit by flushing the caliper with brake fluid. After flushing, wipe dry with a lintless rag. Flush the caliper a second time and dry.

12. Carefully reclamp the caliper in the padded vise jaws. Dip the new piston seal in clean brake fluid and install in caliper bore mounting groove. Use your fingers to work the seal into the groove until properly seated.

13. Coat the caliper piston and piston boot with clean brake fluid. Install the boot on the caliper piston. Install the piston into the caliper bore. Push the piston past the seal until bottomed in the caliper bore. Use even pressure around the edges of the piston to avoid cocking when installing the piston.

14. Position the lip of the dust boot into the counter bore of the caliper. Use a seal driver or suitable tool to install the boot edge.

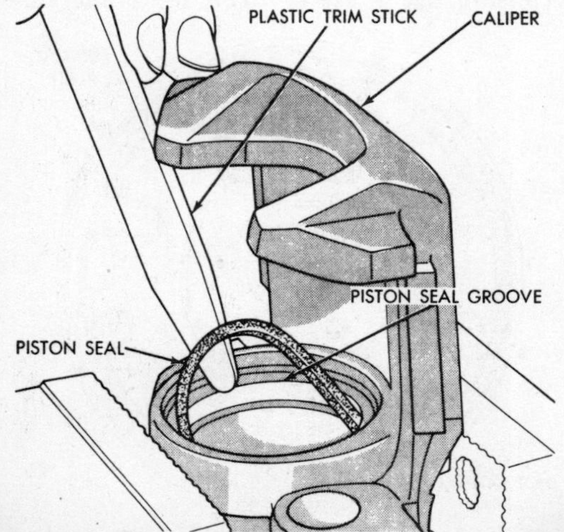

Removing the caliper piston seal

15. Compress the edges of the new guide pin bushing with your fingers and install into position on the caliper. Press in on the bushing while working it into the caliper until fully seated. Be sure the bushing flanges extend evenly over the caliper casting on both sides when installed.

16. Install the brake pads and the caliper. Bleed the brakes after caliper service.

Brake Disc (Rotor)

REMOVAL AND INSTALLATION

1. Loosen the wheel lugs slightly. Raise and support the front of the vehicle on jackstands. Remove the front wheel and tire assembly. Relieve the brake system pressure if equipped with ABS.

2. Remove the disc brake caliper and outer brake pad.

3. Remove the disc brake rotor.

4. Service as necessary. Place the rotor in position and install the caliper assembly. Refer to Brake Pad Removal and Installation for detailed procedures, if necessary.

INSPECTION

If excessive run out, wobble or thickness variation is present, feedback through the brake pedal will be felt when the brakes are applied. Pedal pulsation, chatter, surge and increased pedal travel can be caused when the disc rotor is worn unevenly or deeply scored. Remove the rotor and have an automotive machine shop measure the wear and check for run out. The machine shop can refinish the braking surfaces if replacement is not necessary.

REAR DRUM BRAKES

CAUTION: *Brake shoes contain asbestos, which has been determined to be a cancer causing agent. Never clean the brake surfaces with compressed air! Avoid inhaling any dust from any brake surface! When cleaning brake surfaces, use a commercially available brake cleaning fluid.*

Brake Drums

REMOVAL AND INSTALLATION

1. Raise and support the rear of the vehicle on jackstands. Remove the wheels and tire assemblies.

2. Remove the brake shoe adjusting slot cover from the rear of backing plate.

3. Insert a thin tool through the adjusting

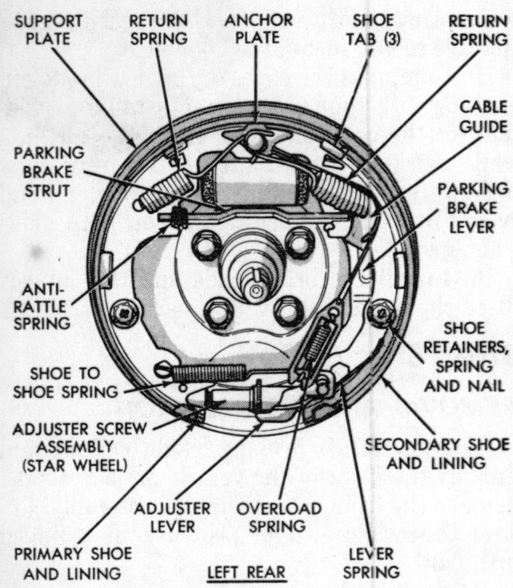

Rear drum brake assembly components

slot and hold the adjusting lever away from the star wheel. Insert an adjusting tool and back off the star wheel by prying downward with the tool.

4. Remove the center hub dust cover, nut, washer, brake drum, hub and wheel bearings.

To install:

5. Inspect the brake lining and drum for wear. Inspect the wheel cylinder for leakage. Service as required.

6. Remove, clean, inspect and repack the wheel bearings. Install the brake drum. Tighten the hub nut to 240-300 inch lbs. and back off the nut until bearing pressure is released. Retighten the nut finger tight, align the cotter pin hole and install the cotter pin.

7. Adjust the rear brakes as described in the beginning of this section.

INSPECTION

Check the brake drum for any cracks, scores, grooves, or an out-of-round condition. Slight scores can be removed with Emory cloth, while extensive scoring or grooves will require machining. Have an automotive machine shop measure the wear and check the drum for run out. The shop will be able to turn the drum on a lathe, if necessary. Never have a drum turned more than 0.060 in. (1.5mm). If the drum is cracked, or worn more than the limit, replace.

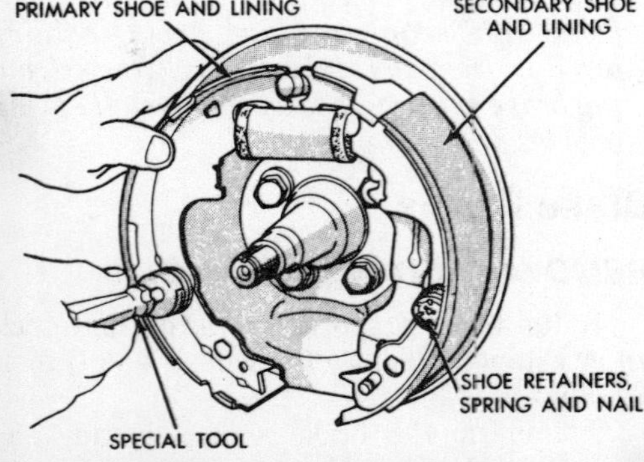

Removing the shoe retainers, springs and pins

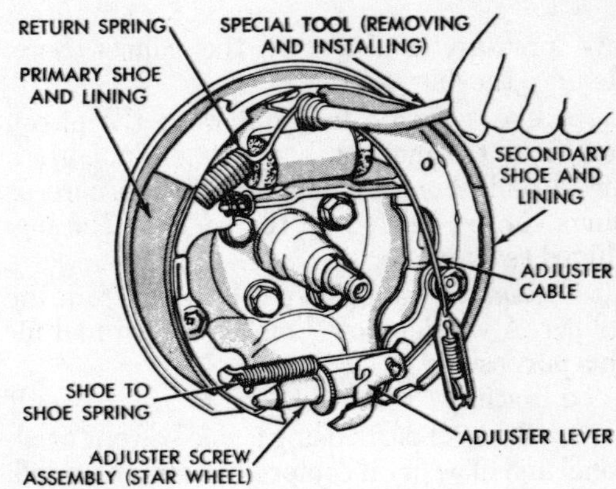

Removing brake shoe return springs

Brake Shoes

REMOVAL AND INSTALLATION

NOTE: *A pair of brake springs pliers or spring removal/installation tool and a retainer cap spring tool are good tools to have on hand for this job.*

1. Raise and support the rear of the vehicle on jackstands. Remove the rear wheels and brake drums.

NOTE: *Remove and install the brake shoes on one side at a time. Use the assembled side for reference.*

CAUTION: *Brake shoes contain asbestos, which has been determined to be a cancer causing agent. Never clean the brake sur-*

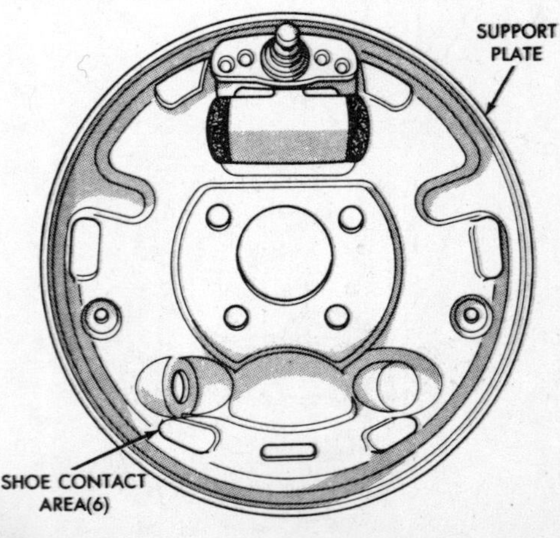

Shoe contact pads on support plate

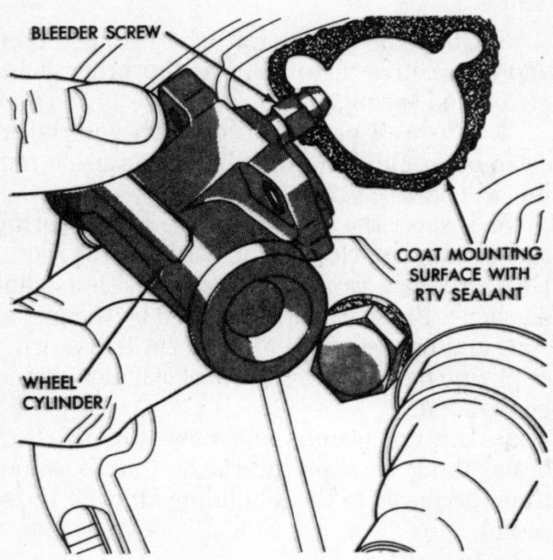

Removing the wheel cylinder from the backing plate

faces with compressed air! Avoid inhaling any dust from any brake surface! When cleaning brake surfaces, use a commercially available brake cleaning fluid.

2. Use a pair of brake spring pliers or appropriate tool and remove the shoe return springs from the top anchor. Take note that the secondary shoe spring is on top of the primary shoe spring. Install in the same position at installation time.
3. Slide the closed eye of the adjuster cable off of the anchor stud. Unhook the spring end and remove the cable, overload spring, cable guide and anchor plate.
4. Remove the adjusting lever from the spring by sliding forward to clear the pivot. Work the lever out from under the spring. Remove the spring from the pivot.
5. Unhook the bottom shoe-to-shoe spring from the secondary (back) shoe and disengage from the primary (front) shoe.
6. Spread the bottom of the brake shoes apart and remove the star wheel adjuster. Remove the parking brake strut and spring assembly.
7. Locate the shoe retainer nail head at the rear of the brake backing plate. Support the nail head with a finger, press in and twist the spring retainer washer with the special retainer tool or a pair of pliers. If you are using pliers, take care not to slip and pinch your fingers.
8. Remove the retainer, spring, inner washer and nail from both shoes. Remove the parking brake lever from the secondary brake shoe. Remove the shoes from the backing plate. Disconnect the parking brake lever from the brake cable.

To install:

9. Clean the backing plate with a safe solvent. Inspect the raised show support pads for rough or rusted contact areas. Clean and smooth as necessary. Clean and inspect the adjuster star wheels, apply a thin film of lubricant to the threads, socket and washer. Replace the star wheel if rust or threads show damage.
10. Inspect the holddown springs, return springs and adjuster spring. If the springs have been subjected to overheating or if their strength is questionable, replace the spring.
11. Inspect the wheel cylinder. If signs of leakage are present (a small amount of fluid inside the end boot is normal) rebuild or replace the cylinder.
12. Lubricate the shoe contact area pads on the backing plate with high temperature resistant white lube.
13. Engage the parking brake lever with the cable and install the lever on the secondary brake shoe. Engage the end of the brake shoe with the wheel cylinder piston and the top anchor. Install the retainer nail, washer, spring and retainer.
14. Position the primary shoe in like manner and install holddown pin assembly. Install the top anchor plate.
15. Install the parking brake strut and spring in position, press the lower part of the brake.
16. Straighten the adjuster cable and install the eye end over the top anchor. Be sure the lower spring end hook is facing inward.
17. Install the primary (front) shoe return spring. Place the cable guide in position on the secondary (rear) shoe (keep cable out of the way) and install the return spring. Check the cable guide and ensure proper mounting position. Squeeze the anchor ends of the return springs with pliers until they are parallel.
18. Carefully install the star wheel between the brake shoes. The wheel end goes closest the secondary (back) shoe. Wind out the star wheel until snug contact between the brake shoes will hold it in position.
19. Install the adjusting lever spring over the pivot pin on the lower shoe web of the secondary shoe. Install the adjuster lever under the spring and over the pivot pin. Slide the lever rearward until it locks in position.
20. Thread the adjuster cable over the guide and hook the end of the overload spring on the adjuster lever. Make sure the cable is float on the guide and the eye end is against the anchor.
21. Check the operation of the adjuster by pulling the cable rearward. The star wheel should rotate upward as the adjuster lever engages the teeth.
22. Back off the star wheel, if necessary, and

install the hub and drum. Adjust the brakes.

23. Repeat the procedures on the other rear wheel.

Wheel Cylinders

REMOVAL AND INSTALLATION

1. Jack up the rear of the vehicle and support it with jackstands.

CAUTION: *On models equipped with ABS, the system pressure must be released before disconnecting any of the hydraulic lines. Failure to do so, can cause personal injury.*

2. Remove the brake drums as previously outlined.
3. Visually inspect the wheel cylinder boots for signs of excessive leakage. Replace any boots that are torn or broken.

NOTE: *A slight amount of fluid on the boots may not be a leak but may be a preservative fluid used at the factory.*

4. If a leak has been discovered, remove the brake shoes and check for contamination. Replace the linings if they are soaked with grease or brake fluid.
5. Disconnect the brake line from the wheel cylinder.
6. Remove the wheel cylinder attaching bolts, then pull the wheel cylinder out of its support.
7. Position the wheel cylinder onto the backing plate and loosely install the mounting bolts. Start the brake line into the cylinder. Tighten the mounting bolts and the brake line. Install the brake shoes and brake drum. Adjust the brake shoes.
8. Bleed the brake system.

OVERHAUL

1. Pry the boots away from the cylinder and remove the boots and pistons.
2. Disengage the boot from the piston.
3. Slide the piston into the cylinder bore and press inward to remove the other boot, piston and spring.
4. Wash all parts (except rubber parts) in clean brake fluid thoroughly. Do not use a rag; lint will adhere to the bore.
5. Inspect the cylinder bores. Light scoring can usually be cleaned up with crocus cloth. Heavier scores can be cleaned up with a cylinder hone. Black stains are caused by the piston cups and are no cause of concern. Bad scoring or pitting means that the wheel cylinder should be replaced.
6. Dip the pistons and new cups in clean brake fluid, or apply lubricant that is sometimes packaged in the rebuilding kit prior to assembly.

To install:

7. Coat the wheel cylinder bore with clean brake fluid.
8. Install the expansion spring with the cup expanders.
9. Install the cups in each end of the cylinder with the open ends facing each other.
10. Assemble new boots on the piston and slide them into the cylinder bore.
11. Press the boot over the wheel cylinder until seated.
12. Apply RTV on the mounting surface of the backing plate. Install the wheel cylinder, and connect brake lines.
13. Install brake shoes, and drum. Adjust and bleed brakes.

Parking Brake

ADJUSTMENT

1. Raise and support the rear of the vehicle on jackstands. Apply and release the parking brake several times.
2. Clean the parking park adjustment bolts with a wire brush and lubricate the threads.

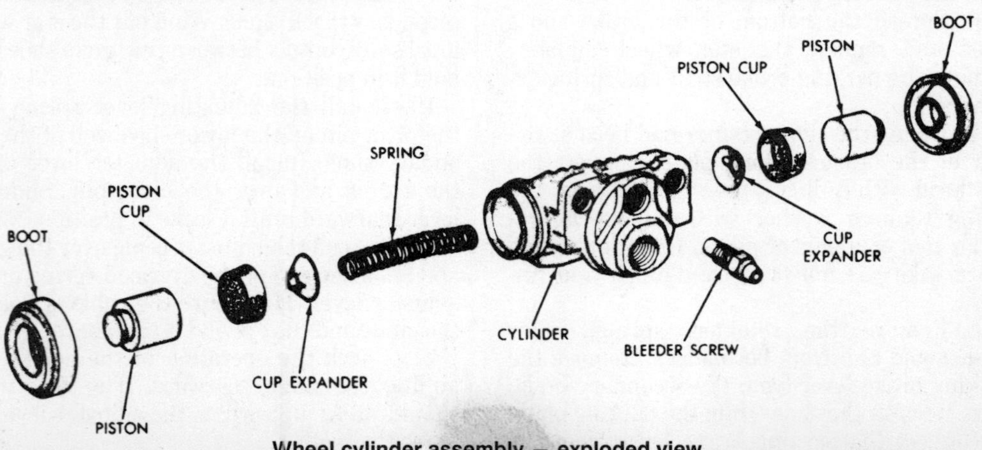

Wheel cylinder assembly — exploded view

Back off the adjusting nut until there is slack in the cable.

3. Check the rear brake adjustment, adjust as necessary.

4. Tighten the parking brake cable adjuster until the slight drag is felt when turning the rear wheel.

5. Loosen the cable until no drag is felt on either rear wheel. Back off adjusting nut two full turns more.

6. Apply and release the parking brake several times to ensure there is not rear wheel drag. Lower the vehicle.

REMOVAL AND INSTALLATION

Front Cable

1. Raise and support the front of the vehicle on jackstands.

2. Back off the adjuster nut until the cable can be released from the connectors.

3. Lift the floor mat for access to the floor pan. Force the seal surrounding the cable from the floor.

4. Pull the cable forward and disconnect from lever clevis. Remove the front cable from support bracket and vehicle.

5. Feed the new cable through the floor pan hole. Attach the front end of the cable to the parking brake lever clevis and support.

6. Engage intermediate cable and adjust.

Intermediate Cable

1. Back off the parking brake adjuster. Disengage the front cable and rear cables from the intermediate cable connector.

2. Remove the intermediate cable. Install the new cable and adjust.

Rear Cables

1. Raise and support the rear of the vehicle on jackstands.

2. Back off the cable adjustment and disconnect the rear cable (that is to be replaced) from the intermediate cable. Remove the rear cable from the mounting clips.

3. Remove the rear wheel and the brake shoes from the side requiring replacement.

4. Disconnect the cable from the rear brake apply lever. Compress the cable lock with a mini-hose clamp and pull the cable from the backing plate.

5. Install the new cable through the brake backing plate. Engage the locks. Attach the cable to the apply lever. Install the brake shoes, drum and wheel assembly.

6. Adjust the service brakes and parking brake.

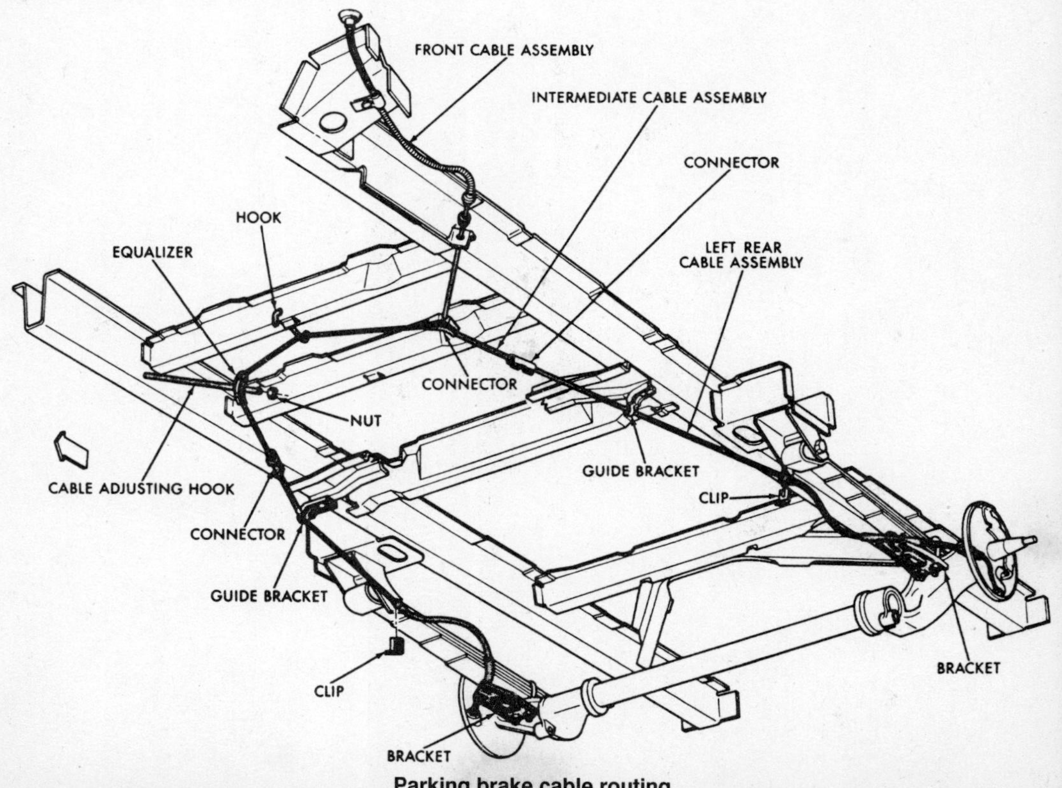

Parking brake cable routing

BRAKE SPECIFICATIONS

Years	Model	Master Cylinder Bore	Brake Disc		Brake Drum		Wheel Cylinder or Caliper Bore Dia.	
			Minimum Thickness	Maximum Runout	Inside Diameter	Maximum Machine O/S	Front	Rear
1984-89	Caravan	0.94	0.80	0.005	9.000	9.060	2.36	0.75
	Voyager	0.94	0.80	0.005	9.000	9.060	2.36	0.75
1990-91	Caravan	0.94	0.80	0.003	7.874 ①	7.934 ②	2.12	0.62
	Voyager	0.94	0.80	0.003	7.874 ①	7.934 ②	2.12	0.62
	Town & Country	0.94	0.80	0.003	7.874 ①	7.934 ②	2.12	0.62

① Heavy Duty: 8.661 in.
② Heavy Duty: 8.721

Body 10

EXTERIOR

Front Doors

REMOVAL AND INSTALLATION

Except 1991 Models

1. Open the front door and remove the inner door panel covering. Disconnect the interior light wiring harness and feed it through the access hole. Disconnect the door swing stop.
2. Open the door wide enough to gain access to the hinge bolts. Place a padded support under the door edge that will hold the door in a level position when the hinges have been unbolted from the frame.
3. Scribe around the door hinge on the door frame. Remove the hinge mounting bolts, lower hinge first, then the upper, from the door frame.
4. Remove the door.
5. Place the door on the padded support and install the hinge mounting bolts until they are snug enough to support the door, but not tight enough to prevent door adjustment. Adjust the door position until correctly aligned and tighten the hinge bolts. Adjust the striker as necessary. Connect the door stop and interior light harness. Install the inner trim panel.

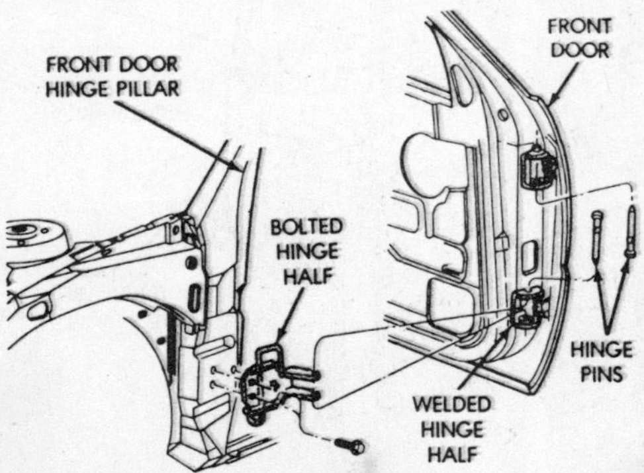

Front door removal and installation

1991 Models

1. Remove the door trim panel, silencer pad and water shield.
2. Disconnect all wire connectors and wire harness hold downs inside of the door, and push the harness through the access hole in the front of the door.
3. Open the door and support it with a jack, an assistant should also be used to hold the door.
4. Using a hammer and punch, drive the bottom hinge pin upward and remove the pin from the hinge.
5. Drive the upper hinge pin from the hinge and remove it. Separate the door from the vehicle.

To install:

6. Install the door assembly on the hinges.
7. Install the hinge pins, by tapping them into position.
8. The door should not require any re-alignment. Install the wiring harness into the door.
9. Install the trim panel.

ALIGNMENT

The front doors should be adjusted so that there is a $^1/_4$ in. (6mm) gap between the edge of the front fender and the edge of the door, and a $^1/_4$ in. (6mm) gap between the back edge of the door and the lock pillar. Adjust the door to position and raise or lower it so that the stamped edge line matches the body panel line. Secure the door in proper position after necessary adjustments.

Front Door Hinge

REMOVAL AND INSTALLATION

1991 Models

1. Raise the front of the vehicle slightly.
2. Remove the wheel and tire assembly.
3. Remove the inner fender, plastic splash shield retaining screws and remove the shield.
4. Support the door assembly. Remove the door retaining pin on the hinge to be replaced.
5. Remove the hinge plate retaining bolts from inside the fender well.
6. Remove the hinge assembly.

To install:

7. Install the hinge plate in position and install the retaining bolts. Do not tighten them completely.
8. Install the hinge pin and check the door alignment, there should be a 1/4 in. (6mm) gap around the sides of the door.
9. Tighten the hinge mounting bolts.
10. Install the inner fender splash shield and install the wheel.
11. Lower the vehicle.

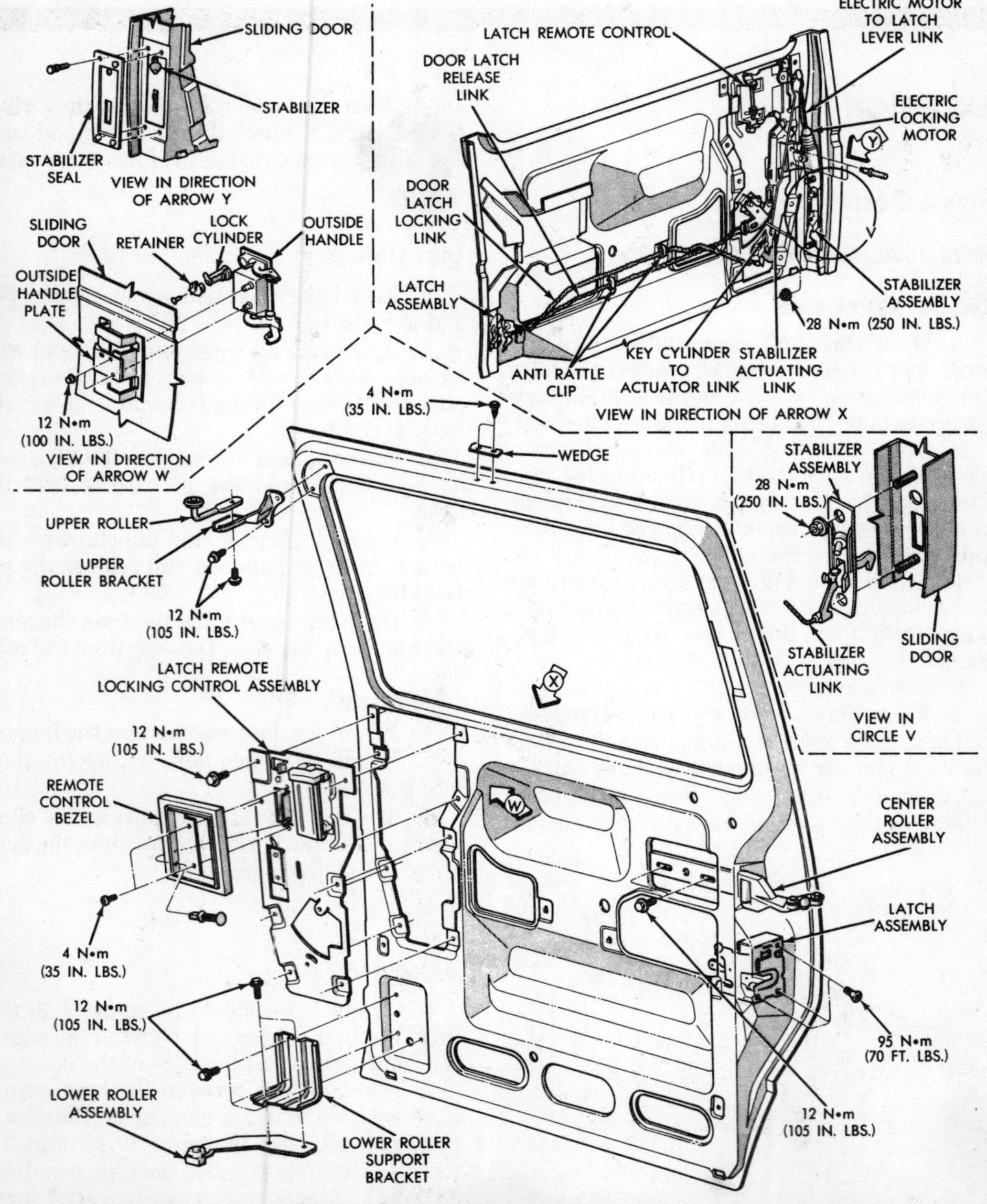

Sliding door assembly — exploded view

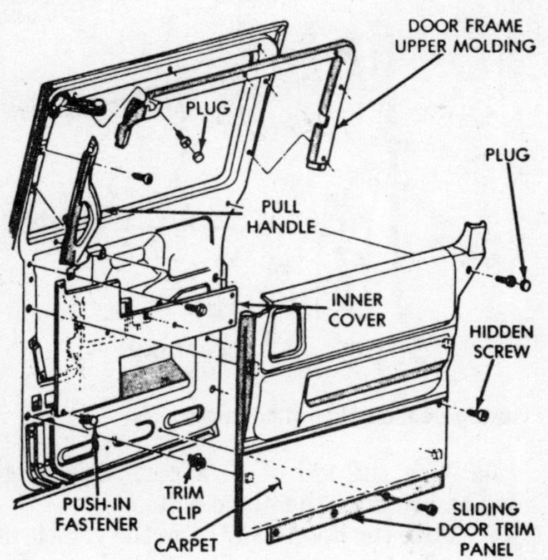

Sliding door trim mounting

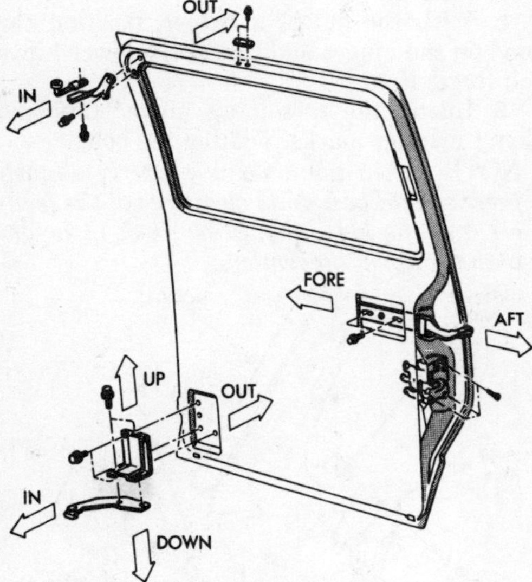

Sliding door adjustments

Sliding Door

REMOVAL AND INSTALLATION

NOTE: *When removing the sliding door as an assembly, it is not necessary to remove or loosen bolts that would change the doors alignment.*

1. Remove the sliding door upper track cover.
2. Remove the upper track over travel stop.
3. Remove the sill plate.
4. Remove the lower track over travel stop.
5. With the help of an assistant, roll the door back and out of its tracks.

To install:

6. Position the door carefully on its tracks and roll it into position.
7. Install the track over travel stops.
8. Install the sill plate.
9. Install the upper track cover.

ALIGNMENT

1. The gap between the back edge of the front door and the front edge of the sliding door should be $^5/_{16}$ in. (8mm). The gap between the sliding door edge and the quarter panel should be $^1/_4$ in. (6mm). The stamped edge line of the front door the sliding door and the quarter panel should be in line.
2. Remove the hinge trim panels and adjust the sliding door in the direction(s) required. Refer to the illustration provided for adjustment direction.

Liftgate

REMOVAL AND INSTALLATION

1. Support the liftgate in the full opened position.
2. Scribe a mark on the liftgate to mark the hinge positions.
3. Place masking tape on the roof edge and liftgate edge to protect the paint surfaces during removal and installation.
4. Remove the liftgate prop fasteners and remove the props.
5. Have a helper on hand to support the liftgate. Remove the hinge mounting bolts and remove the liftgate.

To install:

6. Raise the liftgate into position and install

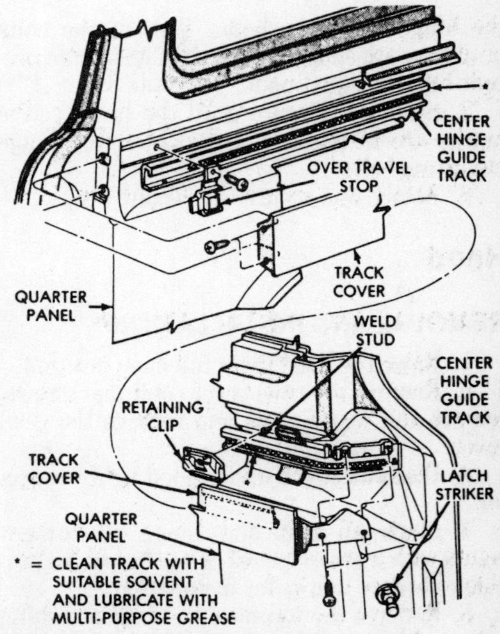

Sliding door center track cover and over travel stop mounting

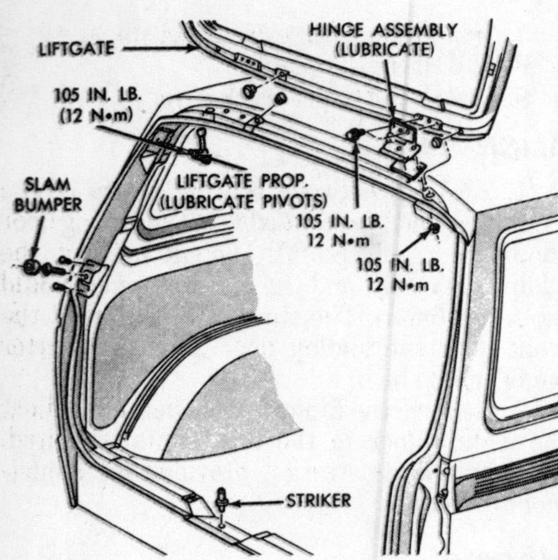

Liftgate assembly mounting

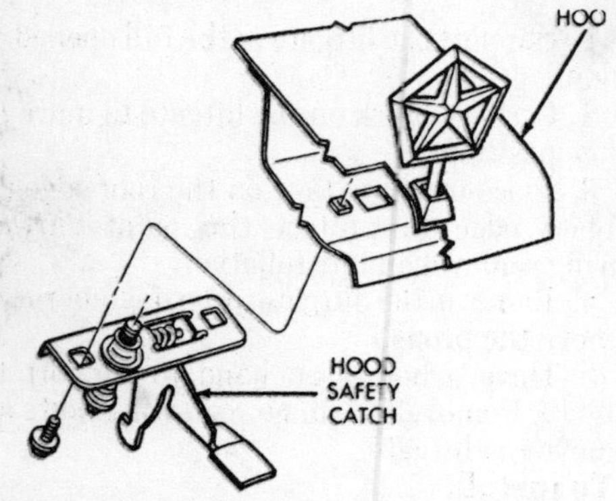

Hood safety catch assembly

the hinge mounting bolts. Tighten the bolts until they are snug, but not tight enough to prevent liftgate adjustment.

7. Shift the liftgate until the hinge scribe marks are in position and tighten the hinge mounting bolts.

8. Attach and secure the liftgate props.

Hood

REMOVAL AND INSTALLATION

1. Raise the hood to its full open position.

2. Remove the cowl cover retaining screws, remove the wiper arms and remove the cowl cover.

3. Disconnect the under hood light connector.

4. Mark all bolt and hinge attachment points with a grease pencil or equivalent, to provide reference marks for installation.

5. Remove the top hood-to-hinge attaching bolts and loosen the bottom bolts until they can be removed by hand.

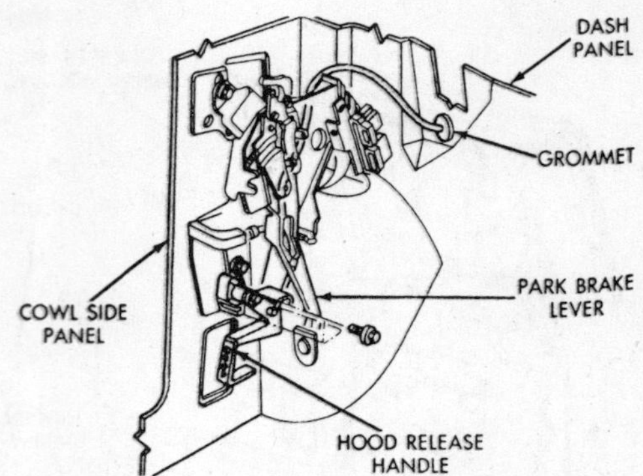

Hood release cable attachment

6. With the aid of a helper, support the hood and remove the hinge bolts.

7. Move the hood away from the vehicle and store it in a way to prevent it from being damaged.

To install:

8. With the aid of a helper, position the hood on the hinges and install the lower hinge bolt finger tight.

9. Install the remaining hinge bolts and align the hinge marks. Tighten the bolts.

NOTE: *When the hood is properly aligned there should be a 4mm clearance at the fenders and the hood should be flush in height with the top of the fenders.*

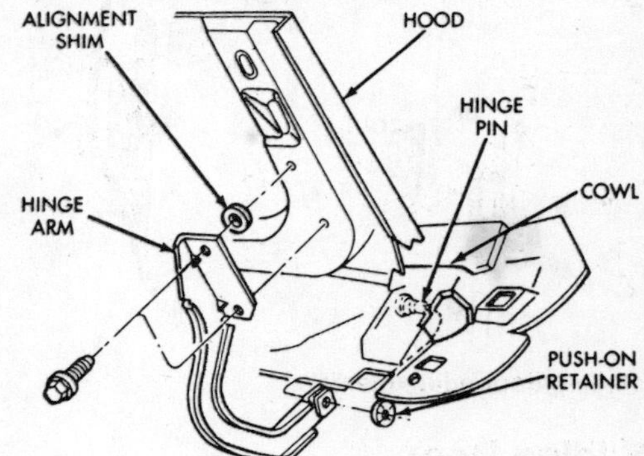

Hood and hinge assembly

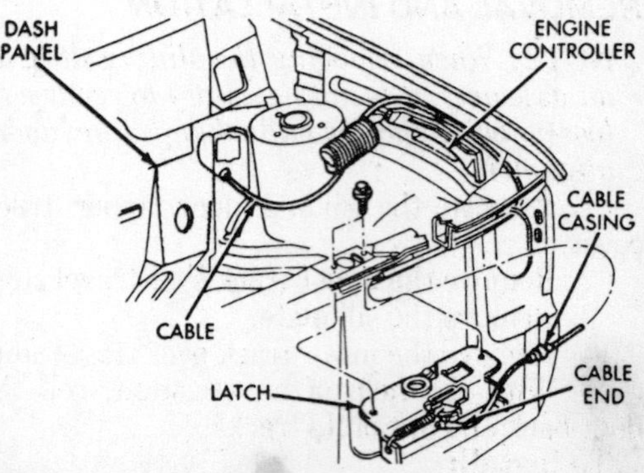

Hood latch components

10. Connect the under hood light and install the cowl cover. Install the wiper arms.

11. Check the hood latch operation.

Outside Mirrors

REMOVAL AND INSTALLATION

1. Remove the door trim panel.
2. Remove the adjustment knob with an Allen wrench. Remove the screw cover plug and the mirror inner bezel mounting screws. Remove the bezel.
3. Remove the mirror mounting nuts and the mirror. If equipped with power mirrors, disconnect the electrical lead.
4. Place the mirror into position and install the mounting nuts. Connect the electrical lead, if equipped.
5. Place the bezel into position and install the mounting screws and cover plug.
6. Install the control knob and trim panel.

INTERIOR

Door Panels

REMOVAL AND INSTALLATION

1. Lower the door glass until it is 3 in. (76mm) from the full down position.
2. Unlock the door and remove the remote door latch control handle bezel by prying the front of the bezel out and rearward.
3. Remove the arrest mounting screw, and on models with electric controls, pry out the power window switch bezel.
4. Remove the window crank handle on models with manual window regulators.
5. Remove the two edge inserts that cover the mounting screws for the door pull strap, and remove the mounting screws and strap.
6. Insert a wide flat tool between the panel and door frame and carefully twist the tool to unfasten the retainer clips from the door.
7. If the vehicle is equipped with power locks, slide the switch bezel through the trim panel.
8. Disconnect the courtesy lamp connector. Remove the door trim panel.
9. Remove the inner plastic cover and service the components as required.

To install:

10. Place sealer along the edges of the plastic liner and put the liner onto the door frame.
11. Potion the trim panel, slide the power lock bezel through the panel, connect the courtesy lamp.
12. Potion the panel clips over their mounting holes and push the panel against the door frame to lock the clips.
13. Install the pull strap, the arrest, widow handle/power switch, remote latch control/bezel.

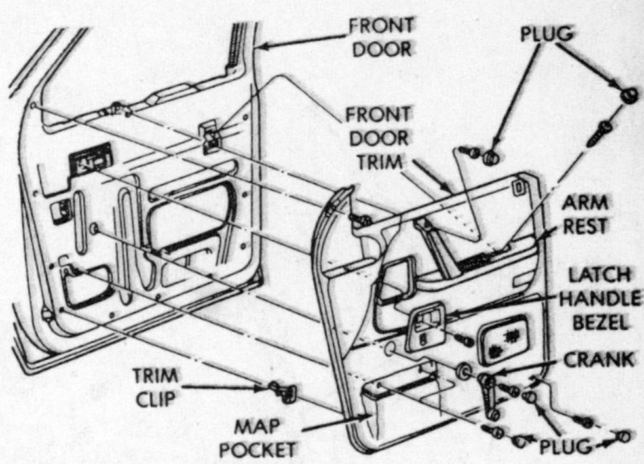

Front door trim panel removal

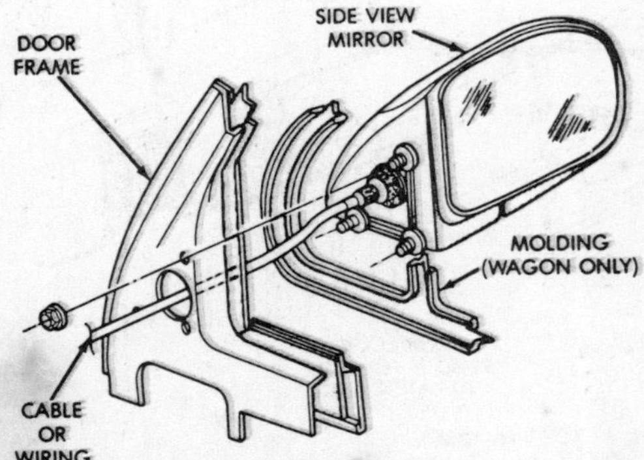

Side view mirror removal

Door Locks/Latch

REMOVAL AND INSTALLATION

This procedure can be used for both the front and sliding doors.

1. Remove the door trim panel and inner cover.
2. Raise the window to the full up position.

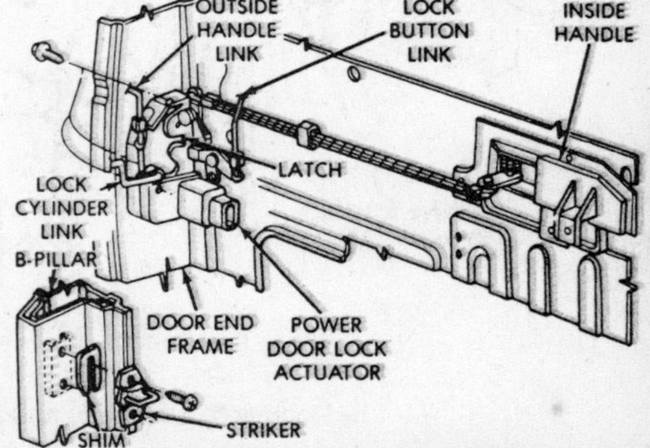

Door latch assembly, striker and linkage mounting – 1984-90 models

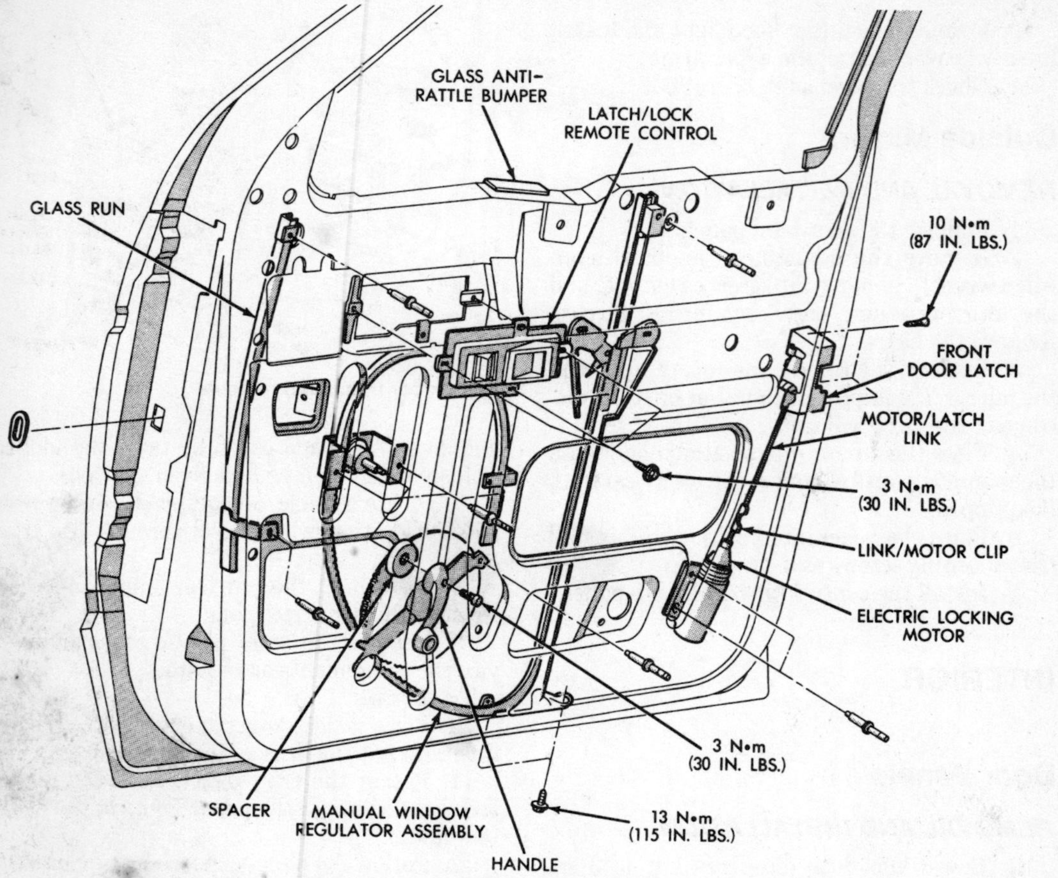

Front door assembly — component view

3. Disconnect all the locking clips from the remote linkage at the latch.

4. Remove the retaining screws at the door edge and remove the latch assembly.

5. Position the latch to the door frame and secure it with the retaining screws.

6. Connect all of the remote linkage to the latch levers.

7. Check latch operation. Install the inner cover and door trim panel.

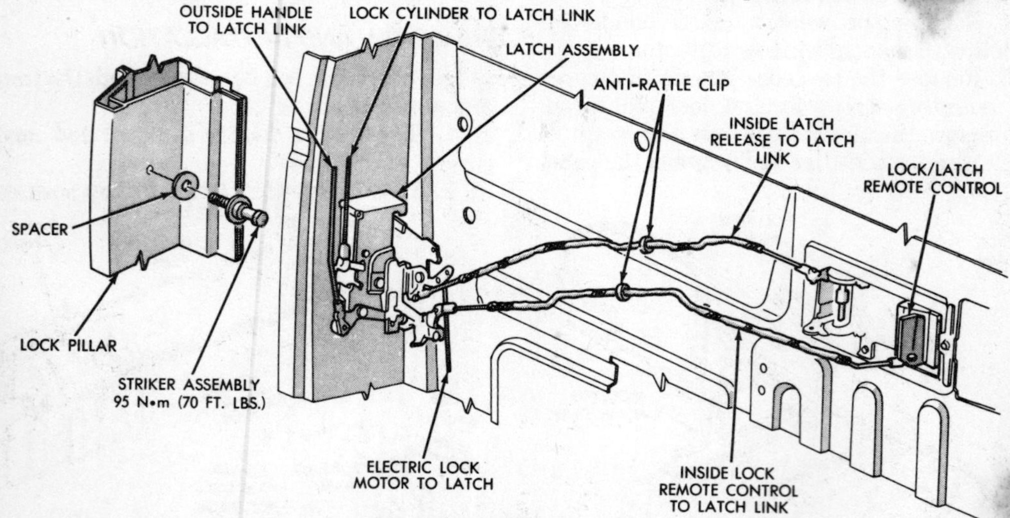

Door latch assembly and striker — 1991 models

Door Glass Regulator

REMOVAL AND INSTALLATION

1. Remove the door trim panel and inner liner.
2. Remove the window glass from the regulator and the door.
3. If equipped with power windows, disconnect the wiring harness and remove the retainer clip.
4. Drill out the regulator mounting rivets. Their are five on vehicles equipped with electric windows, and six if equipped with manual windows.
5. Remove the regulator through the larger access hole. Rotate the regulator through the hole as required for removal.

To install:

6. Install the regulator to the mounting

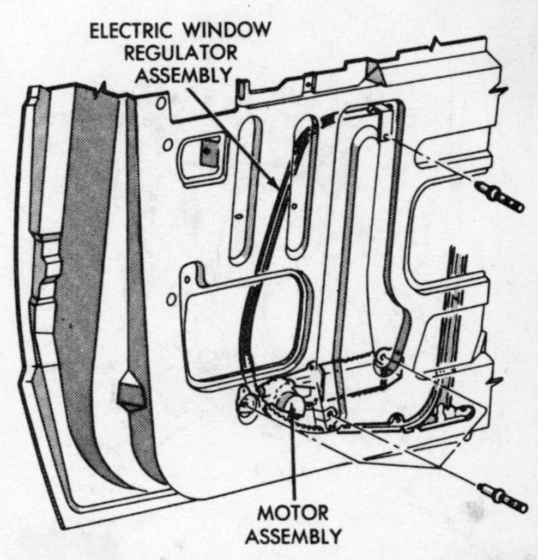

Electric window regulator assembly — 1984-90 models

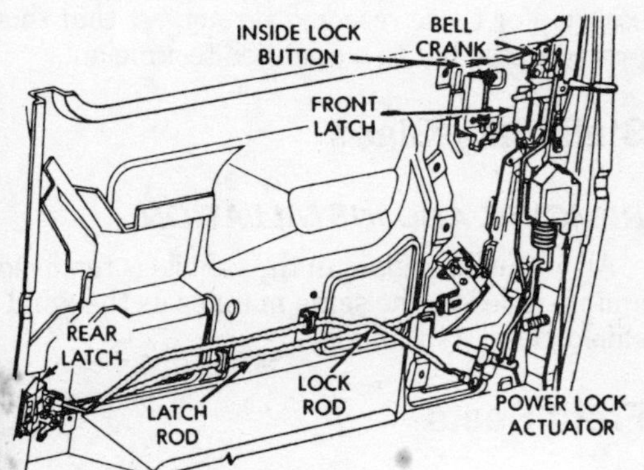

Sliding door latch and linkage

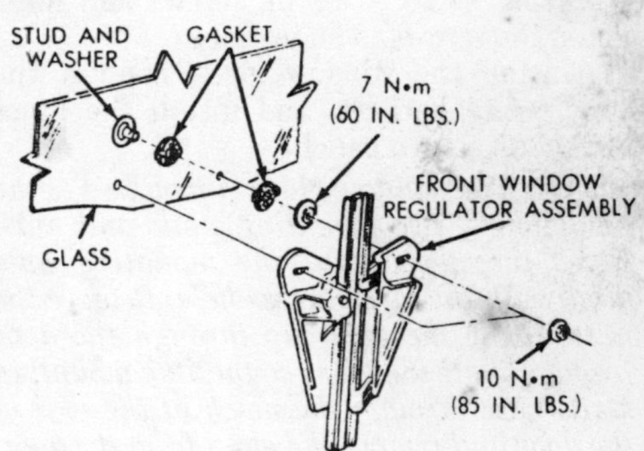

Front door glass mounting

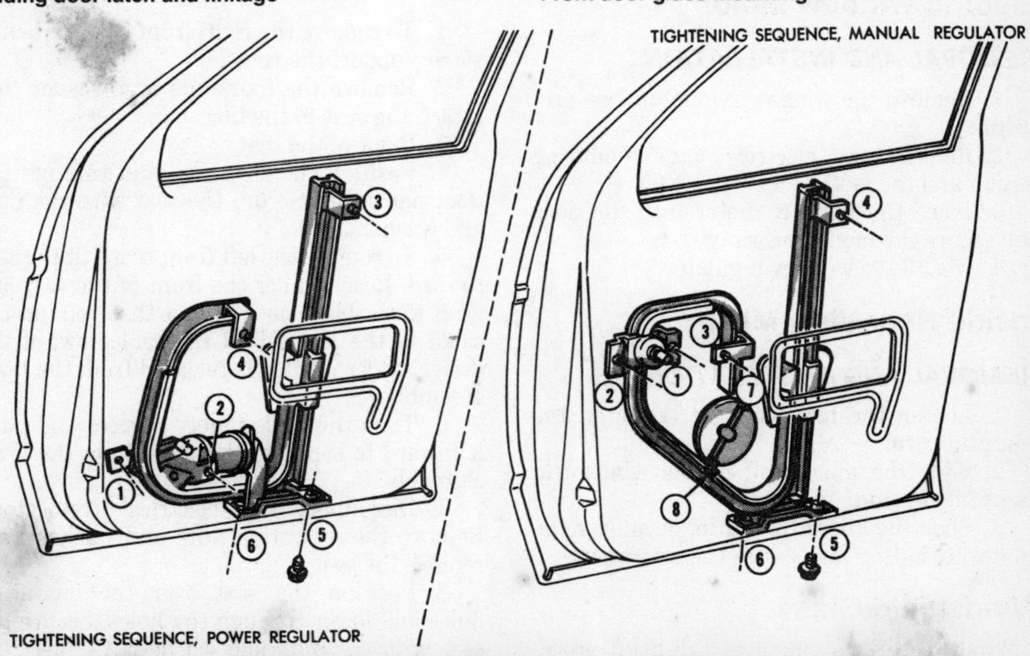

Window regulator tightening sequence — 1984-90 models

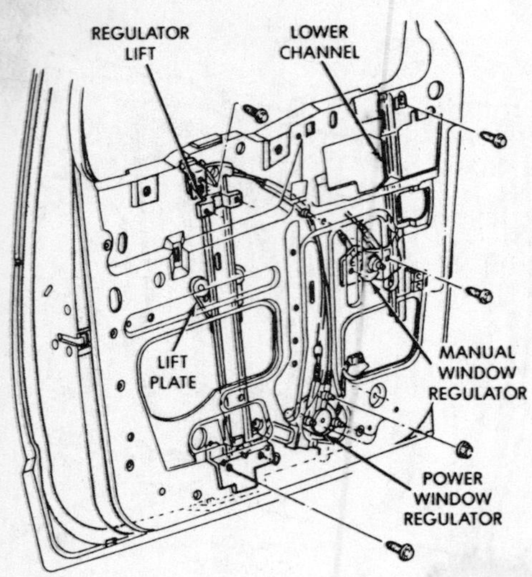

Window regulator components – 1991 models

holes using 1/4-20 × 1/2 in. screws and nuts. Tighten the screws to 90 inch lbs.

7. Install the window glass, connect the motor wiring harness, and install the inner liner and door trim panel.

NOTE: *The window glass is mounted to the regulator by two mounting studs and nuts. Raise the glass until the mounting nuts align with the large access hole. Remove the nuts. Raise the glass up through the door frame. Rotate the glass so that the mounting studs pass through the notch at the rear of the door and remove the glass from the door.*

Electric Window Motor

REMOVAL AND INSTALLATION

1. Remove the window regulator. See procedure.
2. Remove the electric motor mounting screws and the motor.
3. Place the window motor into the door and secure the mounting screws.
4. Install the window regulator.

Inside Rear View Mirror

REMOVAL AND INSTALLATION

1. Loosen the mounting set screw on the mounting arm.
2. Slide the mirror off of the windshield mounting button.
3. Slide the mirror mounting arm over the mounting button and secure the set screw.

Windshield Glass

Windshield replacement is a difficult procedure and must be performed according to FMVSS standards. Many special tools are necessary. For these reasons, we suggest that this procedure be left to a qualified technician.

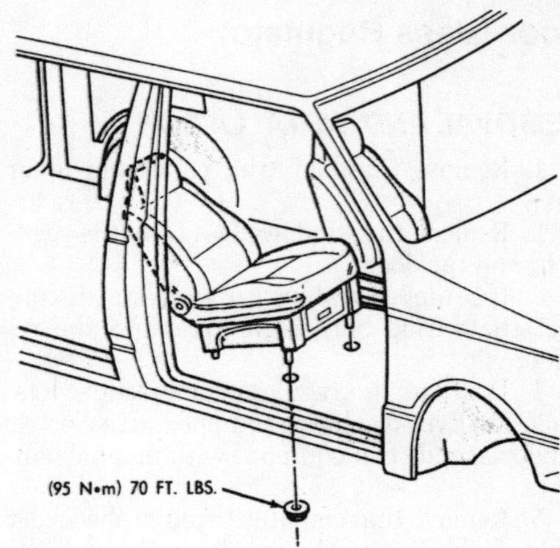

Front seat and riser removal

Stationary Glass

REMOVAL AND INSTALLATION

All of the fixed glass in the vehicle is removed and installed in the same manner as the windshield glass.

Front Seats

REMOVAL AND INSTALLATION

1. To remove the right front seat; raise and safely support the vehicle.
2. Remove the four nuts and washer that attach the seat to the floor pan.
3. Remove the seat.
4. Position the seat over and through the floor pan holes. Secure the seat with the nuts and washers.
5. To remove the left front seat: tilt the seat reward. Reach under the front of the seat and grab the cable near the clip that retains the cable to the lever. Pull the cable toward the driver's door until it is released from the lever assembly.
6. Turn the cable ninety degrees and push it inward to separate the cable from the lever assembly.
7. Disconnect the electrical connectors. Remove the mounting nuts and washers and remove the seat.
8. Position the seat over the mounting holes and lower through the holes. Secure the seat with the nuts and washers. Connect the electrical wiring and cable.

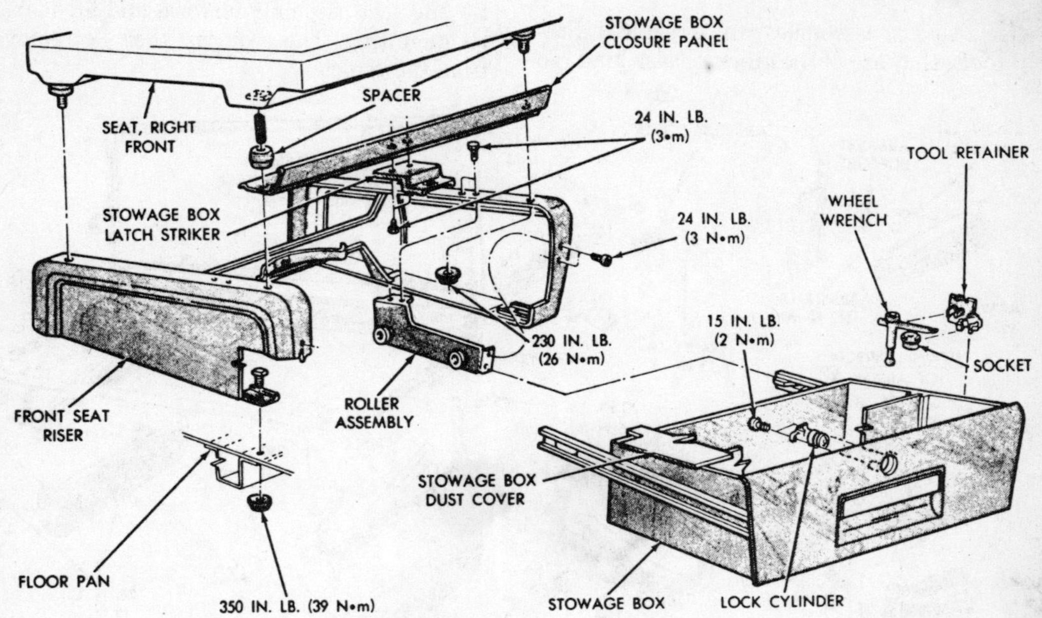

Right front seat track and riser assembly

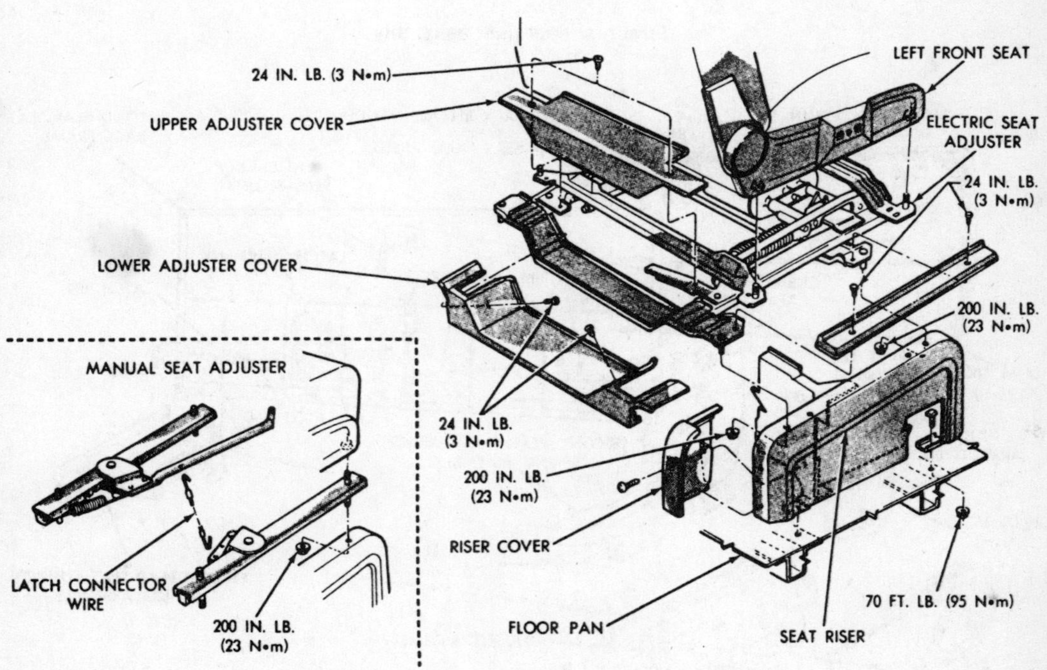

Left front seat track and riser assembly

Rear Seat Assembly

The rear seat assemblies can be removed without tools, they are of the quick release kind. To remove the assembly, pull the latch handle and tilt the seat assembly forward and lift it from its mounting. The seat can then be removed from the vehicle.

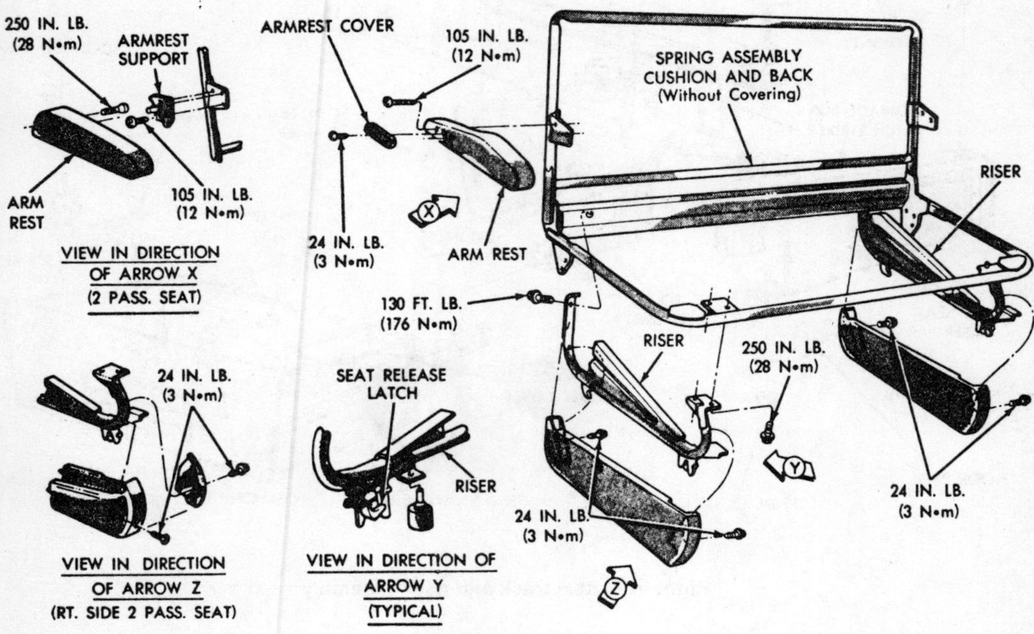

First rear seat riser assembly

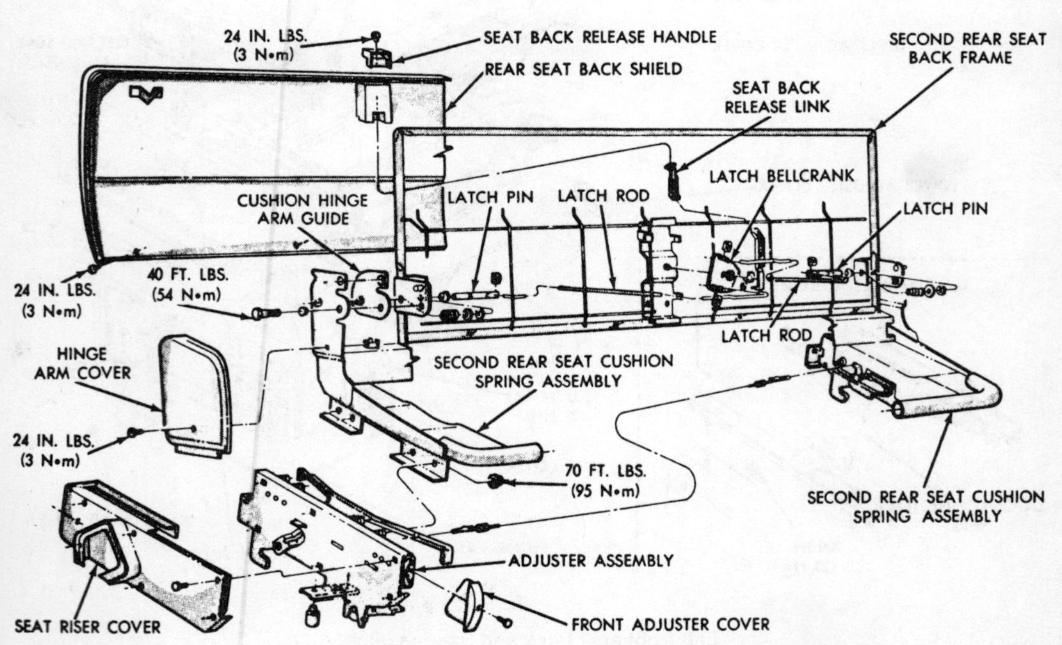

Second rear seat riser and track assembly

11 Mechanic's Data

General Conversion Table

Multiply By	To Convert	To	
	LENGTH		
2.54	Inches	Centimeters	.3937
25.4	Inches	Millimeters	.03937
30.48	Feet	Centimeters	.0328
.304	Feet	Meters	3.28
.914	Yards	Meters	1.094
1.609	Miles	Kilometers	.621
	VOLUME		
.473	Pints	Liters	2.11
.946	Quarts	Liters	1.06
3.785	Gallons	Liters	.264
.164	Cubic inches	Liters	61.02
16.39	Cubic inches	Cubic cms.	.061
28.32	Cubic feet	Liters	.0353
	MASS (Weight)		
28.35	Ounces	Grams	.035
.4536	Pounds	Kilograms	2.20
—	To obtain	From	Multiply by

Multiply By	To Convert	To	
	AREA		
6.45	Square inches	Square cms.	.155
.836	Square yds.	Square meters	1.196
	FORCE		
4.448	Pounds	Newtons	.225
.138	Ft. lbs.	Kilogram/meters	7.23
1.356	Ft. lbs.	Newton-meters	.737
.113	In. lbs.	Newton-meters	8.844
	PRESSURE		
.068	Psi	Atmospheres	14.7
6.89	Psi	Kilopascals	.145
	OTHER		
1.104	Horsepower (DIN)	Horsepower (SAE)	.9861
.746	Horsepower (SAE)	Kilowatts (KW)	1.34
1.609	Mph	Km/h	.621
.425	Mpg	Km/L	2.35
—	To obtain	From	Multiply by

Tap Drill Sizes

National Coarse or U.S.S.

Screw & Tap Size	Threads Per Inch	Use Drill Number
No. 5	40	39
No. 6	32	36
No. 8	32	29
No. 10	24	25
No. 12	24	17
1/4	20	8
5/16	18	F
3/8	16	5/16
7/16	14	U
1/2	13	27/64
9/16	12	31/64
5/8	11	17/32
3/4	10	21/32
7/8	9	49/64

National Coarse or U.S.S.

Screw & Tap Size	Threads Per Inch	Use Drill Number
1	8	7/8
1 1/8	7	63/64
1 1/4	7	1 7/64
1 1/2	6	1 11/32

National Fine or S.A.E.

Screw & Tap Size	Threads Per Inch	Use Drill Number
No. 5	44	37
No. 6	40	33
No. 8	36	29
No. 10	32	21

National Fine or S.A.E.

Screw & Tap Size	Threads Per Inch	Use Drill Number
No. 12	28	15
1/4	28	3
6/16	24	1
3/8	28	Q
7/16	20	W
1/2	20	29/64
9/16	18	33/64
5/8	18	37/64
3/4	16	11/16
7/8	14	13/16
1 1/8	12	1 3/64
1 1/4	12	1 11/64
1 1/2	12	1 27/64

Drill Sizes In Decimal Equivalents

Inch	Decimal	Wire	mm	Inch	Decimal	Wire	mm	Inch	Decimal	Wire & Letter	mm	Inch	Decimal	Letter	mm	Inch	Decimal	mm
1/64	.0156		.39		.0730	49			.1614		4.1		.2717		6.9		.4331	11.0
	.0157		.4		.0748		1.9		.1654		4.2		.2720	I		7/16	.4375	11.11
	.0160	78			.0760	48			.1660	19			.2756		7.0		.4528	11.5
	.0165		.42		.0768		1.95		.1673		4.25		.2770	J		29/64	.4531	11.51
	.0173		.44	5/64	.0781		1.98		.1693		4.3		.2795		7.1	15/32	.4688	11.90
	.0177		.45		.0785	47			.1695	18			.2810	K			.4724	12.0
	.0180	77			.0787		2.0	11/64	.1719		4.36	9/32	.2812		7.14	31/64	.4844	12.30
	.0181		.46		.0807		2.05		.1730	17			.2835		7.2		.4921	12.5
	.0189		.48		.0810	46			.1732		4.4		.2854		7.25	1/2	.5000	12.70
	.0197		.5		.0820	45			.1770	16			.2874		7.3		.5118	13.0
	.0200	76			.0827		2.1		.1772		4.5		.2900	L		33/64	.5156	13.09
	.0210	75			.0846		2.15		.1800	15			.2913		7.4	17/32	.5312	13.49
	.0217		.55		.0860	44			.1811		4.6		.2950	M			.5315	13.5
	.0225	74			.0866		2.2		.1820	14			.2953		7.5	35/64	.5469	13.89
	.0236		.6		.0886		2.25		.1850	13		19/64	.2969		7.54		.5512	14.0
	.0240	73			.0890	43			.1850		4.7		.2992		7.6	9/16	.5625	14.28
	.0250	72			.0906		2.3		.1870		4.75		.3020	N			.5709	14.5
	.0256		.65		.0925		2.35	3/16	.1875		4.76		.3031		7.7	37/64	.5781	14.68
	.0260	71			.0935	42			.1890		4.8		.3051		7.75		.5906	15.0
	.0276		.7	3/32	.0938		2.38		.1890	12			.3071		7.8	19/32	.5938	15.08
	.0280	70			.0945		2.4		.1910	11			.3110		7.9	39/64	.6094	15.47
	.0292	69			.0960	41			.1929		4.9	5/16	.3125		7.93		.6102	15.5
	.0295		.75		.0965		2.45		.1935	10			.3150		8.0	5/8	.6250	15.87
	.0310	68			.0980	40			.1960	9			.3160	O			.6299	16.0
1/32	.0312		.79		.0981		2.5		.1969		5.0		.3189		8.1	41/64	.6406	16.27
	.0315		.8		.0995	39			.1990	8			.3228		8.2		.6496	16.5
	.0320	67			.1015	38			.2008		5.1		.3230	P		21/32	.6562	16.66
	.0330	66			.1024		2.6		.2010	7			.3248		8.25		.6693	17.0
	.0335		.85		.1040	37		13/64	.2031		5.16		.3268		8.3	43/64	.6719	17.06
	.0350	65			.1063		2.7		.2040	6		21/64	.3281		8.33	11/16	.6875	17.46
	.0354		.9		.1065	36			.2047		5.2		.3307		8.4		.6890	17.5
	.0360	64			.1083		2.75		.2055	5			.3320	Q		45/64	.7031	17.85
	.0370	63		7/64	.1094		2.77		.2067		5.25		.3346		8.5		.7087	18.0
	.0374		.95		.1100	35			.2087		5.3		.3386		8.6	23/32	.7188	18.25
	.0380	62			.1102		2.8		.2090	4			.3390	R			.7283	18.5
	.0390	61			.1110	34			.2126		5.4		.3425		8.7	47/64	.7344	18.65
	.0394		1.0		.1130	33			.2130	3		11/32	.3438		8.73		.7480	19.0
	.0400	60			.1142		2.9		.2165		5.5		.3445		8.75	3/4	.7500	19.05
	.0410	59			.1160	32		7/32	2188		5.55		.3465		8.8	49/64	.7656	19.44
	.0413		1.05		.1181		3.0		.2205		5.6		.3480	S			.7677	19.5
	.0420	58			.1200	31			.2210	2			.3504		8.9	25/32	.7812	19.84
	.0430	57			.1220		3.1		.2244		5.7		.3543		9.0		.7874	20.0
	.0433		1.1	1/8	.1250		3.17		.2264		5.75		.3580	T		51/64	.7969	20.24
	.0453		1.15		.1260		3.2		.2280	1			.3583		9.1		.8071	20.5
	.0465	56			.1280		3.25		.2283		5.8	23/64	.3594		9.12	13/16	.8125	20.63
3/64	.0469		1.19		.1285	30			.2323		5.9		.3622		9.2		.8268	21.0
	.0472		1.2		.1299		3.3		.2340	A			.3642		9.25	53/64	.8281	21.03
	.0492		1.25		.1339		3.4	15/64	.2344		5.95		.3661		9.3	27/32	.8438	21.43
	.0512		1.3		.1360	29			.2362		6.0		.3680	U			.8465	21.5
	.0520	55			.1378		3.5		.2380	B			.3701		9.4	55/64	.8594	21.82
	.0531		1.35		.1405	28			.2402		6.1		.3740		9.5		.8661	22.0
	.0550	54		9/64	.1406		3.57		.2420	C		3/8	.3750		9.52	7/8	.8750	22.22
	.0551		1.4		.1417		3.6		.2441		6.2		.3770	V			.8858	22.5
	.0571		1.45		.1440	27			.2460	D			.3780		9.6	57/64	.8906	22.62
	.0591		1.5		.1457		3.7		.2461		6.25		.3819		9.7		.9055	23.0
	.0595	53			.1470	26			.2480		6.3		.3839		9.75	29/32	.9062	23.01
	.0610		1.55		.1476		3.75	1/4	.2500	E	6.35		.3858		9.8	59/64	.9219	23.41
1/16	.0625		1.59		.1495	25			.2520		6.		.3860	W			.9252	23.5
	.0630		1.6		.1496		3.8		.2559		6.5		.3898		9.9	15/16	.9375	23.81
	.0635	52			.1520	24			.2570	F		25/64	.3906		9.92		.9449	24.0
	.0650		1.65		.1535		3.9		.2598		6.6		.3937		10.0	61/64	.9531	24.2
	.0669		1.7		.1540	23			.2610	G			.3970	X			.9646	24.5
	.0670	51		5/32	.1562		3.96		.2638		6.7		.4040	Y		31/64	.9688	24.6
	.0689		1.75		.1570	22		17/64	.2656		6.74	13/32	.4062		10.31		.9843	25.0
	.0700	50			.1575		4.0		.2657		6.75		.4130	Z		63/64	.9844	25.0
	.0709		1.8		.1590	21			.2660	H			.4134		10.5	1	1.0000	25.4
	.0728		1.85		.1610	20			.2677		6.8	27/64	.4219		10.71			

AIR/FUEL RATIO: The ratio of air to gasoline by weight in the fuel mixture drawn into the engine.

AIR INJECTION: One method of reducing harmful exhaust emissions by injecting air into each of the exhaust ports of an engine. The fresh air entering the hot exhaust manifold causes any remaining fuel to be burned before it can exit the tailpipe.

ALTERNATOR: A device used for converting mechanical energy into electrical energy.

AMMETER: An instrument, calibrated in amperes, used to measure the flow of an electrical current in a circuit. Ammeters are always connected in series with the circuit being tested.

AMPERE: The rate of flow of electrical current present when one volt of electrical pressure is applied against one ohm of electrical resistance.

ANALOG COMPUTER: Any microprocessor that uses similar (analogous) electrical signals to make its calculations.

ARMATURE: A laminated, soft iron core wrapped by a wire that converts electrical energy to mechanical energy as in a motor or relay. When rotated in a magnetic field, it changes mechanical energy into electrical energy as in a generator.

ATMOSPHERIC PRESSURE: The pressure on the Earth's surface caused by the weight of the air in the atmosphere. At sea level, this pressure is 14.7 psi at 32°F (101 kPa at 0°C).

ATOMIZATION: The breaking down of a liquid into a fine mist that can be suspended in air.

AXIAL PLAY: Movement parallel to a shaft or bearing bore.

BACKFIRE: The sudden combustion of gases in the intake or exhaust system that results in a loud explosion.

BACKLASH: The clearance or play between two parts, such as meshed gears.

BACKPRESSURE: Restrictions in the exhaust system that slow the exit of exhaust gases from the combustion chamber.

BAKELITE: A heat resistant, plastic insulator material commonly used in printed circuit boards and transistorized components.

BALL BEARING: A bearing made up of hardened inner and outer races between which hardened steel balls roll.

BALLAST RESISTOR: A resistor in the primary ignition circuit that lowers voltage after the engine is started to reduce wear on ignition components.

BEARING: A friction reducing, supportive device usually located between a stationary part and a moving part.

BIMETAL TEMPERATURE SENSOR: Any sensor or switch made of two dissimilar types of metal that bend when heated or cooled due to the different expansion rates of the alloys. These types of sensors usually function as an on/off switch.

BLOWBY: Combustion gases, composed of water vapor and unburned fuel, that leak past the piston rings into the crankcase during normal engine operation. These gases are removed by the PCV system to prevent the buildup of harmful acids in the crankcase.

BRAKE PAD: A brake shoe and lining assembly used with disc brakes.

BRAKE SHOE: The backing for the brake lining. The term is, however, usually applied to the assembly of the brake backing and lining.

BUSHING: A liner, usually removable, for a bearing; an anti-friction liner used in place of a bearing.

BYPASS: System used to bypass ballast resistor during engine cranking to increase voltage supplied to the coil.

CALIPER: A hydraulically activated device in a disc brake system, which is mounted straddling the brake rotor (disc). The caliper contains at least one piston and two brake pads. Hydraulic pressure on the piston(s) forces the pads against the rotor.

CAMSHAFT: A shaft in the engine on which are the lobes (cams) which operate the valves. The camshaft is driven by the crankshaft, via a belt, chain or gears, at one half the crankshaft speed.

CAPACITOR: A device which stores an electrical charge.

CARBON MONOXIDE (CO): A colorless, odorless gas given off as a normal byproduct of combustion. It is poisonous and extremely dangerous in confined areas, building up slowly to toxic levels without warning if adequate ventilation is not available.

CARBURETOR: A device, usually mounted on the intake manifold of an engine, which mixes the air and fuel in the proper proportion to allow even combustion.

CATALYTIC CONVERTER: A device installed in the exhaust system, like a muffler, that converts harmful byproducts of combustion into carbon dioxide and water vapor by means of a heat-producing chemical reaction.

CENTRIFUGAL ADVANCE: A mechanical method of advancing the spark timing by using fly weights in the distributor that react to centrifugal force generated by the distributor shaft rotation.

CHECK VALVE: Any one-way valve installed to permit the flow of air, fuel or vacuum in one direction only.

CHOKE: A device, usually a movable valve, placed in the intake path of a carburetor to restrict the flow of air.

CIRCUIT: Any unbroken path through which an electrical current can flow. Also used to describe fuel flow in some instances.

CIRCUIT BREAKER: A switch which protects an electrical circuit from overload by opening the circuit when the current flow exceeds a predetermined level. Some circuit breakers must be reset manually, while most reset automatically

COIL (IGNITION): A transformer in the ignition circuit which steps up the voltage provided to the spark plugs.

COMBINATION MANIFOLD: An assembly which includes both the intake and exhaust manifolds in one casting.

COMBINATION VALVE: A device used in some fuel systems that routes fuel vapors to a charcoal storage canister instead of venting them into the atmosphere. The valve relieves fuel tank pressure and allows fresh air into the tank as the fuel level drops to prevent a vapor lock situation.

COMPRESSION RATIO: The comparison of the total volume of the cylinder and combustion chamber with the piston at BDC and the piston at TDC.

CONDENSER: 1. An electrical device which acts to store an electrical charge, preventing voltage surges.

2. A radiator-like device in the air conditioning system in which refrigerant gas condenses into a liquid, giving off heat.

CONDUCTOR: Any material through which an electrical current can be transmitted easily.

CONTINUITY: Continuous or complete circuit. Can be checked with an ohmmeter.

COUNTERSHAFT: An intermediate shaft which is rotated by a mainshaft and transmits, in turn, that rotation to a working part.

CRANKCASE: The lower part of an engine in which the crankshaft and related parts operate.

CRANKSHAFT: The main driving shaft of an engine which receives reciprocating motion from the pistons and converts it to rotary motion.

CYLINDER: In an engine, the round hole in the engine block in which the piston(s) ride.

CYLINDER BLOCK: The main structural member of an engine in which is found the cylinders, crankshaft and other principal parts.

CYLINDER HEAD: The detachable portion of the engine, fastened, usually, to the top of the cylinder block, containing all or most of the combustion chambers. On overhead valve engines, it contains the valves and their operating parts. On overhead cam engines, it contains the camshaft as well.

DEAD CENTER: The extreme top or bottom of the piston stroke.

DETONATION: An unwanted explosion of the air/fuel mixture in the combustion chamber caused by excess heat and compression, advanced timing, or an overly lean mixture. Also referred to as "ping".

EASY STEP-BY-STEP TIPS FROM PROS

CHILTON'S

AUTO BODY REPAIR TIPS

Tools and Materials • Step-by-Step Illustrated Procedures
How To Repair Dents, Scratches and Rust Holes
Spray Painting and Refinishing Tips

With a little practice, basic body repair procedures can be mastered by any do-it-yourself mechanic. The step-by-step repairs shown here can be applied to almost any type of auto body repair.

TOOLS & MATERIALS

You may already have basic tools, such as hammers and electric drills. Other tools unique to body repair — body hammers, grinding attachments, sanding blocks, dent puller, half-round plastic file and plastic spreaders — are relatively inexpensive and can be obtained wherever auto parts or auto body repair parts are sold. Portable air compressors and paint spray guns can be purchased or rented.

Auto Body Repair Kits

The best and most often used products are available to the do-it-yourselfer in kit form, from major manufacturers of auto body repair products. The same manufacturers also merchandise the individual products for use by pros.

Kits are available to make a wide variety of repairs, including holes, dents and scratches and fiberglass, and offer the advantage of buying the materials you'll need for the job. There is little waste or chance of materials going bad from not being used. Many kits may also contain basic body-working tools such as body files, sanding blocks and spreaders. Check the contents of the kit before buying your tools.

BODY REPAIR TIPS

Safety

Many of the products associated with auto body repair and refinishing contain toxic chemicals. Read all labels before opening containers and store them in a safe place and manner.

- Wear eye protection (safety goggles) when using power tools or when performing any operation that involves the removal of any type of material.
- Wear lung protection (disposable mask or respirator) when grinding, sanding or painting.

Sanding

1 Sand off paint before using a dent puller. When using a non-adhesive sanding disc, cover the back of the disc with an overlapping layer or two of masking tape and trim the edges. The disc will last considerably longer.

2 Use the circular motion of the sanding disc to grind *into* the edge of the repair. Grinding or sanding away from the jagged edge will only tear the sandpaper.

3 Use the palm of your hand flat on the panel to detect high and low spots. Do not use your fingertips. Slide your hand slowly back and forth.

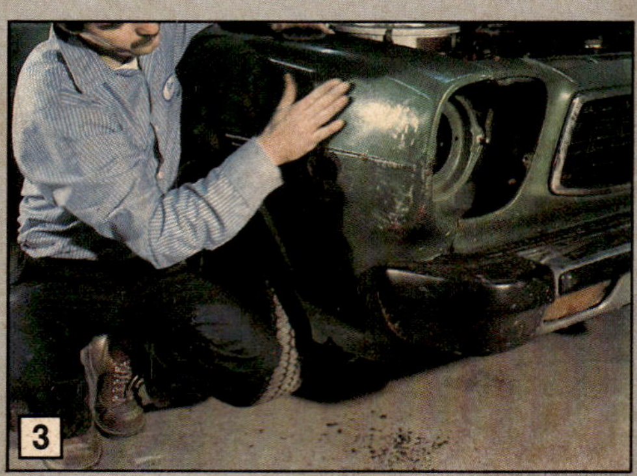

WORKING WITH BODY FILLER

Mixing The Filler

Cleanliness and proper mixing and application are extremely important. Use a clean piece of plastic or glass or a disposable artist's palette to mix body filler.

1 Allow plenty of time and follow directions. No useful purpose will be served by adding more hardener to make it cure (set-up) faster. Less hardener means more curing time, but the mixture dries harder; more hardener means less curing time but a softer mixture.

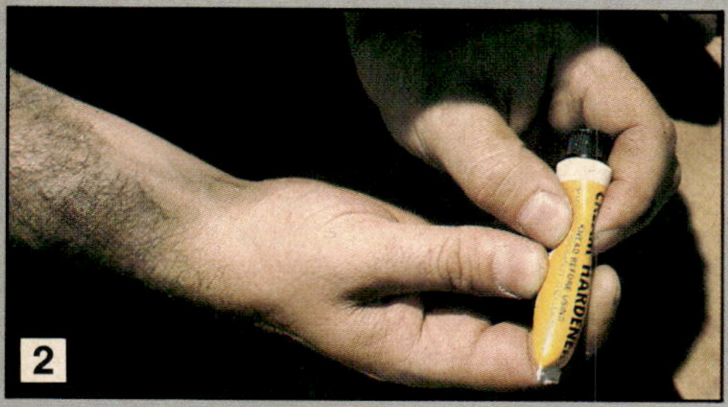

2 Both the hardener and the filler should be thoroughly kneaded or stirred before mixing. Hardener should be a solid paste and dispense like thin toothpaste. Body filler should be smooth, and free of lumps or thick spots.

Getting the proper amount of hardener in the filler is the trickiest part of preparing the filler. Use the same amount of hardener in cold or warm weather. For contour filler (thick coats), a bead of hardener twice the diameter of the filler is about right. There's about a 15% margin on either side, but, if in doubt use less hardener.

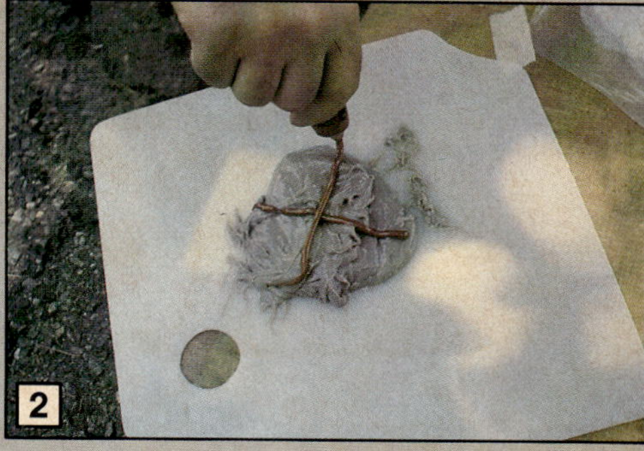

3 Mix the body filler and hardener by wiping across the mixing surface, picking the mixture up and wiping it again. Colder weather requires longer mixing times. Do not mix in a circular motion; this will trap air bubbles which will become holes in the cured filler.

Applying The Filler

1 For best results, filler should not be applied over 1/4″ thick.

Apply the filler in several coats. Build it up to above the level of the repair surface so that it can be sanded or grated down.

The first coat of filler must be pressed on with a firm wiping motion.

Apply the filler in one direction only. Working the filler back and forth will either pull it off the metal or trap air bubbles.

REPAIRING DENTS

Before you start, take a few minutes to study the damaged area. Try to visualize the shape of the panel before it was damaged. If the damage is on the left fender, look at the right fender and use it as a guide. If there is access to the panel from behind, you can reshape it with a body hammer. If not, you'll have to use a dent puller. Go slowly and work the metal a little at a time. Get the panel as straight as possible before applying filler.

1 This dent is typical of one that can be pulled out or hammered out from behind. Remove the headlight cover, headlight assembly and turn signal housing.

2 Drill a series of holes ½ the size of the end of the dent puller along the stress line. Make some trial pulls and assess the results. If necessary, drill more holes and try again. Do not hurry.

3 If possible, use a body hammer and block to shape the metal back to its original contours. Get the metal back as close to its original shape as possible. Don't depend on body filler to fill dents.

4 Using an 80-grit grinding disc on an electric drill, grind the paint from the surrounding area down to bare metal. Use a new grinding pad to prevent heat buildup that will warp metal.

5 The area should look like this when you're finished grinding. Knock the drill holes in and tape over small openings to keep plastic filler out.

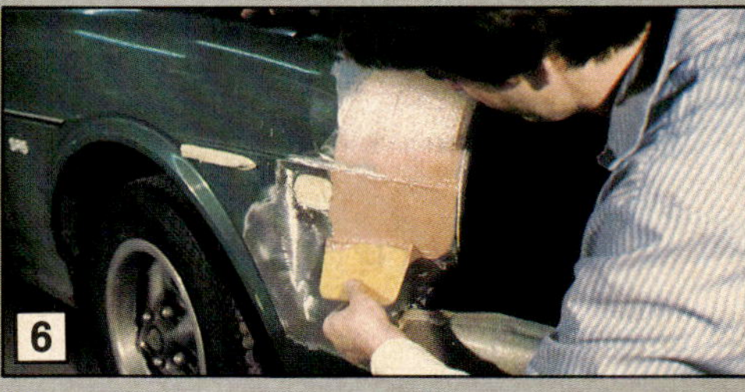

6 Mix the body filler (see Body Repair Tips). Spread the body filler evenly over the entire area (see Body Repair Tips). Be sure to cover the area completely.

7 Let the body filler dry until the surface can just be scratched with your fingernail. Knock the high spots from the body filler with a body file ("Cheese-grater"). Check frequently with the palm of your hand for high and low spots.

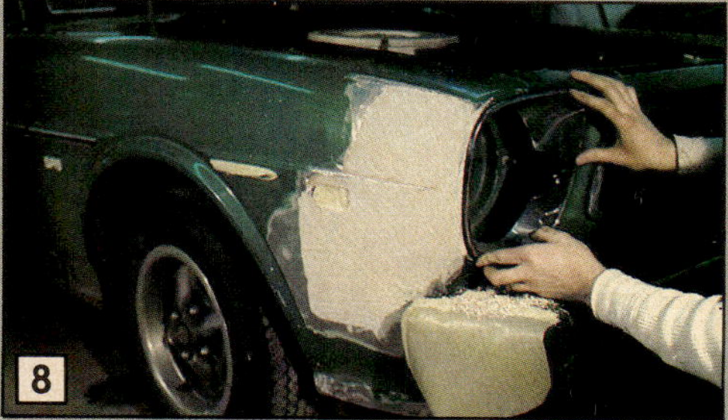

8 Check to be sure that trim pieces that will be installed later will fit exactly. Sand the area with 40-grit paper.

9 If you wind up with low spots, you may have to apply another layer of filler.

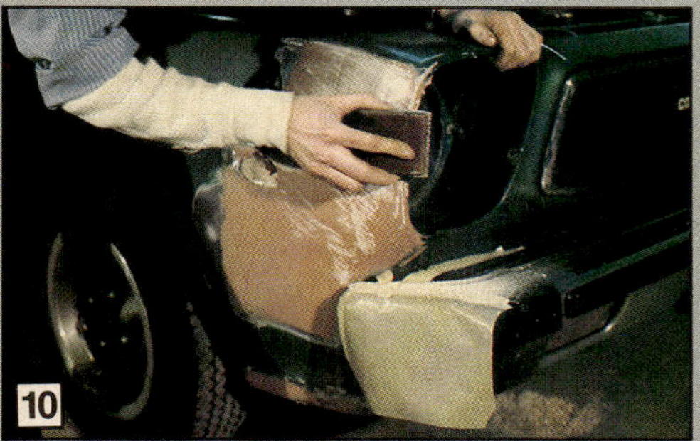

10 Knock the high spots off with 40-grit paper. When you are satisfied with the contours of the repair, apply a thin coat of filler to cover pin holes and scratches.

11 Block sand the area with 40-grit paper to a smooth finish. Pay particular attention to body lines and ridges that must be well-defined.

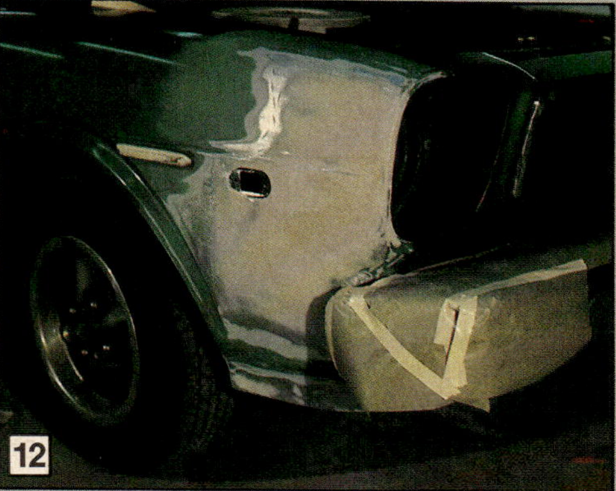

12 Sand the area with 400 paper and then finish with a scuff pad. The finished repair is ready for priming and painting (see Painting Tips).

Materials and photos courtesy of Ritt Jones Auto Body, Prospect Park, PA.

REPAIRING RUST HOLES

There are many ways to repair rust holes. The fiberglass cloth kit shown here is one of the most cost efficient for the owner because it provides a strong repair that resists cracking and moisture and is relatively easy to use. It can be used on large and small holes (with or without backing) and can be applied over contoured areas. Remember, however, that short of replacing an entire panel, no repair is a guarantee that the rust will not return.

1 Remove any trim that will be in the way. Clean away all loose debris. Cut away all the rusted metal. But be sure to leave enough metal to retain the contour or body shape.

2 Grind away all traces of rust with a 24-grit grinding disc. Be sure to grind back 3-4 inches from the edge of the hole down to bare metal and be sure all traces of paint, primer and rust are removed.

3 Block sand the area with 80 or 100 grit sandpaper to get a clear, shiny surface and feathered paint edge. Tap the edges of the hole inward with a ball peen hammer.

4 If you are going to use release film, cut a piece about 2-3″ larger than the area you have sanded. Place the film over the repair and mark the sanded area on the film. Avoid any unnecessary wrinkling of the film.

5 Cut 2 pieces of fiberglass matte to match the shape of the repair. One piece should be about 1″ smaller than the sanded area and the second piece should be 1″ smaller than the first. Mix enough filler and hardener to saturate the fiberglass material (see Body Repair Tips).

6 Lay the release sheet on a flat surface and spread an even layer of filler, large enough to cover the repair. Lay the smaller piece of fiberglass cloth in the center of the sheet and spread another layer of filler over the fiberglass cloth. Repeat the operation for the larger piece of cloth.

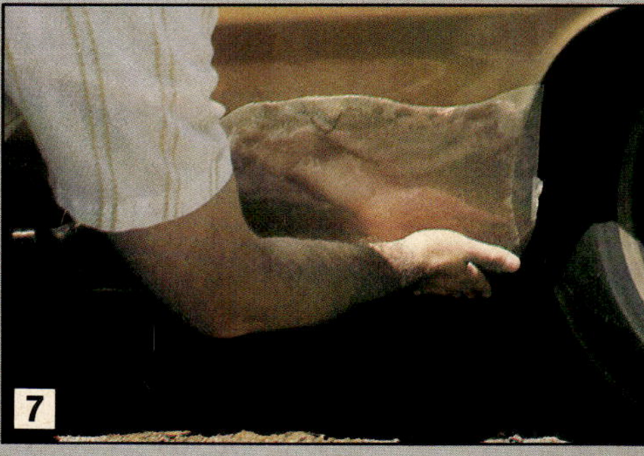

7 Place the repair material over the repair area, with the release film facing outward. Use a spreader and work from the center outward to smooth the material, following the body contours. Be sure to remove all air bubbles.

8 Wait until the repair has dried tack-free and peel off the release sheet. The ideal working temperature is 60°-90° F. Cooler or warmer temperatures or high humidity may require additional curing time. Wait longer, if in doubt.

9

9 Sand and feather-edge the entire area. The initial sanding can be done with a sanding disc on an electric drill if care is used. Finish the sanding with a block sander. Low spots can be filled with body filler; this may require several applications.

10

10 When the filler can just be scratched with a fingernail, knock the high spots down with a body file and smooth the entire area with 80-grit. Feather the filled areas into the surrounding areas.

11

11 When the area is sanded smooth, mix some topcoat and hardener and apply it directly with a spreader. This will give a smooth finish and prevent the glass matte from showing through the paint.

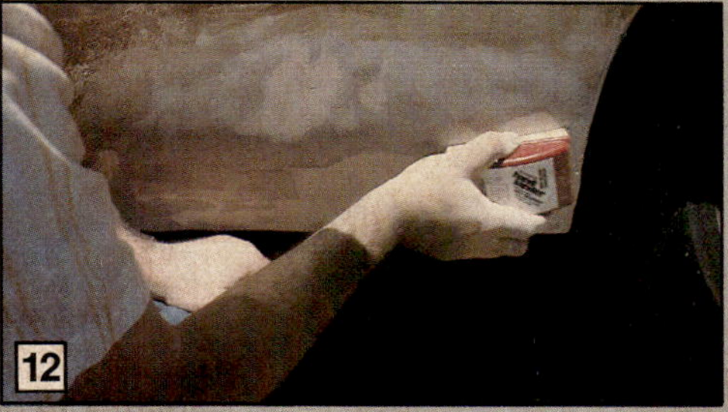

12

12 Block sand the topcoat smooth with finishing sandpaper (200 grit), and 400 grit. The repair is ready for masking, priming and painting (see Painting Tips).

Materials and photos courtesy Marson Corporation, Chelsea, Massachusetts

PAINTING TIPS

Preparation

1 SANDING — Use a 400 or 600 grit wet or dry sandpaper. Wet-sand the area with a ¼ sheet of sandpaper soaked in clean water. Keep the paper wet while sanding. Sand the area until the repaired area tapers into the original finish.

2 CLEANING — Wash the area to be painted thoroughly with water and a clean rag. Rinse it thoroughly and wipe the surface dry until you're sure it's completely free of dirt, dust, fingerprints, wax, detergent or other foreign matter.

3 MASKING — Protect any areas you don't want to overspray by covering them with masking tape and newspaper. Be careful not get fingerprints on the area to be painted.

4 PRIMING — All exposed metal should be primed before painting. Primer protects the metal and provides an excellent surface for paint adhesion. When the primer is dry, wet-sand the area again with 600 grit wet-sandpaper. Clean the area again after sanding.

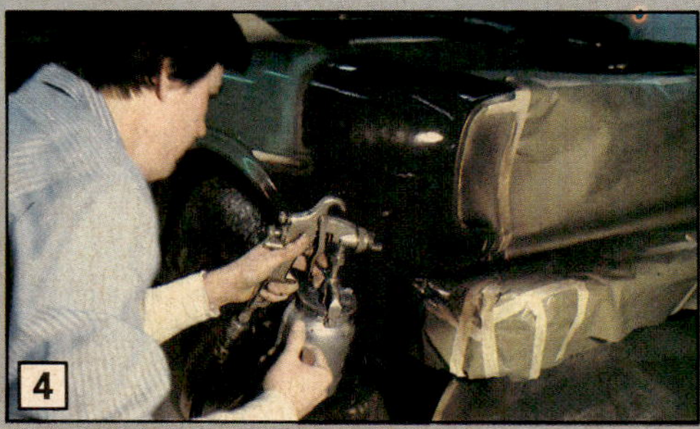

4

Painting Techniques

Paint applied from either a spray gun or a spray can (for small areas) will provide good results. Experiment on an old piece of metal to get the right combination before you begin painting.

SPRAYING VISCOSITY (SPRAY GUN ONLY) — Paint should be thinned to spraying viscosity according to the directions on the can. Use only the recommended thinner or reducer and the same amount of reduction regardless of temperature.

AIR PRESSURE (SPRAY GUN ONLY) — This is extremely important. Be sure you are using the proper recommended pressure.

TEMPERATURE — The surface to be painted should be approximately the same temperature as the surrounding air. Applying warm paint to a cold surface, or vice versa, will completely upset the paint characteristics.

THICKNESS — Spray with smooth strokes. In general, the thicker the coat of paint, the longer the drying time. Apply several thin coats about 30 seconds apart. The paint should remain wet long enough to flow out and no longer; heavier coats will only produce sags or wrinkles. Spray a light (fog) coat, followed by heavier color coats.

DISTANCE — The ideal spraying distance is 8″-12″ from the gun or can to the surface. Shorter distances will produce ripples, while greater distances will result in orange peel, dry film and poor color match and loss of material due to overspray.

OVERLAPPING — The gun or can should be kept at right angles to the surface at all times. Work to a wet edge at an even speed, using a 50% overlap and direct the center of the spray at the lower or nearest edge of the previous stroke.

RUBBING OUT (BLENDING) FRESH PAINT — Let the paint dry thoroughly. Runs or imperfections can be sanded out, primed and repainted.

Don't be in too big a hurry to remove the masking. This only produces paint ridges. When the finish has dried for at least a week, apply a small amount of fine grade rubbing compound with a clean, wet cloth. Use lots of water and blend the new paint with the surrounding area.

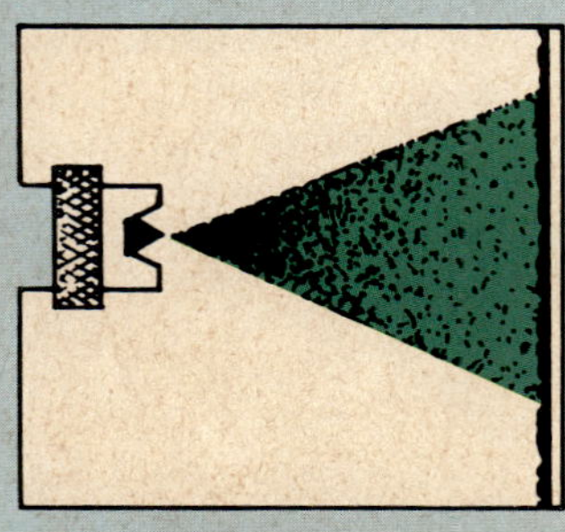

WRONG

Thin coat. Stroke too fast, not enough overlap, gun too far away.

CORRECT

Medium coat. Proper distance, good stroke, proper overlap.

WRONG

Heavy coat. Stroke too slow, too much overlap, gun too close.

DIAPHRAGM: A thin, flexible wall separating two cavities, such as in a vacuum advance unit.

DIESELING: A condition in which hot spots in the combustion chamber cause the engine to run on after the key is turned off.

DIFFERENTIAL: A geared assembly which allows the transmission of motion between drive axles, giving one axle the ability to turn faster than the other.

DIODE: An electrical device that will allow current to flow in one direction only.

DISC BRAKE: A hydraulic braking assembly consisting of a brake disc, or rotor, mounted on an axle, and a caliper assembly containing, usually two brake pads which are activated by hydraulic pressure. The pads are forced against the sides of the disc, creating friction which slows the vehicle.

DISTRIBUTOR: A mechanically driven device on an engine which is responsible for electrically firing the spark plug at a predetermined point of the piston stroke.

DOWEL PIN: A pin, inserted in mating holes in two different parts allowing those parts to maintain a fixed relationship.

DRUM BRAKE: A braking system which consists of two brake shoes and one or two wheel cylinders, mounted on a fixed backing plate, and a brake drum, mounted on an axle, which revolves around the assembly. Hydraulic action applied to the wheel cylinders forces the shoes outward against the drum, creating friction, slowing the vehicle.

DWELL: The rate, measured in degrees of shaft rotation, at which an electrical circuit cycles on and off.

ELECTRONIC CONTROL UNIT (ECU): Ignition module, amplifier or igniter. See Module for definition.

ELECTRONIC IGNITION: A system in which the timing and firing of the spark plugs is controlled by an electronic control unit, usually called a module. These systems have no points or condenser.

ENDPLAY: The measured amount of axial movement in a shaft.

ENGINE: A device that converts heat into mechanical energy.

EXHAUST MANIFOLD: A set of cast passages or pipes which conduct exhaust gases from the engine.

FEELER GAUGE: A blade, usually metal, of precisely predetermined thickness, used to measure the clearance between two parts. These blades usually are available in sets of assorted thicknesses.

F-HEAD: An engine configuration in which the intake valves are in the cylinder head, while the camshaft and exhaust valves are located in the cylinder block. The camshaft operates the intake valves via lifters and pushrods, while it operates the exhaust valves directly.

FIRING ORDER: The order in which combustion occurs in the cylinders of an engine. Also the order in which spark is distributed to the plugs by the distributor.

FLATHEAD: An engine configuration in which the camshaft and all the valves are located in the cylinder block.

FLOODING: The presence of too much fuel in the intake manifold and combustion chamber which prevents the air/fuel mixture from firing, thereby causing a no-start situation.

FLYWHEEL: A disc shaped part bolted to the rear end of the crankshaft. Around the outer perimeter is affixed the ring gear. The starter drive engages the ring gear, turning the flywheel, which rotates the crankshaft, imparting the initial starting motion to the engine.

FOOT POUND (ft.lb. or sometimes, ft. lbs.): The amount of energy or work needed to raise an item weighing one pound, a distance of one foot.

FUSE: A protective device in a circuit which prevents circuit overload by breaking the circuit when a specific amperage is present. The device is constructed around a strip or wire of a lower amperage rating than the circuit it is designed to protect. When an amperage higher than that stamped on the fuse is present in the circuit, the strip or wire melts, opening the circuit.

GEAR RATIO: The ratio between the number of teeth on meshing gears.

GENERATOR: A device which converts mechanical energy into electrical energy.

HEAT RANGE: The measure of a spark plug's ability to dissipate heat from its firing end. The higher the heat range, the hotter the plug fires. **HUB:** The center part of a wheel or gear.

HYDROCARBON (HC): Any chemical compound made up of hydrogen and carbon. A major pollutant formed by the engine as a byproduct of combustion.

HYDROMETER: An instrument used to measure the specific gravity of a solution.

INCH POUND (in.lb. or sometimes, in. lbs.): One twelfth of a foot pound.

INDUCTION: A means of transferring electrical energy in the form of a magnetic field. Principle used in the ignition coil to increase voltage.

INJECTION PUMP: A device, usually mechanically operated, which meters and delivers fuel under pressure to the fuel injector.

INJECTOR: A device which receives metered fuel under relatively low pressure and is activated to inject the fuel into the engine under relatively high pressure at a predetermined time.

INPUT SHAFT: The shaft to which torque is applied, usually carrying the driving gear or gears.

INTAKE MANIFOLD: A casting of passages or pipes used to conduct air or a fuel/air mixture to the cylinders.

JOURNAL: The bearing surface within which a shaft operates.

KEY: A small block usually fitted in a notch between a shaft and a hub to prevent slippage of the two parts.

MANIFOLD: A casting of passages or set of pipes which connect the cylinders to an inlet or outlet source.

MANIFOLD VACUUM: Low pressure in an engine intake manifold formed just below the throttle plates. Manifold vacuum is highest at idle and drops under acceleration.

MASTER CYLINDER: The primary fluid pressurizing device in a hydraulic system. In automotive use, it is found in brake and hydraulic clutch systems and is pedal activated, either directly or, in a power brake system, through the power booster.

MODULE: Electronic control unit, amplifier or igniter of solid state or integrated design which controls the current flow in the ignition primary circuit based on input from the pick-up coil. When the module opens the primary circuit, the high secondary voltage is induced in the coil.

NEEDLE BEARING: A bearing which consists of a number (usually a large number) of long, thin rollers.

OHM:(Ω) The unit used to measure the resistance of conductor to electrical flow. One ohm is the amount of resistance that limits current flow to one ampere in a circuit with one volt of pressure.

OHMMETER: An instrument used for measuring the resistance, in ohms, in an electrical circuit.

OUTPUT SHAFT: The shaft which transmits torque from a device, such as a transmission.

OVERDRIVE: A gear assembly which produces more shaft revolutions than that transmitted to it.

OVERHEAD CAMSHAFT (OHC): An engine configuration in which the camshaft is mounted on top of the cylinder head and operates the valves either directly or by means of rocker arms.

OVERHEAD VALVE (OHV): An engine configuration in which all of the valves are located in the cylinder head and the camshaft is located in the cylinder block. The camshaft operates the valves via lifters and pushrods.

OXIDES OF NITROGEN (NOx): Chemical compounds of nitrogen produced as a byproduct of combustion. They combine with hydrocarbons to produce smog.

OXYGEN SENSOR: Used with the feedback system to sense the presence of oxygen in the exhaust gas and signal the computer which can reference the voltage signal to an air/fuel ratio.

PINION: The smaller of two meshing gears.

PISTON RING: An open ended ring which fits into a groove on the outer diameter of the piston. Its chief function is to form a seal between the piston and cylinder wall. Most automotive pistons have three rings: two for compression sealing; one for oil sealing.

PRELOAD: A predetermined load placed on a bearing during assembly or by adjustment.

PRIMARY CIRCUIT: Is the low voltage side of the ignition system which consists of the ignition switch, ballast resistor or resistance wire, bypass, coil, electronic control unit and pick-up coil as well as the connecting wires and harnesses.

PRESS FIT: The mating of two parts under pressure, due to the inner diameter of one being smaller than the outer diameter of the other, or vice versa; an interference fit.

RACE: The surface on the inner or outer ring of a bearing on which the balls, needles or rollers move.

REGULATOR: A device which maintains the amperage and/or voltage levels of a circuit at predetermined values.

RELAY: A switch which automatically opens and/or closes a circuit.

RESISTANCE: The opposition to the flow of current through a circuit or electrical device, and is measured in ohms. Resistance is equal to the voltage divided by the amperage.

RESISTOR: A device, usually made of wire, which offers a preset amount of resistance in an electrical circuit.

RING GEAR: The name given to a ring-shaped gear attached to a differential case,or affixed to a flywheel or as part a planetary gear set.

ROLLER BEARING: A bearing made up of hardened inner and outer races between which hardened steel rollers move.

ROTOR: 1. The disc-shaped part of a disc brake assembly, upon which the brake pads bear; also called, brake disc.

2. The device mounted atop the distributor shaft, which passes current to the distributor cap tower contacts.

SECONDARY CIRCUIT: The high voltage side of the ignition system, usually above 20,000 volts. The secondary includes the ignition coil, coil wire, distributor cap and rotor, spark plug wires and spark plugs.

SENDING UNIT: A mechanical, electrical, hydraulic or electromagnetic device which transmits information to a gauge.

SENSOR: Any device designed to measure engine operating conditions or ambient pressures and temperatures. Usually electronic in nature and designed to send a voltage signal to an on-board computer, some sensors may operate as a simple on/off switch or they may provide a variable voltage signal (like a potentiometer) as conditions or measured parameters change.

SHIM: Spacers of precise, predetermined thickness used between parts to establish a proper working relationship.

SLAVE CYLINDER: In automotive use, a device in the hydraulic clutch system which is activated by hydraulic force, disengaging the clutch.

SOLENOID: A coil used to produce a magnetic field, the effect of which is to produce work.

SPARK PLUG: A device screwed into the combustion chamber of a spark ignition engine. The basic construction is a conductive core inside of a ceramic insulator, mounted in an outer conductive base. An electrical charge from the spark plug wire travels along the conductive core and jumps a preset air gap to a grounding point or points at the end of the conductive base. The resultant spark ignites the fuel/air mixture in the combustion chamber.

SPLINES: Ridges machined or cast onto the outer diameter of a shaft or inner diameter of a bore to enable parts to mate without rotation.

TACHOMETER: A device used to measure the rotary speed of an engine, shaft, gear, etc., usually in rotations per minute.

THERMOSTAT: A valve, located in the cooling system of an engine, which is closed when cold and opens gradually in response to engine heating, controlling the temperature of the coolant and rate of coolant flow.

TOP DEAD CENTER (TDC): The point at which the piston reaches the top of its travel on the compression stroke.

TORQUE: The twisting force applied to an object.

TORQUE CONVERTER: A turbine used to transmit power from a driving member to a driven member via hydraulic action, providing changes in drive ratio and torque. In automotive use, it links the driveplate at the rear of the engine to the automatic transmission.

TRANSDUCER: A device used to change a force into an electrical signal.

TRANSISTOR: A semi-conductor component which can be actuated by a small voltage to perform an electrical switching function.

TUNE-UP: A regular maintenance function, usually associated with the replacement and adjustment of parts and components in the electrical and fuel systems of a vehicle for the purpose of attaining optimum performance.

TURBOCHARGER: An exhaust driven pump which compresses intake air and forces it into the combustion chambers at higher than atmospheric pressures. The increased air pressure allows more fuel to be burned and results in increased horsepower being produced.

VACUUM ADVANCE: A device which advances the ignition timing in response to increased engine vacuum.

VACUUM GAUGE: An instrument used to measure the presence of vacuum in a chamber.

VALVE: A device which control the pressure, direction of flow or rate of flow of a liquid or gas.

VALVE CLEARANCE: The measured gap between the end of the valve stem and the rocker arm, cam lobe or follower that activates the valve.

VISCOSITY: The rating of a liquid's internal resistance to flow.

VOLTMETER: An instrument used for measuring electrical force in units called volts. Voltmeters are always connected parallel with the circuit being tested.

WHEEL CYLINDER: Found in the automotive drum brake assembly, it is a device, actuated by hydraulic pressure, which, through internal pistons, pushes the brake shoes outward against the drums.

A

B

C

G

H

I

J

K

L

M

N

O

P

R

S

Chilton's Repair & Tune-Up Guides

The Complete line covers domestic cars, imports, trucks, vans, RV's and 4-wheel drive vehicles.

RTUG Title	Part No.
AMC 1975-82 Covers all U.S. and Canadian models	7199
Aspen/Volare 1976-80 Covers all U.S. and Canadian models	6637
Audi 1970-73 Covers all U.S. and Canadian models.	5902
Audi 4000/5000 1978-81 Covers all U.S. and Canadian models including turbocharged and diesel engines	7028
Barracuda/Challenger 1965-72 Covers all U.S. and Canadian models	5807
Blazer/Jimmy 1969-82 Covers all U.S. and Canadian 2- and 4-wheel drive models, including diesel engines	6931
BMW 1970-82 Covers U.S. and Canadian models	6844
Buick/Olds/Pontiac 1975-85 Covers all U.S. and Canadian full size rear wheel drive models	7308
Cadillac 1967-84 Covers all U.S. and Canadian rear wheel drive models	7462
Camaro 1967-81 Covers all U.S. and Canadian models	6735
Camaro 1982-85 Covers all U.S. and Canadian models	7317
Capri 1970-77 Covers all U.S. and Canadian models	6695
Caravan/Voyager 1984-85 Covers all U.S. and Canadian models	7482
Century/Regal 1975-85 Covers all U.S. and Canadian rear wheel drive models, including turbocharged engines	7307
Champ/Arrow/Sapporo 1978-83 Covers all U.S. and Canadian models	7041
Chevette/1000 1976-86 Covers all U.S. and Canadian models	6836
Chevrolet 1968-85 Covers all U.S. and Canadian models	7135
Chevrolet 1968-79 Spanish	7082
Chevrolet/GMC Pick-Ups 1970-82 Spanish	7468
Chevrolet/GMC Pick-Ups and Suburban 1970-86 Covers all U.S. and Canadian $^1/_2$, $^3/_4$ and 1 ton models, including 4-wheel drive and diesel engines	6936
Chevrolet LUV 1972-81 Covers all U.S. and Canadian models	6815
Chevrolet Mid-Size 1964-86 Covers all U.S. and Canadian models of 1964-77 Chevelle, Malibu and Malibu SS; 1974-77 Laguna; 1978-85 Malibu; 1970-86 Monte Carlo; 1964-84 El Camino, including diesel engines	6840
Chevrolet Nova 1986 Covers all U.S. and Canadian models	7658
Chevy/GMC Vans 1967-84 Covers all U.S. and Canadian models of $^1/_2$, $^3/_4$, and 1 ton vans, cutaways, and motor home chassis, including diesel engines	6930
Chevy S-10 Blazer/GMC S-15 Jimmy 1982-85 Covers all U.S. and Canadian models	7383
Chevy S-10/GMC S-15 Pick-Ups 1982-85 Covers all U.S. and Canadian models	7310
Chevy II/Nova 1962-79 Covers all U.S. and Canadian models	6841
Chrysler K- and E-Car 1981-85 Covers all U.S. and Canadian front wheel drive models	7163
Colt/Challenger/Vista/Conquest 1971-85 Covers all U.S. and Canadian models	7037
Corolla/Carina/Tercel/Starlet 1970-85 Covers all U.S. and Canadian models	7036
Corona/Cressida/Crown/Mk.II/Camry/Van 1970-84 Covers all U.S. and Canadian models	7044
Corvair 1960-69 Covers all U.S. and Canadian models	6691
Corvette 1953-62 Covers all U.S. and Canadian models	6576
Corvette 1963-84 Covers all U.S. and Canadian models	6843
Cutlass 1970-85 Covers all U.S. and Canadian models	6933
Dart/Demon 1968-76 Covers all U.S. and Canadian models	6324
Datsun 1961-72 Covers all U.S. and Canadian models of Nissan Patrol; 1500, 1600 and 2000 sports cars; Pick-Ups; 410, 411, 510, 1200 and 240Z	5790
Datsun 1973-80 Spanish	7083
Datsun/Nissan F-10, 310, Stanza, Pulsar 1977-86 Covers all U.S. and Canadian models	7196
Datsun/Nissan Pick-Ups 1970-84 Covers all U.S and Canadian models	6816
Datsun/Nissan Z & ZX 1970-86 Covers all U.S. and Canadian models	6932
Datsun/Nissan 1200, 210, Sentra 1973-86 Covers all U.S. and Canadian models	7197
Datsun/Nissan 200SX, 510, 610, 710, 810, Maxima 1973-84 Covers all U.S. and Canadian models	7170
Dodge 1968-77 Covers all U.S. and Canadian models	6554
Dodge Charger 1967-70 Covers all U.S. and Canadian models	6486
Dodge/Plymouth Trucks 1967-84 Covers all $^1/_2$, $^3/_4$, and 1 ton 2- and 4-wheel drive U.S. and Canadian models, including diesel engines	7459
Dodge/Plymouth Vans 1967-84 Covers all $^1/_2$, $^3/_4$, and 1 ton U.S. and Canadian models of vans, cutaways and motor home chassis	6934
D-50/Arrow Pick-Up 1979-81 Covers all U.S. and Canadian models	7032
Fairlane/Torino 1962-75 Covers all U.S. and Canadian models	6320
Fairmont/Zephyr 1978-83 Covers all U.S. and Canadian models	6965
Fiat 1969-81 Covers all U.S. and Canadian models	7042
Fiesta 1978-80 Covers all U.S. and Canadian models	6846
Firebird 1967-81 Covers all U.S. and Canadian models	5996
Firebird 1982-85 Covers all U.S. and Canadian models	7345
Ford 1968-79 Spanish	7084
Ford Bronco 1966-83 Covers all U.S. and Canadian models	7140
Ford Bronco II 1984 Covers all U.S. and Canadian models	7408
Ford Courier 1972-82 Covers all U.S. and Canadian models	6983
Ford/Mercury Front Wheel Drive 1981-85 Covers all U.S. and Canadian models Escort, EXP, Tempo, Lynx, LN-7 and Topaz	7055
Ford/Mercury/Lincoln 1968-85 Covers all U.S. and Canadian models of FORD Country Sedan, Country Squire, Crown Victoria, Custom, Custom 500, Galaxie 500, LTD through 1982, Ranch Wagon, and XL; MERCURY Colony Park, Commuter, Marquis through 1982, Gran Marquis, Monterey and Park Lane; LINCOLN Continental and Towne Car	6842
Ford/Mercury/Lincoln Mid-Size 1971-85 Covers all U.S. and Canadian models of FORD Elite, 1983-85 LTD, 1977-79 LTD II, Ranchero, Torino, Gran Torino, 1977-85 Thunderbird; MERCURY 1972-85 Cougar,	6696

continued on next page

RTUG Title	Part No.
1983-85 Marquis, Montego, 1980-85 XR-7; LINCOLN 1982-85 Continental, 1984-85 Mark VII, 1978-80 Versailles	
Ford Pick-Ups 1965-86 Covers all $^{1}/_{2}$, $^{3}/_{4}$ and 1 ton, 2- and 4-wheel drive U.S. and Canadian pick-up, chassis cab and camper models, including diesel engines	6913
Ford Pick-Ups 1965-82 Spanish	7469
Ford Ranger 1983-84 Covers all U.S. and Canadian models	7338
Ford Vans 1961-86 Covers all U.S. and Canadian $^{1}/_{2}$, $^{3}/_{4}$ and 1 ton van and cutaway chassis models, including diesel engines	6849
GM A-Body 1982-85 Covers all front wheel drive U.S. and Canadian models of BUICK Century, CHEVROLET Celebrity, OLDSMOBILE Cutlass Ciera and PONTIAC 6000	7309
GM C-Body 1985 Covers all front wheel drive U.S. and Canadian models of BUICK Electra Park Avenue and Electra T-Type, CADILLAC Fleetwood and deVille, OLDSMOBILE 98 Regency and Regency Brougham	7587
GM J-Car 1982-85 Covers all U.S. and Canadian models of BUICK Skyhawk, CHEVROLET Cavalier, CADILLAC Cimarron, OLDSMOBILE Firenza and PONTIAC 2000 and Sunbird	7059
GM N-Body 1985-86 Covers all U.S. and Canadian models of front wheel drive BUICK Somerset and Skylark, OLDSMOBILE Calais, and PONTIAC Grand Am	7657
GM X-Body 1980-85 Covers all U.S. and Canadian models of BUICK Skylark, CHEVROLET Citation, OLDSMOBILE Omega and PONTIAC Phoenix	7049
GM Subcompact 1971-80 Covers all U.S. and Canadian models of BUICK Skyhawk (1975-80), CHEVROLET Vega and Monza, OLDSMOBILE Starfire, and PONTIAC Astre and 1975-80 Sunbird	6935
Granada/Monarch 1975-82 Covers all U.S. and Canadian models	6937
Honda 1973-84 Covers all U.S. and Canadian models	6980
International Scout 1967-73 Covers all U.S. and Canadian models	5912
Jeep 1945-87 Covers all U.S. and Canadian CJ-2A, CJ-3A, CJ-3B, CJ-5, CJ-6, CJ-7, Scrambler and Wrangler models	6817
Jeep Wagoneer, Commando, Cherokee, Truck 1957-86 Covers all U.S. and Canadian models of Wagoneer, Cherokee, Grand Wagoneer, Jeepster, Jeepster Commando, J-100, J-200, J-300, J-10, J20, FC-150 and FC-170	6739
Laser/Daytona 1984-85 Covers all U.S. and Canadian models	7563
Maverick/Comet 1970-77 Covers all U.S. and Canadian models	6634
Mazda 1971-84 Covers all U.S. and Canadian models of RX-2, RX-3, RX-4, 808, 1300, 1600, Cosmo, GLC and 626	6981
Mazda Pick-Ups 1972-86 Covers all U.S. and Canadian models	7659
Mercedes-Benz 1959-70 Covers all U.S. and Canadian models	6065
Mereceds-Benz 1968-73 Covers all U.S. and Canadian models	5907
Mercedes-Benz 1974-84 Covers all U.S. and Canadian models	6809
Mitsubishi, Cordia, Tredia, Starion, Galant 1983-85 Covers all U.S. and Canadian models	7583
MG 1961-81 Covers all U.S. and Canadian models	6780
Mustang/Capri/Merkur 1979-85 Covers all U.S. and Canadian models	6963
Mustang/Cougar 1965-73 Covers all U.S. and Canadian models	6542
Mustang II 1974-78 Covers all U.S. and Canadian models	6812
Omni/Horizon/Rampage 1978-84 Covers all U.S. and Canadian models of DODGE omni, Miser, 024, Charger 2.2; PLYMOUTH Horizon, Miser, TC3, TC3 Tourismo; Rampage	6845
Opel 1971-75 Covers all U.S. and Canadian models	6575
Peugeot 1970-74 Covers all U.S. and Canadian models	5982
Pinto/Bobcat 1971-80 Covers all U.S. and Canadian models	7027
Plymouth 1968-76 Covers all U.S. and Canadian models	6552
Pontiac Fiero 1984-85 Covers all U.S. and Canadian models	7571
Pontiac Mid-Size 1974-83 Covers all U.S. and Canadian models of Ventura, Grand Am, LeMans, Grand LeMans, GTO, Phoenix, and Grand Prix	7346
Porsche 924/928 1976-81 Covers all U.S. and Canadian models	7048
Renault 1975-85 Covers all U.S. and Canadian models	7165
Roadrunner/Satellite/Belvedere/GTX 1968-73 Covers all U.S. and Canadian models	5821
RX-7 1979-81 Covers all U.S. and Canadian models	7031
SAAB 99 1969-75 Covers all U.S. and Canadian models	5988
SAAB 900 1979-85 Covers all U.S. and Canadian models	7572
Snowmobiles 1976-80 Covers Arctic Cat, John Deere, Kawasaki, Polaris, Ski-Doo and Yamaha	6978
Subaru 1970-84 Covers all U.S. and Canadian models	6982
Tempest/GTO/LeMans 1968-73 Covers all U.S. and Canadian models	5905
Toyota 1966-70 Covers all U.S. and Canadian models of Corona, MkII, Corolla, Crown, Land Cruiser, Stout and Hi-Lux	5795
Toyota 1970-79 Spanish	7467
Toyota Celica/Supra 1971-85 Covers all U.S. and Canadian models	7043
Toyota Trucks 1970-85 Covers all U.S. and Canadian models of pick-ups, Land Cruiser and 4Runner	7035
Valiant/Duster 1968-76 Covers all U.S. and Canadian models	6326
Volvo 1956-69 Covers all U.S. and Canadian models	6529
Volvo 1970-83 Covers all U.S. and Canadian models	7040
VW Front Wheel Drive 1974-85 Covers all U.S. and Canadian models	6962
VW 1949-71 Covers all U.S. and Canadian models	5796
VW 1970-79 Spanish	7081
VW 1970-81 Covers all U.S. and Canadian Beetles, Karmann Ghia, Fastback, Squareback, Vans, 411 and 412	6837

Chilton's Repair Manuals are available at your local retailer or by mailing a check or money order for **$15.95** per book plus **$3.50** for 1st book and **$.50** for each additional book to cover postage and handling to:

Chilton Book Company
Dept. DM
Radnor, PA 19089

NOTE: When ordering be sure to include your name & address, book part No. & title.